Praise for *Head Rush Ajax*

"If you thought Ajax was rocket science, this book is for you. *Head Rush Ajax* puts dynamic, compelling experiences within reach for every web developer."

— **Jesse James Garrett, Adaptive Path**

"THE book for all of those web developers who want to get that Ajax attitude that everyone is talking about."

— **Valentin Crettaz, CTO Condris Technologies, Switzerland**

"*Head Rush Ajax* is the book if you want to cut through all the hype and learn how to make your web apps sparkle... your users will love you for it!"

— **Kristin Stromberg, Aguirre International**

"This stuff is brain candy; I can't get enough of it."

— **Pauline McNamara, Center for New Technologies and Education, Fribourg University, Switzerland**

"If you know some HTML, a dollop of CSS, a little JavaScript, and a bit of PHP, but you're mystified about what all the Ajax hype is about, this is the book for you. *Head Rush Ajax* cuts through the hype and explains how to take your beginner web applications to the next level. Before you know it, you'll be writing next-generation web applications, and you'll actually understand how they work!

You'll have a blast learning Ajax with *Head Rush Ajax*. By the time you've reached the end of this book, all those web technologies that didn't quite fit together in your head will all snap into place and you'll have The Ajax Power! You'll know the secrets behind some of the most popular web applications on the Internet. You'll impress your friends and co-workers with your knowledge of how those interactive maps and web forms **really** work.

I can't imagine learning Ajax without Katie and Alex and Rufus and Jenny... all the friends you'll make on your fun-filled, exciting journey through *Head Rush Ajax*. And when you're done, not only will you be able to write next-generation web applications, you'll actually understand how they work."

— **Elisabeth Freeman, Director, Technology**
The Walt Disney Internet Group
Co-author of Head First Design Patterns and Head First HTML with CSS & XHTML

More praise for *Head Rush Ajax*

"After much research, I recently purchased *Head Rush Ajax*... and just wanted to tell you that this is perhaps the best produced technical book I have ever read or purchased. I was able to incorporate Ajax into an existing product before reaching Chapter 3! Kudos to you and the people that helped being this book to publication."

— **Steve Dorris, President, Provident Technologies, Inc.**

"You should be able to come away from this book with an integral and global knowledge of Ajax, aware of its capabilities and familiar with its implementation."

— **Brett Merkey, Web GUI Developer**
Client Experience Team, Nielsen Media Research

"Programmers are flooded with choices about which technologies to pursue in order to maintain a marketable skillset. Even in a particular area of programming like web applications, one must choose carefully where to invest time. Ajax, to the regret of some and delight of others, has emerged as a means of providing rich, responsive web applications that are highly cross-platform. However, when arriving home after a 10-hour day at the office programming, who has the energy to plow through yet another new facet of emerging technology? If a developer is going to invest their free time in self-driven career development, should it not be at least *remotely* enjoyable? Judging from the content of O'Reilly's new release *Head Rush Ajax*, their answer is yes."

— **Barry Hawkins**

"A great book that can be used for anybody wanting to learn advanced JavaScript (DOM), Ajax, or even to learn more about XML and JSON. A book for everyone."

— **Frank Stepnaski**

"The author starts at the very beginning of the Ajax story and does a great job explaining what the various technologies are that make Ajax work. He uses a few different (comical but effective) example applications to teach the topics. You'll create apps like a snowboard sales report, a pizza ordering site, a top-5 CDs site. They're good examples because they're simple enough to just get the points across without losing you in the details. The book is not dependent on any particular server technology. It would be applicable for developers using asp, Java, php, etc. Toward the end of the book, there is a comparison of JSON and XML. Finally, in an appendix, there is a nice collection of various Ajax and web-related toolkits."

— **Jim Anderton**

Praise for other Head First books

"I *heart* *Head First HTML with CSS & XHTML* – it teaches you everything you need to learn in a 'fun coated' format!"

— **Sally Applin, UI Designer and Fine Artist, http://sally.com.**

"Oh, great. You made an XHTML book simple enough a CEO can understand it. What will you do next? Accounting simple enough my developer can understand it? Next thing you know we'll be collaborating as a team or something."

—**Janice Fraser, CEO, Adaptive Path**

"From the awesome Head First Java folks, this book uses every conceivable trick to help you understand and remember. Not just loads of pictures: pictures of humans, which tend to interest other humans. Surprises everywhere. Stories, because humans love narrative. (Stories about things like pizza and chocolate. Need we say more?) Plus, it's darned funny."

— **Bill Camarda, READ ONLY**

"This book's admirable clarity, humor, and substantial doses of clever make it the sort of book that helps even non-programmers think well about problem-solving."

— **Cory Doctorow, co-editor of Boing Boing**
and author of "Down and Out in the Magic Kingdom"
and "Someone Comes to Town, Someone Leaves Town"

"I feel like a thousand pounds of books have just been lifted off of my head."

— **Ward Cunningham, inventor of the Wiki**
and founder of the Hillside Group

"This book is close to perfect, because of the way it combines expertise and readability. It speaks with authority and it reads beautifully. It's one of the very few software books I've ever read that strikes me as indispensable. (I'd put maybe 10 books in this category, at the outside.)"

— **David Gelernter, Professor of Computer Science,**
Yale University and author of "Mirror Worlds" and "Machine Beauty"

"A Nose Dive into the realm of patterns, a land where complex things become simple, but where simple things can also become complex. I can think of no better tour guides than the Freemans."

— **Miko Matsumura, Industry Analyst, The Middleware Company**
Former Chief Java Evangelist, Sun Microsystems

"Just the right tone for the geeked-out, casual-cool guru coder in all of us. The right reference for practical development strategies—gets my brain going without having to slog through a bunch of tired, stale professor-speak."

— **Travis Kalanick, Founder of Scour and Red Swoosh**
Member of the MIT TR100

Other related books from O'Reilly

Ajax Design Patterns (2006)
Ajax Hacks
CSS: The Definitive Guide
CSS Pocket Reference
CSS Cookbook
Dynamic HTML: The Definitive Reference
HTML & XHTML: The Definitive Guide
HTML Pocket Reference
JavaScript: The Definitive Guide
JavaScript Pocket Reference
JavaScript & DHTML Cookbook
PHP in a Nutshell
PHP Cookbook
PHP Pocket Reference

Other books in O'Reilly's Head First Series

Head First Design Patterns
Head First Java
Head First Servlets and JSP
Head First EJB
Head First HTML with CSS & XHTML ← This one in particular will really help you out in your Ajax apps.
Head First Objects (2006)

Head Rush Ajax

Wouldn't it be wonderful if there was an Ajax book that we could **both** understand? One that actually taught programmers and web designers how to create dynamic web sites? It's probably just a fantasy...

Brett McLaughlin

O'REILLY®

Beijing • Cambridge • Köln • Paris • Sebastopol • Taipei • Tokyo

Head Rush Ajax

by Brett McLaughlin

Printed in the United States of America.

Published by O'Reilly Media, Inc., 1005 Gravenstein Highway North, Sebastopol, CA 95472.

O'Reilly Media books may be purchased for educational, business, or sales promotional use. Online editions are also available for most titles (safari.oreilly.com). For more information, contact our corporate/institutional sales department: (800) 998-9938 or corporate@oreilly.com.

Associate Publisher: Mike Hendrickson

Series Creators: Kathy Sierra, Bert Bates

Editor: Mike Loukides

Cover Concept: Ellie Volckhausen, Eric Freeman

Cover Designers: Mike Kohnke, Karen Montgomery, Elisabeth Freeman, Eric Freeman

Ajax Junkie: Brett McLaughlin

Page Viewers: Dean and Robbie

Printing History:

March 2006: First Edition.

In other words, if you use anything in *Head Rush Ajax* to, say, manage and monitor your atomic weapon shipping lanes, you're on your own. We do, however, encourage you to visit the Head First Labs, where we're creating our own world-changing concoctions.

Despite the ominous nature of the PROJECT: CHAOS organization, no applications were irreparably harmed in the making of this book.

ISBN: 0-596-10225-9

[M] [05/06]

To my boys, Dean and Robbie, for reminding me that books can indeed be fun and enjoyable...

...and for my wife, Leigh, for reminding me that people hate big fat books that have nothing to say.

Meet your author

Brett McLaughlin ↘

Brett is a guitar player who is still struggling with the realization that you can't pay the bills if you're into acoustic fingerstyle blues and jazz, and high-end custom instruments. He's just recently discovered, to his delight, that writing books that help people become better programmers *does* pay the bills. He's very happy about this, as are his wife Leigh, and his young kids, Dean and Robbie.

Before Brett wandered into Head First land, he developed enterprise Java applications for Nextel Communications and Allegiance Telecom. When that became fairly mundane, Brett took on application servers, working on the internals of the Lutris Enhydra servlet engine and EJB container. Along the way, Brett got hooked on open source software, and helped found several cool programming tools, like Jakarta Turbine and JDOM.

When Lutris folded, Brett decided to take on writing and editing full-time, and has been an editor at O'Reilly Media, Inc., ever since. Now that he's found the Head First series, he doesn't plan on ever going back to a "normal" career again. Brett manages the bestselling Head First series, and writes Head First and Head Rush books on the side.

In addition to his work on Head First, Brett's a bestselling author, and has written *Java and XML*, *Java 5.0: A Developer's Notebook*, *Home Theater Hacks*, *Java and XML Data Binding*, and *Building Java Enterprise Applications, Volume I*. As if that's not enough, by the time you've got this book in your hands, Brett will probably have already started his next Head First book... but that's still a bit of a secret, so we'll tell you more on that later.

Write to him at brett@oreilly.com or visit him online at http://www.newInstance.com. If Brett's not teaching his kids to play an instrument or watching "24" or "Arrested Development" with his wife, he'll probably answer you pretty quickly.

That's actually Bert Bates's guitar... Bert is one of the Head First series creators.

Thanks to Harold Davis, another HF author, for the great pic.

Table of Contents (summary)

Table of Contents (the real thing)

Intro

Your brain on Ajax. Here *you* are trying to *learn* something, and your *brain* is doing you a favor by making sure the learning doesn't *stick*. Your brain's thinking, "Better leave room for more important things, like which wild animals to avoid and whether naked snowboarding is a bad idea." So how *do* you trick your brain into thinking that your life depends on knowing how to program asynchronously?

web applications for a new generation

1 Using Ajax

Put a new shine on your web applications.

Tired of clunky web interfaces and waiting around for a page to reload? Well, it's about time to give your web apps that pine-scented desktop application feel. What are we talking about? Just the newest thing to hit the Web: **Ajax**—asynchronous JavaScript and XML—and your ticket to building **rich Internet applications** that are more *interactive*, *responsive*, and *easy to use*.

Didn't you say that Ajax will let me update the screen without all that reloading? Something about updating just part of the page?

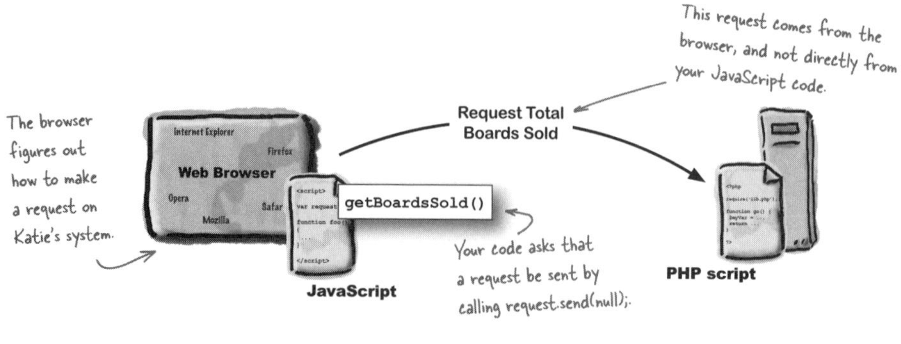
This request comes from the browser, and not directly from your JavaScript code.
The browser figures out how to make a request on Katie's system.
Internet Explorer
Firefox
Web Browser
Opera
Safari
Mozilla
Request Total Boards Sold
getBoardsSold()
Your code asks that a request be sent by calling request.send(null);.
JavaScript
PHP script

Making Ajax Requests

2 Speaking the Language

It's time to learn how to speak asynchronously.

If you're planning on writing the next killer application, you need to understand Ajax inside and out. In this chapter, you'll get the inside scoop on **asynchronous JavaScript**: you'll learn how to send requests on different browsers, master **ready states** and **status codes**, and even pick up a few extra dynamic HTML tricks along the way. By the time you're done, you'll be making requests and handling responses like a pro... and by the way, did we mention your users **won't have to wait** around on you while you're learning?

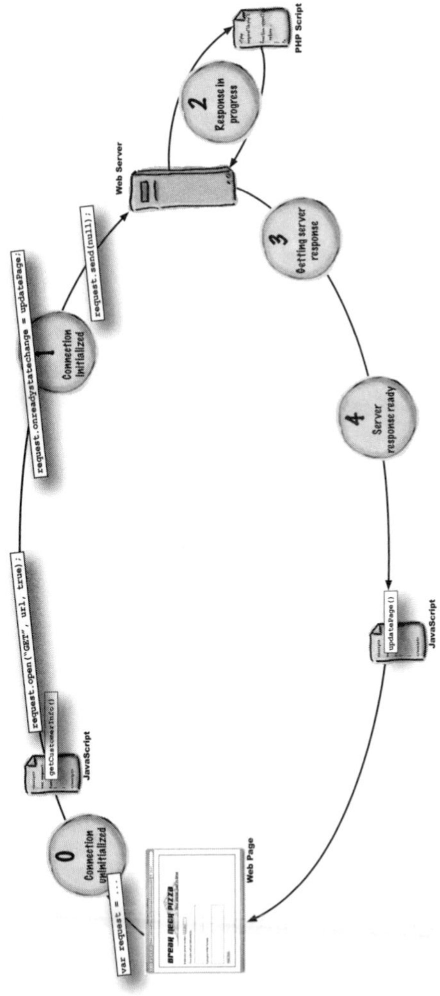

Asynchronous Apps

3 She Blinded Me with Asynchrony

Waiting room? I'm sorry, we don't have one of those.

This is the Web, not a doctor's office, and nobody wants to sit around reading a six-month old magazine while a server does its thing. You've seen how Ajax will let you get rid of page reloads, but it's time to add **responsive** to the list of highlights for your web apps. In this chapter, you'll learn how to send your users' requests to a server, and let your users **keep on working** while they're waiting on a response. In fact... strike that. There'll be **no waiting** in this chapter at all. Turn the page, and let's get started.

4 Web Page Forestry

Wanted: easy-to-update web pages.

It's time to take things into your own hands, and start writing code that updates your web pages on the fly. Using the **Document Object Model**, your pages can take on new life, respond to users' actions, and help you ditch unnecessary page reloads forever. By the time you're done with this chapter, you'll be able to add, remove, and update content virtually anywhere on your web page. So turn the page, and let's take a stroll through the Webville Tree Farm.

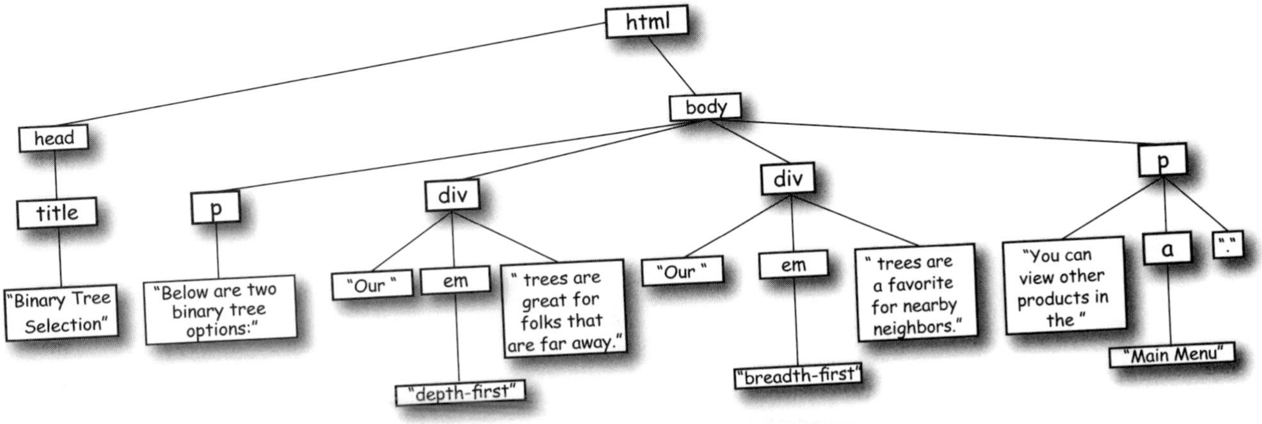

4.5 Developing DOM Applications

A Second Helping

Hungry for more DOM?

In the last chapter, you got a crash course in the coolest way to update your web pages: the **Document Object Model**. We figured you might be wanting even more, though, so in this chapter you'll use what you've just learned to write a nifty DOM-based application. Along the way, you'll pick up some **new event handlers**, learn how to **change a node's style**, and create a **user-friendly, dynamic application**. This is the chapter where we take your DOM skills to a whole new level.

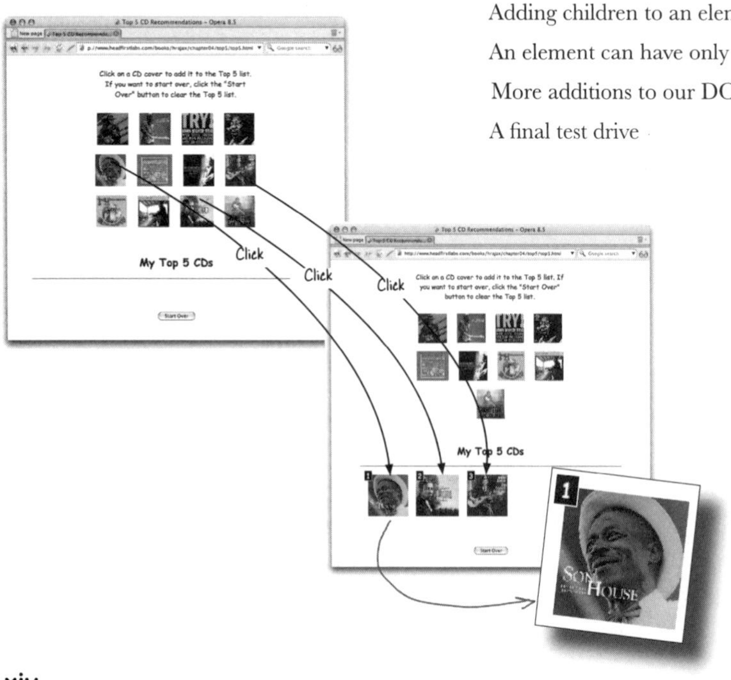

Click on a CD cover to add it to the Top 5 list. If you want to start over, click the "Start Over" button to clear the Top 5 list.
My Top 5 CDs
Click
Click
Click
My Top 5 CDs
1

POST Requests

5 Saying More with POST

This is what you've been waiting for.

You asked for it, and now you're going to get it: we're finally going to **ditch send(null)**, and learn how to **send more data** to a server. It will take a little extra work on your part, but by the time you're finished with this chapter, you'll be saying a lot more than "no data" to the server in your asynchronous requests. So fasten your seatbelts, and let's take a cruise through the land of content types and request headers; **we're in POST-country** now.

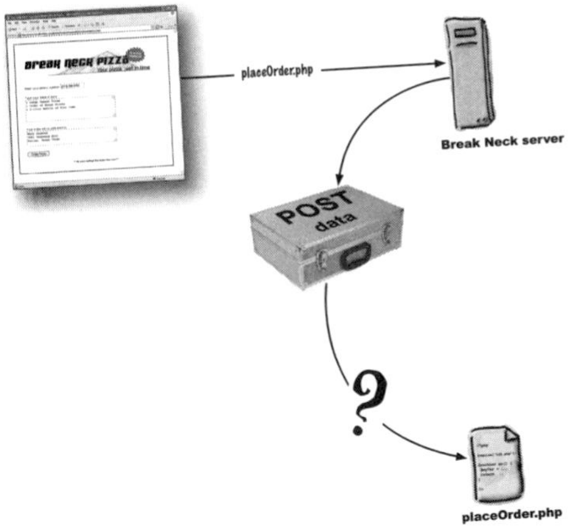

XML Requests and Responses

6 More Than Words Can Say

Ever feel like nobody is listening to you?

Sometimes plain old English just doesn't cut it when you're **trying to communicate**. You've been using text for all of your requests and responses so far, but it's time to break out of our plain-text shells. In this chapter, we'll **dive into XML**, and teach our servers to say a lot more than they ever could with plain text. As if that's not enough, you'll teach your requests XML, too, even though that's not always a good idea (more on that inside). Get ready... once you've finished this chapter, *your requests and responses will never be the same*.

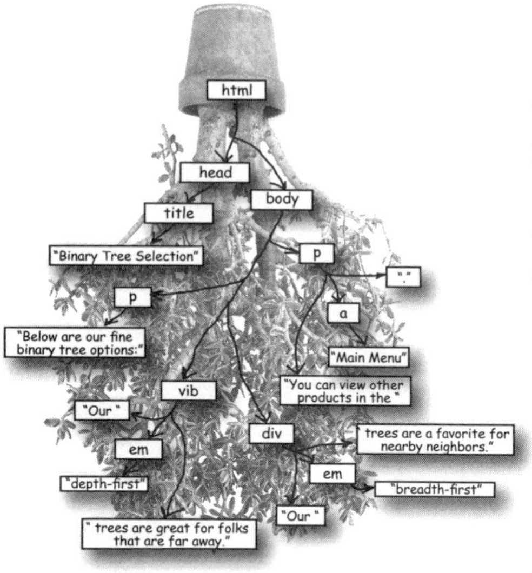

JSON vs. XML

7 A Fight to the Finish

It's time to go back to elementary school.

Remember the days when differences were resolved with harsh words, flying fists, and poor kung fu imitations? Remember when nothing thrilled your soul like hearing "**Fight!**" screamed in the halls of the cafeteria? In this chapter, we're going back to those days, and leaving friendly words and the golden rule behind. **XML and JSON**, two different formats for **sending and receiving data** in your asynchronous requests, are ready to let their differences be settled in the squared circle. Get your scorecard ready, and let's take it to the ring!

totals[1].bootsSold
{"totals": [
{"location":"Vail", "boardsSold":642, "bootsSold":86, "bindingsSold":19},
{"location":"Santa Fe", "boardsSold":236, "bootsSold" 45, "bindingsSold":32},
{"location":"Boulder", "boardsSold":453, "bootsSold":90, "bindingsSold" 16,
{"location":"Denver", "boardsSold" 379 "bootsSold":94, "bindingsSold":
]};
totals[0]
totals[1]
totals[2]
totals[3]
totals[3].boardsSold
totals[2].bindingsSold

Appendix 1: Extras

a.1

A Few Special Bonus Gifts

Just for you: a parting gift from Head First Labs.

In fact, you'll find **five special bonus gifts** in this appendix. We wish we could stick around and tell you about a lot more, but it's time for you to take what's you've learned and head out into the cold, cruel world of web programming on your own. We'd hate for you to take off without **a little more preparation**, though, so take a look at the top five things we just couldn't squeeze into this book.

Appendix 2: ajax and DOM utilities

a.2

It's time for a little bonus credit.

Within the pages of this appendix, you'll find some of the utility code that was a little advanced for when you ran across it earlier in the book. By now, though, you should be ready to tackle these Ajax and DOM utility functions head-on.

i

Index

Intro

You won't ***believe*** the things I learned from reading Head Rush Ajax. I just finished learning how to...

In this section, we answer the burning question: "So, why DID they put that in an Ajax book?"

Who is this book for?

If you can answer "yes" to all of these:

1. Do you know **HTML**, some **CSS**, and some **JavaScript**? (You don't need to be a guru.)
2. Do you want to **learn, understand, and *remember*** Ajax, with a goal of developing more responsive web applications?
3. Do you prefer **stimulating dinner party conversation** to dry, dull, academic lectures?

this book is for you.

Who should probably back away from this book?

If you can answer "yes" to any ***one*** of these:

1. Are you **completely new** to HTML or CSS or JavaScript? (You don't need to be advanced, but you should definitely have some experience. If not, go get a copy of *Head First HTML and CSS*, today, and then come back and get *this* book.)
2. Are you a kick-butt Ajax developer looking for **a *reference* book?**
3. Are you **afraid to try something different**? Would you rather have a root canal than mix stripes with plaid? Do you believe that a technical book can't be serious if browsers are anthropomorphized?

this book is ***not*** for you.

[Note from marketing: this book is for anyone who can afford it.]

We know what you're thinking.

"How can *this* be a serious programming book?"

"What's with all the graphics?"

"Can I actually *learn* it this way?"

"Do I smell pizza?"

And we know what your *brain* is thinking.

Your brain thinks THIS is important.

Your brain craves novelty. It's always searching, scanning, *waiting* for something unusual. It was built that way, and it helps you stay alive.

So what does your brain do with all the routine, ordinary, normal things you encounter? Everything it *can* to stop them from interfering with the brain's *real* job—recording things that *matter*. It doesn't bother saving the boring things; they never make it past the "this is obviously not important" filter.

How does your brain *know* what's important? Suppose you're out for a day hike and a tiger jumps in front of you; what happens inside your head and body?

Neurons fire. Emotions crank up. *Chemicals surge.*

And that's how your brain knows...

This must be important! Don't forget it!

But imagine you're at home, or in a library. It's a safe, warm, tiger-free zone. You're studying. Getting ready for an exam. Or trying to learn some tough technical topic your boss thinks will take a week, ten days at the most.

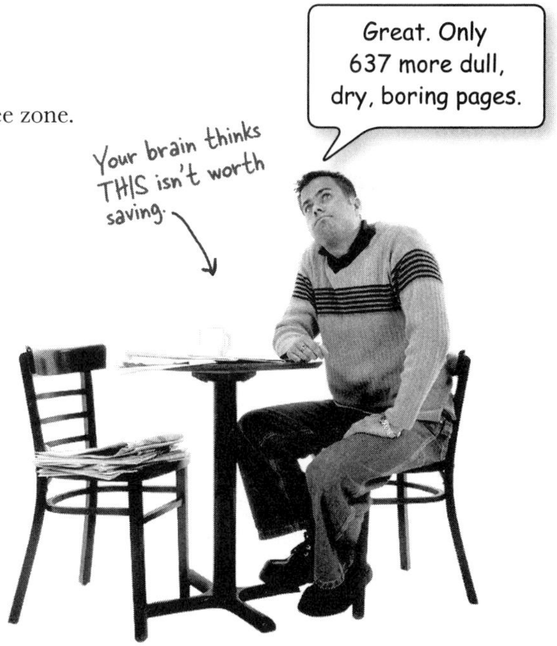
Great. Only 637 more dull, dry, boring pages.
Your brain thinks THIS isn't worth saving.

Just one problem. Your brain's trying to do you a big favor. It's trying to make sure that this *obviously* non-important content doesn't clutter up scarce resources. Resources that are better spent storing the really *big* things. Like tigers. Like the danger of fire. Like how you should never again snowboard in shorts.

And there's no simple way to tell your brain, "Hey brain, thank you very much, but no matter how dull this book is, and how little I'm registering on the emotional Richter scale right now, I really *do* want you to keep this stuff around."

We think of a "Head Rush" reader as a learner.

So what does it take to *learn* something? First, you have to *get* it, then make sure you don't *forget* it. It's not about pushing facts into your head. Based on the latest research in cognitive science, neurobiology, and educational psychology, *learning* takes a lot more than text on a page. We know what turns your brain on.

Some of the Head Rush learning principles:

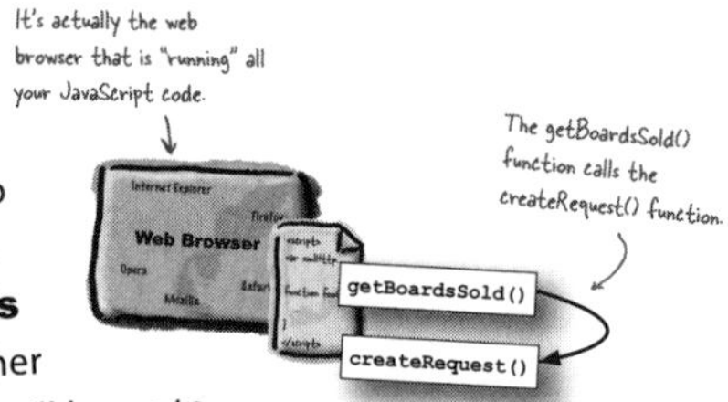
It's actually the web browser that is "running" all your JavaScript code.
The getBoardsSold() function calls the createRequest() function.
Web Browser
getBoardsSold()
createRequest()

Make it visual. Images are far more memorable than words alone, and make learning much more effective (up to 89% improvement in recall and transfer studies). It also makes things more understandable. **Put the words within or near the graphics** they relate to, rather than on the bottom or on another page, and learners will be up to *twice* as likely to solve problems related to the content.

Use a conversational and personalized style. In recent studies, students performed up to 40% better on post-learning tests if the content spoke directly to the reader, using a first-person, conversational style rather than taking a formal tone. Tell stories instead of lecturing. Use casual language. Don't take yourself too seriously. Which would *you* pay more attention to: a stimulating dinner party companion, or a lecture?

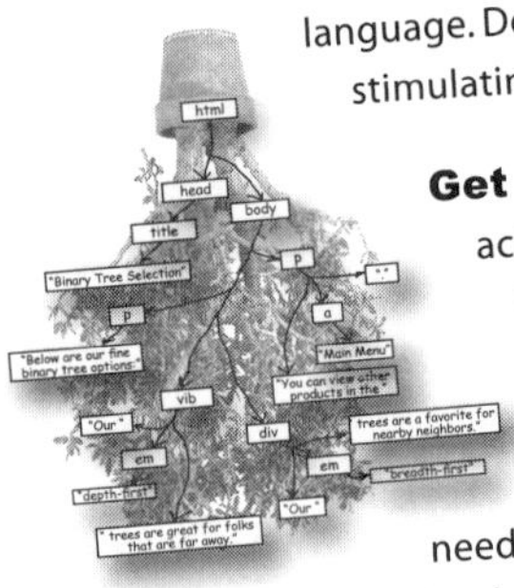
html
head
body
title
"Binary Tree Selection"

Get the learner to think more deeply. In other words, unless you actively flex your neurons, nothing much happens in your head. A reader has to be motivated, engaged, curious, and inspired to solve problems, draw conclusions, and generate new knowledge. And for that, you need challenges, exercises, thought-provoking questions, and activities that involve both sides of the brain, and multiple senses.

Be the Architect

Get—and keep—the reader's attention. We've all had the "I really want to learn this but I can't stay awake past page one" experience. Your brain pays attention to things that are out of the ordinary, interesting, strange, eye-catching, unexpected. Learning a new, tough, technical topic doesn't have to be boring. Your brain will learn much more quickly if it's not.

Touch their emotions. We now know that your ability to remember something is largely dependent on its emotional content. You remember what you care about. You remember when you feel something. No, we're not talking heart-wrenching stories about a boy and his dog. We're talking emotions like surprise, curiosity, fun, "what the...?", and the feeling of "I Rule!" that comes when you solve a puzzle, learn something everybody else thinks is hard, or realize you know something that "more-technical-than-thou" Bob from engineering *doesn't*.

Metacognition: thinking about thinking

If you really want to learn, and you want to learn more quickly and more deeply, pay attention to how you pay attention. Think about how you think. Learn how you learn.

I wonder how I can trick my brain into remembering this stuff...

Most of us did not take courses on metacognition or learning theory when we were growing up. We were *expected* to learn, but rarely *taught* to learn.

But we assume that if you're holding this book, you want to learn Ajax. And you probably don't want to spend a lot of time. And since you're going to develop applications, you need to *remember* what you read. And for that, you've got to understand it. To get the most from this book, or *any* book or learning experience, take responsibility for your brain. Your brain on *this* content.

The trick is to get your brain to see the new material you're learning as Really Important. Crucial to your well-being. As important as a tiger. Otherwise, you're in for a constant battle, with your brain doing its best to keep the new content from sticking.

So just how *DO* you get your brain to treat Ajax like it's a hungry tiger?

There's the slow, tedious way, or the faster, more effective way. The slow way is about sheer repetition. You obviously know that you *are* able to learn and remember even the dullest of topics if you keep pounding the same thing into your brain. With enough repetition, your brain says, "This doesn't *feel* important to him, but he keeps looking at the same thing *over* and *over* and *over*, so I suppose it must be."

The faster way is to do ***anything that increases brain activity,*** especially different *types* of brain activity. The things on the previous page are a big part of the solution, and they're all things that have been proven to help your brain work in your favor. For example, studies show that putting words *within* the pictures they describe (as opposed to somewhere else in the page, like a caption or in the body text) causes your brain to try to makes sense of how the words and picture relate, and this causes more neurons to fire. More neurons firing = more chances for your brain to *get* that this is something worth paying attention to, and possibly recording.

A conversational style helps because people tend to pay more attention when they perceive that they're in a conversation, since they're expected to follow along and hold up their end. The amazing thing is, your brain doesn't necessarily *care* that the "conversation" is between you and a book! On the other hand, if the writing style is formal and dry, your brain perceives it the same way you experience being lectured to while sitting in a roomful of passive attendees. No need to stay awake.

But pictures and conversational style are just the beginning.

Here's what WE did:

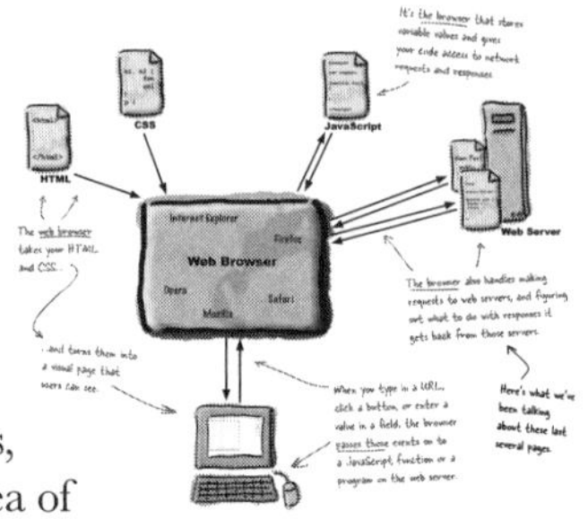

We used ***pictures***, because your brain is tuned for visuals, not text. As far as your brain's concerned, a picture really *is* worth 1,024 words. And when text and pictures work together, we embedded the text *in* the pictures because your brain works more effectively when the text is *within* the thing the text refers to, as opposed to in a caption or buried in the text somewhere.

We used ***repetition***, saying the same thing in different ways and with different media types, and *multiple senses*, to increase the chance that the content gets coded into more than one area of your brain.

We used concepts and pictures in ***unexpected*** ways because your brain is tuned for novelty, and we used pictures and ideas with at least *some* ***emotional*** *content*, because your brain is tuned to pay attention to the biochemistry of emotions. That which causes you to *feel* something is more likely to be remembered, even if that feeling is nothing more than a little ***humor***, ***surprise***, or ***interest.***

We used a personalized, ***conversational style***, because your brain is tuned to pay more attention when it believes you're in a conversation than if it thinks you're passively listening to a presentation. Your brain does this even when you're *reading*.

We included more than 40 ***activities***, because your brain is tuned to learn and remember more when you ***do*** things than when you *read* about things. And we made the exercises challenging-yet-do-able, because that's what most people prefer.

We used ***multiple learning styles***, because *you* might prefer step-by-step procedures, while someone else wants to understand the big picture first, and someone else just wants to see a code example. But regardless of your own learning preference, *everyone* benefits from seeing the same content represented in multiple ways.

We include content for ***both sides of your brain***, because the more of your brain you engage, the more likely you are to learn and remember, and the longer you can stay focused. Since working one side of the brain often means giving the other side a chance to rest, you can be more productive at learning for a longer period of time.

And we included ***stories*** and exercises that present ***more than one point of view,*** because your brain is tuned to learn more deeply when it's forced to make evaluations and judgments.

We included ***challenges***, with exercises, and by asking ***questions*** that don't always have a straight answer, because your brain is tuned to learn and remember when it has to *work* at something. Think about it—you can't get your *body* in shape just by *watching* people at the gym. But we did our best to make sure that when you're working hard, it's on the *right* things. That ***you're not spending one extra dendrite*** processing a hard-to-understand example, or parsing difficult, jargon-laden, or overly terse text.

We used ***people***. In stories, examples, pictures, etc., because, well, because *you're* a person. And your brain pays more attention to *people* than it does to *things*.

We used an ***80/20*** approach. We assume that if you're going for a Ph.D in Ajax, this won't be your only book. So we don't talk about *everything*. Just the stuff you'll actually *need*.

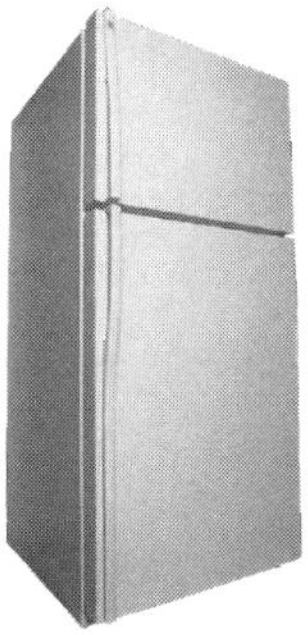

Here's what YOU can do to bend your brain into submission

So, we did our part. The rest is up to you. These tips are a starting point; listen to your brain and figure out what works for you and what doesn't. Try new things.

Cut this out and stick it on your refridgerator.

1. **Slow down. The more you understand, the less you have to memorize.**
   Don't just *read*. Stop and think. When the book asks you a question, don't just skip to the answer. Imagine that someone really *is* asking the question. The more deeply you force your brain to think, the better chance you have of learning and remembering.

2. **Do the exercises. Write your own notes.**
   We put them in, but if we did them for you, that would be like having someone else do your workouts for you. And don't just *look* at the exercises. **Use a pencil.** There's plenty of evidence that physical activity *while* learning can increase the learning.

3. **Read the "Frequently Asked Questions."**
   That means all of them. They're not optional side-bars—***they're part of the core content!*** Don't skip them.

4. **Don't do all your reading in one place.**
   Stand-up, stretch, move around, change chairs, change rooms. It'll help your brain (and body) *feel* something, and keep your learning from being too connected to a particular place. Remember, you won't be taking the exam in your bedroom.

5. **Make this the last thing you read before bed. Or at least the last *challenging* thing.**
   Part of the learning (especially the transfer to long-term memory) happens *after* you put the book down. Your brain needs time on its own, to do more processing. If you put in something new during that processing-time, some of what you just learned will be lost.

6. **Drink water. Lots of it.**
   Your brain works best in a nice bath of fluid. Dehydration (which can happen before you ever feel thirsty) decreases cognitive function. Beer, or something stronger, is called for when you pass the exam.

7. **Talk about it. Out loud.**
   Speaking activates a different part of the brain. If you're trying to understand something, or increase your chance of remembering it later, say it out loud. Better still, try to explain it out loud to someone else. You'll learn more quickly, and you might uncover ideas you didn't know were there when you were reading about it.

8. **Listen to your brain.**
   Pay attention to whether your brain is getting overloaded. If you find yourself starting to skim the surface or forget what you just read, it's time for a break. Once you go past a certain point, you won't learn faster by trying to shove more in, and you might even hurt the process.

9. **Feel something!**
   Your brain needs to know that this *matters*. Get involved with the stories. Make up your own captions for the photos. Groaning over a bad joke is *still* better than feeling nothing at all.

Read Me

This is a learning experience, not a reference book. We deliberately stripped out everything that might get in the way of learning whatever it is we're working on at that point in the book. And the first time through, you need to begin at the beginning, because the book makes assumptions about what you've already seen and learned.

We assume you are familiar with HTML and CSS.

It would take an entire book to teach you HTML and CSS (in fact, that's exactly what it took: *Head First HTML with CSS & XHTML*). We chose to focus this book on Ajax programming, rather than rehash lots of markup and style that you could learn about in other places.

We assume you've at least seen JavaScript code before.

It would take an entire book to teach you... oh, wait, we've already said that. Seriously, JavaScript is a lot more than a simple scripting language, and we aren't going to cover all the ways you can use JavaScript in this book. You'll learn about all the ways that JavaScript is related to Ajax programming, and learn how to use JavaScript extensively to add interaction to your web pages and make requests to a server.

However, if you've never written a line of JavaScript, aren't at all familiar with functions or curly braces, or have never programmed in any language before, you might want to pick up a good JavaScript book and browse through it. If you want to plow into this book, feel free—but we will be moving fairly quickly over the basics.

We don't cover server-side programming in this book.

It's now common to find server-side programs written in Java, PHP, Ruby, Python, Perl, Ruby on Rails, C#, and a whole lot more. Ajax programming works with all of these languages, and we have tried to represent several of them in this book's examples.

To keep you focused on learning Ajax, though, we do not spend much time explaining the server-side programs used; we'll show you the server-side code with some notes, but that's as far as we go. We believe that your Ajax applications can be written to work with any kind of server-side program; we also believe that you're smart enough to apply the lessons learned from an example that uses PHP to one that uses Ruby on Rails or a Java servlet.

We encourage you to use more than one browser with this book.

As much as it sucks, different web browsers handle your HTML, your CSS, and your JavaScript in completely different ways. If you want to be a complete Ajax programmer, you should always test your asynchronous applications on lots of modern browsers. All the examples in this book were tested on recent versions of Firefox, Opera, Safari, Internet Explorer, and Mozilla. If you find problems, though, let us know... we promise it's an accident.

We often use tag names for element names.

Rather than saying "the **a** element," or "the 'a' element," we use a tag name, like "the **<a>** element." While this may not be technically correct (because **<a>** is an opening tag, not a full blown element), it does make the text more readable.

The activities are NOT optional.

The exercises and activities are not add-ons; they're part of the core content of the book. Some of them are to help with memory, some are for understanding, and some will help you apply what you've learned. ***Don't skip the exercises.***

The redundancy is intentional and important.

One distinct difference in a Head First book is that we want you to *really* get it. And we want you to finish the book remembering what you've learned. Most reference books don't have retention and recall as a goal, but this book is about learning, so you'll see many of the concepts come up more than once.

The examples are as lean as possible.

Our readers tell us that it's frustrating to wade through 200 lines of an example looking for the two lines they need to understand. Most examples in this book are shown within the smallest possible context, so that the part you're trying to learn is clear and simple. Don't expect all of the examples to be robust, or even complete—they are written specifically for learning, and aren't always fully functional.

We've placed all the example files on the Web so you can download them. You'll find them at **`http://www.headfirstlabs.com/books/hrajax/`**.

The 'Brain Power' exercises don't have answers.

For some of them, there is no right answer, and for others, part of the learning experience of the Brain Power activities is for you to decide if and when your answers are right. In some of the Brain Power exercises you will find hints to point you in the right direction.

Tech Reviewers

I'm so phenomenally lucky to have a killer team of reviewers. **Johannes de Jong** probably thinks that he didn't do much, and of course he'd be very, very wrong. Johannes started the review, kept it running, and made jokes about whiskey at all the right times. **Pauline McNamara** manages to be in every Head First (and now Head Rush) book, probably because she's such an uber-reviewer. She co-managed the review, and was always technically correct and yet still "cool." Go figure! **Valentin Crettaz** found every grammatical mistake I've ever made, and even kept my diagrams technically accurate. What a combination. **Kristin Stromberg** came to the fray late, and just devoured the chapters. Her feedback was right on point, and really helped make the book more fun, engaging, and enjoyable. You should thank her... seriously! **Andrew Monkouse** made some great Ajax-specific comments that really kept me on my Ajax toes. Nice work, Andrew! And a special thanks, and shout out, to **Bear Bibeault**. Bear, I know life got in the way, but I appreciate your involvement all the same, man!

I hope you like this book, guys—this book is yours as much as it is mine.

Eric and Beth Freeman

It seems like these books end up being as much about friendships as about writing and teaching. If it weren't for **Beth Freeman** and **Eric Freeman**, my life wouldn't be as rich as it is. They brought me into the Head First family, trusted me, and taught me (about strange faux meat as well as ferries and crazy stories). Beth wrote Chapter 3, and Eric worked on the cover and a lot of the new Head Rush elements. Guys, more than your help, I really value your friendship. See ya soon.

And there's a lot more...*

At O'Reilly:

Mike Hendrickson has managed to be the guy who kept this project going, through every conceivable obstable. Mike, this book wouldn't have happened without you. You've seen me through some ragged times, and I'm sure there are more coming. Good to know you'll be there for me when things get tense.

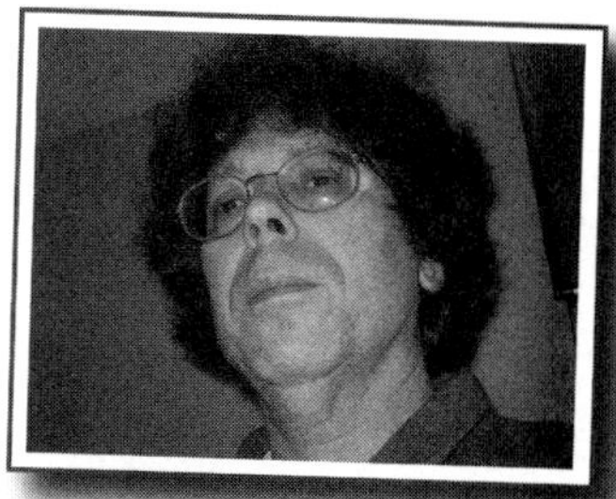

Mike Loukides

Sometimes you know that a chapter is almost right, but there's some nagging detail that is missing. Those are the times when I turn to my editor, **Mike Loukides**; he always sees to know just what's missing. This is our fourth book together, and we're already planning the fifth and sixth.

My heartfelt thanks go out to my team of O'Reilly co-conspirators: **Greg Corrin** led the way on marketing, and in particular kicked butt the last week of writing. **Ellie Volkhausen** did that first cover design so long ago, and **Mike Kohnke** and **Karen Montgomery** took the cover to another level for Head Rush. Thanks to **Colleen Gorman** for doing another amazing copyedit—you just keeping doing these Head First books, and I love that. **Sue Willing, Ron Bilodeau**, and **Marlowe Shaeffer** took care of making sure the printer was happy, and that's no small task.

Greg Corrin

It's really no accident that the name "O'Reilly" is on the cover. **Tim O'Reilly** took a chance, and keeps taking chances, on this series. Tim, you'll never know how honored I am to be a part of this series.

Kathy Sierra

Bert Bates

Kathy Sierra and Bert Bates:

You simple can't do one of these books without spending serious time talking to **Kathy Sierra** and **Bert Bates**, the geniuses who created the Head First series. Bert and Kathy both did hard time the last week of this project, staying up late chatting with me on how to make each page just that little bit better. The book wouldn't be the same without you guys, and your friendship is worth even more than that!

* The large number of acknowledgments is because we're testing the theory that everyone mentioned in a book acknowledgment will buy at least one copy, probably more, what with relatives and everything. If you'd like to be in the acknowledgment of our *next* book, and you have a large family, write to us.

1 Web Applications for a New Generation

Using Ajax

Put a new shine on your web applications. Tired of clunky web interfaces and waiting around for a page to reload? Well, it's about time to give your web apps that pine-scented desktop application feel. What are we talking about? Just the newest thing to hit the Web: **Ajax**—asynchronous JavaScript and XML—and your ticket to building **rich Internet applications** that are more *interactive*, *responsive*, and *easy to use*. So, grab your trial-size Ajax, included with every copy of Head Rush Ajax: we're about to put some polish on your web apps.

The Web, ~~Reloaded~~

Actually, we're getting rid of page reloads in this chapter...

Are your customers tired of waiting around when they place an order on your site? Are you getting complaints that every time a button is pushed, the page reloads? Then it's time to get with the program, and take your programming to the next level. Welcome to the next generation of web apps, where **JavaScript**, some **dynamic HTML**, and a little bit of **XML** can make your applications feel like dynamic, responsive desktop apps.

Let's take a look at the kind of applications you (and your customers) are used to:

The old way (think 1999)

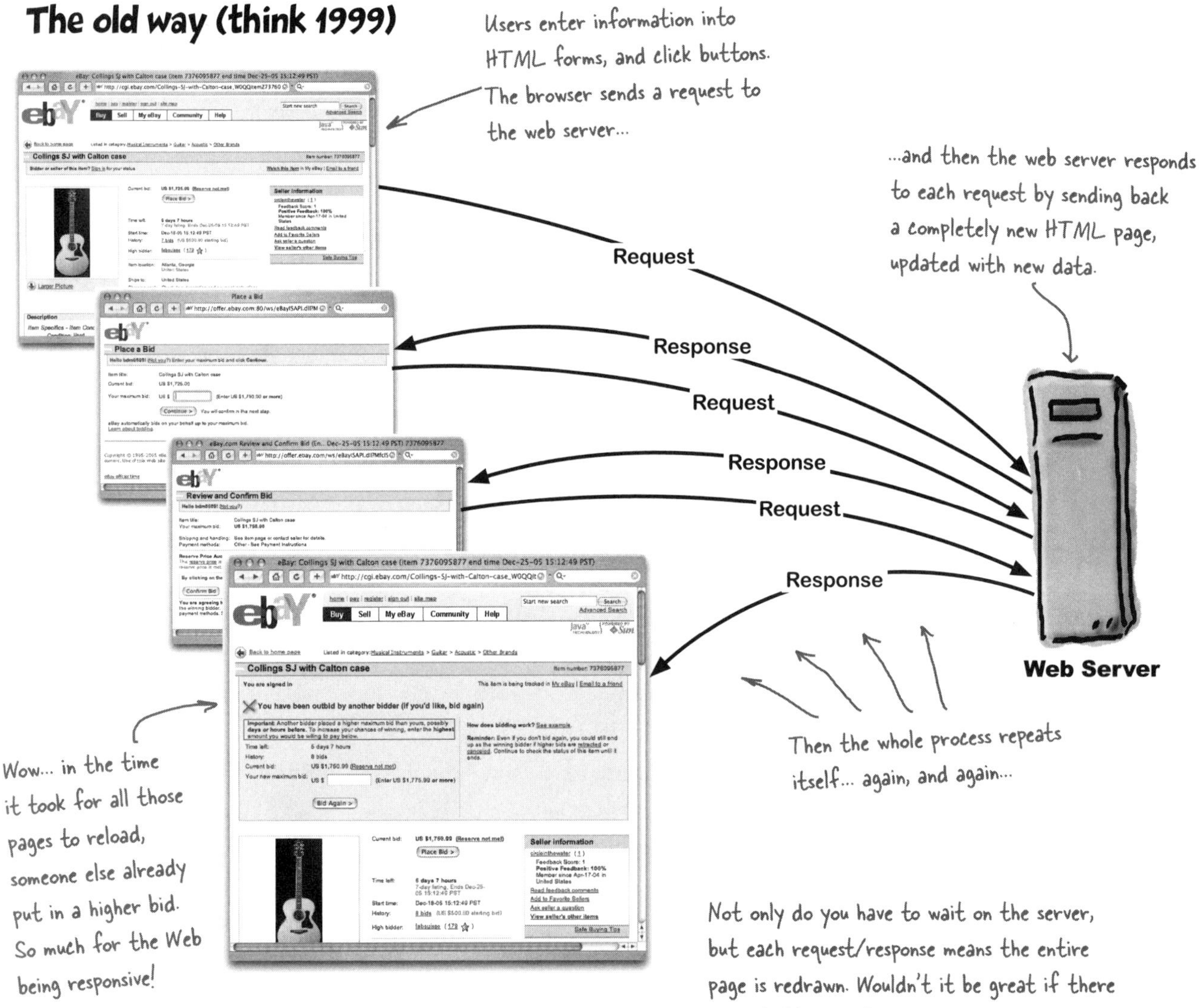

Users enter information into HTML forms, and click buttons. The browser sends a request to the web server...
...and then the web server responds to each request by sending back a completely new HTML page, updated with new data.
Request
Response
Request
Response
Request
Response
Web Server
Then the whole process repeats itself... again, and again...
Wow... in the time it took for all those pages to reload, someone else already put in a higher bid. So much for the Web being responsive!

Not only do you have to wait on the server, but each request/response means the entire page is redrawn. Wouldn't it be great if there was a better way?

Welcome to the new millenium!

Anybody can program using the same old request/response model. But if you want **faster apps** that feel like you're **working on a desktop**, you need something new—you need **Ajax**, a completely different approach to web programming:

No more waiting around...

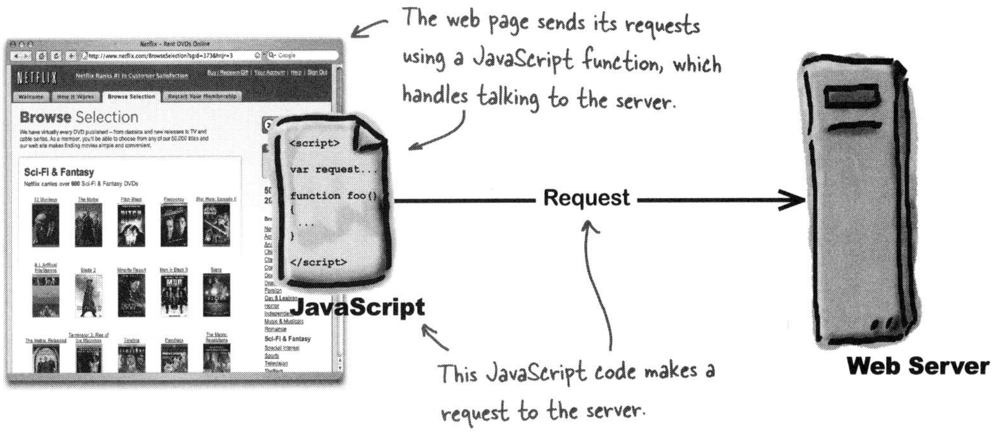

...when you're using Ajax apps

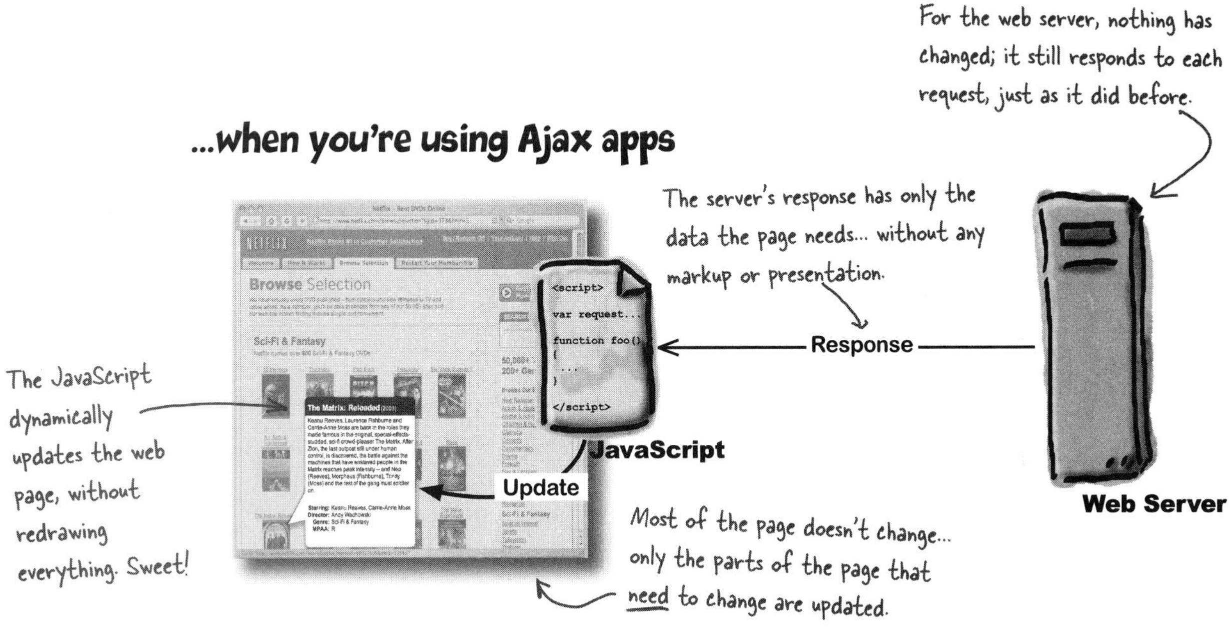

For the web server, nothing has changed; it still responds to each request, just as it did before.
The server's response has only the data the page needs... without any markup or presentation.
Response
JavaScript
Update
Web Server
The JavaScript dynamically updates the web page, without redrawing everything. Sweet!
Most of the page doesn't change... only the parts of the page that need to change are updated.

Not so fast, buddy... you said these new apps would be more responsive. But we're still waiting around for that JavaScript code to finish running, right?

Ajax apps are asynchronous, too

If you haven't guessed by now, we're talking about how you can use Ajax to build killer web apps. So far, you've seen how Ajax applications can talk to a web server without the browser reloading and redrawing the entire page all the time. But there's a lot more to Ajax than improved user interfaces.

On top of ditching those annoying page reloads, the JavaScript in an Ajax application talks to the web server *asynchronously*. In other words, the JavaScript makes a request to the server, but you can still type in web forms, and even click buttons—all while the web server is still working in the background. Then, when the server's done, your code can update just the part of the page that's changed. But *you're* never waiting around. That's the power of **asynchronous requests**! Combine that with updating pages **without reloading** them, and you've got Ajax applications.

Don't worry if you didn't get all this; we'll talk a lot more about asynchronous programming in the coming chapters.

FREQUENTLY ASKED QUESTIONS

Q: OK, I'm confused. So now we're *not* using a request/response model?

A: Actually, your pages are still making requests and getting responses. You're just using a different approach in how you make those requests and handle the responses—now you use JavaScript to make the actual request, instead of just submitting a web form.

Q: Why not just submit the form normally? What does using Ajax really do for us?

A: The JavaScript code in an Ajax application sends your requests to be processed by the server, *but doesn't wait for an answer.* Even better, JavaScript can also work with the server's response, instead of reloading the entire page when the server is finished with your request.

Q: So how does the page ever get back a response?

A: That's where the asynchronous part of Ajax comes in. When the server sends back a response, JavaScript can update a page with new values, change an image, or even take the user to a whole new web page. And the user never has to wait around while all this is going on.

Q: So I should use Ajax for all of my requests?

A: There are still plenty of times when you'll want to use traditional web programming. For instance, when a form is totally filled out, you can let the user click a Submit button, and then send the entire form to your web server, without using Ajax.

But, you'll use Ajax for most of your dynamic page processing, like changing images, updating fields, and responding to users. If you only need to update part of a page, then Ajax is the way to go.

Q: You said something about XML?

A: Sometimes, your JavaScript will use XML to talk back and forth with the server. But you don't always need to use XML for your requests. We'll spend a lot more time looking at when and how you'll use XML in later chapters.

Q: And AJAX is just an acronym for Asynchronous JavaScript and XML?

A: Actually, it's "Ajax", and it's not an acronym. Although it sort of looks like one... and it does fit... hmmm. Well, don't ask us, we didn't come up with the term!

Jesse James Garrett, who came up with the term "Ajax", said he didn't mean for it to be an acronym. Go figure!

Umm, excuse me... if you're done with all this theory, I think I could use some of that Ajax over here.

Now that I'm selling my custom snowboards online, I put together a web form that keeps up with my sales. But every time I want an update, the whole screen reloads. You think all this Ajax stuff can help?

Katie, snowboard queen and web entrepreneur.

Here's the current, non-Ajax version of Katie's app, which is just a web form that submits requests to a PHP script.

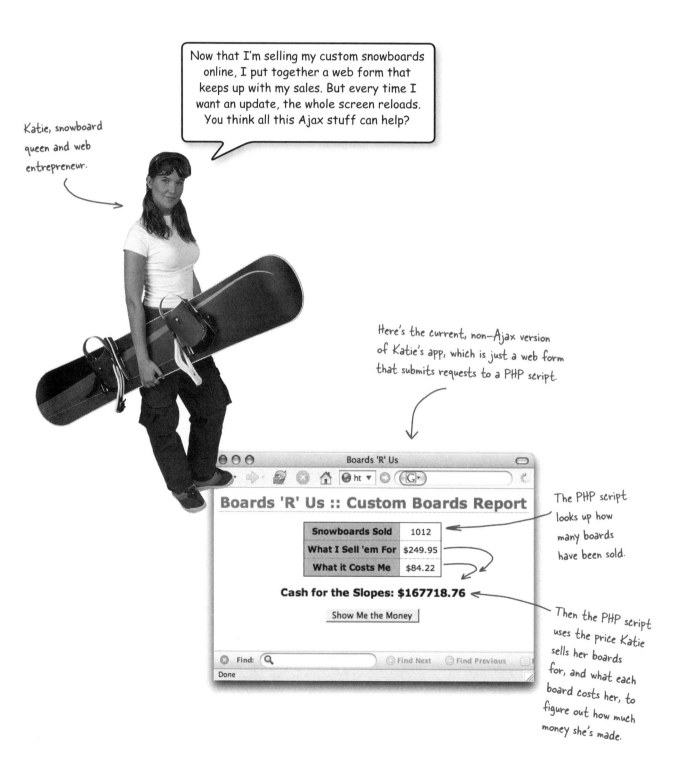

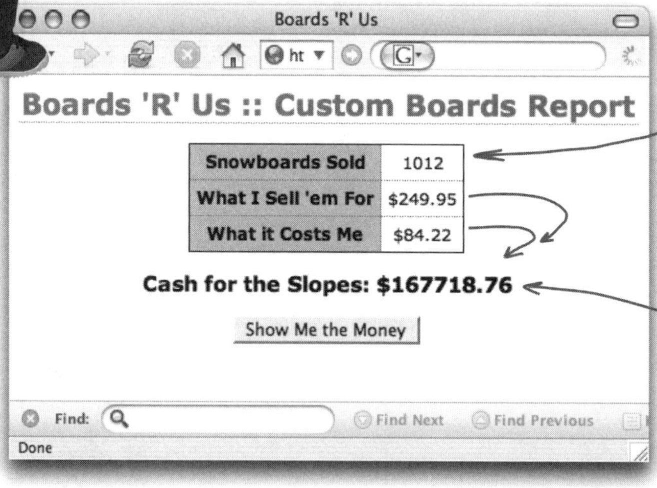

The PHP script looks up how many boards have been sold.

Then the PHP script uses the price Katie sells her boards for, and what each board costs her, to figure out how much money she's made.

"Reloads? We don't need no stinking reloads."

There's nothing more annoying than an application that redraws the whole page everytime you push a button or type in a value. In Katie's report, only a few numbers are changing, but the entire page has to be redrawn.

First, let's figure out why all that reloading is going on...

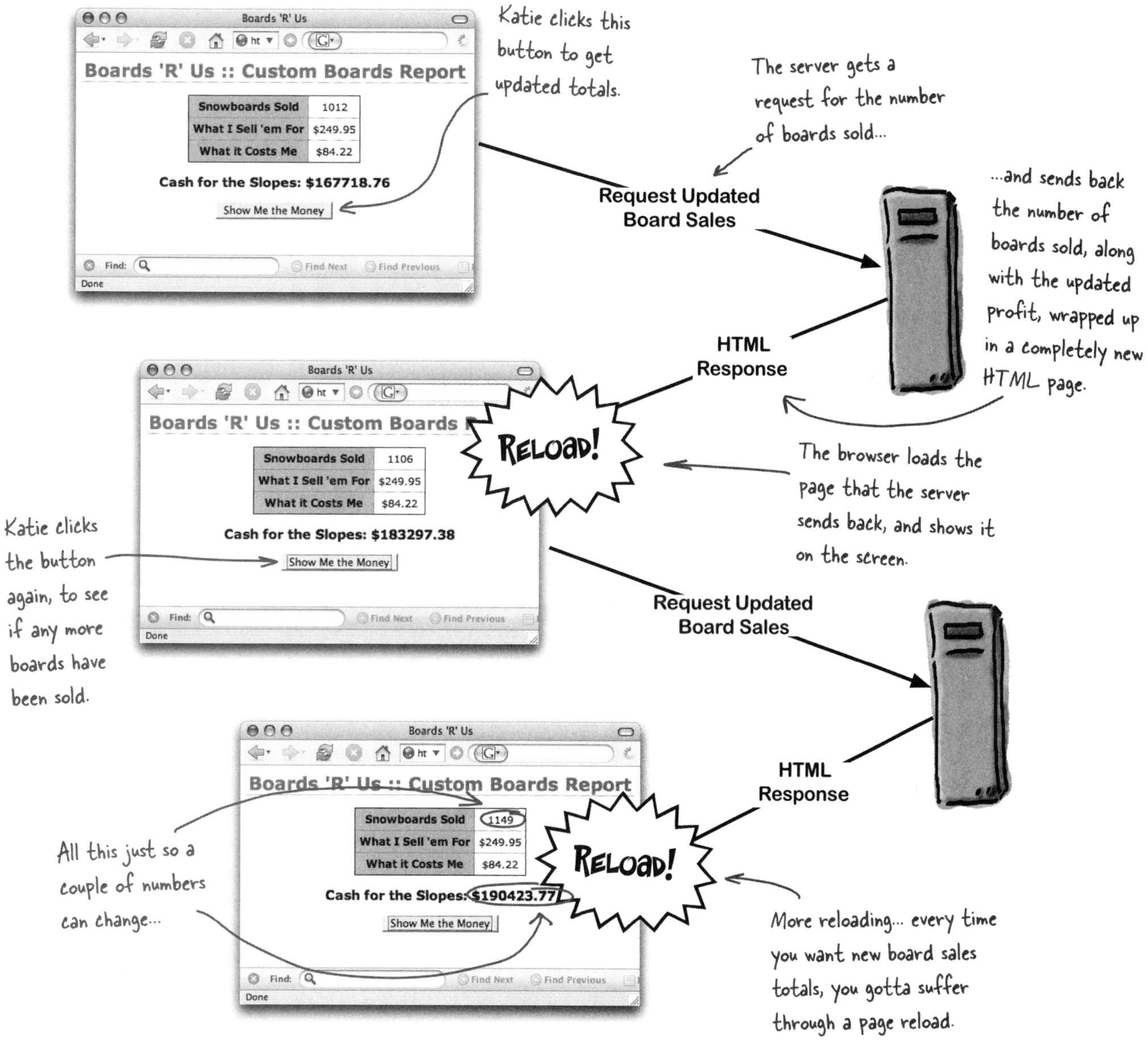
Boards 'R' Us
Boards 'R' Us :: Custom Boards Report
Snowboards Sold 1012
What I Sell 'em For $249.95
What it Costs Me $84.22
Cash for the Slopes: $167718.76
Show Me the Money
Katie clicks this button to get updated totals.
The server gets a request for the number of boards sold...
Request Updated Board Sales
...and sends back the number of boards sold, along with the updated profit, wrapped up in a completely new HTML page.
HTML Response
Boards 'R' Us :: Custom Boards
Snowboards Sold 1106
What I Sell 'em For $249.95
What it Costs Me $84.22
Cash for the Slopes: $183297.38
Show Me the Money
RELOAD!
The browser loads the page that the server sends back, and shows it on the screen.
Katie clicks the button again, to see if any more boards have been sold.
Request Updated Board Sales
HTML Response
Boards 'R' Us :: Custom Boards Report
Snowboards Sold 1149
What I Sell 'em For $249.95
What it Costs Me $84.22
Cash for the Slopes: $190423.77
Show Me the Money
RELOAD!
All this just so a couple of numbers can change...
More reloading... every time you want new board sales totals, you gotta suffer through a page reload.

Ajax to the rescue

Do you see what the problem is? Every time Katie wants to find out the latest number of boards sold, the entire screen is redrawn, and she's left with the Internet version of snow blindness.

Didn't you say that Ajax will let me update the screen without all that reloading? Something about updating just part of the page?

Use Ajax to fix the web report...

Let's change Katie's report to use Ajax to send the request for updated board sales. Then we can get the response from the server, and update the web page using JavaScript and dynamic HTML. No more page reloading, and Katie will be a happy snowboarder again.

Maybe you'll even score a free board...

Work It Through

You're going to need a couple of JavaScript functions to turn Katie's report into an Ajax-powered app. Below are the names of three JavaScript functions. Draw a line connecting each function name to what you think it will do in the final version of the Boards app.

getBoardsSold()

updatePage()

createRequest()

Create a new object for talking to the web server.

Ask the server for the latest snowboard sales figures.

Set the number of boards sold and the cash that Katie's made to the most current values.

Answers on page 9.

Reworking the Boards 'R' Us report

Let's use Ajax to revamp Katie's web report. With Ajax, we can get rid of all those page reloads, and cut down on how much data the server has to send to the report. Here's what you're going to do in the rest of this chapter:

1 Create a new object to make requests to the server

First, you'll need a JavaScript function to create an object that will let you make requests to the server, and get a response back. Let's call this new function **`createRequest()`**.

2 Write a JavaScript function to request new board sales totals

Next, you'll use the object you just created in Step 1 to make a request to the web server. We can put this code in another function, called **`getBoardsSold()`**, and run it when Katie clicks the "Show Me the Money" button.

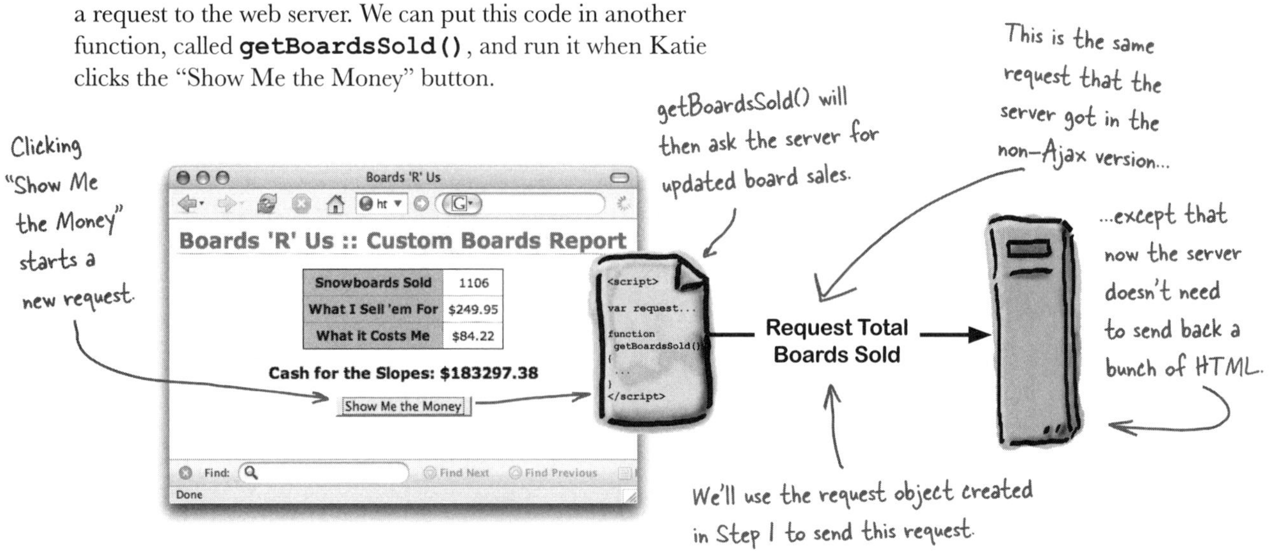

❸ Update Katie's report with new numbers using JavaScript

Now you can update the report with the current number of boards sold, and figure out how much cash Katie's made. Let's take care of this another new JavaScript function that we'll write; we'll call this function **updatePage()**.

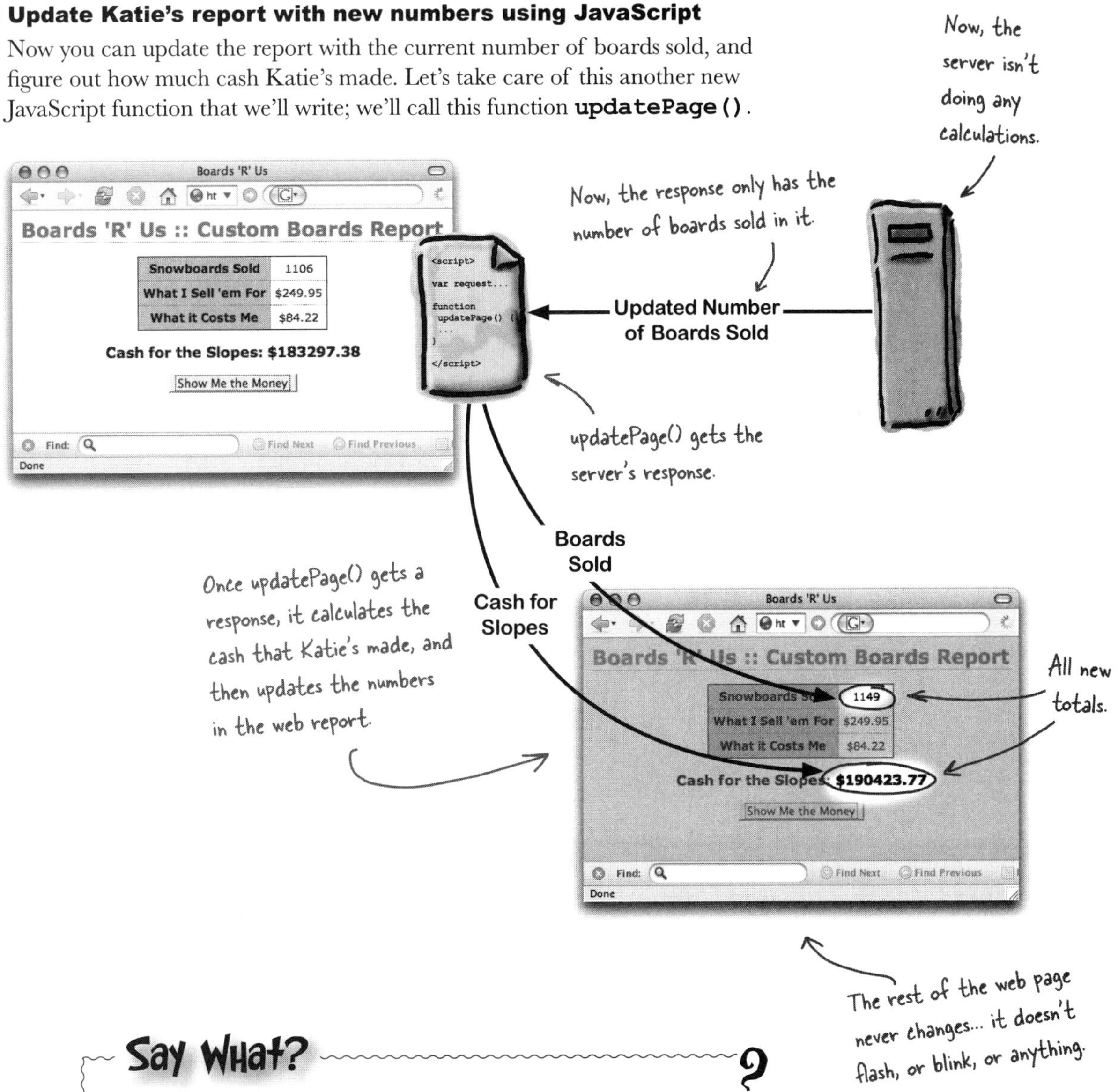

Now, the server isn't doing any calculations.
Now, the response only has the number of boards sold in it.
Updated Number of Boards Sold
updatePage() gets the server's response.
Boards Sold
Cash for Slopes
Once updatePage() gets a response, it calculates the cash that Katie's made, and then updates the numbers in the web report.
All new totals.
The rest of the web page never changes... it doesn't flash, or blink, or anything.
Boards 'R' Us
Boards 'R' Us :: Custom Boards Report
Snowboards Sold 1106
What I Sell 'em For $249.95
What it Costs Me $84.22
Cash for the Slopes: $183297.38
Show Me the Money
Snowboards Sold 1149
Cash for the Slopes: $190423.77

Say What?

Don't worry if you don't understand everything that's going on... especially with the actual request. We're going to cover all of this in detail in this book. For now, just get an idea of the basics of how an Ajax application works. Pay careful attention to how the web page uses JavaScript to make a request, and how the server only returns a single number, and not HTML.

We'll get to coding in just a few pages. First, let's take a short detour...

The highlight reel: Chapter 1

So you're probably thinking, "What's a highlight reel doing at the beginning of the chapter? That's not normal." You're right... but **this is Head Rush, remember?** Before you go any further, stop and read each of these highlights out loud.

Then, go on to the next page, and get ready to load these concepts into your brain. We'll work through each of these in detail throughout this chapter.

- **Asynchronous applications make requests using a JavaScript object, and not a form submit.**

- **Your requests and responses are handled by the web browser, not directly by your JavaScript code.**

- **Once the web browser gets a response to your asynchronous request, it will "call back" your JavaScript with the server's response.**

We're not kidding... don't go any further until you've read these OUT LOUD. Trust us, nobody will think you're weird (well, maybe someone will, but then they'll be impressed with how smart you're becoming, too!)

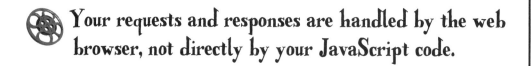

HTML Refresher

Feeling a little rusty on your **<div>**s and **<span>**s? We're going to dive into some HTML on the next page, so before we do, here's a quick refresher course on two of the coolest HTML elements you'll ever run across.

<div>

A **<div>** is a container element that can hold related elements, and allow you to style all those elements with one CSS rule.

```
<div id="menu">
 <a href="home.html">home</a>
 <a href="books.html">writing</a>
 <a href="links.html">resources</a>
 <a href="lib.html">library</a>
</div>
```

You can refer to a <div>'s id in your CSS to style everything within the <div> at one time.

Use a <div> to group together elements with a similar purpose.

<span>

<span> lets you separate a bit of inline text from its surroundings. You can style your **<span>** elements using CSS, and set off text easily.

<span> elements can set off text, but don't start new paragraphs or blocks.

```
<ul>
 <li><span class="cd">Buddha Bar</span>,
   <span class="artist">Claude Challe</span></li>
 <li><span class="cd">When It Falls</span>,
   <span class="artist">Zero 7</span></li>
 ...
```

<span> elements don't create a new block of text, but can still be styled with CSS.

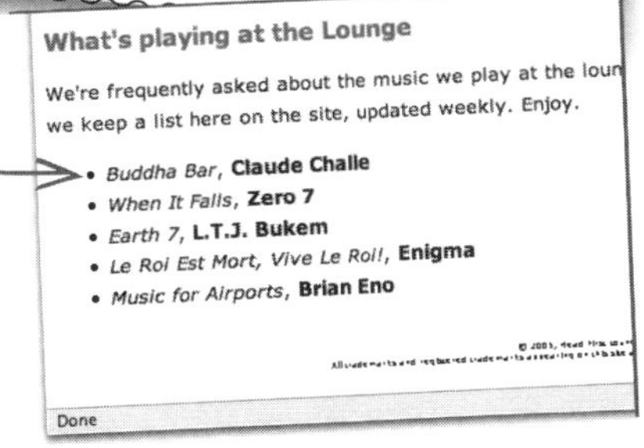

Reviewing the Boards 'R' Us HTML

First things first... Katie already has a web page, so let's take a look at it. Then you can begin to add in all the JavaScript code we've been talking about.

Here's what Katie's page looks like so far:

```
<html>
 <head>
  <title>Boards 'R' Us</title>
  <link rel="stylesheet" type="text/css" href="boards.css" />
 </head>

 <body>
  <h1>Boards 'R' Us :: Custom Board Reports</h1>
  <div id="boards">
   <table>
    <tr><th>Snowboards Sold</th>
     <td><span id="boards-sold">1012</span></td></tr>
    <tr><th>What I Sell 'em For</th>
     <td>$<span id="price">249.95</span></td></tr>
    <tr><th>What it Costs Me</th>
     <td>$<span id="cost">84.22</span></td></tr>
   </table>
   <h2>Cash for the Slopes:
    $<span id="cash">167718.76</span></h2>
   <form method="GET" action="getUpdatedBoardSales.php">
    <input value="Show Me the Money" type="submit" />
   </form>
  </div>
 </body>
</html>
```

Katie's read "Head First HTML with CSS & XHTML", so she's all over this stuff...

You'll need <script> tags here...

Katie's using an external CSS stylesheet.

Here's the total sales figure you'll need to update...

...and then you can figure out a new net profit, too.

Here's that button Katie pushes for updated totals. Right now, it submits the form, but you're going to change that soon.

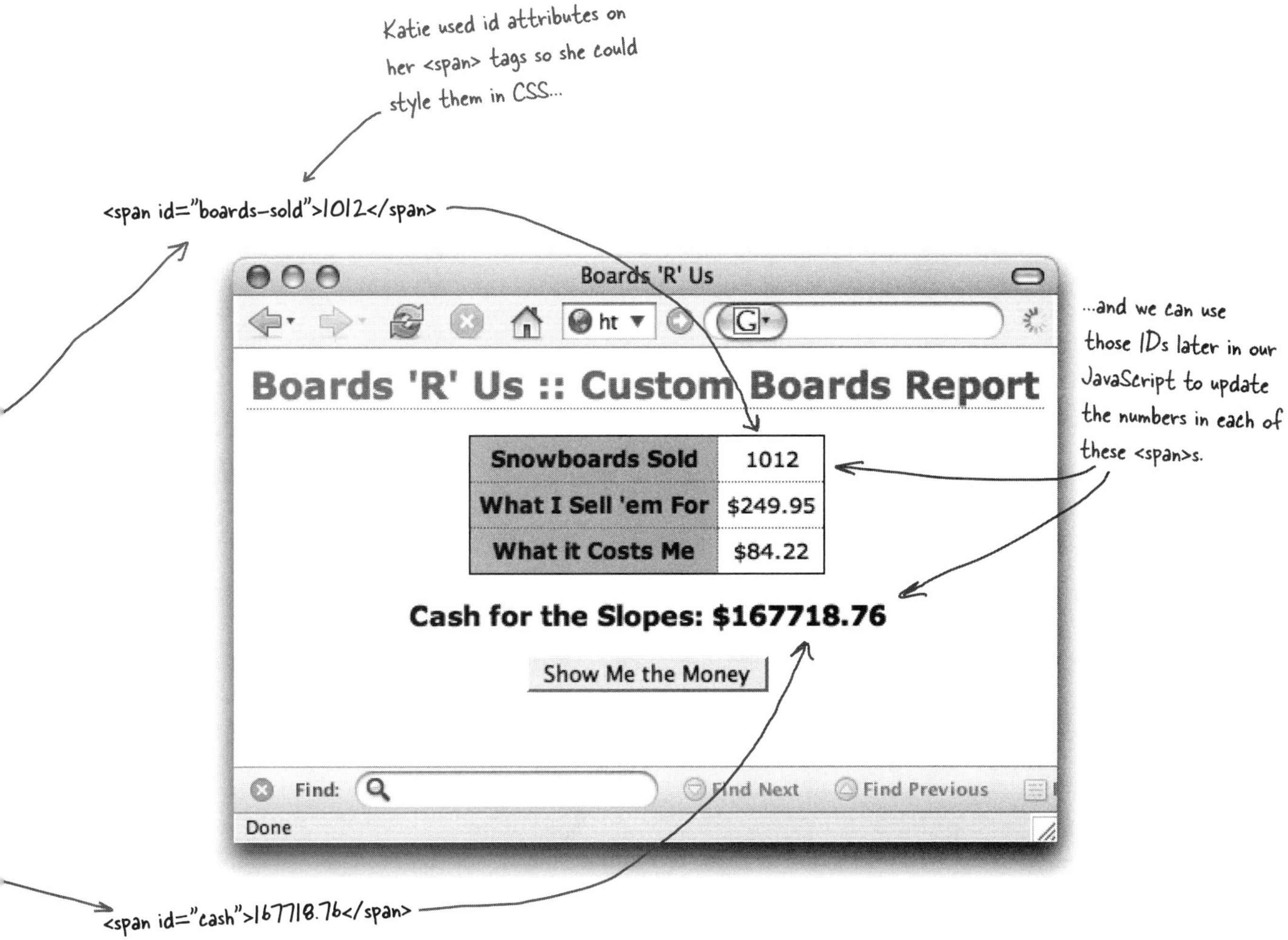
Katie used id attributes on her <span> tags so she could style them in CSS...
<span id="boards-sold">1012</span>
Boards 'R' Us
Boards 'R' Us :: Custom Boards Report
Snowboards Sold
1012
What I Sell 'em For
$249.95
What it Costs Me
$84.22
Cash for the Slopes: $167718.76
Show Me the Money
Find:
Find Next
Find Previous
Done
...and we can use those IDs later in our JavaScript to update the numbers in each of these <span>s.
<span id="cash">167718.76</span>

Just Do It

It's time to take some action. Download the examples for the book at **`http://www.headfirstlabs.com`**, and find the **`chapter01/boards/`** folder. Open up the **`boards.html`** file in your web browser. It should look just like Katie's page above.

Step 1: Creating a request object

Let's get back to updating Katie's web report. First up, you need a function that creates a new object to make requests to the server. This turns out to be a bit tricky, because different browsers have different ways of creating this object. To help you out, we've written some "pre-assembled" JavaScript for you. Whenever you see the Pre-Assembled JavaScript logo, it means you'll have to take some code on faith, like this code below that creates an object to make requests to the server. Trust us though—you'll learn all about this code in more detail in the chapters to come. For now, just type it in and see what it can do.

If you don't want to type this in yourself, you can find this code in create-request.txt, in the chapter01/boards examples folder...

...but you should really type this code in yourself. It will help your brain get used to writing and thinking about Ajax apps.

```
var request = null;

function createRequest() {
  try {
    request = new XMLHttpRequest();
  } catch (trymicrosoft) {
    try {
      request = new ActiveXObject("Msxml2.XMLHTTP");
    } catch (othermicrosoft) {
      try {
        request = new ActiveXObject("Microsoft.XMLHTTP");
      } catch (failed) {
        request = null;
      }
    }
  }

  if (request == null)
    alert("Error creating request object!");
}
```

Annotations:

- Here's a variable to hold the request object.
- This line tries to create a new request object.
- This is the type of the request object.
- These two lines try and create the request object, too, but in a way that works on Internet Explorer.
- If something goes wrong, this makes sure the request variable is still set to null.
- Now, you can check if request is still null. If it is, something went wrong in the code...
- ...and we can spit out an error message to users with JavaScript's alert() function.

Pre-Assembled JavaScript

Go ahead and add this code into the <head> element of your HTML in boards.html. Don't forget, you'll need to add the <script> and </script> tags, too.

```
<head>
 <title>Boards 'R' Us</title>
 <link rel="stylesheet" type="text/css" href="boards.css" />
 <script language="javascript" type="text/javascript">

 </script>
</head>
```

All that pre-assembled JavaScript goes in here.

These tell the browser that you're adding some scripting, and that you're using JavaScript as the scripting language.

Frequently Asked Questions

Q: Am I supposed to understand exactly what that code does yet?

A: No, you don't need to understand all of this code yet. For now, just get a general idea of how this looks; we'll explain it in detail in Chapter 2.

Q: What is null? I saw that in the pre-assembled JavaScript, and wasn't sure what that means.

A: `null` is a special value, and actually means an *empty value*, or a non-existent reference. In other words, it's sort of like an aniti-value. But don't confuse `null` with "0" or "false"—those both are *non*-empty values, and aren't the same as a `null` value.

Q: Is the request object called "XMLHttpRequest" or "ActiveXObject"?

A: It could be either. We'll talk a lot more about this in the next chapter, but the short answer is that you have to use different object names for different types of web browsers.

Q: So do my users have to use a certain browser to use my Ajax apps?

A: No, as long as your users have JavaScript enabled in their web browser, this code should work without any problems.So your Ajax apps will run just fine on Firefox, Mozilla, Internet Explorer, Safari, Netscape, and Opera.

Q: What if someone has JavaScript disabled in their browser?

A: Unfortunately, Ajax applications require JavaScript to run. So users who have JavaScript disabled aren't going to be able to use your Ajax applications.

JavaScript is usually enabled in browsers by default, so anyone who has disabled JavaScript probably knows what they're doing, and could turn it back on if they wanted to use your Ajax app.

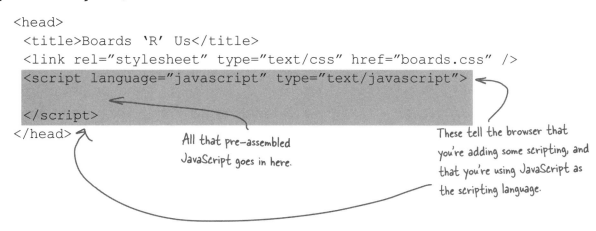

createRequest() getBoardsSold() updatePage()

Step 2: Requesting updated sales

Now that you can get a request object with **`createRequest()`**, you're ready for the next step: writing the **`getBoardsSold()`** JavaScript function. This function will use the new object to request the total number of boards sold from the server. Let's figure out what this function needs to do, and then we can get back to coding Katie's app. Remember our diagram? Here's the step we're working on:

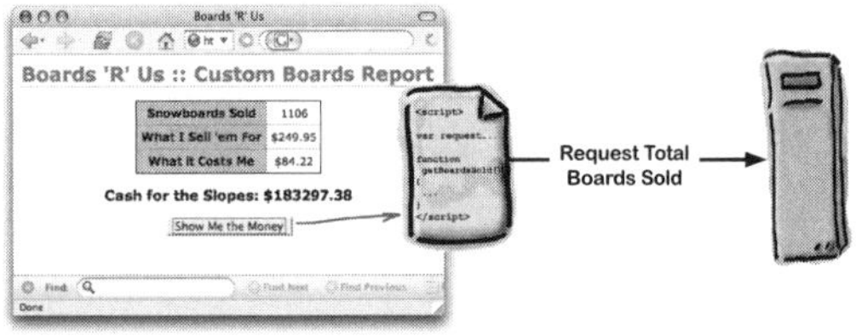

Here's what you'll need to do to make **`getBoardsSold()`** work:

You can use the pre-assembled JavaScript from the last two pages to take care of this.

(a) Create a new request object by calling the createRequest() function.

Katie already has this URL in her form, so this should be simple enough.

(b) Figure out what URL you need to connect to so you can get updated board sales.

(c) Set up the request object to make a connection.

Here's where you'll use that request object you created in createRequest().

(d) Request an updated number of boards sold.

You can use this number later, in Step 3, when you update the page with new values. You'll tackle this in just a little while.

Just Do It

Open up your **`boards.html`** file, and add a new JavaScript function called **`getBoardsSold()`**, right after **`createRequest()`**. Then, see if you can add a line of JavaScript in **`getBoardsSold()`** to create a new request object (that's Step "a" from above). If you're stuck, check the answers in the back of this chapter, on page 61.

Be sure and make these changes to your copy of **`boards.html`** before you go to the next page.

Adding the getBoardsSold() function

If you did the exercise on the previous page, you should have some code in your **boards.html** page that looks something like this:

```
<script language="javascript" type="text/javascript">
  var request = null;

  function createRequest() {
    // pre-assembled JavaScript
  }

  function getBoardsSold() {
    createRequest();
  }
</script>
```

Remember, all of the JavaScript code is between the <script> and </script> tags.

This is your request variable; once your code calls createRequest(), this variable will point to a new request object.

Here's createRequest(), which you should have added a few pages back.

This is the new JavaScript function...

...and here's where the request object is created, using the pre-assembled JavaScript.

Sending the request to the right URL

So what's next? You've got an object that you can use to request the board sales from the server, but how do you make that request? First, you need to tell the object where to send the request—in other words, it needs to know what program on Katie's server to send the request to. So you need to tell it the URL of the script running on the web server.

And where do we get that URL? You can find it in Katie's web form:

```
<form method="GET" action="getUpdatedBoardSales.php">
  <input value="Show Me the Money" type="submit" />
</form>
```

Here's the URL of the PHP script we need to make a request to.

Here's the <form> part of Katie's web report HTML.

But doesn't the PHP script return a bunch of HTML right now? I thought we only wanted the number of boards sold for the Ajax version of the app.

This is bonus credit for those of you who are into PHP. If you don't know PHP, it's OK... just take a quick look, and keep going. You don't need to understand this script to learn Ajax or follow the examples in the book.

PHP ...at a glance

Here's a quick look at the PHP that Katie's using for her Boards app. Remember, we're not going to explain how this all works... but here's what's going on when a request is made for updated board sales.

```
<?php

// Connect to database
$conn = @mysql_connect("mysql.headfirstlabs.com",
                       "secret", "really-secret");
if (!$conn)
  die("Error connecting to MySQL: " . mysql_error());

if (!mysql_select_db("headfirst", $conn))
  die("Error selecting Head First database: " . mysql_error());

$select = 'SELECT boardsSold';
$from   = '  FROM boardsrus';
$queryResult = @mysql_query($select . $from);
if (!$queryResult)
  die('Error retrieving total boards sold from database.');

while ($row = mysql_fetch_array($queryResult)) {
  $totalSold = $row['boardsSold'];
}
$price = 249.95;
$cost = 84.22;
$cashPerBoard = $price - $cost;
$cash = $totalSold * $cashPerBoard;

mysql_close($conn);

?>

<html>
 <head>  <title>Boards 'R' Us</title>
  <link rel="stylesheet" type="text/css" href="boards.css" />
 </head>

 <body>
  <h1>Boards 'R' Us :: Custom Boards Report</h1>
```

The first part of the script makes a connection to the Boards 'R' Us database.

This part of the script handles getting the latest sales totals from the database.

If you wanted, you could store these values in the database, too.

The amount of profit on each board is figured out here.

Here comes all that HTML we've been talking about...

```
  <div id="boards">
   <table>
    <tr><th>Snowboards Sold</th>
     <td><span id="boards-sold">
<?php
  print $totalSold;
?>
    </span></td></tr>
    <tr><th>What I Sell 'em For</th>
     <td>$<span id="price">
<?php
  print $price;
?>
    </span></td></tr>
    <tr><th>What it Costs Me</th>
     <td>$<span id="cost">
<?php
  print $cost;
?>
     </span></td></tr>
   </table>
   <h2>Cash for the Slopes:
    $<span id="cash">
<?php
  print $cash;
?>
    </span></h2>
   <form method="GET" action="getUpdatedBoardSales.php">
    <input value="Show Me the Money" type="submit" />
   </form>
  </div>
 </body>
</html>
```

Lots and lots more HTML output by the PHP script...

The PHP outputs the values it got from the database along with the HTML for the report.

What the Heck?

All this code does is look up how many boards have been sold, figure out the total cash Katie's made, and then return an HTML form with the updated totals sales and cash figures.

It's also OK if you don't know PHP, or haven't worked with databases before. In just a few pages, we'll give you a version of the script that runs without a database, so you can run Katie's web report for yourself.

What the server *used* to do...

Remember how the non-Ajax version of Katie's report works? Every time a request is made to the PHP script, it has to return the number of boards sold, along with an entirely new HTML page. Flip back a page, and notice that over half the PHP script is just HTML! Here's another look at what's going on:

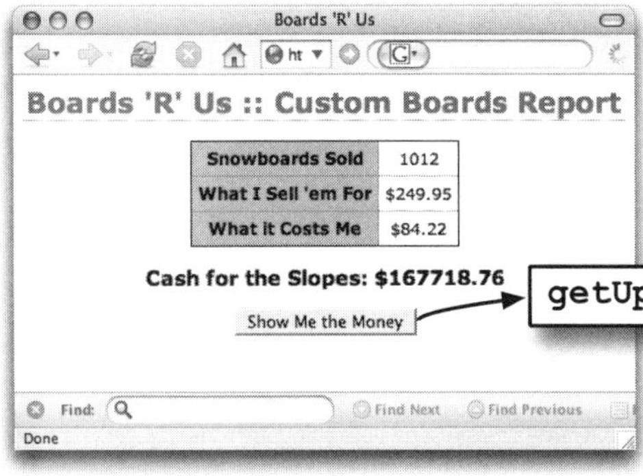

The URL for Katie's script, from her web form.

getUpdatedBoardSales.php

All of the HTML that the server has to return for each request.

Katie's server, having to deal with a lot of HTML content..

```
<html>
 <head>
  <title>Boards 'R' Us</title>
  <link rel="stylesheet" type="text/css" href="boards.css" />
 </head>

 <body>
  <h1>Boards 'R' Us :: Custom Boards Report</h1>
  <div id="boards">
   <table>
    <tr><th>Snowboards Sold</th>
     <td><span id="boards-sold">1149</span></td></tr>
    <tr><th>What I Sell 'em For</th>
     <td>$<span id="price">249.95</span></td></tr>
    <tr><th>What it Costs Me</th>
     <td>$<span id="cost">84.22</span></td></tr>
   </table>
   <h2>Cash for the Slopes:
    $<span id="cash">190423.27</span></h2>
   <form method="GET" action="getUpdatedBoardSales.php">
    <input value="Show Me the Money" type="submit" />
   </form>
  </div>
 </body>
</html>
```

All of this HTML, and the only thing that changed is the number of boards sold, and the updated cash total!

What the server should do now

When you're writing Ajax apps, the server doesn't need to send all that HTML back in its response. Since you'll use JavaScript to update the web page, all you need from the server is the raw data. In Katie's app, that means that all we want is the number of boards sold. Then, you can figure out the cash that Katie has made with some simple JavaScript.

A much happier, stress-free server.

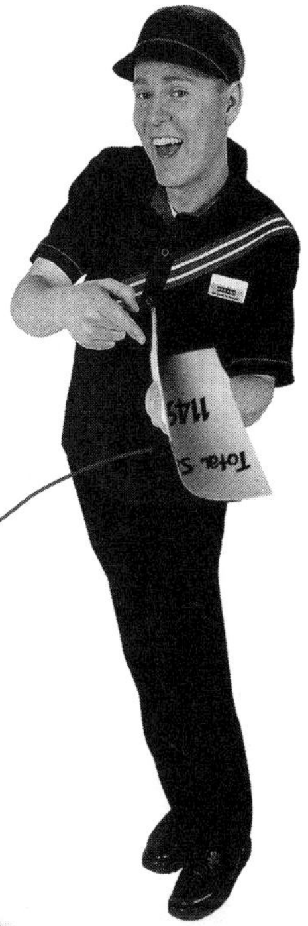

`getUpdatedBoardSales-ajax.php`

The URL to the new, Ajax-ready version of the PHP.

1149

Katie's server doesn't have nearly as much information to send back to her web form.

The total number of boards sold.

That's all the server sends back now? I'll bet my report will run faster with Ajax! I'll have my PHP guy take care of changing the server-side script right away.

PHP ...at a second glance

Katie's PHP script got a lot simpler when all it needed to do was return the total number of boards sold. Take a look:

```
<?php

// Connect to database
$conn = @mysql_connect("mysql.headfirstlabs.com",
                       "secret", "really-secret");
if (!$conn)
  die("Error connecting to MySQL: " . mysql_error());

if (!mysql_select_db("headfirst", $conn))
  die("Error selecting Head First database: " . mysql_error());

$select = 'SELECT boardsSold';
$from   = '  FROM boardsrus';
$queryResult = @mysql_query($select . $from);
if (!$queryResult)
  die('Error retrieving total boards sold from database.');

while ($row = mysql_fetch_array($queryResult)) {
  $totalSold = $row['boardsSold'];
}

echo $totalSold;

mysql_close($conn);

?>
```

Almost everything in the first part of the script is the same as the old version.

Now, instead of a bunch of HTML, the script just returns a single number: the number of boards sold.

* Notice that the code figuring out the cash that Katie made went away. Your JavaScript will take care of those calculations now.

Just Do It

It's time to give Katie's PHP script an Ajax upgrade. Open up the examples, and find **getUpdatedBoardSales-ajax.php** in the **chapter01/boards/** directory. This is a version of **getUpdatedBoardSales.php** that only returns the number of boards sold, without any HTML in the response. It also works without a database, so you don't need to set one up to use this PHP script. Make sure this file is in the same directory as your **boards.html** file; we'll be using this new version of the script in just a moment.

The new script's URL

Now that you've got a PHP script that only returns the number of boards sold, instead of a bunch of HTML, we just need to make a request to that script. Remember, you want to send your request to the new version of the PHP script, and only returns the sales total, not an entire HTML page.

Store the URL of this new PHP script in a JavaScript variable, like this:

```
function getBoardsSold() {
  createRequest();
  var url = "getUpdatedBoardSales-ajax.php";
}
```

Here's your JavaScript function.

This takes care of creating the new request object.

This is the URL of the Ajax-ready version of the PHP script.

createRequest() getBoardsSold() updatePage()

Initializing the connection

You've got a request object, and a variable with the URL to connect to. Now you just need to tell the request object how to connect to the server, and give it that URL as the address to connect to. Here's how you do that:

```
function getBoardsSold() {
  createRequest();
  var url = "getUpdatedBoardSales-ajax.php";
  request.open("GET", url, true);
}
```

Here's where you start to use that request object created in the createRequest() function.

This line handles initializing the connection, and tells the request object how to connect to the server.

Let's break that down a bit...

The open() method initializes a connection...

```
request.open(
```

...and then "GET" indicates how to send data to the server.

```
"GET",
```

This is the URL for the PHP script running on Katie's web server.

```
url,
```

This means that the request should be asynchronous... in other words, this lets JavaScript know that it doesn't need to wait around for a response from the script. Katie's report won't freeze while the server is answering the request.

```
true);
```

These are some pretty advanced concepts. Give yourself a high five if you came up with any of these questions on your own.

LESS FREQUENTLY ASKED QUESTIONS

Q: I thought that it was better to use "POST" for web page requests.

A: POST is usually used when you are sending a server lots of data, or are completing a form submit that involves money, or placing an order. Since we're not sending any data to the PHP script, and there's no purchase being made here. it's easier to use a GET request; we'll look at POST requests a little later on.

Q: Should I ever use open() to make a synchronous request, and set that last value to "false"?

A: Sure. Sometimes you don't *want* the user to be able to keep using your page while the server is answering a request. For instance, if a user is placing an order, you probably don't want to let them do anything else until you confirm that their order was accepted.

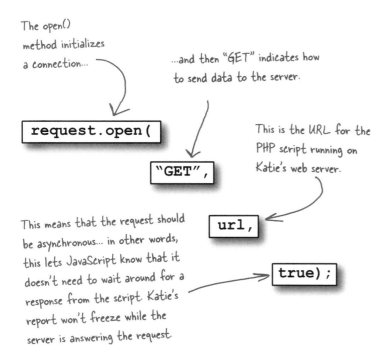

The Great Code-Comment Coupling Contest

In an effort to save programmers time and prevent confusion, code fragments are marrying their comment counterparts across the globe, providing love, companionship, and self-documentation for all.

Below, you'll find several lines of Ajax-related JavaScript. Pair each line of code up with the comment that describes what it does.

The Code

```
request.open("POST", url, true);
```

```
var request = new XMLHttpRequest();
```

```
var url = "/servlet/GetMileageServlet";
```

```
request.open("GET", url, false);
```

The Comments

/* Create a new object to talk HTTP to a web server */

/* Create a new variable and assign it the URL to a Java servlet */

/* Initialize a synchronous connection using GET */

/* Initialize an asynchronous connection using POST */

Mr. Code...

...and Mrs. Comment

So how's it coming? Are we any closer to getting my web report back online? I'd love to know how many boards I've sold.

Remember our checklist for getBoardsSold()?

You're making pretty good progress in your code. Why don't you check off what you've got done?

- ☐ Create a new request object by calling the createRequest() function.
- ☐ Figure out what URL you need to connect to so you can get updated board sales.
- ☐ Set up the request object to make a connection.
- ☐ Request an updated number of boards sold.

The Great Code-Comment Coupling Contest

Did you pair up the happy couples? Make sure you got all of these right, and if not, take your time and figure out what you missed, and why.

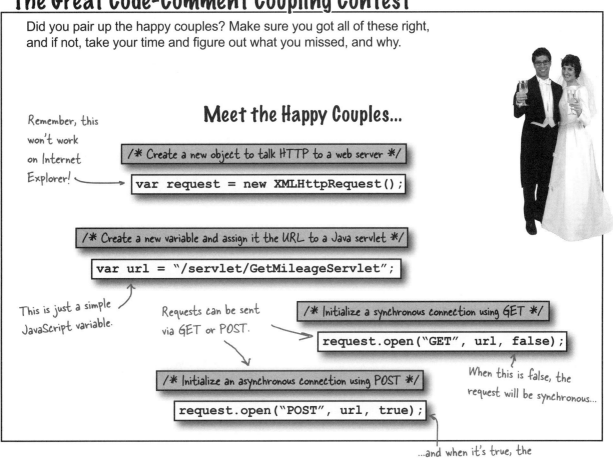

Meet the Happy Couples...

Remember, this won't work on Internet Explorer!

```
/* Create a new object to talk HTTP to a web server */
var request = new XMLHttpRequest();
```

```
/* Create a new variable and assign it the URL to a Java servlet */
var url = "/servlet/GetMileageServlet";
```

This is just a simple JavaScript variable.

Requests can be sent via GET or POST.

```
/* Initialize a synchronous connection using GET */
request.open("GET", url, false);
```

When this is false, the request will be synchronous...

```
/* Initialize an asynchronous connection using POST */
request.open("POST", url, true);
```

...and when it's true, the request is asynchronous.

Here's our checklist from page 28... only one item left to go.

- ☑ Create a new request object by calling the createRequest() function.
- ☑ Figure out what URL you need to connect to so you can get updated board sales.
- ☑ Set up the request object to make a connection.
- ☐ Request an updated number of boards sold.

We're working on this last task now.

Connecting to the web server

All right! You've got a request object, a URL, and your connection is initialized and ready to go. Now you just need to make the connection, and request the updated number of boards sold. To do that, just call **`send()`** on the **`request`** object:

```
function getBoardsSold() {
  createRequest();
  var url = "getUpdatedBoardSales-ajax.php";
  request.open("GET", url, true);
  request.send(null);
}
```

You're sending the request here...

...and this means that you're not sending any data in the request. The script doesn't need any data; it just returns the total board sales, every time it's run.

Rotate your brain (and this page) a bit, and don't miss this key point.

Asynchronous applications make requests using a JavaScript object, and not a form submit.

Are you kidding me? We did all this work, and you're telling me I'm sending **null** to the server? This is what you call next-generation programming?

The server doesn't need any data.

In this particular app, you don't need to provide the server with any information. Each request to the PHP script asks for the same thing: a single number, the total number of boards that Katie has sold. So you don't need to send the server anything but **`null`** in your request.

Remember, null means an "empty value", which is exactly what you want to send the server: nothing.

Reviewing what we've done

We've still got plenty left to do, but let's take a moment to see what's already done. Grab a cup of joe, let your brain relax, and review the first two steps in turning Katie's report into an Ajax-powered app.

This was the original task we had to complete...

1 Create a new object to make requests to the server

You added a new function, called **`createRequest()`**, that creates a new request object. The code even works on different browsers.

...and here's what you did.

2 Write a JavaScript function to request new board sales totals

You wrote another new function, called **`getBoardsSold()`**. This function used **`createRequest()`** to create a new request object. Then, you set up a variable pointing to the Ajax version of a PHP script on Katie's server, initialized the connection, and sent the request to the server.

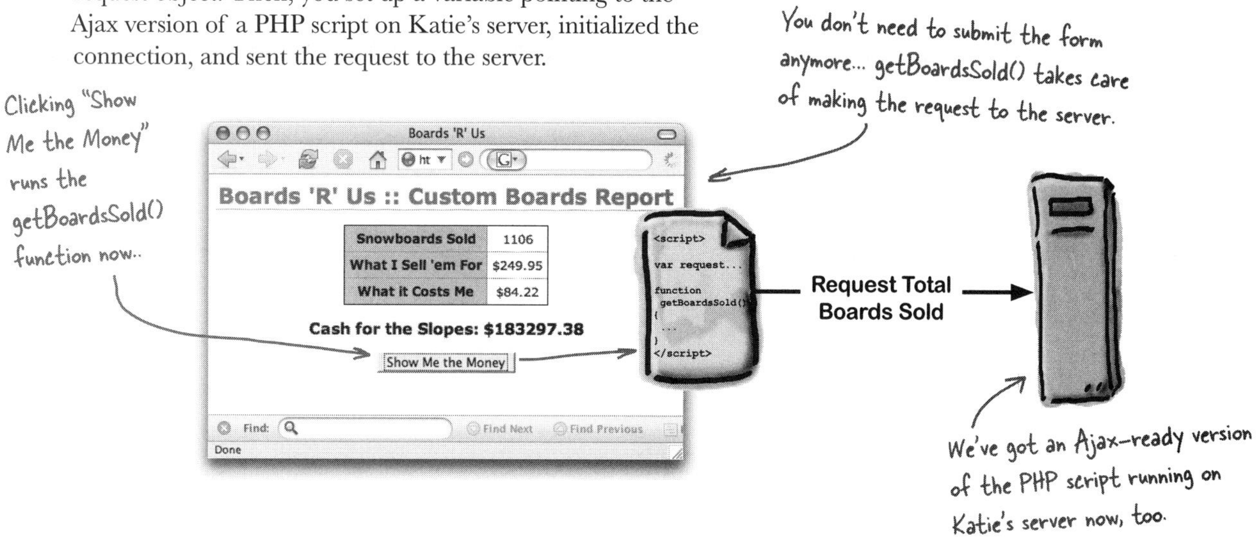

Wait a second... doesn't the "Show Me the Money" button still submit the form to the older version of the PHP script? And how does getBoardsSold() get run? I don't think we're done with Step 2 yet...

There are still some missing pieces

We've got to make sure that Katie's web form no longer gets submitted to the non-Ajax version of her PHP script, or she's going to end up with more page reloads, and all our hard work won't be noticed!

And not only that, but we've got to make sure that our new **`getBoardsSold()`** function gets called from the web form. It looks like we're definitely not ready to start updating the page yet... but what do we need to do next?

There are two major tasks we still need to take care of; use the space below to write out what you think needs to happen to finish off Step 2.

STOP! Don't go on to the next page until you've written something in these blanks.

Back to the HTML

Do you see what you need to do? When Katie clicks the "Show Me the Money" button, the web form submits everything to the PHP script. But we don't want the web form to get submitted, because we're using Ajax to handle requests to the server. This shouldn't be too hard to fix, though.

Let's go back to the HTML for the Boards 'R' Us report:

```
<body>
 <h1>Boards 'R' Us :: Custom Boards Report</h1>
 <div id="boards">
  <table>
   <tr><th>Snowboards Sold</th>
    <td><span id="boards-sold">1012</span></td></tr>
   <tr><th>What I Sell 'em For</th>
    <td>$<span id="price">249.95</span></td></tr>
   <tr><th>What it Costs Me</th>
    <td>$<span id="cost">84.22</span></td></tr>
  </table>
  <h2>Cash for the Slopes:
   $<span id="cash">167718.76</span></h2>
  <form method="GET" action="getUpdatedBoardSales.php">
   <input value="Show Me the Money" type="submit" />
  </form>
 </div>
</body>
```

This is just the HTML in the <body> tag... we've left the rest of the file off.

This button shouldn't submit the form anymore...

```
<input value="Show Me the Money" type="button" />
```

...so you can change it to be just a normal input button.

Frequently Asked Questions

Q: Couldn't we remove the action from the <form> tag, instead of changing the button type?

A: That's a good idea, *in addition* to changing the button type. If you *only* remove the action, though, the "Show Me the Money" button will still try and submit the form... but with no `action` on the `<form>` tag, all you'll get is a page reload. So be sure to also change the button type from "submit" to "button".

Running getBoardsSold() from the web form

The JavaScript's ready, and the button no longer tries to submit the form... but right now, **`getBoardsSold()`** never runs, either. This shouldn't be too hard to fix, though:

Can't we just run the getBoardsSold() function whenever someone clicks on "Show Me the Money"?

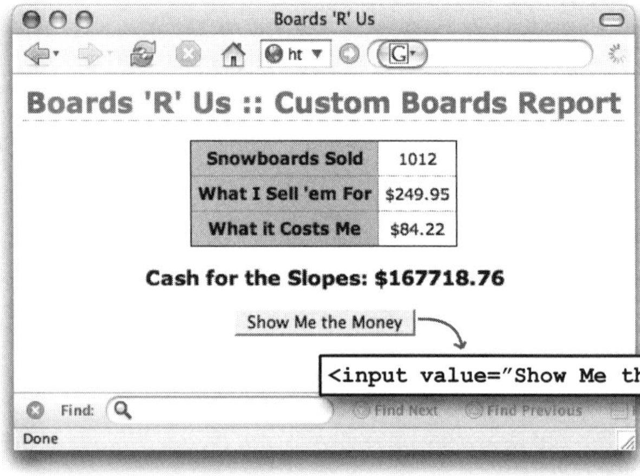

Any time this button is clicked...

```
<input value="Show Me the Money" type="button" />
```

...this JavaScript function needs to get called.

```
function getBoardsSold() { ... }
```

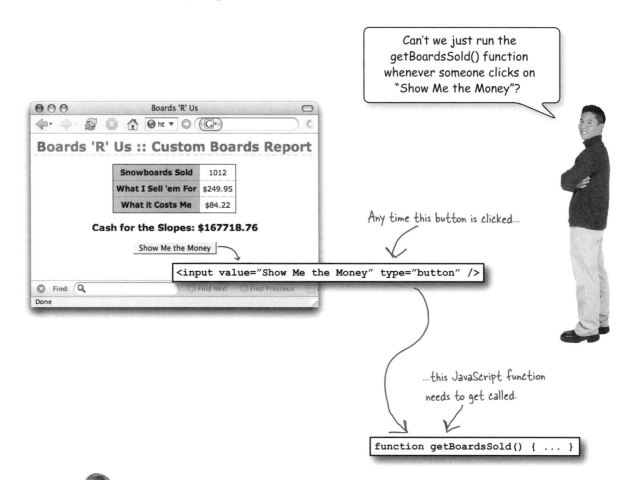

A Question For JavaScript

JavaScript, we need to run a function from our HTML. Can you help us out?

"Oh, well I'm incredibly flexible when it comes to calling functions from a web page. Just use one of my **event handlers** in your HTML. You can use **`onBlur()`** for when someone leaves a field, or **`onClick()`**, for when a user clicks... how about **`onChange()`**, for when a value changes... or there's **`onFocus()`**... wait, wait, I've got more... what do you mean, out of time?"

Adding an event handler

Any time Katie clicks the "Show Me the Money" button, the **`getBoardsSold()`** function should run. You can use a JavaScript **event handler** to take care of this. An event handler connects a piece of JavaScript code—like the **`getBoardsSold()`** function—to a certain event, like when someone clicks a button on a web page.

In the Boards app, let's use an event handler to connect the "Show Me the Money" button to the **`getBoardsSold()`** function. Since you want to attach the event to a button click, use the **`onClick`** handler, like this:

Since this form should never get submitted in the Ajax version of the report, you can remove the "action" attribute if you want.

```
<form method="GET" action="getUpdatedBoardSales.php">
 <input value="Show Me the Money" type="button"
        onClick="getBoardsSold();" />
</form>
```

"onClick" means that anytime Katie clicks this button...

...this function will get run.

Reviewing the highlight reel

Remember our highlight reel? Have you been keeping up with what we've covered, and what you've still got to look forward to? Let's take a quick look at what you've learned in this chapter so far:

This is why we changed the "Show Me the Money" button to call a JavaScript function, instead of having it submit Katie's web form.

We used createRequest() to create this request object.

- **Asynchronous applications make requests using a JavaScript object, and not a form submit.**
- **Your requests and responses are handled by the web browser, not directly by your JavaScript code.**
- **Once the web browser gets a response to your asynchronous request, it will run a callback function.**

We haven't gotten to these two concepts yet.

createRequest() getBoardsSold() updatePage()

Step 3: Coding updatePage()

So now you've taken care of talking to the server, and you're ready to get the server's response, and update the Boards report with new numbers. It's time to write **updatePage()**. Remember what this function is supposed to do?

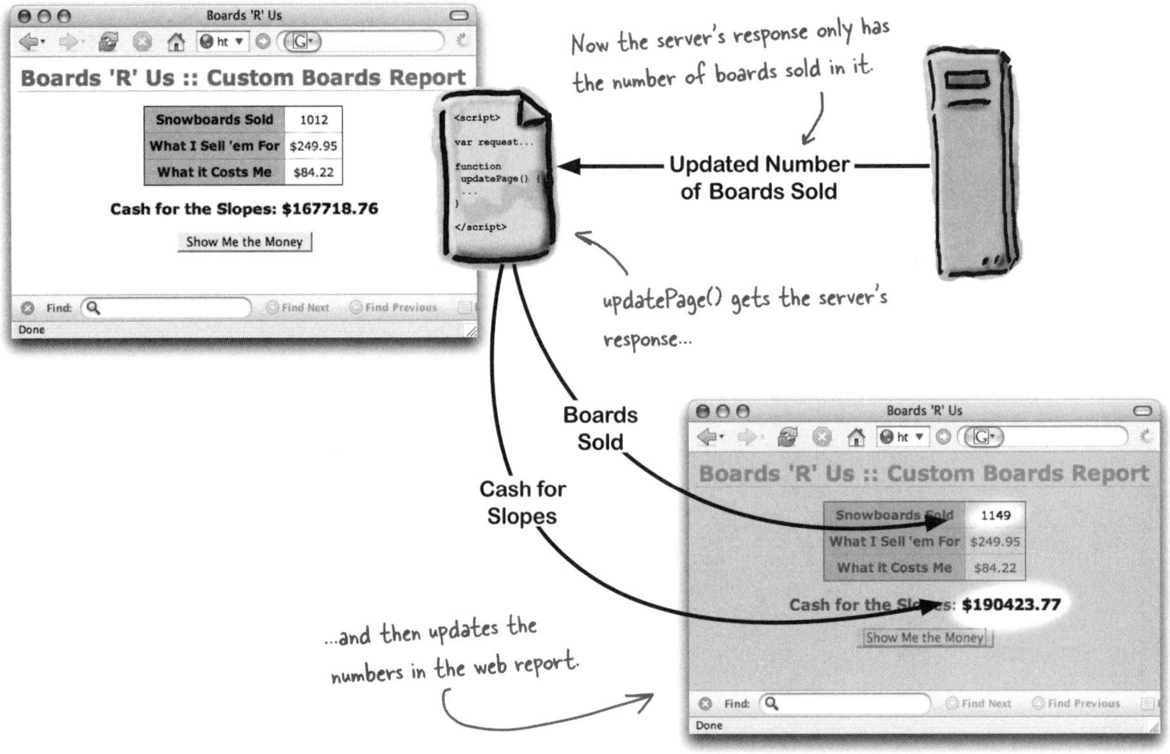

BRAIN POWER

How can your updatePage() function get the response from Katie's PHP script? Remember, the request to the script was made in getBoardsSold()... and this is supposed to be an *asynchronous* application. That means Katie shouldn't have to wait around while the server is getting new sales totals.

So how *does* updatePage() get the response from the server? Think about this for a minute or two, and then turn the page.

I think we should call the updatePage() function at the end of getBoardsSold(). Then updatePage() can get the response from the server, right?

```
function getBoardsSold() {
  createRequest();
  var url =
    "getUpdatedBoardSales-ajax.php";
  request.open("GET", url, true);
  request.send(null);
  updatePage();
}
```

This won't work... since send() doesn't wait on a response from the server, updatePage() would run before the server has finished with your request.

Ajax is asynchronous JavaScript

Remember, **getBoardsSold()** makes an *asynchronous* request. That means that the JavaScript doesn't wait around for an answer from the server.

In fact, the **getBoardsSold()** function will probably finish running before the **getUpdatedBoardSales-ajax.php** script even has a chance to finish processing your request.

So if getBoardsSold() finishes running before the server responds, where does the response go? And how can we make sure that updatePage() runs when the server's finished with our request?

Where does the response go?

You've uncovered the trickiest part of asynchronous web programming: if asynchronous code doesn't wait around for a response from the server, how do we *use* that response? And where does the server's response go in the first place?

You already know about web pages, which can use event handlers to call JavaScript functions. And you've seen how asynchronous JavaScript can make requests to a web server. To complete the asynchronous picture, though, there's another important piece of the puzzle...

How we see web apps...

To figure out what's going on, we're going to have to step back a bit, and think about web applications in general. When you think about a web appl, you probably think about an HTML page, some JavaScript code, a bit of CSS for style, and maybe a web server running some scripts or a servlet. All these pieces work together, like this:

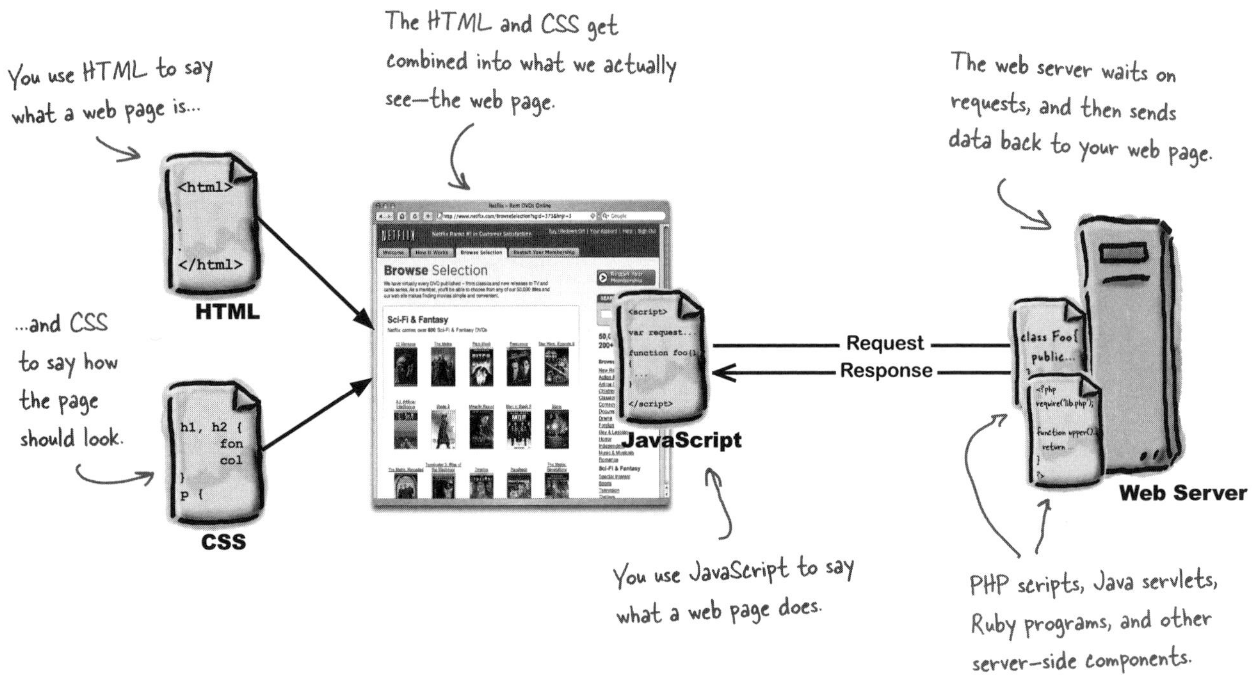

But there's more going on than meets the eye...

Who Am I

It's time to test those higher-order thinking skills. There's an important character in the Ajax play that you haven't met yet, and he's ready to make his grand entrance. See if you can upstage this new character by figuring out who he is *before* you turn the page. We've managed to collect a few quotes from the mystery character to help you out.

- **"Singing? Well, a lot of people don't realize this, but I am classically trained. And I love Wagner."**
- **"Give me your tired, your poor, your huddled brackets yearning to be styled."** ← Yes, our mystery character tends to be a bit overly dramatic at times.
- **"Sure, I love water sports. In fact, I was an extra in 'Point Break', and almost got a lead role in 'Blue Crush'."**
- **"I'm as tough as they come... I've even been involved in a few wars over the years."**

WHO AM I? ____________________

Write who you think the mystery character is in this blank, and then turn the page to see if you were right.

Introducing the web browser

Behind the scenes, something has to connect all these pieces together. That "something" is the web browser. The browser takes your HTML and CSS, and turns those angle brackets and semicolons into a page with graphics, buttons, and text.

It's also the web browser that runs your JavaScript code... behind the scenes, the browser takes care of important jobs like storing the values of your variables, creating new types, and handling any network requests that your code might make.

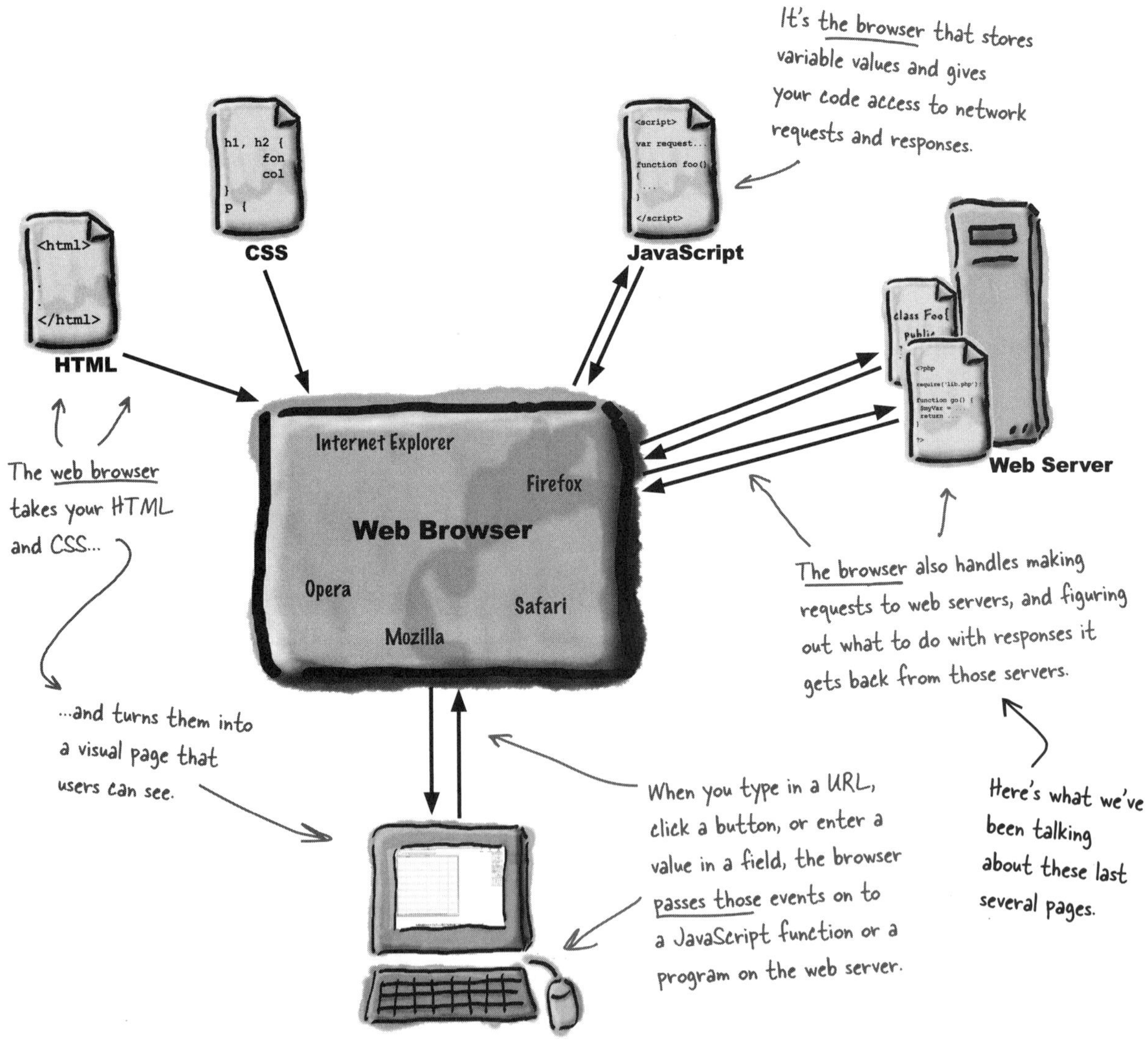

So now you're telling me that my code *isn't* making requests to the server? That it's really the web browser doing all that? I'm so confused...

The browser just helps out

The browser isn't doing anything that tricky. When your JavaScript needs to make a request, you write code like this:

```
function getBoardsSold() {
  createRequest();
  var url = "getUpdatedBoardSales-ajax.php";
  request.open("GET", url, true);
  request.send(null);
}
```

All the browser does is handle the low-level network stuff that makes this code work. Since network connections work differently on each operating system (think Linux and Windows and Mac OS X), the browser handles the stuff specific to each system. That way, your JavaScript will work on any system—and the browser takes care of turning your code into something each user's particular computer understands.

Take a look back at page 40, and notice that it's *the browser* that actually handles sending requests and getting responses from the server. Your code tells the browser **what to do**, and then the browser takes care of actually **doing it**.

Your requests and responses are handled by the web browser, not directly by your JavaScript code.

BRAIN POWER

Why do you think it's so important that the web browser handle requests in asynchronous applications? Remember, a web server can only respond to whomever made the original request to that server.

The browser gives the server's response to your JavaScript

Since the browser handles sending requests, it's also responsible for getting responses back from the server. Let's see what the browser is doing in the Boards app:

① The browser displays the Boards app to Katie

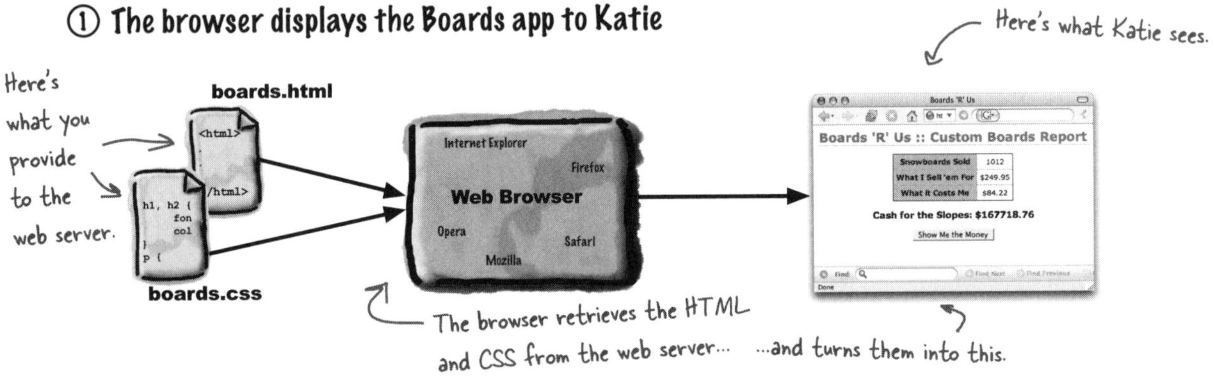

② The browser runs the getBoardsSold() function

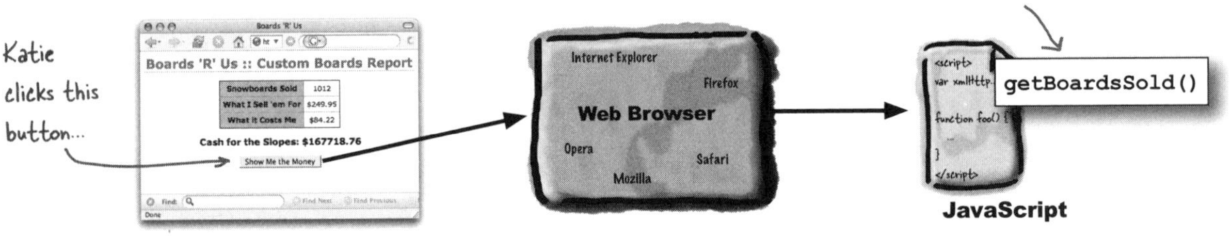

③ The browser runs the createRequest() function

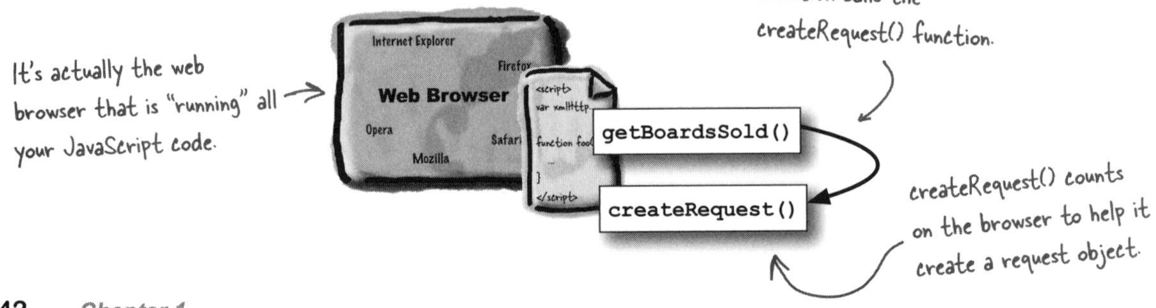

④ The browser sends a request to Katie's web server

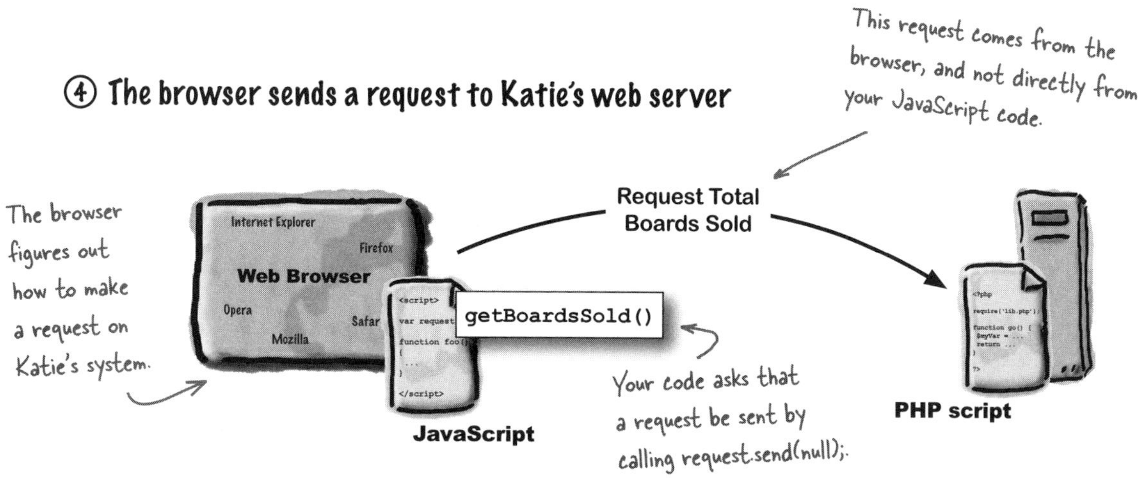
This request comes from the browser, and not directly from your JavaScript code.
The browser figures out how to make a request on Katie's system.
Internet Explorer
Firefox
Web Browser
Opera
Safari
Mozilla
getBoardsSold()
JavaScript
Request Total Boards Sold
Your code asks that a request be sent by calling request.send(null);.
PHP script

⑤ The browser returns "control" to Katie

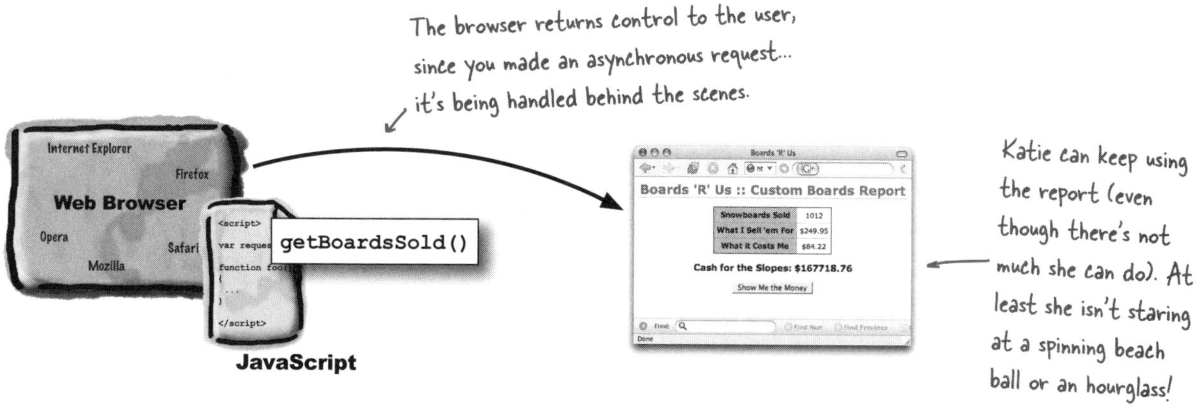
The browser returns control to the user, since you made an asynchronous request... it's being handled behind the scenes.
Internet Explorer
Firefox
Web Browser
Opera
Safari
Mozilla
getBoardsSold()
JavaScript
Boards 'R' Us :: Custom Boards Report
Snowboards Sold 1012
What I Sell 'em For $249.95
What it Costs Me $84.22
Cash for the Slopes: $167718.76
Show Me the Money
Katie can keep using the report (even though there's not much she can do). At least she isn't staring at a spinning beach ball or an hourglass!

⑥ The browser gets a response from the server

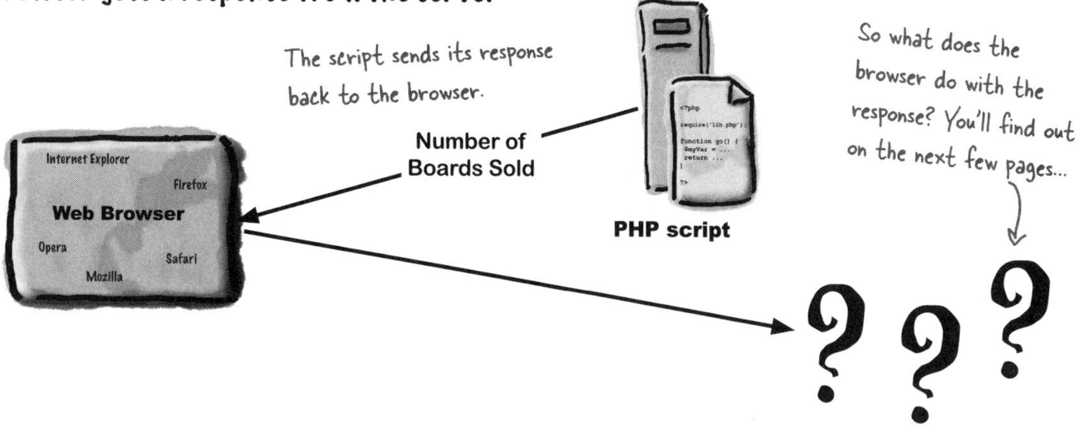
The script sends its response back to the browser.
Number of Boards Sold
PHP script
Internet Explorer
Firefox
Web Browser
Opera
Safari
Mozilla
So what does the browser do with the response? You'll find out on the next few pages...
? ? ?

What should the browser do with the server's response?

The browser gets the response from the server, but won't do anything with that response unless you tell it to. So we need to figure out a way to let the browser know to run our **`updatePage()`** function once it gets a response.

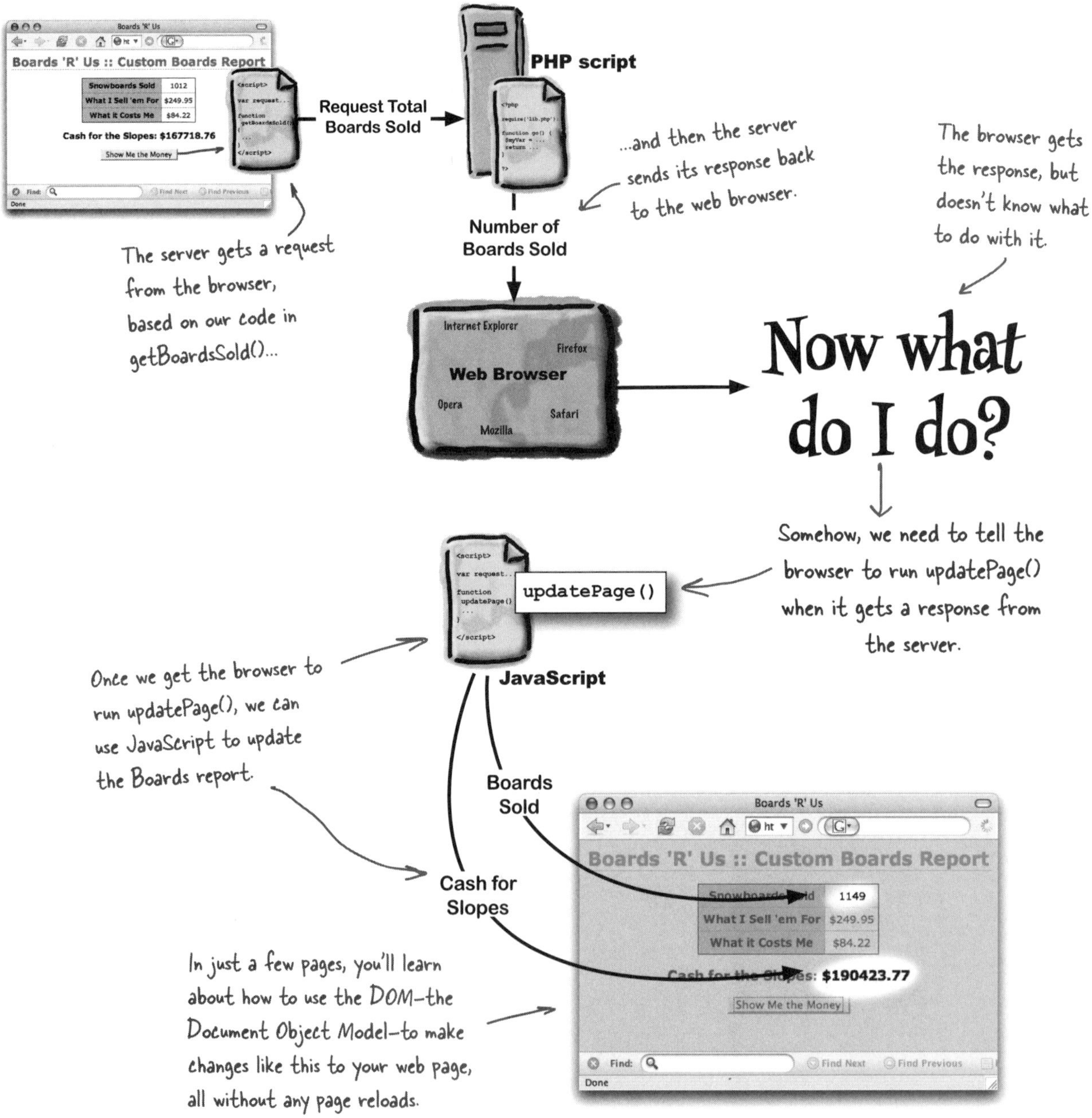

Boards 'R' Us :: Custom Boards Report
Snowboards Sold 1012
What I Sell 'em For $249.95
What it Costs Me $84.22
Cash for the Slopes: $167718.76
Show Me the Money
Request Total Boards Sold
PHP script
The server gets a request from the browser, based on our code in getBoardsSold()...
...and then the server sends its response back to the web browser.
Number of Boards Sold
The browser gets the response, but doesn't know what to do with it.
Internet Explorer
Firefox
Web Browser
Opera
Safari
Mozilla
Now what do I do?
Somehow, we need to tell the browser to run updatePage() when it gets a response from the server.
updatePage()
JavaScript
Once we get the browser to run updatePage(), we can use JavaScript to update the Boards report.
Boards Sold
Cash for Slopes
Boards 'R' Us :: Custom Boards Report
1149
What I Sell 'em For $249.95
What it Costs Me $84.22
$190423.77
Show Me the Money
In just a few pages, you'll learn about how to use the DOM—the Document Object Model—to make changes like this to your web page, all without any page reloads.

Espresso Talk

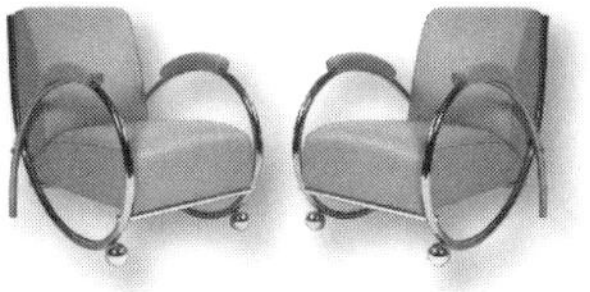

Tonight's coffee-loving, jittery-handed guests:
Web Browser and an HTML Page

Browser: Hi there, HTML. Good to see you again. I was just talking with your buddy, CSS.

HTML Page: Oh yeah? I've been hanging out with him a lot more these days. It seems people must be reading up on using CSS in their pages... we both love it, though.

Browser: Yeah, I'm a big fan. Although it does mean I have to do some extra work, since I've got to take two files and combine them together.

HTML Page: *You* have to do work? What do you mean? I'm the one who had to say farewell to old friends like "align" and "font face". I don't see what any of this has to do with you.

Browser: Are you kidding? You markup language types... always in the dark. XHTML is the exact same way... without me, nobody would even see you guys!

HTML Page: What, just because you're the program that lets people look at us? Look, the only reason you even exist is to let people view my markup.

Browser: Boy, you just don't have a clue, do you? People can "see" HTML with a text editor... but nobody cares about your angle brackets and <head> tags. People want what I make out of you... a visual page, with images and tables and links.

HTML Page: Delusions of grandeur... geez. Yeah, I'm sure people are beating down your door to see how many different ways you can display the *same* web page. Yeah, I just *love* web browsers, and how they're always screwing up how I look.

Browser: The browser wars are coming to an end, you big uninformed bucket of brackets. Besides, if people would just write standardized web pages, there'd hardly be any problems.

HTML Page: Oh, really? That's not what JavaScript has been telling me. He was just complaining the other day about having to use two different types of objects for making a simple request to a server.

Browser: Hey, two is a lot better than five or six... and with some of the new releases of browsers like Internet Explorer and Mozilla, I'll bet we'll be using just one type of request object before you know it.

HTML Page: You sure seem to think you have all the answers.

Browser: Maybe not all the answers, but I *do* have all the responses. And that's just one more thing you need me for.

HTML Page: All the responses? What are you talking about?

Browser: Maybe you should ask your friend JavaScript about that. Everyone seems to think that it's web pages and code that make requests...

HTML Page: Exactly!

Browser: ...but it's really me, behind the scenes, making sure that pages look right, requests get sent, and responses are heard. Without me, you'd just be a bunch of funny characters in a text file.

HTML Page: *...grumble...grumble...*

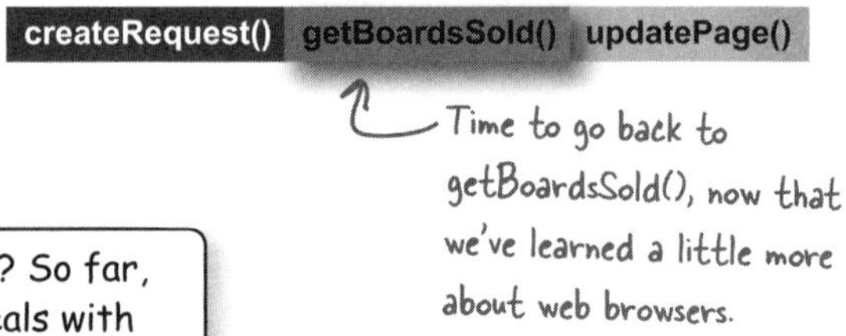
createRequest() getBoardsSold() updatePage()
Time to go back to getBoardsSold(), now that we've learned a little more about web browsers.

So how do we talk to the browser? So far, all the code we've written just deals with that JavaScript request object. Wait a second... that's it! Can we use the request object to talk to the browser?

Sending instructions to the browser

Remember, we've got to tell the browser what to do with the server's response to our request *before* we make the request... because once the request is made, **getBoardsSold()** finishes running, and our JavaScript code won't know what's going on with the request. Fortunately, the request object we've been using has a property just for this purpose:

```
function getBoardsSold() {
  createRequest();
  var url = "getUpdatedBoardSales-ajax.php";
  request.open("GET", url, true);
  request.onreadystatechange = updatePage;
  request.send(null);
}
```

Be sure you set this property before you call send(), or this function won't get run.

If you put the name of a function here, the browser will run that function when it gets a response from the server.

JavaScript requires that you leave off the parentheses on the function name here.

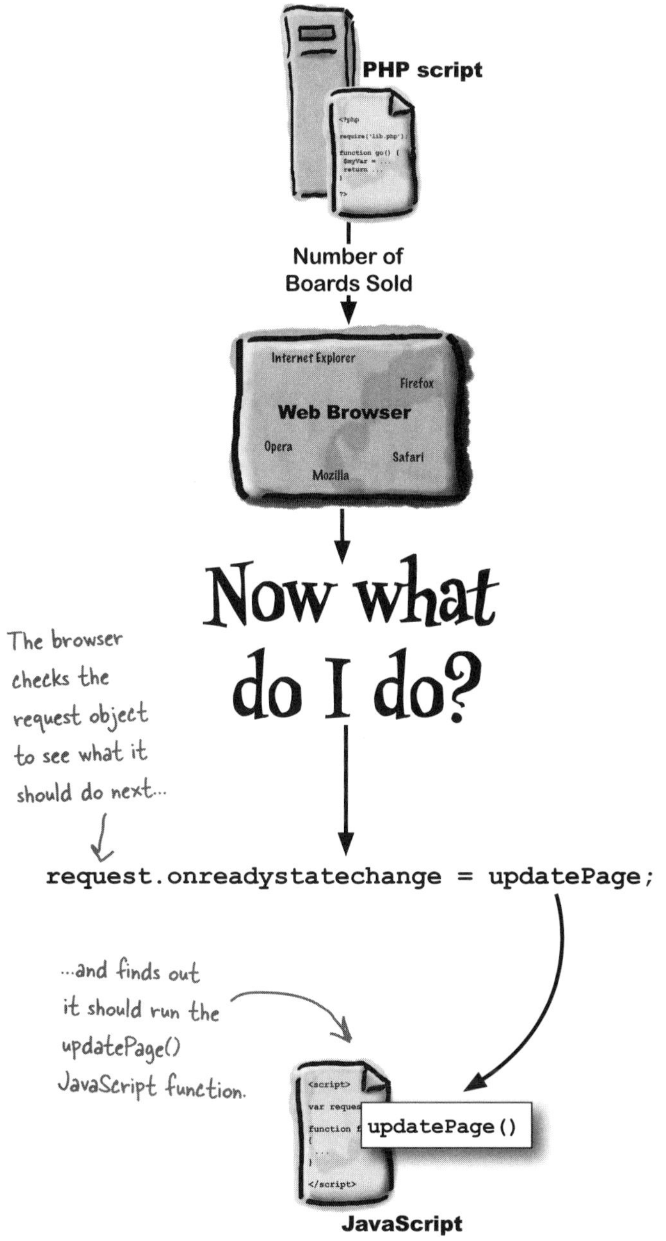

PHP script
Number of Boards Sold
Internet Explorer
Firefox
Web Browser
Opera
Safari
Mozilla
Now what do I do?
The browser checks the request object to see what it should do next...
request.onreadystatechange = updatePage;
...and finds out it should run the updatePage() JavaScript function.
updatePage()
JavaScript

Frequently Asked Questions

Q: The server talks to the browser, the browser talks to the JavaScript, the JavaScript updates our page... I'm lost. Can you run that by me again?

A: Remember, these are *asynchronous* requests. When your code tells the browser to send a request to the server, the server has to respond with an answer—but your code doesn't wait around to find out what that answer is. So when the server responds, it's left to the web browser to figure out what to do next. Since there's no running code waiting for a response, the browser runs the function you assigned to the request object's **`onreadystatechange`** property.

Q: Remind me again what onreadystatechange is all about? That seems sort of confusing to me.

A: It's actually not as difficult as it might look. That property just tells the browser that when the request's state changes—like when the PHP script responds to the browser—the browser should call the JavaScript function indicated in the request object. In this case, that's the **`updatePage`** function.

Q: So are there things besides the script finishing up that can result in updatePage() being called?

A: Yup. Web requests can be in several different "ready states", and each time the ready state changes, **`updatePage()`** is called. We'll dig into this much more in the next chapter, so keep this in mind.

Once the web browser gets a response to your asynchronous request, it will "call back" your JavaScript with the server's response.

Getting the server's response

We're finally ready to code **`updatePage()`**... right? Since you've set up the **`onreadystatechange`** property of the request object, the web browser will run **`updatePage()`** when the server responds to the request. But something's still missing...

I see how we can get the browser to run updatePage() when the server responds, but what about the data that the server responds *with*? How do we get access to that in updatePage()?

You can get the server's response using the responseText property of your JavaScript request object.

The browser helps out again

You've already seen how to tell the browser to run the **`updatePage()`** function when the server responds, but the browser—and that request object you've been using—does even more to help you out.

Once the browser gets a response from the server, it figures out what to do next by checking the request object's **`onreadystatechange`** property. And, since you're going to want the data the server returned, the browser puts that data in another property of the request object: a property called **`responseText`**.

So any time you want to figure out what the server returned in its response, just access the request object's **`responseText`** property.

In fact, the browser sets quite a few properties on the request object before it runs your JavaScript function. Stay tuned to find out what these other properties do...

Work It Through

You've already seen two of the properties from the request object we've been using. Now it's time to put what you've learned to the test. Below on the left are several properties of a request object, and on the right are descriptions of these properties. See if you can match the property name to its purpose.

responseText	The HTTP status code returned from the server.
readyState	The function for the browser to run when the server responds to your request.
onreadystatechange	A number indicating what state the request is in: loading, in progress, finished processing, etc.
status	The data returned from the server in response to your request.

You haven't seen some of these properties yet, but go ahead and take a guess at what each does.

createRequest() getBoardsSold() updatePage()

Planning the updatePage() function

The browser stores the server's response in the request object, and then runs **updatePage()**. We're *finally* ready to start coding this function. Let's see what we need to do:

First: Get the updated number of boards sold

The server returns this number to the browser, and then the browser puts this value in the request object's **responseText** property:

```
function updatePage() {
  var newTotal = request.responseText;
}
```

This is the property of the request object that the browser uses to pass on response data from the server.

Here's the request object again.

Second: Get the HTML elements you need to update

There are two elements you have to update: the number of boards sold, and the cash that Katie has made. You can use JavaScript's **getElementById()** method to grab each of these based on their **id** attributes.

```
function updatePage() {
  var newTotal = request.responseText;
  var boardsSoldEl = document.getElementById("boards-sold");
  var cashEl = document.getElementById("cash");
}
```

Assign each element to a variable, so you can easily reference them in your code later.

document represents the entire HTML page...

...and getElementById() finds the element with the ID you pass into the function.

These are the names of the HTML elements we want to get.

Remember how Katie added id attributes to her <span> elements so she could style them with CSS? Those same id attributes make it easy to access each of the <span> elements in our JavaScript code.

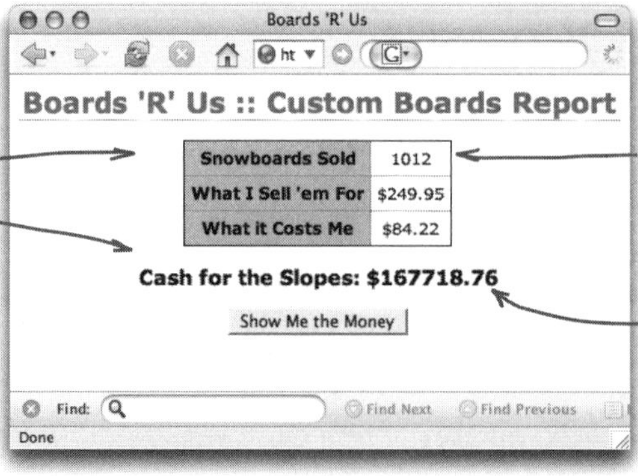

<span id="boards-sold">1012</span>

<span id="cash">167718.76</span>

Third: Add a reference to Katie's text utilities

Now you're ready to update the total number of snowboards sold. It's going to take a little bit of advanced JavaScript to update the text in those **<span>** elements. We'll cover these techniques in Chapter 4, when we talk about the Document Object Model, but for now, Katie has some PRE-ASSEMBLED JavaScript in a JavaScript utility file, called **text-utils.js**. This file has some handy functions you can use, but you need to let the Boards app know where to find these utilities first. You can add in a reference to Katie's JavaScript utilities using the **<script>** tag in your HTML, like this:

You can find text-utils.js in the chapter01/boards directory of this chapter's examples.

This is all in the <head> of your HTML page.

```
<head>
 <title>Boards 'R' Us</title>
 <link rel="stylesheet" type="text/css" href="boards.css" />
 <script type="text/javascript" src="text-utils.js"> </script>
 <script language="javascript" type="text/javascript">
```

Here's the beginning of all the JavaScript code you've written in this chapter.

Add this line, and then you can use all the utility functions from text-utils.js in your updatePage() function.

Fourth: Update the report with the updated board sales

The **text-utils.js** file has a function in it called **replaceText()**. You can use this utility function to update Katie's report with the new number of boards sold:

All the functions in text-utils.js use the DOM—the Document Object Model—to update a web page on the fly.

```
function updatePage() {
  var newTotal = request.responseText;
  var boardsSoldEl = document.getElementById("boards-sold");
  var cashEl = document.getElementById("cash");
  replaceText(boardsSoldEl, newTotal);
}
```

This function is defined in text-utils.js. We'll talk more about these functions later in the book.

This is the element whose text will be replaced...

...and this is the value to replace the text with.

When this code runs, the web report will get updated with the new total for board sales.

Just Do It

You're ready to finish up the updatePage() function on your own. Below is the code for updatePage(), but there are plenty of blanks left to be filled in. Try and figure out the code that belongs in each blank, and write in your answers.

Once you think you've got all the code filled in, be sure to compare your answers to ours on the next page.

```
function updatePage() {
  var newTotal = request.responseText;
  var boardsSoldEl = document.getElementById("boards-sold");
  var cashEl = document.getElementById("cash");
  replaceText(boardsSoldEl, newTotal);

  /* Figure out how much cash Katie has made */
  var priceEl = document.getElementById("_____________");
  var price = getText(___________);
  var __________ = document.______________("cost");
  var cost = getText(costEl);
  var cashPerBoard = ____________ - _________;
  var cash = ___________ * ____________;

  /* Update the cash for the slopes on the form */
  cash = Math.round(cash * 100) / 100;
  replaceText(cashEl, _____________);
}
```

getText() is from text-utils.js. It will take any element, and return the text within that element.

This little trick makes sure that the cash total has only two decimal places, like a normal dollar value.

Frequently Asked Questions

Q: You've mentioned the Document Object Model a couple of times. What's that? And what does it have to do with Katie's web report?

A: The Document Object Model, called the DOM for short, is how web browsers store and represent HTML pages. By working with the DOM, you can dynamically update a web page, like you're doing with Katie's report. We'll look at the DOM in detail in Chapter 4, but for now, you can just use the `text-utils.js` utility file, and not worry too much about the details of the DOM.

Just Do It Solutions

You're ready to finish up the updatePage() function on your own. Below is the code for updatePage(), but there are plenty of blanks left to be filled in. Try and figure out the code that belongs in each blank, and write in your answers.

```
function updatePage() {
  var newTotal = request.responseText;
  var boardsSoldEl = document.getElementById("boards-sold");
  var cashEl = document.getElementById("cash");
  replaceText(boardsSoldEl, newTotal);

  /* Figure out how much cash Katie has made */
  var priceEl = document.getElementById("price");
  var price = getText(priceEl);
  var costEl = document.getElementById("cost");
  var cost = getText(costEl);
  var cashPerBoard = price - cost;
  var cash = cashPerBoard * newTotal;

  /* Update the cash for the slopes on the form */
  cash = Math.round(cash * 100) / 100;
  replaceText(cashEl, cash);
}
```

getText() is from text-utils.js. It will take any element, and return the text within that element.

This little trick makes sure that the cash total has only two decimal places, like a normal dollar value.

createRequest() getBoardsSold() updatePage()

Make sure the server is finished

Right now, your **updatePage()** function assumes that the server is finished when it runs... but that's not the case! To understand what's going on with your request, it's time to learn about **ready states**. Your request object has a ready state that tells the browser quite a bit about what **state** the request is in.

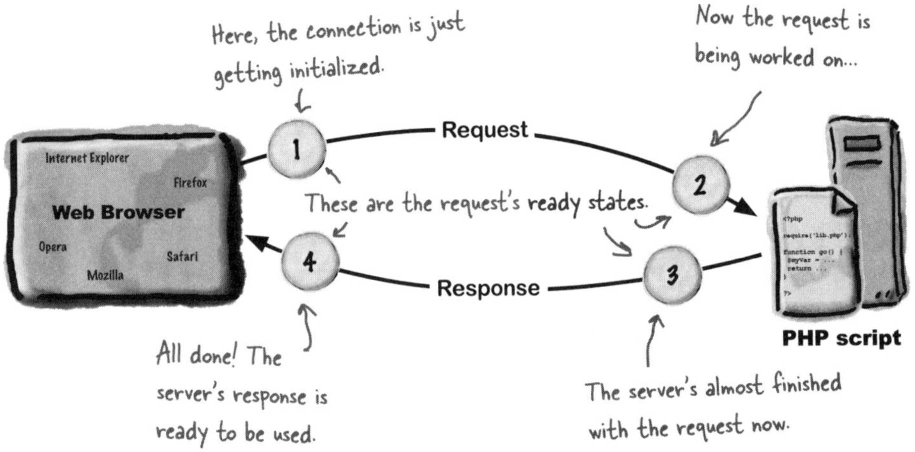
Here, the connection is just getting initialized.
Now the request is being worked on...
Request
Internet Explorer
Firefox
Web Browser
Opera
Safari
Mozilla
1
2
3
4
These are the request's ready states.
Response
PHP script
All done! The server's response is ready to be used.
The server's almost finished with the request now.

A ready state tells the browser what stage a request is in.

Ready states are connected to your request object's onreadystatechange property

Do you remember the property you used in **getBoardsSold()** to tell the browser what to do when the server sent back a response? Take a look to refresh your memory:

```
function getBoardsSold() {
  createRequest();
  var url = "getUpdatedBoardSales-ajax.php";
  request.open("GET", url, true);
  request.onreadystatechange = updatePage;
  request.send(null);
}
```

This property sets the function that the browser should run every time that the request's ready state changes.

This property affects every ready state, not just the one indicating that the server is finished with a request.

Checking for the right ready state

You already know that the browser will run your **updatePage()** function when it gets a response from the server. But, there's a twist: the browser actually runs **updatePage()** *every time* the ready state changes, and not just when the server is finished sending back a response. Look at the diagram on page 54 again, and notice that as the request is progressing, the ready state number changes.

It looks like when the server is finished with our request, the ready state is "4", so we can check for that number in our code. That way, we can make sure that we only try and update Katie's report when we know that the server has sent us back a response.

readyState is the property on the request object that stores the current ready state.

When the request object's readyState is set to 4, the server is done with the request.

This function will get run every time the ready state changes.

```
function updatePage() {
  if (request.readyState == 4) {
    var newTotal = request.responseText;
    var boardsSoldEl = document.getElementById("boards-sold");
    var cashEl = document.getElementById("cash");
    replaceText(boardsSoldEl, newTotal);

    /* Figure out how much cash Katie has made */
    ...

    /* Update the cash total on the web form */
    ...

  }
}
```

Here's that code you wrote a few pages back.

All this code only runs when the request's ready state is 4, and the server's done with the reqest.

Don't forget the closing bracket.

When the server is finished with your request, the ready state of the request will be "4"... that means that it's safe to use the data that the server sent back (and that the browser stored in your request object).

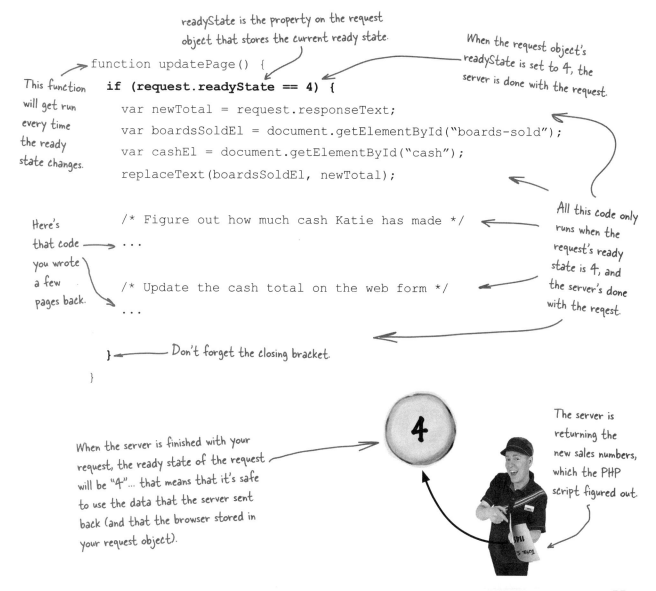

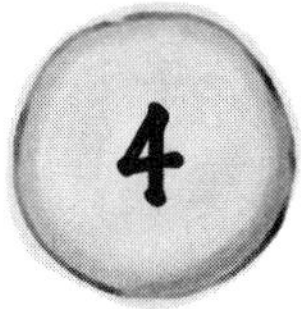

The server is returning the new sales numbers, which the PHP script figured out.

Just Do It

Open up your **`boards.html`** file, and add in all this new JavaScript. Make sure your **`updatePage()`** function has the JavaScript that checks the request object's ready state, as well as code to update the total board sales and figure out how much cash Katie has made. You also need to make sure you've got a copy of **`text-utils.js`** in the same directory as your **`boards.html`** and **`boards.css`** files.

Frequently Asked Questions

Q: At the end of the updatePage() function, on page 52, I don't understand why you multiplied the cash that Katie's made by 100, and then divided it by 100. Won't you get the same number you started with?

A: JavaScript can be a little weird about multiplying numbers. A lot of times, it will add a bunch of decimal places to a product. So instead of getting 59.95, JavaScript might come up with 59.9499995. That's clearly not what Katie wants to see on her report.

To fix a number like 59.9499995, first multiply it by 100, to get 5994.99995. Then you can use **`Math.round()`** to round this to the nearest integer, which is 5995. Finally, divide this result by 100, and you'll get 59.95... just what Katie wants.

Q: What does the getText() function do? I see we're using it in the updatePage() function, on page 52.

A: **`getText()`** is another utility function, like **`replaceText()`**. You pass it an element from a web page, and it will return the text within that element. In Katie's report, **`getText()`** gets the price Katie sells her boards for, and how much it costs Katie to make a board, both from **`<span>`** elements in Katie's HTML.

Q: So what about all those utility functions in text-utils.js? Do I need to worry about those?

A: As long as you reference the **`text-utils.js`** file with a **`<script>`** tag, your code will work fine. Those functions use the DOM quite a bit, and we'll explain all of them in Chapter 4.

We've also included all the code from **`text-utils.js`** in Appendix I, but don't worry if you don't understand it all now. By the time you're done with this book, all those utility functions will make sense to you.

Q: And the DOM is how we work with an HTML page?

A: That's right. Web browsers use the DOM to represent an HTML web page. Your JavaScript can use the DOM to update values in a page on the fly.

In fact, you've already been using the DOM a bit! Every time you use the JavaScript **`document`** object, or call the **`getElementById()`** function, you're using the DOM.

Q: And the readyState property... can you explain that again?

A: **`readyState`** is a property of the request object, and lets you know what stage your request is in. We'll spend a lot of time on this in the next chapter, but for now, you just need to know that when the **`readyState`** is 4, the server is finished with your request.

Showing Katie some Ajax magic

It's time to see what all this hard work has done for Katie's web report. Make sure you've added all the JavaScript we've talked about in this chapter, and double-check that the "Show Me the Money" button runs **`getBoardsSold()`**, instead of submitting the form. Then, load up **`boards.html`** in your web browser, and let's see what Ajax can do!

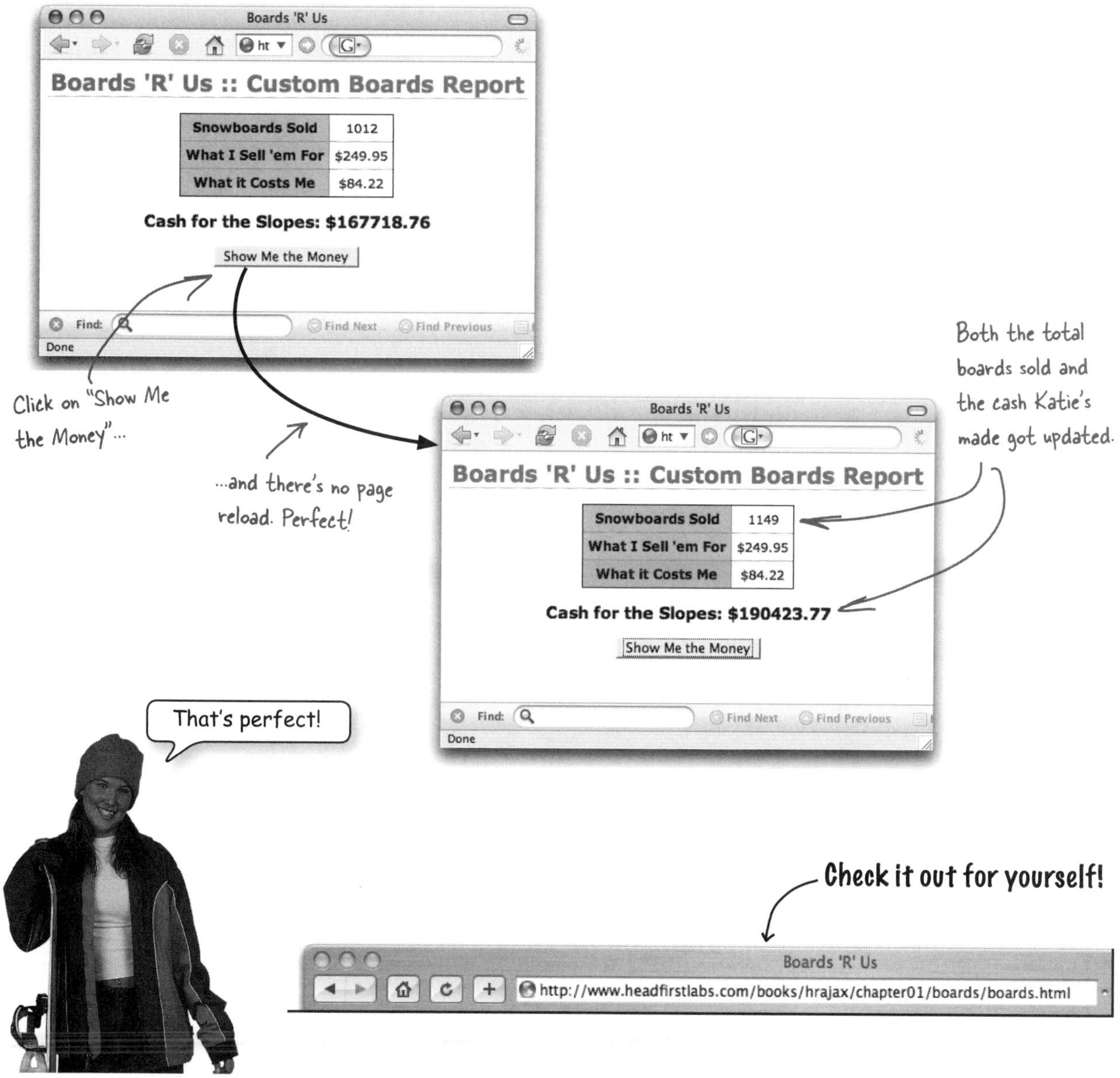

AJAX
1ST PRIZE

You did it! You took a boring sales report, and turned it into a dynamic Ajax application!

Nice work. Katie's web report is back online, Katie knows how much cash she's making—without having to wait on her server or suffer a bunch of page reloads—and with all that profit, Katie's even offered to give you free snowboarding lessons.

Reviewing the highlight reel

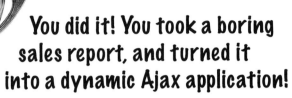

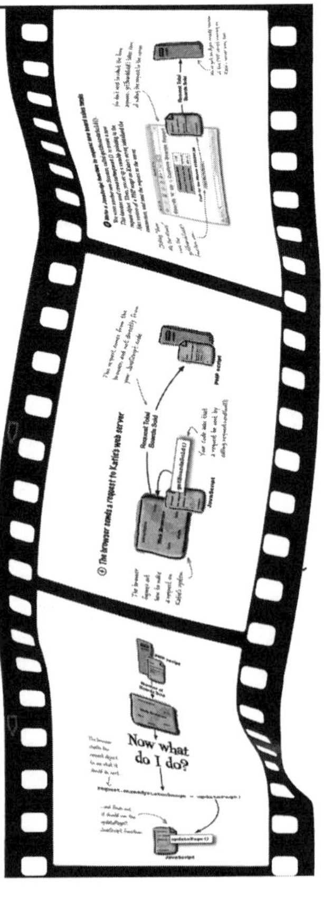
Now what do I do?

- Asynchronous applications make requests using a JavaScript object, and not a form
- Your requests and responses are handled by the web browser, not directly by your JavaScript code.
- Once the web browser gets a response to your asynchronous request, it will "call back" your JavaScript with the server's response.

Wait! Stop the presses!

Everything works on Katie's Mac, but on my Windows machine, I only get new sales totals the first time I click "Show Me the Money". After that, I just get the same numbers over and over... what's up with that?

Katie's brother and business manager. He's a die-hard Windows guy, even though Katie is a Mac-lover.

Here's the report after clicking "Show Me the Money" once... it's got new figures.

The first time using Internet Explorer, everything works great...

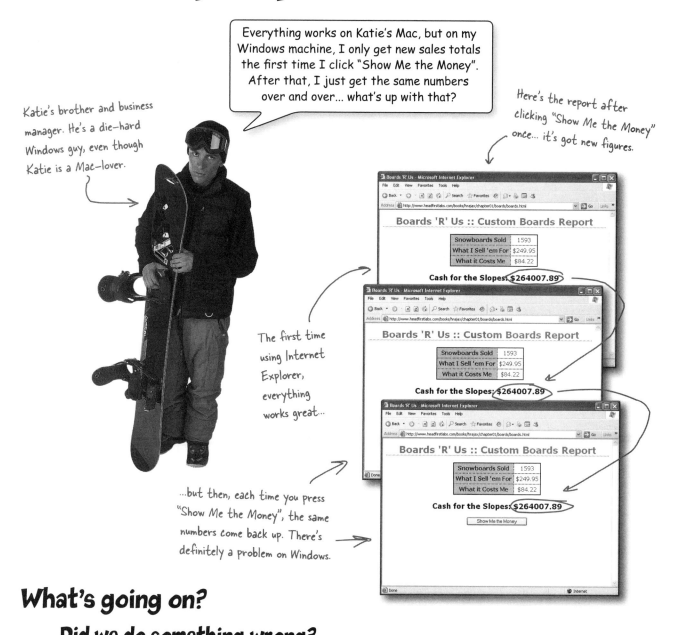

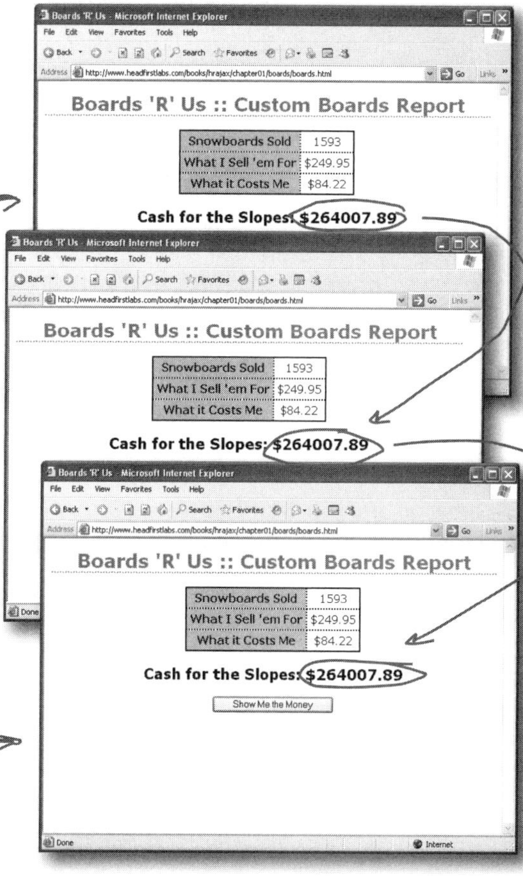

...but then, each time you press "Show Me the Money", the same numbers come back up. There's definitely a problem on Windows.

What's going on?

Did we do something wrong?

Do Ajax apps not work on Internet Explorer?

For answers to these questions and more, you'll have to wait for Chapter 2...

60 Second Review

- Traditional web programming involves making requests to a server, and getting back a response, usually with updated data wrapped up in a completely new HTML page.
- Ajax apps use asynchronous JavaScript.
- Ajax applications can make requests and get responses without reloading an entire page.
- Asynchronous JavaScript doesn't wait on a server to respond to a request. Users can keep using a page, even while the server is still working on the request.
- Web browsers turn HTML and CSS into pages you can see on your screen, and take care of running any JavaScript in the page.
- In Ajax applications, servers usually send back just the data you request, without any additional HTML markup and presentation.
- You can use JavaScript to make both synchronous and asynchronous requests to a web server.
- JavaScript offers several event handlers to call JavaScript code when certain events happen; onChange() and onClick() are two common examples.
- The browser always knows what ready state a request is in, and makes that available to your JavaScript functions.
- You can have the browser run a JavaScript function every time a request's ready state changes using the onreadystatechange property in your request object.
- When the ready state of a request is "4", the request has been processed, and the server has a response ready.

Exercise Solutions

Just Do It Solutions

Open up your **boards.html** file, and add a new JavaScript function called **getBoardsSold()**, right after **createRequest()**. Then, see if you can add a line of JavaScript in **getBoardsSold()** to create a new request object (that's Step "a" from page 18).

```
<script language="javascript" type="text/javascript">
  var request = null;

  function createRequest() {
    try {
      request = new XMLHttpRequest();
    } catch (trymicrosoft) {
      try {
        request = new ActiveXObject("Msxml2.XMLHTTP");
      } catch (othermicrosoft) {
        try {
          request = new ActiveXObject("Microsoft.XMLHTTP");
        } catch (failed) {
          request = null;
        }
      }
    }

    if (request == null)
      alert("Error creating request object!");
  }

  function getBoardsSold() {
    createRequest();
  }
</script>
```

All this is the pre-assembled JavaScript you should have typed in.

Here's the start of your getBoardsSold() function...

...which uses createRequest() to get a new request object created.

WHO AM I

It's time to test those higher-order thinking skills. There's an important character in the Ajax play that you haven't met yet, and he's ready to make his grand entrance. See if you can upstage this new character by figuring out who he is *before* you turn the page. We've helped you understand what each quote refers to with a few notes below.

➡ **"Singing? Well, a lot of people don't realize this, but I am classically trained. And I love Wagner."**

Here's the Opera web browser bragging a bit about her singing chops.

➡ **"Give me your tired, your poor, your huddled brackets yearning to be styled."**

That's definitely a web browser, asking for HTML content.

➡ **"Sure, I love water sports. In fact, I was an extra in 'Point Break', and almost got a lead role in 'Blue Crush'."**

Surfing... browsers are all about the surfing.

➡ **"I'm as tough as they come... I've even been involved in a few wars over the years."**

Netscape vs. IE, anyone? Remember the browser wars?

WHO AM I? The Web Browser

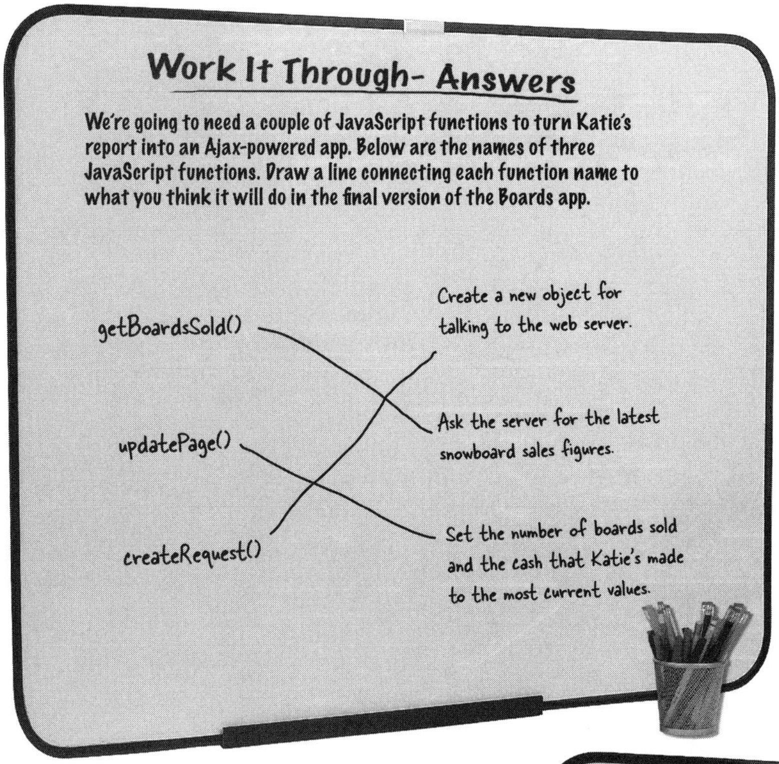
Work It Through- Answers
We're going to need a couple of JavaScript functions to turn Katie's report into an Ajax-powered app. Below are the names of three JavaScript functions. Draw a line connecting each function name to what you think it will do in the final version of the Boards app.
getBoardsSold()
updatePage()
createRequest()
Create a new object for talking to the web server.
Ask the server for the latest snowboard sales figures.
Set the number of boards sold and the cash that Katie's made to the most current values.

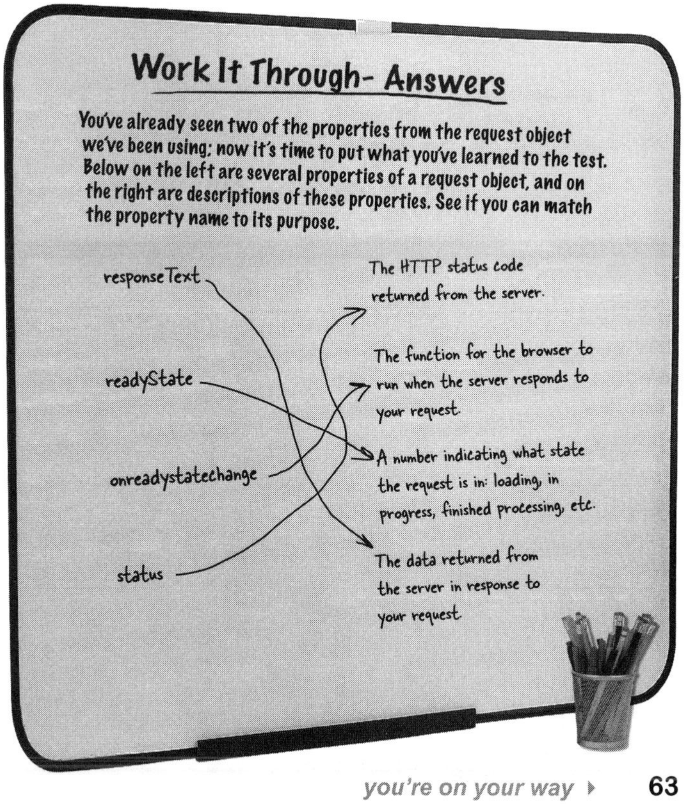
Work It Through- Answers
You've already seen two of the properties from the request object we've been using; now it's time to put what you've learned to the test. Below on the left are several properties of a request object, and on the right are descriptions of these properties. See if you can match the property name to its purpose.
responseText
readyState
onreadystatechange
status
The HTTP status code returned from the server.
The function for the browser to run when the server responds to your request.
A number indicating what state the request is in: loading, in progress, finished processing, etc.
The data returned from the server in response to your request.

2 Making Ajax Requests

Speaking the Language

I really thought we were getting somewhere, but then she said all she wanted to do was talk!

It's time to learn how to speak asynchronously.

If you're planning on writing the next killer application, you need to understand Ajax inside and out. In this chapter, you'll get the inside scoop on **asynchronous JavaScript**: you'll learn how to send requests on different browsers, master **ready states** and **status codes**, and even pick up a few extra dynamic HTML tricks along the way. By the time you're done, you'll be making requests and handling responses like a pro... and by the way, did we mention your users **won't have to wait** around on you while you're learning?

Break Neck Pizza Delivery

30-minute pizza delivery? Old skool. Try Break Neck Pizza, revolutionizing high speed pizza delivery through its patented "just in time" cooking process along with its distributed network of bicycle messengers. Better yet, Break Neck only takes orders via its web site (no human interaction required). Next time you need a pizza in under ten minutes, they're the ones to call.

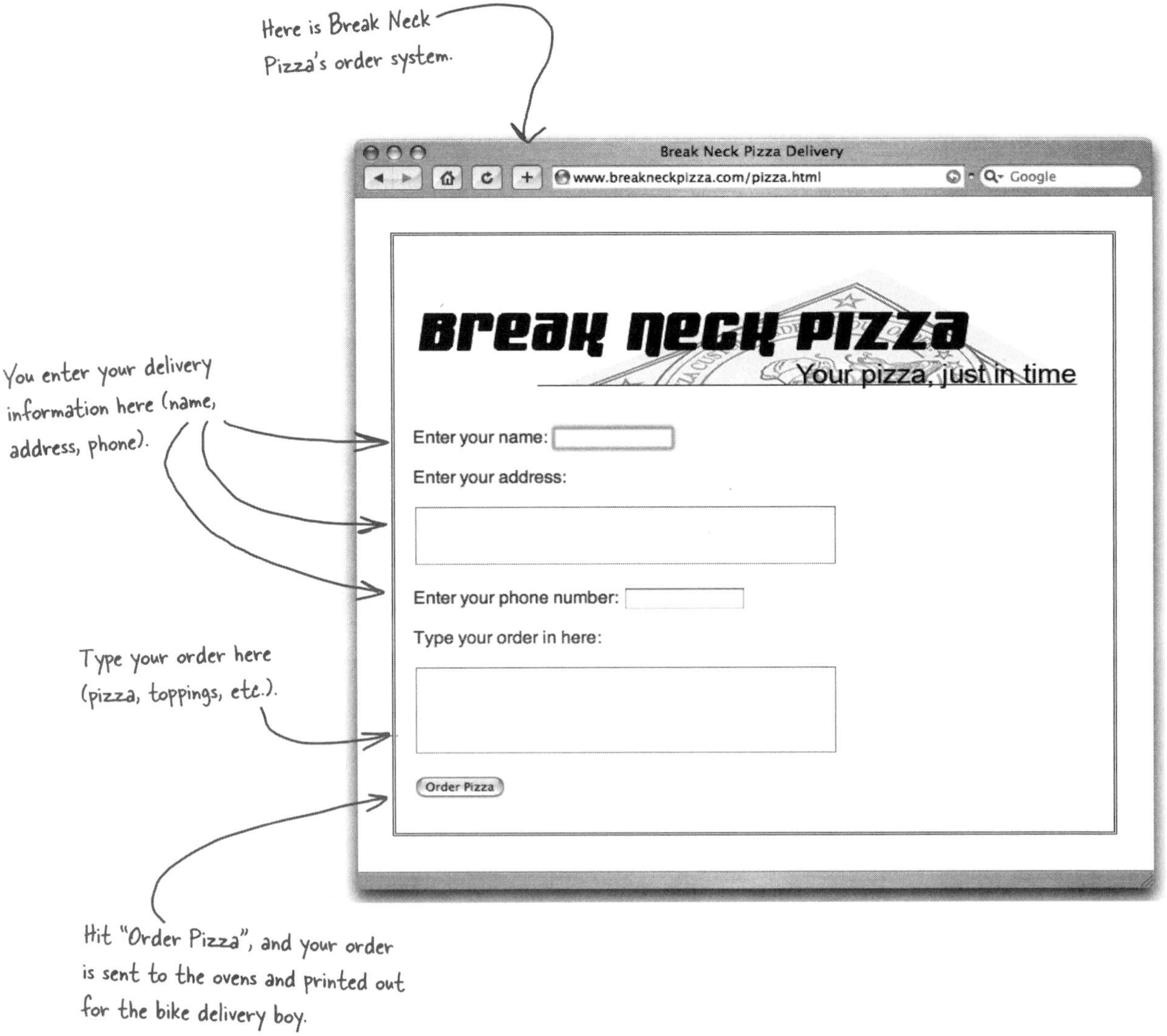
Here is Break Neck Pizza's order system.
Break Neck Pizza Delivery
www.breakneckpizza.com/pizza.html
Google
Break Neck Pizza
Your pizza, just in time
Enter your name:
Enter your address:
Enter your phone number:
Type your order in here:
Order Pizza
You enter your delivery information here (name, address, phone).
Type your order here (pizza, toppings, etc.).
Hit "Order Pizza", and your order is sent to the ovens and printed out for the bike delivery boy.

Ten minutes? I'm lucky if I can deliver a pizza in an hour when customers enter the wrong address in the order form. Can't you web geniuses do something about this?
Alex, Break Neck's top delivery guy.

What's the deal?

When customers submit their orders, there's nothing that makes sure that their address is correct—the order is just sent straight to Alex. If the customer makes a mistake and types his address incorrectly, Alex ends up at the wrong house, and then wastes a lot of time looking for the right one. On top of that, the pizza gets cold, and customers get angry.

Somehow, we need to be able to get the customer's correct address to Alex. But we can't count on the customer to enter his address correctly every time. *How would you make sure Alex gets the right address?*

Solving the pizza delivery problem

Fortunately, web developers have been solving these sorts of problems for years. Instead of letting users enter their own address (and type something incorrectly), let's look up the customer's address in the Break Neck customer database. Then, Alex will always get the right delivery address. Here's what we can do:

1 The customer enters their phone number

A customer enters his phone number, and the phone number gets sent to Break Neck's web server.

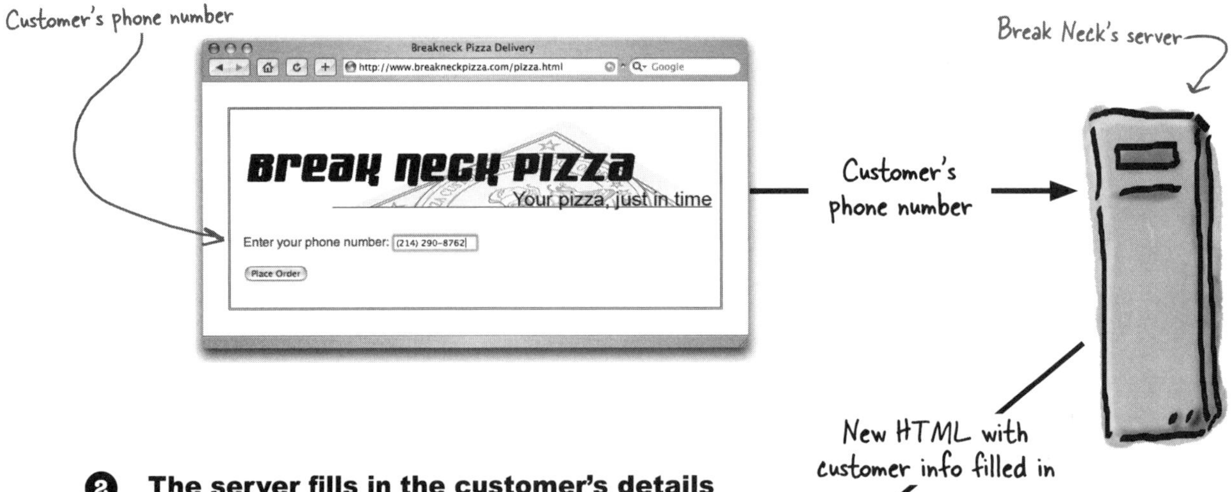

2 The server fills in the customer's details

The server sends back a new form, with the customer's name, phone number, and address already entered into the HTML.

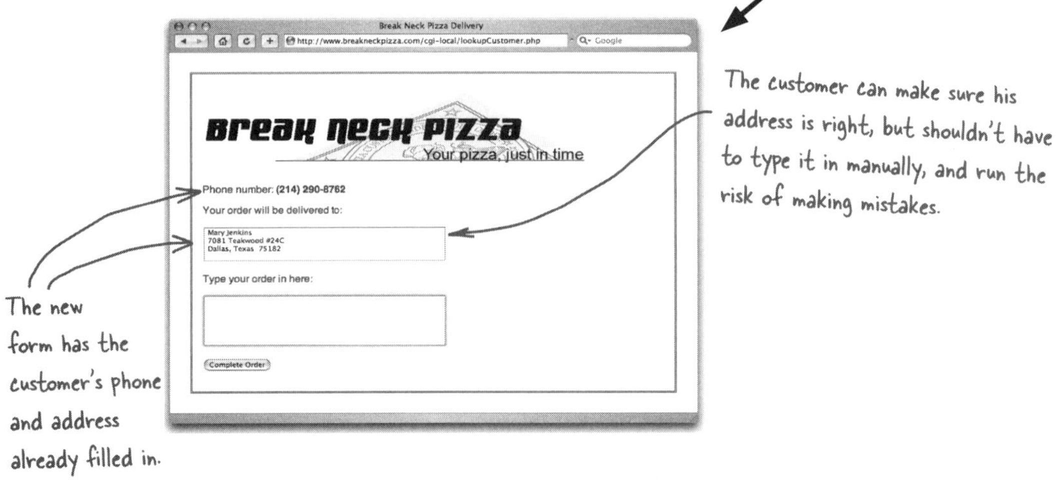

3 The customer enters their order

With the customer's details filled in, he can enter his pizza order into the form, and click "Complete Order".

Umm... hello? I thought this was an *Ajax* book... why aren't we using asynchronous requests here? And the customer has to wait around while the server looks up his address? That's not very **Break Neck**!

No kidding!

It looks like Ajax is just the thing to help out Break Neck. Let's look up that address *without* making the customer wait around for the server... and solve Alex's delivery woes, all at the same time.

Break Neck Pizza, Ajax-style

Instead of starting with old 1990s development ideas, let's look at what the Break Neck app *should* do. Then you can use your new asynchronous programming skills to make sure Break Neck's order form is a responsive, customer-friendly means of getting great pizza, fast. Here's how things should work:

The customer starts out by entering his phone number.
Break Neck Pizza
Your pizza, just in time
Enter your phone number:
Your order will be delivered to:
Type your order in here:
The order form then fills in the customer's address automatically.
The customer enters their pizza order into the form, without waiting on their address to get filled in.
Yeah, come on over, the pizza's already here. Unbelievable... it can't have been ten minutes, and I didn't even have to enter my address.
Once the customer has entered in his order, he clicks "Order Pizza"...
...and Alex, the delivery boy, can get the hot pizza right to the customer's front door.

Work It Through

Just like the Boards 'R' Us application in Chapter 1, you're going to need several JavaScript functions to make the Break Neck app work. Below on the left are the names of two JavaScript functions, and on the right are several lines of JavaScript. Draw arrows from the lines of code to the function each line of code should go into.

request.send(null);

if (request.readyState == 4) { ... }

getCustomerInfo()

request.open("GET", url, true);

request.onreadystatechange = updatePage;

updatePage()

var phone =
    document.getElementById("phone").value;

if (request.status == 200) { ... }

We've done one to help you get started. You don't need to write any code... just draw lines from the code to what function that code goes in.

→ Answers on page 125.

Diagramming the Break Neck app

Now that you know how customers will use the Break Neck app, let's take a look at what actually has to happen behind the scenes.

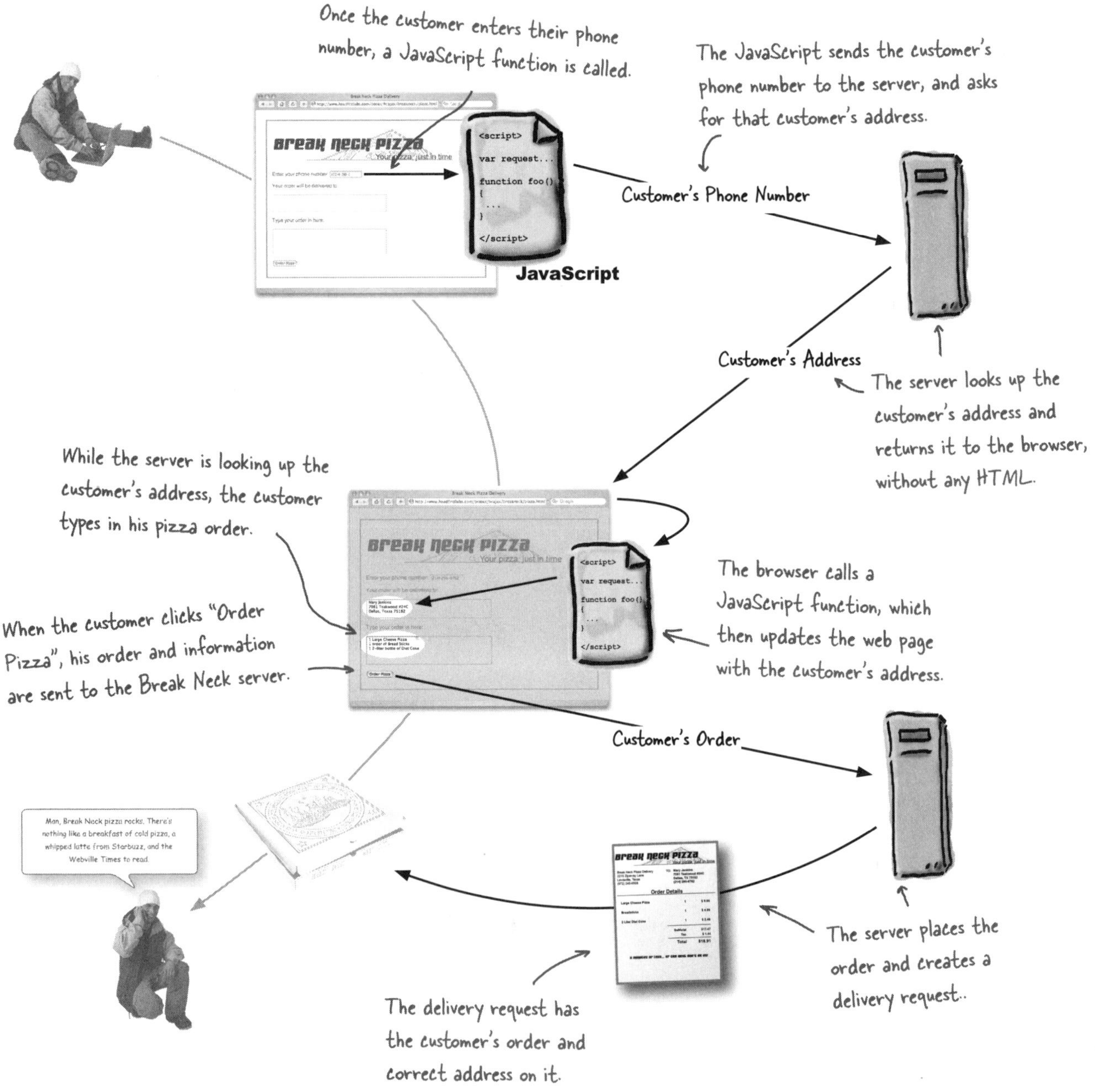

Be the Architect

You've seen what the Break Neck order form should do, and you've also got an idea of what has to happen behind the scenes to turn Break Neck into a customer-friendly web app. Now it's your turn to take charge.

Below is the basic flow diagram for the Break Neck app. Your job is to add notes to this diagram, indicating what steps you need to take to turn this diagram into reality. Write what functions you might need to write, and relate them to the drawing. We've added a few notes of our own to help you get started, and given you some sample notes at the bottom to give you some ideas.

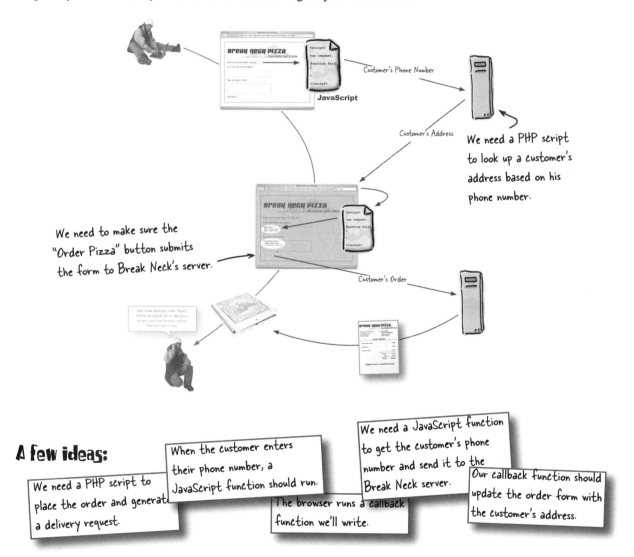

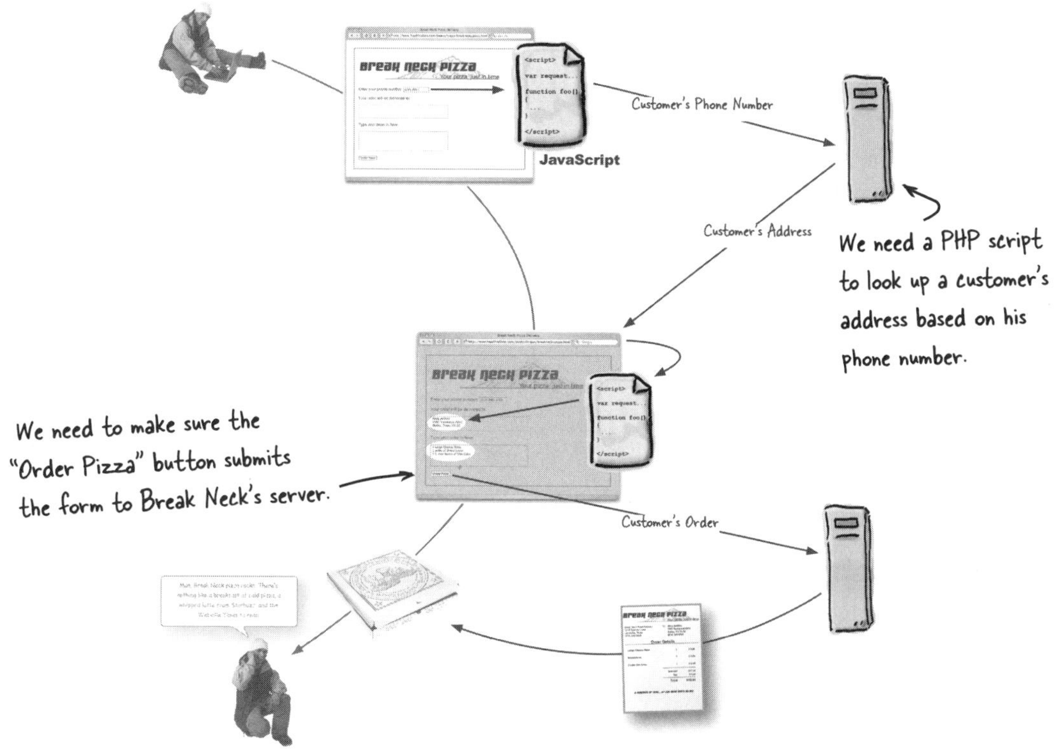
JavaScript
Customer's Phone Number
Customer's Address
We need a PHP script to look up a customer's address based on his phone number.
We need to make sure the "Order Pizza" button submits the form to Break Neck's server.
Customer's Order

A few ideas:

We need a PHP script to place the order and generate a delivery request.

When the customer enters their phone number, a JavaScript function should run.

The browser runs a callback function we'll write.

We need a JavaScript function to get the customer's phone number and send it to the Break Neck server.

Our callback function should update the order form with the customer's address.

Step 1: Get the customer's phone number

It looks like the first thing we need to do with the Break Neck app is make sure we can get the customer's phone number. That's going to take some HTML, a bit of JavaScript, and a lot of help from the web browser.

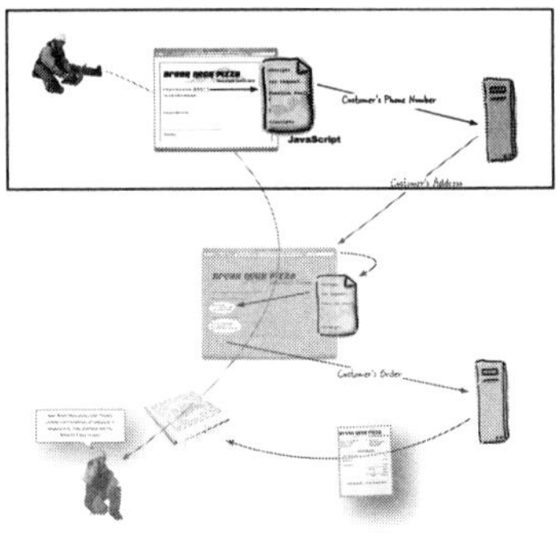

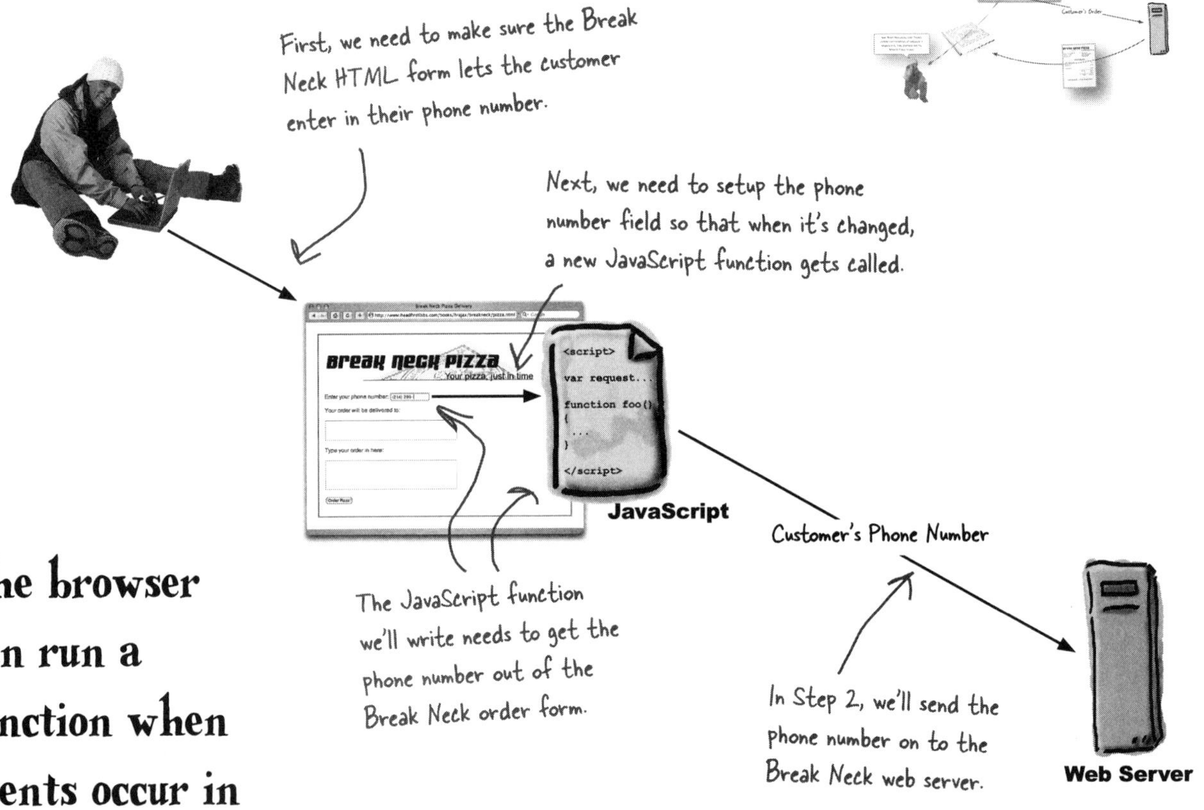

The browser can run a function when events occur in a web page, and give your JavaScript access to user-entered information in the page.

HTML 101: accepting user input

The Break Neck order form already has fields for the customer to enter in their phone number, address, and pizza order. Let's take a quick look at the HTML for the order form, and then figure out how to connect this HTML to the JavaScript you'll be writing:

```
<html>
 <head>
  <title>Break Neck Pizza Delivery</title>
  <link rel="stylesheet" type="text/css" href="breakneck.css" />
 </head>
 <body>
  <p>
   <img src="breakneck-logo.gif"
        alt="Break Neck Pizza" />
  </p>
  <form method="POST" action="placeOrder.php">
   <p>Enter your phone number:
    <input type="text" size="14" name="phone" />
   </p>
   <p>Your order will be delivered to:</p>
   <p><textarea name="address" rows="4" cols="50">
      </textarea></p>
   <p>Type your order in here:</p>
   <p><textarea name="order" rows="6" cols="50"></textarea></p>
   <p><input type="submit" value="Order Pizza" /></p>
  </form>
 </body>
</html>
```

All the style for the Break Neck app is in an external CSS stylesheet.

This is the URL for placing the pizza order once the form is completely filled out.

Here's where the customer enters his phone number.

You'll fill this in with the address that the server returns, but let's leave it as a field so a customer can enter a different address if the want.

A normal "submit" button is used for placing the order, using a form POST.

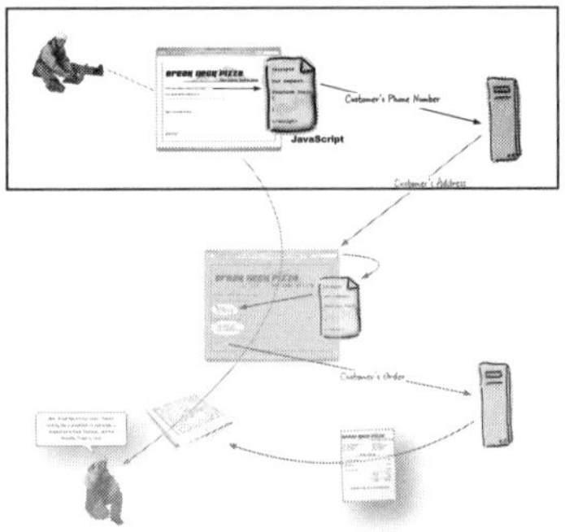

Event handlers connect HTML to JavaScript

Remember event handlers from Chapter 1? You used the **onClick** handler to connect a button on an HTML page to a JavaScript function. Let's take a quick peek back at Chapter 1:

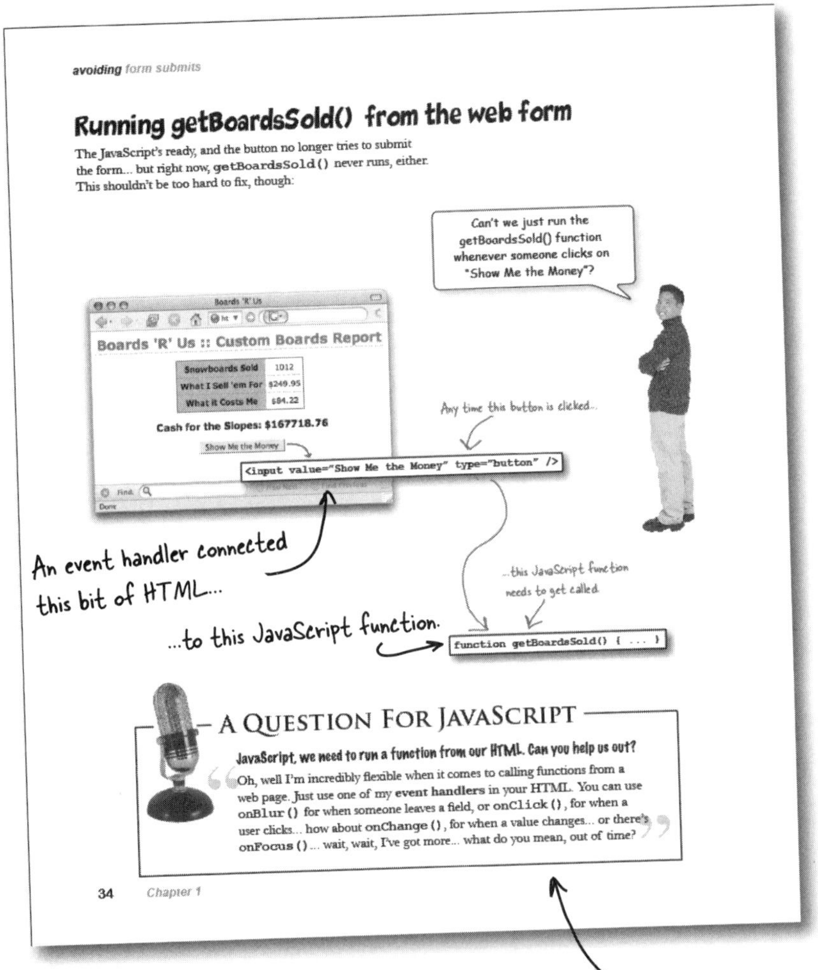

avoiding form submits

Running getBoardsSold() from the web form

The JavaScript's ready, and the button no longer tries to submit the form... but right now, getBoardsSold() never runs, either. This shouldn't be too hard to fix, though:

A Question for JavaScript

JavaScript, we need to run a function from our HTML. Can you help us out?

"Oh, well I'm incredibly flexible when it comes to calling functions from a web page. Just use one of my **event handlers** in your HTML. You can use onBlur() for when someone leaves a field, or onClick(), for when a user clicks... how about onChange(), for when a value changes... or there's onFocus()... wait, wait, I've got more... what do you mean, out of time?"

34 Chapter 1

Remember this? We used event handlers to connect the "Show Me the Money" button in the Boards app to a JavaScript function.

An event handler connected this bit of HTML...

...to this JavaScript function.

We need to use one of these event handlers to connect the phone number field to a JavaScript function.

Aren't you getting a little ahead of things? How can we write an event handler if we haven't even written a JavaScript function yet?

Plan first, code later

Sometimes, it's better to do a little planning before you jump in and start writing code. In this case, we can go ahead and decide what we'll call the JavaScript function that makes a request to the Break Neck server, even though you haven't started coding it yet. Let's name this function **`getCustomerInfo()`**, since that's exactly what the function is going to do: ask the server for the customer's information.

And now that you know the name of this function, you can go ahead and update the HTML in the Break Neck form to run **`getCustomerInfo()`** when a phone number is entered... even though you won't code the function for a few more pages.

You might want to flip back to your application blueprints on page 73, and add the name of this JavaScript function to your notes.

Speaking of planning...

Looking for answers to the Be the Architect exercise back on page 73? You'll find them... throughout this entire chapter.
As you read through the chapter, you'll see how we decided to build the Break Neck Pizza order app. See how your decisions match up with ours, and think about how you might do things differently.

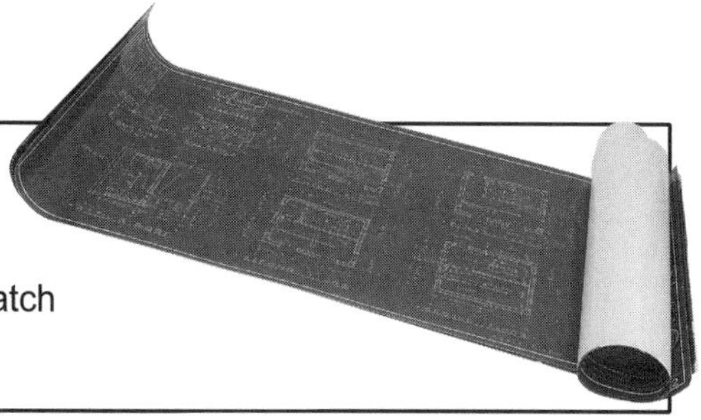

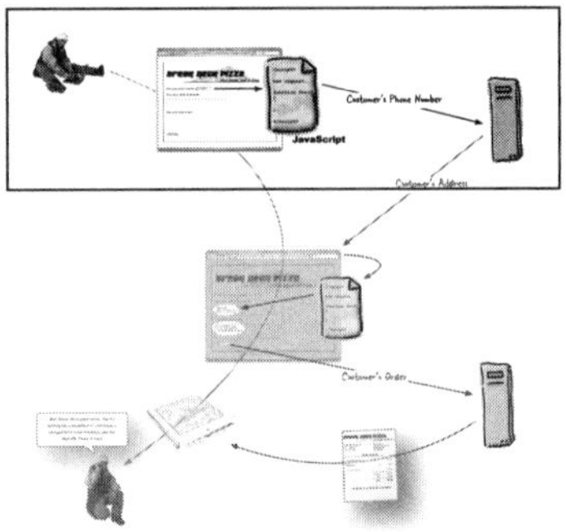

Event handler roundup

You have lots of different ways to attach your JavaScript code to your HTML pages. Here are just a few of the more popular event handlers, and a brief review of how each works. Take a close look; you'll be using one of these on the next page...

onChange

The **onChange** event is triggered any time the value in a form field changes, like when you type in a new value, or clear the existing one.

```
<input type="text"
       name="street"
  onChange="updateMap();" />
```

Here's how you'd specify an onChange event in HTML.

Triggered when:

- ___ Field is entered
- ___ Field is exited
- ✓ Field is changed

onFocus

```
<input type="text" name="state"
       onFocus="popupStates();" />
```

Here's the onFocus event handler in action.

Any JavaScript attached to the **onFocus** event is run when a field or other page component gets the focus, by tabbing into the field or by clicking on the component.

Triggered when:

- ✓ Field is entered
- ___ Field is exited
- ___ Field is changed

onBlur

onBlur is used to run code when a user leaves a field, by tabbing out of the field or by clicking on another form component.

Triggered when:

- ___ Field is entered
- ✓ Field is exited
- ___ Field is changed

This code runs when the zipCode field loses focus.

```
<input type="text"
       name="zipCode"
  onBlur="validateZip();" />
```

Code Magnets

By now, you should be ready to update the Break Neck pizza form. First, you need to add an event handler to run the getCustomerInfo() function that you'll write in just a few pages. Remember, this function should run every time a customer enters a new phone number.

Next, you need to add id attributes to the order form; you'll need these later, when you want access the form's fields in your JavaScript. While you're at it, why don't you clear the form every time it's loaded, too?

Below is the HTML for the current version of the web form. To update this form, attach the HTML and JavaScript magnets from the bottom of the page to the correct blanks in the markup.

```
<body _____________________>
 <p>
  <img src="breakneck-logo.gif" alt="Break Neck Pizza" />
 </p>
 <form method="POST" action="placeOrder.php">
  <p>Enter your phone number:
   <input type="text" size="14" name="phone" ___________
          __________="getCustomerInfo();" />
  </p>
  <p>Your order will be delivered to:</p>
  <p><textarea name="address" _________________
             rows="4" cols="50"></textarea></p>
  <p>Type your order in here:</p>
  <p><textarea name="order" _________________
             rows="6" cols="50"></textarea></p>
  <p><input type="submit" ________________
          value="Order Pizza" /></p>
 </form>
</body>
```

```
onBlur
id="pizza-location"
id="address"
onChange
id="order"
onFocus
id="phone"
onSubmit
id="submit"
onLoad="document.forms[0].reset();"
onClick
```

Code Magnets Solutions

Here's how we finished off the Break Neck web form. Make sure your answers match ours before going on to the next page.

```
<body onLoad="document.forms[0].reset();">
 <p>
  <img src="breakneck-logo.gif" alt="Break Neck Pizza" />
 </p>
 <form method="POST" action="placeOrder.php">
  <p>Enter your phone number:
   <input type="text" size="14" name="phone" id="phone"
       onChange="getCustomerInfo();" />
  </p>
  <p>Your order will be delivered to:</p>
  <p><textarea name="address" id="address"
              rows="4" cols="50"></textarea></p>
  <p>Type your order in here:</p>
  <p><textarea name="order" id="order"
              rows="6" cols="50"></textarea></p>
  <p><input type="submit" id="submit"
           value="Order Pizza" /></p>
 </form>
</body>
```

This clears the first form (forms[0]) in the HTML document.

onChange makes sure that anytime the phone number changes, getCustomerInfo() will be run.

Here are the magnets that were left over.

`onBlur` `onFocus` `onSubmit` `onClick` `id="pizza-location"`

? Frequently Asked Questions

Q: I used the onBlur handler, instead of onChange. Wouldn't that work also?

A: **`onBlur`** will run whenever the customer leaves the phone number field, so that's also a good option. But with **`onBlur`**, **`getCustomerInfo()`** will get run even if the customer *didn't* change the phone number. **`onChange`** will only run when the number changes, so it's probably a better choice.

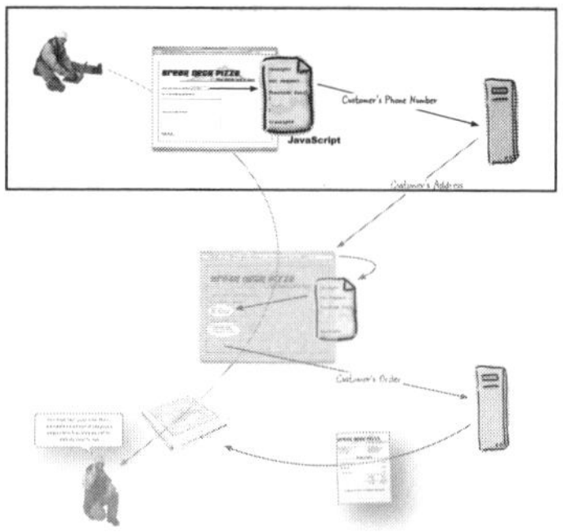

On to the JavaScript

Now you're ready to dig into some JavaScript. You know the name of the function that you'll be using to get the customer's phone number: **`getCustomerInfo()`**. This function needs to send the customer's phone number to Break Neck's server, and ask for that customer's address.

Let's start out with just the function name:

```
function getCustomerInfo() {
  ...
}
```

Here's where all your code will go.

The first thing we need to do is get the customer's phone number from the HTML form.

BRAIN POWER

Do you think there could be any problems with event handlers that run JavaScript code that then makes asynchronous requests? What would happen if the pizza form sent a request for an address, and then sent another request before the first response was returned? What do you think the customer would see happen on the order form?

Just Do It

Open up the examples for Head Rush Ajax that you downloaded from http://www.headfirstlabs.com. Go into the chapter02/breakneck/ folder, and you'll find pizza.html. This is the Break Neck order form, but you need to make some changes to bring it up to speed.

First, make sure the HTML matches the answers from the Code Magnets exercise, on page 80. Next, you need to add <script> tags to the <head> section of the HTML, just like you did for the Boards app back in Chapter 1. Finally, go ahead and enter in the empty getCustomerInfo() function. We'll be filling this function in over the next several pages.

Be sure not to go on to the next page until you've got your version of pizza.html updated.

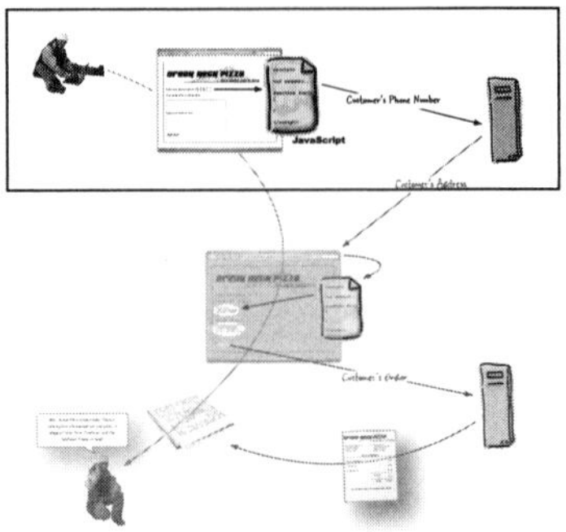

Use the DOM to get the phone number

You can use the Document Object Model, or DOM, from your JavaScript to get the phone number that the customer entered into the Break Neck order form. We'll spend a lot more time looking at the Document Object Model in Chapter 4. For now, just think of the DOM as the way you ask the web browser to get information from, or send information to, a web page.

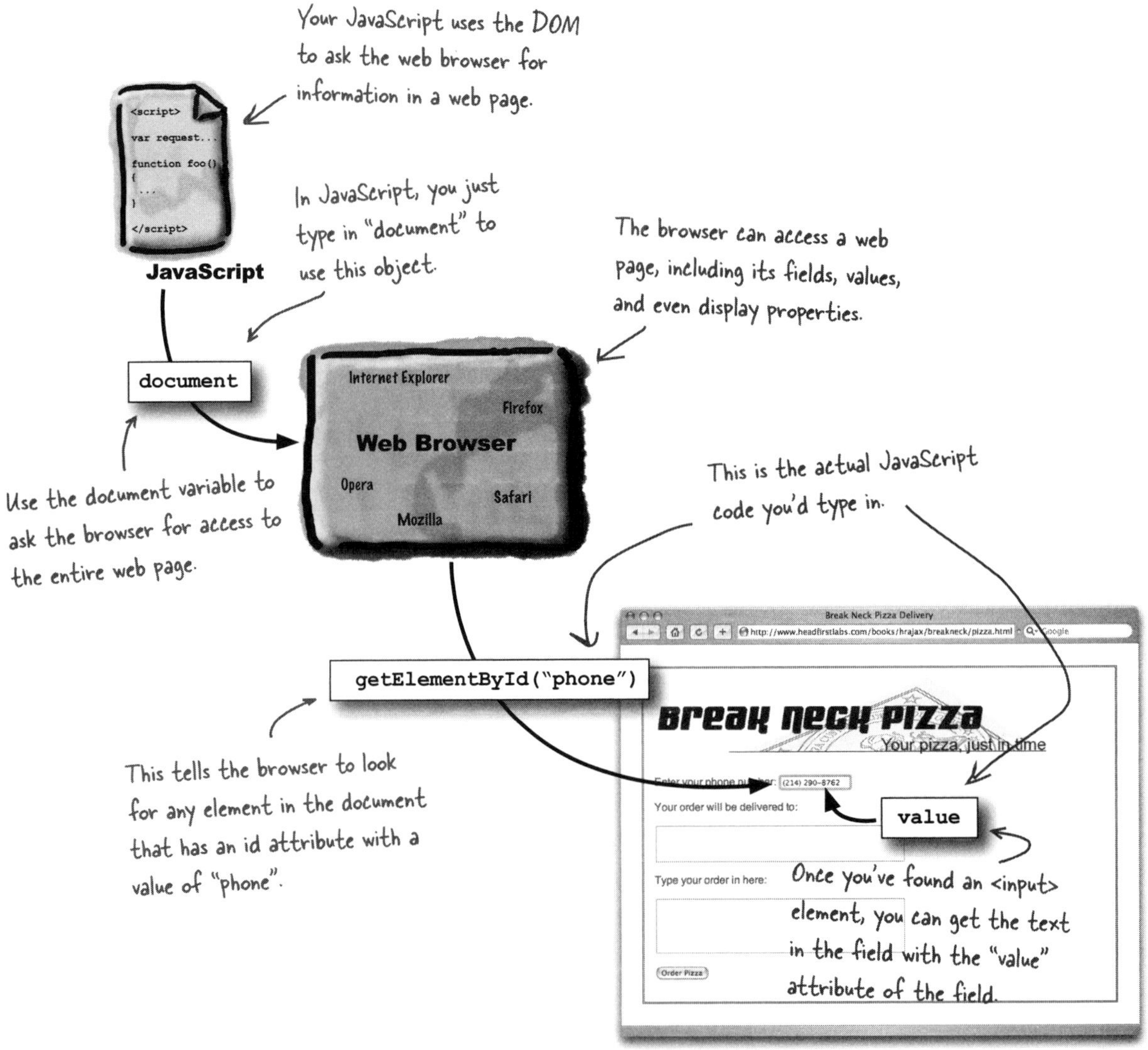

Connecting the DOM dots

Let's use the DOM to get the customer's phone number. Below, we've connected the pieces of DOM code you saw on the last page, and added them to the empty **`getCustomerInfo()`** function:

```
function getCustomerInfo() {
  var phone = document.getElementById("phone").value;
}
```

Let's store the phone number in a new variable.

This just combines the pieces of JavaScript you saw on the last page into a single line of code.

Go ahead and add this line of code into your version of pizza.html.

The entire HTML page is represented by the "document" object in JavaScript.

```
<html>
 <head>
  <title>Break Neck Pizza Delivery</title>
  <link rel="stylesheet" type="text/css" href="breakneck.css" />
  <script language="javascript" type="text/javascript">
    function getCustomerInfo() {
      var phone = document.getElementById("phone").value;
    }
  </script>
 </head>

 <body>
  <p><img src="breakneck-logo.gif" alt="Break Neck Pizza" /></p>
  <form method="POST" action="placeOrder.php">
   <p>Enter your phone number:
    <input type="text" size="14"
           name="phone" id="phone" onChange="getCustomerInfo()" />
   </p>
   <p>Your order will be delivered to:</p>
   <p><textarea name="address" rows="4" cols="50" id="address">
      </textarea></p>
   <p>Type your order in here:</p>
   <p><textarea name="order" rows="6" cols="50" id="order">
      </textarea></p>
   <p><input type="submit" value="Order Pizza" /></p>
  </form>
 </body>
</html>
```

getElementById("phone") looks for an element with an "id" attribute...

...with a value of "phone".

That's it for *Step 1!* On to *Step 2*...

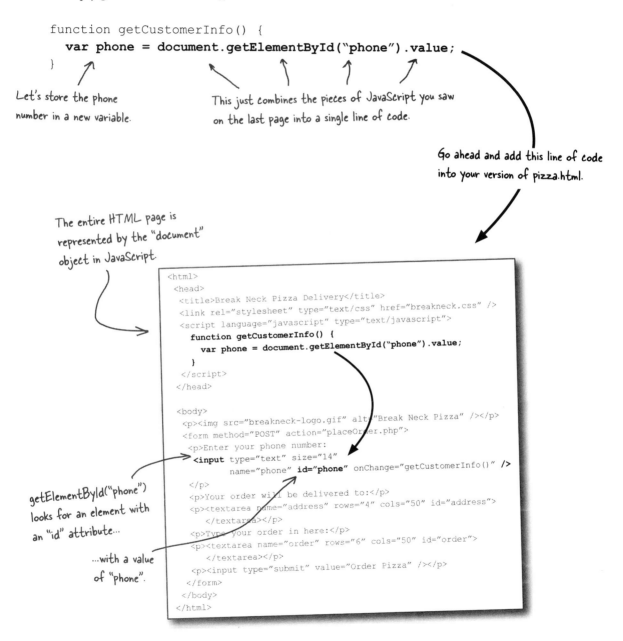

Step 2: Request the customer's address

Next up is sending the phone number we got in Step 1 to Break Neck's web server, and asking for the customer's address based on that phone number.

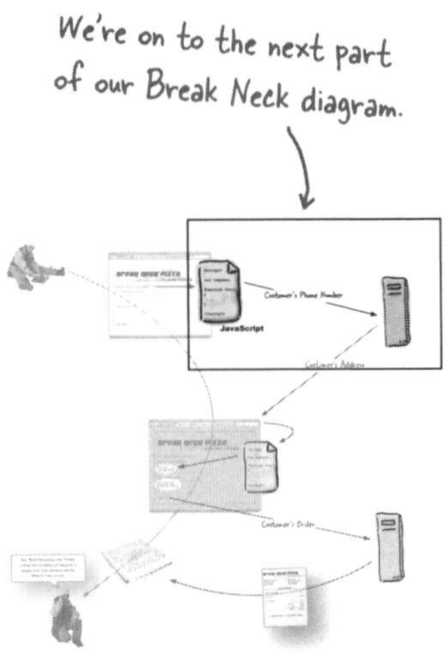

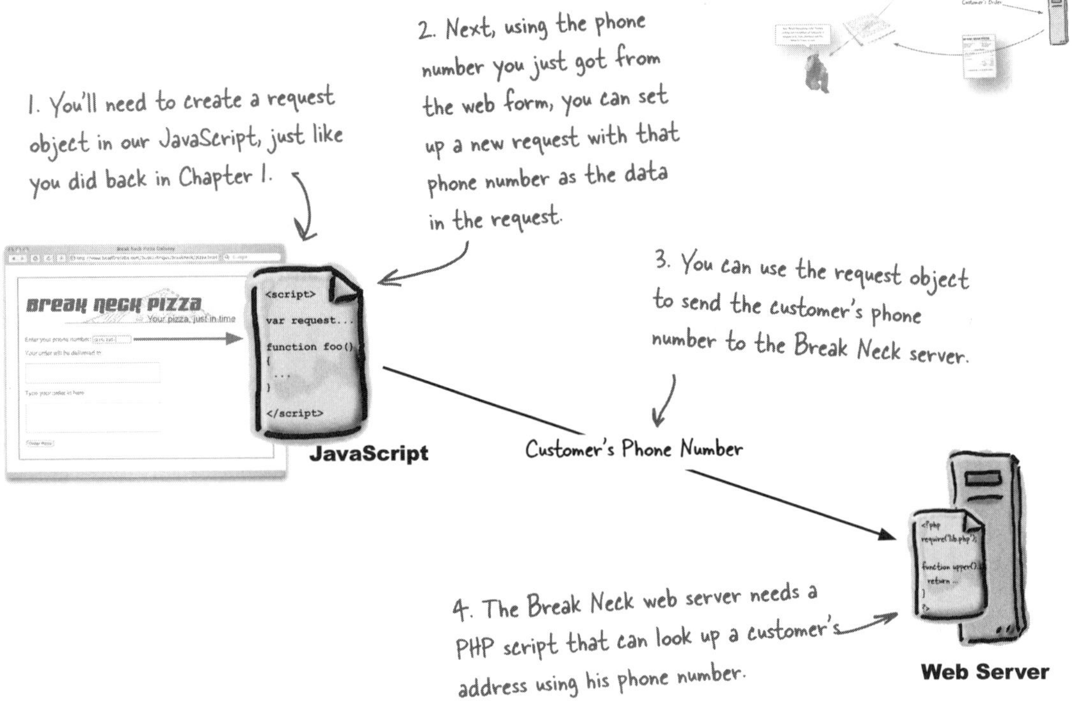

Where's ~~Waldo~~ the Web Browser?

Is the browser involved at all in this step? If you think it is, add a note to this page saying what you think the browser does.

getCustomerInfo() at a glance

You should be pretty comfortable with making a GET request after fixing up Katie's Boards 'R' Us app back in Chapter 1. Here's similar code for **`getCustomerInfo()`**; most of this JavaScript should look similar to the code you wrote Chapter 1:

```
function getCustomerInfo() {
  var phone = document.getElementById("phone").value;
  createRequest();
  var url = "lookupCustomer.php?phone=" +
            escape(phone);
  request.open("GET", url, true);
  request.onreadystatechange = updatePage;
  request.send(null);
}
```

You've already set up the Break Neck form to call this function whenever the phone number field is changed.

This is the code to get the phone number, using the DOM, that you wrote in Step 1.

You wrote this function in Chapter 1; it creates a new request object.

Here's the URL for the script on the server...

...and this sends the phone number as a request parameter.

This sets up the request object to make a GET request.

This tells the browser what function to run when the request's ready state changes.

This last line sends the request, with no additional data other than what is in the request URL.

Say What?

It's OK if you've still got some questions about this code. We're going to look at each line in detail throughout the chapter, so don't feel like you have to understand it all now.

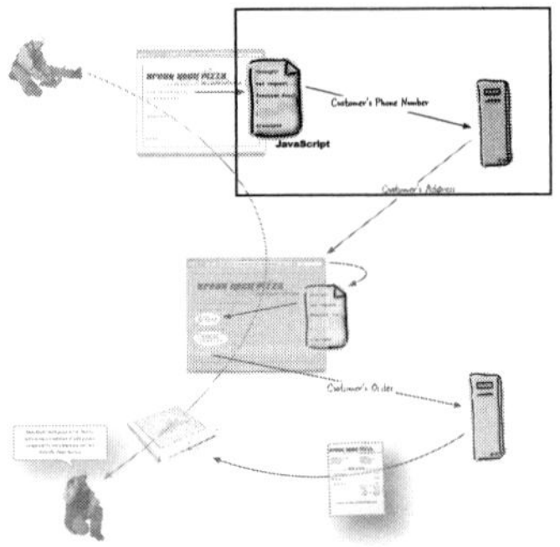

Creating a request object

This step is all about making a request to the Break Neck server. For that, we need a request object that our JavaScript function can use. Luckily, though, you already wrote code that creates a request object back in Chapter 1, in the **createRequest()** function.

You should remember **createRequest()** from Chapter 1. Let's take a look at that JavaScript again, and make sure it's ready to use in the Break Neck app:

Here's the top part of pizza.html, updated with the createRequest() function from Chapter 1.

Since requset isn't created inside a function, __all__ your functions can use the request variable.

This was all pre-assembled JavaScript in Chapter 1.

Remember, we had to use different code for different browsers.

Our error checking here makes sure nothing went wrong.

We've pulled this code out of its pre-assembled box... you're going to learn exactly what each line of this JavaScript does over the next few pages.

```html
<html>
 <head>
  <title>Break Neck Pizza Delivery</title>
  <link rel="stylesheet" type="text/css" href="breakneck.css" />
  <script language="javascript" type="text/javascript">
   var request = null;

   function createRequest() {
     try {
       request = new XMLHttpRequest();
     } catch (trymicrosoft) {
       try {
         request = new ActiveXObject("Msxml2.XMLHTTP");
       } catch (othermicrosoft) {
         try {
           request = new ActiveXObject("Microsoft.XMLHTTP");
         } catch (failed) {
           request = null;
         }
       }
     }

     if (request == null)
       alert("Error creating request object!");
   }

   function getCustomerInfo() {
     var phone = document.getElementById("phone").value;
     createRequest();
     var url = "lookupCustomer.php?phone=" + escape(phone);
     request.open("GET", url, true);
     request.onreadystatechange = updatePage;
     request.send(null);
   }
  </script>
 </head>
```

Plans change

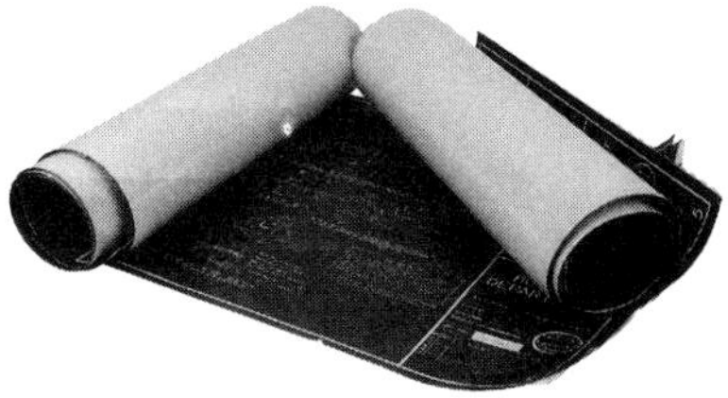

Remember your plans for the Break Neck app from page 73? Well, you've learned a lot since then, and now's your chance to make a few changes. Flip back to your original plans, and see if there are any changes you might want to make... there's still a lot of work left to do before we finish up with Break Neck.

Use the space below to write updated notes about what you think needs to happen to ensure Break Neck crushes its competitors. If you still like what you had back on page 73, you can write those notes in on these plans, and give yourself a pat on the back for getting things right the first time.

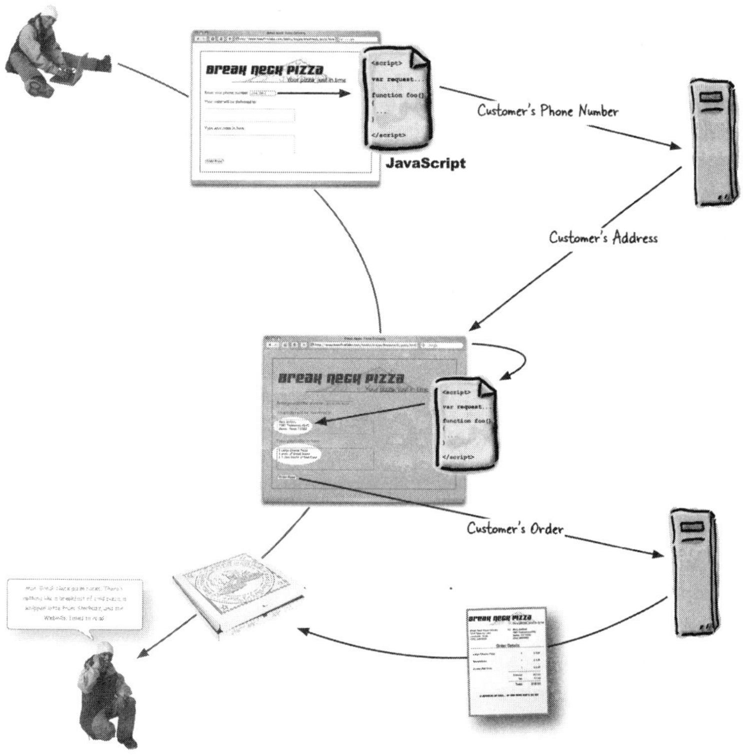

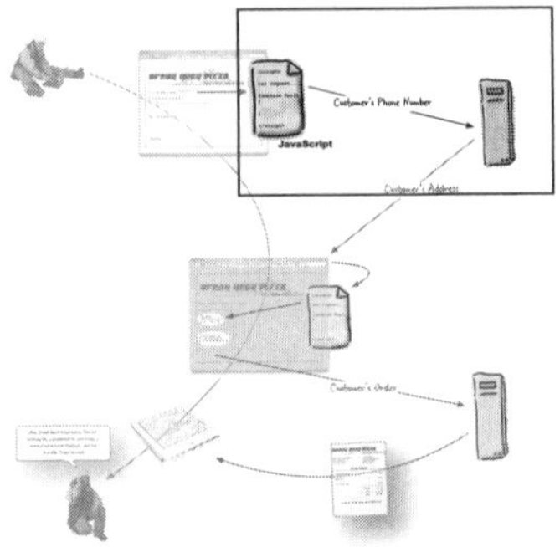

Supporting multiple browsers

It's time to break into this pre-assembled JavaScript, and figure out exactly what's going on. Let's walk through exactly what each piece of **`createRequest()`** does, step-by-step.

1 Declare a request variable

First, we declare a new variable to represent the request object, so we can use that variable in the rest of our JavaScript.

```
var request = null;
```

Remember, this variable is not declared in a function... it's just nested inside pizza.html's <script> tags.

Since this variable isn't declared inside a function, any of your JavaScript functions can use it.

We want our request variable to point at a JavaScript request object.

2 Try and create XMLHttpRequest for non-Microsoft browsers

Next, we define a new function called **`createRequest()`**. The first thing this function does is try and create a new request object using the **`XMLHttpRequest`** type, which works on almost all browsers except Internet Explorer:

```
function createRequest() {
  try {
    request = new XMLHttpRequest();
  } catch (trymicrosoft) {
    // Try something different
    //   for Microsoft
    //   (check out step 3)
  }

  if (request == null)
    alert("Error creating XMLHttpRequest!");
}
```

XMLHttpRequest works on Safari, FireFox, Mozilla, Opera, and most non-Microsoft browsers.

If that fails, let's try something else.

At the end of all this, spit out an error if the request variable is still null.

3 Try and create an ActiveXObject for Microsoft browsers

In the **catch** block, we try to create a request object using one of the Microsoft-compatible types... by trying each type in *its* own **try/catch** block:

```
try {
  request =
    new ActiveXObject("Msxml2.XMLHTTP");
} catch (othermicrosoft) {
  try {
    request =
      new ActiveXObject("Microsoft.XMLHTTP");
  } catch (failed) { request = null; }
}
```

Most versions of IE support this...

...but for some, you'll need this other type.

Uh oh... if the code gets here, we've got a problem. Make sure request is still set to null.

Here's our request variable again.

ActiveXObject works on Internet Explorer.

WARNING! IE 5 on the Mac still won't work, even with this IE-specific code. If you're using IE on the Mac, though... well, what can we say?

Now put it all together...

```
var request = null;
function createRequest() {
  try {
    request = new XMLHttpRequest();
  } catch (trymicrosoft) {
    try {
      request = new ActiveXObject("Msxml2.XMLHTTP");
    } catch (othermicrosoft) {
      try {
        request = new ActiveXObject("Microsoft.XMLHTTP");
      } catch (failed) {
        request = null;
      }
    }
  }
  if (request == null)
    alert("Error creating XMLHttpRequest!");
}
```

For non-Microsoft browsers like Safari and Firefox.

For the Internet Explorer fans.

Error handling in case something went wrong.

Don't forget about the big picture... we're still working on getting a request to the Break Neck web server.

Just Do It

It's time to get a taste of the browser wars for yourself. Add the getCustomerInfo() and createRequest() JavaScript from the last several pages into your copy of pizza.html. Then, comment out the parts of createRequest() that create the request object for the type of browser you're using.

If you're using InternetExplorer, comment out the code that deals with ActiveXObject; if you're using a non-Microsoft browser, comment out the lines that create the XMLHttpRequest type. Now load pizza.html in your browser, and enter in a phone number. You should get an error message, like this:

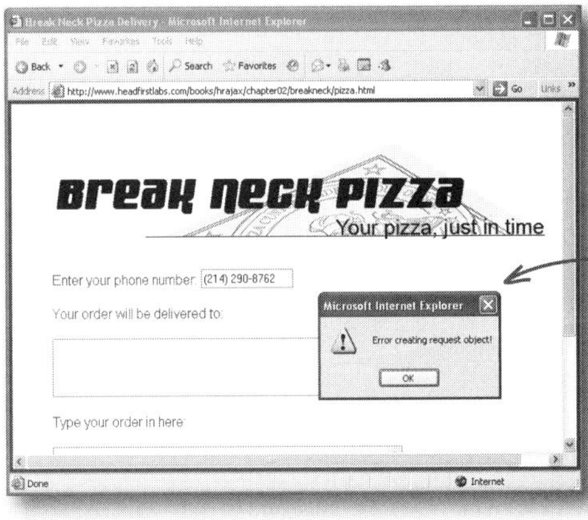

Here's Internet Explorer, reporting an error because the ActiveXObject part of createRequest() was commented out.

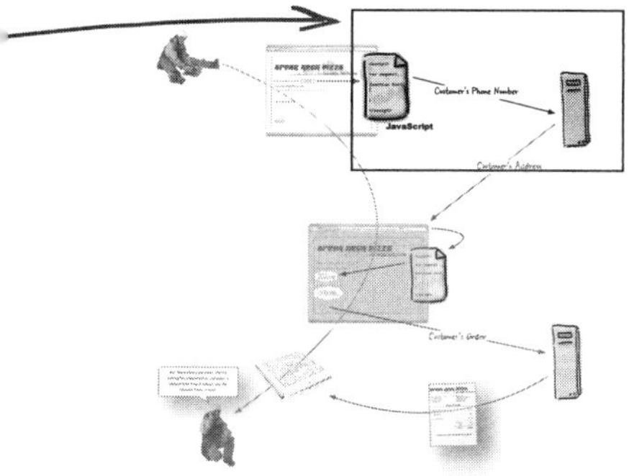

I just tried this, and it really sucks that I had to enter my phone number in to find out that things weren't working. Couldn't you have told me that before I bothered typing my number in?

Don't annoy the customer!

In the Break Neck app, customers only have to fill out one field before **`getCustomerInfo()`** gets called, and your code tries to create a new request object. Then, if something's wrong, the customer gets an error message.

But imagine how annoying it would be to fill out an entire form, and *then* find out that something's wrong... what a waste of time!

It looks like we need to find a way to let users know about any problems much earlier... like *before* they start typing into the Break Neck form.

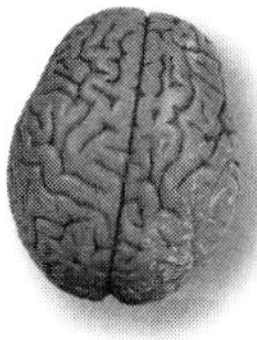

BRAIN POWER

Look back at Step 1 on page 88, and think about how we handled creating the request variable. Does this give you any ideas about how you could let customers know about any problems before they start using the Break Neck order form?

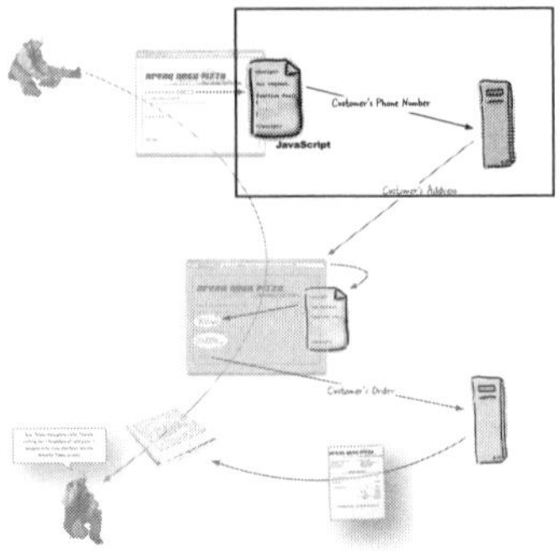

Well, we've got to run the createRequest() function somehow, right? How else can we create the request object?

JavaScript doesn't have to be in a function

Remember how we declared the **request** variable, but didn't put that line of code in a function?

```
<head>
 <title>Break Neck Pizza Delivery</title>
 ...
 <script language="javascript" type="text/javascript">
  var request = null;
 </script>
</head>
```

This code will run automatically when the page loads.

Any JavaScript in your web page that's not in a function gets run **statically**. That means that as the web browser is loading your page, it will automatically run any JavaScript it finds that is not in a function, *before* anyone can type into your form or click any buttons on the page.

So if we move *all* of the code in **createRequest()** out of a function, *all* the code that tries to create the request object will run as soon as the Break Neck form loads. If there are errors, customers will know right away... and **getCustomerInfo()** won't need to run **createRequest()** anymore—the request object will be ready to use, or the customer will have already received an error message.

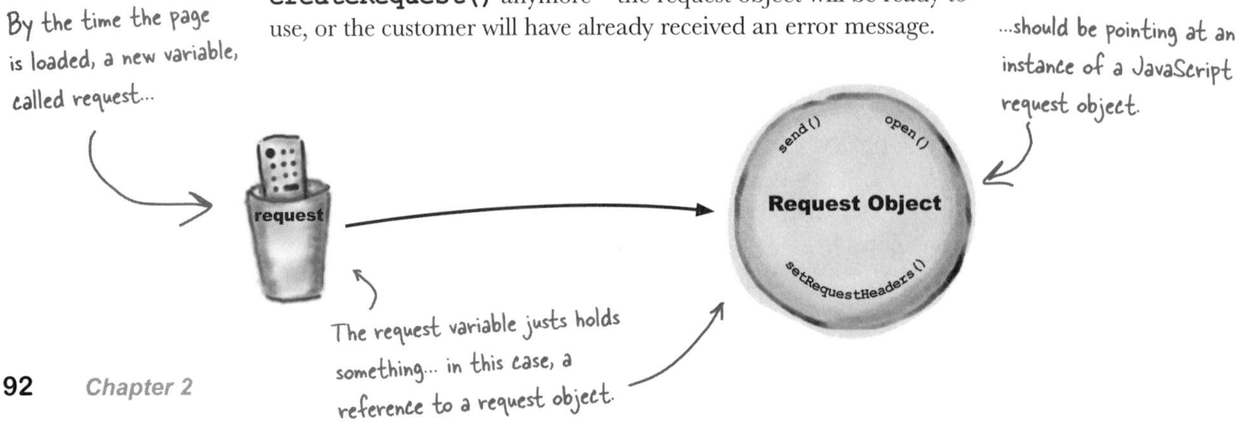
By the time the page is loaded, a new variable, called request...
request
Request Object
send()
open()
setRequestHeaders()
...should be pointing at an instance of a JavaScript request object.
The request variable justs holds something... in this case, a reference to a request object.

Just Do It

Now that you've learned about static JavaScript, creating request objects, and better error handling, you need to make some more changes to pizza.html. Open up your HTML, and move all the code in createRequest() outside of the function, right after the line of JavaScript that looks like this:

```
<script language="javascript" type="text/javascript">
 var request = null;

</script>
```

All the code that is in createRequest() should go here.

Next, remove the createRequest() function altogether, and also remove the line in getCustomerInfo() that ran the createRequest() function. You can test your changes by commenting out the JavaScript that creates a request object for the type of browser you're using. If there are any errors, they should show up immediately, before you get a chance to use the Break Neck order form. Once you're done testing, remove all your comments, and make sure pizza.html runs on both Microsoft and non-Microsoft browsers. Save your changes, and you're ready to turn the page.

Any errors get reported before the order form ever gets loaded. Much better!

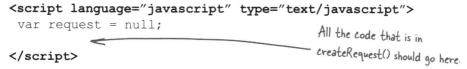

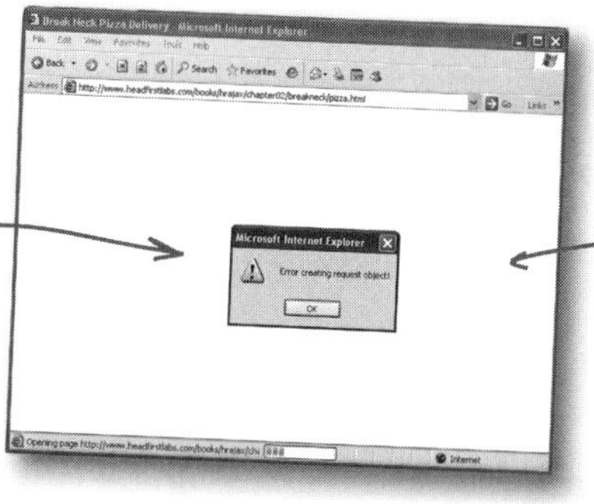

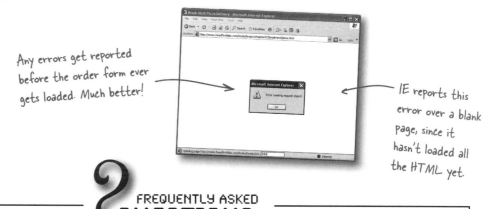

IE reports this error over a blank page, since it hasn't loaded all the HTML yet.

FREQUENTLY ASKED QUESTIONS

Q: So the browser runs any JavaScript that's not in a function before the HTML in the page is displayed?

A: Any JavaScript that's in the **<head>** section of your HTML will get run before the page loads. However, you can insert JavaScript anywhere in an HTML page... even between elements like **<p>** or **<form>** in the middle of the page. JavaScript in those sections runs when the browser gets to that part of the page. But, all static JavaScript will get run before anyone can actually use your page, and that's what's important here.

Q: And tell me again why we have to use ActiveXObject to make Break Neck work on Internet Explorer?

A: Remember the browser wars? It's still common to have the same object called different things in different browsers. Fortunately, Internet Explorer 7.0 is supposed to move to a standard naming scheme, and replace their **`ActiveXObject`** object with a new object, called **`XMLHttpRequest`**. Of course, you'll still have to support those older versions of Internet Explorer, so your code won't change too much.

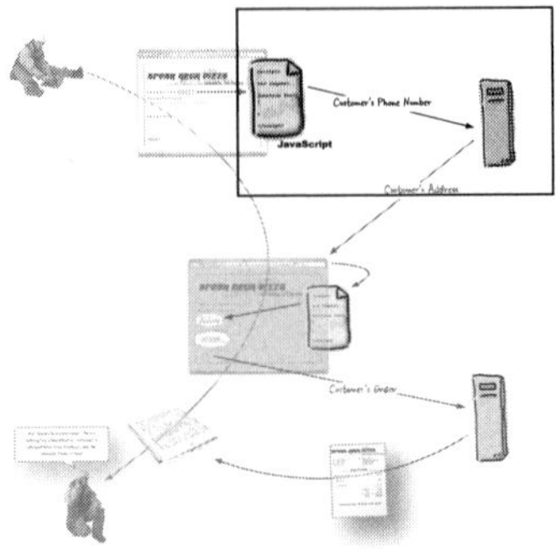

Back to getCustomerInfo()

With the request object taken care of, let's get back to coding **getCustomerInfo()**. Remember where we left this function?

```
function getCustomerInfo() {
  var phone = document.getElementById("phone").value;
  createRequest();
  var url = "lookupCustomer.php?phone=" +
            escape(phone);
  request.open("GET", url, true);
  request.onreadystatechange = updatePage;
  request.send(null);
}
```

Get rid of this line... now our request object is created in static JavaScript.

This is the code you wrote back in Step 1.

Next up is getting the PHP script working on the Break Neck server.

Talking to the server-side guys

Here's what we need to have the server-side guys take care of for us:

1. **Create a new PHP script to lookup a customer's address based on their phone number.**
2. **Name the script lookupCustomer.php.**
3. **Figure out how the script will accept the customer's phone number.**
4. **Make sure the script doesn't return any HTML... we just want the customer's address.**

Draw a line connecting each of these four points to the statement in the Team Chat on the next page which deals with that point.

Break Neck's PHP script

Let's ask Frank over in the server-side group to write us a PHP script to look up customer addresses. Then you can send the customer's phone number to this script, and get the customer's address as a response.

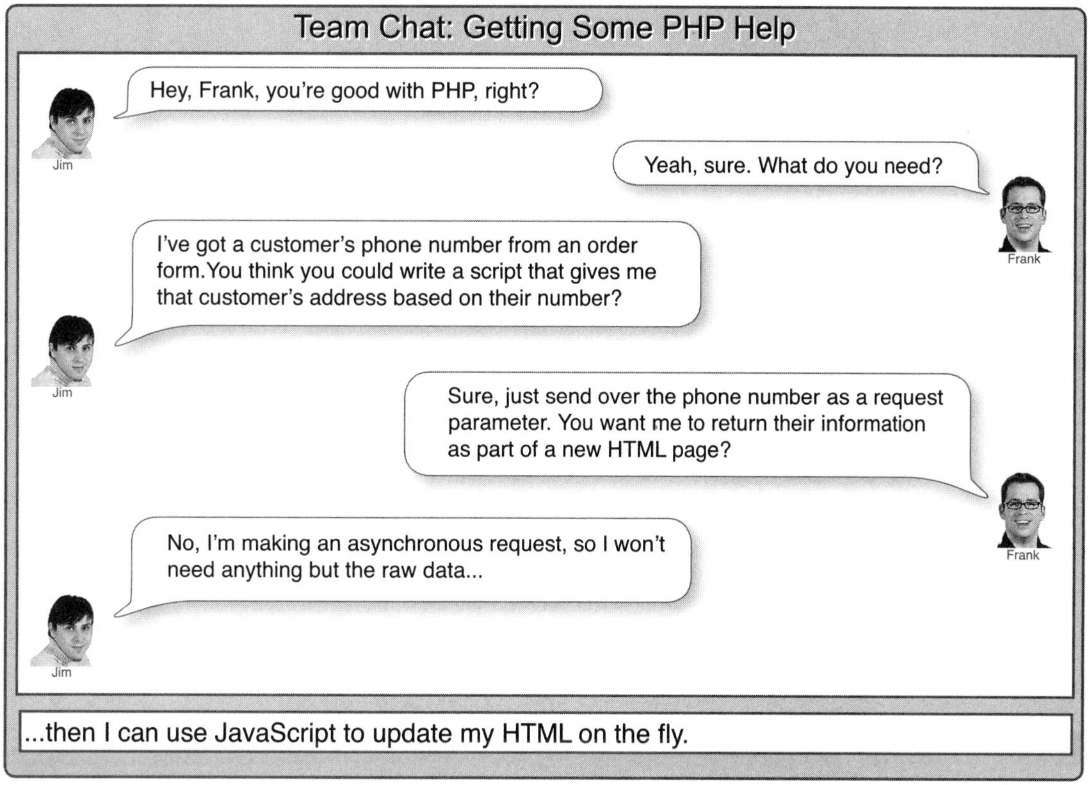

Team Chat: Getting Some PHP Help
Hey, Frank, you're good with PHP, right?
Jim
Yeah, sure. What do you need?
Frank
I've got a customer's phone number from an order form. You think you could write a script that gives me that customer's address based on their number?
Jim
Sure, just send over the phone number as a request parameter. You want me to return their information as part of a new HTML page?
Frank
No, I'm making an asynchronous request, so I won't need anything but the raw data...
Jim
...then I can use JavaScript to update my HTML on the fly.

Just Do It

In the book's examples, look in the chapter02/breakneck directory, and find the lookupCustomer.php script. This is a PHP script that will run without a database server; keep this file on your computer, or FTP it to your web site—you'll be using it in just a sec.

Remember, you don't need to understand all this PHP... this is just for bonus credit.

PHP ...at a glance

Here's the script that Frank wrote to take a phone number from the order form, and look up a customer's address:

```
<?php

// Connect to database
$conn = @mysql_connect("mysql.headfirstlabs.com",
                       "secret", "really-secret");
if (!$conn)
  die("Error connecting to MySQL: " . mysql_error());

if (!mysql_select_db("headfirst", $conn))
  die("Error selecting Head First database: " . mysql_error());

$phone = preg_replace("/[\. \(\)\-]/", "", $_REQUEST['phone']);
$select = 'SELECT *';
$from   = '  FROM hraj_breakneck';
$where  = ' WHERE phone = \'' . $phone . '\'';

$queryResult = @mysql_query($select . $from . $where);
if (!$queryResult)
  die('Error retrieving customer from the database.');

while ($row = mysql_fetch_array($queryResult)) {
  echo $row['name'] . "\n" .
       $row['street1'] . "\n" .
       $row['city'] . ", " .
       $row['state'] . " " .
       $row['zipCode'];
}

mysql_close($conn);

?>
```

Here's all the standard database connection code.

This bit of code removes any special phone characters, like "(", ")", and the "-".

Using the phone number you sent as part of the request, the script looks up the customer's address...

...and then echoes the address back to the requesting program.

* The version of lookupCustomer.php in the examples doesn't use a database, and just returns a random address, so you don't need MySQL running to get Break Neck working on your own computer.

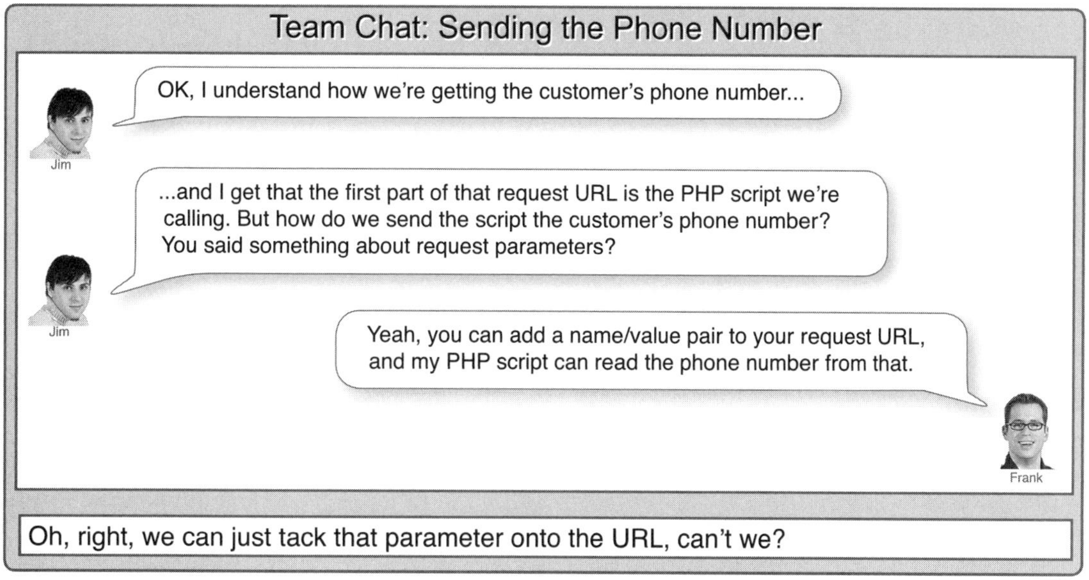

Team Chat: Sending the Phone Number
OK, I understand how we're getting the customer's phone number...
Jim
...and I get that the first part of that request URL is the PHP script we're calling. But how do we send the script the customer's phone number? You said something about request parameters?
Jim
Yeah, you can add a name/value pair to your request URL, and my PHP script can read the phone number from that.
Frank
Oh, right, we can just tack that parameter onto the URL, can't we?

This is the script name; you've already got this part down cold.

Use a "?" to separate the script from any parameters.

Then give a name to the parameter, like "phone"...

...and put the customer's phone number from the order form here.

lookupCustomer.php | **?** | **phone=** | (214) 290-8762

```
function getCustomerInfo() {
  var phone = document.getElementById("phone").value;
  var url = "lookupCustomer.php?phone=" + escape(phone);
  request.open("GET", url, true);
  request.onreadystatechange = updatePage;
  request.send(null);
}
```

We're storing the entire request URL in a JavaScript variable.

Using the escape() function makes sure none of the tricky characters in the phone number cause problems for the web browser when it sends this request.

Request URLs deliver data to the server

The simple little request URL in **getCustomerInfo()** has a lot of responsibility. Let's take a closer look, and see exactly what that request URL is doing:

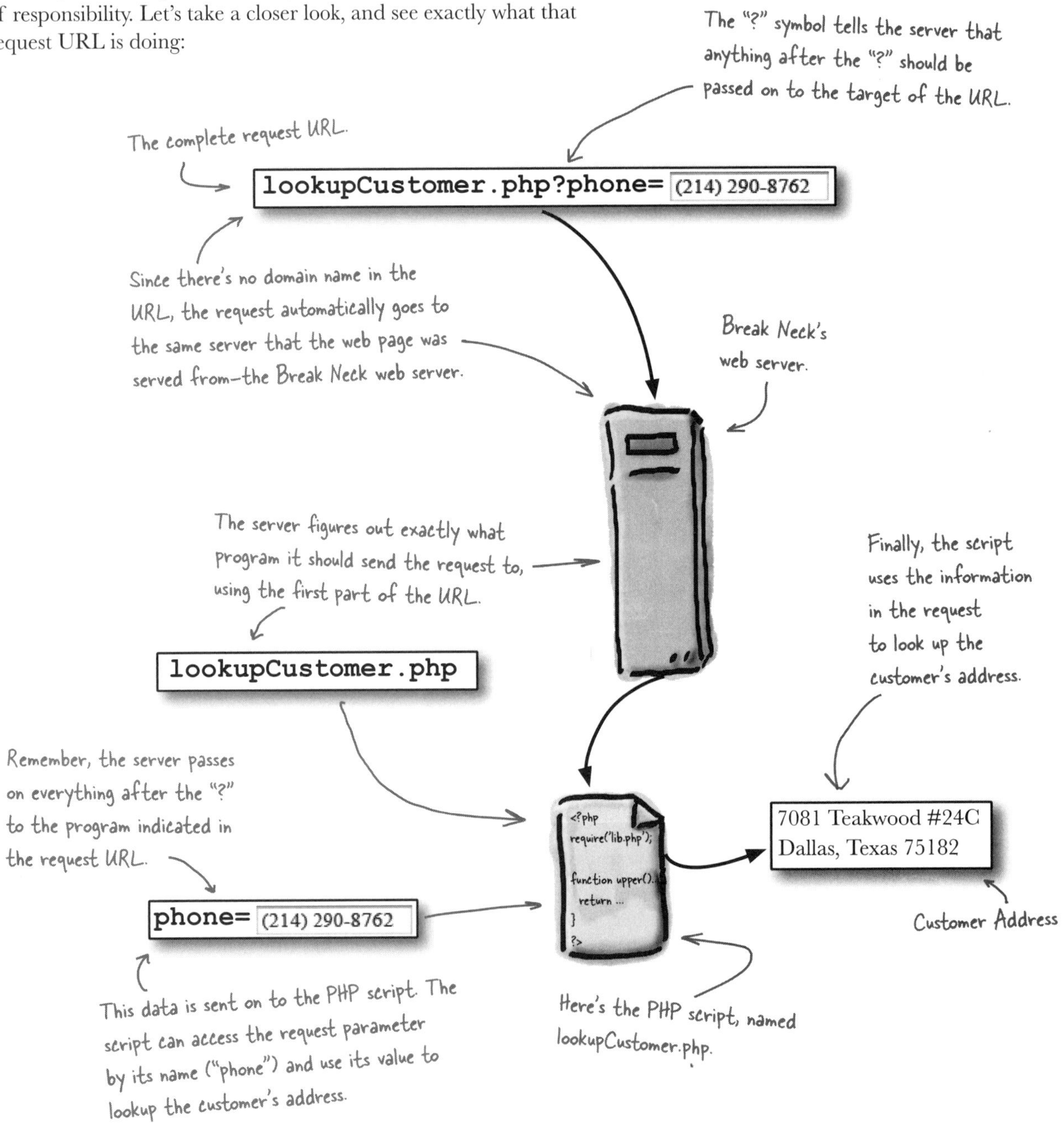

The "?" symbol tells the server that anything after the "?" should be passed on to the target of the URL.
The complete request URL.
lookupCustomer.php?phone= (214) 290-8762
Since there's no domain name in the URL, the request automatically goes to the same server that the web page was served from–the Break Neck web server.
Break Neck's web server.
The server figures out exactly what program it should send the request to, using the first part of the URL.
lookupCustomer.php
Finally, the script uses the information in the request to look up the customer's address.
Remember, the server passes on everything after the "?" to the program indicated in the request URL.
<?php
require('lib.php');
function upper()...
return ...
}
?>
7081 Teakwood #24C
Dallas, Texas 75182
Customer Address
phone= (214) 290-8762
This data is sent on to the PHP script. The script can access the request parameter by its name ("phone") and use its value to lookup the customer's address.
Here's the PHP script, named lookupCustomer.php.

Just Do It

Now that you've got the request URL figured out, you can initialize a connection using the request object's **open()** method. You should remember how the **open()** method works from Chapter 1. Below is the line of JavaScript that initializes a connection, with each parameter you give to **open()** on a separate line. In each blank, write in what the parameter for that line tells the request object to do.

```
request.open(
  "GET",      ________________________________________
  url,        ________________________________________
  true        ________________________________________
);
```

Giving instructions to the browser

Next we need to tell the browser what to do when it gets a response from the server. Remember, the browser will run the function we tell it about every time the ready state changes.

```
function getCustomerInfo() {
  var phone = document.getElementById("phone").value;
  var url = "lookupCustomer.php?phone=" + escape(phone);
  request.open("GET", url, true);
  request.onreadystatechange = updatePage;
  request.send(null);
}
```

Here's the name of the function that the browser should run whenever the ready state of the request object changes.

Be sure you set the onreadystatechange property before calling send(), so the browser knows what to do when it gets a response.

Frequently Asked Questions

Q: If we aren't calling createRequest() in our getCustomerInfo() method anymore, how can we be sure that there's a request object available?

A: Remember, all the JavaScript code that creates the request object is run statically, before the browser lets customers start entering information in the order form. If there are problems, the browser will display an error to the customer.

By the time `getCustomerInfo()` is called, the request object has been created and is available through the `request` variable, or the customer will already know there's a problem. So all you need to do in your code is use the `request` variable.

Q: Why are we sending the phone number as part of the URL? Couldn't we use the send() method to pass the phone number on to the PHP script on the server?

A: You can definitely use the `send()` method to pass data to a server, but that requires using the POST method for your request, as well as specifying a content type for your data. Then you'll need to format your request as a name/value pair in the `send()` method. If that sounds like a lot of extra work just to send a simple phone number, then you're right! For the Break Neck order form, it's much easier to use a GET request, and simply add the phone number onto the request URL. That way, you don't need to worry about POST requests or content types. And since you're passing the phone number along as part of the request URL, you pass null to `request.send()`, just like you did in Chapter 1.

Remember, POST requests are usually best for sensitive data like a credit card, or requests that involve a lot of data. We'll revisit POST requests and more interesting uses of `send()` when we look at XML requests and responses in Chapter 5.

Q: Can you tell me a little bit more about these "tricky characters" that we need to worry about in the request URL's phone parameter?

A: Sure. Think about a typical phone number, like "(214) 290-8762". In addition to the numbers, dash, and parentheses in the entry, there are also spaces. When the request object sends this data to the web server, it uses a request URL; it's the same as if you typed that URL right into the address line of your web browser.

But if you try and enter spaces as part of a URL in a web browser, you're going to get errors, or part of your URL will be ignored. The request object has the same problem. The JavaScript `escape()` function solves this problem, by replacing characters like a space with something that will work as part of a request URL. For example, `escape()` replaces your space character with `%20`. Scripts and server-side programs know when they see `%20` to convert that back to a space, so your data gets sent correctly.

Send the request to the server

All that's left to complete this step is to actually send the request. This is a piece of cake, as you saw in Chapter 1. Let's look at the last line of **`getCustomerInfo()`** now:

```
function getCustomerInfo() {
  var phone = document.getElementById("phone").value;
  var url = "lookupCustomer.php?phone=" + escape(phone);
  request.open("GET", url, true);
  request.onreadystatechange = updatePage;
  request.send(null);
}
```

Make sure you set up the function for the browser to run when the ready state changes before you call send().

This sends the request to the Break Neck web server.

We sent the customer's phone number as part of the request URL, so we don't need to send any other data to the server.

So I'm still waiting to find out more about when that ready state changes.

Just Do It

Make sure you're keeping your version of pizza.html up to date. Open up pizza.html, and add the getCustomerInfo() function if you haven't already. You should also have lookupCustomer.php in the same directory as your pizza.html and breakneck.css files.

Podcasting Studio

HeadRush: We're here today with the ever-popular Web Browser. Browser, we've been really looking forward to talking with you today.

Web Browser: Thanks for having me, HeadRush.

HeadRush: Let's begin by talking about requests and ready states. We get more questions on that topic than almost anything else these days.

Web Browser: Sure, I'd love to talk about that. In fact, ready states are one of the few areas where people actually notice me. Most of the time, everyone would rather talk about JavaScript and PHP.

HeadRush: Well, those are awfully important programming languages...

Web Browser: Sure, sure, but what good is JavaScript without me and Callback? I mean, without us, JavaScript is just a bunch of funny looking lines of text.

HeadRush: Wait a second... Callback? Who's that? I'm not really familiar with that term.

Web Browser: Callback? Oh, I bet you've heard of him, and just don't realize it. You know that function I'm supposed to run whenever a request's ready state changes?

HeadRush: Yeah, that's the one you assign to the request object's onreadystatechange property, right?

Web Browser: Exactly. Well, that's Callback. He's a special type of function: a callback function. But I usually just say, "Callback!", and he comes running.

HeadRush: OK, I'm with you. Callback... because you call him back?

Web Browser: Yes, you've got the idea now. I find out that something's happened with the request, and I "call back" that function. Then he can take care of all the details of handling the server's response.

HeadRush: So once you call back the ... err ... callback, then you're done?

Web Browser: No, not at all. In fact, I have to give Callback a holler several times for a typical request. And not only that, but I make sure he knows about anything the server said.

HeadRush: Oh, right, by using the request object.

Web Browser: Yup, you've got it down. I use the responseText property to let Callback know what the server said. I take care of the responseXML property, too, but I think that might be another chapter...

HeadRush: Yes, we're not quite there yet, but we'll get to that later. So when a callback function runs, it can get the server's response by using the responseText property?

Web Browser: Wait a second there... you're forgetting about something. I let Callback know *every time* something goes on in the request, not just when I've got a response. Callback knows better than to just use the request object without making sure the request is finished up. Otherwise, we'd end up in a big mess.

HeadRush: Because the server isn't done with the request...

Web Browser: ...and I haven't put the server's response into the request object. Speaking of which, I've got to take care of a ready state changing right now. Gotta run... cya later!

Step 3: Retrieve the customer's address

In this step, we need to use the address that the Break Neck PHP script will return in response to the request we made in Step 2. Then, we can have the browser run a JavaScript function once it has a response from the Break Neck server, and pass along the address from the script.

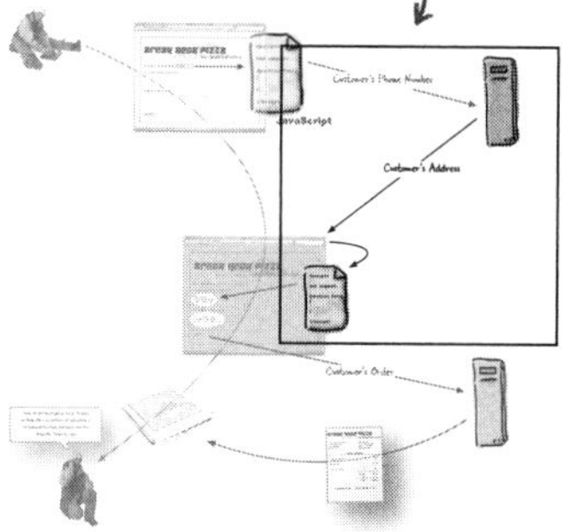

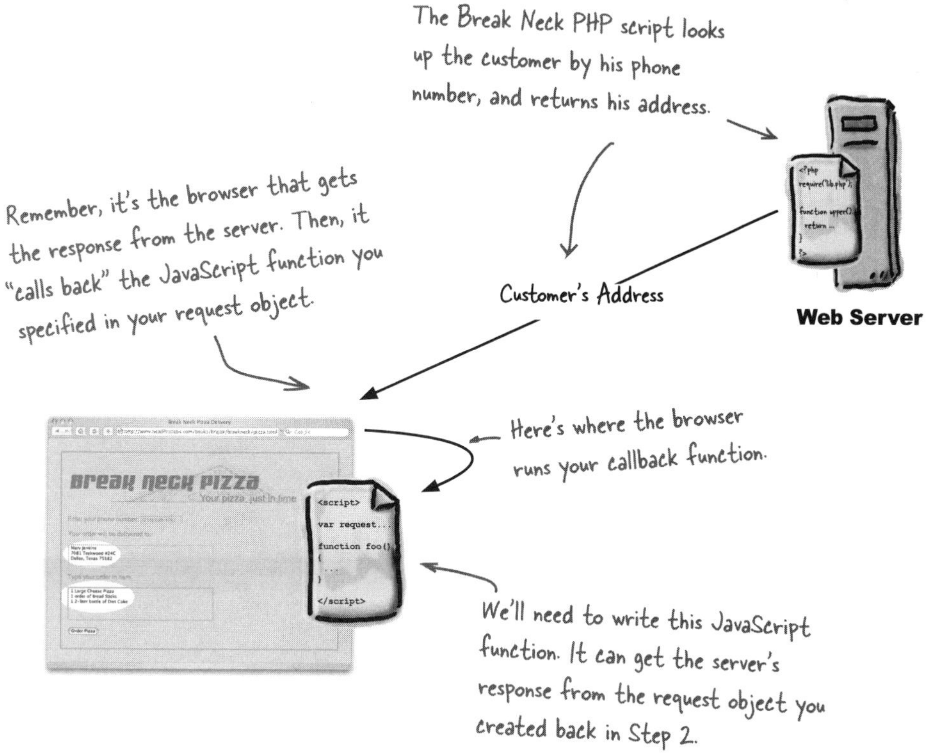

The browser runs your callback function every time the ready state of your request object changes.

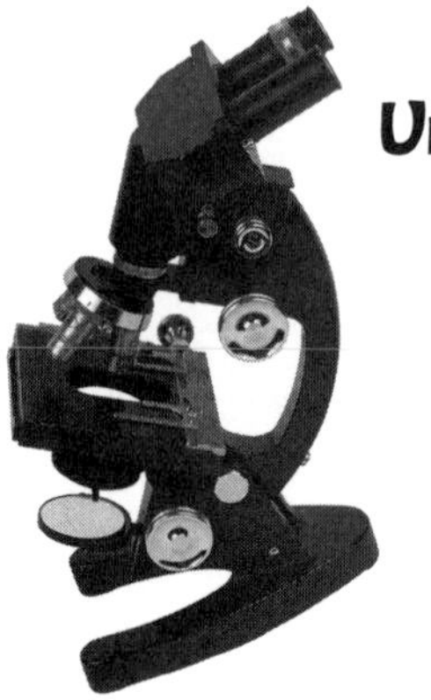

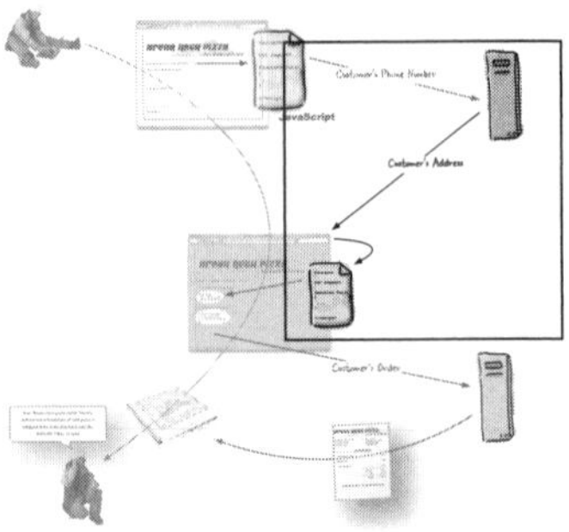

Under the Microscope:
HTTP Ready States

So when exactly does the ready state of a request change? Here's a close-up look at the ready state of a request, and how it changes as a request is processed by a web server.

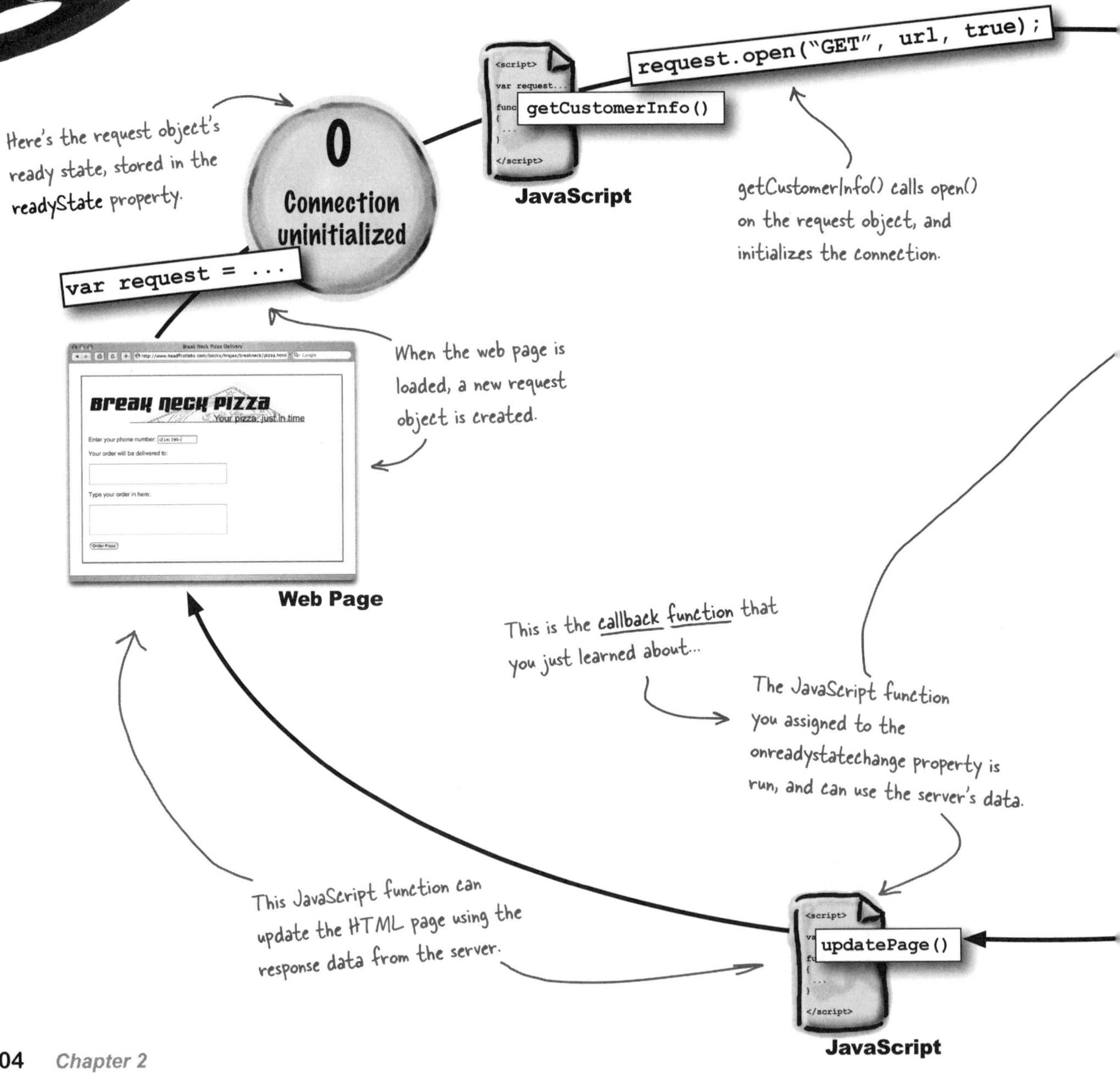

request.open("GET", url, true);
getCustomerInfo()
JavaScript
getCustomerInfo() calls open() on the request object, and initializes the connection.
Here's the request object's ready state, stored in the readyState property.
0
Connection uninitialized
var request = ...
When the web page is loaded, a new request object is created.
Break Neck Pizza
Your pizza, just in time
Enter your phone number:
Your order will be delivered to:
Type your order in here:
Order Pizza
Web Page
This is the callback function that you just learned about...
The JavaScript function you assigned to the onreadystatechange property is run, and can use the server's data.
This JavaScript function can update the HTML page using the response data from the server.
updatePage()
JavaScript

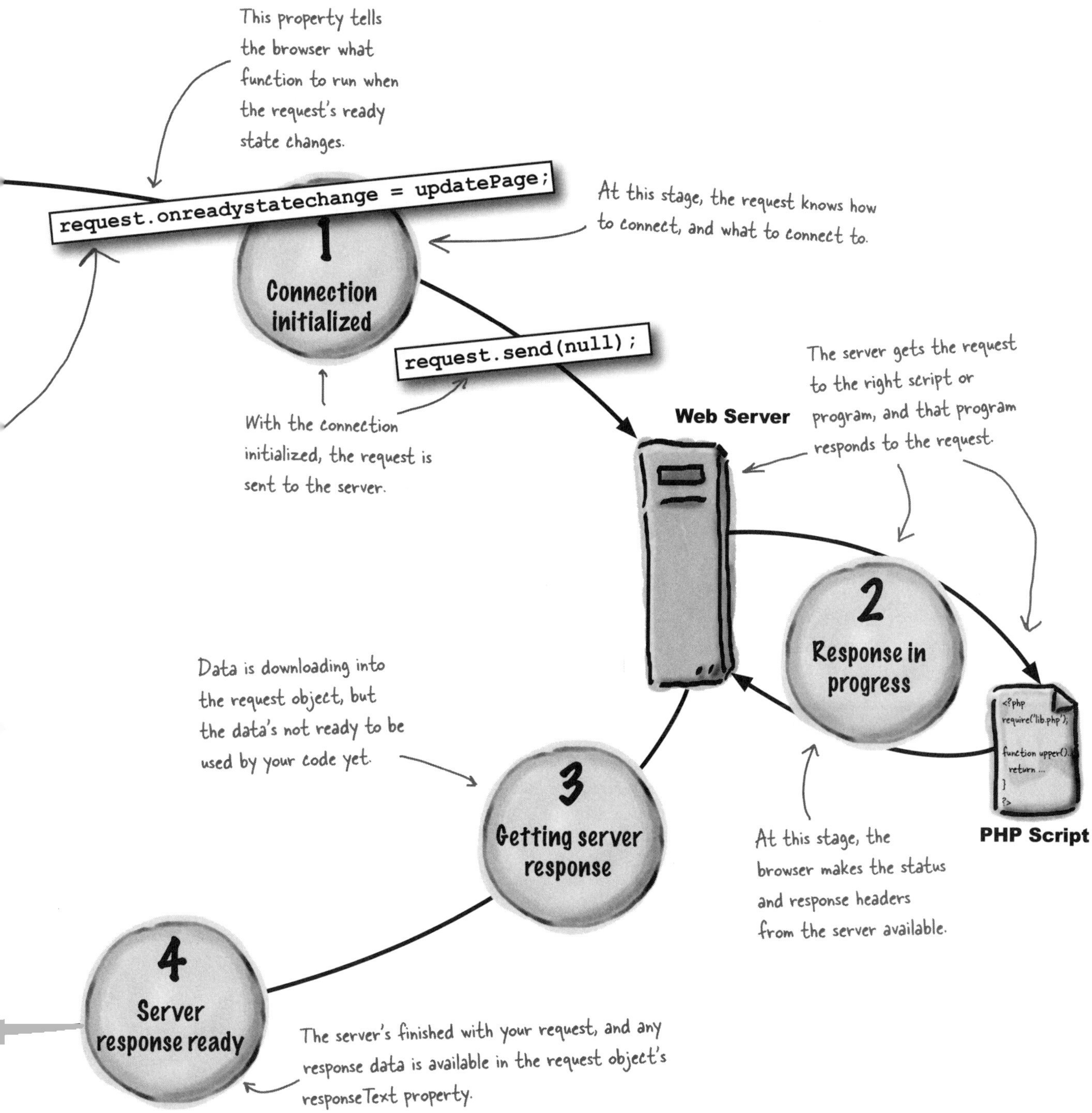
This property tells the browser what function to run when the request's ready state changes.
request.onreadystatechange = updatePage;
At this stage, the request knows how to connect, and what to connect to.
1
Connection initialized
request.send(null);
With the connection initialized, the request is sent to the server.
Web Server
The server gets the request to the right script or program, and that program responds to the request.
2
Response in progress
PHP Script
At this stage, the browser makes the status and response headers from the server available.
Data is downloading into the request object, but the data's not ready to be used by your code yet.
3
Getting server response
4
Server response ready
The server's finished with your request, and any response data is available in the request object's responseText property.

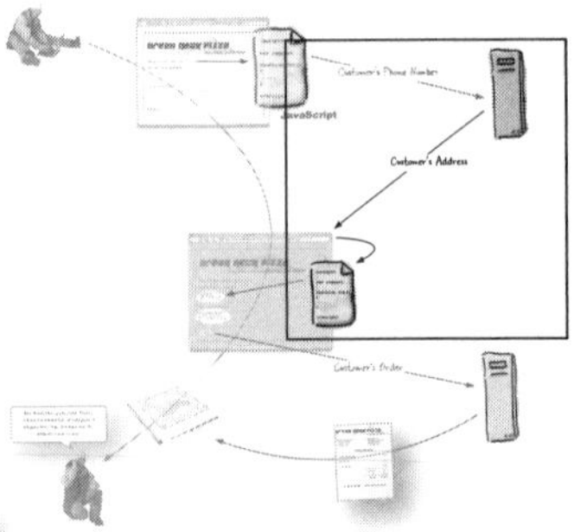

So that's why we check to make sure the ready state is 4 before doing anything in our callback function, right? Otherwise, our JavaScript might try and update the page before the server is finished.

Right—because updatePage() runs every time the ready state changes.

As long as you remember the name of the property you use to set the callback function, you'll remember that the callback is run more than one time. Do you remember what the property was called?

It's **`onreadystatechange`**. So when the ready state changes from 1 to 2, for example, your callback function, **`updatePage()`**, gets run. In other words, **`updatePage()`** will run several times: when the ready state changes from 1 to 2, when it changes again from 2 to 3, and one more time, when the ready state changes from 3 to 4.

But the server only guarantees that it's got data you can use when the ready state is 4. So you need to check the current ready state before trying to update the order form, or the page might end up with bad or missing data.

Checking the ready state

Now that you've got **`getCustomerInfo()`** working, and the browser knows to call **`updatePage()`** when the request's ready state changes, it's time to write the callback function for the Break Neck app. Let's start out by checking that ready state, and making sure the request has been completed before doing anything to the HTML.

Add a new function to your **`pizza.html`** file, called **`updatePage()`**, and start with this code:

You HAVE to make sure the name of this function matches up to the function name you assigned to onreadystatechange in getCustomerInfo().

This if statement makes sure that none of the rest of the code runs unless the ready state is "4", which means the server's finished, and it's safe to use the response data.

```
function updatePage() {
  if (request.readyState == 4) {
    /* Get the response from the server */
    /* Update the order form */
  }
}
```

Remember, you declared the request variable in your static JavaScript, so any function can use it.

You'll write code to take care of both of these things over the next few pages.

Frequently Asked Questions

Q: How does the server run the callback function when the ready state changes? I didn't think the server could call JavaScript code that's in an HTML page.

A: You're right...it's the browser that actually runs the callback function. When the server is done with a request, it lets the browser know. At that point, the server's finished, and it's the browser's job to figure out what to do next. The browser looks up the function specified in the **`onreadystatechange`** property of the request object, and calls that function. So it's the browser running your JavaScript code, not the server.

Q: Will we ever need to write code that does something when the ready state *isn't* 4?

A: Not very often. Remember, these are asynchronous requests, so your users aren't waiting around on the server, and don't really need to know what state the request is in. You'll usually code your callback to only take action when the server is finished with the request, and the ready state is 4.

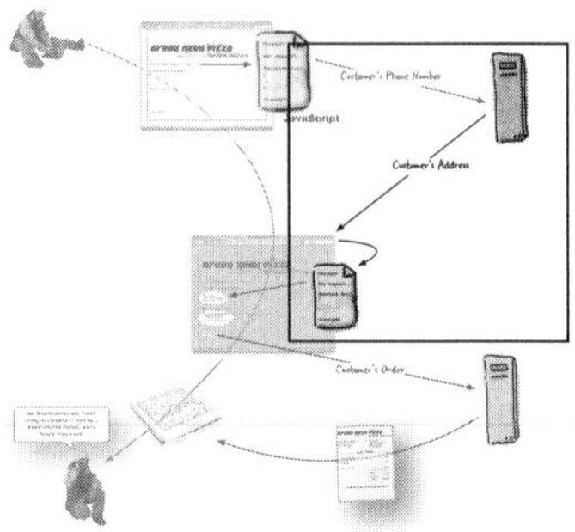

What is the browser doing?

You've seen what the Break Neck server is doing, and you're written a lot of new JavaScript, but what's the browser doing as all these ready states are changing?

Let's take a look and find out:

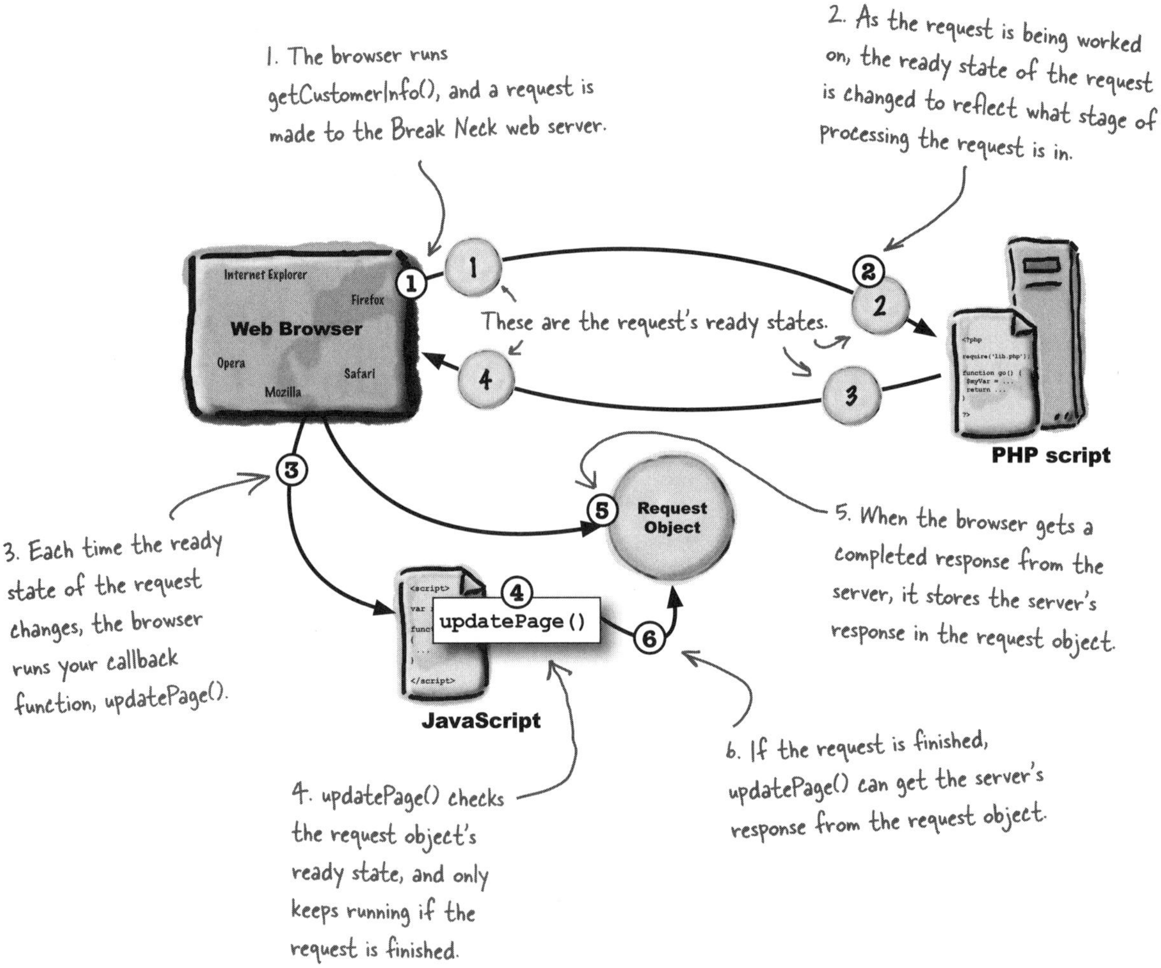

1. The browser runs getCustomerInfo(), and a request is made to the Break Neck web server.

2. As the request is being worked on, the ready state of the request is changed to reflect what stage of processing the request is in.

These are the request's ready states.

PHP script

Web Browser

Internet Explorer
Firefox
Opera
Safari
Mozilla

5. When the browser gets a completed response from the server, it stores the server's response in the request object.

3. Each time the ready state of the request changes, the browser runs your callback function, updatePage().

JavaScript

updatePage()

Request Object

6. If the request is finished, updatePage() can get the server's response from the request object.

4. updatePage() checks the request object's ready state, and only keeps running if the request is finished.

The browser makes a server's response available to your code through the JavaScript request object.

Get the server's response from the request object

If the ready state is "4", the browser will have put the server's response in the request object's **`responseText`** property:

The server is returning the customer's address. →

```
function updatePage() {
  if (request.readyState == 4) {
    /* Get the response from the server */
    var customerAddress = request.responseText;

    /* Update the HTML web form */
  }
}
```

↑ The browser will store the server's reponse in the responseText property.

Blueprints, revisited

You haven't fogotten about the diagram and notes you drew up for developing the Break Neck application, have you? Take a moment to look back at what you wrote down on pages 73, and see how that compares to the steps we've taken so far. This is your chance to make a few more changes before we hit the home stretch.

In the space below, write down what you think still needs to happen to complete the Break Neck application.

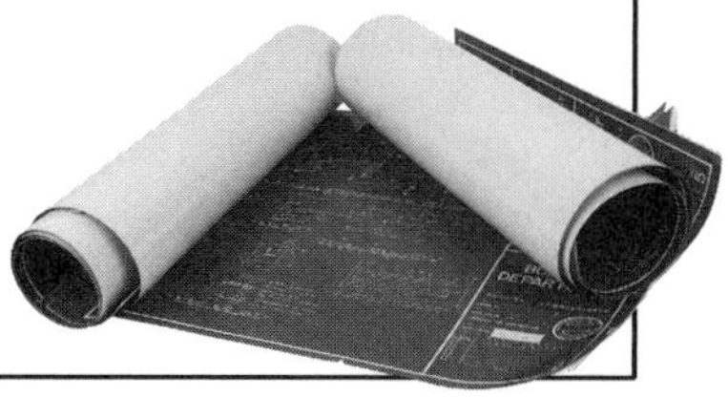

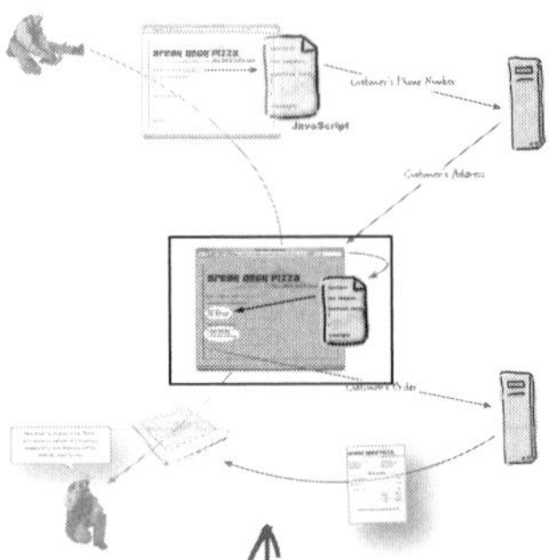

Step 4: Update the order form

Once you've got the customer's address, you need to update the pizza order form. You'll need the browser again, as well as some help from the Document Object Model.

We're getting close to being done with the Break Neck app!

If you make a change to a web page using the Document Object Model, the browser updates the web page immediately.

Your JavaScript callback function can use the browser and the Document Object Model to update the order form.

You've already gotten the customer's address in Steps 2 and 3...

...and can use the DOM to update the web form, similar to how you got the customer's phone number earlier.

Finishing off the callback function

With the address from the server, all that's left is to update the web form. Since the address is stored in a form field, you can use the DOM again, similar to how you got the value of the phone number field in **`getCustomerInfo()`** way back on page 82.

```
function updatePage() {
  if (request.readyState == 4) {
    /* Get the response from the server */
    var customerAddress = request.responseText;

    /* Update the HTML web form */
    document.getElementById("address").value =
      customerAddress;
  }
}
```

Here's where those id attributes come in handy again.

Since address is a form field, you can access the text in it using the "value" property.

Just set the field's value to the customer's address.

You're using the DOM again... this time to set a value in the web form.

FREQUENTLY ASKED QUESTIONS

Q: Why don't we have to use that JavaScript utility file from Chapter 1 to update the address field?

A: In Chapter 1, we were updating the text in a **`<span>`** element. Since **`<span>`** isn't an HTML element that you usually type in, it doesn't have a value property; the same is true for most other HTML elements, like **`<p>`**, **`<em>`**, and **`<div>`**.

For form fields, though, you usually *do* need to enter a value. To make that easier, you can just use the **`value`** property on a form field element, and get and set its text value directly.

Q: Couldn't we just use a <div> for the customer's address? Why are we using a field, anyway?

A: Even though the Break Neck server looks up the customer's address, there are times when a customer might want their pizza delivered to some other address (like for that big Super Bowl party). So the customer's address is filled in for them, but they can still enter a different address if they want.

Don't worry, though—we're going to talk about **`<span>`**, **`<div>`**, and updating your HTML a lot more in Chapter 4.

Test driving the Break Neck app

Make sure you've added all the JavaScript we've talked about into **`pizza.html`**. Then, open up the page in your web browser, and enter in a phone number. It looks like everything is working! The server answers your request, and fills in the form with your address from the customer database.

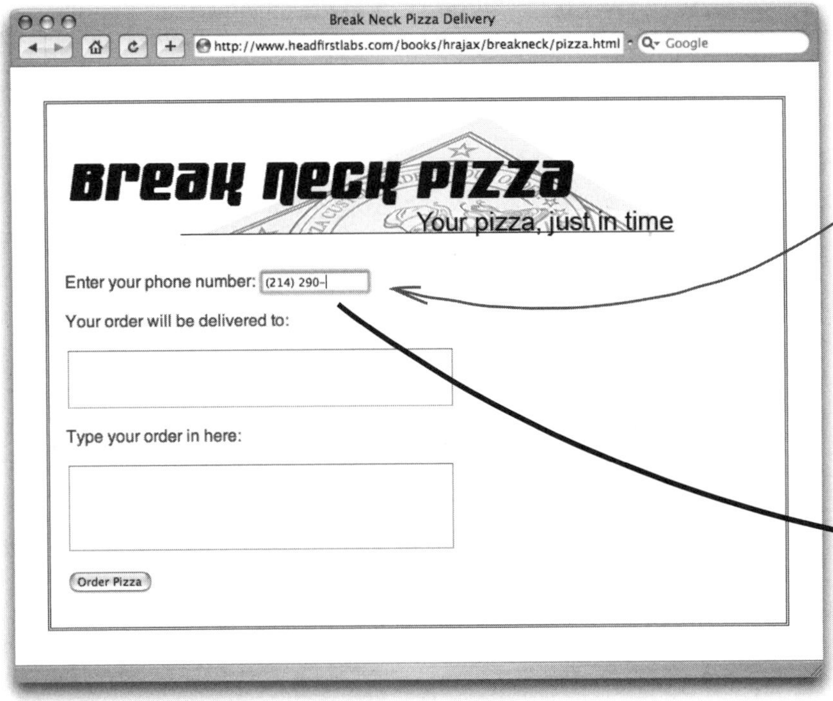

Enter in a phone number. (The version of lookupCustomer.php you downloaded from the Head First Labs site will accept any phone number you enter.)

As soon as you leave the phone number field, the page should automatically fill in the customer's address and order.

Remember, none of this involves a customer having to click a button or submit the pizza form.

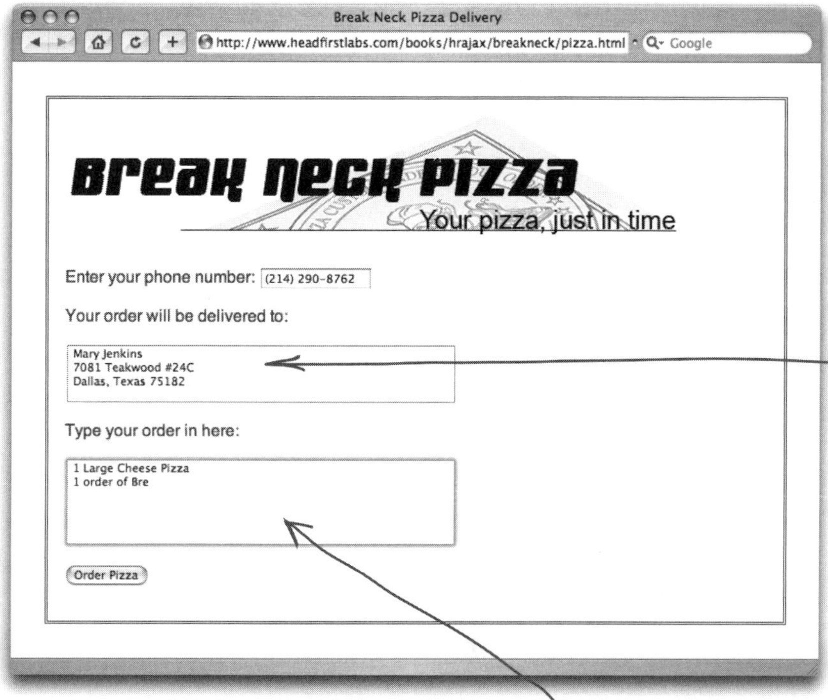

The customer's address, which the Break Neck PHP script looked up, got filled in.

The customer can start working on their order while the server is getting their address.

So we're ready to start accepting orders again, right?

Wait just a second...

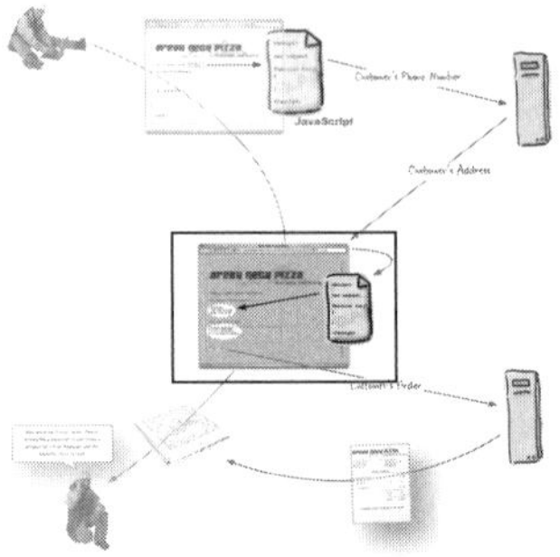

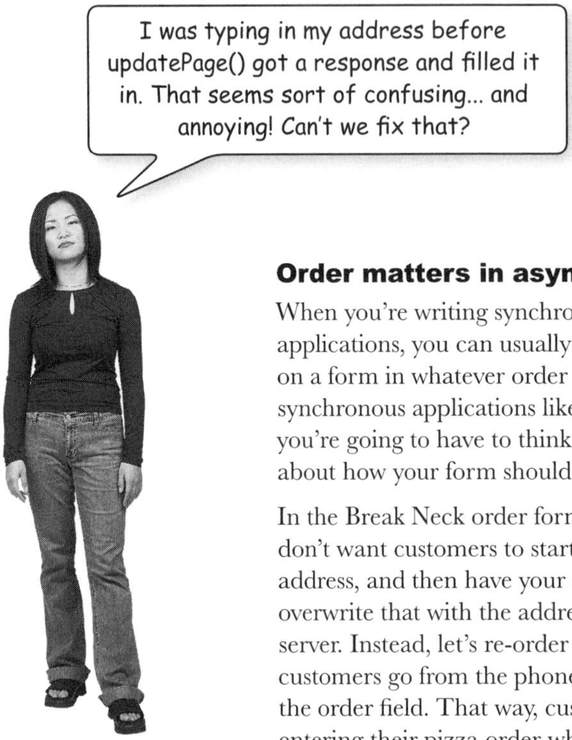
I was typing in my address before updatePage() got a response and filled it in. That seems sort of confusing... and annoying! Can't we fix that?

Order matters in asynchronous apps

When you're writing synchronous applications, you can usually put your fields on a form in whatever order you like. But for synchronous applications like Break Neck, you're going to have to think a little harder about how your form should look.

In the Break Neck order form, you probably don't want customers to start entering their address, and then have your callback function overwrite that with the address from the server. Instead, let's re-order the form, so customers go from the phone number field to the order field. That way, customers can start entering their pizza order while their address is being looked up.

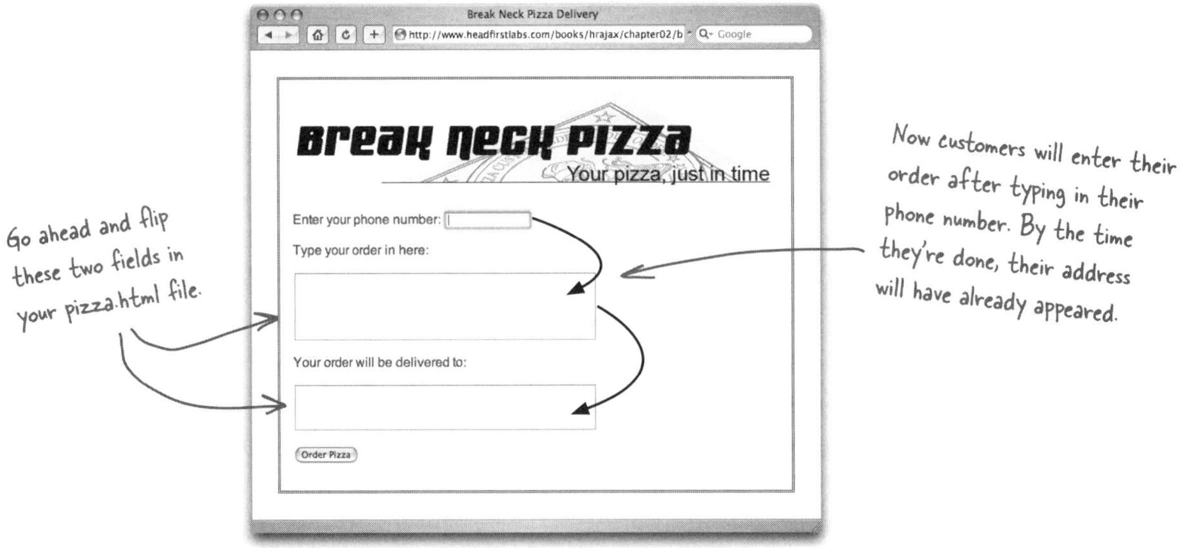
Break Neck Pizza Delivery
http://www.headfirstlabs.com/books/hrajax/chapter02/b
Break Neck Pizza
Your pizza, just in time
Enter your phone number:
Type your order in here:
Your order will be delivered to:
Order Pizza
Go ahead and flip these two fields in your pizza.html file.
Now customers will enter their order after typing in their phone number. By the time they're done, their address will have already appeared.

> And what about that Windows problem from back in Chapter 1? Don't we need to fix that so Break Neck runs on Macs and PCs?

What's going on in Windows?

Internet Explorer is a pretty smart browser, and tries to do lots of things to help make your browsing a better and faster experience. For instance, it will cache a lot of your images, so if you visit a page with lots of graphics, and then come back later, you'll see the graphics come up really quickly.

IE tries to do something similar with URLs. If you make a request to a server-side program, IE keeps track of the URL you requested. Then, if you make a request to the same URL—without any different data—IE figures you're going to get the same response. So, instead of re-sending the request, it just gives you the result from the first time you made the request.

The Opera browser does the same thing that IE does in this situation: it caches URLs.

Since we first saw this problem in the Boards 'R' Us app, let's start by fixing that app on Windows. Then, we can take what we learned and fix up Break Neck Pizza, too.

BRAIN POWER

Why would Internet Explorer's and Opera's caching of requests cause a problem in the Boards 'R' Us application? Will this also create trouble for customers using the Break Neck pizza order form? And what should we do to try and fix this problem?

When browsers cache request URLs...

Let's take a closer look at exactly what browsers like Internet Explorer and Opera are doing, and figure out why that creates trouble for our asynchronous apps.

① Your code makes a request to a web server

Most Ajax apps start by running a JavaScript function based on an event (like a phone number being entered in). The JavaScript builds a request URL, and sends a request to that URL.

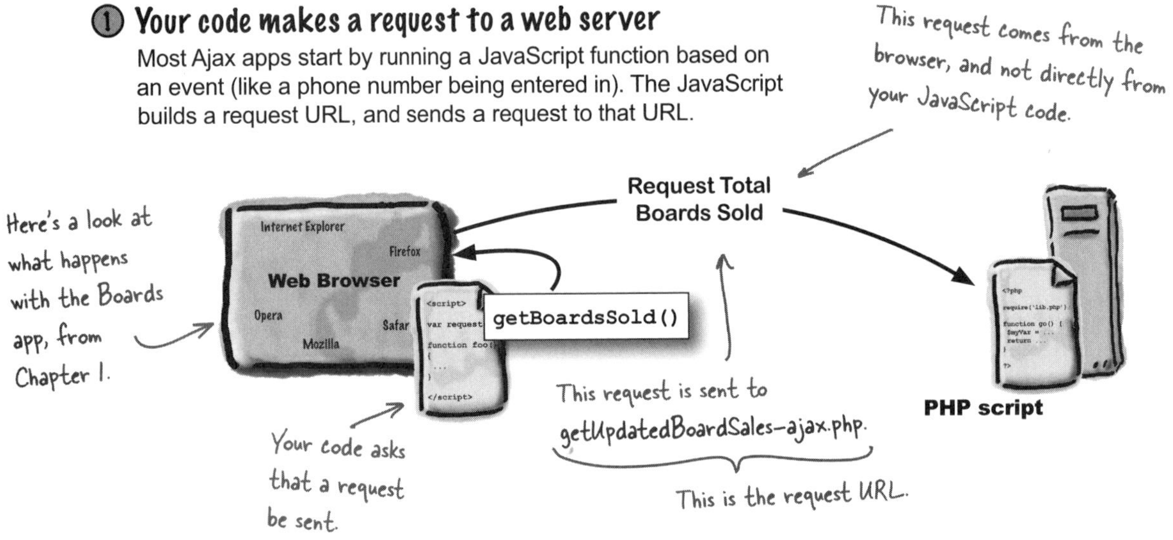

This request comes from the browser, and not directly from your JavaScript code.
Request Total Boards Sold
Here's a look at what happens with the Boards app, from Chapter 1.
Internet Explorer
Firefox
Web Browser
Opera
Safari
Mozilla
getBoardsSold()
PHP script
Your code asks that a request be sent.
This request is sent to getUpdatedBoardSales-ajax.php.
This is the request URL.

② The server sends back a response

When a response is sent back to the browser, the callback function you specified is run. But, if the browser is caching request URLs, it takes a note of the URL, and the answer from the server, and saves those two values for later.

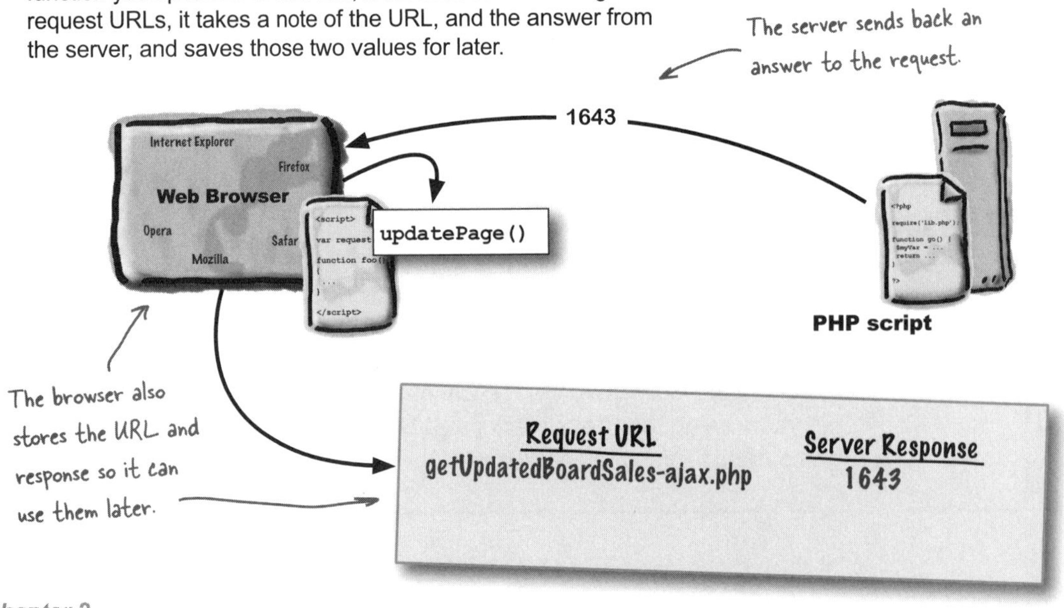

The server sends back an answer to the request.
1643
Internet Explorer
Firefox
Web Browser
Opera
Safari
Mozilla
updatePage()
PHP script
The browser also stores the URL and response so it can use them later.
Request URL
getUpdatedBoardSales-ajax.php
Server Response
1643

At this point, everybody loves you. You're a hero!

3 **You've got a dynamic application!**

Your JavaScript callback function can update the web page with new values based on the server's response, all without having to submit any forms or redraw the page.

4 Your code makes another request to the web server

Since everyone loves your app, it gets a lot of repeat use. So in the Boards app, Katie's boyfriend clicks the "Show Me the Money" button a second time.

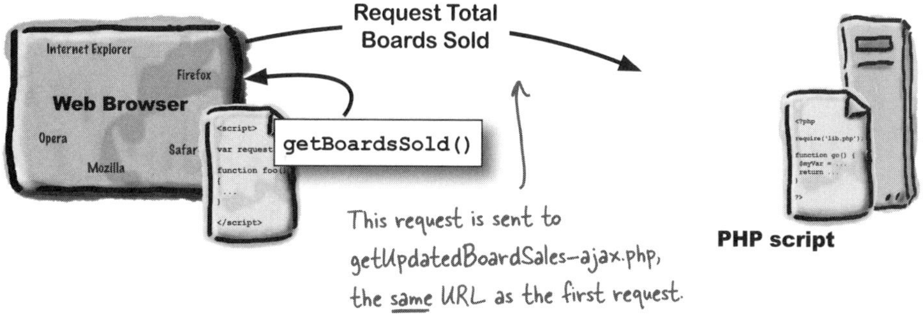

5 The browser gives your code a response

The browser sees that it already has an answer for the request URL you supplied, so it figures it can save you some time. Instead of sending the response to the server, it gives you the response it has in its caching table.

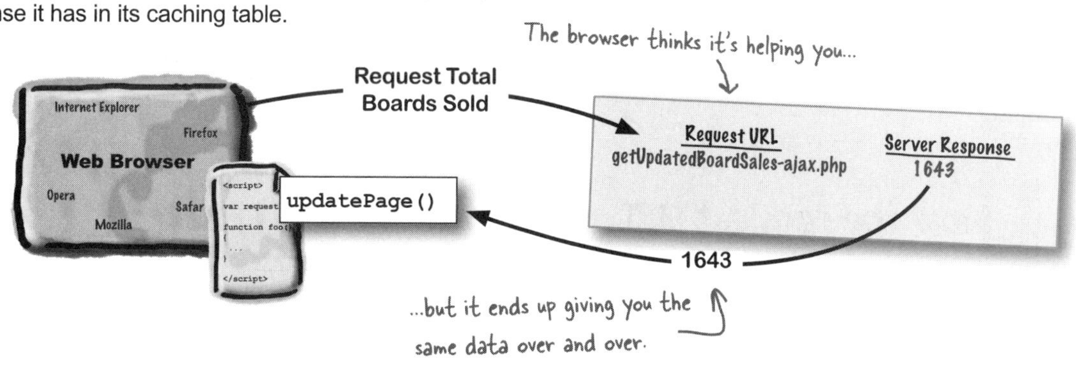

Now, everyone hates you. You're an idiot, and all this Ajax stuff was a waste of time.

6 **You've got a crappy application!**

Suddenly, your dynamic application is returning the same data, over and over. Your callback is getting stale data from the server, and your web page isn't getting updated with fresh information.

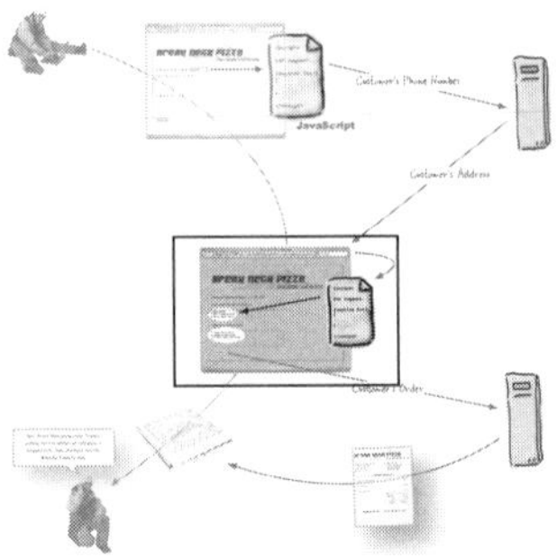

So to get around the caching, we have to change our request URL every time. But... if we're talking to the same script, and we're not sending in data in the Boards app, how can we make the URL different?

Sometimes it takes a hack...

The browser doesn't care *how* the request URL is different; it just cares that it's different. So, we can add a dummy parameter onto the request URL, and give it a different value every time we send the request. And, since we don't want to write a random number generator, or do any extra work, we can just grab the current time (in seconds), and add that to the request URL.

Let's take a look at how we can fix up **getBoardsSold()** from Chapter 1:

Remember back in the old days, when our request object was created in a function?

```
function getBoardsSold() {
  createRequest();
  var url = "getUpdatedBoardSales-ajax.php";
  url = url + "?dummy=" + new Date().getTime();
  request.open("GET", url, true);
  request.onreadystatechange = updatePage;
  request.send(null);
}
```

This first line sets the URL normally, and the second line adds a dummy value to the URL.

Our dummy parameter has the current time as its value.

Now the request URL changes...

```
getUpdatedBoardSales-ajax.php?dummy=1139262723388
getUpdatedBoardSales-ajax.php?dummy=1139262774440
getUpdatedBoardSales-ajax.php?dummy=1139262797519
```

Now, no two request URLs are the same...

...because each time the request URL is built, the time is slightly different.

Just Do It

Go back to your copy of **`boards.html`**, from the Chapter 1 examples, and update the **`getBoardsSold()`** function. Try your new version of the Boards app out on Windows using Internet Explorer, or on Opera (on the Mac or Windows). Do you have any problems with caching using this new version?

Frequently Asked Questions

Q: Can't I just turn off caching in my browser, and avoid all this extra code?

A: No, most of the options you have in your browser control caching of pages you directly load, by either typing a URL in the address bar or clicking a hyperlink on a web page. The requests that your JavaScript make are behind the scenes, and IE and Opera don't give you much control over how they handle those requests.

And even if you could turn off caching, many of your users will still have caching on in their browser. So you've got to work around caching, even if you can turn it off on your own web browser.

Q: So just by sticking that "dummy" parameter on the end, I can get around caching?

A: It's more than just the parameter, or the name of the parameter. It's changing the request URL itself. We used the name "dummy" to make it clear that the parameter isn't pointing to any data that's important to the application, but you could use any name for the parameter that you wanted to.

Q: Won't there still be a problem if two requests are made within the same minute? The time would be the same for both requests then, right?

A: No, `getTime()` returns the time elapsed since January 1st, 1970, and it returns that time in milliseconds. So unless you can manage to click "Show Me the Money" twice in the same millisecond, the request URL will be different each time.

Q: What happens to the dummy parameter when the PHP script receives the request?

A: Nothing. The PHP script doesn't need that parameter, so it just ignores it.

Q: So now we just need to make this same change to getCustomerInfo() in pizza.html?

A: That's not a bad idea... is it? Turn the page and let's talk about that some more.

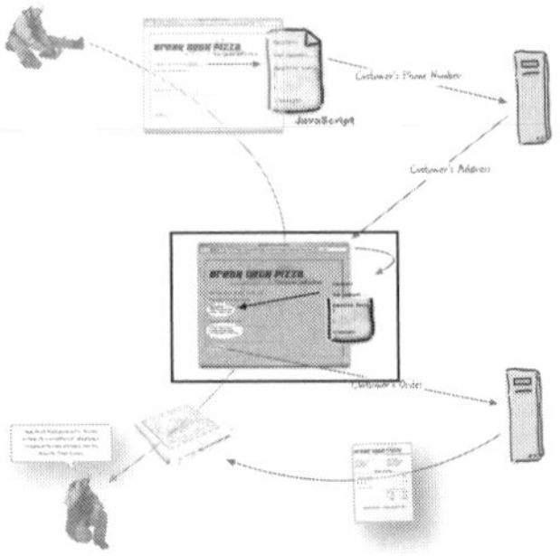

I don't think we don't need to worry about caching in the Break Neck app. If the phone number is different, the request URL will be different. And if it's the same phone number, we don't need fresh data from the server; the customer's address is the same each time.

Good thinking!

You don't always need to worry about caching. In the Break Neck app, the request URL will be unique for each phone number, so there won't be any caching problems there.

If a customer enters the same phone number, caching probably would keep the request from going to the Break Neck server... but in that case, the server really *would* be returning the same customer data—the customer's address—each time. So in that situation, caching actually saves your customer's time.

Be sure you don't end up adding code that you don't need to your applications. In the Break Neck app, there's no need to make any changes to the code you've already got.

This means we're done with Step 4! On to Step 5...

Step 5: Place the customer's pizza order

The customer enters their order into the form, and they'll see their address filled in, Ajax style, by the JavaScript function you wrote in Step 4. All that's left is to let the user submit his order, and get the pizza cooking.

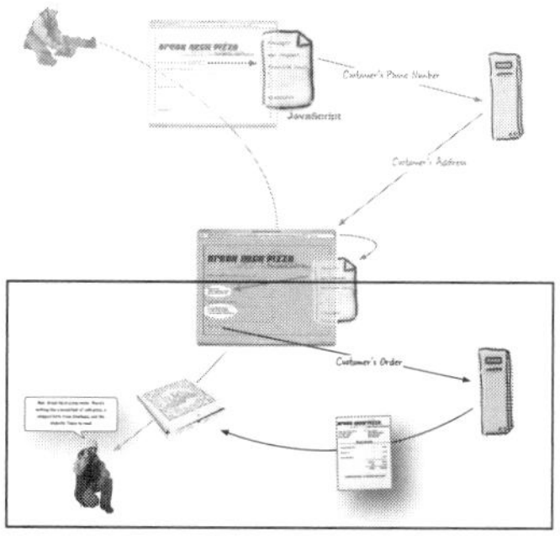

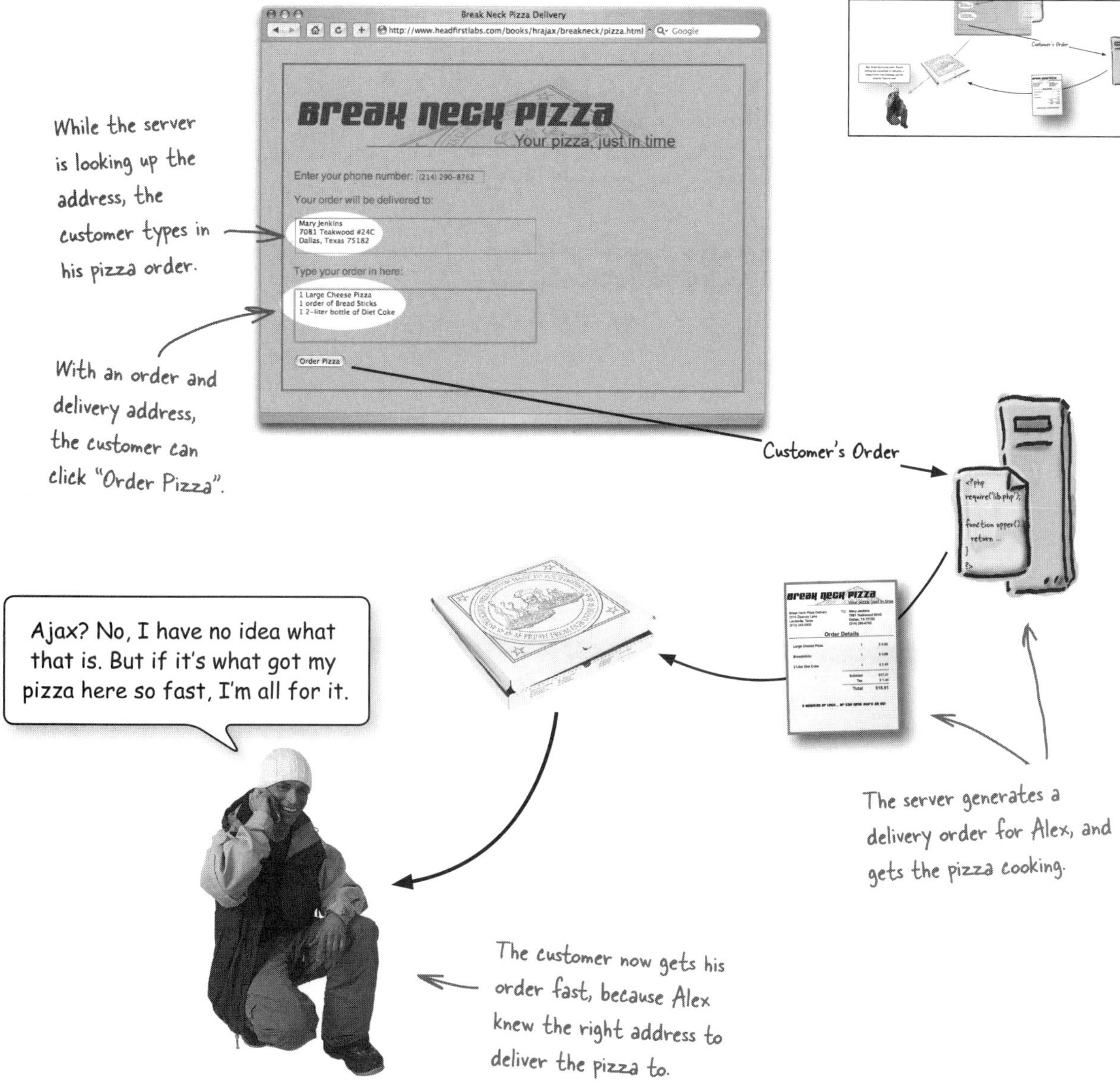
Break Neck Pizza Delivery
http://www.headfirstlabs.com/books/hrajax/breakneck/pizza.html
Break Neck Pizza
Your pizza, just in time
Enter your phone number: (214) 290-8762
Your order will be delivered to:
Mary Jenkins
7081 Teakwood #24C
Dallas, Texas 75182
Type your order in here:
1 Large Cheese Pizza
1 order of Bread Sticks
1 2-liter bottle of Diet Coke
Order Pizza
While the server is looking up the address, the customer types in his pizza order.
With an order and delivery address, the customer can click "Order Pizza".
Customer's Order
Ajax? No, I have no idea what that is. But if it's what got my pizza here so fast, I'm all for it.
The server generates a delivery order for Alex, and gets the pizza cooking.
The customer now gets his order fast, because Alex knew the right address to deliver the pizza to.

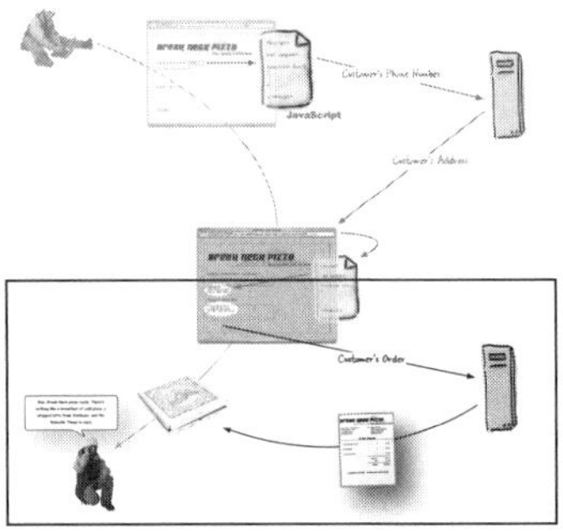

Back to Break Neck's order form

With all the JavaScript sorted out, let's get back to the pizza order form. Once the customer enters their phone number, types in their pizza order, and verifies their address, all that's left is to send the order to Break Neck.

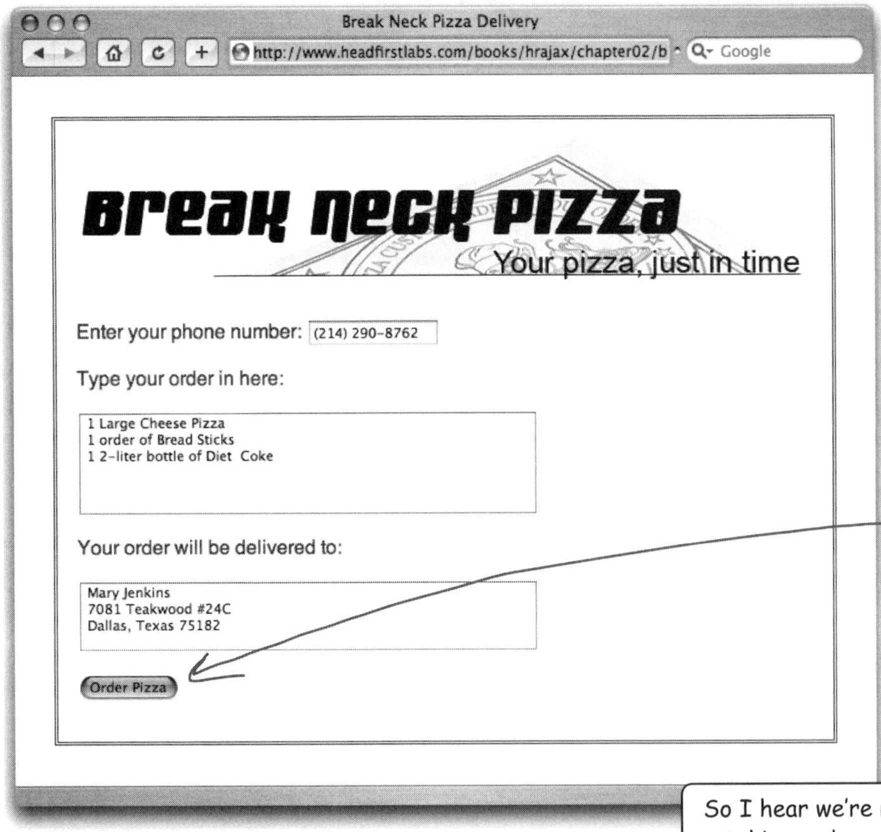

You've already got this part done... the customer can send their order to Break Neck's servers by clicking the "Order Pizza" button.

So I hear we're ready to start taking order again... I sure hope this works!

The final test drive

The customer enters their phone number...

...and then the JavaScript gets their order details and address from the server...

...and fills in the web form.

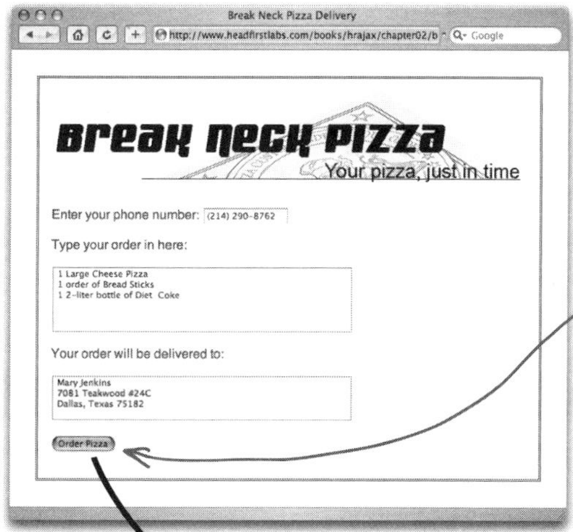

The customer makes sure the order and address are right, and places the order...

...and 10 minutes later, it's pizza time!

Check it out for yourself!

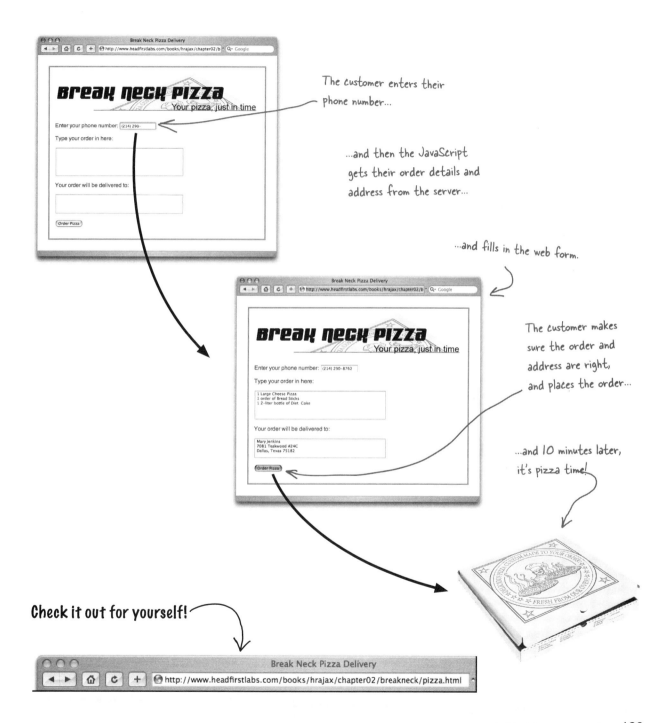

I think it's time to quit delivering pizzas and start writing Ajax apps. This asynchronous programming stuff is sweet! I bet I could even program an app to make my morning coffee.

60 Second Review

- For Microsoft browsers, the Ajax request object is ActiveXObject, using either Msxml2.XMLHTTP or Microsoft.XMLHTTP as the type of the object.
- For non-Microsoft browsers, including FireFox, Safari, and Opera, the Ajax request object is XMLHttpRequest.
- Static JavaScript is JavaScript that is not in a function, and is run by the browser when it loads your page.
- You can use static JavaScript to make sure certain pieces of code run before users start working with your web page.
- A request's ready state indicates what is happening with the request: whether it's being initialized, the server has been contacted, the server is finished, etc.
- When the ready state of a request is "4", the server has finished processing the request, and any response data is safe to use.
- Every time a request's ready state changes, the callback function registered with the request is run by the web browser.
- You need to use the DOM to update the text in HTML display elements like <div> and <span>; you can use the value property to set the text of form field elements like <input> and <textarea>.
- Make sure the ordering of your fields works with your application's JavaScript, and not against it, to help avoid confusing your users.
- You need to use a different request URL for each request to work around caching browsers like Opera and Internet Explorer.

Exercise Solutions

Work It Through

Just like the Boards 'R' Us application in Chapter 1, you're going to need several JavaScript functions to make the Break Neck application work. Below on the left are the names of two JavaScript functions, and on the right are several lines of JavaScript. Draw arrows from the lines of code to the function each line will go into.

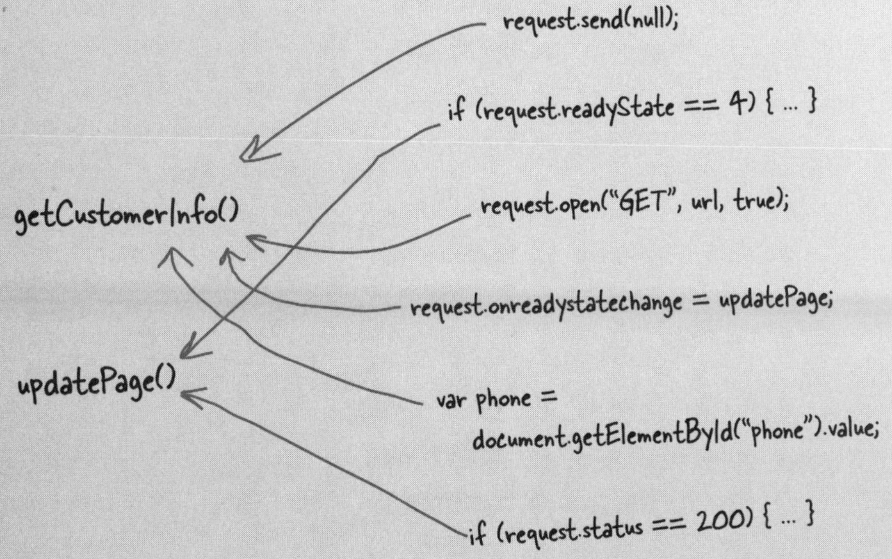

request.send(null);
if (request.readyState == 4) { ... }
getCustomerInfo()
request.open("GET", url, true);
request.onreadystatechange = updatePage;
updatePage()
var phone =
document.getElementById("phone").value;
if (request.status == 200) { ... }

TOP SECRET

Eyes Only

Duplication strictly prohibited

WELCOME TO PROJECT: CHAOS

Congratulations! Your wealth of experience and expertise in building web applications have made you a prime candidate for PROJECT: CHAOS. While the world sleeps on oblivious to our work, we are the men and women who ensure that faulty code will always keep programmers awake late at night, that moonlit walks by the beach will be interrupted by the ring of a cell phone, and that evenings started with a rose and a kiss end at the office, rather than in the bedroom.

We have determined that the Break Neck Pizza order form's interactivity could provide unprecedented levels of customer satisfaction, and greatly reduce the frustration of pizza lovers throughout this region of the world. Further, the application's asynchrony could catch on, turning the Internet into a dynamic, user-friendly place for browsing. This is simply ***not*** acceptable!

To receive your assignment, and understand how you can aid in combatting the rise of these "next generation" applications, you are to be sitting at a table for two, at precisely 10:14 PM, in your local Starbuzz Coffee Shop. Place a blue feather between the pages of a paperback copy of Neal Stephenson's "Snow Crash".

You will be contacted; do not attempt to contact us, or the consequences will be more serious than you can imagine.

The napkin handed to you by the strange looking man with the gun.

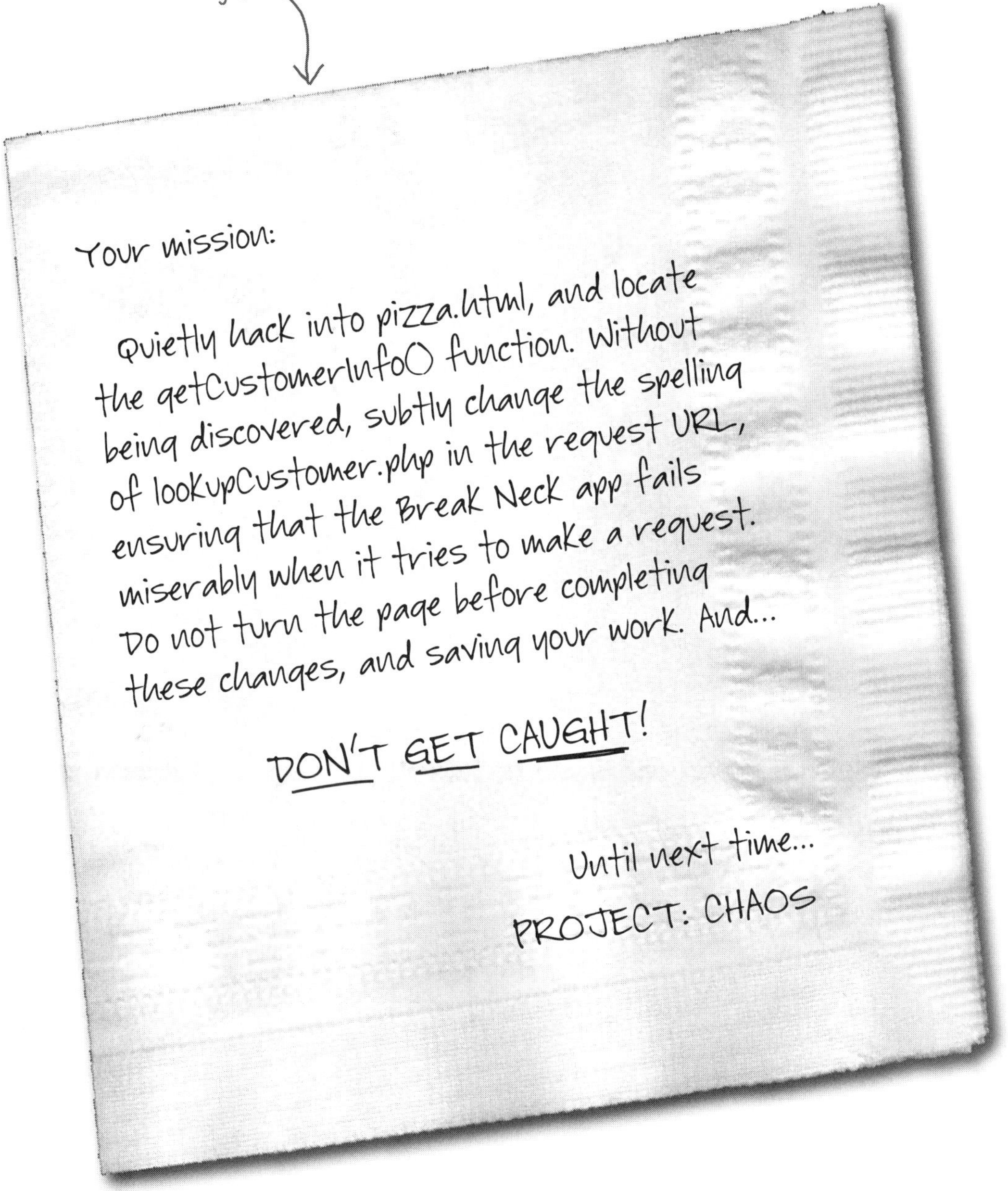

Your mission:

Quietly hack into pizza.html, and locate the getCustomerInfo() function. Without being discovered, subtly change the spelling of lookupCustomer.php in the request URL, ensuring that the Break Neck app fails miserably when it tries to make a request. Do not turn the page before completing these changes, and saving your work. And...

DON'T GET CAUGHT!

Until next time...

PROJECT: CHAOS

Problems at Break Neck...

It seems that something is going wrong with the Break Neck app. Try opening **pizza.html** up in your browser, and enter a phone number. What happens?

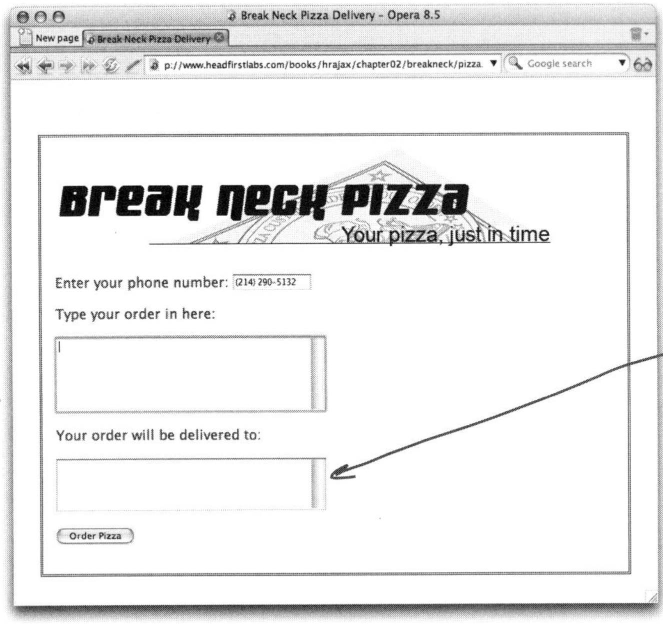

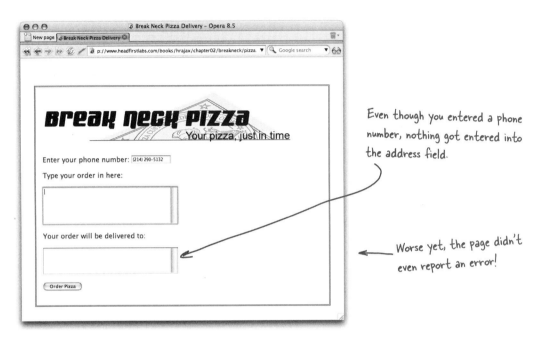

Even though you entered a phone number, nothing got entered into the address field.

Worse yet, the page didn't even report an error!

Obviously, the Break Neck app failed because ... someone ... changed the request URL to be invalid. But why didn't the browser tell us something went wrong with our request?

Checking the request's status

Even though you probably didn't realize it, the browser *did* try to tell you something went wrong. The browser uses a property of your request object, called **status**, that you can use to determine whether something went wrong.

Here's how you can check the status of a request:

You've seen most of this code in Chapter 2... this is the updatePage() callback function.

The server sends a status of "200" when everything is OK.

Here's a new property of the request object. It reports the status code from the server.

```
function updatePage() {
  if (request.readyState == 4) {
    if (request.status == 200) {
      var customerAddress = request.responseText;
      document.getElementById("address").value = customerAddress;
    } else
      alert("Error! Request status is " + request.status);
  }
}
```

In case the status isn't OK, let's output an error message to the screen with the request's status.

Just Do It

Add the code shown above to your **updatePage()** function in **pizza.html**. Now reload your page in a web browser, and enter a phone number. When you change the phone number field, and then move to another field, what happens? Write down the server's status code in the blank:

____

Now fix the request URL in **getCustomerInfo()** so that it points to the correct script on the Break Neck server. Reload your page, and see what happens. Did you get another status code? Write down what happened when you used the correct URL:

____

Wait a second. If there's a mistake in the request URL, is the server even getting our request?

The request URL is a relative URL

Remember the first part of the request URL from **`getCustomerInfo()`**?

```
lookupCustomer.php
```

We've left off the "phone" request parameter to make this a little shorter.

This is a *relative URL*, and doesn't include the domain name of the server that the request should be sent to. So what domain does the browser send this request to? The browser will automatically use the same domain that it requested the **`pizza.html`** web page from. So if you entered http://www.breakneckpizza.com/pizza.html to view the Break Neck order form, your web browser would turn the relative URL above into an *absolute URL*, like this:

```
http://www.breakneckpizza.com/lookupCustomer.php
```

So the request gets sent to the same server that your browser downloaded the pizza order form from. Even if the program to run on the server is ... mis-spelled ... the request will still get sent by your browser to the right server.

This program could be a Java servlet, or a PHP script, or a Ruby component, or any other bit of code running on the the server.

This is an absolute URL. It has a domain name...

...and a path to a program or file on the server.

```
http://www.boardsrus.com/getUpdatesBoardSales.php
```

This is an relative URL. It has no domain name...

...and just the path to the program or file on the server.

```
/getUpdatesBoardSales.php
```

OK, so I see how it's getting to the server. But if the server can't find the program in the request URL to run, why does the browser still run our callback? Shouldn't it report an error or something?

The browser always runs your callback... ...and it did report an error.

The browser will always run your callback, because that gives you a chance to respond to whatever the server did to handle your request. Since you're using an asynchronous request, the **callback** is the only way you have to write code that can **deal with a server's response**. To help you out with dealing with that response, the browser gives you both the state of your request, and the status of your request.

There's a different between the **state** of your request, and the **status** of the same request. Your request's ready state tells the browser what stage of processing the request is in: initialization, processing, completed, etc.. But just because a request is complete doesn't mean that the request was successful... that involves the *status* of the request.

A server reports any *problems* with a request by using a **status code**. The status code indicates what happened *during* the request, and whether things went as you intended. So even if a request was completed, you still need to make sure the status code for the request indicates that everything went OK.

Servers return a ready state and a status code

The server is sending a lot of information back in its response... maybe more than you realized. Here's a look at how the server returns both a ready state *and* a status code:

1. Your request object sends a request to a web server.

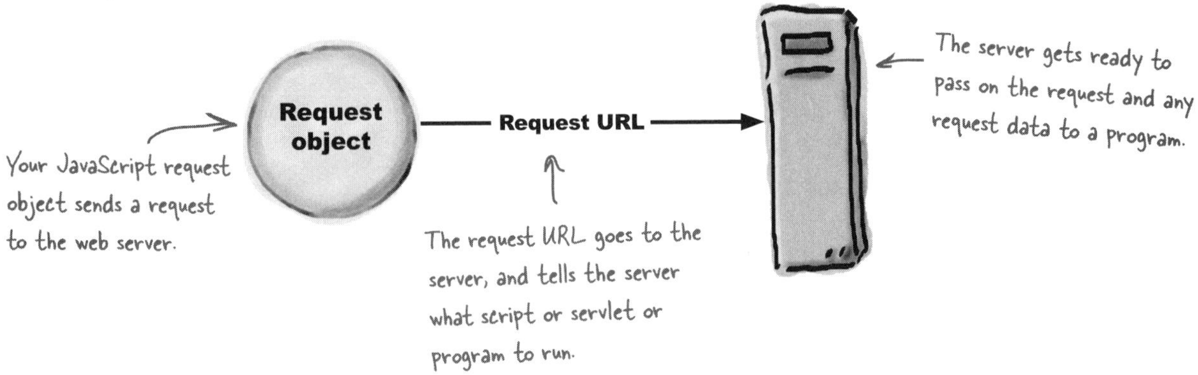

Request object
Request URL
The server gets ready to pass on the request and any request data to a program.
Your JavaScript request object sends a request to the web server.
The request URL goes to the server, and tells the server what script or servlet or program to run.

2. The web server tries to locate the program in the request URL.

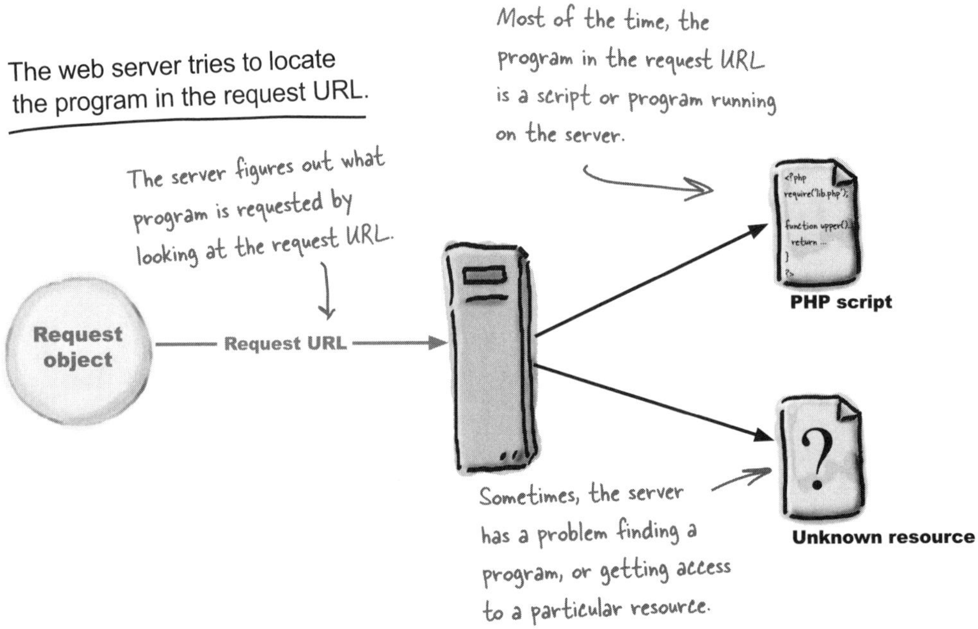

3 The server figures out what status code it should return.

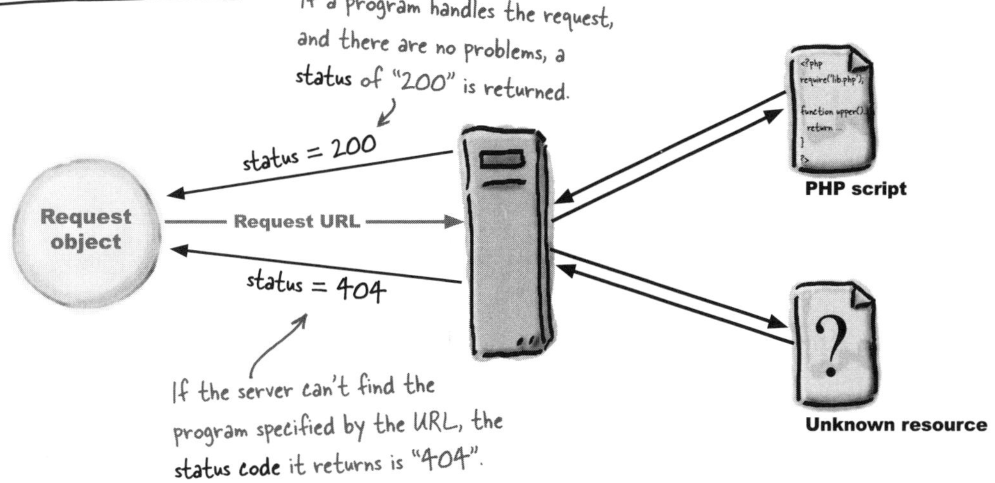

4 The server returns both a ready state and a status code.

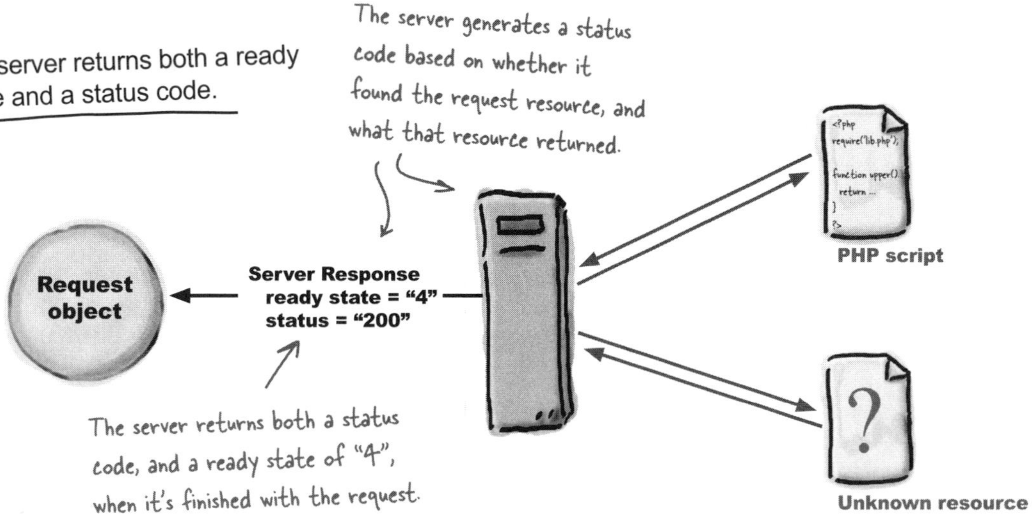

The server generates a status code based on whether it found the request resource, and what that resource returned.
Request object
Server Response
ready state = "4"
status = "200"
The server returns both a status code, and a ready state of "4", when it's finished with the request.
PHP script
Unknown resource

Frequently Asked Questions

Q: I thought the ready state told us the server was finished with our request. Why do we need to check a status code, too?

A: The ready state lets you know that the server is finished processing your request; that's why you should always check it before running any code in your callback function. Then, once you know your request has been completely processed, you need to make sure no errors occurred; that's what the request's status tells you. You need *both* the ready state and status code to really be sure your request was handled, and it's safe to update the page with the response data from the server.

Q: So we want the ready state to be "4", and the status to be "200", right?

A: Right. A ready state of "4" means the request has been completely processed, and a status code of "200" means that there were no errors.

Q: Are there any other status codes I need to worry about?

A: Well, you already saw the 404 status code, which means the server couldn't find the program you requested. 403 is another common status code, and means that you tried to request a program or resource that you're forbidden from accessing, at least without authentication.

There are lots of other status codes, too. There's a complete list online at http://www.w3.org/Protocols/rfc2616/rfc2616-sec10.html.

Q: Do I need to write JavaScript to handle each one of those codes?

A: Most of the time, all you need to check for is the 200 status code, and print an error if the status is something else.

You could try and write some fancy JavaScript that retries the request, but if your request failed, it's usually a problem with your web page or your JavaScript that needs to be fixed. Printing out messages to the screen is only going to confuse your users.

Q: And even with a bad request URL, the server will respond to my request and my callback will get run?

A: Remember, since we're using relative request URLs, the domain name of the request will be the same as the domain name of the server hosting your web page. So if your web page is at http://www.breakneckpizza.com/pizza.html, your request URL's domain name will be http://www.breakneckpizza.com. You can then add anything after the domain name, like directories or the name of a script or web application.

Remember, there's a difference between the server, and a program running *on* the server. As long as your request has your web server's domain in it, you'll get a response—even if the response is that the program you asked to run on that server is missing or unavailable.

Seasoned members of PROJECT: CHAOS use HTTP: The Definitive Guide to decode their HTTP status codes.

Back to Break Neck...

Before you abandon the ranks of PROJECT: CHAOS, make sure you've added code to your updatePage() function that checks your request's status code. You should also fix any errors in the request URL from getCustomerInfo(). Save your changes, and then load pizza.html again, and make sure things are working correctly.

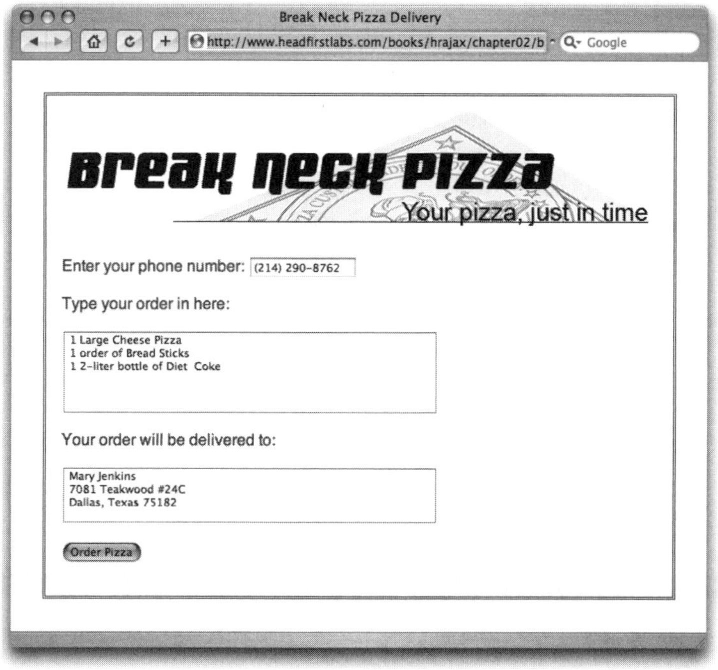

Make sure that the pizza order form is working correctly, that your request looks up the customer's address, and that you can place pizza orders.

Don't think you've heard the last of PROJECT: CHAOS... we'll be back!

3 Asynchronous Apps

She Blinded Me with Asynchrony

Waiting room? I'm sorry, we don't have one of those.

This is the Web, not a doctor's office, and nobody wants to sit around reading a six-month old magazine while a server does its thing. You've seen how Ajax will let you get rid of page reloads, but it's time to add **responsive** to the list of highlights for your web apps. In this chapter, you'll learn how to send your users' requests to a server, and let your users **keep on working** while they're waiting on a response. In fact... strike that. There'll be **no waiting** in this chapter at all. Turn the page, and let's get started.

What does asynchronous really mean?

Asynchronous means that you don't have to **wait around** while a web server is responding to your request. That means you're not stuck: you can go on doing what you want, and have the server let you know when it's finished with your request. Let's take a view of this from 10,000 feet by first looking at what a synchronous request is, and compare it to an asynchronous request.

A synchronous request for cola

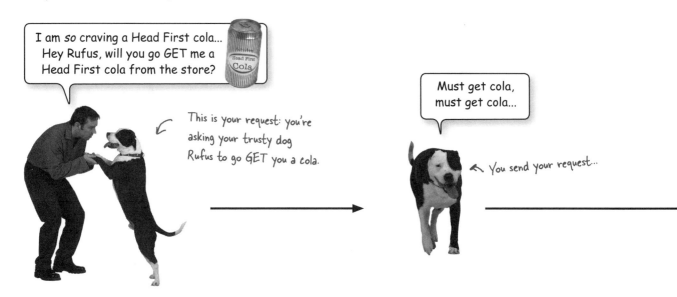

An asynchronous request for cola

Now, compare that to this *asynchronous* request...

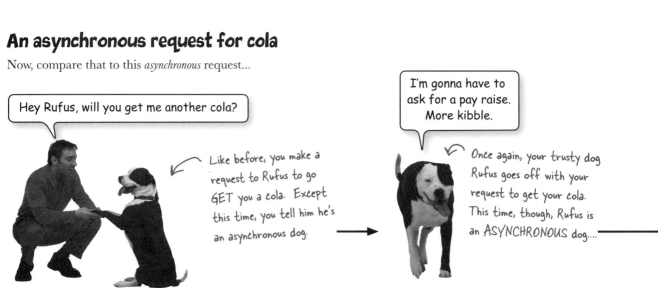

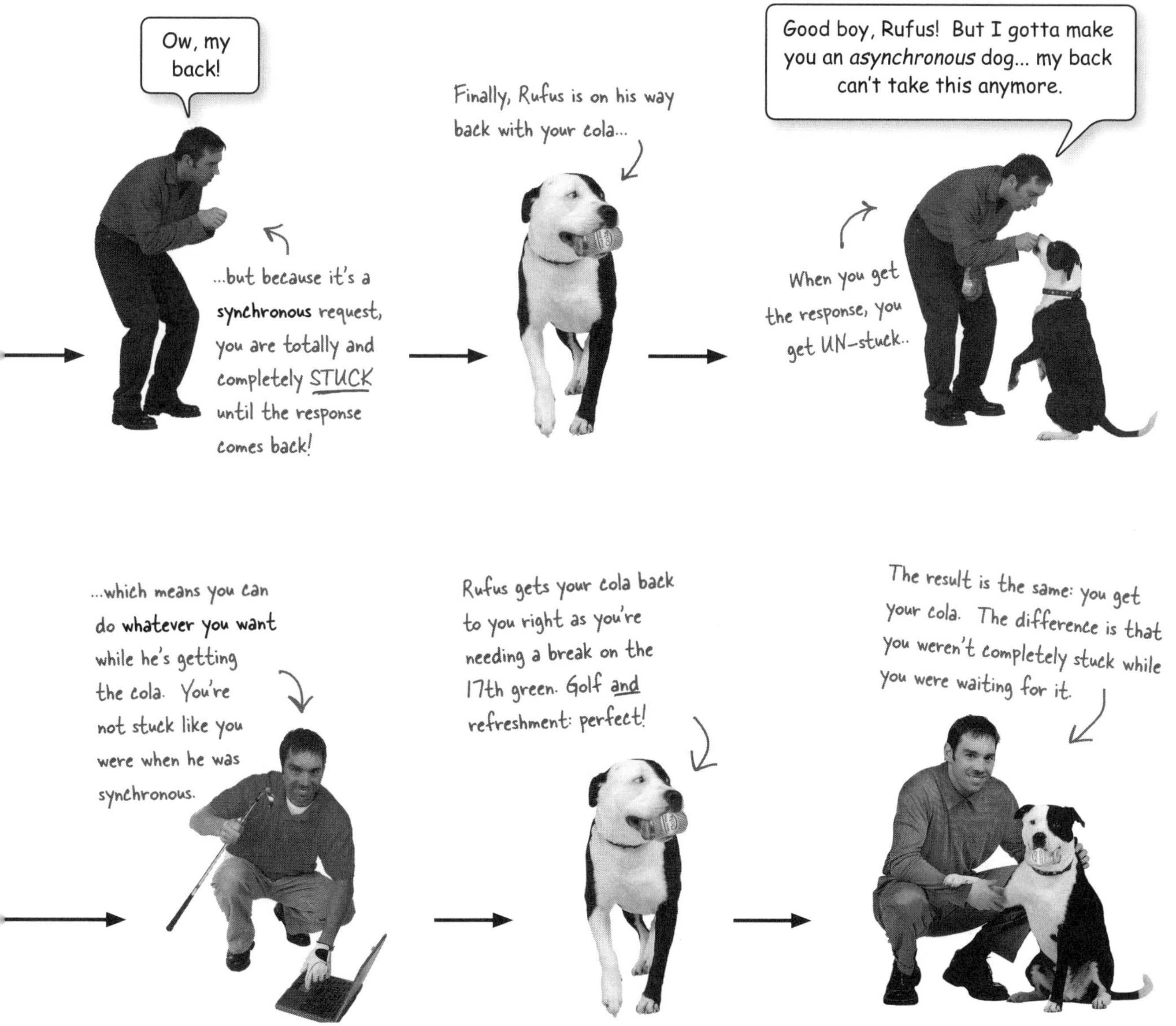
Ow, my back!
...but because it's a synchronous request, you are totally and completely STUCK until the response comes back!
Finally, Rufus is on his way back with your cola...
When you get the response, you get UN-stuck..
Good boy, Rufus! But I gotta make you an asynchronous dog... my back can't take this anymore.
...which means you can do whatever you want while he's getting the cola. You're not stuck like you were when he was synchronous.
Rufus gets your cola back to you right as you're needing a break on the 17th green. Golf and refreshment: perfect!
The result is the same: you get your cola. The difference is that you weren't completely stuck while you were waiting for it.

Break Neck Pizza is an asynchronous app

Take another look at the Break Neck Pizza Ajax application. You type in your phone number, and then move to the pizza order or address. The page's JavaScript then gets your phone number from the form, and sends the request for your address to the web server. If your address takes a long time to look up, you'll notice that you can go ahead and enter your pizza order *without having to wait for the server to return your address.*

```
function getCustomerInfo() {
  var phone = document.getElementById("phone").value;
  var url = "lookupCustomer.php?phone=" + escape(phone);
  request.open("GET", url, true);
  request.onreadystatechange = updatePage;
  request.send(null);
}
```

Remember, this parameter is how you tell the request object to send your request asynchronously.

Here's the JavaScript function in pizza.html that sends a request to the Break Neck web server.

Here's where we send the request to the Break server.

Customer's Phone Number

Since this is an asynchronous request, from the time the browser sends the request to get your address to the time it gets a response, you can still go on using the web page. You won't be stuck.

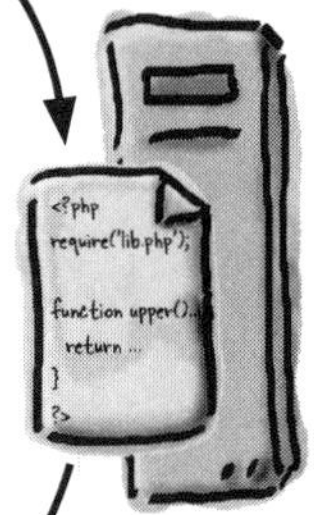

Customer's Address and Order

And here's the callback function that's run when the response comes back from the server.

```
function updatePage() {
  if (request.readyState == 4) {
    if (request.status == 200) {
      var customerAddress = request.responseText;
      document.getElementById("address").value = customerAddress;
    }
  }
}
```

But it was probably too fast for you to notice...

Break Neck Pizza isn't called "break neck" for nothing—the request to get your address and the response from the server happens so fast that you probably don't have time to start typing in your order—much less improve your golf game—before your address pops up.

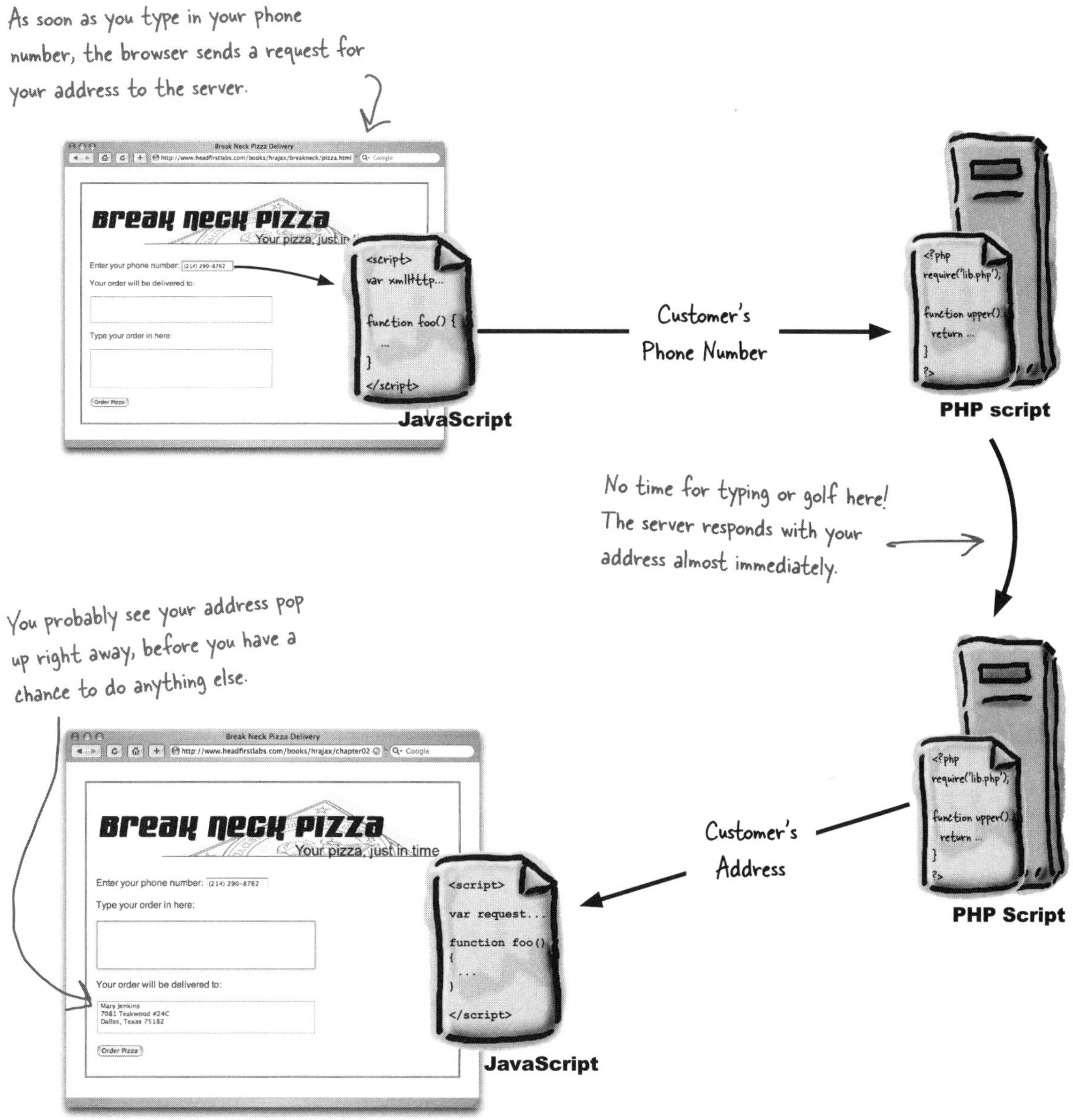

As soon as you type in your phone number, the browser sends a request for your address to the server.
Break Neck Pizza
Enter your phone number:
Your order will be delivered to:
Type your order in here:
Order Pizza
JavaScript
Customer's Phone Number
PHP script
No time for typing or golf here! The server responds with your address almost immediately.
You probably see your address pop up right away, before you have a chance to do anything else.
Break Neck Pizza
Your pizza, just in time
Enter your phone number:
Type your order in here:
Your order will be delivered to:
Mary Jenkins
7081 Teakwood #24C
Dallas, Texas 75182
Order Pizza
JavaScript
Customer's Address
PHP Script

So what's the point of an "asynchronous" application if the server responds so fast that it doesn't make a difference anyway?

What does asynchronous get you?

Both of the applications you've built so far are asynchronous. Still, the server responded so fast to your requests that you probably didn't notice any benefit from the asynchronous part of these applications.

But what happens if it takes a really long time to get the data back from the server? Or what if you really *do* need to do two things at one time? You'd like to keep using the application while that's happening, right?

That's when you'll really see the benefits of the "asynchronous" part of Ajax. In fact, you're going to build another application—an Ajax-powered coffee maker—where being asynchronous makes a big difference. Ready? Let's get started.

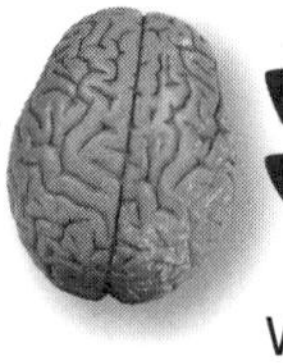

BRAIN POWER

What applications do you use on the Web that would be better if they were asynchronous?

Building an Ajax-powered coffee maker

Two coffee makers... ...and a whole office of caffeine addicts.

As the official "coffee pot manager," it's your job to make sure that the caffeine needs of your officemates are met... and quickly, at that. All your mates are caffeine addicts, and they get a bit testy if there's no fresh coffee on hand. Good thing that there are two coffee makers; even if one order is being brewed, your co-workers can place another order, and have it filled by the second coffee maker.

You're going to build an Ajax application to allow your co-workers to order their coffee online.

You don't want anyone coming after you with empty coffee cups, so let's write an Ajax application for ordering coffee and keeping track of the status of both coffee makers. Here's what it will look like:

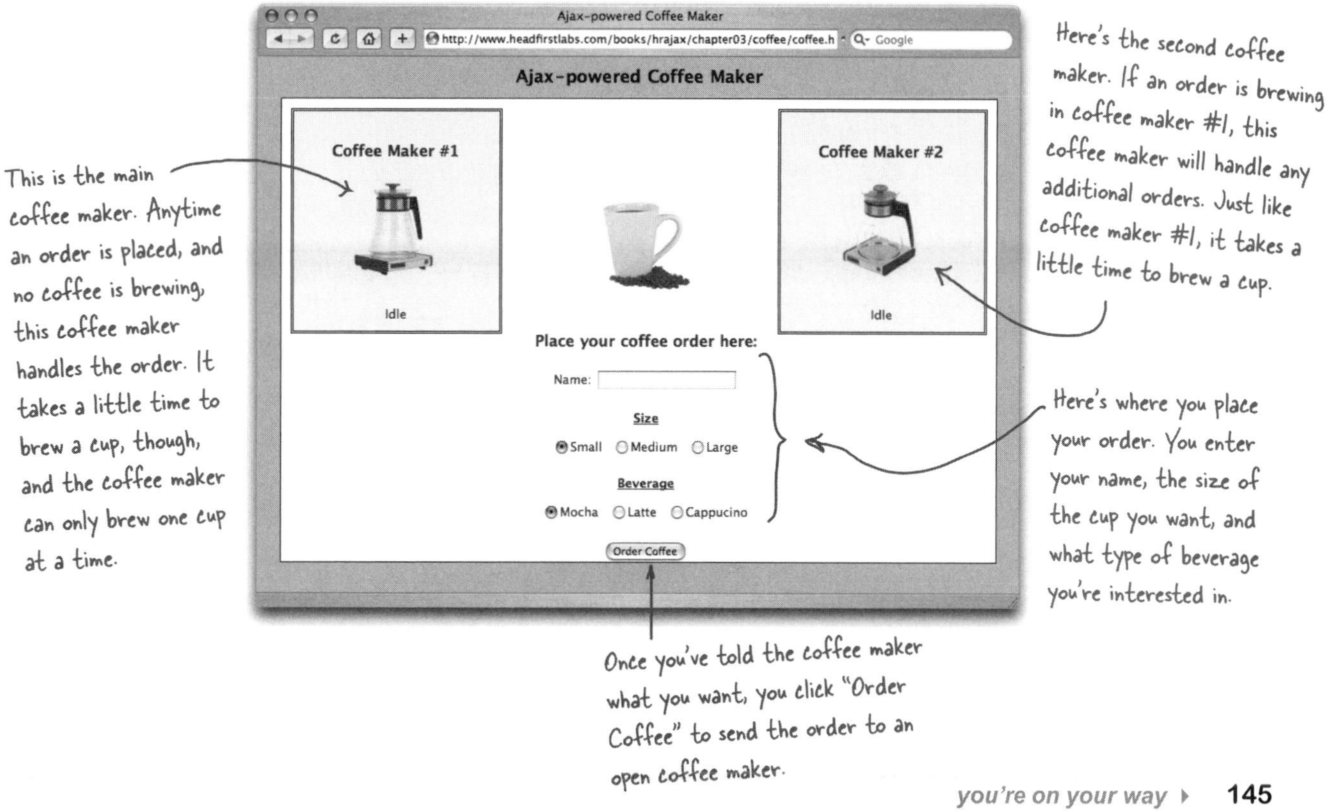
Ajax-powered Coffee Maker
http://www.headfirstlabs.com/books/hrajax/chapter03/coffee/coffee.h
Google
Ajax-powered Coffee Maker
Coffee Maker #1
Idle
Coffee Maker #2
Idle
Place your coffee order here:
Name:
Size
Small
Medium
Large
Beverage
Mocha
Latte
Cappucino
Order Coffee
This is the main coffee maker. Anytime an order is placed, and no coffee is brewing, this coffee maker handles the order. It takes a little time to brew a cup, though, and the coffee maker can only brew one cup at a time.
Here's the second coffee maker. If an order is brewing in coffee maker #1, this coffee maker will handle any additional orders. Just like coffee maker #1, it takes a little time to brew a cup.
Here's where you place your order. You enter your name, the size of the cup you want, and what type of beverage you're interested in.
Once you've told the coffee maker what you want, you click "Order Coffee" to send the order to an open coffee maker.

Three ingredients for asynchronous coffee

There are three basic parts to the Ajax-powered coffee maker:

① Coffee maker HTML

First, you'll need the HTML for the coffee maker web page. The page needs to take orders, and report on the status of the two coffee makers.

We'll have to create the controls for ordering coffee in the HTML page.

② JavaScript code

Second, you'll need some JavaScript, including:

- Code to create a request object.
- A function to send an order to the coffee-making script.
- A function to serve a drink when it's been brewed.
- Event handlers to connect the web form buttons to these JavaScript functions.

③ Server-side coffee-making script

You'll also need a server-side coffee-making script, which will brew coffee anytime it gets a request.

This is the PHP script that makes coffee. You'll send all the coffee orders to this script for brewing.

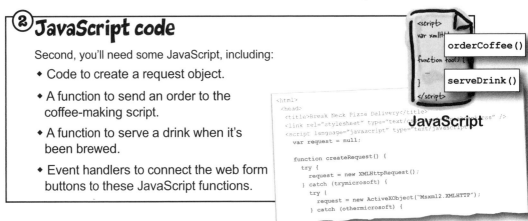

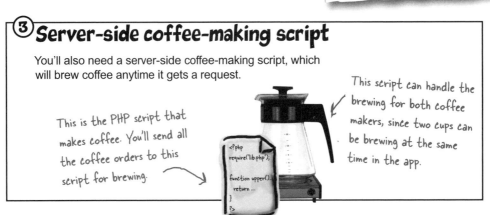

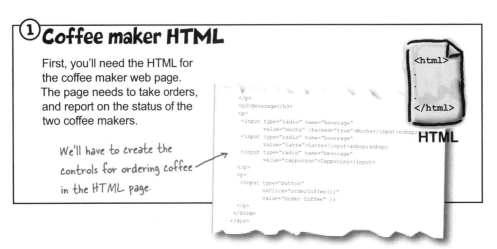

PHP script

This script can handle the brewing for both coffee makers, since two cups can be brewing at the same time in the app.

Connecting the parts of the coffee maker

You've seen the three basic parts of the coffee maker app. But let's go a little further, and see how these parts combine into a coffee-making wonder. Obviously, we've got an HTML form, some JavaScript, and a coffee-making script on the server. So how does all this fit together?

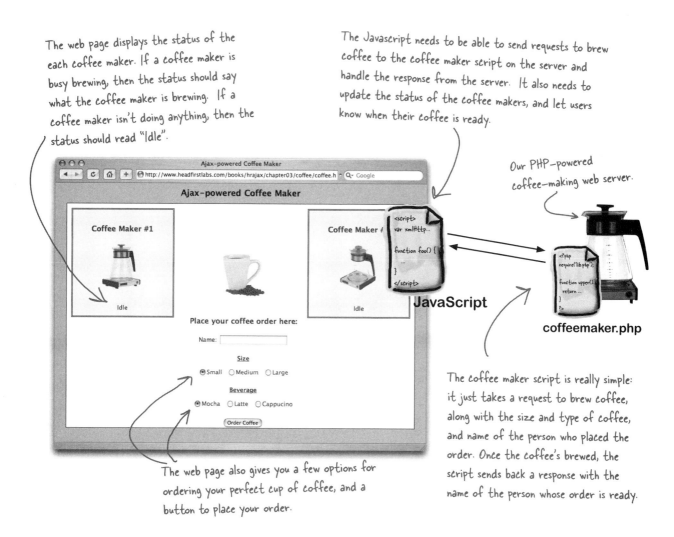

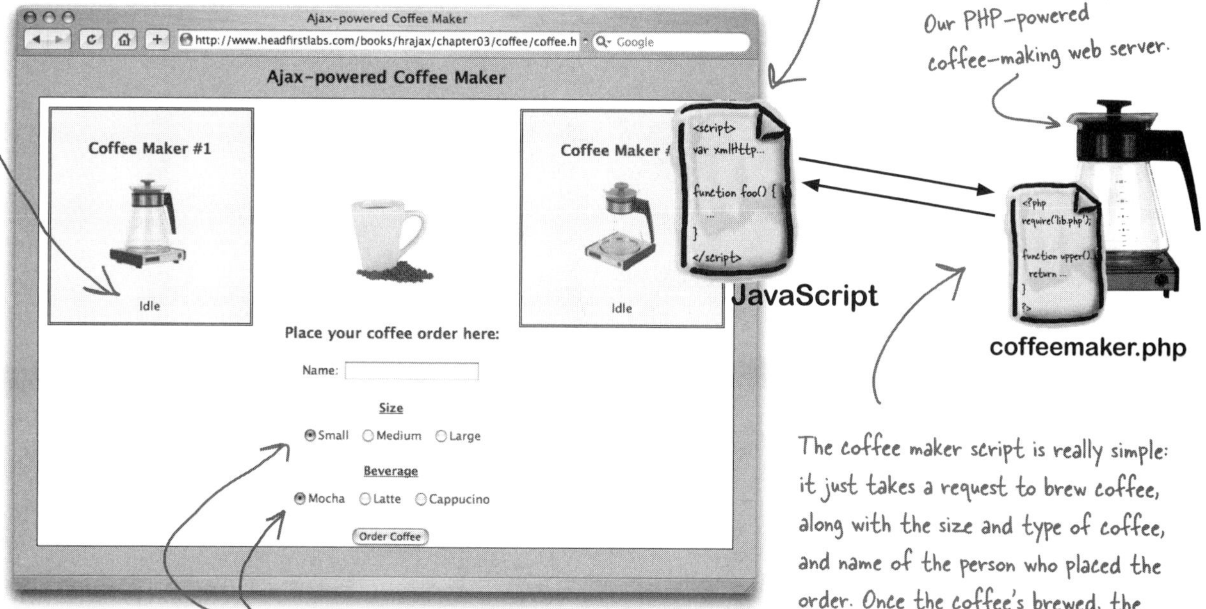

The web page displays the status of the each coffee maker. If a coffee maker is busy brewing, then the status should say what the coffee maker is brewing. If a coffee maker isn't doing anything, then the status should read "Idle".
The Javascript needs to be able to send requests to brew coffee to the coffee maker script on the server and handle the response from the server. It also needs to update the status of the coffee makers, and let users know when their coffee is ready.
Our PHP-powered coffee-making web server.
Ajax-powered Coffee Maker
Coffee Maker #1
Idle
Idle
Place your coffee order here:
Name:
Size
Small
Medium
Large
Beverage
Mocha
Latte
Cappucino
Order Coffee
JavaScript
coffeemaker.php
The coffee maker script is really simple: it just takes a request to brew coffee, along with the size and type of coffee, and name of the person who placed the order. Once the coffee's brewed, the script sends back a response with the name of the person whose order is ready.
The web page also gives you a few options for ordering your perfect cup of coffee, and a button to place your order.

How is the coffee maker going to work?

You should have a good idea of what you'll need to build the coffee-making app. Now you just need to be sure you know what the app will **do**. Before diving into the actual HTML and JavaScript, let's take a closer look at how the coffee maker will handle requests to make a cup of coffee.

1. Let's say that Jim wants to get a caffeine fix. He enters his name into the web form, selects Large and Mocha, and then clicks "Order Coffee". This causes your JavaScript to run, which then sends a request to the first coffee maker.

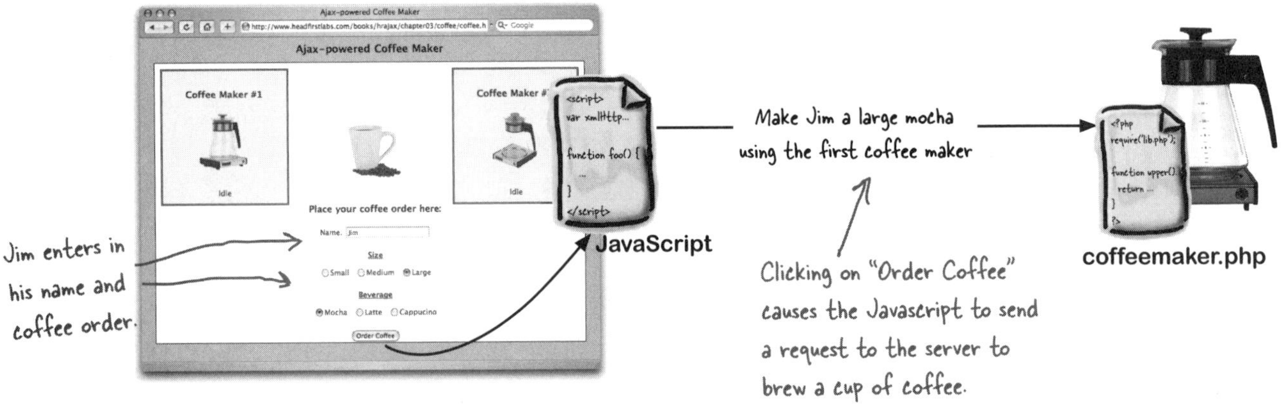
Ajax-powered Coffee Maker
Coffee Maker #1
Idle
Coffee Maker #2
Idle
Place your coffee order here:
Name: Jim
Size
Small Medium Large
Beverage
Mocha Latte Cappucino
Order Coffee
Jim enters in his name and coffee order.
JavaScript
Make Jim a large mocha using the first coffee maker
Clicking on "Order Coffee" causes the Javascript to send a request to the server to brew a cup of coffee.
coffeemaker.php

2. While the first coffee maker is brewing coffee for Jim, Mary decides she needs some cappucino to keep her going. Good thing this is an asynchronous application—she can order a drink from the second coffee maker, even though the server is still brewing coffee in response to Jim's earlier request.

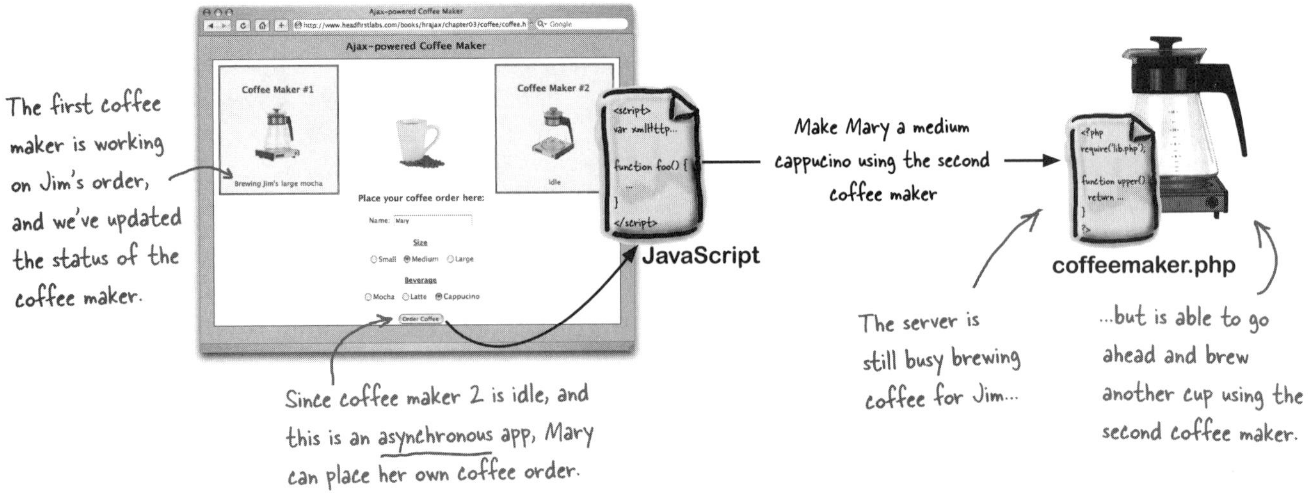
Ajax-powered Coffee Maker
Coffee Maker #1
Brewing Jim's large mocha
Coffee Maker #2
Idle
Place your coffee order here:
Name: Mary
Size
Small Medium Large
Beverage
Mocha Latte Cappucino
Order Coffee
The first coffee maker is working on Jim's order, and we've updated the status of the coffee maker.
JavaScript
Make Mary a medium cappucino using the second coffee maker
coffeemaker.php
The server is still busy brewing coffee for Jim...
...but is able to go ahead and brew another cup using the second coffee maker.
Since coffee maker 2 is idle, and this is an asynchronous app, Mary can place her own coffee order.

3. The coffee maker is finally done brewing Jim's mocha, and sends a response back to your page. The browser runs your Javascript callback, which updates the status of the first coffee maker to "Idle" and lets Jim know that his order is ready .

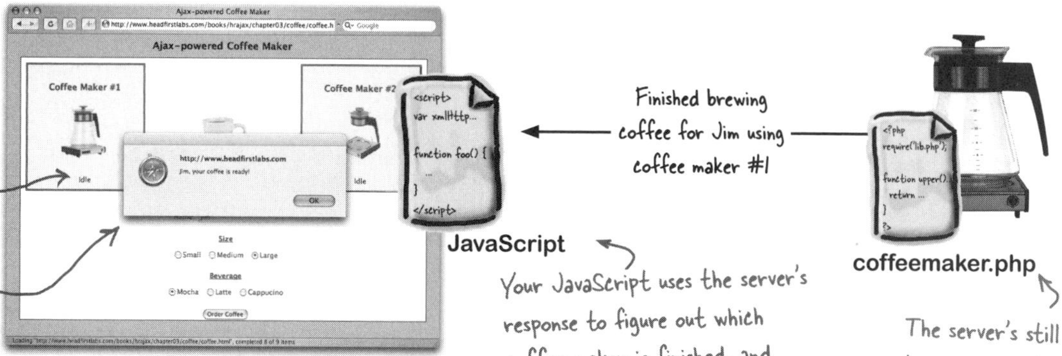

Your JavaScript sets the status of coffee maker #1 back to "Idle"...

...and lets Jim know that his coffee is ready.

Finished brewing coffee for Jim using coffee maker #1

Your JavaScript uses the server's response to figure out which coffee maker is finished, and whose coffee is ready.

The server's still brewing Mary's coffee, but finished up with Jim's cup.

4. Now, Jim has has mocha, Mary's capuccino is almost ready, and the first coffee maker's available again to brew more coffee. Even better, nobody had to wait around for their caffeine fix.

Productivity is up, coffee mugs are full, and you're on your way to scoring a raise for your Ajax expertise.

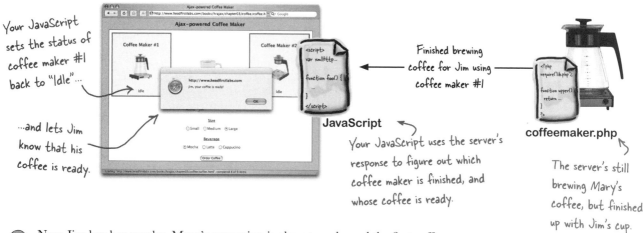

Even your boss is smiling now.

Just Do It

In the book's examples, find the **chapter03/coffee** directory. We've already written the PHP for the coffee maker and named the script **coffeemaker.php**. You'll also see an HTML file, **coffee.html**, and some CSS for the page, in **coffee.css**. Your job is to finish off the HTML in **coffee.html**, and to write the JavaScript to put all this coffee brewing and pouring into action. But first, turn the page for a little brain teaser...

Coffee Conundrum

What do you think would happen if you implemented the coffee maker application as a **synchronous** application instead of an **asynchronous** application? Try this exercise and see if you can figure it out.

The answer comes later in the chapter, so you'll have to keep going to know if you got it right!

1 Sara places an order for a small latte and gets the first coffee maker brewing.

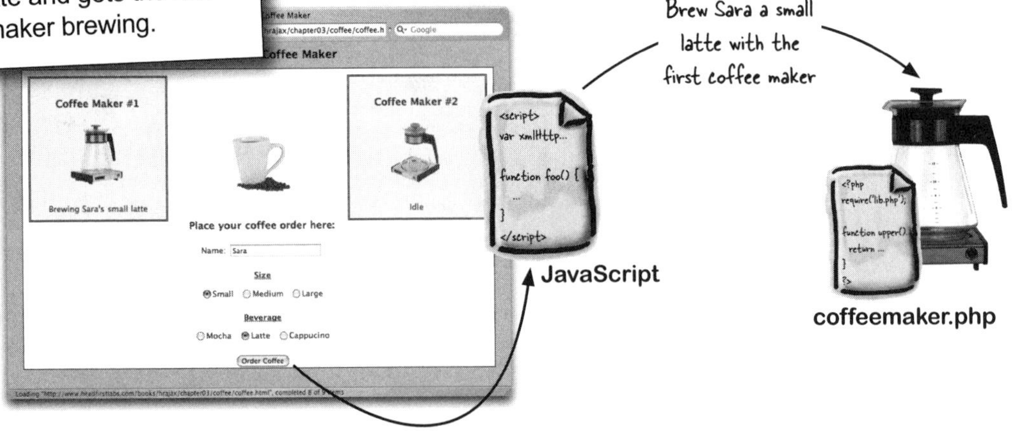

Brew Sara a small latte with the first coffee maker

2 Your officemate needs some coffee. Can she use the second coffee maker while the first coffee maker is brewing Sara's order? Remember, this is a **synchronous** application (at least for now).

The first coffee maker is still brewing coffee for Sara.

Brewing

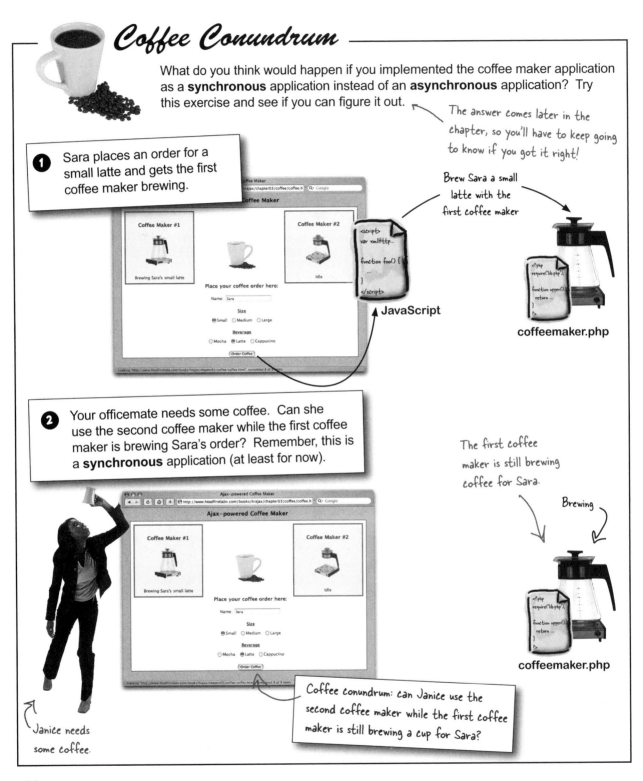

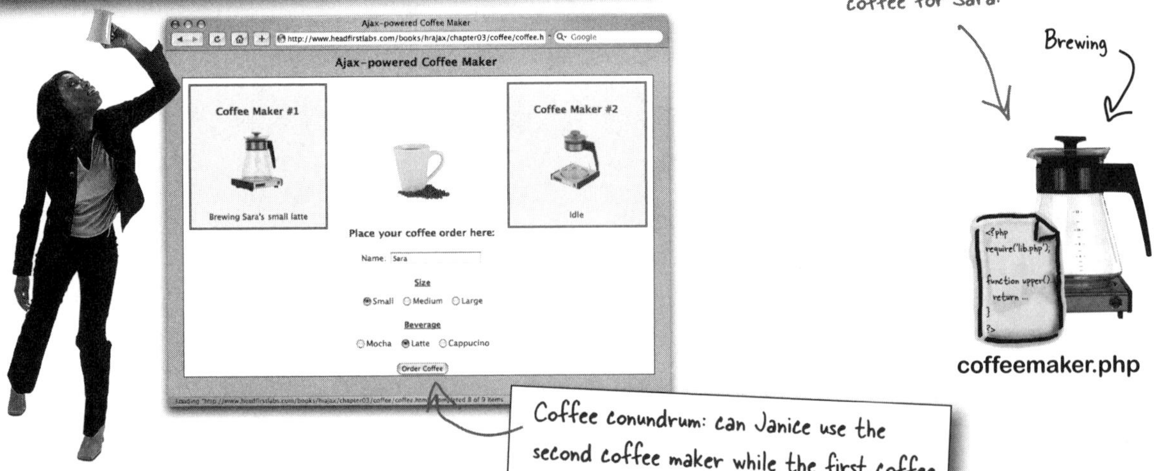

Coffee conundrum: can Janice use the second coffee maker while the first coffee maker is still brewing a cup for Sara?

Janice needs some coffee.

The back-and-forth of Ajax development

In Chapters 1 and 2, you were able to start working on an application and develop it piece by piece until you were done. In this chapter, we're going to have to go back and forth a bit between the three parts of the coffee maker app. This is called **iterative development**, because you keep working on the same pieces over and over.

You'll see this graphic at the top of most of the pages in this chapter. It will remind you which part of the coffee maker app we're working on.
The part of the app we're focusing on will be pulled out, and the arrow will point to that part, too.
HTML form
JavaScript
PHP script
Even when we start working on the JavaScript or PHP, we'll still have to come back to the HTML to make improvements or changes.

Most applications are developed iteratively: you keep coming back to things you've already worked on, and adding to and improving them.

The coffee maker HTML

Enough coffee talk; it's time to build the asynchronous coffee maker application. First, let's take a look at the HTML for the coffee maker application, in **coffee.html**. We've gone ahead and written the HTML for placing and order and the first coffee maker (you're going to do the second coffee maker later). Let's see what you've got to work with:

```
<html>
 <head>
  <title>Ajax-powered Coffee Maker</title>
  <link rel="stylesheet" type="text/css" href="coffee.css" />
 </head>
 <body>
  <div id="header">
   <h1>Ajax powered Coffee Maker</h1>
  </div>

  <div id="wrapper">
   <div id="coffeemaker1">
    <h2>Coffee Maker #1</h2>
    <p><img src="images/CoffeeMaker1.gif"
            alt="Coffee Maker #1" /></p>
    <div id="coffeemaker1-status">Idle</div>
   </div>

   <div id="coffeeorder">
    <p><img src="images/coffeeMugWithBeans.jpg" alt="Coffee Pot 1" /></p>
    <h2>Place your coffee order here:</h2>
    <div id="controls1">
     <form>
      <p>Name: <input type="text" name="name" id="name" /></p>
      <h3>Size</h3>
      <p>
       <input type="radio" name="size"
              value="small" checked="true">Small</input>
         
       <input type="radio" name="size"
              value="medium">Medium</input>
         
       <input type="radio" name="size"
              value="large">Large</input>
      </p>
```

All this is standard stuff. We've linked to an external style sheet and included a title with the name of the application.

Here's the HTML for the first coffee maker. The status indicates if the coffee maker is idle or brewing someone's order. Notice we're using a <div> element to hold the status text.

This <div> is for ordering a cup of coffee.

Here's where you enter your name, so the coffee maker knows who it's brewing coffee for.

Here's where you can select the size of the cup you want: Small, Medium, or Large.

...continued on the next page...

```
    <h3>Beverage</h3>
    <p>
     <input type="radio" name="beverage"
            value="mocha" checked="true">Mocha</input>
       
     <input type="radio" name="beverage"
            value="latte">Latte</input>
       
     <input type="radio" name="beverage"
            value="cappucino">Cappucino</input>
    </p>
    <p>
     <input type="button"
            onClick="____________________"
            value="Order Coffee" />
    </p>
   </form>
  </div>
 </div>

 <div id="_______________">
  <h2>Coffee Maker #2</h2>
  <p><img src="images/CoffeeMaker2.gif" alt="Coffee Maker #2" /></p>
  <div id="____________________">Idle</div>
 </div>

 <p id="clear"></p>
</div>
</body>
</html>
```

This is the last of the coffee order options: you can select the type of coffee you want.

Here's the button to place a coffee order. We'll come back to this and fill in the JavaScript onClick event handler a bit later.

Later in the chapter, we'll come back and finish the HTML for the second coffee maker.

This is a little HTML and CSS trick to make sure the coffee ordering options all fit into the main white part of the form.

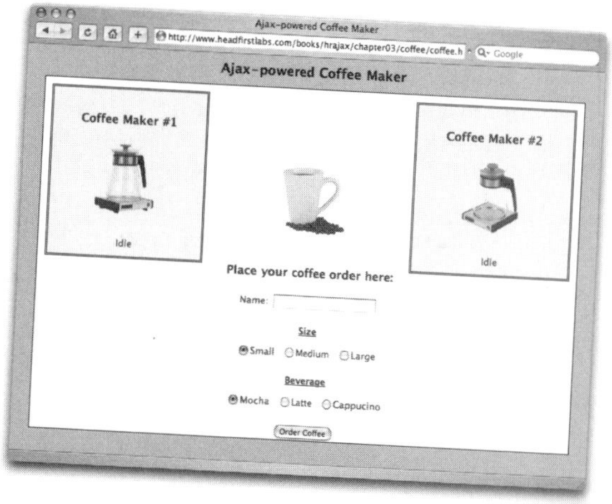

Before we start working on the Javascript, I was thinking... Wouldn't it be better to put our Javascript in a separate file instead of always mixing it in with our HTML?

Yes, let's put your JavaScript in a separate file.

Instead of putting all the JavaScript for the coffee maker directly in the HTML, let's put it in a separate file. Then we can link to it using a **`<script>`** element in the **`<head>`** of the HTML for the coffee maker. Just like separating your HTML and CSS is a good idea, separating your Javascript from your HTML is also a good idea: it keeps the logic (the Javascript) of your application separate from the app's structure and presentation (the HTML and CSS).

You know, I think we should actually make *two* files—one for the JavaScript that's the same in all our Ajax applications, and one for the JavaScript that's specific to the coffee maker. Then we can use the common JavaScript file any time we write a new application.

You're probably tired of typing the same JavaScript over and over for each application... we can take care of that by creating *two* files for our JavaScript: one for the JavaScript that stays *the same* for every Ajax application, and one for the JavaScript that's *specific* to an application. Let's call the JavaScript file containing the code that's common to every application **`ajax.js`**, and the file containing the code specific to this Coffee Maker application **`coffee.js`**. Go ahead and update your HTML with two **`<script>`** elements linking to the two JavaScript files you're about to create:

```
<html>
 <head>
  <title>Ajax-powered Coffee Maker</title>
   <link rel="stylesheet" type="text/css"
         href="coffee.css" />
   <script type="text/javascript" src="ajax.js"> </script>
   <script type="text/javascript" src="coffee.js"> </script>
 </head>
<body>
  ...
</body>
</html>
```

Here are the two <script> elements you need to link to the two JavaScript files. Be sure to add the empty space and the </script> tag, or some browsers won't load the JavaScript you point to.

Just Do It

Here's an outline of the Javascript you're going to need for the Coffee Maker application. For each bit of JavaScript, indicate whether the code should go into the "ajax.js" file or the "coffee.js" file.

Write the name of the file where the code belongs on each line.

```
try {
  request = new XMLHttpRequest();
} catch (trymicrosoft) {
  try {
    request = new ActiveXObject("Msxml2.XMLHTTP");
  } catch (othermicrosoft) {
    try {
      request = new ActiveXObject("Microsoft.XMLHTTP");
    } catch (failed) {
      request = null;
    }
  }
}
```
____

```
function getBeverage() {
   // Figure out what beverage was selected
}
```
____

```
function serveDrink() {
   // When the coffee maker is done, serve the drink
}
```
____

```
if (request == null)
  alert("Error creating request object!");
```
____

```
function orderCoffee() {
   // Take an order from the web form
}
```
____

```
function sendRequest(url) {
   // Send a request to the Coffee Maker
}
```
____

```
var request = null;
```
____

```
function getSize() {
   // Figure out what size cup was selected
}
```
____

HTML form
JavaScript
PHP script

? Frequently Asked Questions

Q: I couldn't figure out whether to put the sendRequest() function into ajax.js or coffee.js. On the one hand, we'll need this function for every Ajax app, but on the other hand, it will have code that's specific to the coffee maker application. Which file does this function go in?

A: You're right—that's a toughie. You could probably go either way on this one. We decided to put the `sendRequest()` function in the `coffee.js` file, even though—as you'll see in a few pages—`sendRequest()` has no coffee maker-specific code in it. We decided to do things this way because we like keeping the `sendRequest()` and `serveDrink()` functions together. Since `serveDrink()` does have some coffee maker-specific code, we put them both into `coffee.js`.

Q: Why do we need a separate function for getting the drink size and type of beverage?

A: As you'll see in a few pages, it takes several lines of JavaScript to get the value of a radio button, which is the control we use for getting the size of a drink and the type of beverage. We like keeping this code separate from the rest of `orderCoffee()`, which will build the request URL and update the coffee makers' status text.

Q: It looks like the request object is created in static code. Why did we do that again?

A: By putting the code that creates the request object into static JavaScript—JavaScript that's not in a function—any errors that occur will be reported *before* the coffee maker can be used. That way, none of your co-workers get their order entered in, and then find out that something went wrong.

Here's what we did...

We put all the code that creates and tests the request object into **`ajax.js`**, and then put all the coffee-related functions into **`coffee.js`**. If you did things differently, that's okay. Just make sure you remember where each function is so you know which file to edit as you build the rest of the application.

<script>
var xmlHttp...
function foo() {
}
</script>

ajax.js

```
var request = false;
try {
  ...
}

if (request == null) {
  ...
}
```

<script>
var xmlHttp...
function foo() {
}
</script>

coffee.js

```
function sendRequest(url) {...}
function serveDrink() {...}
function orderCoffee() {...}
function getSize() { ... }
function getBeverage() {...}
```

Welcome to iterative development... we're going back to finish up the HTML now, even though we've started on the JavaScript.

Just Do It

Now that you know the name of your JavaScript functions, you can finish up the rest of the HTML for the coffee maker.

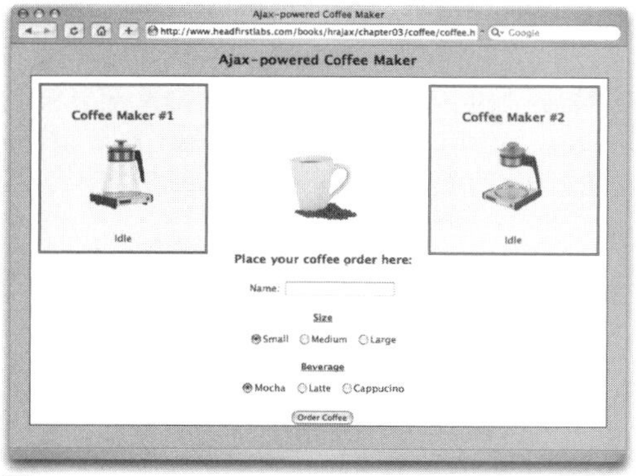

This is your coffee.html file.

```
  <h3>Beverage</h3>
  <p>
   <input type="radio" name="beverage"
          value="mocha"
          checked="true">Mocha</input>
     
   <input type="radio" name="beverage"
          value="latte">Latte</input>
     
   <input type="radio" name="beverage"
          value="cappucino">Cappucino</input>
  </p>
  <p>
   <input type="button"
          onClick="___________________"
          value="Order Coffee" />
  </p>
 </form>
 </div>
</div>

<div id="______________">
 <h2>Coffee Maker #2</h2>
 <p><img src="images/CoffeeMaker2.gif"
        alt="Coffee Maker #2" /></p>
 <div id="____________________">Idle</div>
</div>
```

1. Fill in the blanks in the HTML on the left for placing a coffee order with the name of the function to run when someone clicks the "Order Coffee"" button.

2. Next, finish the HTML for the second coffee maker. Remember, all your element's id values should be unique. We're depending on the id names in the JavaScript, so make sure you check your answer with ours (on the next page) before moving on.

If you're stuck, look back at the HTML for the first coffee maker, and use that as a model for filling in the blanks on the second coffee maker HTML.

Just Do It Solutions

Now that you know the name of your JavaScript functions, you can finish up the rest of the HTML for the coffee maker.

```
  <h3>Beverage</h3>
  <p>
   <input type="radio" name="beverage"
          value="mocha"
          checked="true">Mocha</input>
     
   <input type="radio" name="beverage"
          value="latte">Latte</input>
     
   <input type="radio" name="beverage"
          value="cappucino">Cappucino</input>
  </p>
  <p>
   <input type="button"
          onClick=" orderCoffee(); "
          value="Order Coffee" />
  </p>
 </form>
 </div>
</div>

<div id="coffeemaker2">
 <h2>Coffee Maker #2</h2>
 <p><img src="images/CoffeeMaker2.gif"
         alt="Coffee Maker #2" /></p>
 <div id="coffeemaker2-status">Idle</div>
</div>
```

orderCoffee() is the JavaScript function you'll write to send a new coffee order to the coffee-making PHP script.

In the first coffee maker, these ids were "coffeemaker1" and "coffeemaker1-status"...

...so in this coffee maker, we just changed all the "1"s to "2"s.

Sending a request for coffee

With the HTML complete, it's back to our JavaScript. Let's write the JavaScript to send a request to the server to make coffee. By now, you're a pro at making requests, so **`orderCoffee()`** should be a piece of cake, right? Let's think through what this function needs to do:

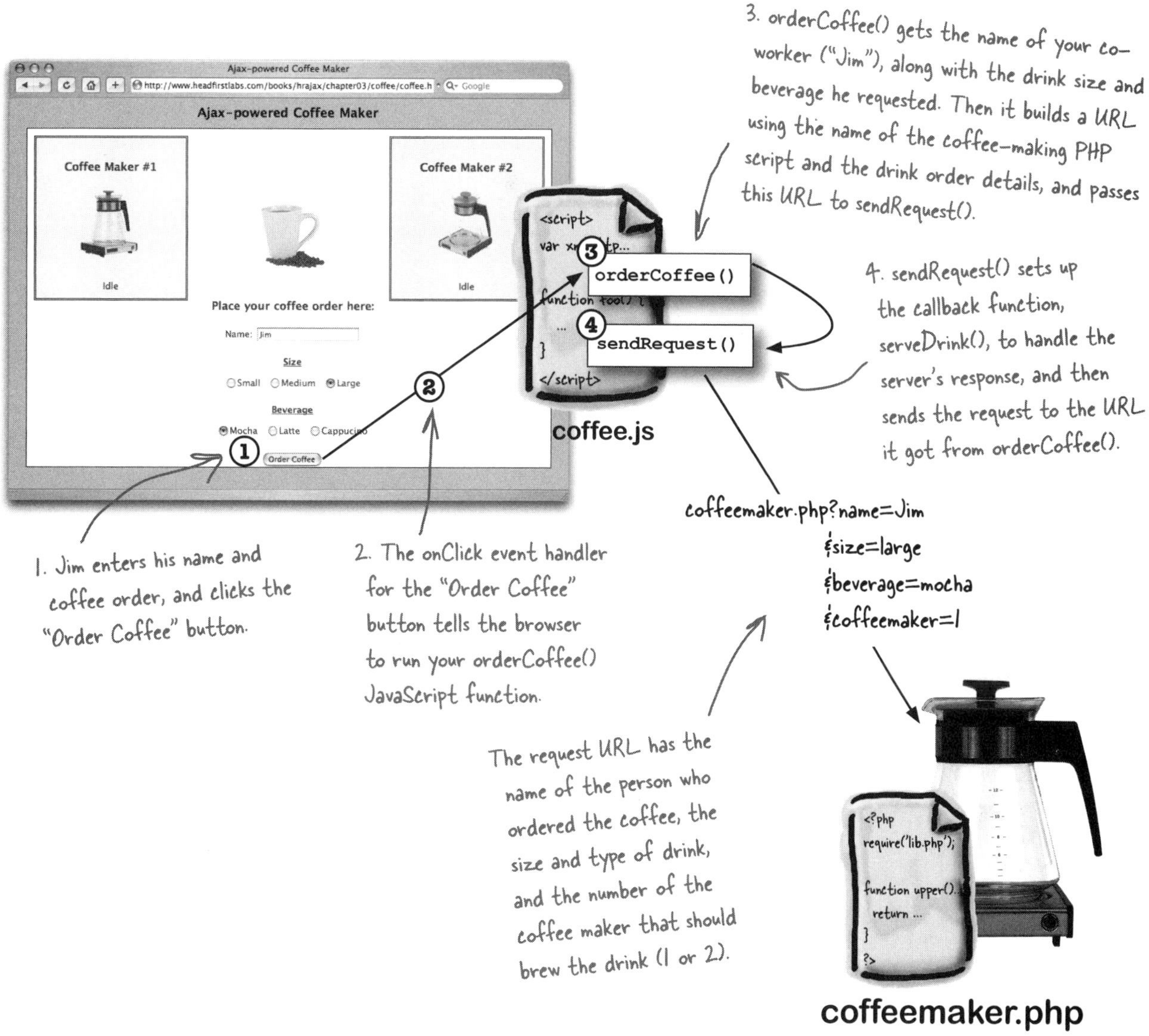

Writing JavaScript to send the request

Now let's write the JavaScript to send the request to the coffee-making script:

All this code should go in your copy of coffee.js.

```
function sendRequest(url) {
  request.onreadystatechange = serveDrink;
  request.open("GET", url, true);
  request.send(null);
}

function orderCoffee() {
  var name = document.getElementById("name").value;
  var beverage = getBeverage();
  var size = getSize();

  var url = "coffeemaker.php?name=" + escape(name) +
                      "&size=" + escape(size) +
                      "&beverage=" + escape(beverage) +
                      "&coffeemaker=1";

  sendRequest(url);
}
```

sendRequest() sets up the callback function for the server response (serveDrink) and sends a GET request to the URL passed in from makeFreshCoffee().

We'll write the functions to get the size and beverage requested in just a few pages.

orderCoffee() builds the request URL, using the coffeemaker.php script and all the information it got from the coffee order form.. It requests the first coffee maker be used to brew the coffee.

coffee.js

Now wait just a second. That's it? You completely forgot something—what if the first coffee maker is already brewing coffee? And what about the second coffee maker? When should we use it?

Which coffee maker should we use?

Each coffee maker can only brew one cup at a time, so what if the first coffee maker is already brewing coffee? Somehow we need to find out if the first coffee maker status is "Idle" before we send a new request. If it's busy, we can try the second coffee maker. And if that one's busy... well, then Jim's gonna have to wait a bit for his coffee.

How do you think we can get the status of each coffee maker? Here's the HTML for the first coffee maker... what do you think we should do?

```
<div id="coffeemaker1">
 <h2>Coffee Maker #1</h2>
 <p><img src="images/CoffeeMaker1.gif"
        alt="Coffee Maker #1" /></p>
 <div id="coffeemaker1-status">Idle</div>
</div>
```

Remember, the second coffee maker HTML is very similar to this.

BRAIN POWER

How do you think we can find out the status of the coffee makers? And how can we update the status when one is brewing coffee, and when the coffee maker finishes brewing?

Keep thinking about this, and we'll come back to it a little later in the chapter.

Getting the beverage and size of the order

Before we figure out how to get and update the status of the two coffee makers, you need to write the code for **`getSize()`** and **`getBeverage()`**.

Let's look back at the coffee order form and see what we're dealing with:

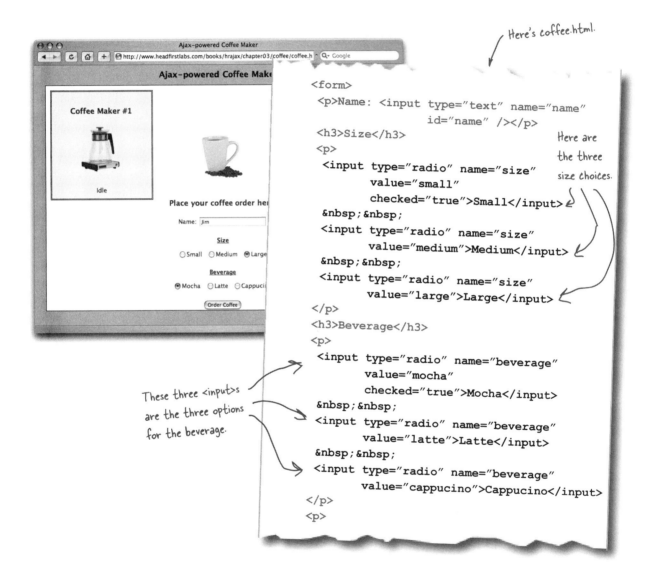

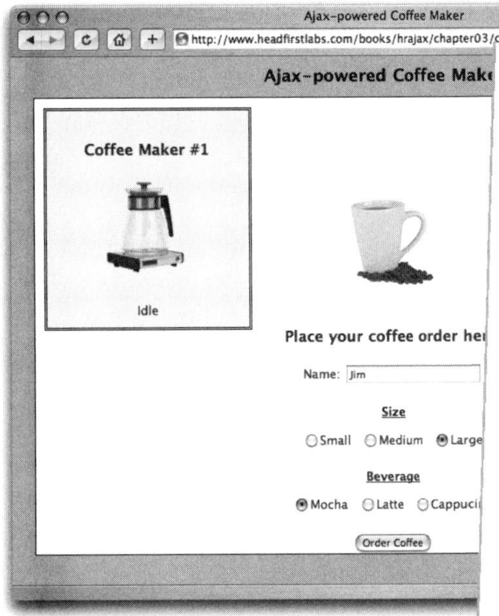

Here's coffee.html.

```
<form>
 <p>Name: <input type="text" name="name"
                 id="name" /></p>
 <h3>Size</h3>
 <p>
  <input type="radio" name="size"
         value="small"
         checked="true">Small</input>
    
  <input type="radio" name="size"
         value="medium">Medium</input>
    
  <input type="radio" name="size"
         value="large">Large</input>
 </p>
 <h3>Beverage</h3>
 <p>
  <input type="radio" name="beverage"
         value="mocha"
         checked="true">Mocha</input>
    
  <input type="radio" name="beverage"
         value="latte">Latte</input>
    
  <input type="radio" name="beverage"
         value="cappucino">Cappucino</input>
 </p>
 <p>
```

Here are the three size choices.

These three <input>s are the three options for the beverage.

But how do we find out what size and beverage Jim selected?

Getting the value of a radio group

The key to getting the size and beverage that Jim selected is realizing that there are three different <input> elements, all named "size" (and "beverage"). So you need to figure out which of these three is currently selected:

```
function getSize() {
  var sizeGroup = document.forms[0].size;
  for (i=0; i<sizeGroup.length; i++) {
    if (sizeGroup[i].checked == true) {
      return sizeGroup[i].value;
    }
  }
}
```

orderCoffee() will call this function to find out what size coffee was ordered.

"document" is the entire web page, and forms[0] is the first form on that page. Then, "size" is the name of the <input> elements that let users select their drink size.

Since there is more than one element named "size", this variable will be a group of elements, not just a single <input> element.

This line loops through all the elements in the "size" grouping...

...and this line checks to see if the current element is checked (selected).

If we've found the option that is checked, then return the value of that item.

The returned value will be either "small", "medium", or "large", which is exactly what the orderCoffee() function needs.

Just Do It

It's your turn to work with radio <input> elements. First, open up coffee.js and add the orderCoffee(), sendRequest(), and getSize() functions that we've looked at over the last few pages.

Next, you need to write the getBeverage() function. You should be able to figure this out from the HTML in coffee.html, and the getSize() function you just looked at. Once you're done, be sure you save coffee.html, and then turn the page.

Espresso Talk

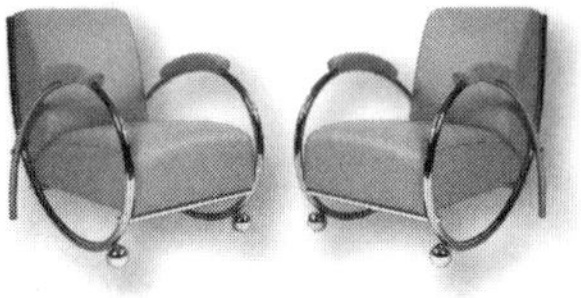

Tonight's overly caffeinated guests:
Asynchronous and Synchronous Application

Synchronous: Hey Mr. Asynchronous, long time no talk.

Asynchronous: No kidding... every time I call you, I get a busy signal. You'd think we weren't even brothers.

Synch: I'm a busy guy, you know? And I don't let anything get in the way of me paying attention to the user I'm serving.

Asynch: I can see that. But what about all your *other* users, waiting around?

Synch: They'll get their turn, too. Remember, I learned from Client-Server himself. He was really great; everyone liked him just fine, and he was the strong, silent type, just like me.

Asynch: I guess. I always thought he seemed a lot more like the my-users-are-all-tired-of-waiting-on-me type.

Synch: You know, you seem to forget who's the older sibling here. I've been around a lot longer than you.

Asynch: Yeah, and so have your users... waiting and waiting...

Synch: Look, nobody gives their users more time and attention than I do. I'm just trying to please them. Meanwhile, you're running around, trying to please *everyone*. That never works!

Asynch: It sounds to me like you're trying to please your USER... like just one. Everybody else has to wait in line.

Synch: Hey, sometimes it's much better to take care of one thing at a time, and then move on to other jobs.

Asynch: Sure, maybe if someone submits like 200 pieces of data. But most of the time, you're just not needed anymore.

Synch: Just because I don't let people interrupt me while I'm working...

Asynch: Hey, I can listen *and* talk, all at the same time. You're the one with a one-track mind...

Synch: One-track mind? I just make sure I finish what I start.

Asynch: Sure, but what if that takes ten seconds? Or ten minutes? Or an hour? Come on, do you really think people enjoy that little hourglass whirling around?

Synch: I don't seem to get many complaints.

Asynch: Yeah, well, I'd love to sit around like this all day, but my users don't like to wait on me. That's more your department.

Synch: Yeah, enjoy your 15 minutes, bro. I've seen fads like you come and go a million times.

Asynch: I bet you thought U2 was a one-hit wonder, too. I'm not going anywhere—except to make the web a hip place again. See you when I see you, Synch...

What JavaScript do we still need to write?

There's a lot of JavaScript that you'll need to write to make the coffee maker work like it's supposed to. Let's take a look at all the functions we've got to code, and review what we still need to do:

This code is done, and in ajax.js. It's the same code that we used in Chapter 2, and creates the request object in static JavaScript.

We can get the user's order, but still need to check the status of the coffee makers and figure out which one to send the order to.

JavaScript code

You'll need some JavaScript, including:

- ~~Code to create a request object.~~
- A function to send an order to the coffee-making script.
- A function to serve a drink when it's been brewed.
- ~~An event handler to connect the "Order Coffee" button to these JavaScript functions.~~

We still have to write this function. It needs to get the server's response, and set the status of the coffee maker that just finished brewing back to "Idle".

We've got this done also. When someone clicks "Order Coffee", our orderCoffee() function runs.

* Don't forget, we've still got to get a coffee-making script running on the server, too. We'll get to that in a little bit.

Getting and setting the text content in a <div>

Let's get back to **orderCoffee()**. We need to get the status of the first coffee maker from the "coffeemaker1-status" **<div>** element, and then if the status is "Idle", send a request to brew coffee using this coffee maker. If the first coffee maker is busy, we should check the second coffee maker, and the "coffeemaker2-status" **<div>**.

On top of all that, you'll need to change the status of whichever coffee maker you use to indicate that it's busy brewing an order. To get or set the text content in a **<div>**, you need to use the browser's Document Object Model, or DOM for short. We're going to go into how to use the DOM in a lot more detail in the next chapter, so for now, just follow along using the PRE-ASSEMBLED JavaScript so we can finish the coffee maker application.

What you want: to get the text in the "coffeemaker1-status" <div>

```
<div id="coffeemaker1">
  <h2>Coffee Maker #1</h2>
  <p><img src="images/CoffeeMaker1.gif"
          alt="Coffee Maker #1" /></p>
  <div id="coffeemaker1-status">Idle</div>
</div>
```

Coffee Maker

To read the status, you need to get the content of the "coffeemaker1-status" <div>. → Idle

We'll need to be able to do the same thing for the second coffee maker, using the "coffeemaker2-status" <div>.

More help from text-utils.js

Remember, PRE-ASSEMBLED JavaScript is code that's ready for you to use. Just type it in and we'll explain it all later—promise!

In Chapter 1, you used the **text-utils.js** JavaScript file to help you update Katie's web report. We're going to use the same JavaScript utility file in the coffee maker. Start out by adding another **<script>** element into the head of your **coffee.html** file referring to **text-utils.js**, like this:

```
<html>
  <head>
    <title>Ajax-powered Coffee Maker</title>
    <link rel="stylesheet" type="text/css" href="coffee.css" />
    <script type="text/javascript" src="ajax.js"> </script>
    <script type="text/javascript" src="text-utils.js"> </script>
    <script type="text/javascript" src="coffee.js"> </script>
  </head>
```

Add this line, and then you can use all the utility functions from text-utils.js in your JavaScript functions.

Checking a coffee maker's status

Now that you can use the utility functions in **text-utils.js**, you can easily check the status of a coffee maker using the **getText()** function, like this:

```
function orderCoffee() {
  var name = document.getElementById("name").value;
  var beverage = getBeverage();
  var size = getSize();

  var coffeemakerStatusDiv1 =
   document.getElementById("coffeemaker1-status");
  var status = getText(coffeemakerStatusDiv1);
  if (status == "Idle") {
    // Update the coffee maker's status

    var url = "coffeemaker.php?name=" + escape(name) +
                              "&size=" + escape(size) +
                              "&beverage=" + escape(beverage) +
                              "&coffeemaker=1";
    sendRequest(url);
  }
}
```

This gets the <div> that holds the status for the first coffee maker.

getText() will return the text in the coffeemaker1-status <div>.

If the first coffee maker is idle, we want to send the coffee order to it, and let it brew the order.

We still need to figure out how to update the coffee maker's status, too.

getText() will return the text within a <div>, or any other element that you give it.

text-utils.js has several JavaScript functions for working with the DOM. We'll cover the DOM in detail in Chapter 4.

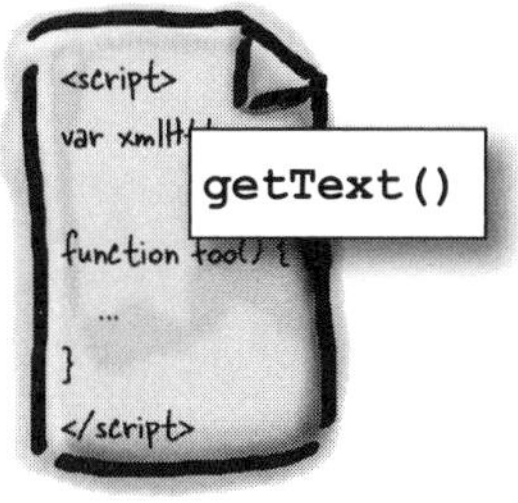

text-utils.js

All the code in text-utils.js is in Appendix 2. You can check it out now, or wait until we've talked more about the DOM in Chapter 4.

Setting the text in a <div>

Now that you know how to get the text in the coffee maker status **<div>**s, you just need to be able to set the text in those status **<div>**s. You can use another utility function in **text-utils.js** for this, called **replaceText()**.

```
function orderCoffee() {
  var name = document.getElementById("name").value;
  var beverage = getBeverage();
  var size = getSize();

  var coffeemakerStatusDiv1 =
   document.getElementById("coffeemaker1-status");
  var status = getText(coffeemakerStatusDiv1);
  if (status == "Idle") {
    replaceText(coffeemakerStatusDiv1, "Brewing " +
                name + "'s " +
                size + " " + beverage);
    var url = "coffeemaker.php?name=" + escape(name) +
                          "&size=" + escape(size) +
                          "&beverage=" + escape(beverage) +
                          "&coffeemaker=1";
    sendRequest(url);
  }
}
```

If the first coffee maker is idle, this will update the coffee maker's status to indicate that it's making a drink...

...and these send the request to the coffee-making PHP script.

getText() will return the text within a <div>, or any other element that you give it.

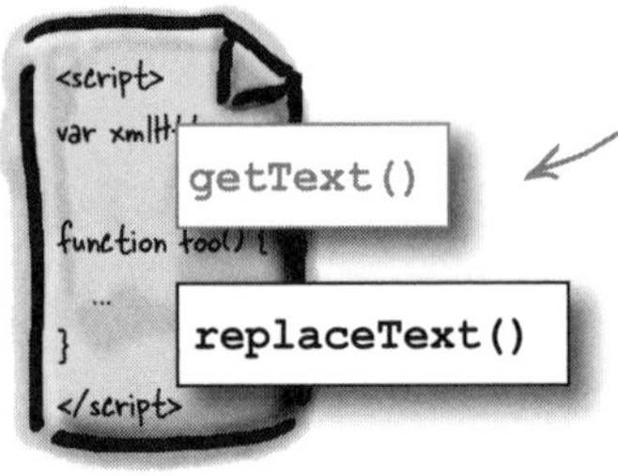

text-utils.js

reaplaceText() takes an element, and the text to put within that element. This will clear out any existing text, so that the text you supply becomes the only text in the element.

We haven't covered the DOM yet, so just get a general idea of what the JavaScript in text-utils.js does. We'll cover the DOM in detail in the next chapter.

JavaScript ...at a glance

Let's take a brief look at text-utils.js. Remember, all of this code will make a lot more sense once you've gone through Chapter 4.

```
function replaceText(el, text) {
  if (el != null) {
    clearText(el);
    var newNode = document.createTextNode(text);
    el.appendChild(newNode);
  }
}

function clearText(el) {
  if (el != null) {
    if (el.childNodes) {
      for (var i = 0; i < el.childNodes.length; i++) {
        var childNode = el.childNodes[i];
        el.removeChild(childNode);
      }
    }
  }
}

function getText(el) {
  var text = "";
  if (el != null) {
    if (el.childNodes) {
      for (var i = 0; i < el.childNodes.length; i++) {
        var childNode = el.childNodes[i];
        if (childNode.nodeValue != null) {
          text = text + childNode.nodeValue;
        }
      }
    }
  }
  return text;
}
```

replaceText() is a general purpose function that takes an element object, like a <div>, and a string of text, and sets the element's content to the text that you pass in.

replaceText() uses clearText() to clear out an element's contents, and then replaceText() sets the element's new text content.

Watch out! clearText() will clear out any content in an element, including nested elements, as well as text.

getText() will return the text content of the element you give to it.

getText() will take all the text in an element, and combine it into a single string, which is what the function returns.

REMEMBER: It's OK if you don't understand this code. We're going to spend a lot of time on the DOM in the next chapter.

Code Magnets

With the help of text-utils.js, sendCoffee() figures out if the first coffee maker is idle, and if it is, uses that coffee maker to brew an order. But what happens if the first coffee maker isn't idle? In that case, your JavaScript needs to see if the second coffee maker is idle, and if it is, use that coffee maker to brew the order. Otherwise, you'll need to let the user know that they'll have to wait for one of the busy coffee makers to finish before their order can be brewed.

Below is the code for sendCoffee(), with several blanks. Your job is to set up the JavaScript to try and use both coffee makers. Place the correct magnets in each blank, and then turn the page:

```
function orderCoffee() {
  var name = document.getElementById("name").value;
  var beverage = getBeverage();
  var size = getSize();

  var coffeemakerStatusDiv1 =
   document.getElementById("coffeemaker1-status");
  var status = getText(coffeemakerStatusDiv1);
  if (status == "Idle") {
    replaceText(coffeemakerStatusDiv1, "Brewing " +
                name + "'s " +
                size + " " + beverage);
    var url = "coffeemaker.php?name=" + escape(name) +
                          "&size=" + escape(size) +
                          "&beverage=" + escape(beverage) +
                          "&coffeemaker=1";
    sendRequest(url);
  } else {
```

All the code on the facing page is part of the "else" block.

The "else" part of this code will run when the first coffee maker's status is not "Idle".

If you're not sure which magnets to use where, look back at the JavaScript that controls the first coffee maker. The JavaScript for the second coffee maker should look very similar.

```
    var ____________________ =
      document.getElementById("________________");
    status = getText(_______________);
    if (status == "_________") {
      replaceText(_____________________,
                  "Brewing " + _______ + "'s " +
                  _______ + " " + ____________);
      var url = "_______________?__________=" + escape(________) +
                                "&__________=" + escape(________) +
                                "&__________=" + escape(________) +
                                "&__________=___";
      _______________(url);
    } else {
      ________("Sorry! Both coffee makers are busy. " +
               "Try again later.");
    }
  }
}
```

You can use a magnet more than once if you need to.

coffeemaker.php
coffeemakerStatusDiv
alert
coffeemakerStatusDiv2
coffeemaker2-status
coffeemaker
beverage
name
alert
size
2
coffeemakerStatusDiv
sendRequest
Idle
1
coffeemaker1-status

Code Magnets Solutions

Below is the portion of orderCoffee() that you should have finished off. Be sure your answers match ours, and save your copy of coffee.js with these changes.

All this code is in the orderCoffee() function.

This code runs when the first coffee maker is already brewing coffee for someone else.

```
if (status == "Idle") {
  ...
} else {
  var coffeemakerStatusDiv2 =
    document.getElementById("coffeemaker2-status");
  status = getText(coffeemakerStatusDiv2);
  if (status == "Idle") {
    replaceText(coffeemakerStatusDiv2
                "Brewing " + name + "'s " +
                size + " " + beverage);
    var url = "coffeemaker.php name=" + escape(name) +
                             "&size=" + escape(size) +
                             "&beverage=" + escape(beverage) +
                             "&coffeemaker=2";
    sendRequest(url);
  } else {
    alert("Sorry! Both coffee makers are busy. " +
          "Try again later.");
  }
}
}
```

Be sure to use the second coffee maker here!

This lets users know when both coffee makers are already busy.

These magnets are all left over.

`coffeemakerStatusDiv` `alert` `1` `coffeemaker1-status` `coffeemakerStatusDiv`

Test drive

Even though there is plenty of work left to do, go ahead and take the coffee maker for a test drive. Be sure you've added the **`sendRequest()`**, **`getSize()`**, **`getBeverage()`**, and **`orderCoffee()`** functions to **`coffee.js`**, and then load **`coffee.html`** in your web browser.

Enter in an order, and see what happens. Then, enter in another order... are both coffee makers being used?

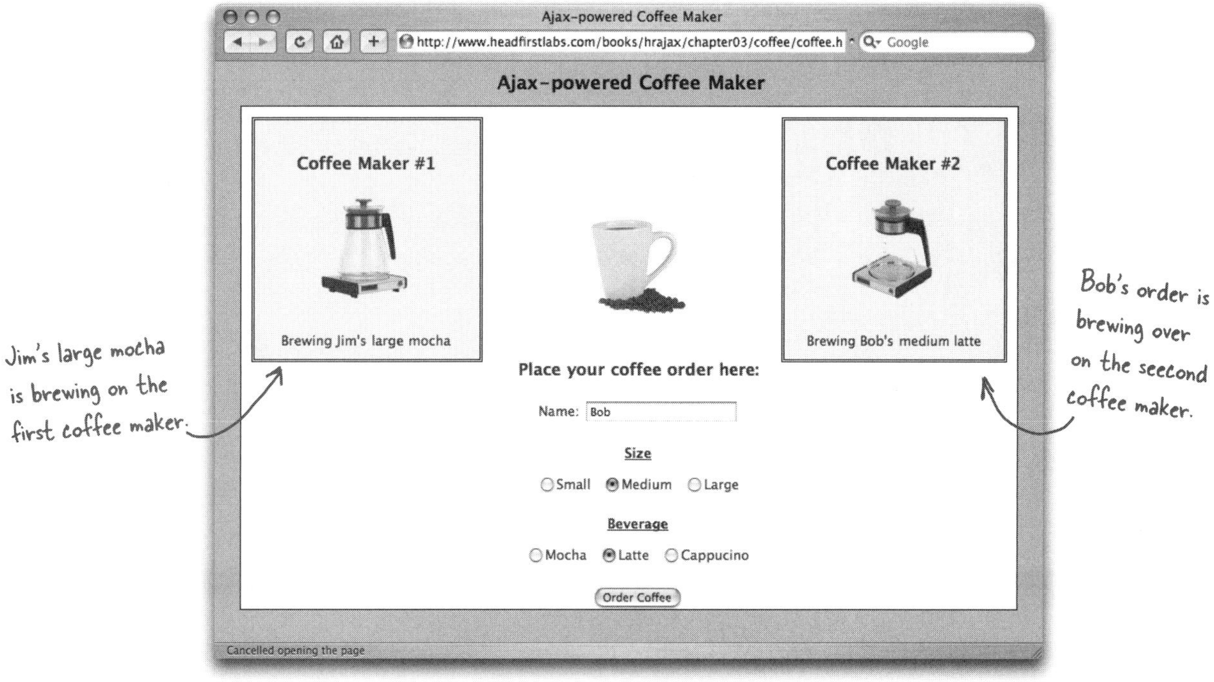

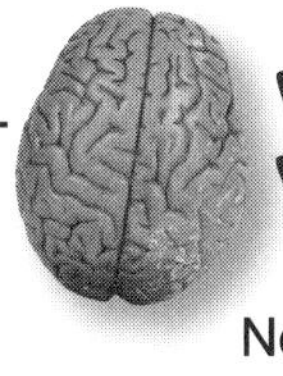

BRAIN POWER

Notice that once an order is placed, the person's name and order details stay filled in. Could this cause problems? What do you think we should do to avoid any confusion?

HTML form
JavaScript
PHP script

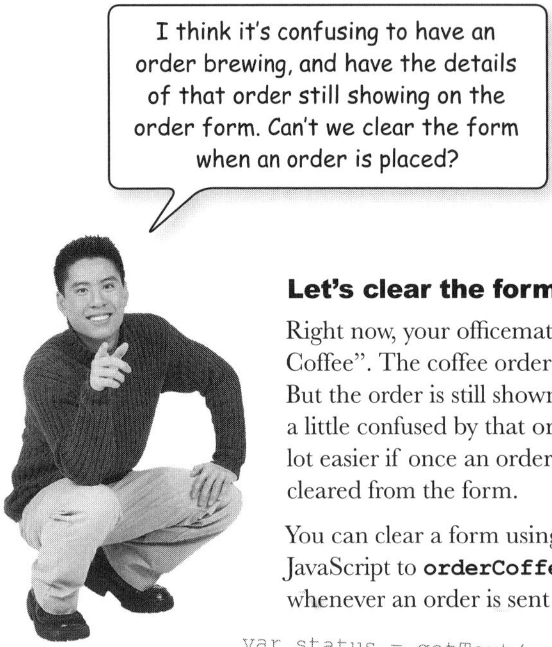
I think it's confusing to have an order brewing, and have the details of that order still showing on the order form. Can't we clear the form when an order is placed?

Let's clear the form when an order is placed

Right now, your officemates enter their coffee order and click "Order Coffee". The coffee order is sent to a coffee maker, and brewing begins. But the order is still shown on the screen, and co-workers could be a little confused by that order still being on the screen. It would be a lot easier if once an order got sent to a coffee maker, the details were cleared from the form.

You can clear a form using the **`reset()`** method. Let's add some JavaScript to **`orderCoffee()`**, in **`coffee.js`**, to clear the order form whenever an order is sent to a coffee maker:

There are two places in coffee.js where you send a request to a coffee maker.

In both places, get the first form on the web page, and call reset() on the form.

```
var status = getText(coffeemakerStatusDiv1);
if (status == "Idle") {
  replaceText(coffeemakerStatusDiv1,
              "Brewing " + name + "'s " +
              size + " " + beverage);
  document.forms[0].reset();
  var url = "coffeemaker.php?name=" + escape(name) +
                            "&size=" + escape(size) +
                            "&beverage=" + escape(beverage) +
                            "&coffeemaker=1";
  sendRequest(url);
} else {
  var coffeemakerStatusDiv2 =
    document.getElementById("coffeemaker2-status");
  status = getText(coffeemakerStatusDiv2);
  if (status == "Idle") {
    replaceText(coffeemakerStatusDiv2,
                "Brewing " + name + "'s " +
                size + " " + beverage);
    document.forms[0].reset();
    var url = "coffeemaker.php?name=" + escape(name) +
                              "&size=" + escape(size) +
                              "&beverage=" + escape(beverage) +
                              "&coffeemaker=2";
```

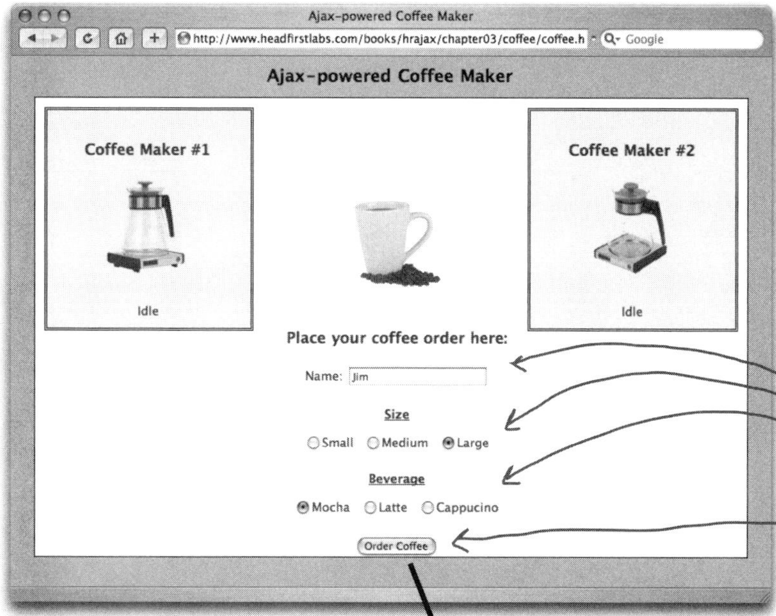
Ajax-powered Coffee Maker
http://www.headfirstlabs.com/books/hrajax/chapter03/coffee/coffee.h
Google
Ajax-powered Coffee Maker
Coffee Maker #1
Idle
Coffee Maker #2
Idle
Place your coffee order here:
Name: Jim
Size
Small Medium Large
Beverage
Mocha Latte Cappucino
Order Coffee
Jim enters his coffee order just like before...
...and then clicks "Order Coffee"...
...which runs the orderCoffee() JavaScript function...

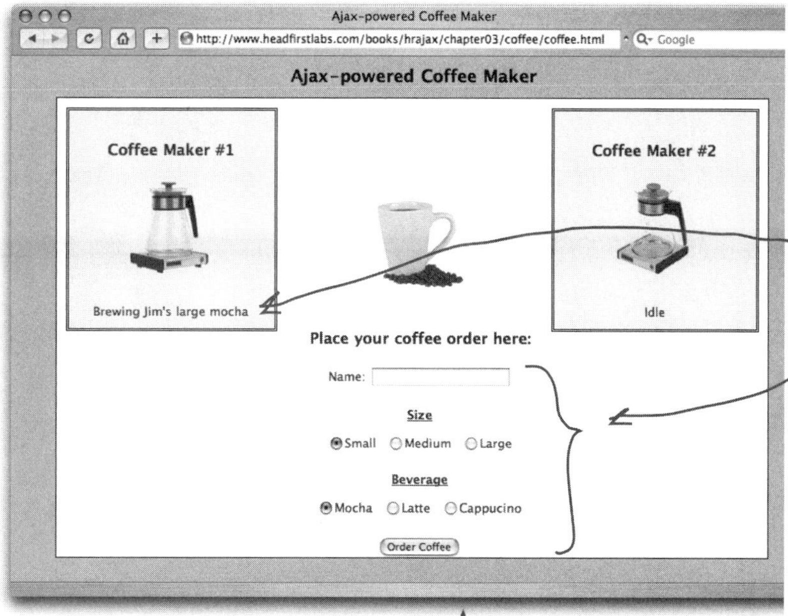
Ajax-powered Coffee Maker
http://www.headfirstlabs.com/books/hrajax/chapter03/coffee/coffee.html
Google
Ajax-powered Coffee Maker
Coffee Maker #1
Brewing Jim's large mocha
Coffee Maker #2
Idle
Place your coffee order here:
Name:
Size
Small Medium Large
Beverage
Mocha Latte Cappucino
Order Coffee
Let's try these changes out.
...which sends the order to the first coffee maker, and then resets the form.
Now, there's no confusion for the next person who wants to order a coffee.

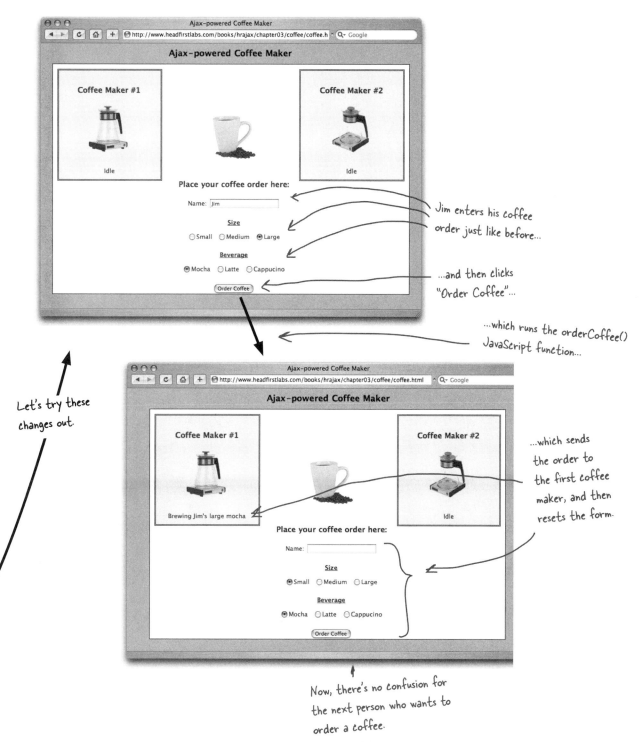

It's time to get the server making some coffee so we can start serving drinks to your hard working co-workers.

PHP ...at a glance

The PHP coffee maker script just loops for a while to simulate coffee brewing. Here's the code we used for coffeemaker.php:

```
<?php

$name = $_REQUEST[‘name’];
$size = $_REQUEST[‘size’];
$beverage = $_REQUEST[‘beverage’];
$coffeemaker = $_REQUEST[‘coffeemaker’];

for ($i = 0; $i < 50000000; $i++) {
  // brewing
}

echo $coffeemaker . $name;
?>
```

The script starts by getting all the data sent as part of the request URL.

Here's where you can plug in your own Internet-enabled coffee maker code.

This loop just kills time... and simulates brewing coffee.

Once brewing is done, the script returns the number of the coffee maker that finished, and the name of the person whose order is ready. So this might look like "1Jim" if the first coffee maker finished an order for Jim, or "2Mary" if the second coffee maker finished an order for Mary.

You can download coffeemaker.php from http://www.headfirstlabs.com, or check out all the code listings in Appendix 2.

What do we do with the server's response?

You've completed **`orderCoffee()`**, and now **`coffeemaker.php`** is done. When you send a request to brew coffee to one of the coffee makers, **`coffeemaker.php`** runs and then returns the coffee maker that completed the order, as well as the name of the person who placed the order.

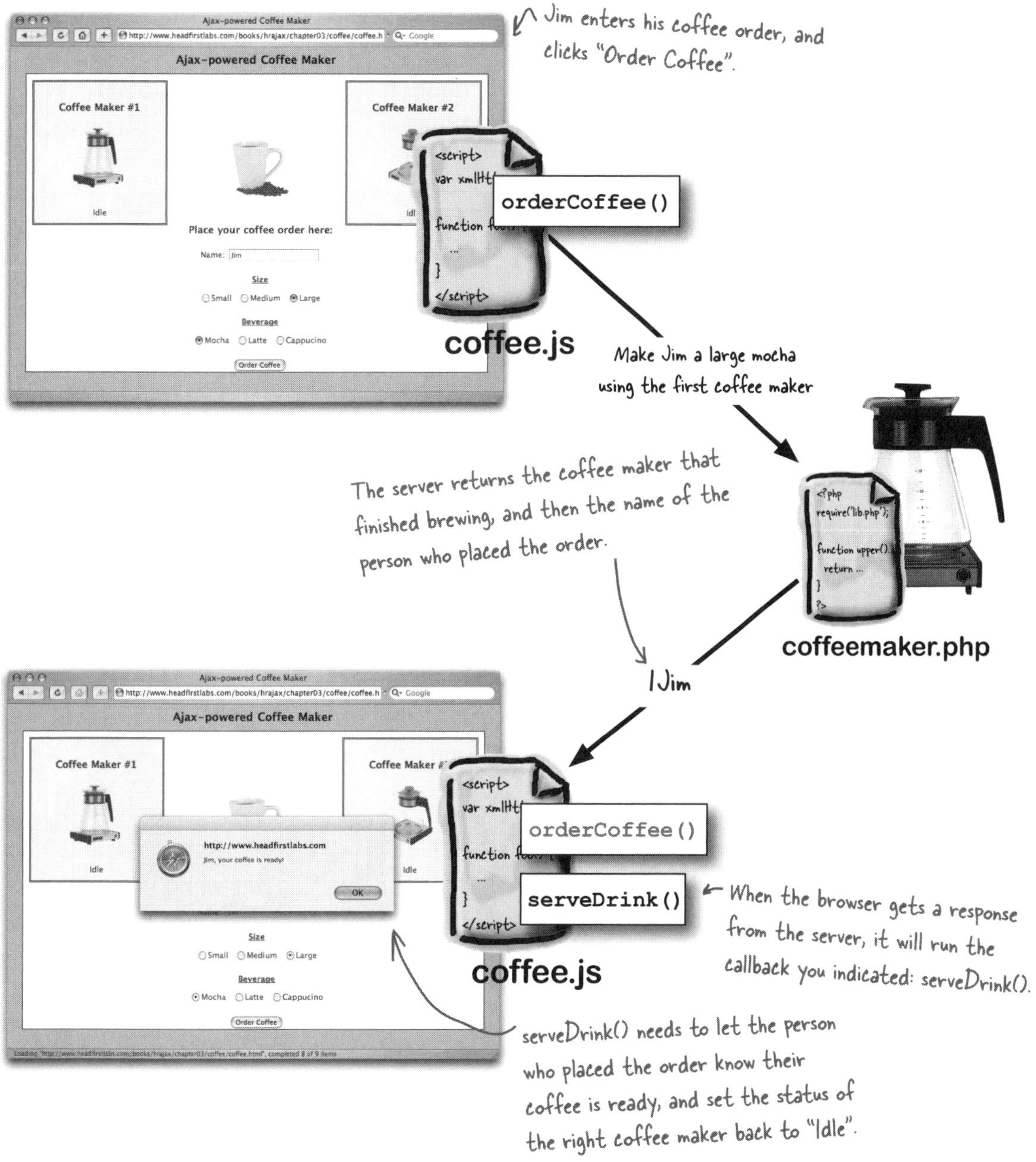
Jim enters his coffee order, and clicks "Order Coffee".
Ajax-powered Coffee Maker
Coffee Maker #1
Coffee Maker #2
Idle
Place your coffee order here:
Size
Beverage
Order Coffee
orderCoffee()
coffee.js
Make Jim a large mocha using the first coffee maker
coffeemaker.php
The server returns the coffee maker that finished brewing, and then the name of the person who placed the order.
1Jim
http://www.headfirstlabs.com
Jim, your coffee is ready!
OK
orderCoffee()
serveDrink()
coffee.js
When the browser gets a response from the server, it will run the callback you indicated: serveDrink().
serveDrink() needs to let the person who placed the order know their coffee is ready, and set the status of the right coffee maker back to "Idle".

Writing the callback function

The only function left to write is **serveDrink()**, which needs to take the response from the server and figure out who placed the order, and which coffee maker was used to brew the order. Then **serveDrink()** can set the coffee maker's status to "Idle" and let the person who placed the order know that their coffee is ready.

Let's start by checking the ready state, the HTTP status code, and then getting the response from the server.

```
function serveDrink() {
  if (request.readyState == 4) {
    if (request.status == 200) {
      var response = request.responseText;

      // Figure out who placed the order, and
      //   which coffee maker was used
    } else
      alert("Error! Request status is " + request.status);
  }
}
```

All of this code should be pretty familiar by now. You'll use this same code in almost every callback function you ever write.

Interpreting the server's response

The server's response looks like this when it's received by the **serveDrink()** callback:

Here's the response from the server-side coffee-making script.

We really need to split this response into two parts.

1Jim

"1" indicates that it's the first coffee maker that brewed this order.

"Jim" is the name of the person who placed this order.

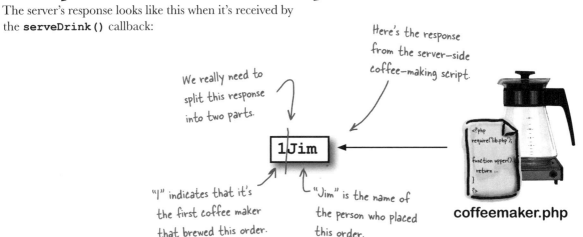

coffeemaker.php

Introducing the JavaScript substring() function

JavaScript has a function that's just perfect for taking a string like the coffee maker is returning, and breaking it up into a few parts. Here's how you use the **`substring()`** function:

substring() is the JavaScript function you can use to break down strings into smaller parts.

startIndex is the position in myString you want your substring to begin at. Remember, "0" is the position of the first character, not "1".

```
var newString = myString.substring(startIndex, endIndex);
```

newString is the smaller substring returned by JavaScript.

myString is the variable that holds the string you want to break up into several smaller parts.

endIndex is the position in myString that you want your substring to end at. The character at this poisition is not included in the substring.

It may help you to think of substring() as creating a string from position startIndex to position (endIndex - 1).

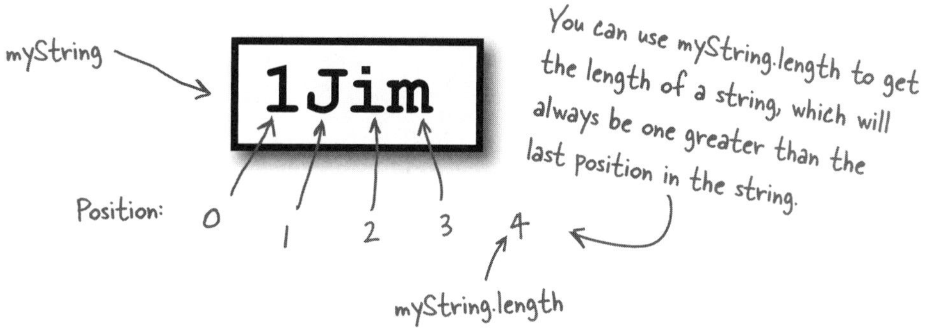

myString
1Jim
Position:
0
1
2
3
4
mySring.length
You can use myString.length to get the length of a string, which will always be one greater than the last position in the string.

substring() practice

Let's spend a little time practicing how to use the JavaScript **substring()** method, using the string you saw on the last two pages.

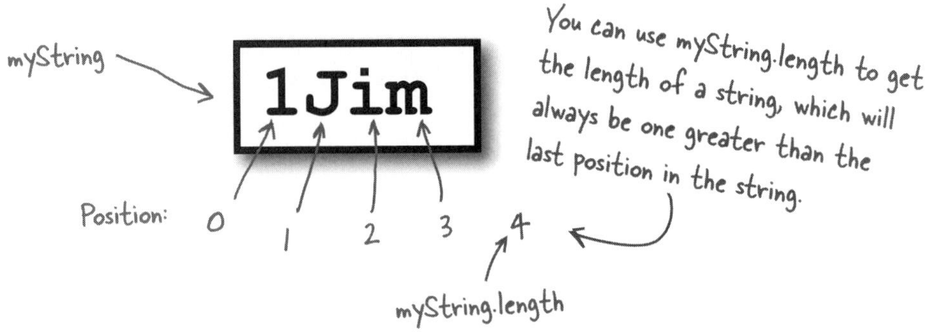

myString
1Jim
Position:
0
1
2
3
4
myString.length
You can use myString.length to get the length of a string, which will always be one greater than the last position in the string.

This substring will start at position 1, end at position 3, and not include the character at position 3.

This substring started at position 1 ("J"), and went to position (3 – 1), which is position 2 ("i").

```
myString.substring(1, 3);
```

→ **Ji**

Since myString.length will be 1 greater than the last position, this will always go to the end of a string.

```
myString.substring(2, myString.length);
```

→ **im**

Position 0 is the first character in the string...

...and myString.length will always return to the end of the string.

This JavaScript would always return the entire string.

```
myString.substring(0, myString.length);
```

→ **1Jim**

Just Do It

You should be ready to write the rest of the JavaScript for serveDrink() on your own now. Below is part of that function's JavaScript; your job is to fill in the blanks and get things working.

You'll need to get the response from the server, then break that response into the number of the coffee maker that brewed this order and the name of the person that placed the coffee order. Next you should set the status of the coffee maker that just finished to "Idle" and let the person that ordered coffee know that his order is ready.

Here's where you can put what you just learned about substring() to use.

```
function serveDrink() {
  if (request.readyState == _______) {
    if (request.status == _______) {
      var response = request.responseText;
      var whichCoffeemaker = response.substring(___, ___);
      var name = response.substring(_____, _________);
      if (whichCoffeemaker == "1") {
        var coffeemakerStatusDiv1 =
          document.getElementById("____________________");
        replaceText(_____________________, "Idle");
      } else {
        var coffeemakerStatusDiv2 =
          document.getElementById("____________________");
        replaceText(______________________, "_______");
      }
      ________(name + ", your coffee is ready!");
    } else
      alert("Error! Request status is " + request.status);
  }
}
```

coffee.js

Finishing up serveDrink()

Let's spend a little time practicing with the JavaScript **substring()** method, using the string you saw on the last two pages.

```
function serveDrink() {
  if (request.readyState == 4) {
    if (request.status == 200) {
      var response = request.responseText;
      var whichCoffeemaker = response.substring(0, 1);
      var name = response.substring(1, response.length);
      if (whichCoffeemaker == "1") {
        var coffeemakerStatusDiv1 =
          document.getElementById("coffeemaker1-status");
        replaceText(coffeemakerStatusDiv1, "Idle");
      } else {
        var coffeemakerStatusDiv2 =
          document.getElementById("coffeemaker2-status");
        replaceText(coffeemakerStatusDiv2, "Idle");
      }
      alert(name + ", your coffee is ready!");
    } else
      alert("Error! Request status is " + request.status);
  }
}
```

These two lines should be pretty routine by now.

We want just the very first position in order to get the number of the coffee maker that finished up.

The name returned by the server starts in the second position ("1"), and goes to the end of the string.

This code updates the status of whichever coffee maker finished brewing.

This last bit just lets the person who placed an order know that his coffee is now ready.

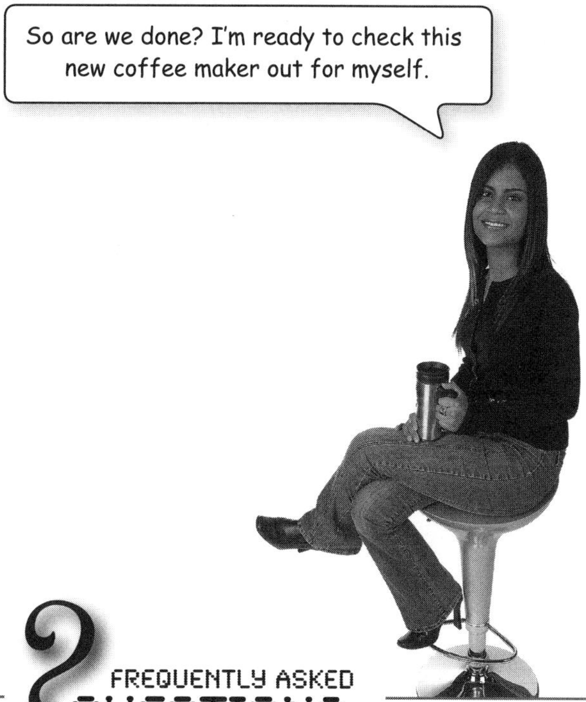

So are we done? I'm ready to check this new coffee maker out for myself.

Frequently Asked Questions

Q: Why didn't we just use form <input> elements for the coffee maker's status? Wouldn't that have been a lot easier than using all this DOM stuff?

A: We certainly could have used form elements to display the status of the coffee makers. The problem with using form elements, though, is that users expect to be able to type into form fields. The status elements we're using are for display only—users are not supposed to change those values themselves. So it makes more sense for them to be non-editable fields that just display text.

That means we have to use the DOM... but as you'll see in the next chapter, the DOM isn't that hard. Once you understand how the browser *really* sees your HTML markup, you'll be writing your own DOM code in no time. So stay tuned...

Q: Isn't there a simpler way to get and set the text of a <div>? I've read about a property called "innerHTML," which would let me just put in the HTML I wanted for the <div>. Couldn't we use that instead?

A: Using the `innerHTML` property is *not* a good way to get and set the contents of an element. It's not part of the DOM specification, and the W3C has deprecated it—future versions of browsers may not even support it. Worse than that, some browsers don't support it now!

It's much safer going with the DOM code we're using here. In the next chapter, we'll get into all the details about how the DOM code works, and once you've written a few functions using the DOM, you'll see it's pretty easy to use. Best of all, the DOM is available anytime you've got a web browser, on any platform.

The final test drive (right?)

It looks like we've got all the JavaScript for the coffee maker app written. Be sure you've followed along with all the examples so far, and saved your changes to **`coffee.html`** and **`coffee.js`**. Then load **`coffee.html`** in your browser, and take the coffee maker for a test drive.

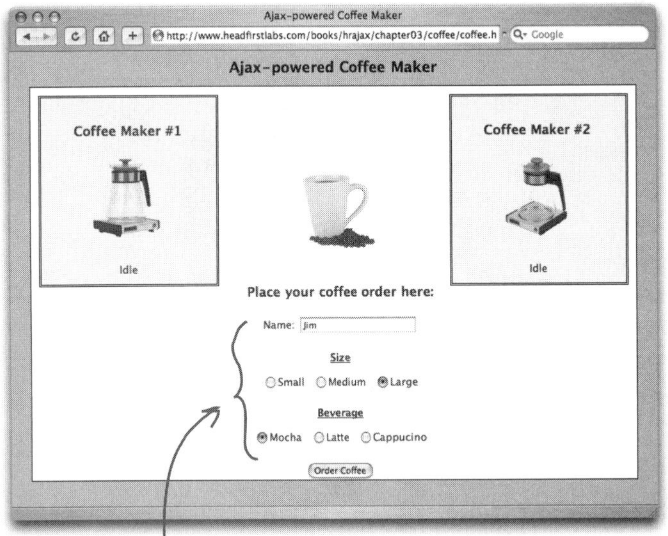

1. Enter an order for Jim: he wants a large mocha. Then click "Order Coffee".

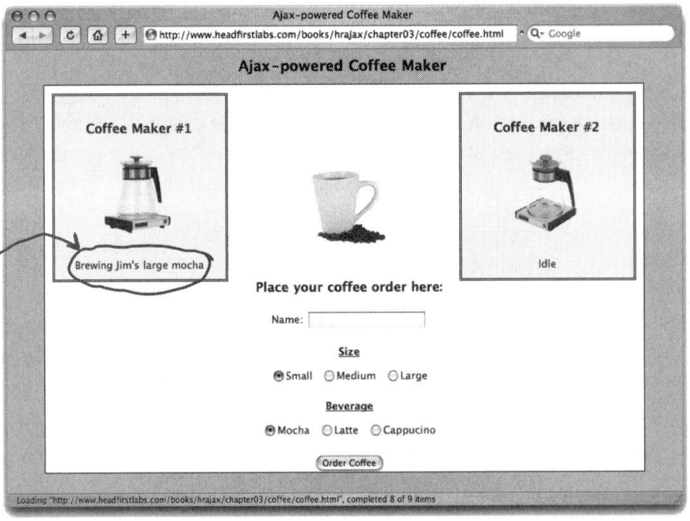

2. Jim's order starts brewing, using the first coffee maker.

3 Now enter another order, for Bob. Bob wants a medium latte. Click "Order Coffee", and Bob's order should start brewing on the second coffee maker.

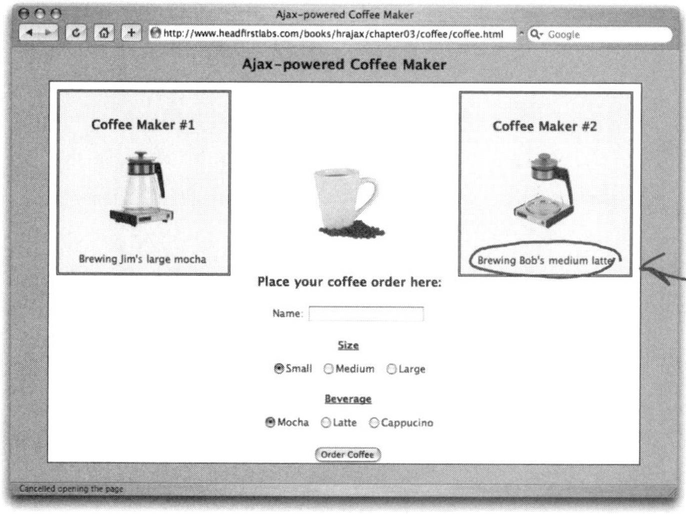

4 Now wait for the coffee makers to finish brewing. Whose order comes up first? Do both orders finish brewing? Is this what you expected to happen?

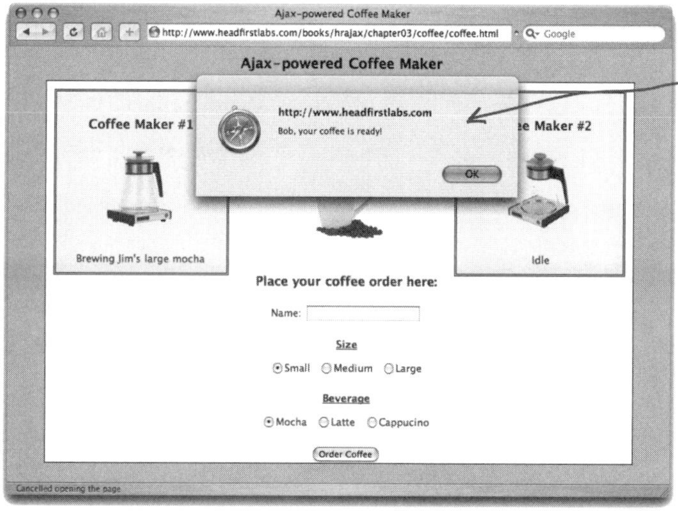

Bob's order comes up first, even though it was ordered second.

So what happened to Jim's coffee order?

A closer look at the request object

To figure out what's going on with Jim's order, let's take a closer look at each step of the test drive on the last two pages, and what our request object is actually doing.

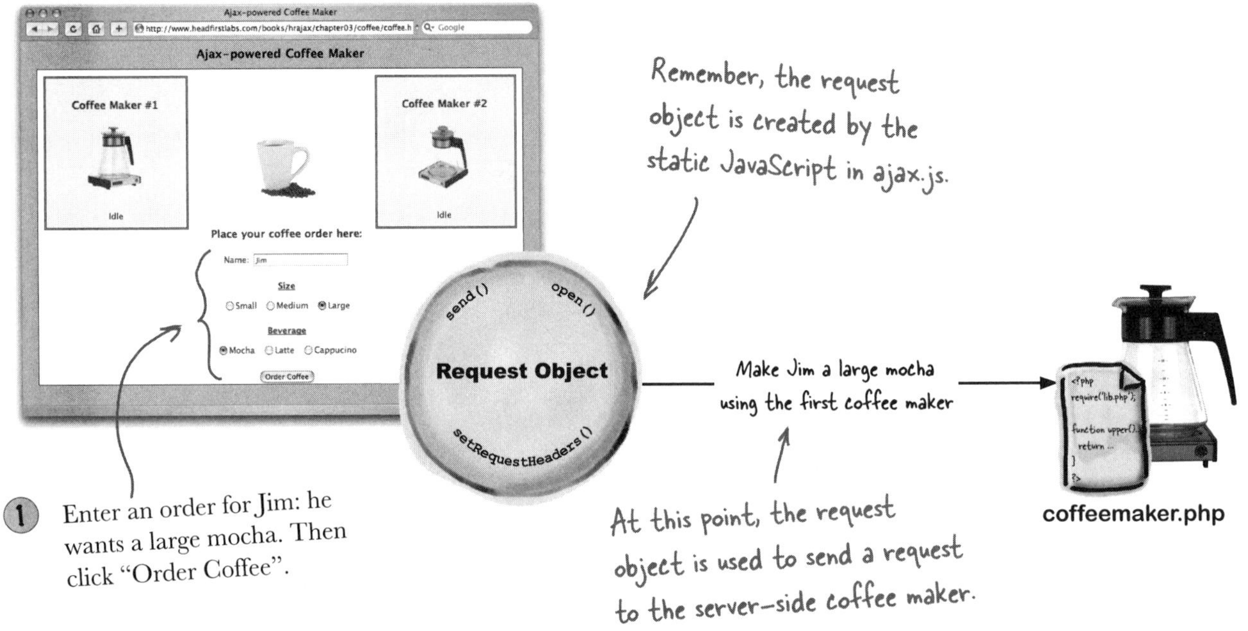

1 Enter an order for Jim: he wants a large mocha. Then click "Order Coffee".

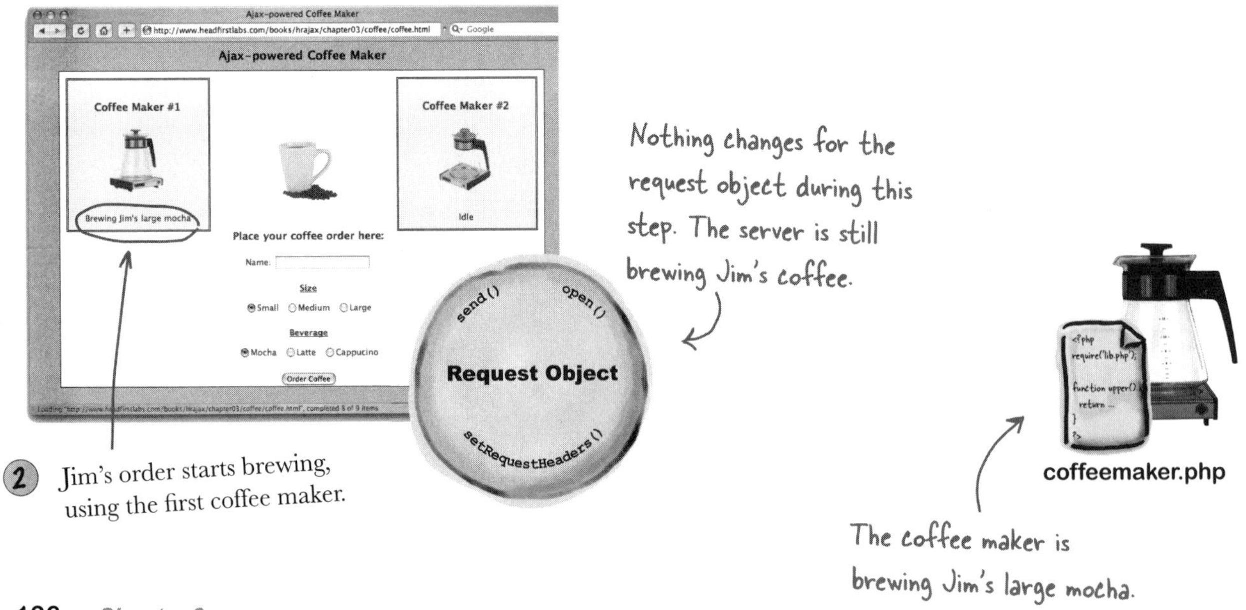

2 Jim's order starts brewing, using the first coffee maker.

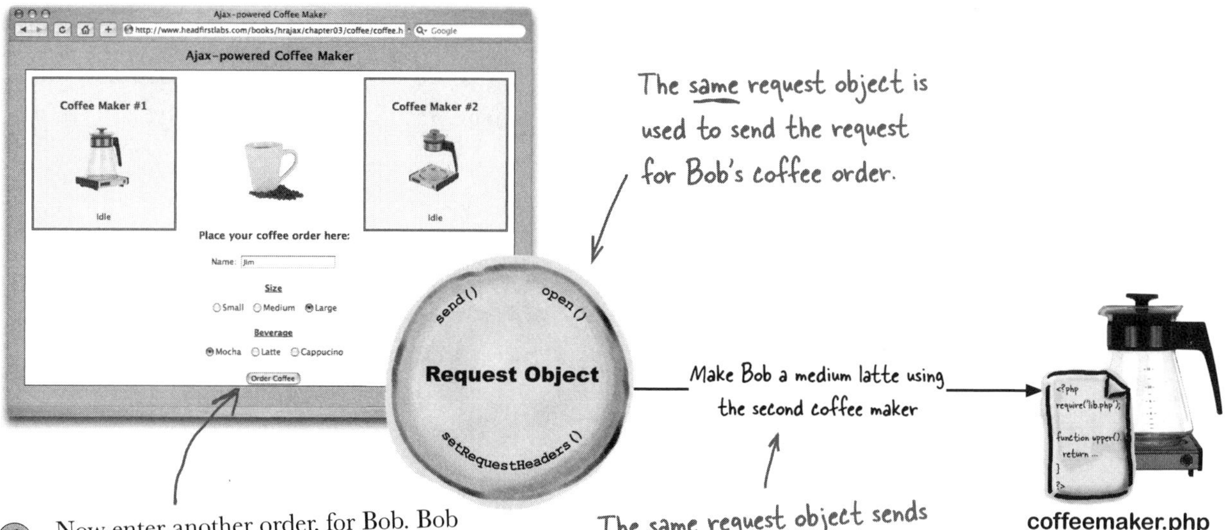

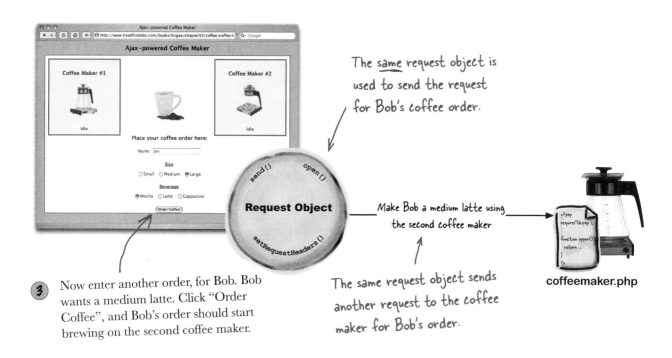

3 Now enter another order, for Bob. Bob wants a medium latte. Click "Order Coffee", and Bob's order should start brewing on the second coffee maker.

But what about Jim's order?

Do you see the problem? Jim's order is still brewing, but now there's no request object attached to that request! The request for Bob's order overwrote the information in the request object related to Jim's order:

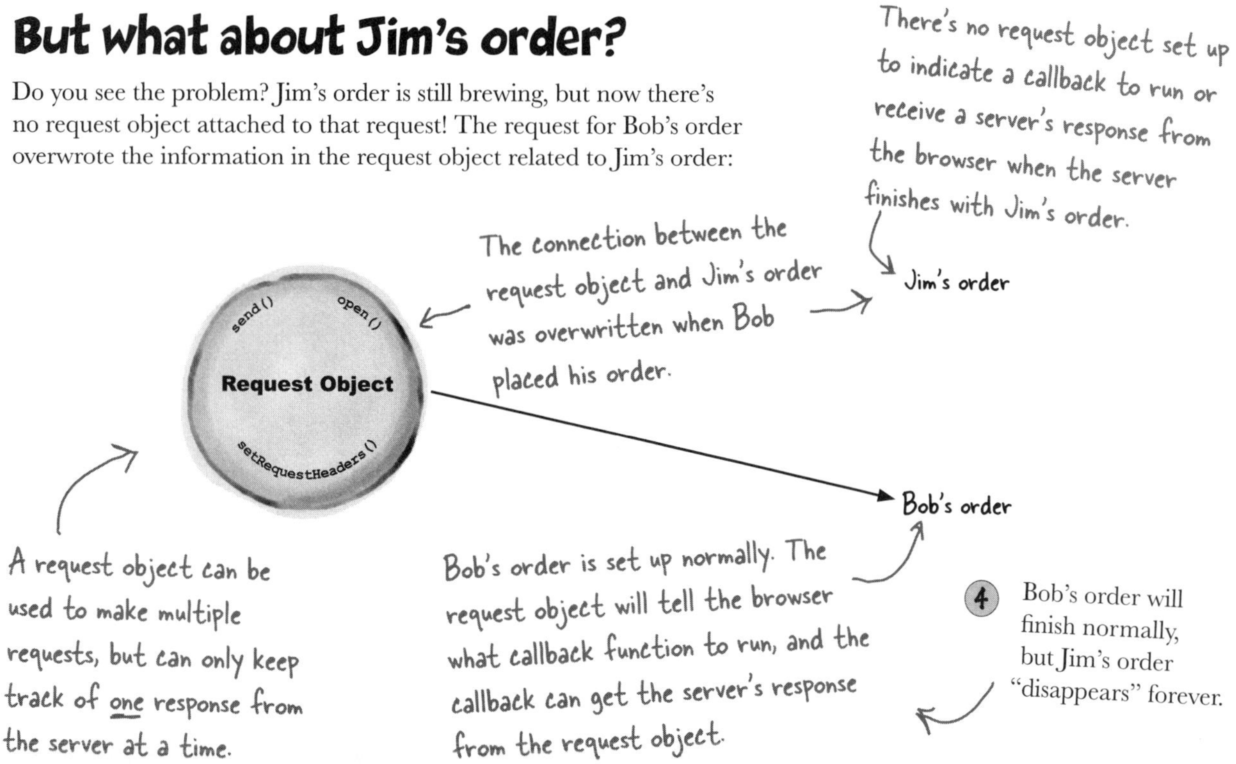

There's no request object set up to indicate a callback to run or receive a server's response from the browser when the server finishes with Jim's order.
The connection between the request object and Jim's order was overwritten when Bob placed his order.
Jim's order
send()
open()
Request Object
setRequestHeaders()
Bob's order
A request object can be used to make multiple requests, but can only keep track of one response from the server at a time.
Bob's order is set up normally. The request object will tell the browser what callback function to run, and the callback can get the server's response from the request object.

4 Bob's order will finish normally, but Jim's order "disappears" forever.

We need two request objects!

It looks like with just one request object, we can't keep up with more than one order at a time. Let's see if we can fix the problems we're running into by using two different request objects:

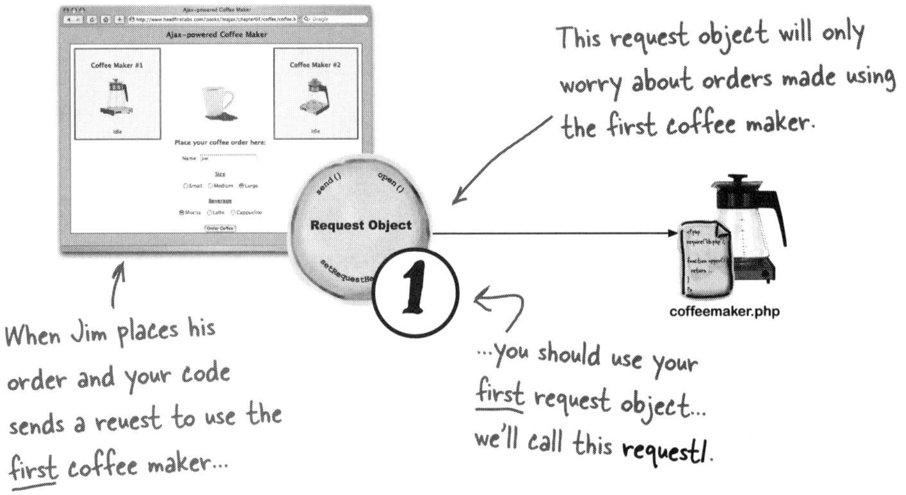

This request object will only worry about orders made using the first coffee maker.
Request Object
1
coffeemaker.php
When Jim places his order and your code sends a reuest to use the first coffee maker...
...you should use your first request object... we'll call this request1.

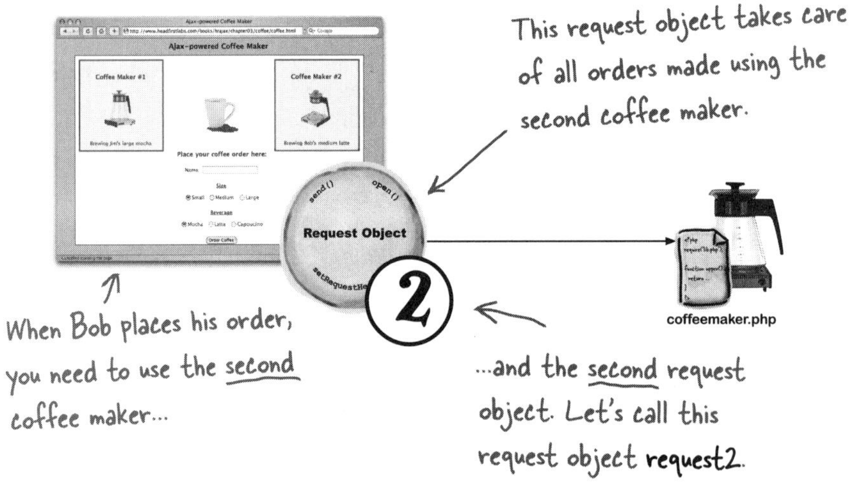

This request object takes care of all orders made using the second coffee maker.
Request Object
2
coffeemaker.php
When Bob places his order, you need to use the second coffee maker...
...and the second request object. Let's call this request object request2.

Now you can keep up with both coffee orders.

Creating two request objects

First, we need to actually create both request objects. Open up **ajax.js** and make the following changes, so that we're creating two request objects instead of just one:

This is your ajax.js file.

```
var request = null;

function createRequest() {
  var request = null;
  try {
    request = new XMLHttpRequest();
  } catch (trymicrosoft) {
    try {
      request = new ActiveXObject("Msxml2.XMLHTTP");
    } catch (othermicrosoft) {
      try {
        request = new ActiveXObject("Microsoft.XMLHTTP");
      } catch (failed) {
        request = null;
      }
    }
  }

  if (request == null) {
    alert("Error creating request object!");
  } else {
    return request;
  }
}

var request1 = createRequest();
var request2 = createRequest();
```

(The line ~~var request = null;~~ is struck through.)

We no longer want to create a single request object. Delete this line.

Now, turn this code back into a function, so we can run it more than once easily.

If the request object is created successfully, return it as the result of the function.

Finally, in static JavaScript, create two request objects. Assign each the return value of the createRequest() function.

ajax.js

When this finishes running, you'll have two request objects—request1 and request2—created and ready to use.

Using two request objects

With two request objects created and ready for use, you'll need to change **`updateCoffee()`** to use both request objects, instead of just one. We can use the first request object, **`request1`**, to send all requests to the first coffee maker, and the second request object, **`request2`**, to send all requests to the second coffee maker...

I think we need to change sendRequest() before we rewrite orderCoffee(). Doesn't sendRequest() need to be updated to use both request objects?

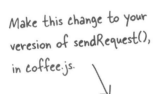

Yes, let's change sendRequest() first

Let's change **`sendRequest()`** to accept a request object as one of the parmeters you send to it—then, it will use that request object to send the request to the URL you supply. That way, we don't have to write the code that sends a request twice... we'll just call **`sendRequest()`**, and be sure to send it the request object we want to use.

Make this change to your veresion of sendRequest(), in coffee.js.

This is the only addition you need to make to sendRequest().

```
function sendRequest(request, url) {
  request.onreadystatechange = serveDrink;
  request.open("GET", url, true);
  request.send(null);
}
```

These lines of code now affect the request object passed in to sendRequest(). Remember, there isn't a single request object anymore.

Both request1 and request2 are set up with the same callback and connection parameters. The only thing different will be the request URL for each.

Updating orderCoffee()

Since **sendRequest()** handles requesting that a coffee maker start brewing an order, you only need to pass in the right request object with orderCoffee(). That means just making two small changes:

Make both of these changes to your version of orderCoffee(), in coffee.js.

```
var status = getText(coffeemakerStatusDiv1);
if (status == "Idle") {
  replaceText(coffeemakerStatusDiv1,
              "Brewing " + name + "'s " +
              size + " " + beverage);
  document.forms[0].reset();
  var url = "coffeemaker.php?name=" + escape(name) +
                      "&size=" + escape(size) +
                      "&beverage=" + escape(beverage) +
                      "&coffeemaker=1";
  sendRequest(request1, url);
} else {
  var coffeemakerStatusDiv2 =
    document.getElementById("coffeemaker2-status");
  status = getText(coffeemakerStatusDiv2);
  if (status == "Idle") {
    replaceText(coffeemakerStatusDiv2,
                "Brewing " + name + "'s " +
                size + " " + beverage);
    document.forms[0].reset();
    var url = "coffeemaker.php?name=" + escape(name) +
                        "&size=" + escape(size) +
                        "&beverage=" + escape(beverage) +
                        "&coffeemaker=2";
    sendRequest(request2, url);
  } else {
    alert("Sorry! Both coffee makers are busy. " +
          "Try again later.");
  }
```

If we're sending an order to the first coffee maker, we always want to use the request1 object.

We always use request2 for requests to the second coffee maker.

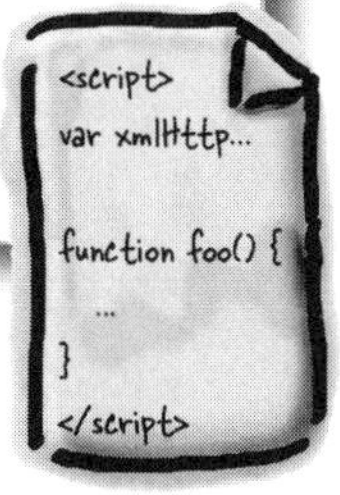

coffee.js

Just Do It

You're almost done with your multi-request coffee-making wonder app... all that's left is to change the serveDrink() callback so that it can handle two request objects, instead of just one. We've gotten started on this code by filling in all the JavaScript to handle the first request object. Your job is to finish off the callback by writing the code to handle dealing with the second request object.

```
function serveDrink() {
  if (request1.readyState == 4) {
    if (request1.status == 200) {
      var response = request1.responseText;
      var whichCoffeemaker = response.substring(0, 1);
      var name = response.substring(1, response.length);
      if (whichCoffeemaker == "1") {
        var coffeemakerStatusDiv1 =
          document.getElementById("coffeemaker1-status");
        replaceText(coffeemakerStatusDiv1, "Idle");
      } else {
        var coffeemakerStatusDiv2 =
          document.getElementById("coffeemaker2-status");
        replaceText(coffeemakerStatusDiv2, "Idle");
      }
      alert(name + ", your coffee is ready!");
      request1 = createRequest();
    } else
      alert("Error! Request status is " + request1.status);
  } else if (request2.readyState == 4) {
    // All your code goes here
  }
}
```

The first half of this code all deals with the "request1" object now.

We have to be sure to "clear" the request object once we're done... this does that by re-creating the request object.

Your job is to write all the code that goes in here.

Frequently Asked Questions

Q: We're using two request objects so we can send requests to both coffee makers, right?

A: We were actually able to make requests to both coffee makers with just one request object. The problem, though, was that we can't get responses from both coffee makers with just a single request object.

When you make a request, and the server works on that request, the browser uses the request object to connect the server's response with your JavaScript code. But if you start another request using the same request object before the first request is complete, the browser can't make that connection anymore. The second request overwrites the first one.

Q: And that's why Bob's coffee got brewed, but Jim's didn't, right? Because his order was placed second, so it overwrote Jim's earlier order?

A: Exactly. And even though the coffee-making script on the server finished Jim's order and returned a response, the browser had no way to connect that response to your JavaScript. The request object was already being reused to handle Bob's order.

By using two request objects, we can make sure that both coffee makers can be used, and that the browser can always get the server's response back to your JavaScript callback function.

Q: So we should always use two request objects in our asyncronous applications?

A: No, not at all. In fact, in a lot of your asynchronous apps, one request object will be plenty. The only time you need more than one request object is when your app needs to make more than one asynchronous request at the same time.

Q: And why did we turn the code that created request objects into a function again? Didn't we just take that code out of a function in Chapter 2?

A: We sure did. But remember, in Chapter 2 we only needed that code to run once: for the single request object. Since we need two request objects for the coffee maker, it was simpler to put the request object creation code in a function, and then call that function twice: once for each request object.

You could have kept the code static—and not put it in a function—but you would have had to change it to refer to `request1` instead of `request`, and then create another copy that referred to `request2`. There's nothing really wrong with this, but we preferred to keep the request object creation code in a single function, and then just call that function as many times as we need it to run.

Q: Why are you calling createRequest() again in serveDrink()?

A: When a server's response is complete, the ready state of the request object is set to "4". But even if you use the response, nothing resets the request object's ready state. So the first line of `serveDrink()`—`if (request1.readyState == 4)`—would always be true after coffee has been brewed using the first coffee maker.

This is a problem if `serveDrink()` is called when the *second* coffee maker finishes brewing, though. Even though it's the second coffee maker—and the *second* request object—that needs to be dealt with, the first request object could still have that ready state of 4. To avoid this, we need to reset the request object.

Q: Wouldn't it be easier to just set the request object's readyState property to 0 in serveDrink()?

A: It sure would... except that `readyState` is a read-only property, and you can't set it directly in your JavaScript. Only the browser can change the `readyState` property of the request object.

To get around that, we just call `createRequest()`, which creates a new request object. That's a bit of a hack, but it's the easiest way to reset the request and make sure only an active request object has a ready state of 4.

Just Do It

You're almost done with your multi-request coffee-making wonder app... all that's left is to change the serveDrink() callback so that it can handle two request objects, instead of just one. Here's the code we wrote for the part of serveDrink() that deals with the second coffee maker. Make sure you have the same code, and save your changes to coffee.js

```
      request1 = createRequest();
    } else
      alert("Error! Request status is " + request1.status);
  } else if (request2.readyState == 4) {
    if (request2.status == 200) {
      var response = request2.responseText;
      var whichCoffeemaker = response.substring(0, 1);
      var name = response.substring(1, response.length);
      if (whichCoffeemaker == "1") {
        var coffeemakerStatusDiv1 =
          document.getElementById("coffeemaker1-status");
        replaceText(coffeemakerStatusDiv1, "Idle");
      } else {
        var coffeemakerStatusDiv2 =
          document.getElementById("coffeemaker2-status");
        replaceText(coffeemakerStatusDiv2, "Idle");
      }
      alert(name + ", your coffee is ready!");
      request2 = createRequest();
    } else
      alert("Error! Request status is " + request2.status);
  }
}
```

Welcome to the world of asynchrony!

It's been a long ride, but you should have everything in place to get your co-workers all the caffeine they want, without any waiting. Be sure you've made the changes to **`ajax.js`** and **`coffee.js`** so that there are two request objects used: one for each coffee maker.

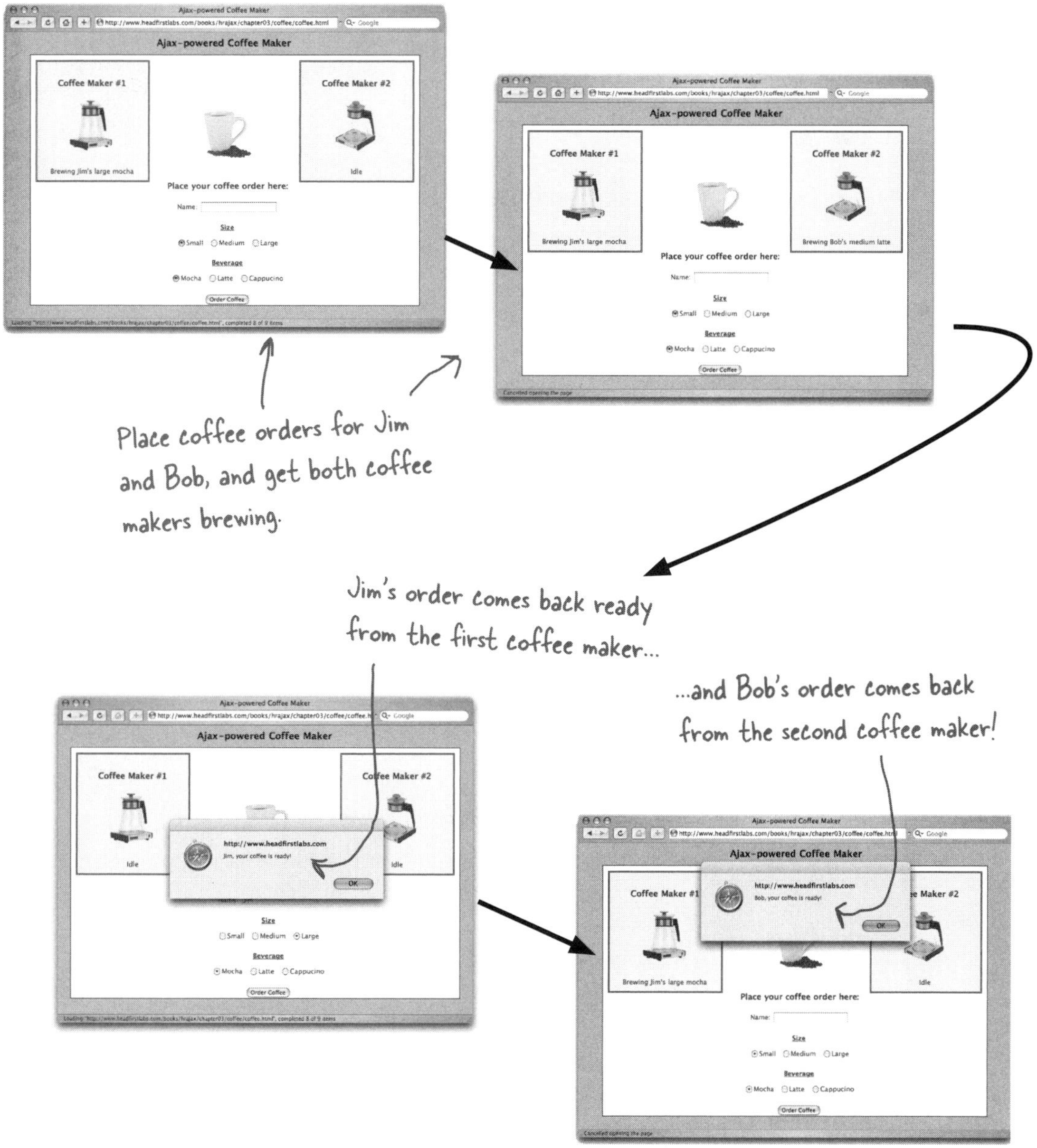

Ajax-powered Coffee Maker
Coffee Maker #1
Coffee Maker #2
Brewing Jim's large mocha
Brewing Bob's medium latte
Place your coffee order here:
Place coffee orders for Jim and Bob, and get both coffee makers brewing.
Jim's order comes back ready from the first coffee maker...
...and Bob's order comes back from the second coffee maker!

That's all fine, but I want to see what happens in this application when it's *not* asynchronous. I want to compare the synchronous and asynchronous versions, and see if the asynchronous version is really that much better.

Skeptical?

So, you want to see for yourself how different the Coffee Maker program is as a *synchronous* application? That's easy to do. All you have to do is change the third argument of the call to **request.open()** in the **sendRequest()** function: switch it from **true** to **false**:

```
function sendRequest(request, url) {
  request.onreadystatechange = serveDrink;
  request.open("GET", url, false);
  request.send(null);
}
```

Change the argument from true to false to tell your application to send the request to the coffee makers on the server synchronously.
Then give it a try. What happens?

A synchronous test drive

When you run the synchronous version of the coffee maker application, you should notice quite a big difference. As soon as you click on "Order Coffee", you're stuck. The button stays highlighted, and if you try to enter another order, you get the spinning beach ball (on Macs) or the hourglass (on Windows), meaning "You'll have to wait—I'm busy!"

As soon as you click on "Order Coffee", you're stuck.

Nothing else can happen until the response comes back from the server. You won't even see the status of the coffee maker change, because that code can't run!

If you try to do something else, like start a new order, you won't see anything happen, because everything is frozen until that response comes back. You just get your system's "wait" icon.

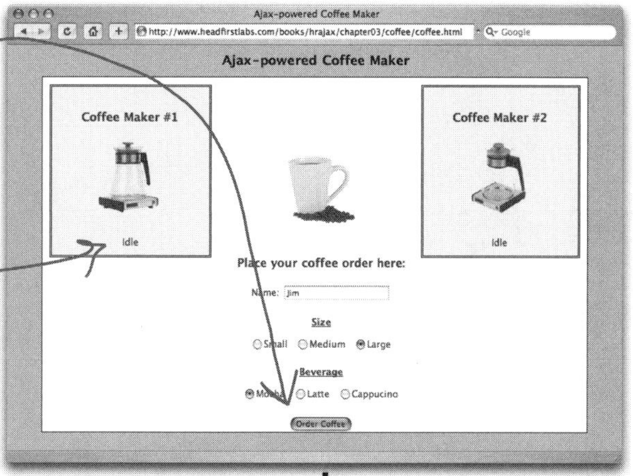

...time passes...

The coffee is finished brewing, the status of the first coffee maker is set to "Idle" (because it's done brewing again), and you never actually see the "Brewing" status.

All that work to add another request object, and now you can't even use it. Synchrony sucks when it comes to coffee makers!

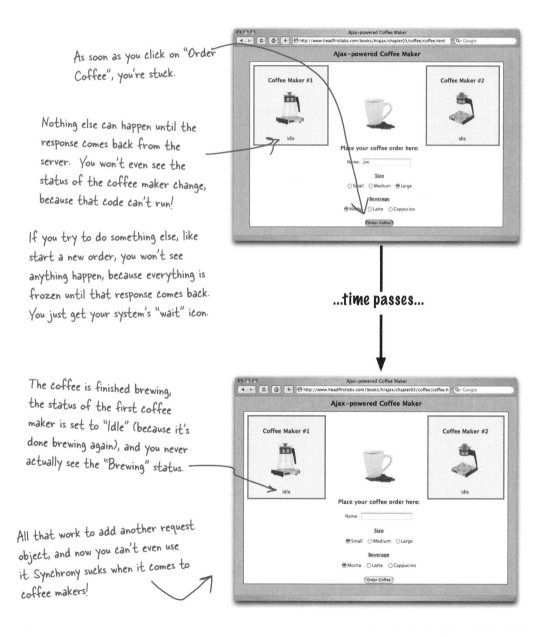

Change that baby back to asynchronous!

Don't forget to change **`sendRequest()`**, in **`coffee.js`**, back to the asynchronous version... nobody wants to wait around on their caffeine fix.

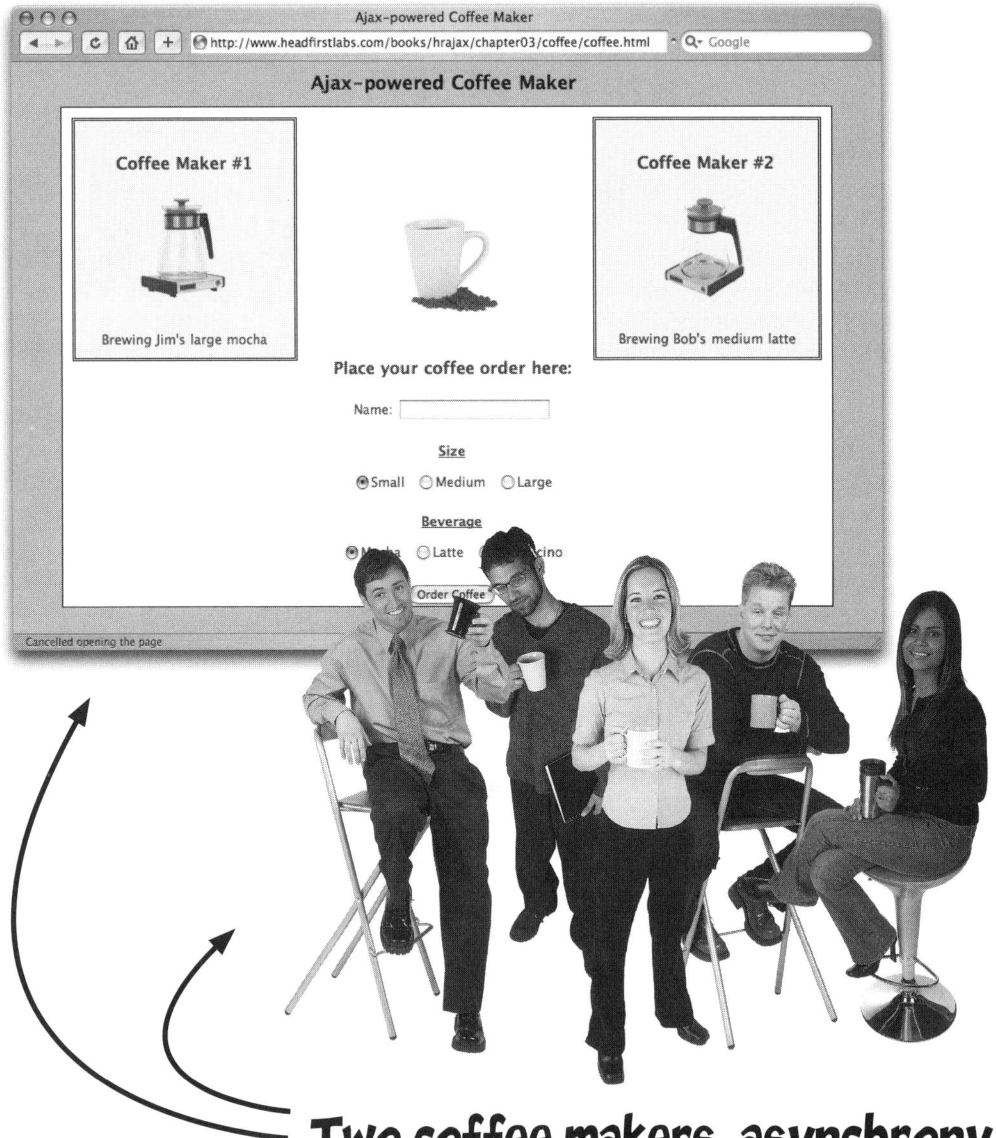

Two coffee makers, asynchrony, and one jittery, wired, happy office.

Check out the coffee maker for yourself!

60 Second Review

- Synchronous requests wait for a response from the server before anything else is allowed to happen.
- Asynchronous requests don't wait for a response, so users can keep pounding away at an asynchronous application while a request is being handled.
- A lot of Ajax applications are asynchronous, but when a web server returns a response quickly, it really doesn't matter whether the app is asynchronous or not.
- Asynchronous applications work best when the server takes a while to send a response back, or when users need to do several things at one time on a web page or form.
- When you call a request object's open() method, the third parameter tells the request whether or not it's asynchronous. A value of "true" means asynchronous; "false" means synchronous.
- The DOM allows you to change a web page without reloading the page.
- The innerHTML property is deprecated, and isn't as safe or stable an approach as using the DOM to change a web page from your JavaScript.
- Once your requests are asynchronous, you don't need any special code in the rest of your application. You write code normally and it runs automatically, without waiting for a server's response.
- It's a good idea to test an application in "synchronous" mode to see the difference being asynchronous really makes.

We're headed to the tree farm in Chapter 4... get ready for some Web Forestry.

Just Do It Solutions

Now that you know the name of your JavaScript functions, you can finish up the rest of the HTML for the coffee maker.

```
  <h3>Beverage</h3>
  <p>
   <input type="radio" name="beverage"
          value="mocha"
          checked="true">Mocha</input>
     
   <input type="radio" name="beverage"
          value="latte">Latte</input>
     
   <input type="radio" name="beverage"
          value="cappucino">Cappucino</input>
  </p>
  <p>
   <input type="button"
          onClick="orderCoffee();"
          value="Order Coffee" />
  </p>
 </form>
 </div>
</div>

<div id="coffeemaker2">
 <h2>Coffee Maker #2</h2>
 <p><img src="images/CoffeeMaker2.gif"
         alt="Coffee Maker #2" /></p>
 <div id="coffeemaker2-status">Idle</div>
</div>
```

orderCoffee() is the JavaScript function you'll write to send a new coffee order to the coffee-making PHP script.

In the first coffee maker, these ids were "coffeemaker1" and "coffeemaker1-status"...

...so in this coffee maker, we just changed all the "1"s to "2"s.

4 the Document Object Model

Web Page Forestry

I've really taken control of my DOM trees. A little pruning here, a bit of snipping there, and my web pages are more dynamic than ever.

Wanted: easy-to-update web pages. It's time to take things into your own hands, and start writing code that updates your web pages on the fly. Using the **Document Object Model**, your pages can take on new life, respond to users' actions, and help you ditch unnecessary page reloads forever. By the time you're done with this chapter, you'll be able to add, remove, and update content virtually anywhere on your web page. So turn the page, and let's take a stroll through the Webville Tree Farm.

OK, so here's the thing: I'm really enjoying getting my head around asynchronous programming... but all my friends are into fancy effects and flashy sites. Isn't that part of what makes Ajax apps so cool?

Jenny, fledgling web programmer.

NetFlix has some nice popups, without requiring any page reloading.

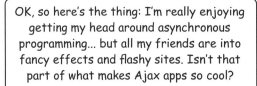

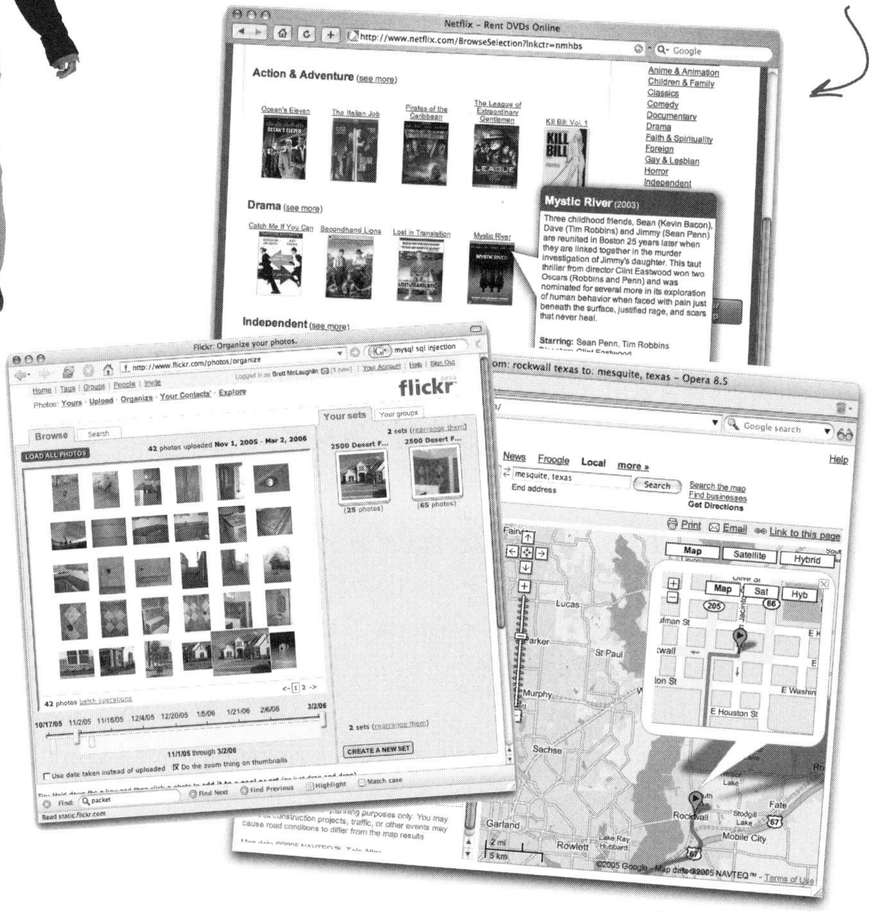

Flickr is a great Ajax app... very responsive, with a killer user interface.

Google Maps is another popular Ajax-driven application.

Need a dynamic application?

Here's the application you'll be building a little later in this chapter.

The DOM lets you look at this web page...

...in this format.

Use the Document Object Model.

The web browser uses the Document Object Model to represent your web page. When you change this model with your JavaScript code, the web page will automatically change, too.

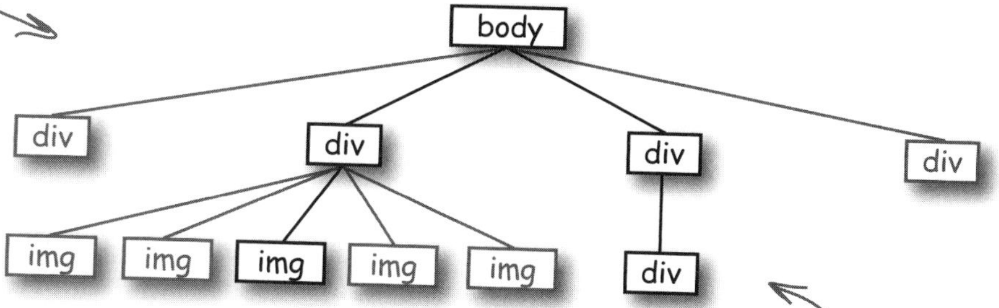

Your JavaScript can work with the DOM much easier than working directly with HTML or CSS.

Meet the DOM

(again)

Although you may not have realized it, you've been using the DOM since way back in Chapter 1. Remember this code from Katie's Boards 'R' Us report?

```
function updatePage() {
  var newTotal = request.responseText;
  var boardsSoldEl = document.getElementById("boards-sold");
  var cashEl = document.getElementById("cash");
  ...
}
```

We've left out the rest of the code from this function.

The document object gives JavaScript access to the DOM tree that the web browser creates.

And here's some similar code from the Break Neck pizza app:

```
function getCustomerInfo() {
  var phone =
    document.getElementById("phone").value;
  var url = "lookupCustomer.php?phone=" +
    escape(phone);
  request.open("GET", url, true);
  request.onreadystatechange = updatePage;
  request.send(null);
}
```

Here's that document object again.

The "document" object gives your JavaScript access to the web browser's DOM tree.

Don't miss this... it's probably the most important thing in the whole chapter!

Under the Microscope: The document object

Everything in the web browser's model of your web page can be accessed using the JavaScript "document" object. You've already seen the getElementById() function, but there's a lot more that you can do with the document object.

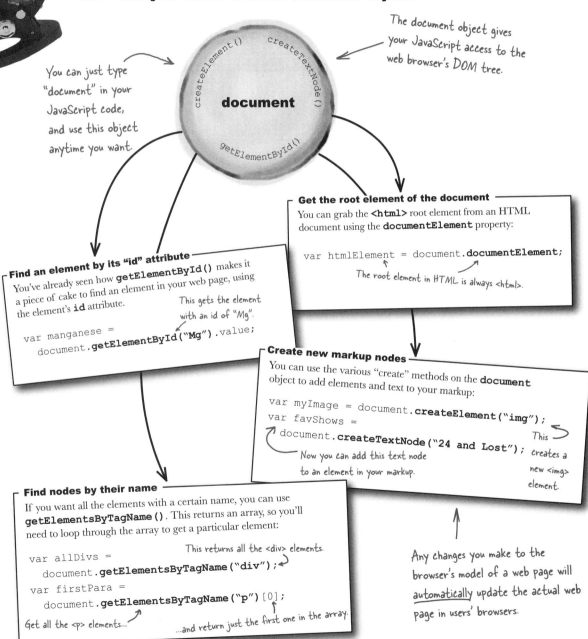

You can just type "document" in your JavaScript code, and use this object anytime you want.

The document object gives your JavaScript access to the web browser's DOM tree.

Get the root element of the document

You can grab the **<html>** root element from an HTML document using the **documentElement** property:

```
var htmlElement = document.documentElement;
```

The root element in HTML is always <html>.

Find an element by its "id" attribute

You've already seen how **getElementById()** makes it a piece of cake to find an element in your web page, using the element's **id** attribute.

```
var manganese =
  document.getElementById("Mg").value;
```

This gets the element with an id of "Mg".

Create new markup nodes

You can use the various "create" methods on the **document** object to add elements and text to your markup:

```
var myImage = document.createElement("img");
var favShows =
  document.createTextNode("24 and Lost");
```

This creates a new <img> element.

Now you can add this text node to an element in your markup.

Find nodes by their name

If you want all the elements with a certain name, you can use **getElementsByTagName()**. This returns an array, so you'll need to loop through the array to get a particular element:

```
var allDivs =
  document.getElementsByTagName("div");
var firstPara =
  document.getElementsByTagName("p")[0];
```

This returns all the <div> elements.

Get all the <p> elements...

...and return just the first one in the array.

Any changes you make to the browser's model of a web page will automatically update the actual web page in users' browsers.

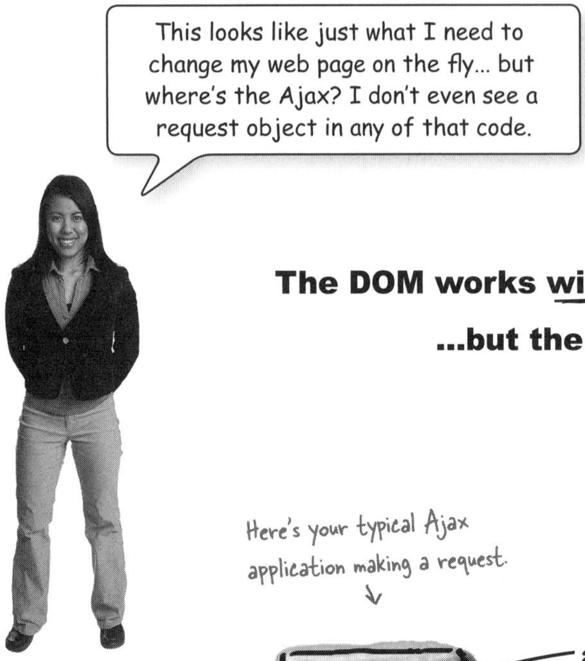

This looks like just what I need to change my web page on the fly... but where's the Ajax? I don't even see a request object in any of that code.

The DOM works with Ajax...

...but the DOM isn't part of Ajax.

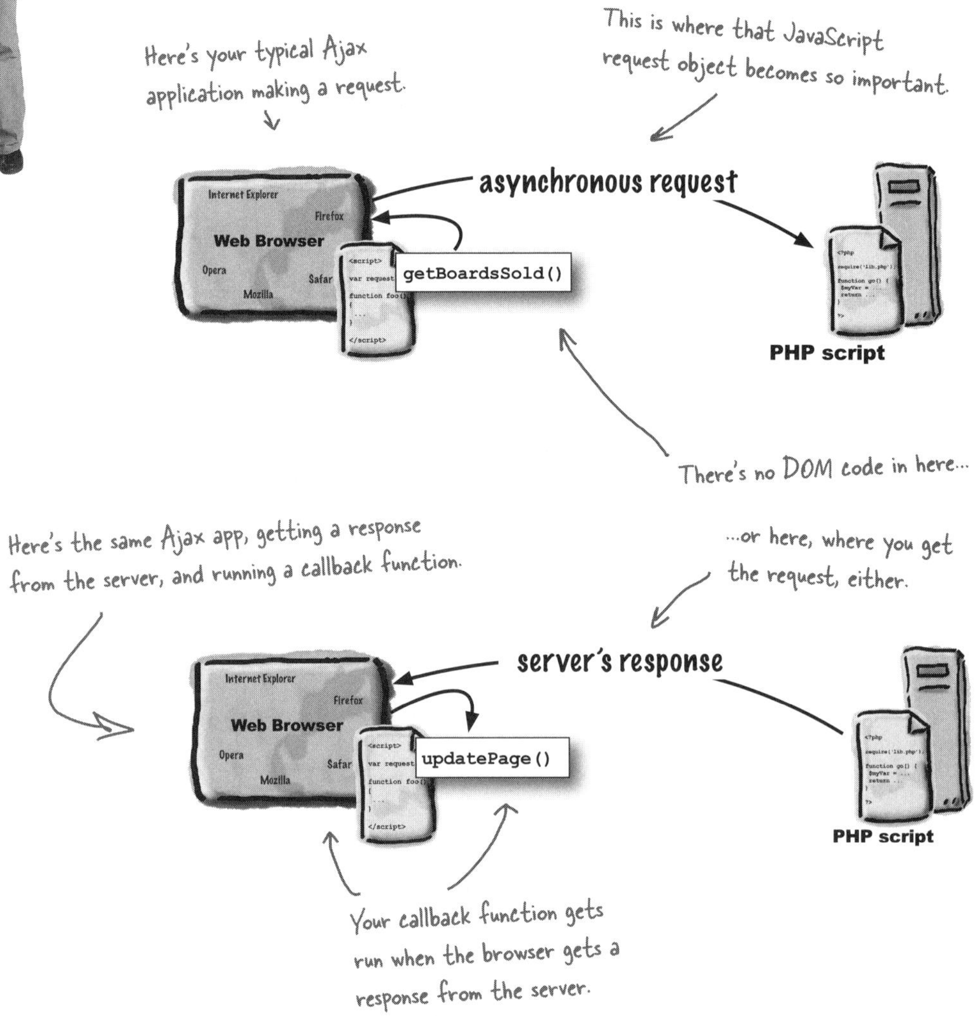

Here's your typical Ajax application making a request.
This is where that JavaScript request object becomes so important.
asynchronous request
Web Browser
Internet Explorer
Firefox
Opera
Safari
Mozilla
getBoardsSold()
PHP script
There's no DOM code in here...
Here's the same Ajax app, getting a response from the server, and running a callback function.
...or here, where you get the request, either.
server's response
updatePage()
PHP script
Your callback function gets run when the browser gets a response from the server.

Once you're ready to update a web page, the asynchronous part of your programming is done.

But your callback still needs a way to actually change the web page that the user is looking at.

When you're ready to update a web page, or just want to build a cool user interface, you need to use the Document Object Model for the page.

Here's the DOM tree for a web page, and some JavaScript that works on the DOM.

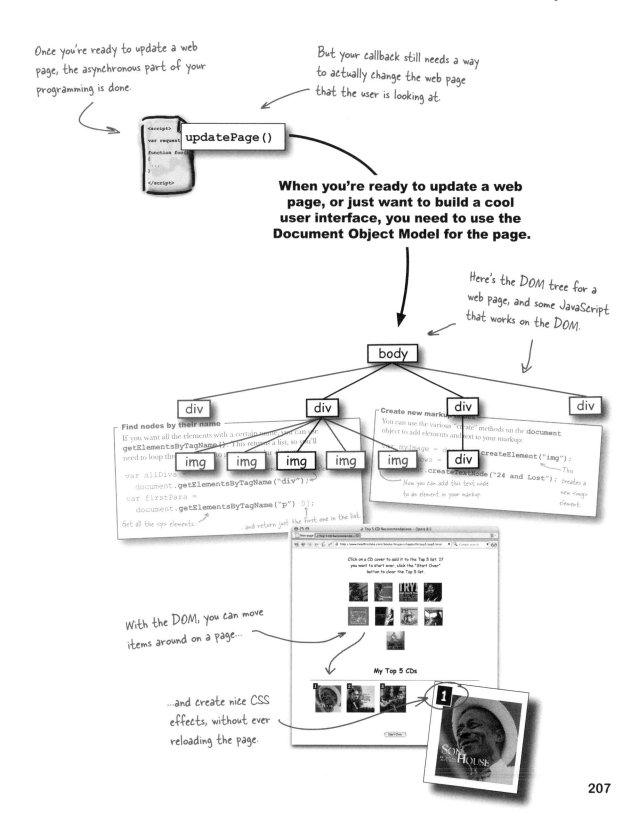

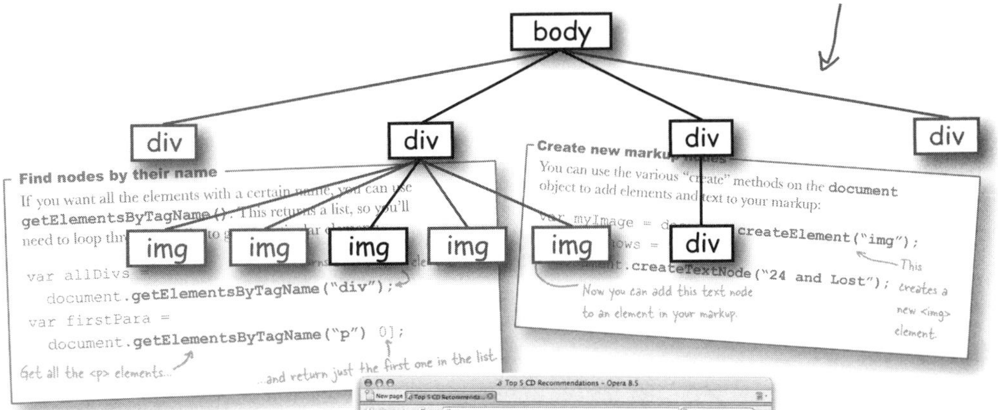

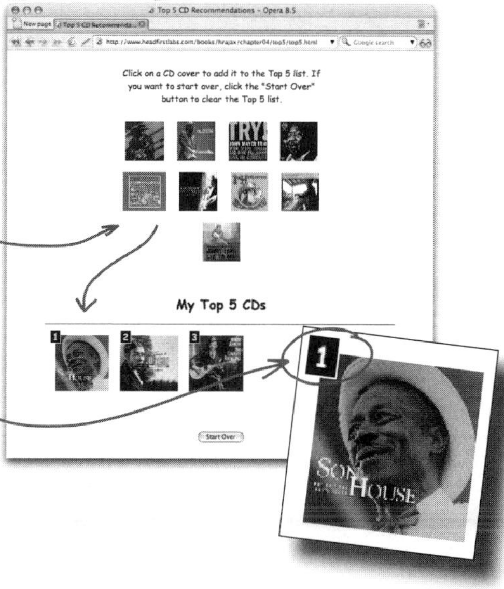

With the DOM, you can move items around on a page...

...and create nice CSS effects, without ever reloading the page.

Using the DOM without Ajax

Since the Document Object Model isn't tied to your asynchronous programming, there's nothing preventing you from using the DOM in *all* your web applications. In fact, we're going to prove it to you...

The Great Chapter 4 Coding Challenge

Write a killer web application that uses the Document Object Model to create a dynamic user interface, without writing any Ajax code.

If you can pull this off, then you'll know that you can use the DOM to make all your applications better, even if they aren't making asynchronous requests.

Alright, I'm psyched! I want to learn more about the DOM. So where can I find out how to use this thing?

Better visit your local tree farm...

WEBVILLE TREE FARM
Hi there, and welcome to the Webville Tree Farm. What can I cut down for you today?

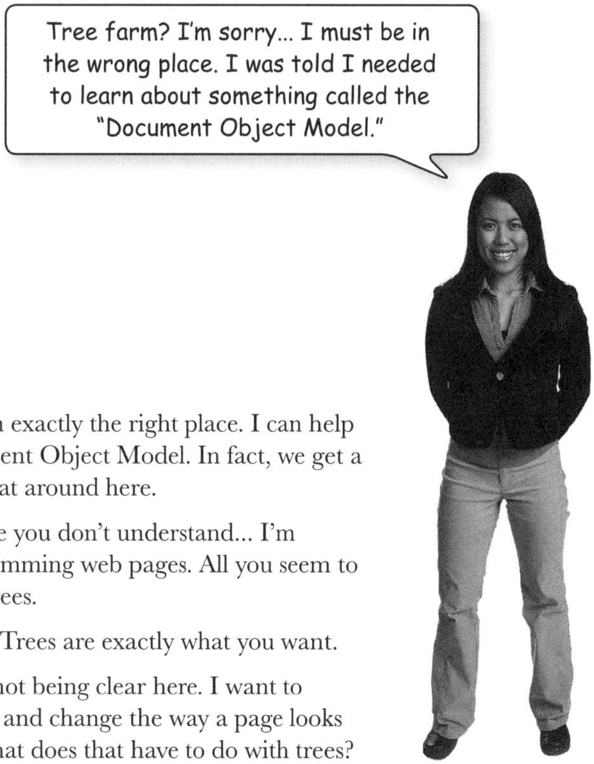
Tree farm? I'm sorry... I must be in the wrong place. I was told I needed to learn about something called the "Document Object Model."

Mike, Webville Tree Farm owner and founder.

Mike: Oh, you're in exactly the right place. I can help you with the Document Object Model. In fact, we get a lot of requests for that around here.

Jenny: Huh? Maybe you don't understand... I'm talking about programming web pages. All you seem to have is a bunch of trees.

Mike: That's right. Trees are exactly what you want.

Jenny: Maybe I'm not being clear here. I want to program web pages, and change the way a page looks using JavaScript. What does that have to do with trees?

Mike: Every web page is, in fact, a tree.

Jenny: Is this some sort of weird simile? How are web pages like trees?

Mike: You aren't listening to me. I didn't say web pages are *like* trees... I said web pages *are* trees. Every time you give a browser a page full of HTML, the browser sees that HTML as a tree.

Jenny: How does that work? I guess I can see how HTML has some structure to it, but I've never heard anything about web browsers and trees before.

Mike: Yeah, most people haven't. But if you're going to change and update web pages with JavaScript, you've gotta get ahold of the tree concept. Here, let me show you what I mean...

Here's the HTML that you give to the browser...

When you're creating a web page, you write HTML to represent the different parts of your page. Then you give that HTML to the browser, and the browser figures out how to represent that HTML on the screen. But if you want to start changing your web page using JavaScript, you need to know exactly how the browser sees your HTML.

First, let's take a look at a simple HTML document:

```
<html>
 <head>
  <title>Webville Tree Farm</title>
 </head>
 <body>
  <h1>Webville Tree Farm</h1>
  <p>Welcome to the Webville Tree Farm. We're still learning
     about CSS, so pardon our plain site. We just bought
     <a href="http://www.headfirstlabs.com/books/hfhtml/">Head
     First HTML with CSS &amp; XHTML</a>, though, so expect
     great things soon.</p>
  <p>You can visit us at the corner of Binary Blvd. and
     DOM Drive. Come check us out today!</p>
 </body>
</html>
```

OK, this is HTML 101. So what in the world does any of this have to do with trees?

...and here's how the browser sees the HTML

The browser has to make some sense of all that markup, and organize it in a way that allows the browser—and your JavaScript code—to work with the page. Here's what the browser turns your text markup into:

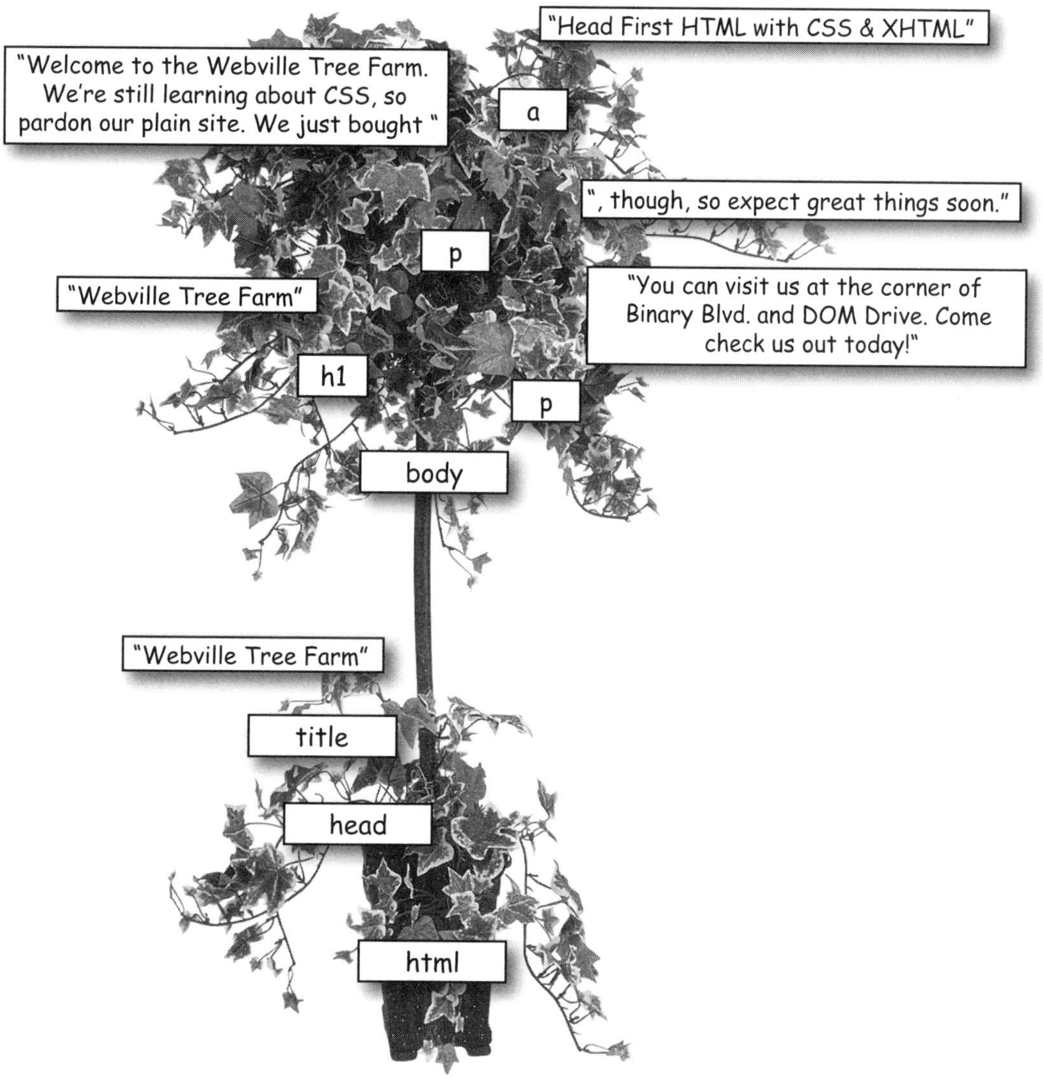

"Head First HTML with CSS & XHTML"
"Welcome to the Webville Tree Farm. We're still learning about CSS, so pardon our plain site. We just bought "
a
", though, so expect great things soon."
p
"Webville Tree Farm"
"You can visit us at the corner of Binary Blvd. and DOM Drive. Come check us out today!"
h1
p
body
"Webville Tree Farm"
title
head
html

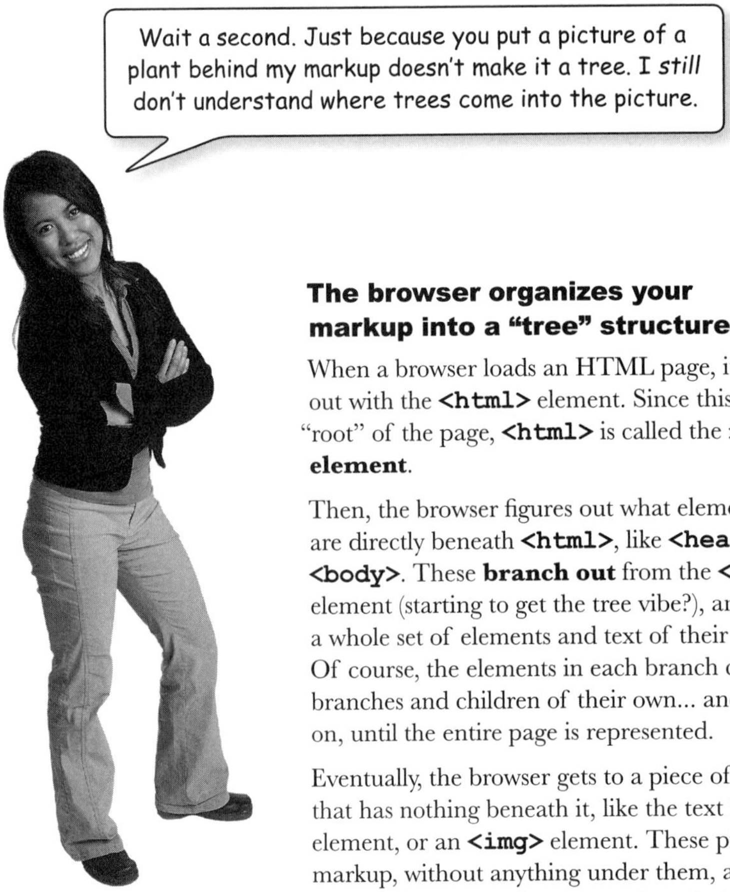
Wait a second. Just because you put a picture of a plant behind my markup doesn't make it a tree. I *still* don't understand where trees come into the picture.

The browser organizes your markup into a "tree" structure.

When a browser loads an HTML page, it starts out with the **<html>** element. Since this is at the "root" of the page, **<html>** is called the **root element**.

Then, the browser figures out what elements are directly beneath **<html>**, like **<head>** and **<body>**. These **branch out** from the **<html>** element (starting to get the tree vibe?), and have a whole set of elements and text of their own. Of course, the elements in each branch can have branches and children of their own... and on and on, until the entire page is represented.

Eventually, the browser gets to a piece of markup that has nothing beneath it, like the text in a **<p>** element, or an **<img>** element. These pieces of markup, without anything under them, are called **leaves**. So your entire page ends up being one big tree to the web browser.

Let's look at that tree structure again, but this time with some lines making the connections between the markup a little clearer.

How the browser sees your HTML (part 2)

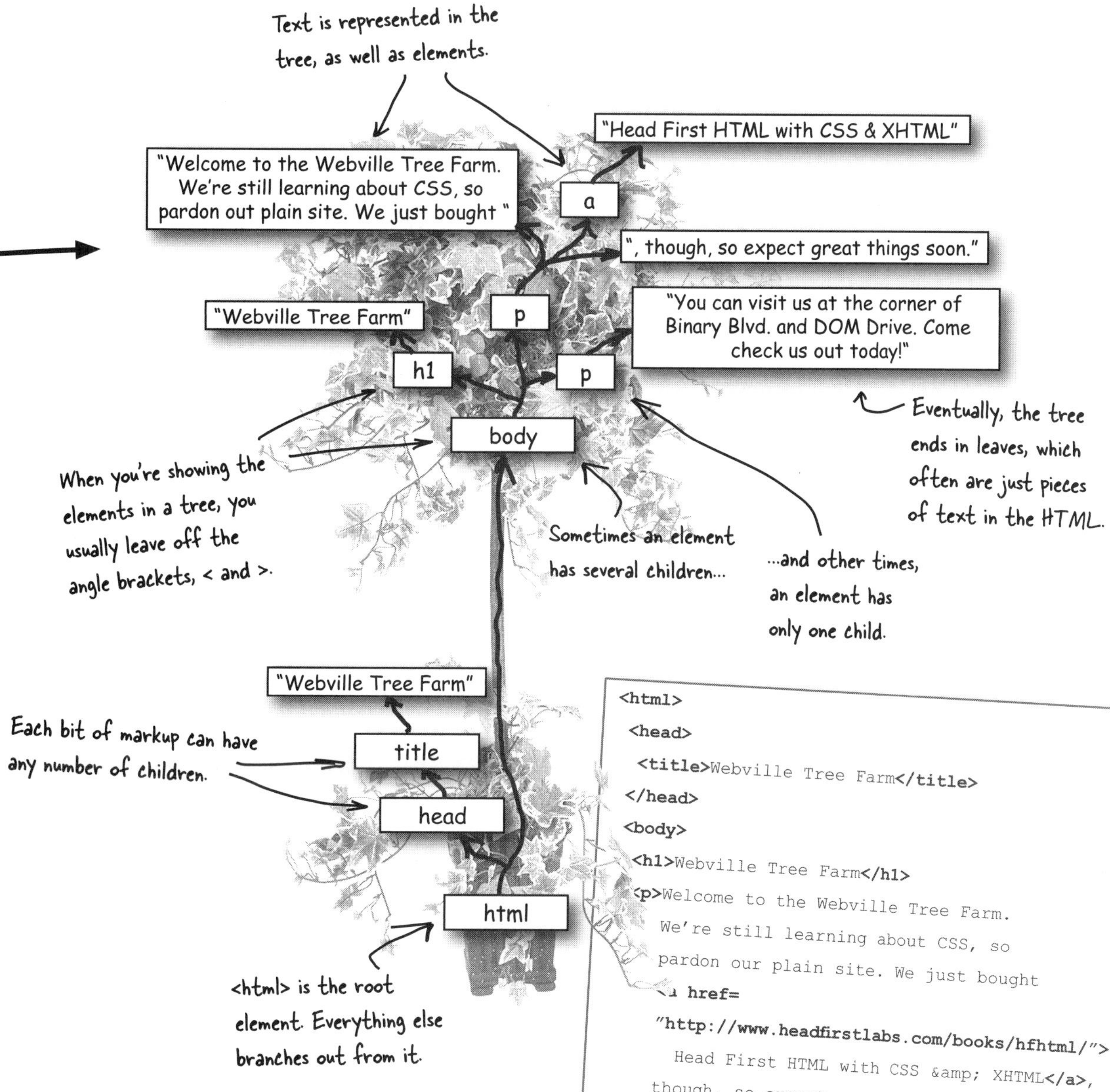

Here's the HTML that this tree represents.

```
<html>
 <head>
  <title>Webville Tree Farm</title>
 </head>
 <body>
  <h1>Webville Tree Farm</h1>
  <p>Welcome to the Webville Tree Farm.
     We're still learning about CSS, so
     pardon our plain site. We just bought
     <a href=
     "http://www.headfirstlabs.com/books/hfhtml/">
      Head First HTML with CSS &amp; XHTML</a>,
     though, so expect great things soon.</p>
  <p>You can visit us at the corner of
     Binary Blvd. and DOM Drive. Come check
     us out today!</p>
 </body>
</html>
```

Frequently Asked Questions

Q: Do I need to reference the ajax.js file we've been using if I want to write JavaScript code that uses the DOM?

A: Nope. In fact, Ajax and the Document Object Model have nothing to do with each other, other than the fact that most Ajax applications happen to use the DOM. But there are lots of non-Ajax apps that have been using the DOM for years. If you've got a web browser that has JavaScript enabled, then you've got all that you need to start changing web pages using the DOM.

Q: And what about text-utils.js? That file had a bunch of DOM utilities in it, right? Do I need that?

A: You used `text-utils.js` in Chapter 1, and then again in Chapter 3. It did contain several utility functions, and those functions used the DOM to make changing a web page fairly easy. In this chapter, though, we're going to dig deeper into the DOM, and learn how to work with it directly, rather than using some pre-assembled JavaScript.

In fact, by the time you're done with this chapter, you'll know exactly what's going on in `text-utils.js`, and be able to make improvements and add additional utility functions for yourself.

Appendix 2 has all the code from text-utils.js listed, along with several notes on how each of the utility functions in that file works. Once you've finished this chapter, you may want to check out Appendix 2... you'll know enough DOM to understand everything in the text-utils.js utility file by then.

Q: It looks like you called some parts of that markup "children." So an element can have "child elements"?

A: Yes. When the browser organizes your HTML into a tree, it begins with the root element. Each piece of content under that root is a branch, but you can also call those bits of content "child elements." In fact, you can use family terms like this going towards the root of the tree, too: the `<head>` element can be called the "parent" of the `<title>` element. Keep this in mind; we'll talk a lot more about parents and children in the rest of this chapter.

Q: It seems like you're using a whole bunch of new terms, like root and branch and child. How am I supposed to keep up with all of this?

A: It's not as hard as it seems. Just keep the idea of a tree in mind, and you shouldn't have any trouble. You've been using terms like root and branch and leaf for years. As for parent and child, anytime you're moving *towards* the root of the tree, you're moving towards a parent; anytime you move *away* from the root, you're moving towards a child. The only term that may be totally new to you is "node", and we're just about to take a look at that...

WRITE YOUR OWN

Web Dictionary

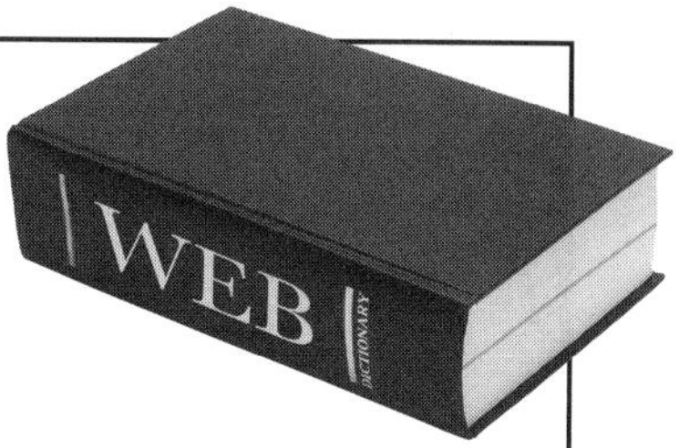

What good is looking at a bunch of definitions? This is Head Rush, and we want your *brain* working, not just your eyes. Below are several entries from a Web Dictionary, with some of the words in each definition removed. Your job is to try and complete each entry by filling in the blanks.

node. Any ______ piece of markup, such as an element or text. The <a> element is an ________ node, while the "Head First HTML with CSS & XHTML" text is a ______ node.

leaf. A piece of markup that has ________, such as an element with __ text content, like <img>, or textual data.
Also known as: **leaf node**

child. Any piece of markup that is __________ by another piece of markup. The text "Head First HTML with CSS & XHTML" is the ______ of the <a> element, and the <p>s in this markup are ________ of the <body> element.
Also known as: **child node, children**

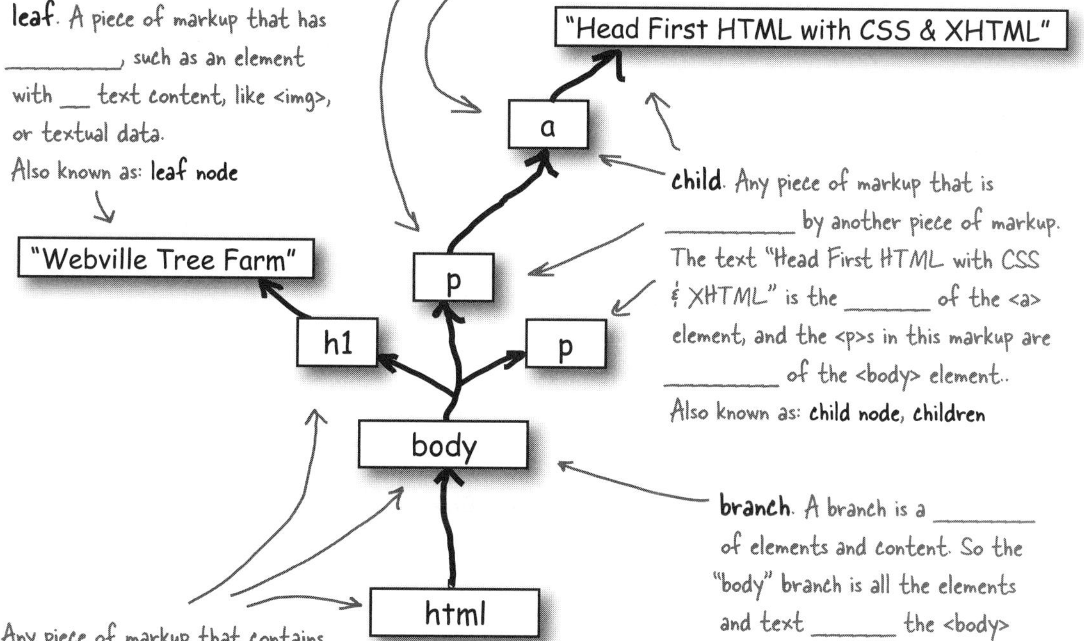

branch. A branch is a ________ of elements and content. So the "body" branch is all the elements and text ______ the <body> element in the tree.

parent. Any piece of markup that contains __________. <h1> is the parent of the text "Webville Tree Farm", and <html> is the parent of the ________ element.
Also known as: **parent element, parent node**

root element. The element in a ________ that ______ all other elements. In HTML, the root element is always ________.

no children	child	children	under	contained
other markup	text	collection	single	document
element	contains	<body>	no	<html>

Here are the words you should use to fill in the blanks.

WRITE YOUR OWN Web Dictionary Solutions

Here's the Web Dictionary with all the blanks filled in. It's OK if you used different words than in our version of the dictionary... just make sure you understand what each entry means, and that you are comfortable with how these pieces work together to form a tree of markup for a web page.

node. Any single piece of markup, such as an element or text. The <a> element is an element node, while the "Head First HTML with CSS & XHTML" text is a text node.

leaf. A piece of markup that has no children, such as an element with no text content, like <img>, or textual data.
Also known as: leaf node

child. Any piece of markup that is contained by another piece of markup. The text "Head First HTML with CSS & XHTML" is the child of the <a> element, and the <p>s in this markup are children of the <body> element.
Also known as: child node, children.

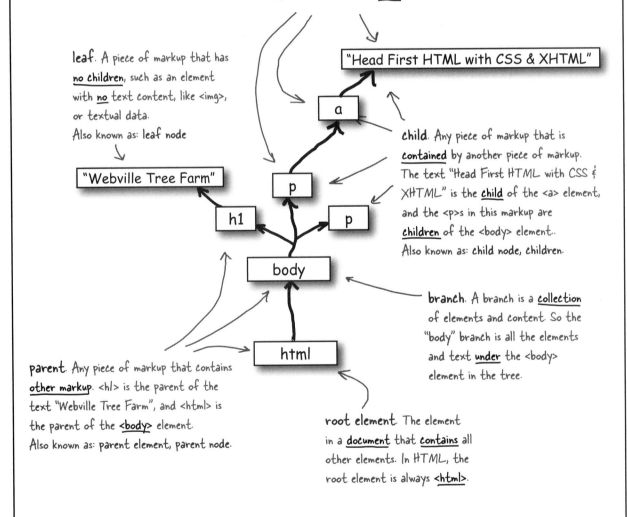

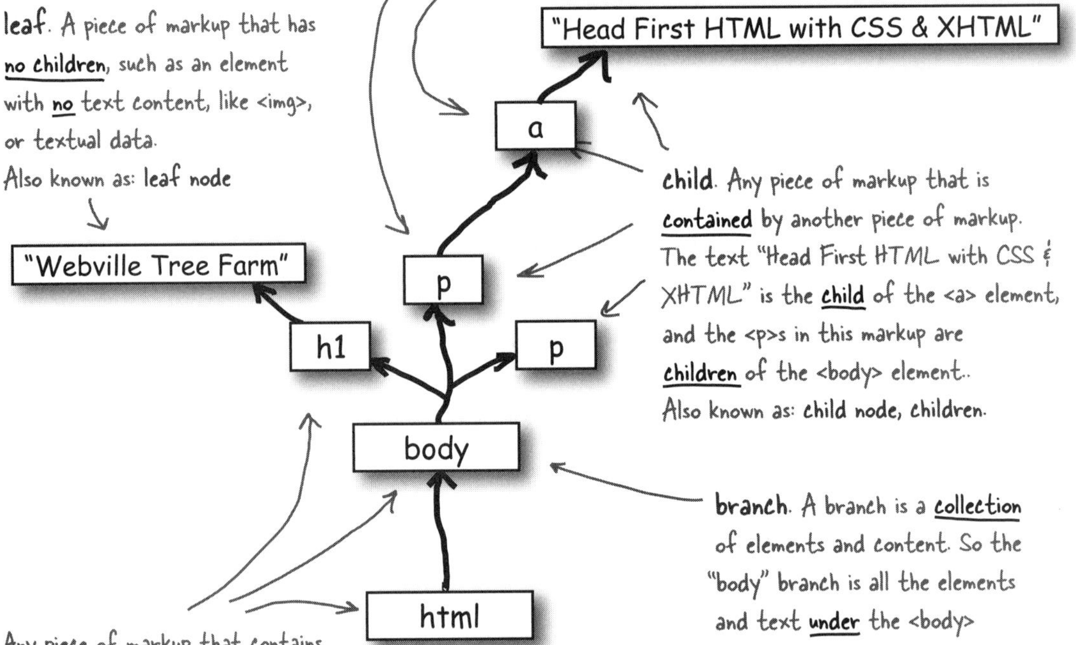

branch. A branch is a collection of elements and content. So the "body" branch is all the elements and text under the <body> element in the tree.

parent. Any piece of markup that contains other markup. <h1> is the parent of the text "Webville Tree Farm", and <html> is the parent of the <body> element.
Also known as: parent element, parent node.

root element. The element in a document that contains all other elements. In HTML, the root element is always <html>.

Tree Magnets

Now that you've got a handy Web Dictionary, it's time to put it to use. Below is the tree view of the HTML we looked at a few pages back. Your job is to take the different tree magnets from the bottom of the page, and attach them to the right parts of this tree. Be careful: some parts of the tree may have more than one magnet that could apply, and you won't need to use all the magnets. Good luck!

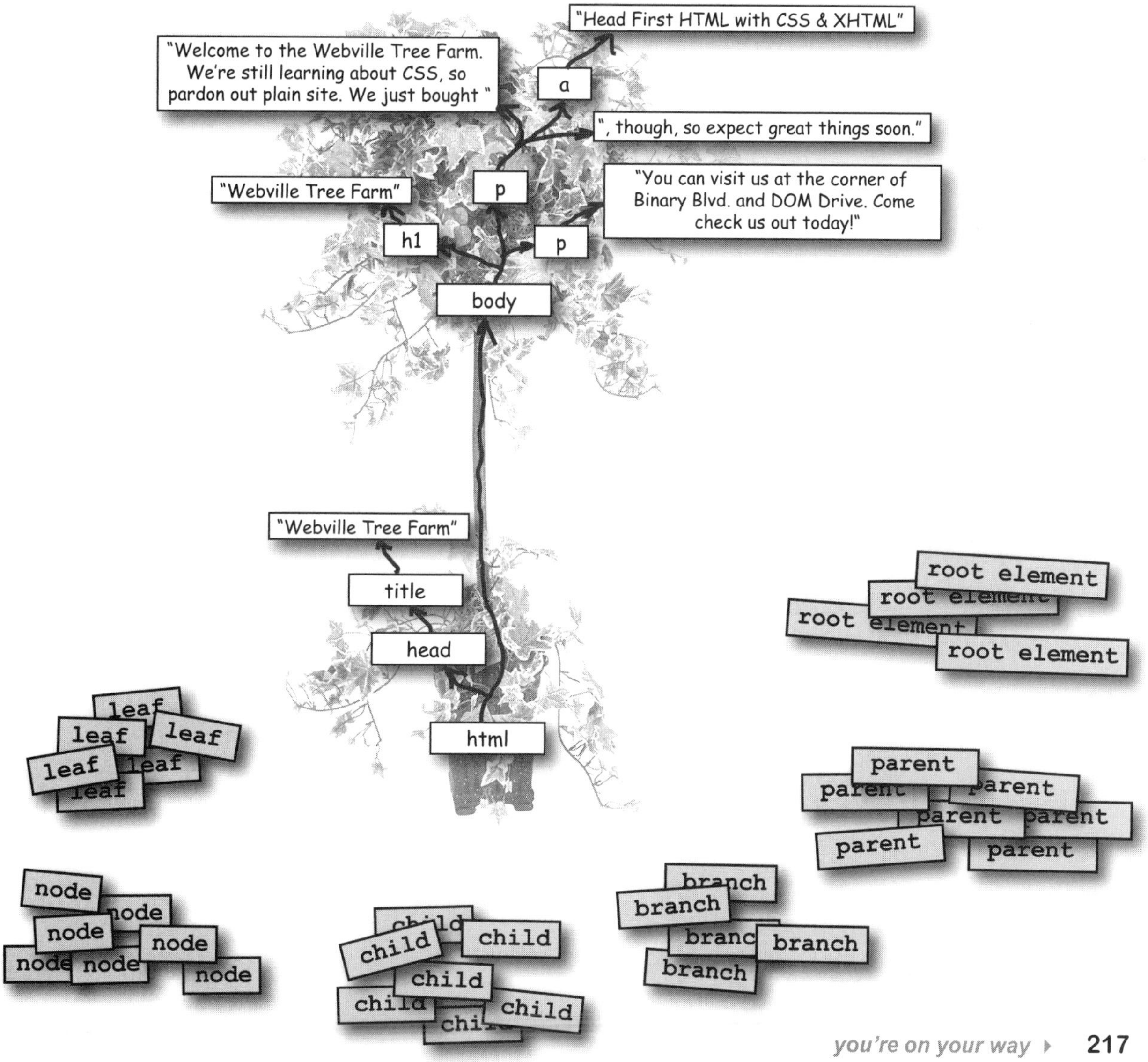

Flip back to page 213 to see what Jenny's talking about.

Order matters to the web browser.

When the browser gets your HTML and represents it as a tree, the browser has to keep up with the order of text and elements in the markup. Otherwise, paragraphs could appear in the wrong order on the page, and the wrong words might be bolded or underlined.

Let's take another look at the markup for the welcome text:

```
<p>
  Welcome to the Webville Tree Farm. We're still
  learning about CSS, so pardon our plain site. We
  just bought <a href=
    "http://www.headfirstlabs.com/books/hfhtml/">
    Head First HTML with CSS &amp; XHTML</a>,
  though, so expect great things soon.
</p>
```

Here's the <p> element that is the parent of all this content.

There's quite a bit of text within the <p>...

...as well as an <a> element that creates a link.

The <a> element has some text of its own, also.

The tree has to match the HTML exactly, or people looking at the web page could get really confused. This tree, for example... that <p> has to know exactly where its child <a> element goes, and how the text fits around that.

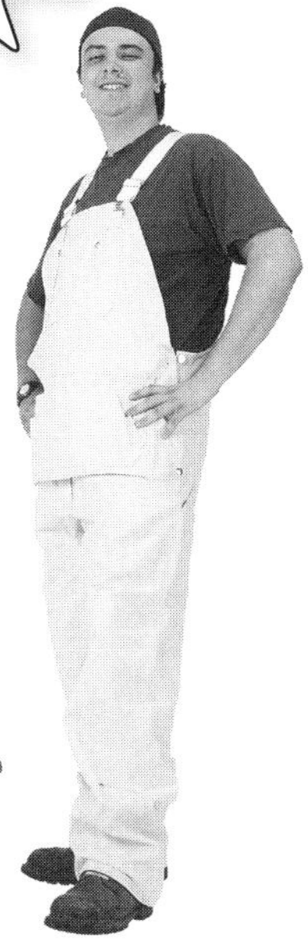

In this case, the easiest way for the browser to keep up with the ordering of the text and link in the HTML is to put the first part of the text in one node under the <p> element, and then add the <a> element node, and then add one more text node, with all the text after the <a>. When you look at the tree view of an HTML page, you usually just read it from left to right, like this:

Yes, this is a mouthful. Read it, check out the diagram below, and then read it again. Don't worry... you'll get it!

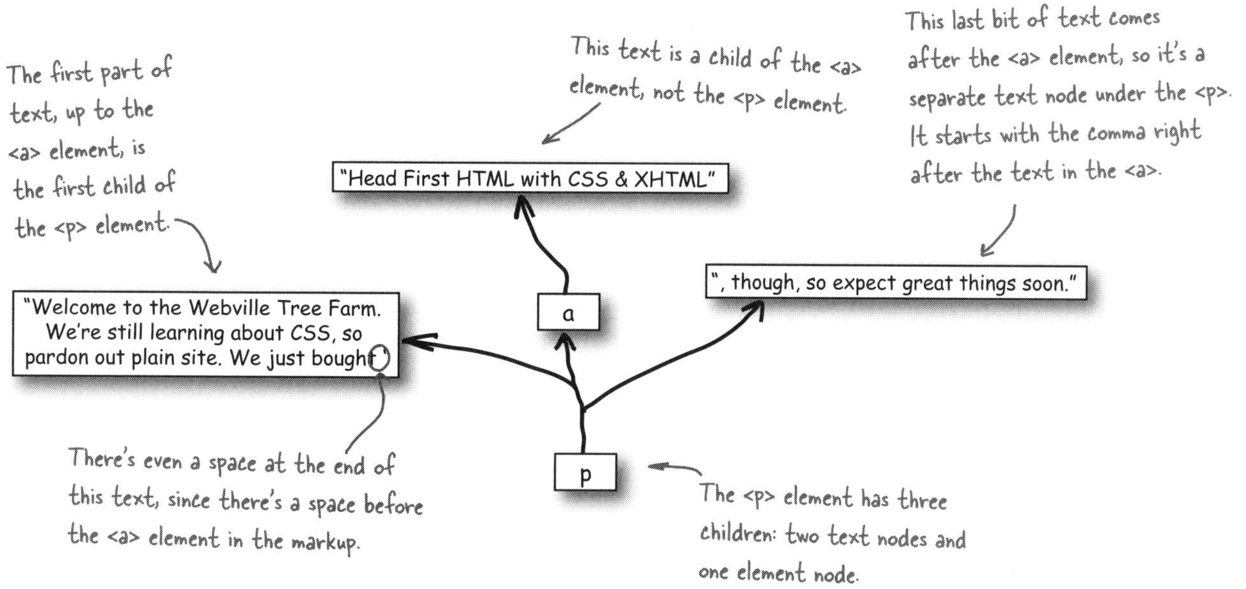

Just Do It

It's time to load markup trees into your brain. Below is a simple HTML document. Your job is to figure out how a web browser organizes this HTML into a tree structure. On the right is a tree, ready for you to fill in its branches and leaves. To get you started, we've provided spaces for each piece of markup; be sure you've filled each space with an element or text from the HTML markup before showing off your tree to anyone else!

```
<html>
 <head>
  <title>Binary Tree Selection</title>
 </head>
 <body>
  <p>Below are two binary tree options:</p>
  <div>
   Our <em>depth-first</em> trees are great for folks that
   are far away.
  </div>
  <div>
   Our <em>breadth-first</em> trees are a favorite for
   nearby neighbors.
  </div>
  <p>You can view other products in the
     <a href="menu.html">Main Menu</a>.</p>
 </body>
</html>
```

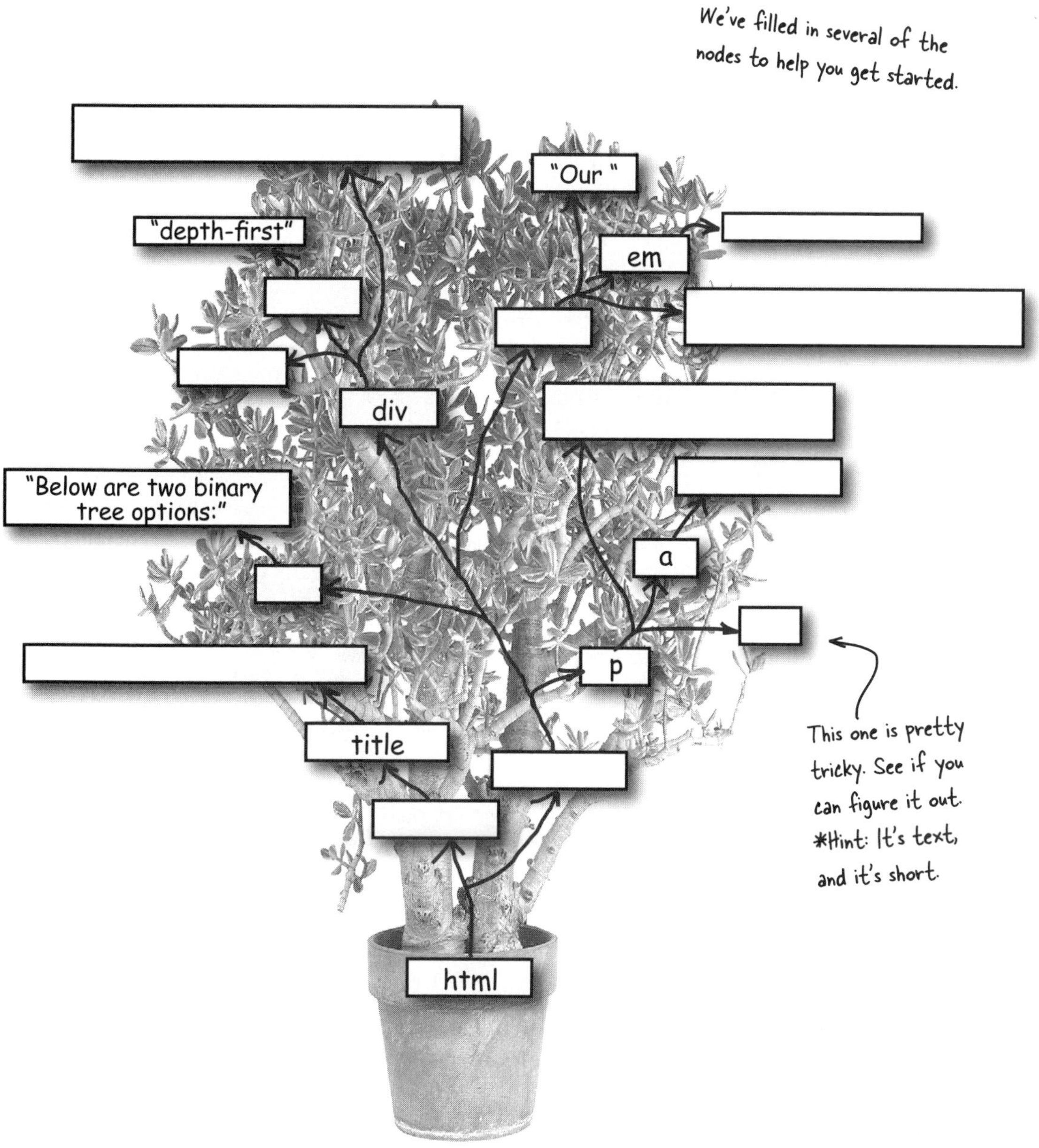
We've filled in several of the nodes to help you get started.
"Our "
"depth-first"
em
div
"Below are two binary tree options:"
a
p
title
html
This one is pretty tricky. See if you can figure it out. *Hint: It's text, and it's short.

We'll look at the answers to this exercise in just a few pages.

Frequently Asked Questions

Q: The ordering of the elements and text in the HTML matters, right?

A: Yes. So for the **<html>** element, the first child is **<head>**, and the second is **<body>**. If these were reversed, the tree would be different, and as a result, the page would be displayed differently in your web browser. So always be sure you're keeping things in the correct order when you're representing HTML as a tree like this.

Q: You keep talking about elements and text. Are those two different things, or is text also a type of element?

A: Elements are the names surrounded in brackets, like **<title>** or **<p>**. Text is the actual characters within elements, like "Webville Tree Farm" or "directions". There are also attributes, like **id="binary"** or **class="greentea"**.

All of these are considered nodes, but elements, attributes, and text are all different kinds of nodes. So you could have a text *node*, but you would never have a text *element*.

Q: What about attributes? You said that there are attribute nodes, but that they really aren't "children" of the element they appear on, are they?

A: Attributes are a bit of a special case. If you have markup like **<div id="depth-first">**, it's really not correct to say that the **id** attribute is a child of the **<div>** element.

Instead, the browser stores the attributes of an element in a special list for each element. So there are attribute nodes, but they're not very easy to represent on a tree. When we look at the DOM in a few pages, you'll see that it handles attributes in a special list for each element.

Q: Don't lots of older HTML pages leave off closing tags, like </p>? How does a web browser handle pages with markup like that?

A: Boy, you're really on top of your HTML, aren't you? You're right, lots of older HTML pages are pretty messy, and have elements that aren't closed or nested properly. In these cases, web browsers do the best they can in creating a tree structure.

Usually, the browser gets it right, but if you ever see a page that doesn't appear quite the way you expected, it might be because the browser guessed wrong in creating the tree structure for that page's HTML. That's just one more reason to be careful when writing HTML.

Q: Will different web browsers all represent a page in the same way?

A: If you're writing standard HTML—and even better, validating your HTML—different browsers will almost always come up with the same tree for an HTML page. This is one of the things that HTML 4.01 and XHTML 1.0 and 1.1 have provided: a standard view of HTML that browsers can rely on.

If you start to get sloppy, though, and forget to close an element, or use older, outdated HTML, then web browsers have to do the best they can to represent your markup. As a result, you'll start to see differences in the tree between different browsers. But as long as you write standard, valid HTML pages, this shouldn't be a problem.

See? If you want to understand web pages, you have to master trees.

OK, I get all this business about a web browser seeing my pages as trees... but how does that really help me? I need to **change** a web page, not **grow** one.

Mike: Often, the root must be watered carefully before one can enjoy the leaf.

Jenny: What the heck does that mean?

Mike: Honestly, I have no idea. I read it somewhere, and thought that it might impress you. Anyway... since web browsers view your pages as trees, you need to be able to write code that works on those trees. And that's where the Document Object Model comes in.

Jenny: OK, now we're talking. That's what I came here to find out about... the Document Object Model.

Mike: The Document Object Model—usually called the DOM for short—is how you can work on the tree that the browser creates from your web page. You can manipulate the DOM with JavaScript, and update the browser's tree. And once you update the tree, the page itself will automatically be changed by the browser, without any page reloading or refreshing.

There's a group called the World Wide Web Consortium (most people call them the W3C for short) that publishes the specifications and standards for the DOM. Just a bit of trivia for you standards gurus out there...

Back to the forest

Remember, web browsers see your web pages as trees of elements, text, attributes, and other markup:

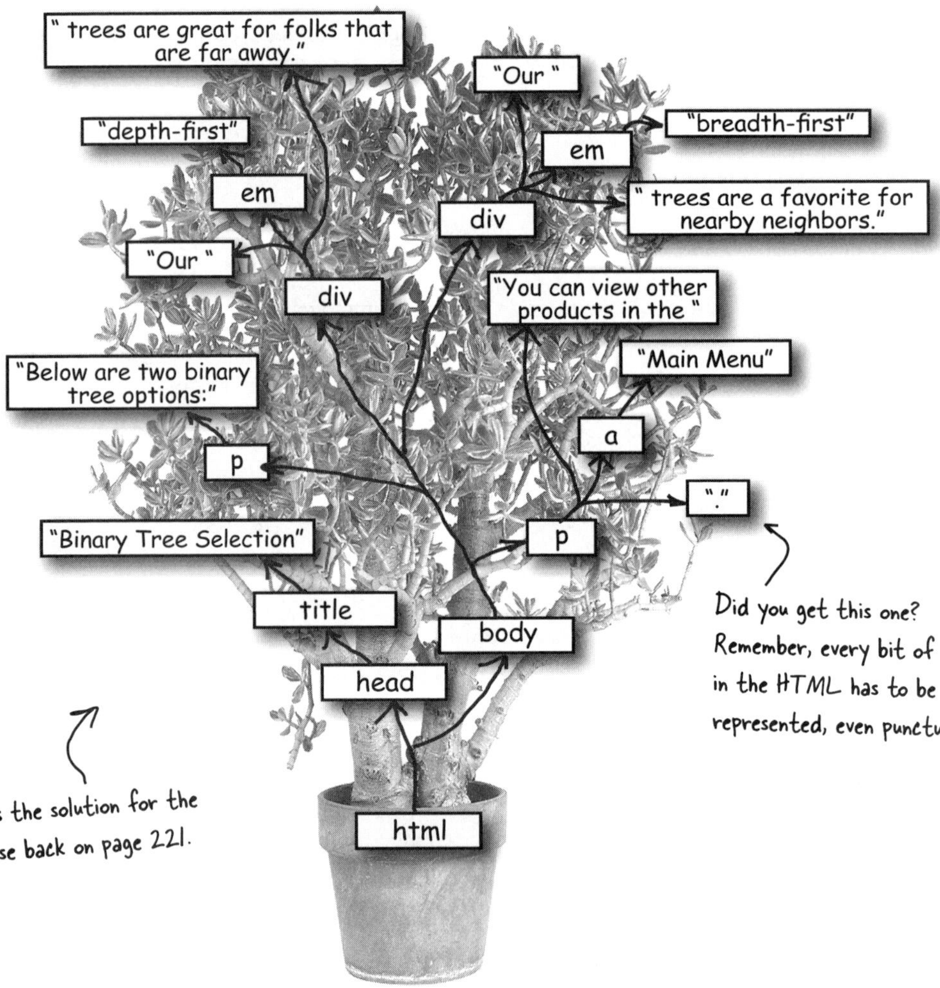

Did you get this one? Remember, every bit of text in the HTML has to be represented, even punctuation.

Here is the solution for the exercise back on page 221.

Browsers see the world upside down

Of course, browsers don't literally store a picture of a tree with your markup on it. If you want to really understand what the browser stores in memory, you need to learn about the DOM. Let's see how the browser takes the tree you just looked at and represents it with objects.

First, the browser flips the entire tree upside down so the **<html>** element is at the top of the tree instead of the bottom:

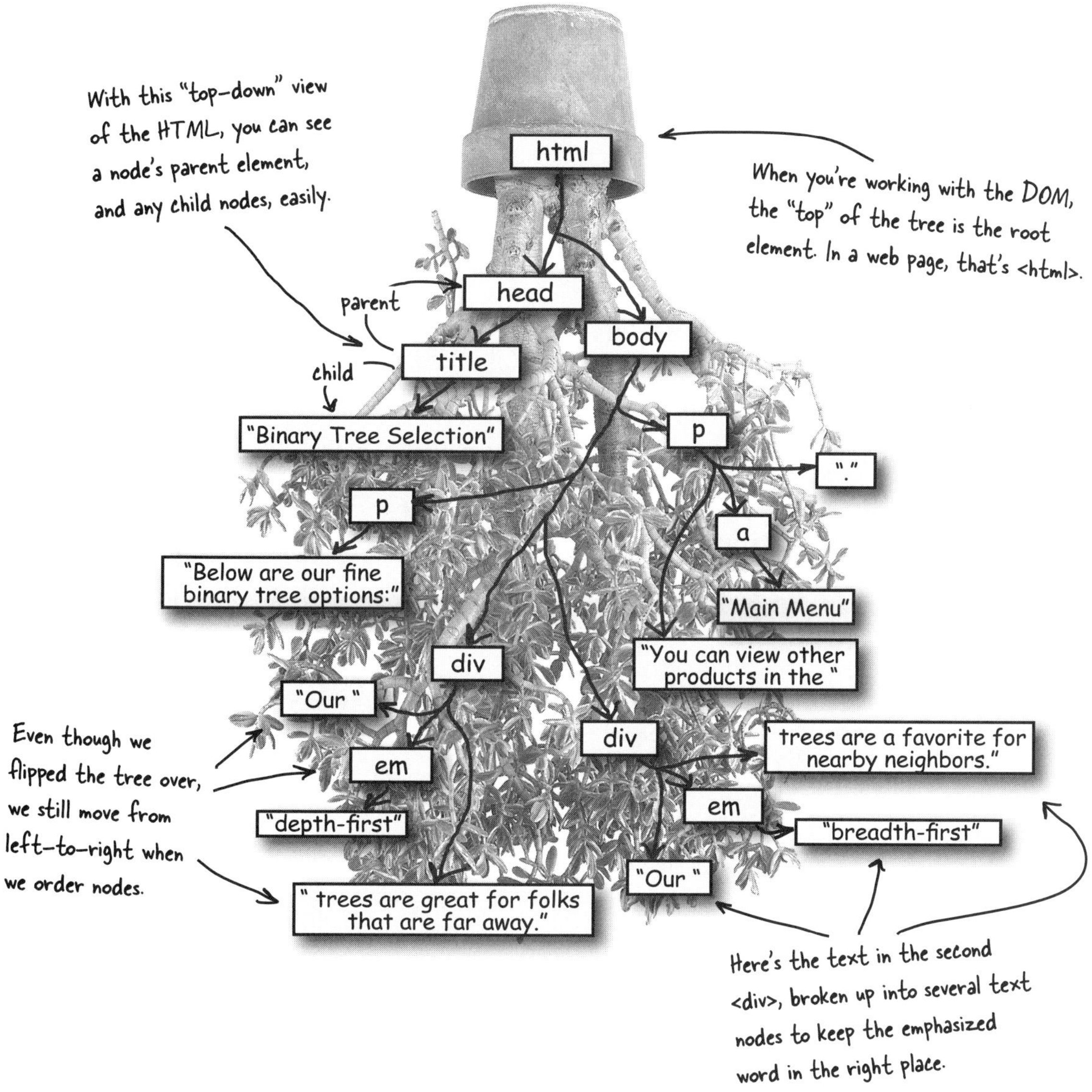

A new type of tree: the DOM tree

Once the browser has your markup with the **<html>** element at the top, it creates a new object for each node in the tree. The result is a bunch of objects, all "connected" together, like you see here:

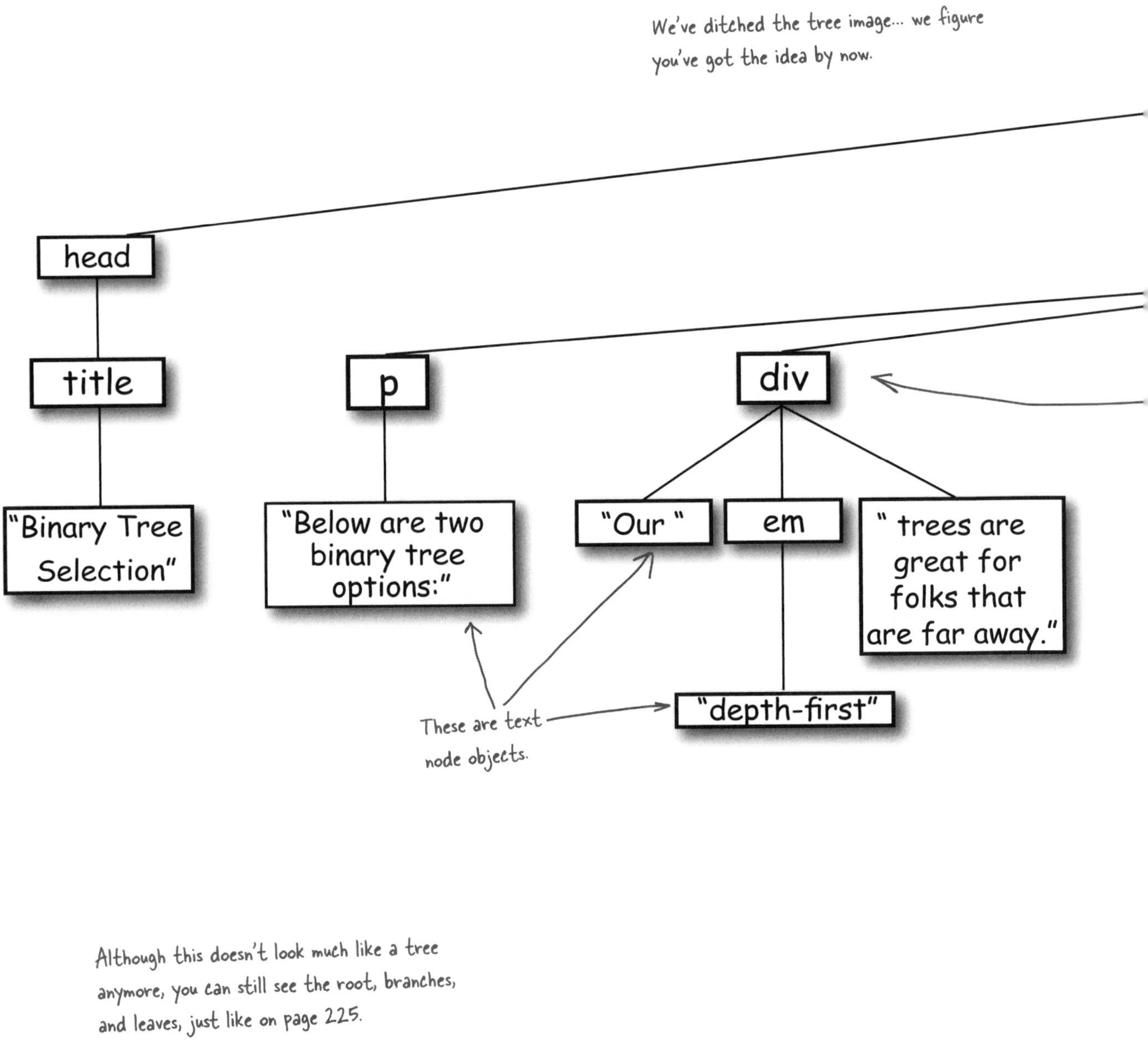
We've ditched the tree image... we figure you've got the idea by now.
head
title
"Binary Tree Selection"
p
"Below are two binary tree options:"
div
"Our "
em
"depth-first"
" trees are great for folks that are far away."
These are text node objects.
Although this doesn't look much like a tree anymore, you can still see the root, branches, and leaves, just like on page 225.

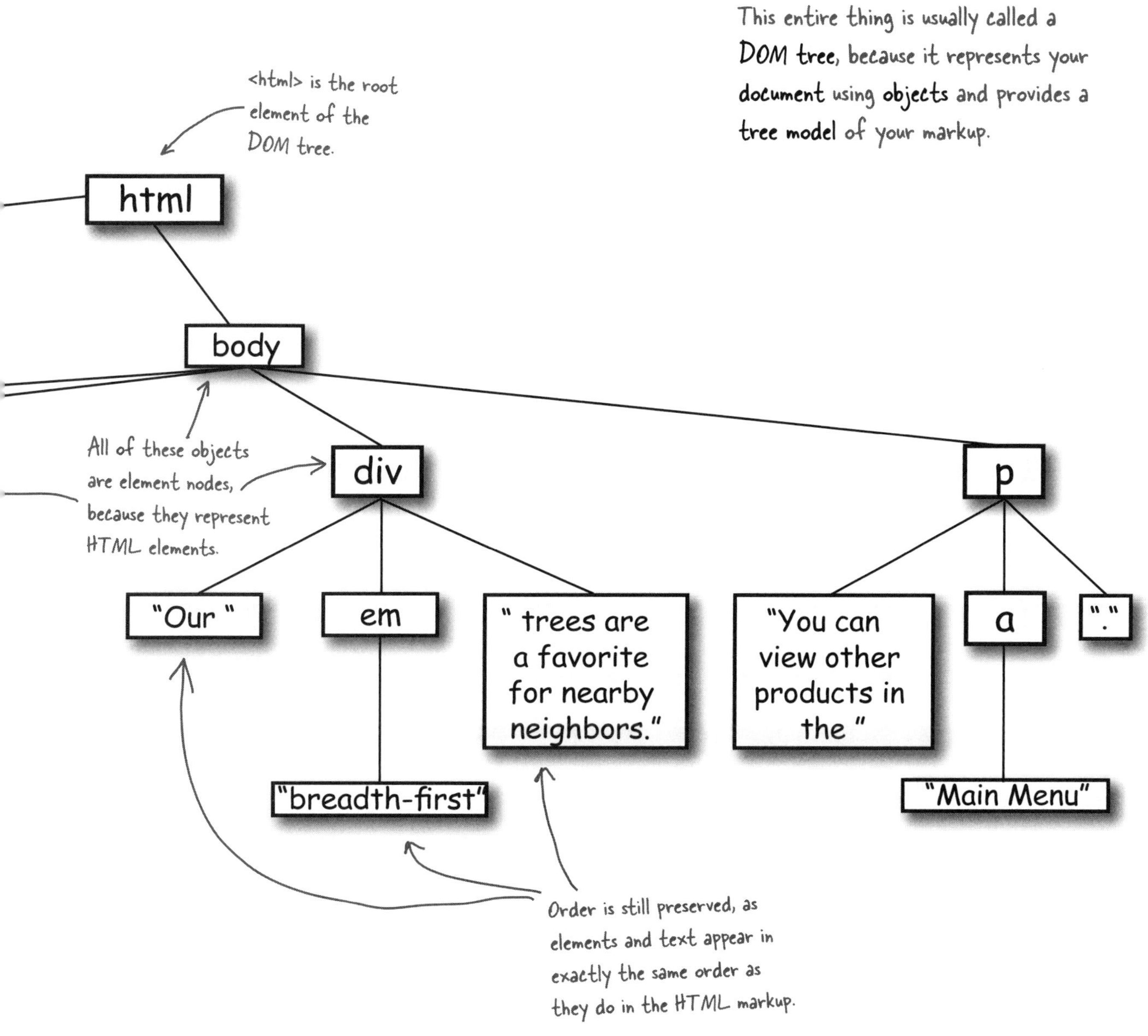
This entire thing is usually called a DOM tree, because it represents your document using objects and provides a tree model of your markup.
<html> is the root element of the DOM tree.
html
body
All of these objects are element nodes, because they represent HTML elements.
div
p
"Our "
em
" trees are a favorite for nearby neighbors."
"You can view other products in the "
a
"."
"breadth-first"
"Main Menu"
Order is still preserved, as elements and text appear in exactly the same order as they do in the HTML markup.

Work It Through

Time to get your dry-erase markers out and dive into the DOM for yourself. Your job is to take the HTML below and draw the DOM tree that a web browser would create to represent this markup.

```
<html>
 <head><title>Gonna Get Me Some Blues</title></head>
 <body>
  <p>Do you have the blues? If not, check out Stefan
     Grossman's <a href="http://www.guitarvideos.com">
     Guitar Workshop</a> for some great DVDs and
     instructional videos.</p>
 </body>
</html>
```

Draw what you think the DOM tree will look like here:

Start out by drawing boxes, with the element names and text inside. Then, connect your boxes together, like this.*

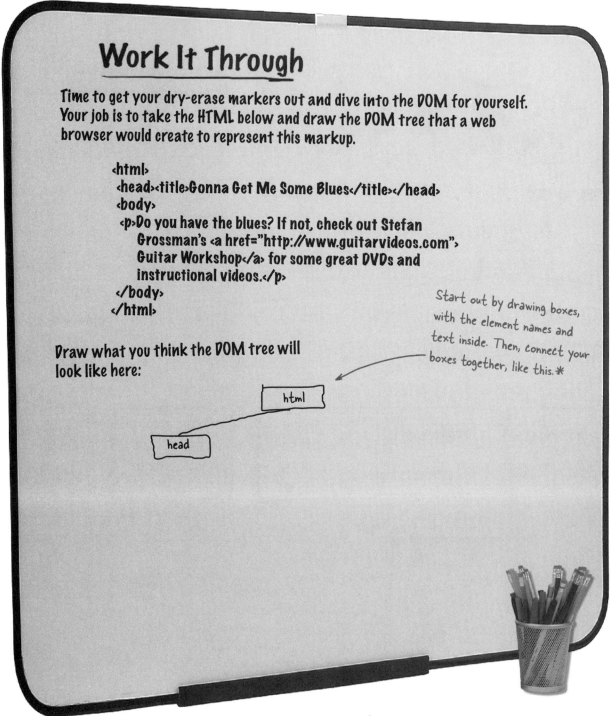

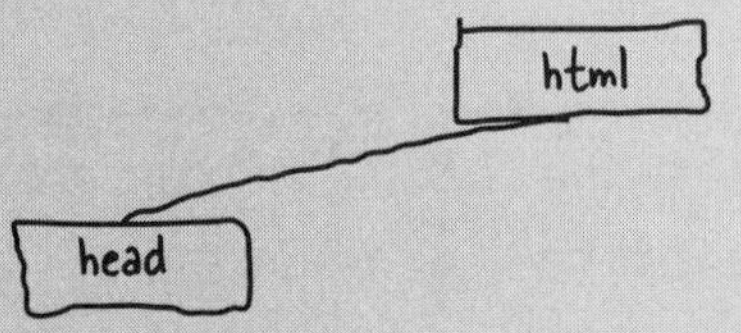

* One of our reviewers pointed out that you don't have to draw the boxes before writing in the element names. After long hours of thought, we concur.

Podcasting Studio

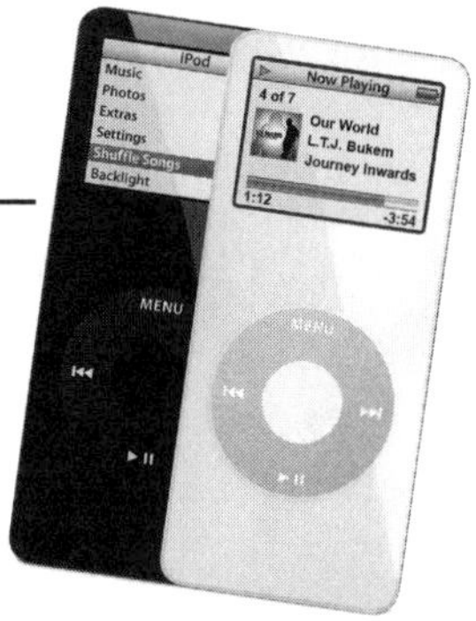

HeadRush: We're here with the Document Object Model, talking about how web browsers really see HTML, and what JavaScript programmers need to know to update their pages on the fly. It's good to have you, ummm... Document... ummm, Mr. Model.... well, what exactly should we call you?

Document Object Model: Most folks just call me the DOM. It's an awful lot of trouble to go around saying "Document Object Model."

HeadRush: Oh, that is easier. So, let me get this straight. You're what a web browser sees when it looks at an HTML page?

DOM: Well, the browser starts out with HTML and CSS and JavaScript files. But web browsers really don't like to work with text, which is all that those files are. It's hard to apply CSS styles and JavaScript event handlers to a bunch of text.

HeadRush: Oh, that makes sense. Because hardly anyone puts their CSS into their HTML files anymore... the CSS is usually in a separate file.

DOM: Right, and most of the time, the JavaScript isn't in the same file as the HTML, either. So the browser uses me, and combines all the HTML, CSS, and JavaScript into one structure. So, for each piece of HTML, the browser creates an object. And I keep all those objects organized and connected.

HeadRush: I can see how that would make it easier for the browser to keep up with all those HTML elements. But I'm not sure I understand how CSS and JavaScript fit into this picture.

DOM: Well, all my objects that represent HTML have helpful methods you can call, and properties you can set. So, for example, you could call addEventListener() on a button, and have the button call a JavaScript function every time it's pushed. All that is easy if browsers use me—and the objects I provide—to model web pages.

HeadRush: OK, I get it. So do you make it easier to change what's on a web page, too?

DOM: You got it. You can add a new text node to an element to make text appear, or remove a <div> element from its parent to make an entire section of a page vanish.

HeadRush: Oh, that is nice. And none of that requires reloading the page?

DOM: Exactly. I exist in memory all on the web browser, so the browser doesn't need to talk to a server or even be connected to the network to use me.

HeadRush: Wow, that's pretty sweet. I'm looking forward to getting to know you better...

Work It Through- Answers

Time to get your dry-erase markers out and dive into the DOM for yourself. Your job is to take the HTML below and draw the DOM tree that a web browser would create to represent this markup.

```
<html>
 <head><title>Gonna Get Me Some Blues</title></head>
 <body>
  <p>Do you have the blues? If not, check out Stefan
     Grossman's <a href="http://www.guitarvideos.com">
     Guitar Workshop</a> for some great DVDs and
     instructional videos.</p>
 </body>
</html>
```

Here's what we drew:

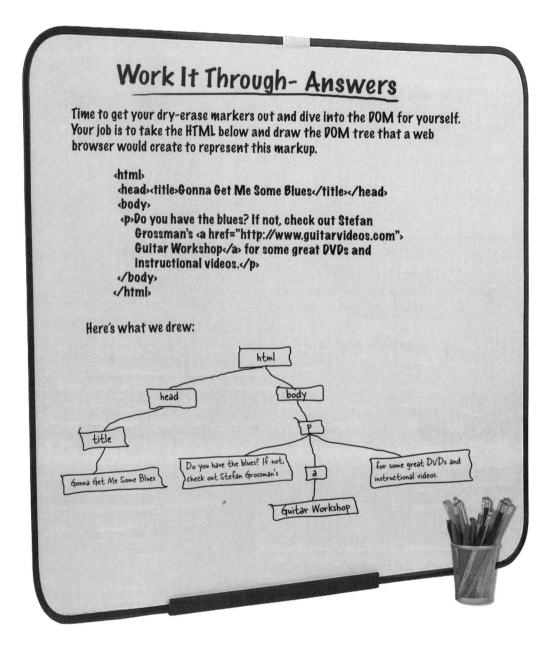

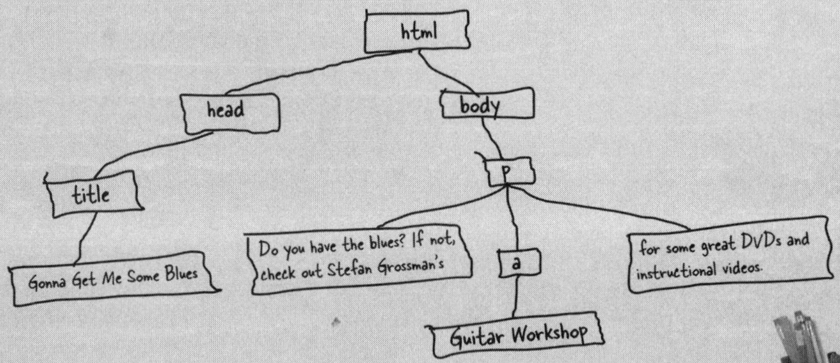

Remember that big huge DOM tree we just looked at?

Here's the DOM tree for the HTML you looked at back on page 220.

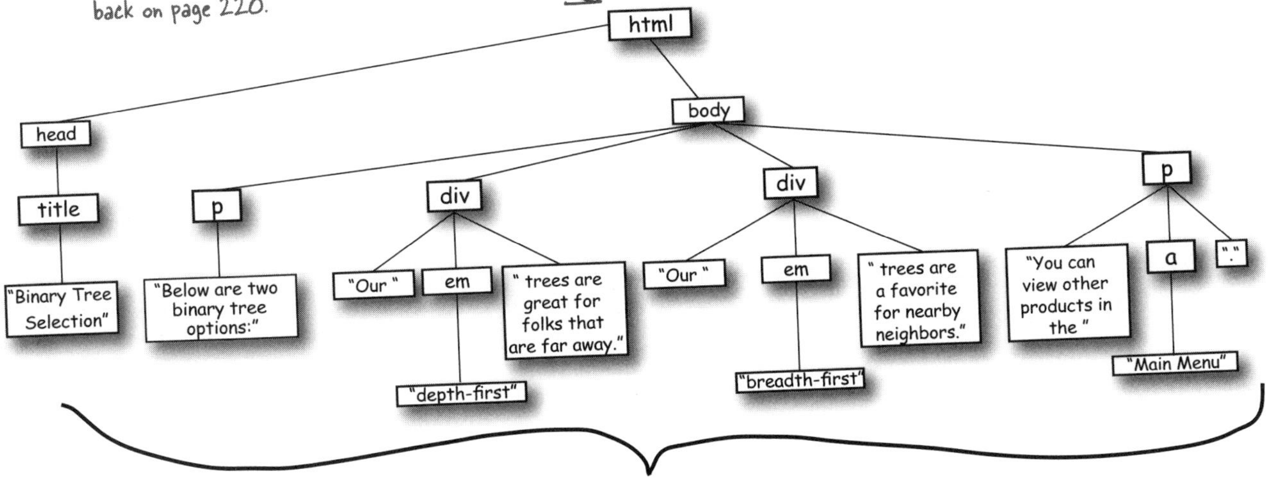

You can get to this whole thing using the "document" variable in your JavaScript.

You've already seen several ways to use the document object in your code... here are a few reminders from earlier in this chapter.

Get the root element of the document

You can grab the **<html>** root element from an HTML document using the **documentElement** property:

```
var htmlElement = document.documentElement;
```

documentElement is a special property of the document object. It always returns the root element of the DOM tree.

Remember, the root element in HTML is always <html>.

Find an element by its "id" attribute

You've already seen how **getElementById()** makes it a piece of cake to find an element in your web page, using the element's **id** attribute.

```
var manganese =
  document.getElementById("Mg").value;
```

This gets the element with an id of "Mg".

Moving around in a DOM tree

You already know how the **document** object can help you find an element with a particular **id** attribute, but there are a lot of other ways you can get around in a DOM tree. Since each node has a parent, and most element nodes have children, you can move up and down in the DOM tree using these connections.

Here's part of the DOM tree from page 226; let's look at how you could move around the tree, starting with one of the **<div>** elements:

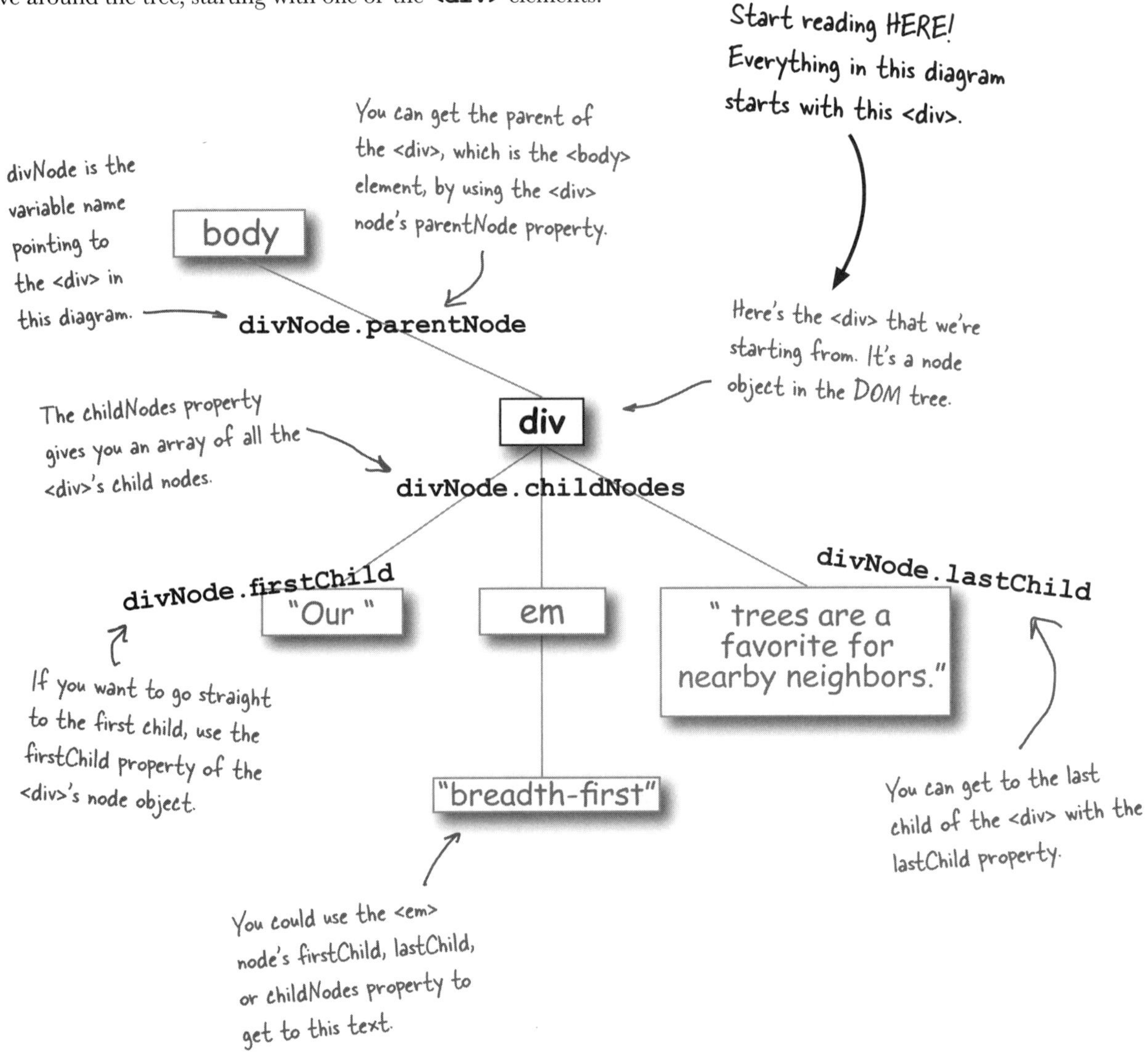

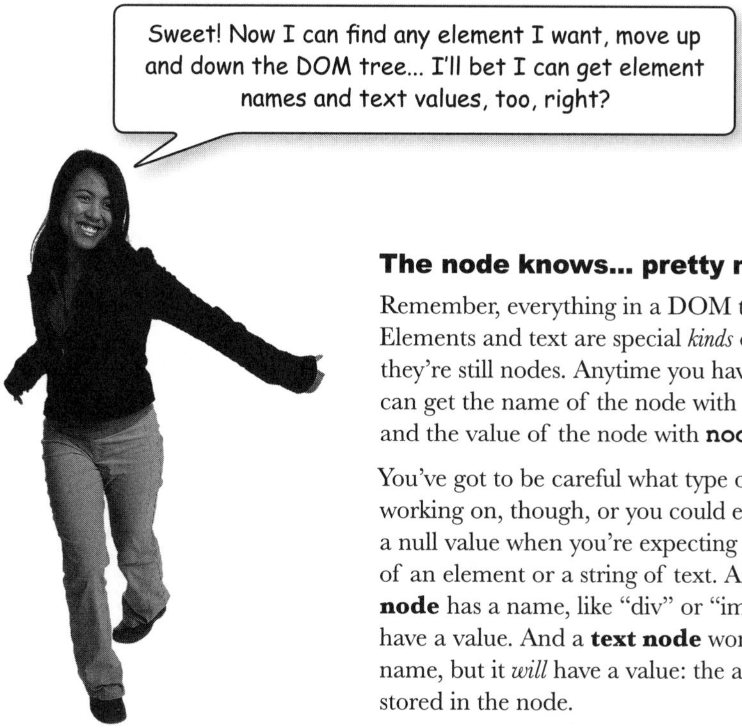

Sweet! Now I can find any element I want, move up and down the DOM tree... I'll bet I can get element names and text values, too, right?

The node knows... pretty much everything.

Remember, everything in a DOM tree is a node. Elements and text are special *kinds* of nodes, but they're still nodes. Anytime you have a node, you can get the name of the node with **`nodeName`**, and the value of the node with **`nodeValue`**.

You've got to be careful what type of node you're working on, though, or you could end up getting a null value when you're expecting the name of an element or a string of text. An **element node** has a name, like "div" or "img", but *won't* have a value. And a **text node** won't have a name, but it *will* have a value: the actual text stored in the node.

Let's take a look and see how this works:

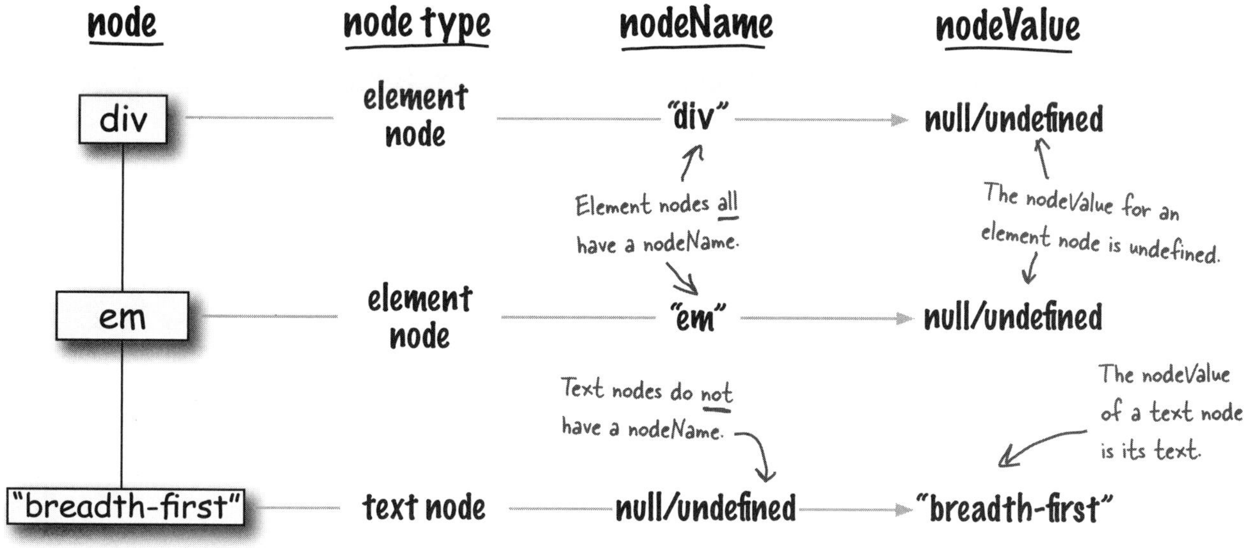

Just Do It

You've got to keep up with what type of node you're working on, and always know where in the DOM tree your variables are pointing. To help you get some practice, here's a bit of JavaScript code, and some HTML. Your job is to figure out what each **`alert()`** prints out. Try this first without running the code on your own... but don't be afraid to type this code in and test it out for yourself if you get stuck.

Write what the alert() prints out here...

```
function guess() {
 var whatAmI;
 var element =
   document.documentElement.lastChild;
 alert("I am a " + element.nodeName);                 ____________________
 var anotherElement =
   document.getElementsByTagName("h1")[0];
 alert("I am a " + anotherElement.nodeValue);         ____________________
 var child = anotherElement.firstChild;
 alert("I am a " + child.nodeValue);                  ____________________
 element =
   document.getElementById("tiger").lastChild;
 alert("I am a " + element.nodeValue);                ____________________
 alert("I am a " +
   element.parentNode
          .getAttributeNode("id").nodeValue);         ____________________
}
```

Here's the HTML to use for the exercise.

```
<html>
 <head>
  <title>Who Am I exercise</title>
 </head>
 <body>
  <h1>I am a cow</h1>
  <div id="ranch">
   I am a <em>horse</em>, but I wish I
   was a <span id="tiger">tiger</span>.
  </div>
  <form>
   <input type="button" value="What Am I?"
          onClick="guess();" />
  </form>
 </body>
</html>
```

Answers on page 240.

Frequently Asked Questions

Q: I understand text, and elements, and branches, but I'm still confused about exactly what a "node" is.

A: *Everything* in a DOM tree is a node: elements, text, attributes, even comments. Since each piece of markup has some common properties, like a parent, and in most cases a name and children, the DOM groups these common properties into a **`Node`** object. Then, each different type of node adds its own unique properties to the common properties in the **`Node`** type.

For example, element nodes have a **`getAttribute()`** and **`setAttribute()`** method, because only elements can have attributes. But element nodes get the **`parent`** and **`childNodes`** properties from the **`Node`** object, since that functionality is shared by several different types of nodes.

Q: But some nodes don't have a name. What happens if you use the nodeName property on something like a text node?

A: If you try to use a property on a node where that property doesn't apply, you'll get a value like "null" or "undefined". That's the DOM's way of telling you that it didn't know what you meant, or at least that what you meant didn't match up with the DOM tree the browser created from your markup.

So if you tried to access the **`nodeName`** property on a text node, you'd get an undefined value because, unlike elements, text nodes don't have names. Or, if you tried to use **`nodeValue`** on an element, you'd get an undefined value, because elements don't have values. An element can have attributes, but any text within the element will be in the element's child text nodes, and not available through the element's **`nodeValue`** property.

I like most of this DOM stuff so far, but all this null value and undefined stuff kind of freaks me out. Can't I just **ask** the node if it's an element, or text, or whatever?

You can! (well, sort of)

Every node has a property called nodeType, along with the nodeName and nodeValue proeprties that you've already seen. The nodeType property returns a number, and that number maps to a value stored in the Node class. There's a value for each type of node, so you can use these values to figure out exactly what kind of node you're working with, like this:

Here's the nodeType property. It returns a number...

...that you can compare to the numbers defined in the Node class.

```
if (someNode.nodeType == Node.ELEMENT_NODE) {
  // Do something with the element node
} else if (someNode.nodeType == Node.TEXT_NODE) {
  // Do something with the text node
}
```

Once you know what type of node you have, you can avoid using properties that would return null values.

There are numbers defined for all the node types, including elements, text, and attributes.

Some browsers don't recognize Node

Unfortunately, some web browsers don't support the Node class in your JavaScript. Your code won't run, and you're back to dealing with errors and null values.

All browsers support the nodeType proeprty...

...but several browsers report an error right here.

```
if (someNode.nodeType == Node.ELEMENT_NODE) {
  // Do something with the element node
} else if (someNode.nodeType == Node.TEXT_NODE) {
  // Do something with the text node
}
```

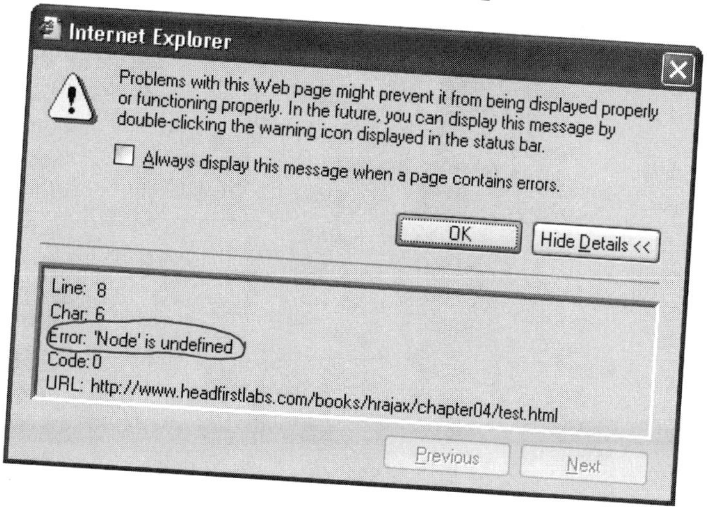

Here's IE reporting that it doesn't recognize the Node object in your code.

FREQUENTLY ASKED QUESTIONS

Q: So as long as my users aren't running Internet Explorer, I can use the Node object, right?

A: Actually, you shouldn't ever use the **Node** object... at least not until all major browsers support the **Node** object. Even if you don't think your users are running IE, it's still the world's most popular browser (by a long-shot). In the next chapter, you"ll see that you can get the same results with a little more work, and end up with code that works on *all* browsers.

Cool! I can definitely see there are some weird things about the DOM, but I think I'm starting to get the hang of it. But what ever happened to that coding challenge you mentioned?

You're ready for the challenge...

The DOM is a pretty big topic, and it's taken us almost 40 pages just to explain how it works. But now you've got some mad DOM skills, and are almost ready to take on building a DOM app... and taking on the coding challenge.

Before you do, though, check out the exercise solutions on the next few pages, and make sure you understsand everything so far. Then, turn to **Chapter 4.5**, and we'll start working on a DOM app all our own.

Yes, you read that right. There's a Chapter 4.5. And you're ready for it now, so close your eyes, chant "D-O-M" a few times, and let's get to coding.*

The Great Chapter 4 Coding Challenge

Write a killer web application that uses the Document Object Model to create a dynamic user interface, without writing any Ajax code.

* OK, we admit it. This chapter just got so stinking big that we broke it into two chapters. But then, the Great Chapter 4 Coding Challenge became the Great Chapter 5 Coding Challenge, and nobody liked that nearly as much. So we called the next Chapter 4.5, and now we can still say ...
...(drum roll) ...
the Great Chapter 4 Coding Challenge. Who said there couldn't be drama in a programming book?

Just Do It *Solutions*

You've got to keep up with what type of node you're working on, and always know where in the DOM tree your variables are pointing. Did your answers match up with ours? Let's take a look:

```
function guess() {
 var whatAmI;
 var element =
   document.documentElement.lastChild;
 alert("I am a " + element.nodeName);
 var anotherElement =
   document.getElementsByTagName("h1")[0];
 alert("I am a " + anotherElement.nodeValue);
 var child = anotherElement.firstChild;
 alert("I am a " + child.nodeValue);
 element =
   document.getElementById("tiger").lastChild;
 alert("I am a " + element.nodeValue);
 alert("I am a " +
   element.parentNode
      .getAttributeNode("id").nodeValue);
}
```

The document element is <html>. It's first child is <head>, and it's last child is <body>.

There's only one <h1> in the document...

...and elements don't have a nodeValue.

The first (and only) child of <h1> is the text node with the text "I am a cow".

You're used to writing code like this by now.

The <span> elements's last child is its text, which is "tiger".

The text node's parent is the <span> element.

You haven't seen this function before, but you can figure it out. It gets the "id" attribute...

...which has a value of "tiger".

Did you get that last one? It's easy to forget that the "element" variable isn't really an element at all! It's a text node, and its parent is the <span> element.
If you thought this last line ended up at the <div>, with an "id" attribute of "ranch", it's OK... just make sure you understand why the alert() printed "tiger" before continuing on.

Don't worry about capitalization on element names... browsers usually put them all in uppercase.

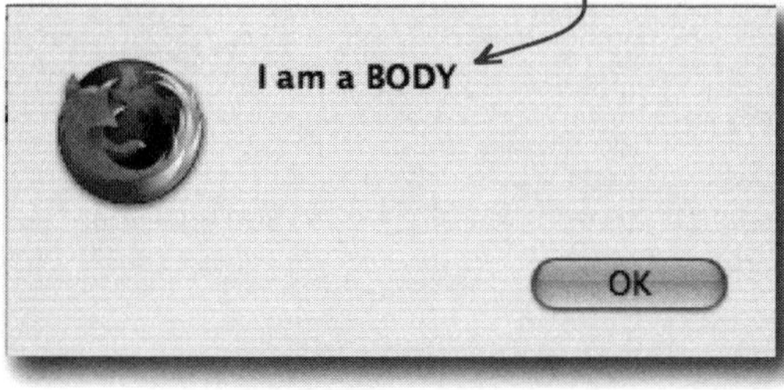
I am a BODY
OK

This just means that there's not a value for this property.

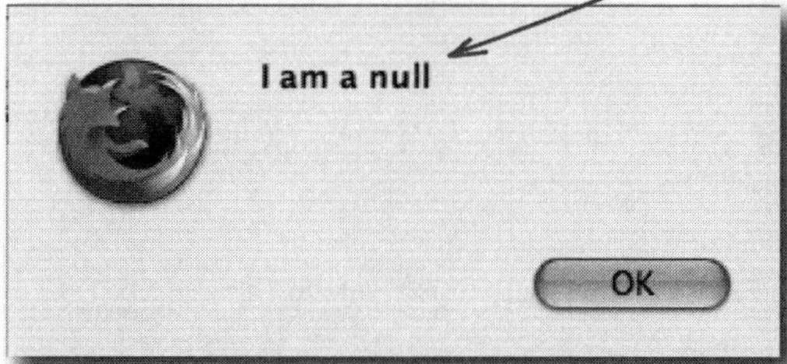
I am a null
OK

I am a I am a cow
OK

```
<html>
  <head>
   <title>Who Am I exercise</title>
  </head>
  <body>
   <h1>I am a cow</h1>
   <div id="ranch">
    I am a <em>horse</em>, but I wish I
    was a <span id="tiger">tiger</span>.
   </div>
   <form>
    <input type="button" value="What Am I?"
           onClick="guess();" />
   </form>
  </body>
```

The HTML for this exercise.

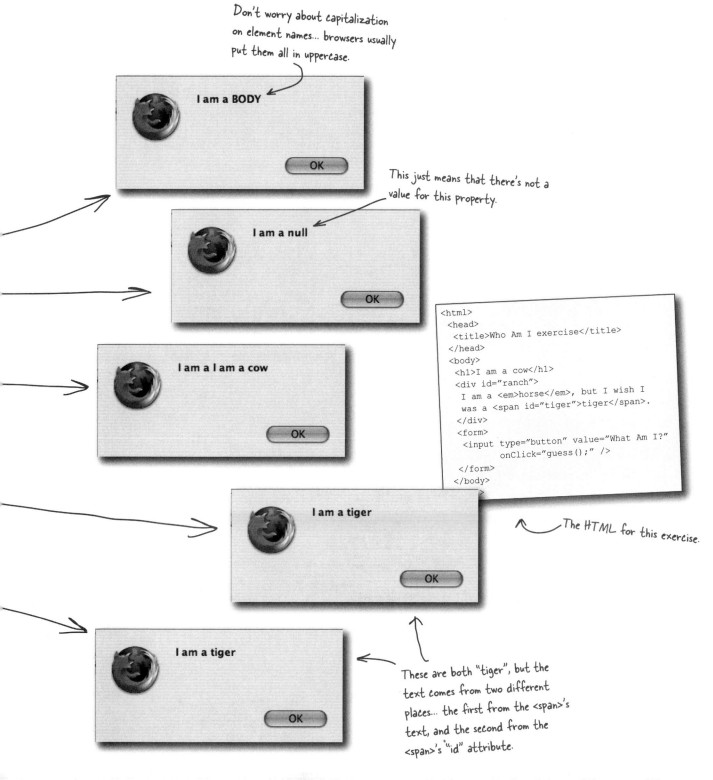

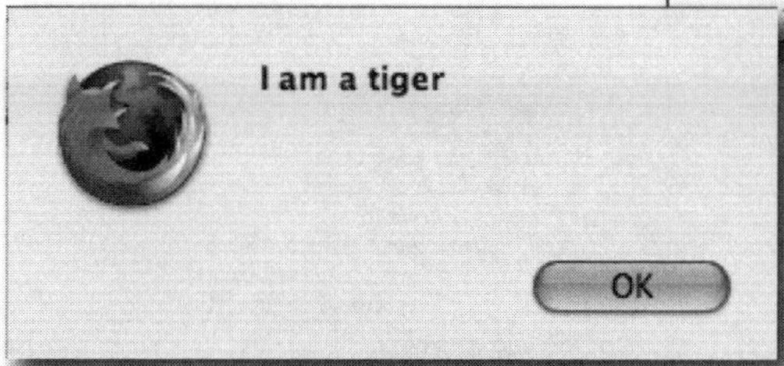
I am a tiger
OK

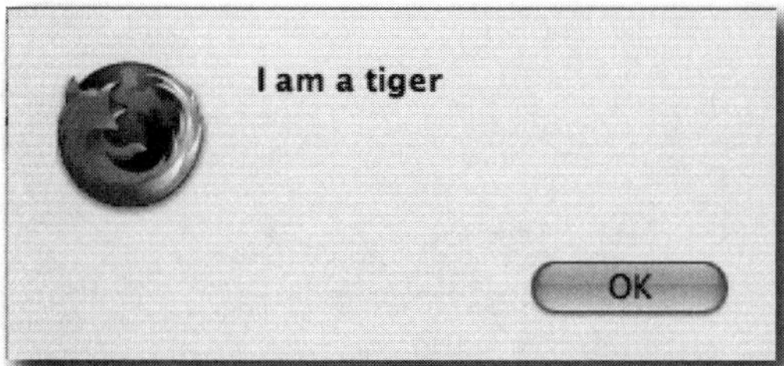
I am a tiger
OK

These are both "tiger", but the text comes from two different places... the first from the <span>'s text, and the second from the <span>'s "id" attribute.

Exercise Solutions

Tree Magnets Solutions

Below is how a web browser would view a simple HTML page. We've added magnets to each part of the tree. See how your answers compared with ours.

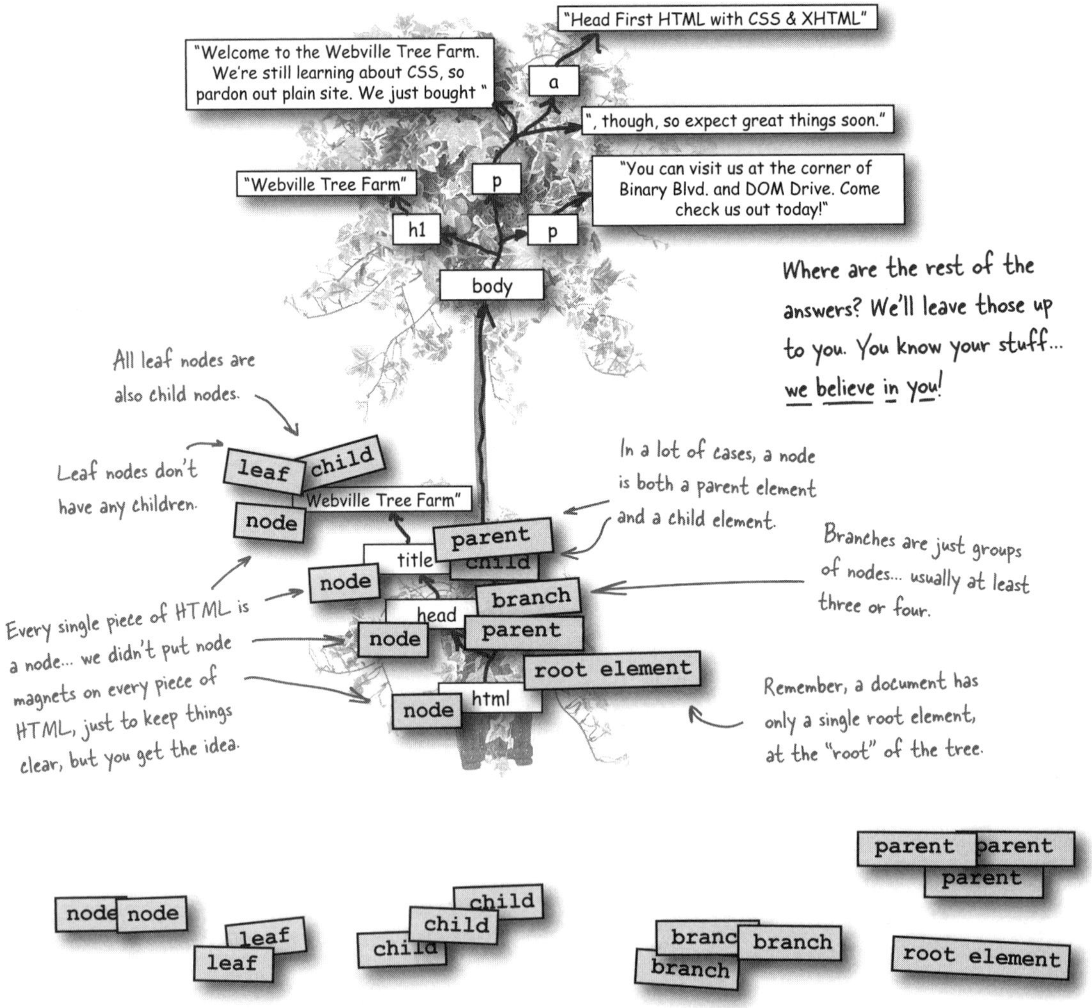

"Head First HTML with CSS & XHTML"
"Welcome to the Webville Tree Farm. We're still learning about CSS, so pardon out plain site. We just bought "
a
", though, so expect great things soon."
"Webville Tree Farm"
p
"You can visit us at the corner of Binary Blvd. and DOM Drive. Come check us out today!"
h1
p
body
All leaf nodes are also child nodes.
Leaf nodes don't have any children.
leaf
child
"Webville Tree Farm"
node
In a lot of cases, a node is both a parent element and a child element.
parent
title
node
Branches are just groups of nodes... usually at least three or four.
branch
head
parent
node
Every single piece of HTML is a node... we didn't put node magnets on every piece of HTML, just to keep things clear, but you get the idea.
root element
html
node
Remember, a document has only a single root element, at the "root" of the tree.
parent
parent
parent
node
node
leaf
leaf
child
child
child
branch
branch
branch
root element

Where are the rest of the answers? We'll leave those up to you. You know your stuff... we believe in you!

4.5 developing DOM applications

A Second Helping

Hungry for more DOM? In the last chapter, you got a crash course in the coolest way to update your web pages: the **Document Object Model**. We figured you might be wanting even more, though, so in this chapter you'll use what you've just learned to write a nifty DOM-based application. Along the way, you'll pick up some **new event handlers**, learn how to **change a node's style**, and create a **user-friendly, dynamic application**. This is the chapter where we take your DOM skills to a whole new level.

Everyone's a critic

If you enjoy music, you've probably got an opinion about what you like to listen to... and what you don't. Let's use what we've been learning about the DOM to build a web page for rating the Top 5 blues CDs of all time.

Rather than spend a bunch of time writing HTML and CSS, we've already taken care of putting a simple page together, and adding some style. Open up the **chapter04/** folder in the source code for the book's examples. You'll see another folder named **top5**, with some files and a sub-folder:

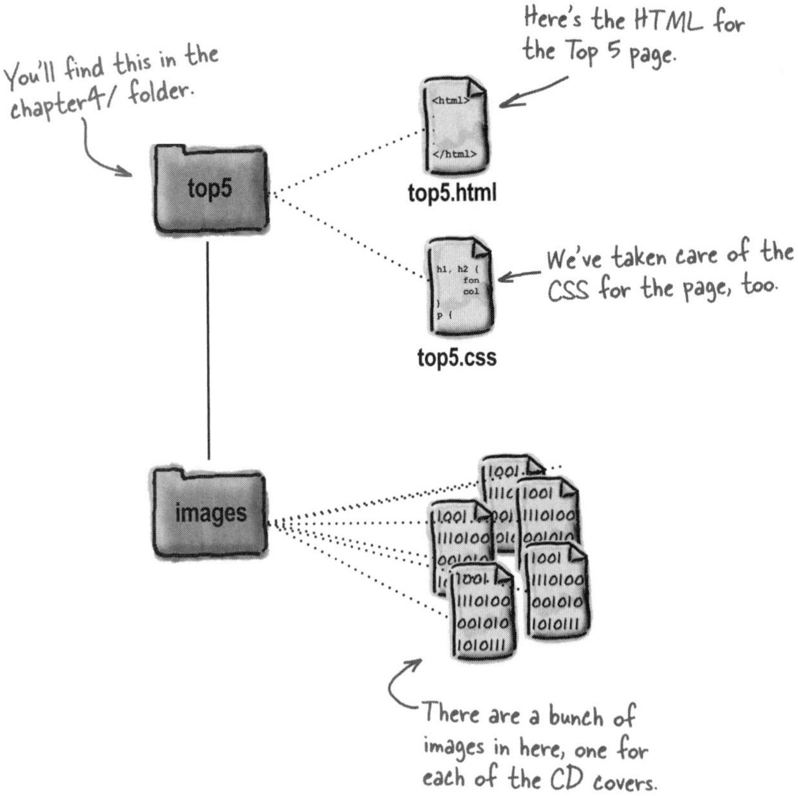

Here's what all this HTML and CSS looks like in a browser...

You can click on any of these CD cover images.

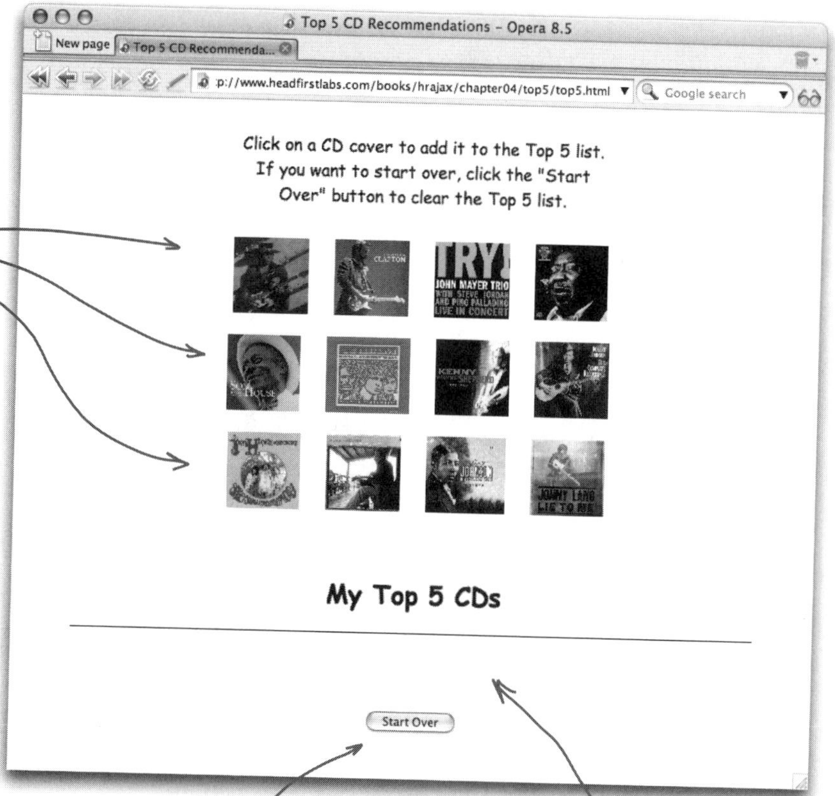
Top 5 CD Recommendations - Opera 8.5
New page
Top 5 CD Recommenda...
p://www.headfirstlabs.com/books/hrajax/chapter04/top5/top5.html
Google search
Click on a CD cover to add it to the Top 5 list. If you want to start over, click the "Start Over" button to clear the Top 5 list.
My Top 5 CDs
Start Over

You can click "Start Over" to move all the CDs back to the top of the page, and create a new list.

When you click on a CD, it should move down into this Top 5 listing area.

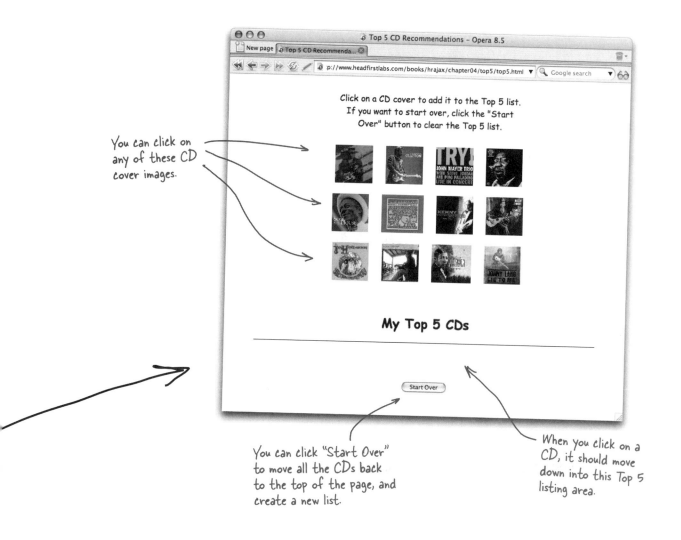

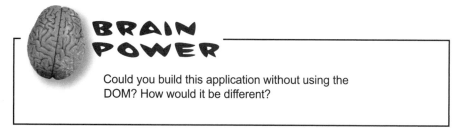

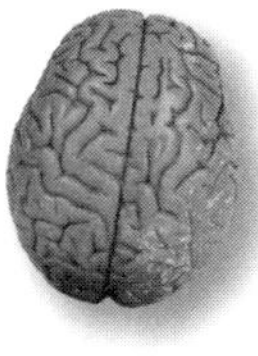

BRAIN POWER

Could you build this application without using the DOM? How would it be different?

Checking out top5.html

Open up **top5.html** and take a look. Most of the file is filled with **<img>** elements to display the CD covers. You'll also see some instructions, a form with a button, and a few **<div>**s:

As usual, this app uses an external CSS stylesheet.

```
<html>
 <head>
  <title>Top 5 CD Recommendations</title>
  <link rel="stylesheet" type="text/css" href="top5.css" />
 </head>
 <body>
  <div id="instructions">
   Click on a CD cover to add it to the Top 5 list. If you want to start
   over, click the "Start Over" button to clear the Top 5 list.
  </div>

  <div id="cds">
   <img class="cover" src="images/vaughan_flood.jpg" />
   <img class="cover" src="images/clapton_cream.jpg" />
   <!-- Lots more images in here... -->
  </div>

  <div id="top5-listings">
   <h2>My Top 5 CDs</h2>
   <div id="top5"></div>
  </div>

  <form>
   <input type="button" value="Start Over" />
  </form>
 </body>
</html>
```

All these id attributes will help when we need to look these elements up in our code.

Nothing tricky here... just lots of <img> elements to show the CD covers to choose from.

Here's where we'll put the CDs that the user chooses.

We'll probably need to run some JavaScript here at some point...

What's the game plan?

With the HTML and CSS already written, all that's left for you to take care of is the JavaScript. Let's figure out what needs to be done, and start writing some code.

1. **Create a new file to store the page's JavaScript code.**
2. **Write a function that adds a CD to the Top 5 list when the CD's cover is clicked on.**
3. **Add a ranking number to each CD, so users can see the order of the Top 5.**
4. **Write a function that clears the user's choices and starts over.**

This is the easy part... let's call the new file top5.js. (Step 1)

We'll have to add an onClick() event handler to each CD cover image to handle this. Then we can create a new function, called addToTop5(). (Step 2)

The DOM makes tasks like this pretty easy. We can put this code in addToTop5(), also. (Step 3)

An onClick event handler on the "Start Over" button can handle this, and run another JavaScript function that you'll write. Let's call this new function startOver(). (Step 4)

Just Do It

Start out by taking care of Step 1. Create a new file and name it **`top5.js`**. Go ahead and create a function called **`addToTop5()`** to handle Step 2, and another function named **`startOver()`** to handle Step 4. We'll write the code for Step 3 as part of the **`addToTop5()`** function, so you don't need a separate function for that step. You can leave all of these functions blank for now; we'll fill each one in as we go through the chapter.

Be sure you've made these changes before you turn the page, and then save your new JavaScript file as **`top5.js`** in the **`top5/`** directory, alongside **`top5.html`** and **`top5.css`**.

The big picture

Did you get all of that done? Check the diagram below, and make sure you have all the files you need for the Top 5 app, and have started on the code like we have.

Here's the top5/ folder you started with, in the chapter04/ examples directory.

top5.js goes in the top5/ folder, along with the HTML and CSS for the page.

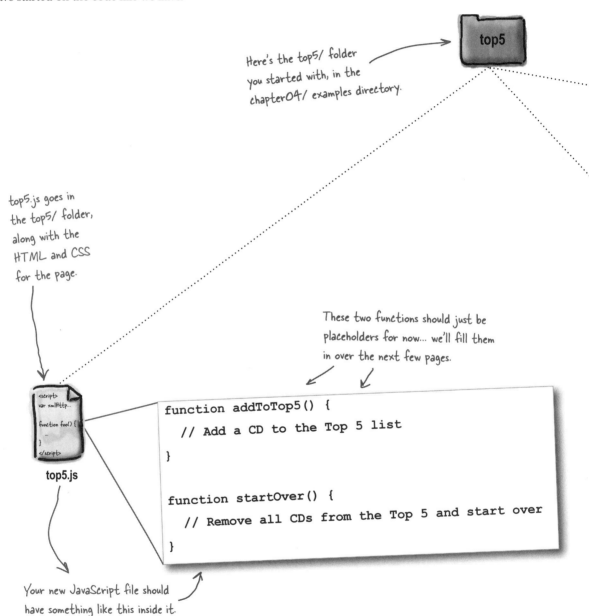

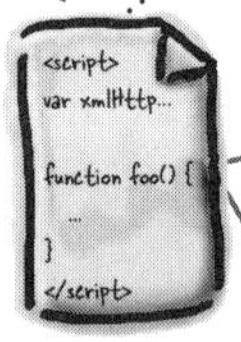

top5.js

These two functions should just be placeholders for now... we'll fill them in over the next few pages.

```
function addToTop5() {
  // Add a CD to the Top 5 list
}


function startOver() {
  // Remove all CDs from the Top 5 and start over
}
```

Your new JavaScript file should have something like this inside it.

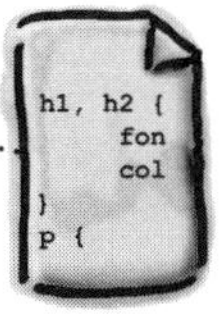

top5.css

We'll have to add some CSS to this file later.

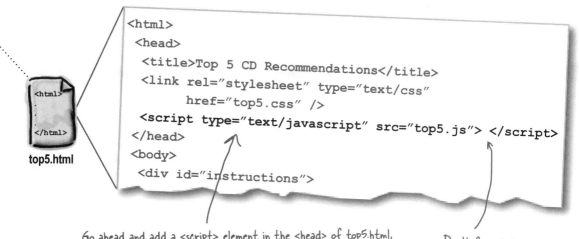

top5.html

```
<html>
 <head>
  <title>Top 5 CD Recommendations</title>
  <link rel="stylesheet" type="text/css"
        href="top5.css" />
  <script type="text/javascript" src="top5.js"> </script>
 </head>
 <body>
  <div id="instructions">
```

Go ahead and add a <script> element in the <head> of top5.html, referring to the new JavaScript file you created.

Don't forget to leave a space in here.

Setting up the CD covers

Any time someone clicks on a CD cover image, we need the Top 5 page to run our **`addToTop5()`** function. That way—once we write the code for **`addToTop5()`**—the CD that was clicked on will get added to the Top 5 list.

There are two different ways we can handle this:

Option 1: Add onClick event handlers to every <img> element in top5.html.

Pros:

- ✓ Easy to do. Just add **`onClick="addToTop5();"`** to each **`<img>`** element in the HTML.
- ✓ Doesn't require writing any JavaScript.

Cons:

- × If you change or add images to the HTML page, you have to remember to add the **`onClick`** event handler.

Option 2: Use JavaScript to programmatically add event handlers to all <img> elements.

Pros:

- ✓ Makes sure all images call **`addToTop5()`**, even if new images are added later.
- ✓ The application can call the function that adds event handlers any time it's needed.

Cons:

- × Requires writing code instead of adding **`onClick`** handlers directly to the HTML.

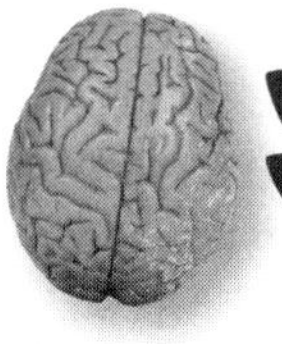

BRAIN POWER

Which option do you think is best? Remember, after you add a CD to the Top 5 listings, you don't want anything to happen if someone clicks on that cover again. Otherwise, you'd be adding a CD to the Top 5 that is *already* in the Top 5. Does this make a difference in how you add the **`onClick`** event to the CD cover **`<img>`** elements?

Option 1: Add onClick event handlers to every <img> element in top5.html.

Here's top5..html, with onClick() handlers set up to run addToTop5() when a CD cover image is clicked.

Top 5 CD Recommendations - Opera 8.5
Click on a CD cover to add it to the Top 5 list. If you want to start over, click the "Start Over" button to clear the Top 5 list.
My Top 5 CDs
Start Over

```
<img class="cover"
     src="images/shepherd_ledbetter.jpg"
     alt="Ledbetter Heights"
     onClick="addToTop5();" />
<img class="cover"
     src="images/johnson_complete.jpg"
     alt="The Complete Recordings"
     onClick="addToTop5();" />
<img class="cover"
```

Every time you click this CD cover, addToTop5() will run.

When the CD is clicked, addToTop5() will use the DOM to move the cover down to the Top 5 listings at the bottom of the page.

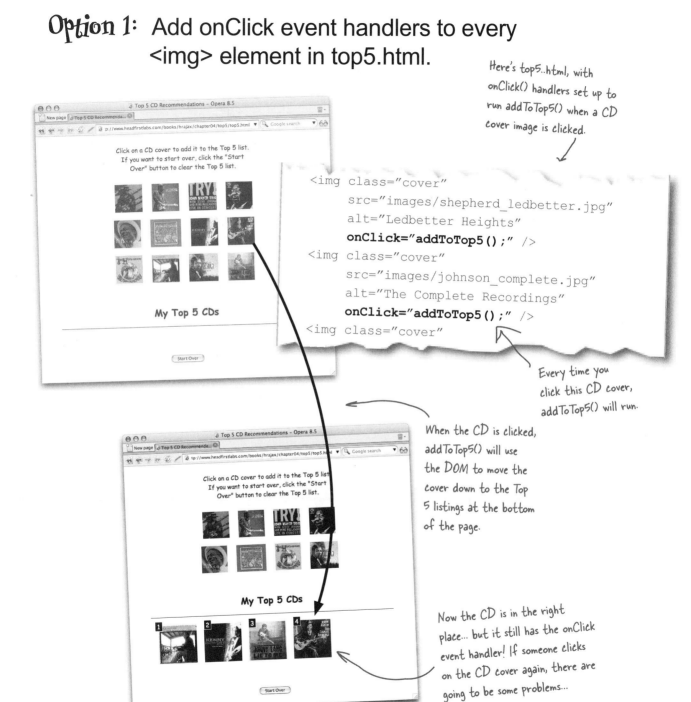

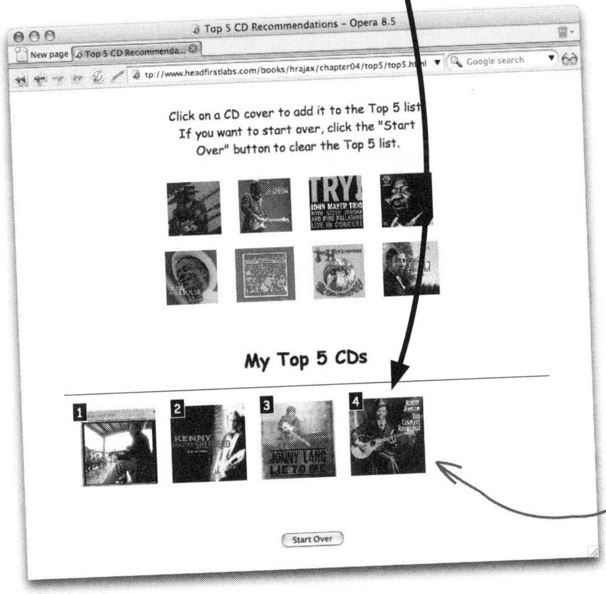
Top 5 CD Recommendations - Opera 8.5
Click on a CD cover to add it to the Top 5 list. If you want to start over, click the "Start Over" button to clear the Top 5 list.
My Top 5 CDs
1
2
3
4
Start Over

Now the CD is in the right place... but it still has the onClick event handler! If someone clicks on the CD cover again, there are going to be some problems...

We better take a look at Option 2...

Create JS file | Add CD to Top 5 | Add CD rankings | Start over

Option 2: Use JavaScript to programmatically add event handlers to all <img> elements.

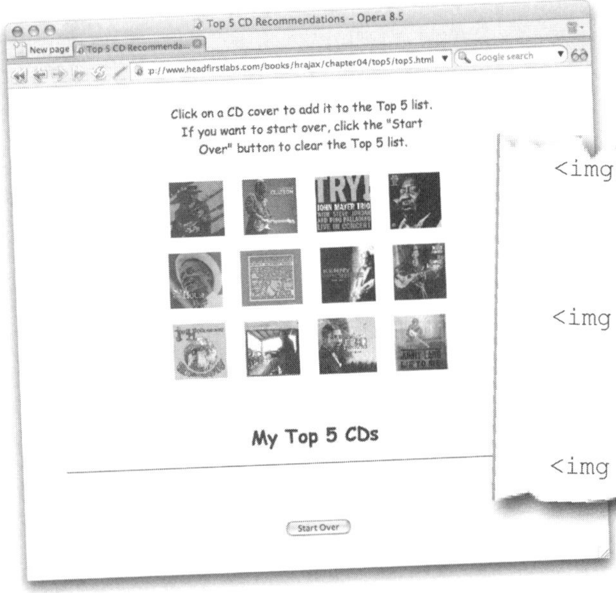
Top 5 CD Recommendations - Opera 8.5
Click on a CD cover to add it to the Top 5 list. If you want to start over, click the "Start Over" button to clear the Top 5 list.
My Top 5 CDs
Start Over

This time, there's nothing in the HTML that sets up an event handler for the CD covers.

```
<img class="cover"
     src="images/shepherd_ledbetter.jpg"
     alt="Ledbetter Heights"
     onClick="addToTop5();" />
<img class="cover"
     src="images/johnson_complete.jpg"
     alt="The Complete Recordings"
     onClick="addToTop5();" />
<img class="cover"
```

(The `onClick="addToTop5();"` lines are struck through.)

Here's part of the DOM for the Top 5 web page. This is the "cds" <div>...

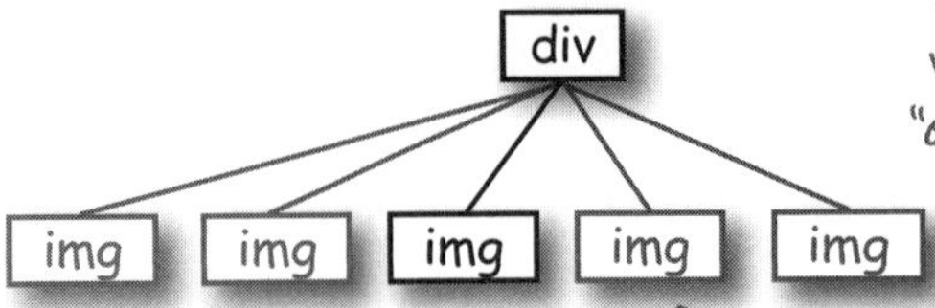
div
img
img
img
img
img

...and here are all the CD covers, represented as <img> elements.

Using JavaScript, we need to set up each <img> element to run addToTop5() when the <img> is clicked on.

NEED ARROWS

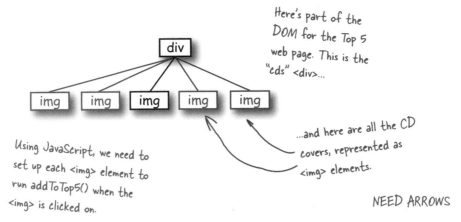

top5.js

```
function addToTop5() {
  // Add a CD to the Top 5 list
}

function startOver() {
  // Remove all CDs from the Top 5 and start over
}
```

I think we should use JavaScript. When we add a CD to the Top 5 listing, we need to remove the event handler on that <img> element... but then if the user clicks "Start Over", we need to move the image back to the "cds" <div>, and then add the handler back. Seems like it would be easier to just handle adding and removing the onClick event with JavaScript.

Nice thinking! We can write a function that adds the onClick event handler to all the <img> elements in the "cds" div. If the CD is added to the Top 5 list, we'll remove the handler, and move the <img> down to the "top5" div.

But if "Start Over" is clicked, we need to put all the CDs back in the top <div>, the one named "cds". Then we can run our function again, and add the handlers back to all these images.

When the app starts, all of these <img> elements need to call addToTop5() when they're clicked on...

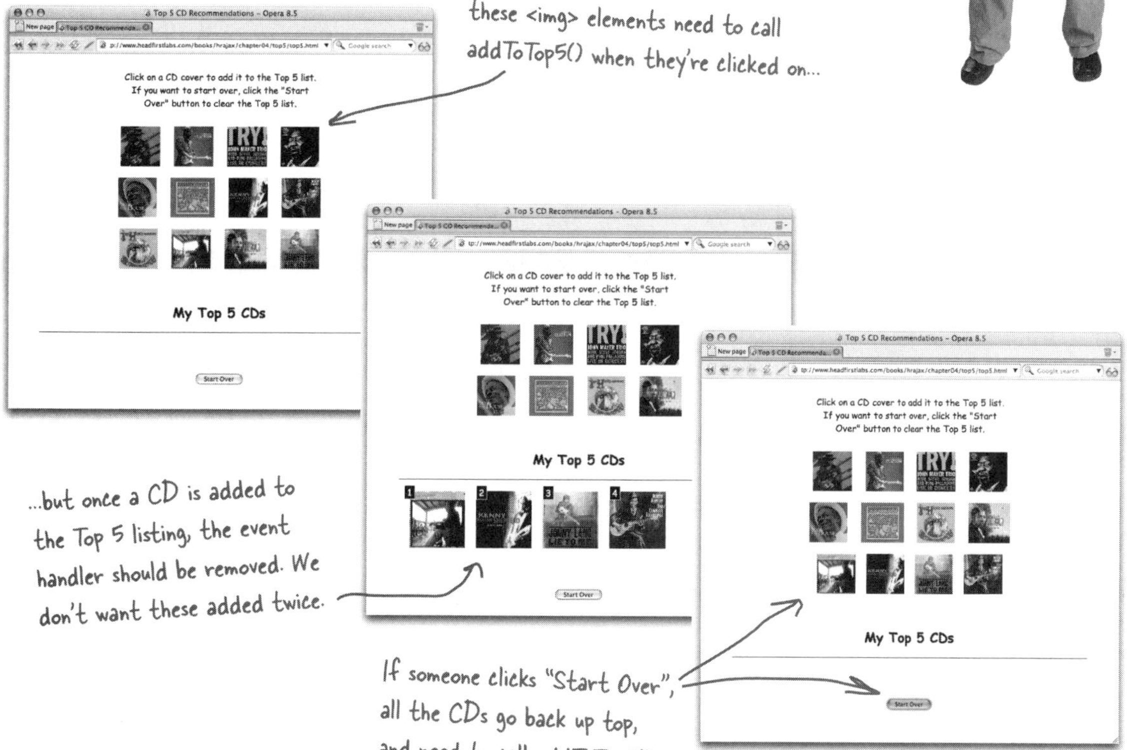
Top 5 CD Recommendations - Opera 8.5
Click on a CD cover to add it to the Top 5 list.
If you want to start over, click the "Start Over" button to clear the Top 5 list.
My Top 5 CDs
Start Over

...but once a CD is added to the Top 5 listing, the event handler should be removed. We don't want these added twice.

If someone clicks "Start Over", all the CDs go back up top, and need to call addToTop5() if they're clicked on again.

Create JS file | Add CD to Top 5 | Add CD rankings | Start over

Adding event handlers

You've already used **onClick** and **onChange** in your HTML to assign a JavaScript function to an event. You can do the same thing with JavaScript code, and get a little practice working with the DOM, too. Let's create a new function, called **addOnClickHandlers()**, that will add event handlers to all the **<img>** elements in the "cds" **<div>**.

This wasn't on our original checklist back on page 247, but it's still part of setting up the CDs to be added to the Top 5 listings.

Add this function to top5.js.

```
function addOnClickHandlers() {

  var cdsDiv = document.getElementById("cds");

  var cdImages = cdsDiv.getElementsByTagName("img");

  for (var i=0; i<cdImages.length; i++) {

    cdImages[i].onclick = addToTop5;

  }

}
```

All the CD covers we want to add handlers to are nested in the "cds" <div>.

This will return an array of all the elements named "img" within the "cds" div.

We can just loop through all the <img> elements, and add an event handler to each.

"onclick" is the JavaScript event that matches up with the HTML onClick event handler...

...and addToTop5 is the function to run on that event.

Q: getElementsByTagName? What's that all about?

A: The JavaScript **document** object, as well as all element nodes, has a method that you can run called **getElementsByTagName()**. That method returns all the nested elements that have the name you supplied. In this case, we want all the **<img>** elements in the "cds" **<div>**, so we call **getElementsByTagName("img")**. Remember, this method only returns matching elements nested within the node you run the method on... in this case, that's the **cdsDiv** node.

Q: What's the difference between using the onclick property in JavaScript, and the onClick attribute in an HTML page?

A: There's really no difference at all. However, as we discussed a few pages back, writing a method to take care of setting up event handlers is a little more flexible... and you can call this method multiple times, which will come in handy in just a bit.

Remember, the browser reads the markup in your HTML file, and then doesn't use that text file anymore. It converts the markup into a DOM tree, so it's reallly the DOM that you're working with here.

Running addOnClickHandlers()

We need to make sure that these event handlers are set up as soon as the page loads. Fortunately for us, the **<body>** element has an event handler called **onLoad()**. We can use that to run a JavaScript function any time the page loads, which is just what we want.

Make this change to your **top5.html** markup:

Be sure and make the changes on the last few pages to top5.js, also.

```
<html>
 <head>
  <title>Top 5 CD Recommendations</title>
  <link rel="stylesheet" type="text/css"
        href="top5.css" />
  <script type="text/javascript" src="top5.js"> </script>
 </head>
 <body onLoad="addOnClickHandlers();">
  <div id="instructions">
```

Any function specified in the onLoad() event handler will run every time the HTML page is loaded in a browser.

addOnClickHandlers() will run when the page loads, and then every time someone clicks on a CD cover, addToTop5() will run.

Frequently Asked Questions

Q: onClick, onChange, and now onLoad... where are all these event handlers coming from? You seem to be pulling them out of thin air!

A: Don't worry if you're not familiar with all of these event handlers... you can look them up in any good JavaScript reference. Now that you're starting to work with JavaScript more, you'll start to learn about the different event handlers, and what each handler does. For now, just trust us... and be on the lookout for *Head First JavaScript*, where you'll get the full scoop on event handlers.

Q: Isn't there an addEventHandler() method that would be better than working with the onclick property directly?

A: **addEventHandler()** is a method that you can use to add event handlers to elements, and works in a similar way to the **onclick** property. However, **addEventHandler()** isn't supported on Internet Explorer, while the **onclick** property works on all modern browsers. Need we say more?

By the way, the property is "onclick", not "onClick". If you use anything but lowercase letters, you'll get an error, so use only lowercase when you're typing event handler properties like this.

Adding a CD to the top 5

Now that clicking on a CD cover runs **addToTop5()**, it's about time to get that function working, isn't it? When a CD is clicked, we need to move that CD from the "cds" **<div>**, near the top of the screen, down to the Top 5 listings. Thanks to the DOM, though, this should be a piece of cake.

Let's start by looking at a bit of the DOM tree for **top5.html**.

```
<html>
 <head>
  <title>Top 5 CD Recommendations</title>
  <link rel="stylesheet" type="text/css" href="top5.css" />
  <script type="text/javascript" src="top5.js"> </script>
 </head>
 <body>
  <div id="instructions">
   Click on a CD cover to add it to the Top 5 list.
   If you want to start over, click the "Start Over"
   button to clear the Top 5 list.
  </div>
  <div id="cds">
   <img class="cover" src="images/vaughan_flood.jpg" />
   <img class="cover" src="images/clapton_cream.jpg" />
   <!-- Lots more images in here... -->
  </div>
  <div id="top5-listings">
   <h2>My Top 5 CDs</h2>
   <div id="top5"></div>
  </div>
  <form>
   <input type="button" value="Start Over" />
  </form>
 </body>
</html>
```

Here's top5.html, from back on page 246. The browser takes this HTML, and turns it into this DOM tree.

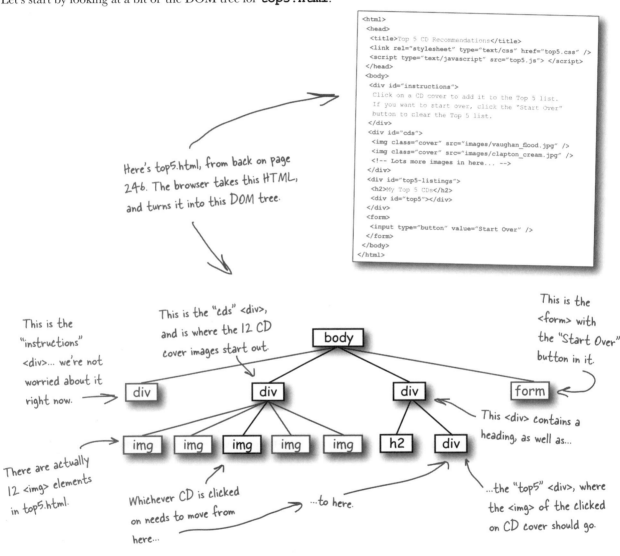

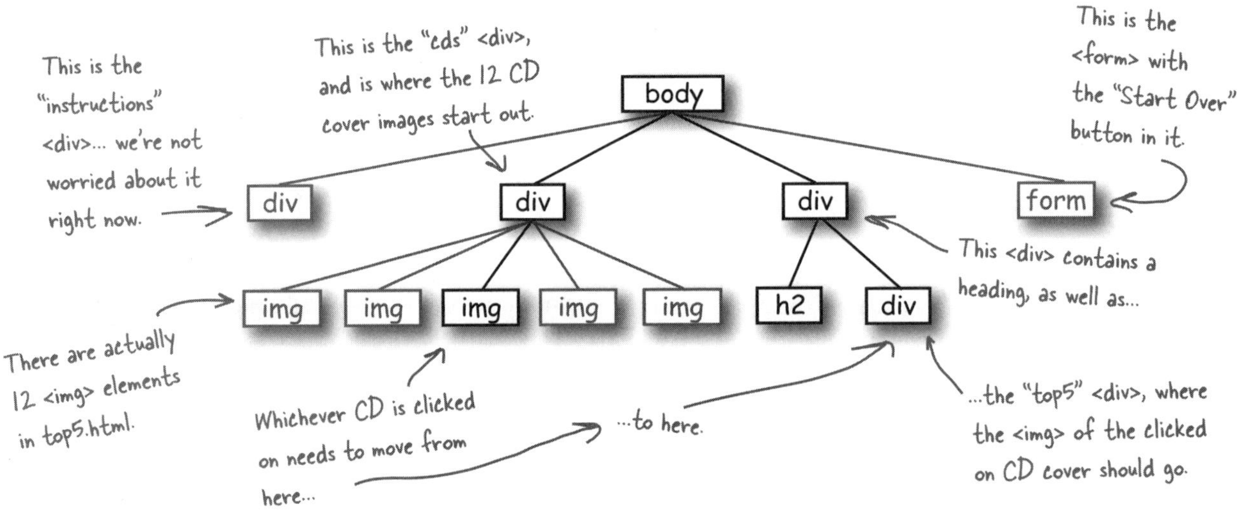

After addToTop5() runs...

When someone clicks on a CD cover image, **addToTop5()** will run. We want that JavaScript function to take the **<img>** element that was clicked on, and move it from the “cds” **<div>** to the “top5” **<div>**. Here’s what the end result should look like:

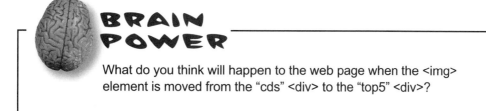

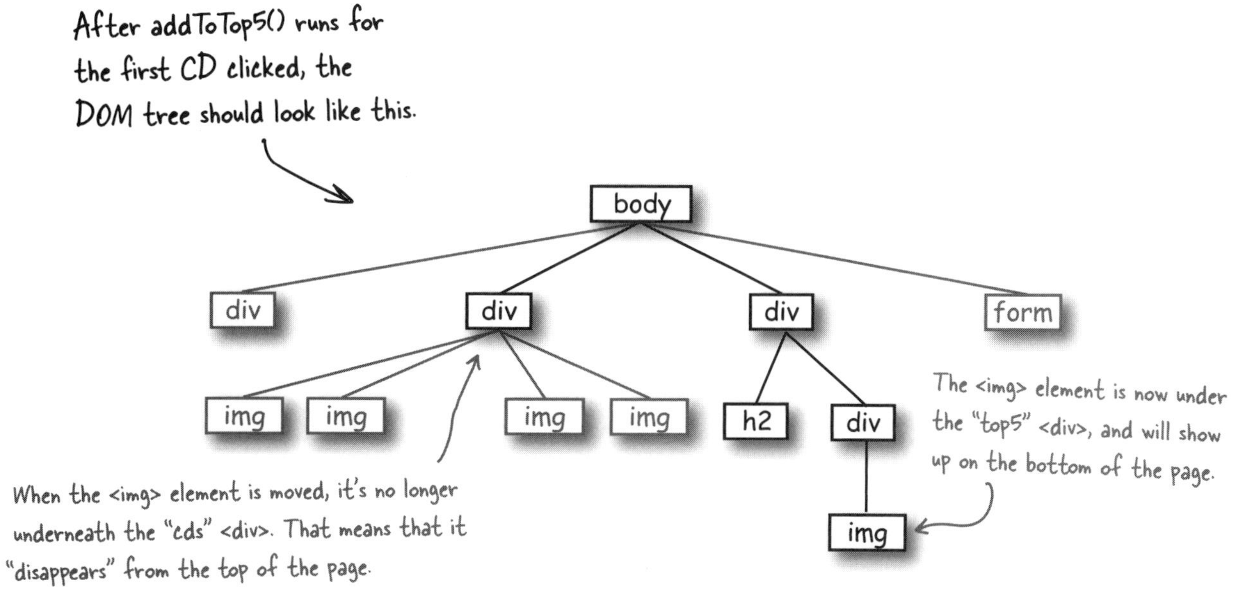

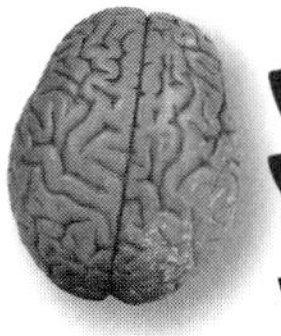

BRAIN POWER

What do you think will happen to the web page when the <img> element is moved from the “cds” <div> to the “top5” <div>?

Pay attention to "this"

The first thing we need to do is figure out which **<img>** was clicked on, so you can add the right CD cover to the "top5" **<div>**. JavaScript lets you know what part of the DOM tree called your function through a special keyword named **this**.

Take a look and see how the **this** keyword works:

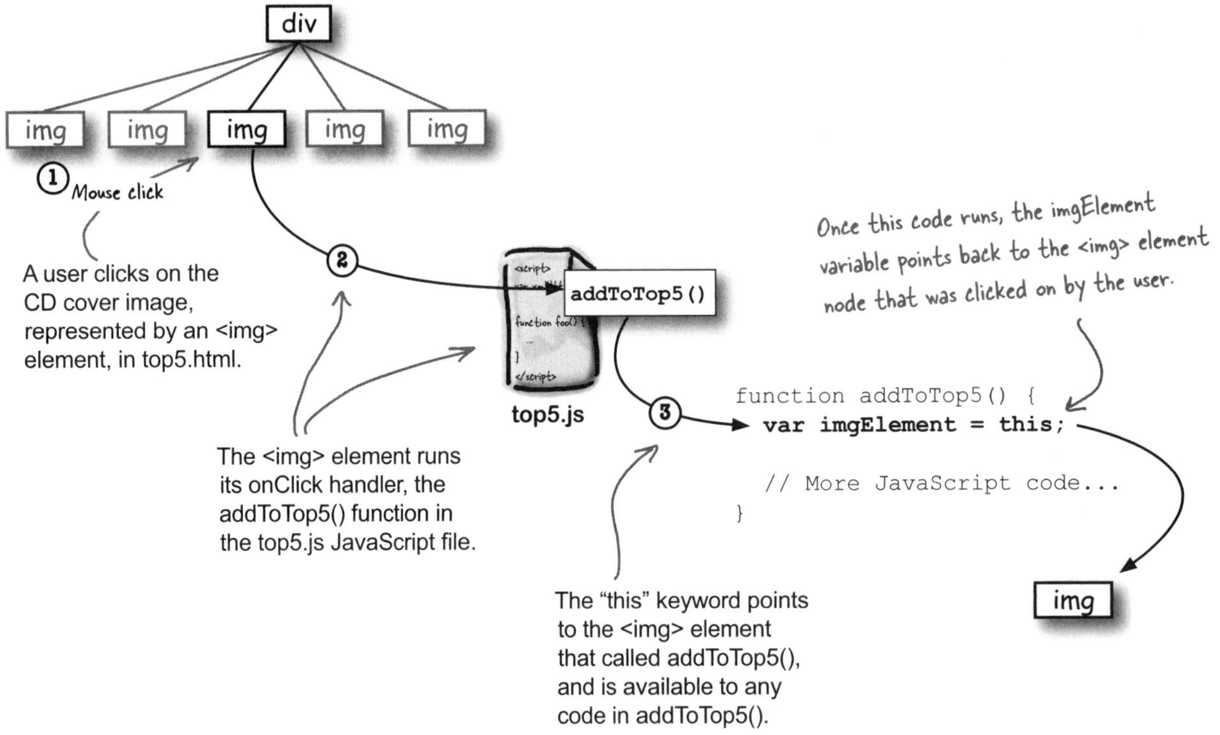

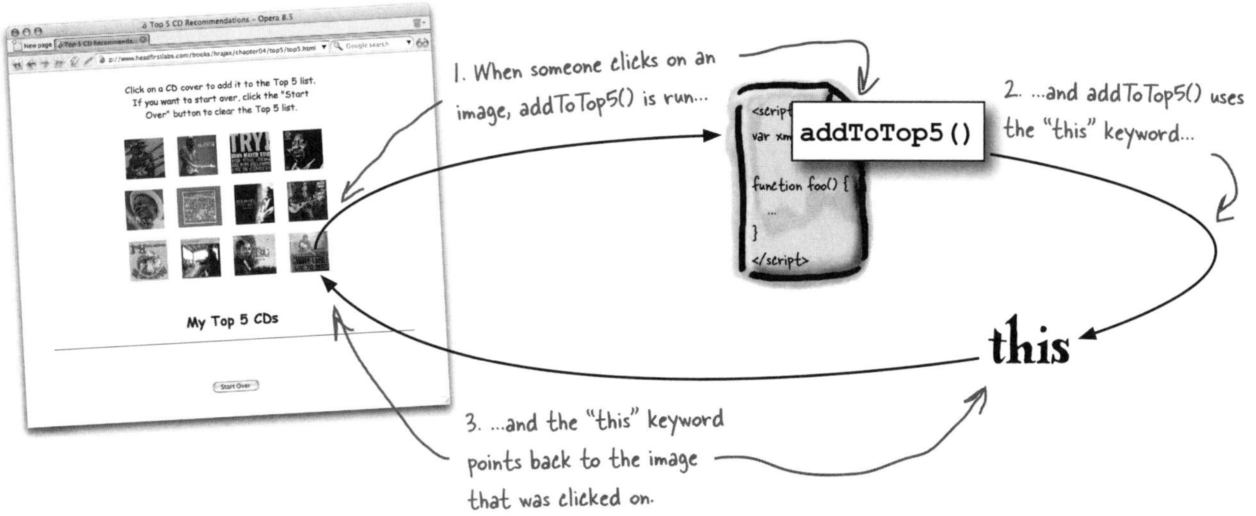

Finding the "top5" <div>

Next, let's get the "top5" **<div>** element from the browser's DOM tree. You'll need to add the **<img>** element that was clicked on to the "top5" **<div>**, and then remove the **<img>**'s **onClick** handler, so it no longer runs **addToTop5()** when it's clicked.

Now you've got the CD cover image and the "top5" <div> that you need to add the cover to.

```
function addToTop5() {
  var imgElement = this;
  var top5Element = document.getElementById("top5");
}
```

Create JS file | Add CD to Top 5 | Add CD rankings | Start over

Adding children to an element

Once you've got the CD cover **<img>** element, and the "top5" **<div>**, you need to add the **<img>** to that **<div>**. There are several ways you can add an element to another element:

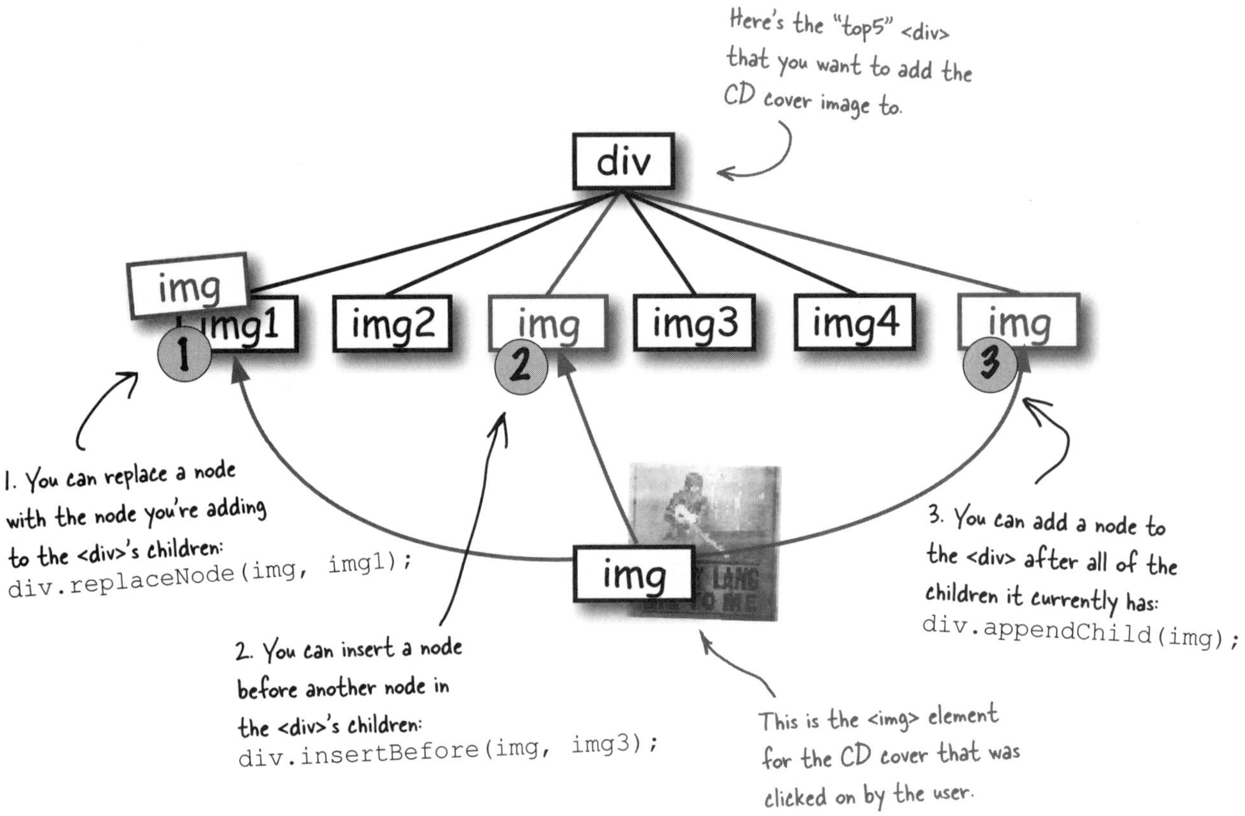

Which approach do you think we should use to add the CD cover to the "top5" <div>?

As you add CDs to the Top 5 list, you want to add newer CDs to the "end" of the list.

Back to event handlers

You're almost ready to write the code for **addToTop5()**... but there's one more detail you need to think about. Once you've moved the CD cover image down into the "top5" **<div>**, you've got to remove the event handler that runs **addToTop5()** when the cover is clicked on.

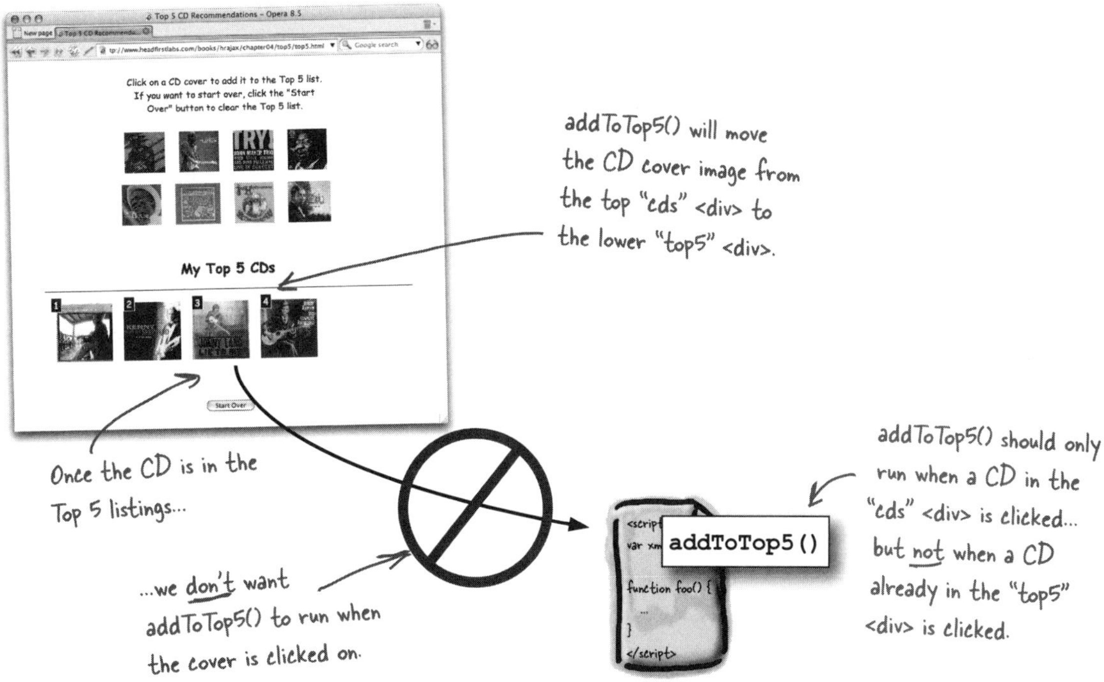

Remember how we added the event handler?

```
function addOnClickHandlers() {
  var cdsDiv = document.getElementById("cds");
  var cdImages = cdsDiv.getElementsByTagName("img");
  for (var i=0; i<cdImages.length; i++) {
    cdImages[i].onclick = addToTop5;
  }
}
```

This is the <img> element for the CD cover...

...and this is the event handler name.

Here's the event handler to run. You can remove this event handler by setting the handler property to null.

Code Magnets

You've learned a lot these last few pages, and now it's time to put all your new DOM and JavaScript tricks into action. Go ahead and finish off the addToTop5() function by pinning the code magnets into the blanks below. Be careful—you might not need all the code magnets.

```
function addToTop5() {
  var imgElement = ___________;
  var top5Element = document.getElementById(___________);

  top5Element.______________________________;
  imgElement.__________ = _______;
}
```

Here's where you add the <img> element to the "top5" <div>, using one of the methods you saw on the last page.

You need to remove the event handler from the CD cover once it's in the Top 5 listings.

Magnets:

- appendChild(imgElement)
- that
- onclick
- this
- insertBefore(imgElement)
- addToTop5
- "top5"
- imgElement
- top5Element
- replaceNode(imgElement)
- top5-listings
- null

Remember, null means "no value", or "remove any current value."

Testing addToTop5()

Be sure you've completed the Code Magnets exercise, and check your answers with ours on page 264. Make these changes to **top5.js**, and then load up **top5.html** into your web browser. Can you click on the CD covers? What happens when you do?

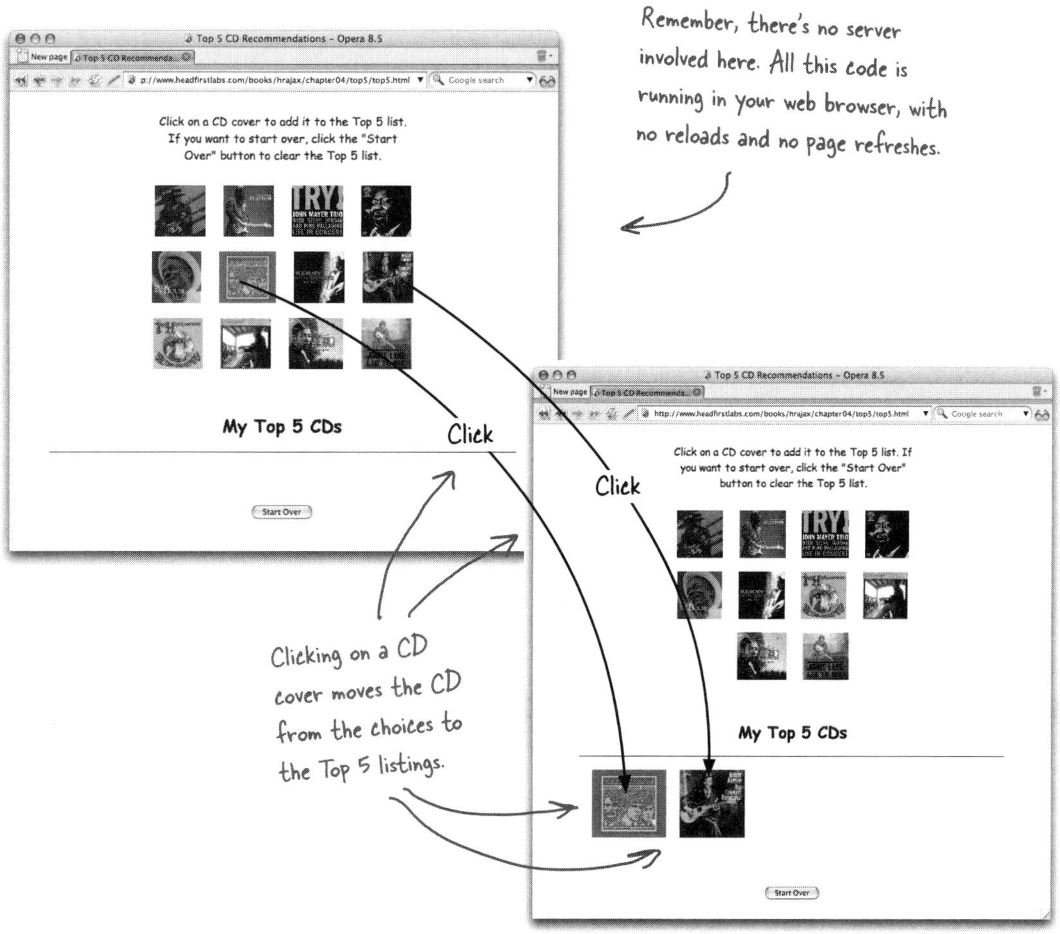
Remember, there's no server involved here. All this code is running in your web browser, with no reloads and no page refreshes.
Top 5 CD Recommendations - Opera 8.5
Click on a CD cover to add it to the Top 5 list. If you want to start over, click the "Start Over" button to clear the Top 5 list.
My Top 5 CDs
Start Over
Click
Click
Clicking on a CD cover moves the CD from the choices to the Top 5 listings.

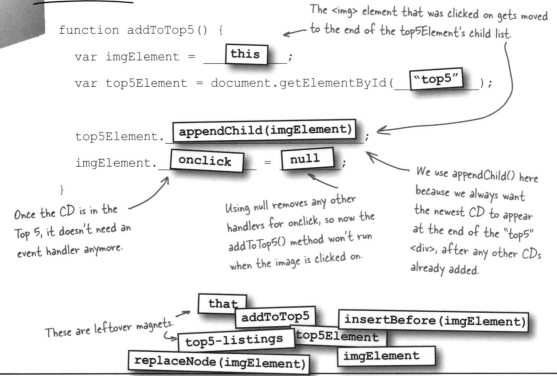

Code Magnets Solutions

Did you have any trouble with the Top 5 CDs test drive? If you did, make sure you put the code magnets in the right blanks, and update your JavaScript code to match.

```
function addToTop5() {
  var imgElement = this;
  var top5Element = document.getElementById("top5");

  top5Element.appendChild(imgElement);
  imgElement.onclick = null;
}
```

The <img> element that was clicked on gets moved to the end of the top5Element's child list.

Once the CD is in the Top 5, it doesn't need an event handler anymore.

Using null removes any other handlers for onclick, so now the addToTop5() method won't run when the image is clicked on.

We use appendChild() here because we always want the newest CD to appear at the end of the "top5" <div>, after any other CDs already added.

These are leftover magnets.

`that` `addToTop5` `insertBefore(imgElement)` `top5-listings` `top5Element` `replaceNode(imgElement)` `imgElement`

Hey, you forgot to show us something... where's the code that removes the CD from the top section when you put it down in the Top 5 listings?

An element can have only one parent

Take a close look at the code for **addToTop5()** so far. First, we get the **<img>** element for the CD cover, and then get a reference to the "top5" **<div>**. So far, no surprises, right?

Next, we take the **<img>**, and add it as a child of the "top5" **<div>**. At that point, the parent of the **<img>** is no longer the "cds" **<div>**... it's the "top5" **<div>**. And since elements have only one parent, it gets moved in the DOM tree:

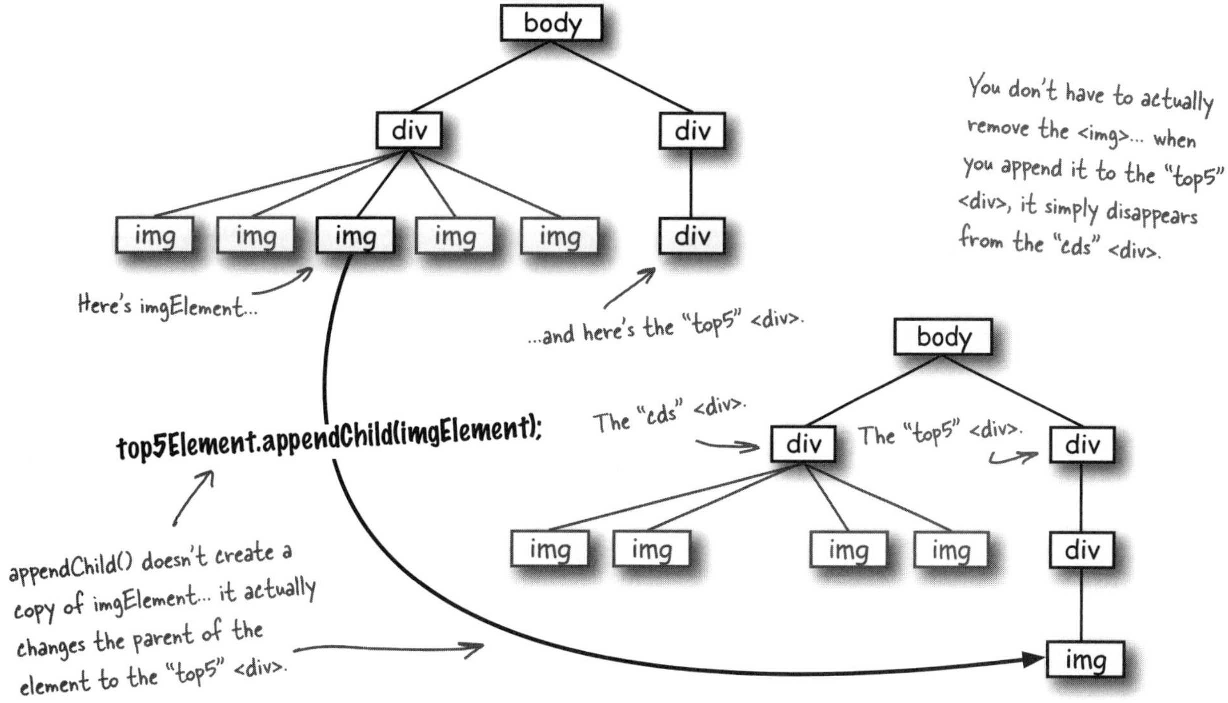

If you're feeling unsure about looping and checking an element's name, peek back at addOnClickHandlers() on page 254.

Exactly!

And now that you know how to loop through an element's child nodes and how to figure out an element's name, this should be pretty easy.

Let's add a new variable to our **addToTop5()** function and set it to the number of CDs in the top 5 listings:

```
function addToTop5() {
  var imgElement = this;
  var top5Element = document.getElementById("top5");
  var numCDs = 0;

  for (var i=0; i<top5Element.childNodes.length; i++) {
    if (top5Element.childNodes[i].nodeName.toLowerCase() == "img") {
      numCDs = numCDs + 1;
    }
  }

  /* Code to move a CD into the Top 5 listings is here */
}
```

Here's the new variable. Start it out at 0.

You need to check each child element of the "top5" <div>.

Just bump the counter up for each CD cover.

We loop through the top5 <div>'s children, and only count up <img> elements... remember, there could be text nodes with just spaces in them, so check each child to see if it's an <img>.

Adding the ranking number

Now that you know how many CDs there are in the Top 5, you can start adding a ranking number to each CD as it's added. Here's a look again at how we want the CD ranking to look.

More additions to our DOM tree

We need a text element for the ranking number. For the current ranking, we can just add one to **numCds**. But getting the formatting of the ranking isn't a JavaScript thing... we handle style with CSS, right?

Let's create a new **<span>** to put the ranking in, and then create some CSS to style the **<span>** just like we want it. So here's what we want the "top5" **<div>** part of the DOM tree to look like:

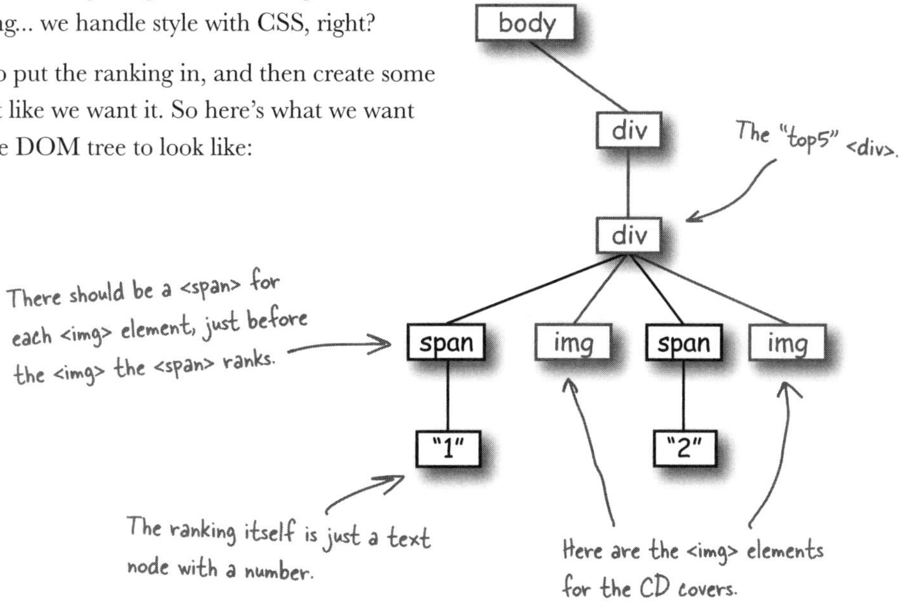

Create JS file | Add CD to Top 5 | Add CD rankings | Start over

What's left to do?

There are several things left to do in order to finish up **addToTop5()**. Let's figure out exactly what needs to be done, and then get to the code on the next page.

1. **Add a new CSS class for CD rankings**

   Here's the CSS you need to overlay the ranking on the CD cover image, and handle the white-on-black coloring. Add this CSS to your **top5.css** file:

```
.rank {
  position:         absolute;
  text-align:       center;
  top:              20px;
  font-size:        small;
  background-color: black;
  color:            white;
  border:           thin solid white;
  width:            20px;
  z-index:            99;
}
```

Add this CSS to your top5.css file before going on.

Let's call this class "rank", and set it up so that CD rankings will overlay the CD cover images with white-on-black text.

2. **Create a new <span> element and set up its CSS class**

This involves your top5.html file.

3. **Create a new text node and set its text to the CD ranking**

We've already got the number of CDs, so we just need to add one to that, and set that new number as the current CD's ranking.

The rest of this all applies to your addToTop5() JavaScript function.

4. **Add the text node to the <span>, and the <span> to the <div>**

This is just connecting the new nodes to the DOM tree, to make sure the CD ranking appears in the web page.

5. **Make sure only 5 CDs can be added to the Top 5 listings**

Since we have a count of the CDs, this is a simple check to make sure there aren't more than 5 at any time.

Just Do It

It's time to fire up your text editor and finish off addToTop5(). Your job is to take care of steps 2 through 5 listed on the last page by adding code to the addToTop5() function. Think you're ready for the challenge?

See if you can fill in all the missing code blanks. We've added some notes to help you out. Be sure to finish this exercise before turning the page.

```
function addToTop5() {
  var imgElement = this;
  var top5Element = document.getElementById("top5");
  var numCDs = 0;

  for (var i=0; i<top5Element.childNodes.length; i++) {
    if (top5Element.childNodes[i].nodeName.toLowerCase() == "img") {
      numCDs = numCDs + 1;
    }
  }
  if (________ >= ____) {
    alert("You already have 5 CDs. Click \"Start Over\" to try again.");
    return;
  }

  top5Element.appendChild(imgElement);
  imgElement.onclick = null;

  var newSpanElement = ___________.createElement(__________);
  _______________.className = "________";
  var newTextElement = document.________________(numCDs + 1);
  newSpanElement.______________(newTextElement);
  ______________.insertBefore(_______________, imgElement);
}
```

Make sure only 5 CDs can be added to the Top 5 listings.

You may have to flip way back to the first few pages of Chapter 4 if you get stuck on this one.

"className" is used to assign a CSS class to an element.

The text can go at the "end" of the <span>'s children (since there aren't any).

What should be the parent of the <span> element?

The first argument to insertBefore() is the node to insert.

Create JS file | Add CD to Top 5 | Add CD rankings | Start over

Completing addToTop5()

Here's the completed **addToTop5()** function. Make sure your answers match ours, and then add all of this new code to **top5.js**.

```
function addToTop5() {
  var imgElement = this;
  var top5Element = document.getElementById("top5");
  var numCDs = 0;

  for (var i=0; i<top5Element.childNodes.length; i++) {
    if (top5Element.childNodes[i].nodeName.toLowerCase() == "img") {
      numCDs = numCDs + 1;
    }
  }
  if (numCDs >= 5) {
    alert("You already have 5 CDs. Click \"Start Over\" to try again.");
    return;
  }

  top5Element.appendChild(imgElement);
  imgElement.onclick = null;

  var newSpanElement = document.createElement("span");
  newSpanElement.className = "rank";
  var newTextElement = document.createTextNode(numCDs + 1);
  newSpanElement.appendChild(newTextElement);
  top5Element.insertBefore(newSpanElement, imgElement);
}
```

Compare numCDs to 5 to prevent too many CDs from being added.

All the create methods are available through the document object.

This sets the "className" attribute of the <span>.

The text node should have the next CD ranking.

Just stick the text node at the end of <span>'s child nodes list.

The <span> goes before this CD's <img> element, under the "top5" <div>.

Testing the CD rankings (again)

Once you've finished up **addToTop5** in your JavaScript, fire up your web browser again. Load the Top 5 web page, and click on some CD covers. You should see rankings show up, overlaid on the top left corner of each CD cover. The absolute positioning in CSS makes sure these appear on top of the cover, adding a nice visual bit of eye candy to the page.

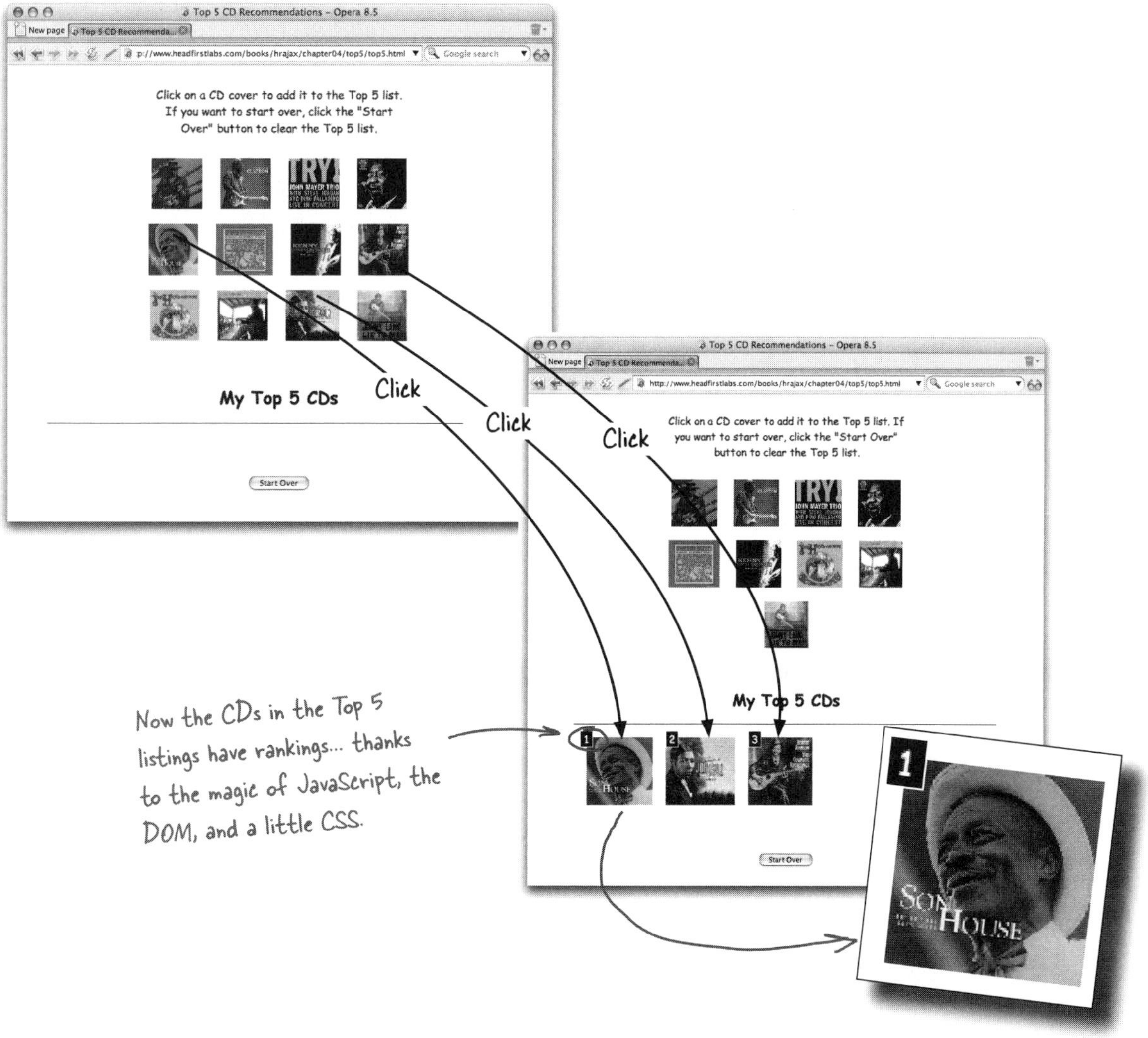
Top 5 CD Recommendations - Opera 8.5
Click on a CD cover to add it to the Top 5 list. If you want to start over, click the "Start Over" button to clear the Top 5 list.
My Top 5 CDs
Start Over
Click
Click
Click
Now the CDs in the Top 5 listings have rankings... thanks to the magic of JavaScript, the DOM, and a little CSS.

Just Do It

It's time to exercise your DOM skills one more time. The startOver() function needs to do several things:

1. Run through each of the children of the "top5" <div>.
2. Any CD cover images need to be added back to the top of the page.
3. And other elements, like <span>s, need to be removed from the page.

See if you can fill in the blanks, and finish off the JavaScript in top5.js.

```
function startOver() {
  var top5Element = document.______________("top5");
  var cdsElement = document.getElementById("______");
  while (_______________.hasChildNodes()) {
    var firstChild = top5Element.______________;
    if (firstChild.______________.toLowerCase() == "img") {
      _____________.appendChild(firstChild);
    } else {
      top5Element.removeChild(_________________);
    }
  }
  ______________________;
}
```

This one is a little tricky. Remember, once all the CD covers are back up top, you should be able to click on them and have addToTop5() get called. Maybe there's a function that does that?

Now you just need to update top5.html, and set the "Start Over" button to call your completed startOver() function:

```
<form><p>
 <input type="button" value="Start Over" onClick="startOver();" />
</p></form>
```

Always remember to connect your HTML buttons and elements to your JavaScript code.

A final test drive

Type in the JavaScript for **`startOver()`** from the last page, and don't forget to add the **`onClick`** handler to your HTML's **`<input>`** button. Then take the Top 5 CD listings page for a final test drive. You should be able to click on CD covers, add them to the Top 5 listings (along with a nice overlapping ranking), remove all the CDs by clicking "Start Over", and then do it all over again.

Top 5 CD Recommendations - Opera 8.5
New page
Top 5 CD Recommenda...
tp://www.headfirstlabs.com/books/hrajax/chapter04/top5/top5.html
Google search
Click on a CD cover to add it to the Top 5 list.
If you want to start over, click the "Start Over" button to clear the Top 5 list.
My Top 5 CDs
1
2
3
4
Start Over

Country blues? Electric guitars? The old Delta or the back alleys in Texas... pick your favorites.

The Great Chapter 4 Coding Challenge

Write a killer web application that uses the Document Object Model to create a dynamic user interface, without writing any Ajax code.

Remember this? You just built a slick web app, without a single line of asynchronous JavaScript. Nice job!

Don't think we've left asynchronous programming altogether... we're getting ready to dive back in as soon as you turn over to Chapter 5.

Check it out for yourself!

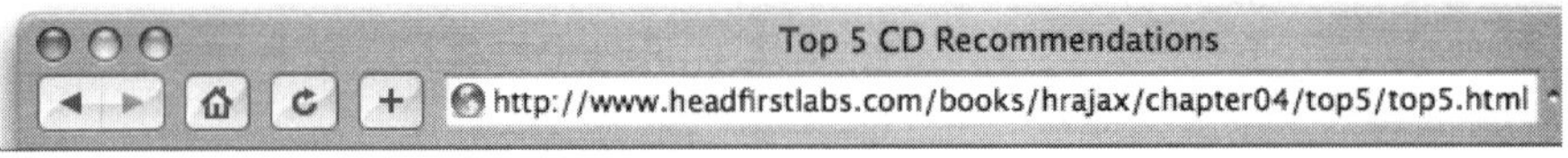

60 Second Review

- The browser represents the HTML, CSS, and JavaScript that makes up a web page as a tree full of objects, using the Document Object Model, or DOM.
- You can view and change the DOM using JavaScript code. Changes you make to the DOM are automatically reflected in the web page that the browser is displaying.
- You can use the JavaScript document object to access the browser's DOM tree for the current web page.
- You can use the DOM from any web application, not just asynchronous ones.
- A DOM tree is made up of different types of nodes: elements nodes, attribute notes, and text nodes.
- Element nodes can have only a single parent. If you change an element's parent, or add the element as the child of another node, you are moving the element in the DOM tree.
- You can add CSS styles and JavaScript event handlers to DOM nodes using JavaScript code.

Just Do It Solutions

It's time to exercise your DOM skills one more time. The startOver() function needs to do several things:

1. Run through each of the children of the "top5" <div>.
2. Any CD cover images need to be added back to the top of the page.
3. And other elements, like <span>s, need to be removed from the page.

```
function startOver() {
  var top5Element = document.getElementById("top5");
  var cdsElement = document.getElementById("cds");
  while (top5Element.hasChildNodes()) {
    var firstChild = top5Element.firstChild;
    if (firstChild.nodeName.toLowerCase() == "img") {
      cdsElement.appendChild(firstChild);
    } else {
      top5Element.removeChild(firstChild);
    }
  }
  addOnClickHandlers();
}
```

Start out by getting the two <div>s you'll need to work with.

Keep working on this <div>'s children until none are left.

If the node is an <img> element, add it back to the top of the page...

...if it's a <span>, or whitespace, or anything else, just remove it from the page.

This calls the addOnClickHandlers() function you wrote earlier, and adds event handlers back to all the CD cover <img> elements.

5 POST Requests

Saying More with POST

This is what you've been waiting for. You asked for it, and now you're going to get it: we're finally going to **ditch send(null)**, and learn how to **send more data** to a server. It will take a little extra work on your part, but by the time you're finished with this chapter, you'll be saying a lot more than "no data" to the server in your asynchronous requests. So fasten your seatbelts, and let's take a cruise through the land of content types and request headers; **we're in POST-country** now.

Repeat business rocks

Remember all the work you did on Break Neck Pizza? Well, it seems like everyone's been loving the Ajax version of the pizza order form. In fact, Break Neck has a few new features they want to add, and they're depending on you once again. Let's see what they need.

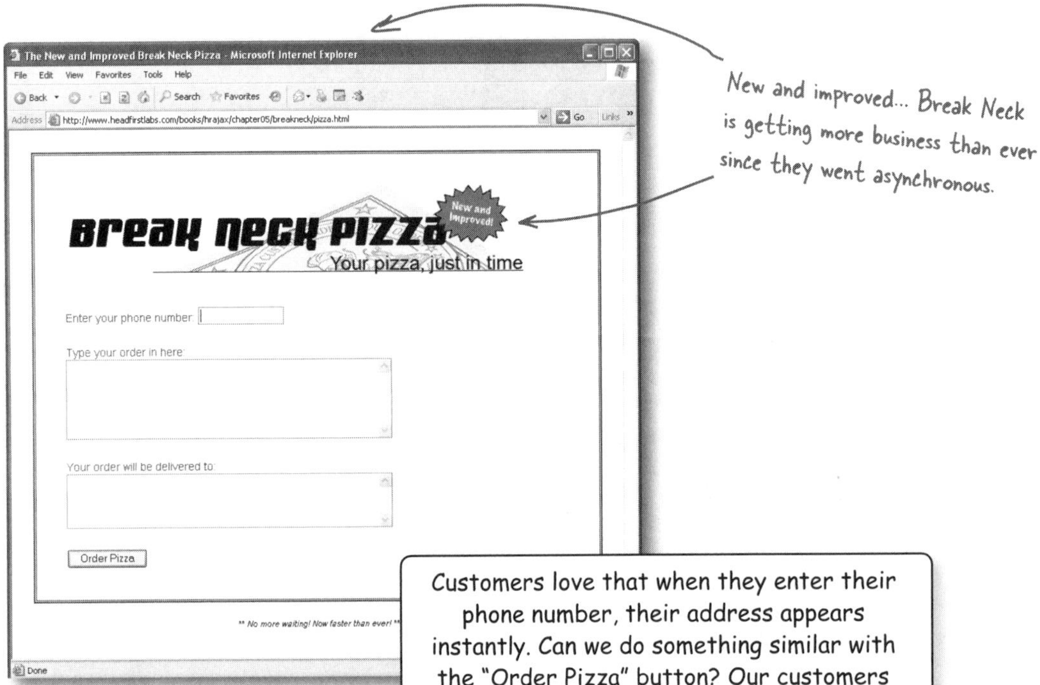
The New and Improved Break Neck Pizza - Microsoft Internet Explorer
http://www.headfirstlabs.com/books/hfajax/chapter05/breakneck/pizza.html
Break Neck Pizza
New and Improved!
Your pizza, just in time
Enter your phone number:
Type your order in here:
Your order will be delivered to:
Order Pizza
** No more waiting! Now faster than ever! **
New and improved... Break Neck is getting more business than ever since they went asynchronous.

Customers love that when they enter their phone number, their address appears instantly. Can we do something similar with the "Order Pizza" button? Our customers just hate waiting around for *anything*!

Submitting a form with Ajax

Break Neck doesn't seem to be asking for anything that complicated. Let's see if we can convert the Break Neck pizza form submission into an asynchronous request. Here's what you'll need to do:

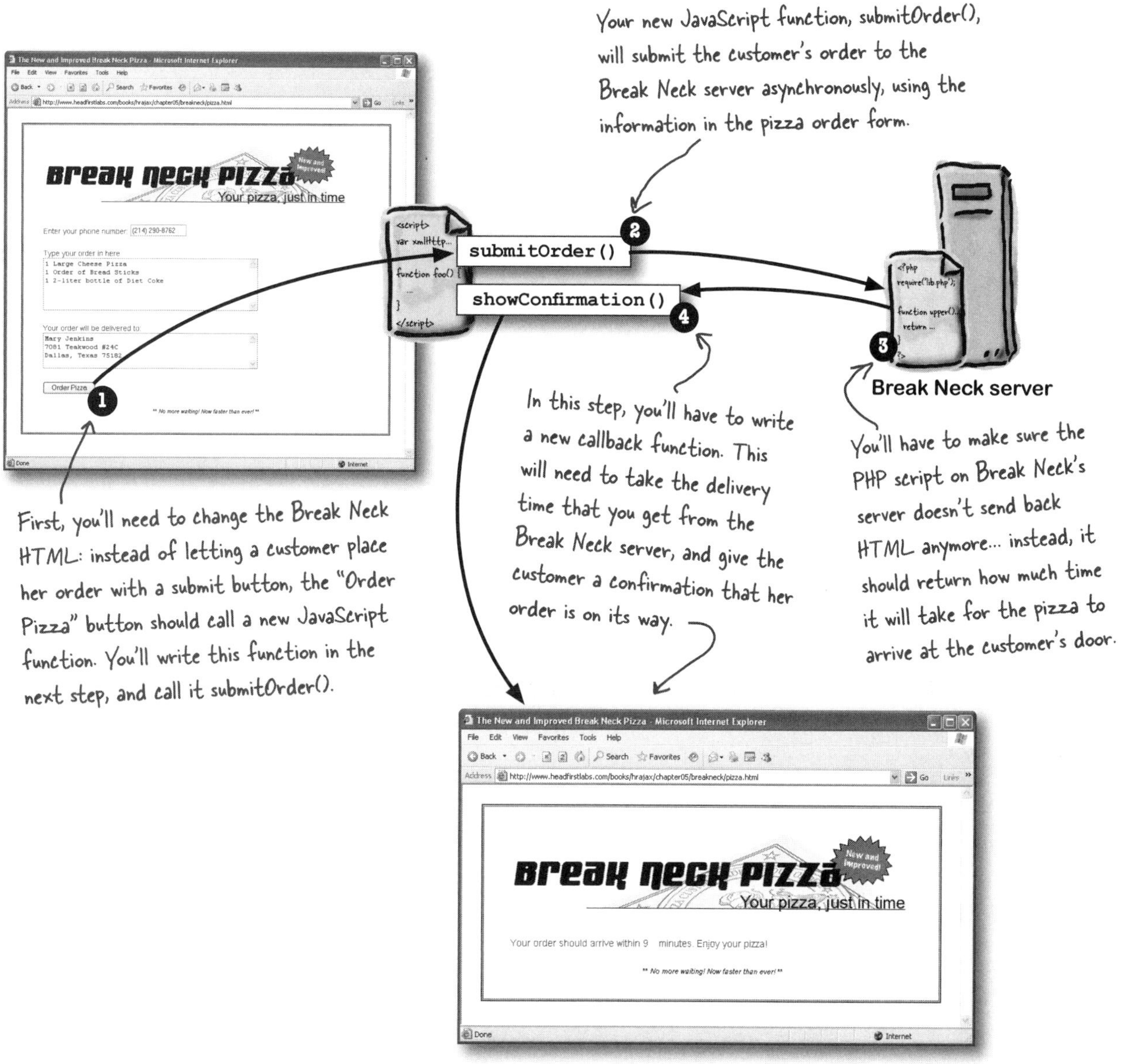

Your new JavaScript function, submitOrder(), will submit the customer's order to the Break Neck server asynchronously, using the information in the pizza order form.
submitOrder()
showConfirmation()
Break Neck server
First, you'll need to change the Break Neck HTML: instead of letting a customer place her order with a submit button, the "Order Pizza" button should call a new JavaScript function. You'll write this function in the next step, and call it submitOrder().
In this step, you'll have to write a new callback function. This will need to take the delivery time that you get from the Break Neck server, and give the customer a confirmation that her order is on its way.
You'll have to make sure the PHP script on Break Neck's server doesn't send back HTML anymore... instead, it should return how much time it will take for the pizza to arrive at the customer's door.
Your order should arrive within 9 minutes. Enjoy your pizza!
** No more waiting! Now faster than ever! **

1. Update the Break Neck HTML

First, we need to change Break Neck's HTML so that it no longer submits the form when a customer clicks "Order Pizza". Let's take a look at the Break Neck order form, and make a few changes:

```
<body onLoad="document.forms[0].reset();">
 <div id="main-page">
  <p><img src="breakneck-logo_new.gif" alt="Break Neck Pizza" /></p>
  <form id="order-form" method="POST" action="placeOrder.php">
   <p>Enter your phone number:
    <input type="text" size="14"
           name="phone" id="phone" onChange="getCustomerInfo();" />
   </p>
   <p>Type your order in here: <br />
   <textarea name="order" rows="6" cols="50" id="order">
     </textarea></p>
   <p>Your order will be delivered to: <br />
   <textarea name="address" rows="4" cols="50" id="address">
     </textarea></p>
   <p><input type="submit" value="Order Pizza" /></p>
   <p><input type="button" value="Order Pizza"
             onClick="submitOrder();" /></p>
  </form>
  <p class="tagline">** No more waiting! Now faster than ever! **</p>
 </div>
</body>
```

(In the listing, `method="POST" action="placeOrder.php"` and the line `<p><input type="submit" value="Order Pizza" /></p>` are crossed out; `type="button"` and `onClick="submitOrder();"` are highlighted.)

The <form> element no longers needs the "action" or "method" attributes.

Here's the old version of the submit button.

This button can change from a "submit" type to a "button" type.

Instead of submitting the form, clicking "Order Pizza" should run the JavaScript function you'll be writing next.

2. Send the order to the server

Next on the Break Neck task list is writing the submitOrder() JavaScript function. This function needs to get the customer's phone number, address, and pizza order from the order form, and send them to the placeOrder.php script on the Break Neck server. The callback function you'll write will be named showConfirmation(), so be sure to tell the browser to run that function when it gets a response from the server.

And, to add a little twist to this puzzle, you can use each code magnet as many times as you need... or not at all. You may also have to use more than one magnet on the same line.

```
function submitOrder() {
  var phone = ________________________("phone").________;
  var ________ = ________.getElementById("________").value;
  var order = _________.getElementById("order").________;
  var _____ = "placeOrder.php?phone=" + _______(phone) +
                        "&address=" + _______(address) +
                        "&order=" + ________(order);
  url = ____ + "&dummy=" + ______________________;
  ___________.open("GET", _____, ______);
  request.____________________ = ________________;
  request.send(______);
}
```

showConfirmation
escape
getTime
getElementById
order
change
value
address
state
document
onClick
doc
submit
url
esc
new Date
request
()
onready
null
submitOrder
.
true

*Hint: The same person, with the same phone and address, might place the exact same order more than once.

Code Magnets Solutions

Next on the Break Neck task list is writing the submitOrder() JavaScript function. Here's where you should have placed the magnets to get this function working. Be sure you don't have any extra parentheses on your callback functions, and double-check all your dots between terms like "document" and "getElementById".

```
function submitOrder() {
  var phone = document.getElementById("phone").value;
  var address = document.getElementById("address").value;
  var order = document.getElementById("order").value;
  var url = "placeOrder.php?phone=" + escape(phone) +
                       "&address=" + escape(address) +
                       "&order=" + escape(order);
  url = url + "&dummy=" + new Date().getTime();
  request.open("GET", url, true);
  request.onreadystatechange = showConfirmation;
  request.send(null);
}
```

Did you get this? We want to prevent browsers like Opera and IE from caching a response, in case customers want to order the same thing more than once.

Make sure you didn't add any parentheses at the end of the name of your callback function.

Just Do It

It's time to make Break Neck an even better place for ordering pizza. Look in the **chapter05/breakneck/** folder in the book's examples, and you'll find the latest version of the Break Neck app, complete with HTML, CSS, and PHP. You'll need to open up **pizza.html**, and change the form to run **submitOrder()** when "Order Pizza" is clicked, instead of submitting directly to the **placeOrder.php** script on the Break Neck server.

As long as you're making improvements to Break Neck, go ahead and move all of the JavaScript out of **pizza.html**. You can use **ajax.js**, which you wrote in Chapter 3, for creating the request object. Then, create a new JavaScript file called **pizza.js**. Move your Break Neck functions—**getCustomerInfo()**, **updatePage()**, and **submitOrder()**—into this file. Don't forget to add **<script>** elements that link to these files in your HTML!

Once you've done all of this, flip to the back of this chapter, and check page 314 to make sure your files look the same as ours do. Once you've got that done, you're ready for Step 3.

Be sure you uses the version of ajax.js you created with just one request object... we don't need two request objects in this chapter.

HTML Form | **Send Order** | **PHP Script** | **Callback**

3. Update placeOrder.php

You're moving along pretty quickly now! Let's get our old pal Frank to update his PHP script. It doesn't need to send us back a bunch of HTML anymore.

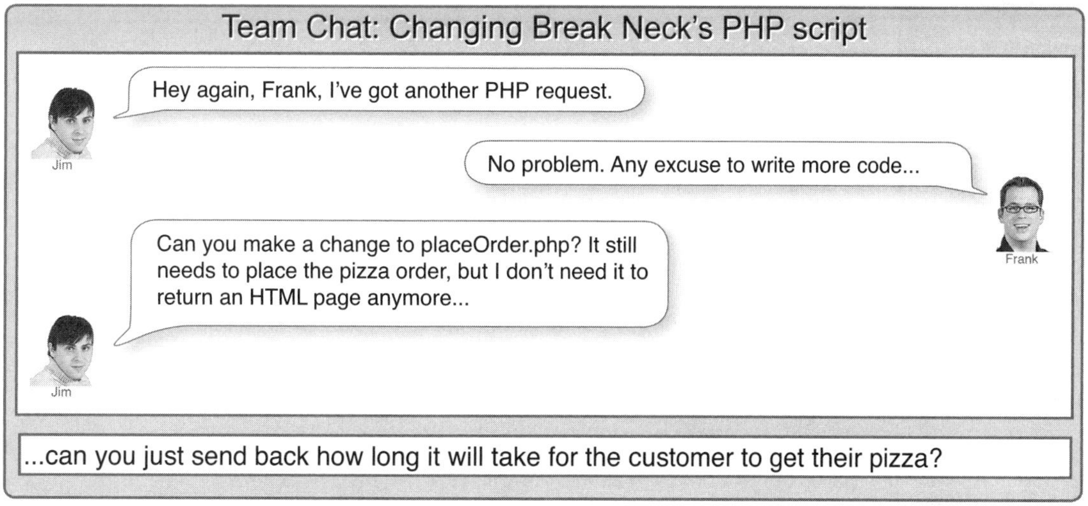

PHP ...at a glance

Frank hardly took any time in updating the placeOrder.php script. It still places an order, but now it doesn't need to return any HTML. Instead, it just gives an estimate for when the pizza will arrive at the customer's front door.

```
<?php

include("order.php");
include("delivery.php");

// Error checking
$order = $_REQUEST['order'];
$address = $_REQUEST['address'];
if (strlen($order) <= 0) {
  header("Status: No order was received.", true, 400);
  echo " ";
  exit;
}

if (strlen($address) <= 0) {
  header("Status: No address was received.", true, 400);
  echo " ";
  exit;
}

// Place the order
$pizzaOrder = new PizzaOrder($order, $address);
$pizzaOrder->cookOrder();
$pizzaOrder->prepOrder();

// Deliver the order
$delivery = new Delivery($pizzaOrder);
$delivery->deliver();
$deliveryTime = $delivery->getDeliveryEstimate();

echo $deliveryTime;
?>
```

Frank's using a couple of other PHP files to handle order and delivery specifics. We won't look at those, but all these files are included in the book's downloadable examples.

These just get the request data.

Make sure we got an order that isn't an empty string.

Some web browsers, like Safari, report a status code of "undefined" unless there is some response from the server. By sending a blank reponse, the correct status code will be reported by those browsers.

This makes sure an address was entered.

This sends a header back to the browser with an error message...

...and an HTTP status code indicating that an error occurred.

The order is created, cooked, and then prepped for delivery.

The entire order is sent to the delivery boy, who takes care of getting it to the customer.

Finally, the script finds out how long it will take for the pizza to arrive, and passes that back to the browser.

When things go wrong

There are lots of things that can go wrong when a customer uses the Break Neck web app. Below are several problems that might come up when a customer uses the pizza order form. In each of the blanks below, write down what you think will happen when each error occurs.

Walt mistypes his phone number into the Break Neck order form, and then enters his address and order manually. ____________________________

Maylee enters her phone number and pizza order, but accidentally changes the street number in the address field. ____________________________

Susan enters her phone number, but accidentally clicks "Order Pizza" before she enters her pizza order. ____________________________

→ Answers on page 291.

4. Write the callback function

Now that the Break Neck PHP script just returns a delivery estimate, we can write a new JavaScript function to display this to the customer. Let's figure out exactly what we need to do.

Here's the main <div> for the page, with an id of "main-page".

What we have: An HTML page with a main <div>, and a <form> within that <div> for taking orders.

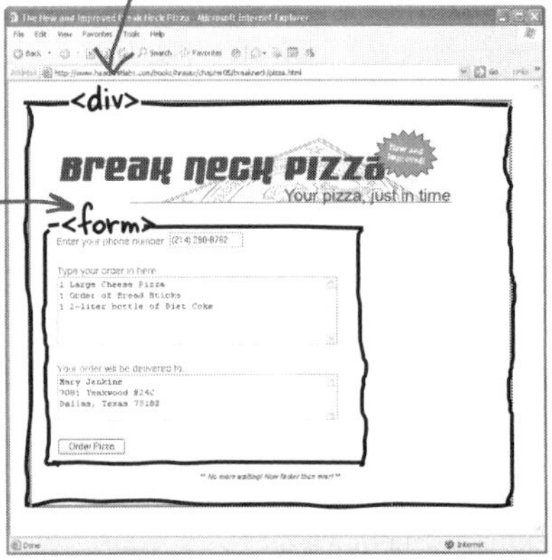

The <form> has an id, "order-form", that we can use to look the <form> element up in the DOM.

What we want: An HTML page with a main <div>, and an order confirmation within that <div>.

This is the same <div> as in the original order form...

...but we've replaced the <form> with a text order confirmation.

What we need to do: Replace the <form> in the main <div> with the order confirmation.

1. Get a reference to the <div> in the page, using its "id" attribute.
2. Get a reference to the <form> in the page, using its "id" attribute.
3. Create a new <p> element, and add a text confirmation of the order to the <p>.
4. Replace the <form> element with the new <p> element (and its text node).

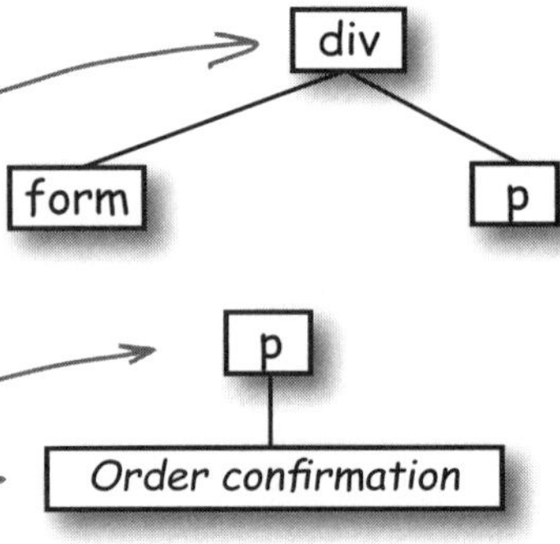

Let's look at this step in a little more detail.

The DOM is connected to what a customer sees

Let's take a closer look at exactly what happens when you replace an element in the DOM:

Here's the part of the DOM tree that we're working on.

Here's what's going on in the browser as we change the DOM tree.

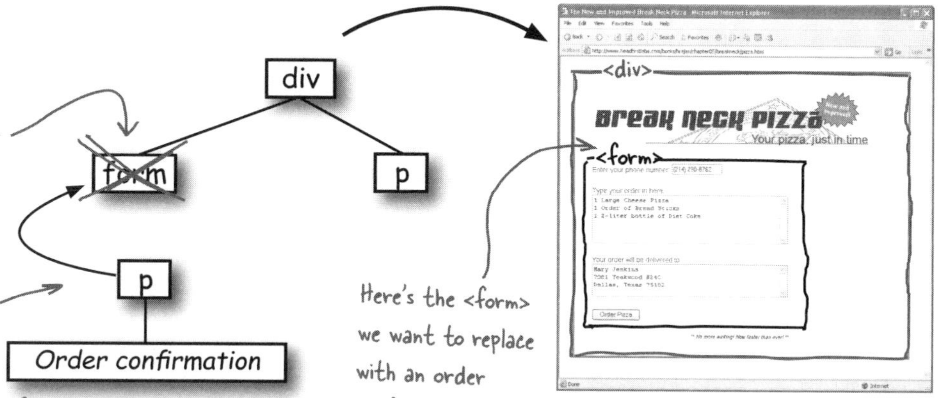

We need to replace the <form> element from the DOM tree...

...and add the <p> in the place of the <form> element.

Here's the <form> we want to replace with an order confirmation.

This won't show up in the web browser until you've added it in to the DOM tree.

Here's the DOM tree after you've replaced the **<form>** element with the new **<p>** element...

Now the <form> is nowhere to be seen. Perfect!

At the end of this process, here's what the DOM tree should look like.

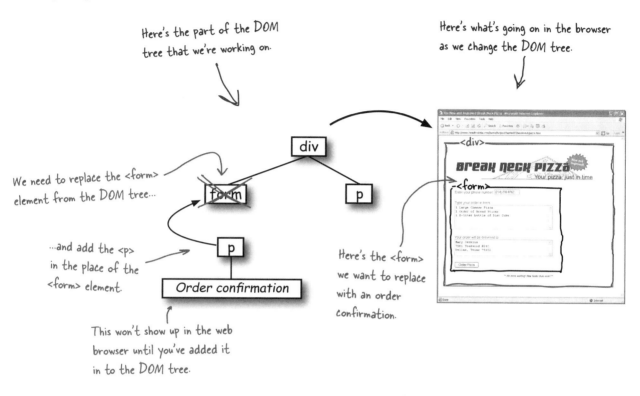

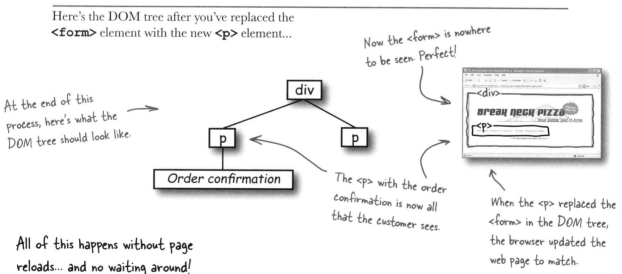

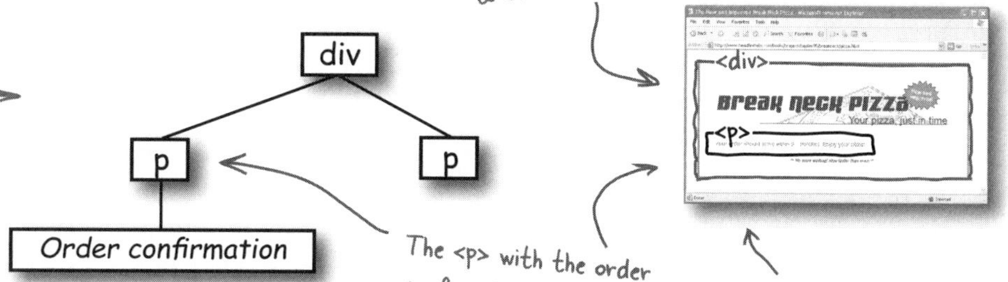

The <p> with the order confirmation is now all that the customer sees.

When the <p> replaced the <form> in the DOM tree, the browser updated the web page to match.

All of this happens without page reloads... and no waiting around!

Just Do It

It's time to take everything you've been learning in these last few chapters, and put it all to work. Below is the **`showConfirmation()`** callback function for the new and improved Break Neck pizza order form. Your job is to complete the code by filling in all the blanks. You'll need to use what you know about asynchronous requests, HTML forms, the DOM, and error handling to get this function working.

```
function showConfirmation() {
  if (request.___________ == _____) {
    if (request.___________ == _____) {
      var response = request.______________;
      // Locate form on page
      var mainDiv = document.getElementById("___________");
      var orderForm = document.getElementById("___________");

      // Create some confirmation text
      pElement = document.______________("p");
      textNode = document.______________(
        "Your order should arrive within " +
        __________ +
        " minutes. Enjoy your pizza!");
      pElement.___________(textNode);

      // Replace the form with the confirmation
      mainDiv.replaceChild(___________, __________);
    } else {
      alert("Error! Request status is " + request._________);
    }
  }
}
```

This callback will get run once the server places the order, and responds with a delivery time.

*HINT: replaceChild() takes two arguments: the first argument is the new node, and the second argument is the node to be replaced.

Once you think you've got this function finished, compare your answers with ours on page 290. Then add this code to your pizza.js file, and let's take Break Neck for a test drive.

Test driving Break Neck

Make sure you've checked your answers to the Just Do It exercise on the last page with ours, and made these changes to your **pizza.js** JavaScript file. Then, load up **pizza.html**, and let's see how things look.

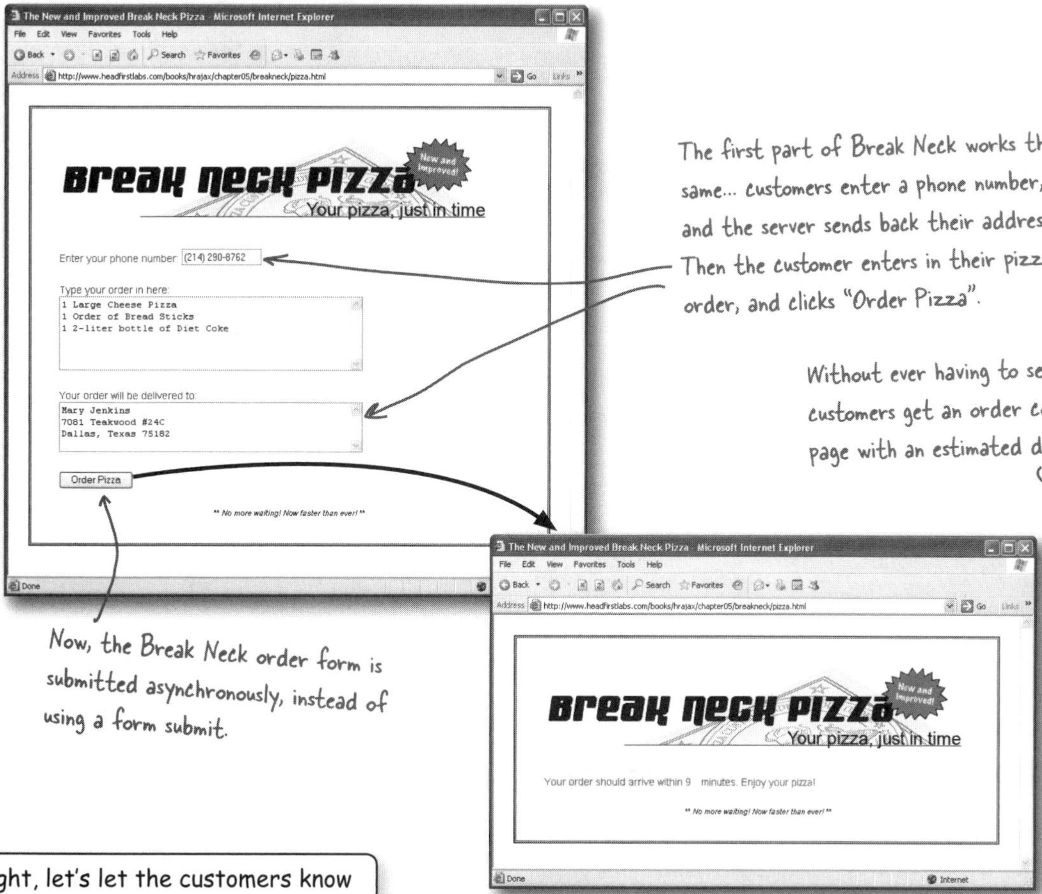

The first part of Break Neck works the same... customers enter a phone number, and the server sends back their address. Then the customer enters in their pizza order, and clicks "Order Pizza".

Without ever having to see a page reload, customers get an order confirmation page with an estimated delivery time.

Now, the Break Neck order form is submitted asynchronously, instead of using a form submit.

Alright, let's let the customers know we've made some improvements!

Not so fast, Alex...

Just Do It Solutions

Below is the completed **showConfirmation()** callback function; make sure your answers match up with ours... and make sure you understand all this code.

```
function showConfirmation() {
  if (request.readyState == 4) {
    if (request.status == 200) {
      var response = request.responseText;
      // Locate form on page
      var mainDiv = document.getElementById("main-page");
      var orderForm = document.getElementById("order-form");

      // Create some confirmation text
      pElement = document.createElement("p");
      textNode = document.createTextNode(
        "Your order should arrive within " +
        response +
        " minutes. Enjoy your pizza!");
      pElement.appendChild(textNode);

      // Replace the form with the confirmation
      mainDiv.replaceChild(pElement, orderForm);
    } else {
      alert("Error! Request status is " + request.status);
    }
  }
}
```

Be sure you check the ready state before checking the request's status.

Remember, this is run after the server places the customer's pizza order. The response from the server will be the estimated time until the pizza is delivered.

The request's responseText gives us the delivery time estimate.

Here, we get a reference to the <form> element node.

Next, use the DOM to create some new text for a <p> element.

Don't forget to add the text node to the <p> element.

The first argument is the new <p> element, and the second argument is the <form> to replace.

If the PHP script sends back an error code, this will print that code out for the customer to see.

When things go wrong *Solutions*

So what do you think went wrong in each of the cases below? See how your answers compared with ours:

Walt mistypes his phone number into the Break Neck order form, and then enters his address and order manually.

As long as Walt typed his address correctly, there won't be a problem. He'll get his pizza.

This really isn't an error at all.

Maylee enters her phone number and pizza order, but accidentally changes the street number in the address field.

Alex will end up delivering the pizza to the wrong address! Nothing we can do about this...

There's not much we can do to prevent this.

Susan enters her phone number, but accidentally clicks "Order Pizza" before she enters her pizza order.

The pizza form will show an alert box with the error code returned from placeOrder.php, which is "400".

In this case, the status code is not "200", so the "else" block of code in showConformation() gets run...

...and the user gets a really useless error message from the web form. Who's going to know what error code "400" means?

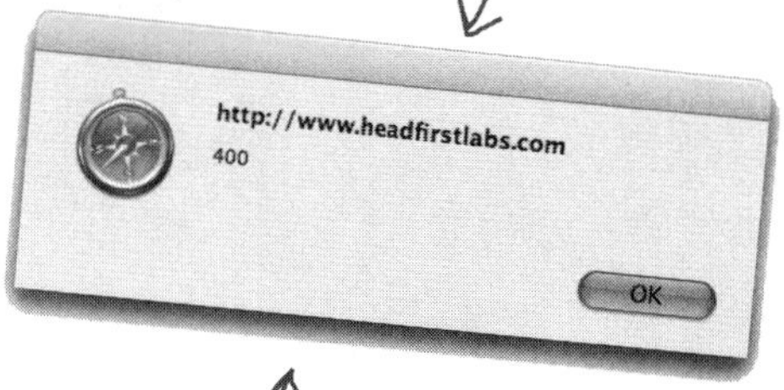

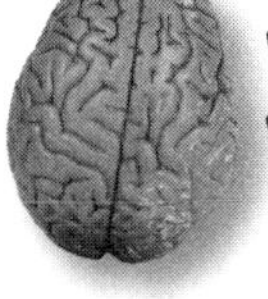

BRAIN POWER

Take a look at the last error, when placeOrder.php returns an error status code to the browser. Is there anything you could do to make the error message that the customer sees any more helpful?

Wait a second... doesn't placeOrder.php return an error message along with any error status codes? If we show that error message to the customer, they'll know what went wrong.

Error messages are a good thing

Flip back to the **`placeOrder.php`** script on page 284, and look at those lines at the top that check and make sure the customer's address and pizza order were received. If there's a problem, the script returns a status code of "400" along with an error message, and stops processing the customer's order.

But, our JavaScript callback, **`showConfirmation()`**, doesn't check for an error message from the script; it just shows the request object's HTTP status code if it's not 200. That's not very helpful...

The PHP code creates a new response header:

```
if (strlen($order) <= 0) {
  header("Status: No order was received.", true, 400);
  exit;
}
if (strlen($address) <= 0) {
  header("Status: No address was received.", true, 400);
  exit;
}
```

"Status" becomes the name of the response header sent back to the browser.

Everything after "Status:" becomes part of the message returned as the value of the response header.

This sends a status code of "400", and "true" means to replace any existing response headers with the same type; in this case, that's "Status".

The server talks back

Anytime the server sends a response to your request, it can give you information about its response using **response headers**.

The server provides the web browser information about a response using response headers.

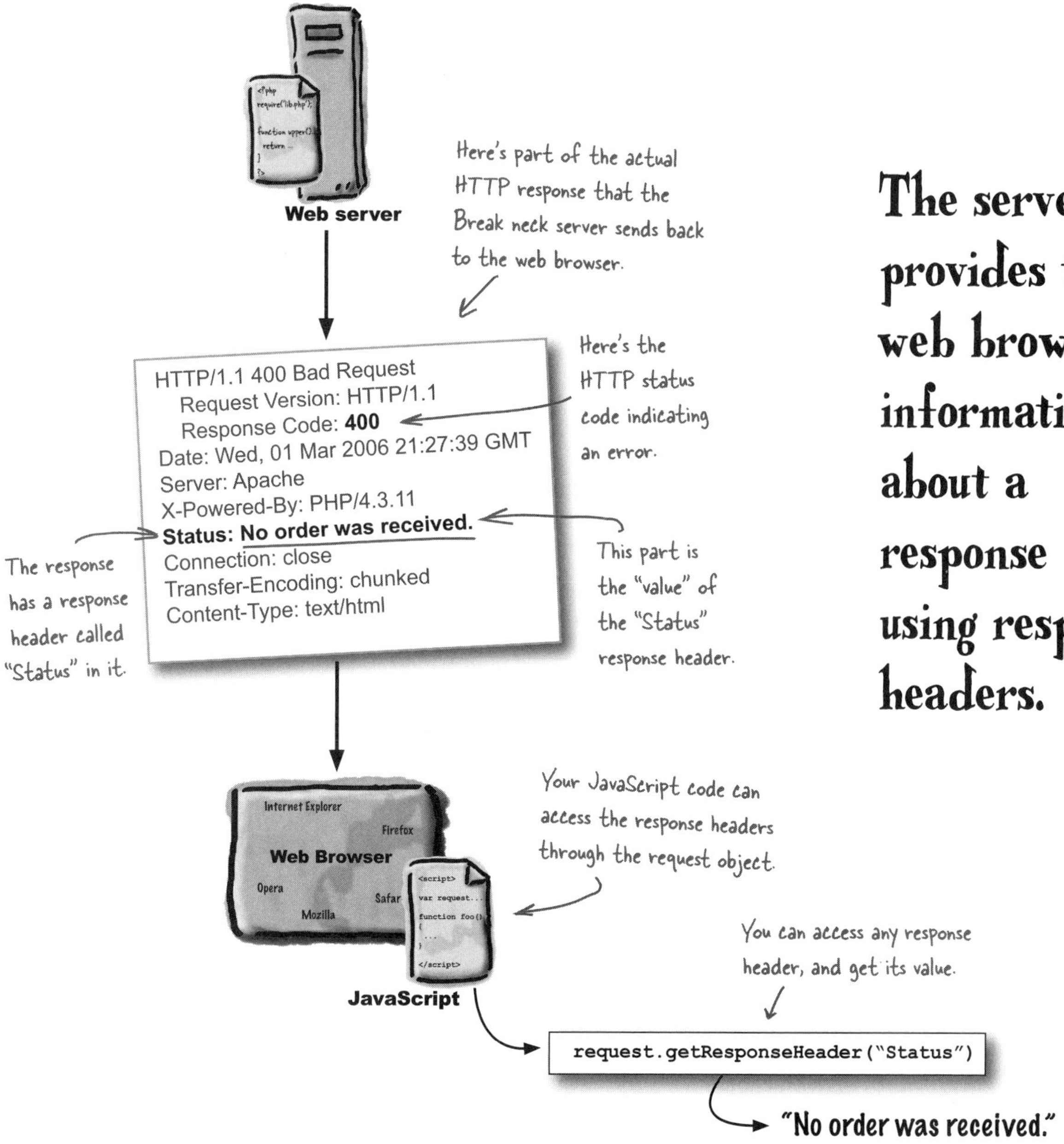

Web server
Here's part of the actual HTTP response that the Break neck server sends back to the web browser.
HTTP/1.1 400 Bad Request
Request Version: HTTP/1.1
Response Code: 400
Date: Wed, 01 Mar 2006 21:27:39 GMT
Server: Apache
X-Powered-By: PHP/4.3.11
Status: No order was received.
Connection: close
Transfer-Encoding: chunked
Content-Type: text/html
Here's the HTTP status code indicating an error.
The response has a response header called "Status" in it.
This part is the "value" of the "Status" response header.
Web Browser
JavaScript
Your JavaScript code can access the response headers through the request object.
You can access any response header, and get its value.
request.getResponseHeader("Status")
"No order was received."

Break Neck error handling

Now that you know how to get a response header from the server, you can improve the Break Neck JavaScript, and let customers know a little more about any errors they run into.

Let's make a few simple changes to **pizza.js**:

```
function showConfirmation() {
  if (request.readyState == 4) {
    if (request.status == 200) {
      var response = request.responseText;
      var mainDiv = document.getElementById("main-page");
      var orderForm = document.getElementById("order-form");

      pElement = document.createElement("p");
      textNode = document.createTextNode(
        "Your order should arrive within " +
        response +
        " minutes. Enjoy your pizza!");
      pElement.appendChild(textNode);

      mainDiv.replaceChild(pElement, orderForm);
    } else {
      var message = request.getResponseHeader("Status");
      if ((message.length == null) || (message.length <= 0)) {
        alert("Error! Request status is " + request.status);
      } else {
        alert(message);
      }
    }
  }
}
```

If placeOrder.php reports an error, the status code will be "400", so the "else" part of this code will run.

This gets the value of the "Status" response header, if there is one.

If there's no "Status" response header, then just print out the error code, like we did in the older versions of the Break Neck app.

If the server or script returned a "Status" response header, then show that to the customer.

OK, so now we're ready to go, right?

Team Chat: One more problem to fix...

Frank: I know it seems like everything is working, but I've still got a few concerns about the Break Neck order form.

Jim: What do you mean? Why mess with something that already works?

Frank: Well, that's the thing. I'm not sure this code really *will* work... at least not in every situation. You're using a GET request when you submit the pizza order form, right?

Jim: Right. All the order details get sent as part of the request URL.

Frank: That's what I thought... and that's where I think there might be a problem. What if someone places a really long order? Their order gets added to the request URL, but if that URL is longer than the browser or server supports...

Anne: Oh, I see what Frank's getting at. The request URL has to include the customer's order, and if that order makes the URL too long, part of the order could get cut off!

Jim: Oh, wow... I hadn't thought about that. So since we're adding the customer's phone number, address, and order to the request URL...

Frank: ...everything has to fit within the maximum URL length. Each browser has a different maximum, and some servers have a maximum length that they'll accept, to. So you just can't be too careful. That's one of the real limitations with using GET requests instead of POST requests.

Jim: Right. I can just see someone placing a huge order during the Super Bowl—20 pizzas, tons of sides, drinks, snacks—and we end up blowing it because part of their order got cut off in the request URL.

So we probably should use POST for our request instead of GET, huh?

GET requests versus POST requests

Losing part of a customer's order would definitely be a problem for Break Neck. But, it looks like using a POST request might help solve the problem.

Let's take a closer look at both types of requests:

GET requests send data in the request URL

GET requests send data to the server as part of the request URL:

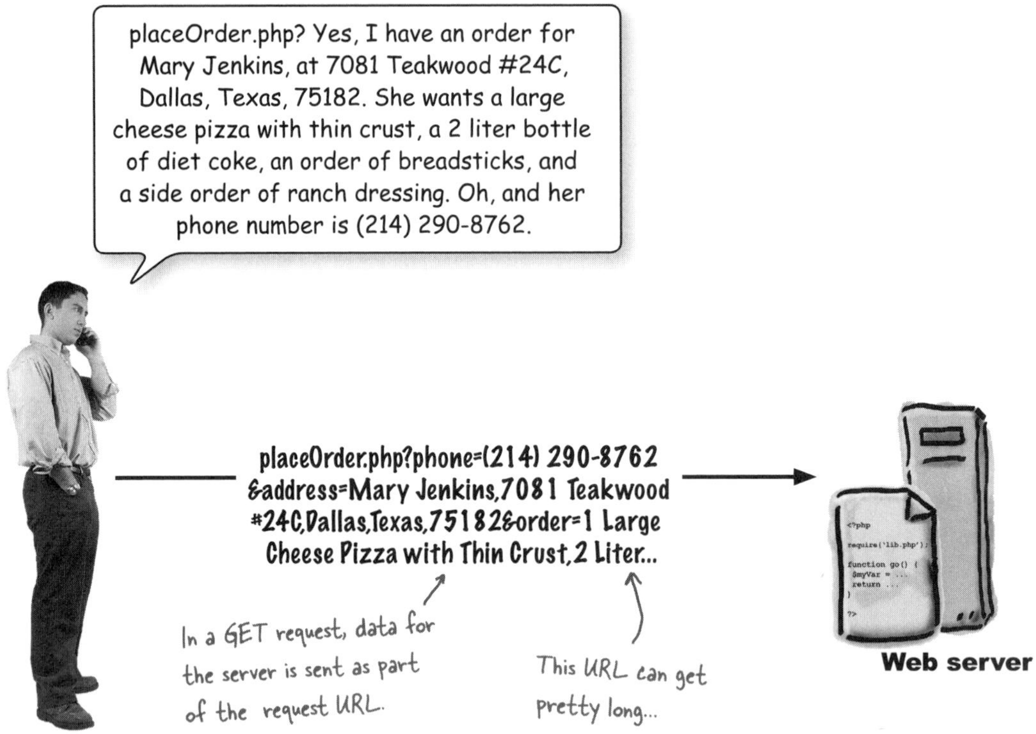
placeOrder.php? Yes, I have an order for Mary Jenkins, at 7081 Teakwood #24C, Dallas, Texas, 75182. She wants a large cheese pizza with thin crust, a 2 liter bottle of diet coke, an order of breadsticks, and a side order of ranch dressing. Oh, and her phone number is (214) 290-8762.
placeOrder.php?phone=(214) 290-8762 &address=Mary Jenkins,7081 Teakwood #24C,Dallas,Texas,75182&order=1 Large Cheese Pizza with Thin Crust,2 Liter...
In a GET request, data for the server is sent as part of the request URL.
This URL can get pretty long...
Web server

* In an actual request, lots of the special characters in this URL would be encoded by the JavaScript escape() function. We've left it unencoded, though, to make it a little easier to understand.

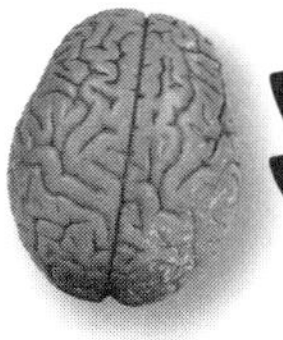

BRAIN POWER

What do you think happens to the data in the GET request if the URL gets too long for a web browser or a web server to handle?

POST requests send data separate from the request URL

In a POST request, data that has to be sent to the server is kept separate from the URL, and there's no length restriction:

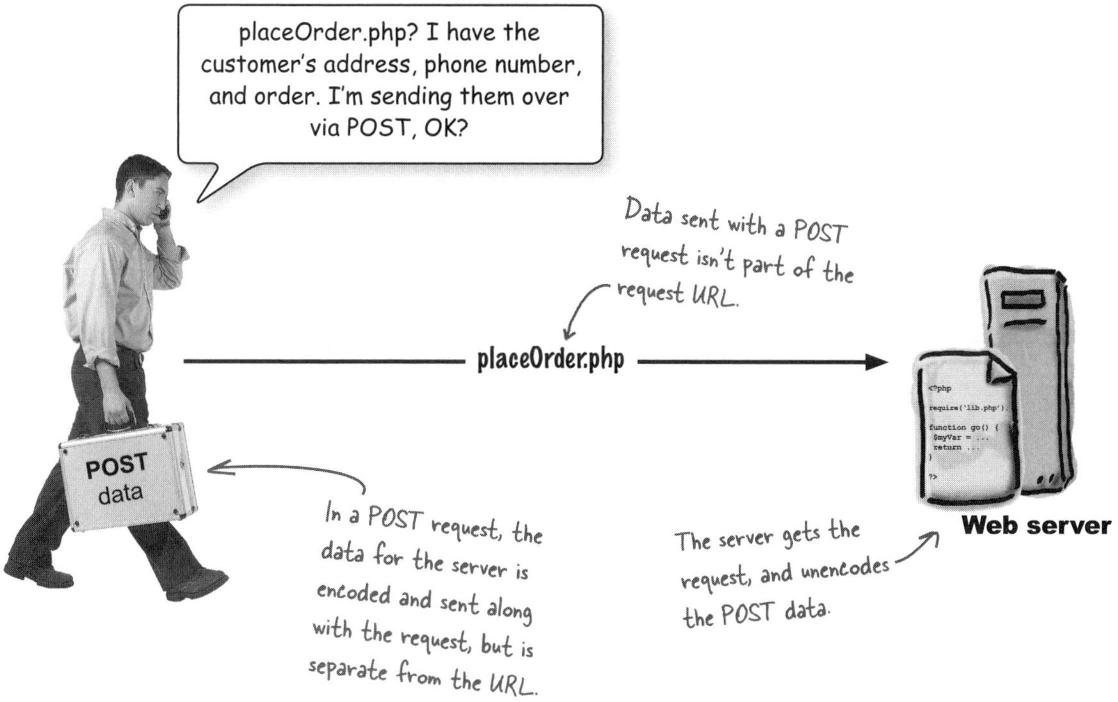

placeOrder.php? I have the customer's address, phone number, and order. I'm sending them over via POST, OK?
Data sent with a POST request isn't part of the request URL.
placeOrder.php
POST data
In a POST request, the data for the server is encoded and sent along with the request, but is separate from the URL.
The server gets the request, and unencodes the POST data.
Web server

Web servers unencode POST data

Once a web server gets a POST request, it figures out what type of data it has received, and then passes that information on to the program in the request URL.

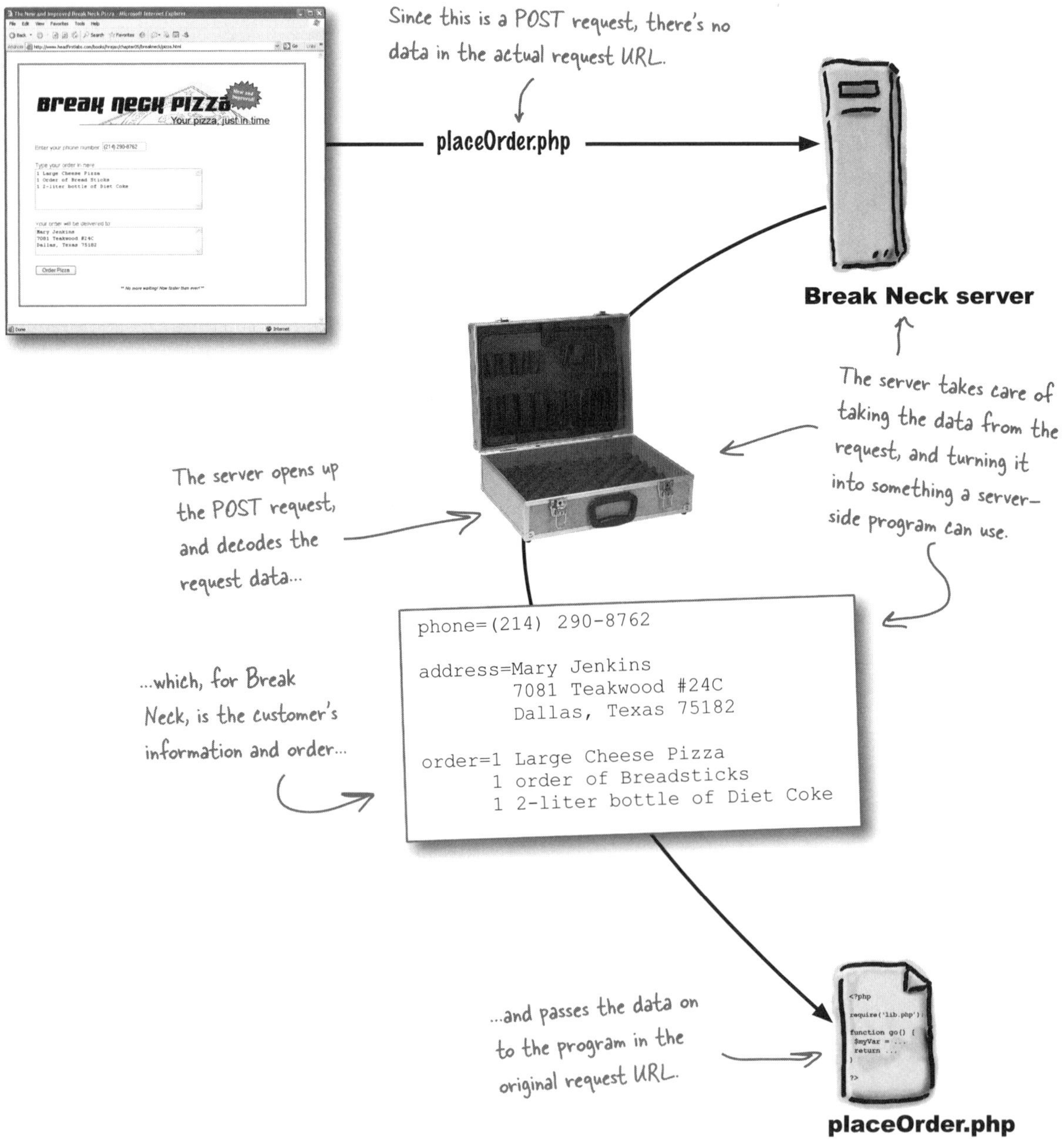
Since this is a POST request, there's no data in the actual request URL.
placeOrder.php
Break Neck server
The server takes care of taking the data from the request, and turning it into something a server-side program can use.
The server opens up the POST request, and decodes the request data...
phone=(214) 290-8762
address=Mary Jenkins
7081 Teakwood #24C
Dallas, Texas 75182
order=1 Large Cheese Pizza
1 order of Breadsticks
1 2-liter bottle of Diet Coke
...which, for Break Neck, is the customer's information and order...
...and passes the data on to the program in the original request URL.
placeOrder.php

Send more data with a POST request

It looks like POST is just what we need to make sure those big orders get to Break Neck's **placeOrder.php** script intact. Let's update the JavaScript in **placeOrder()** to use a POST request instead of a GET request:

Back to Step 2... gotta update submitOrder() again.

submitOrder() is in pizza.js.

```
function submitOrder() {
    var phone = document.getElementById("phone").value;
    var address = document.getElementById("address").value;
    var order = document.getElementById("order").value;
    var url = "placeOrder.php?phone=" + escape(phone) +
              "&address=" + escape(address) +
              "&order=" + escape(order);
    url = url + "&dummy=" + new Date().getTime();
    request.open("POST", url, true);
    request.onreadystatechange = showConfirmation;
    request.send("phone=" + escape(phone) +
              "&address=" + escape(address) +
              "&order=" + escape(order));
}
```

Start out by removing all the form data from the request URL.

Don't lose this semicolon at the end of the line.

Since we're using POST, we don't need this dummy parameter anymore.

Tell the open() method that you want to use POST instead of GET.

Use send() to send the pizza order to the Break Neck server.

Use name/value pairs in send(), just like you did at the end of the request URL in the GET version of this code.

Just Do It

Go ahead and open up your copy of **pizza.js**, and find the **submitOrder()** function. Change the function's code so that it sends the customer's order to **placeOrder.php** using a POST request instead of a GET request. Once your code matches ours from above, save **pizza.js**, and go ahead and turn the page for some Q-and-A before we take Break Neck for another test drive.

Hold on a second... just because we're using a POST request, caching isn't an issue? I'd like a little more explanation than that.

Browsers cache GET requests

Browsers know exactly what data you're sending them in a GET request... all the data is in the request URL. So when the web browser thinks a request is the same—because the same data is in the URL—it tries to "help out" and return any cached answer it has for that request.

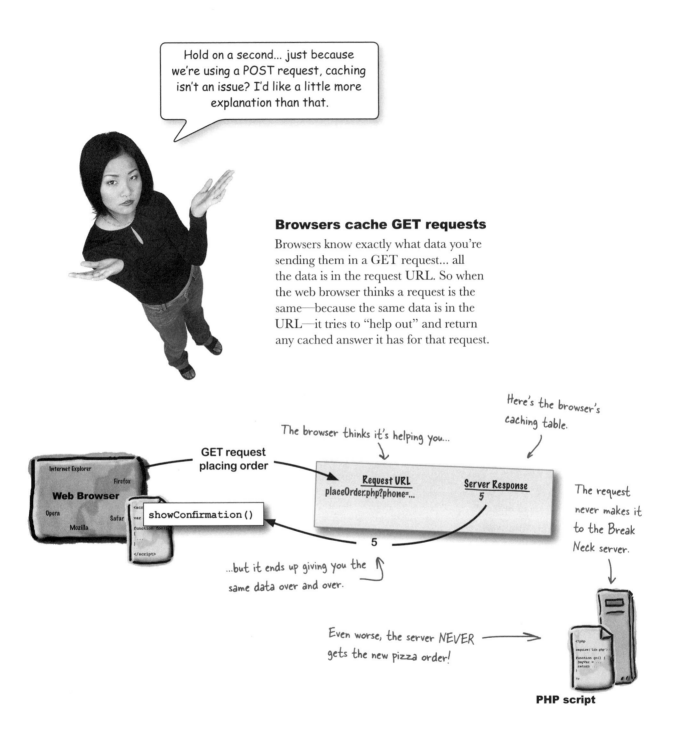

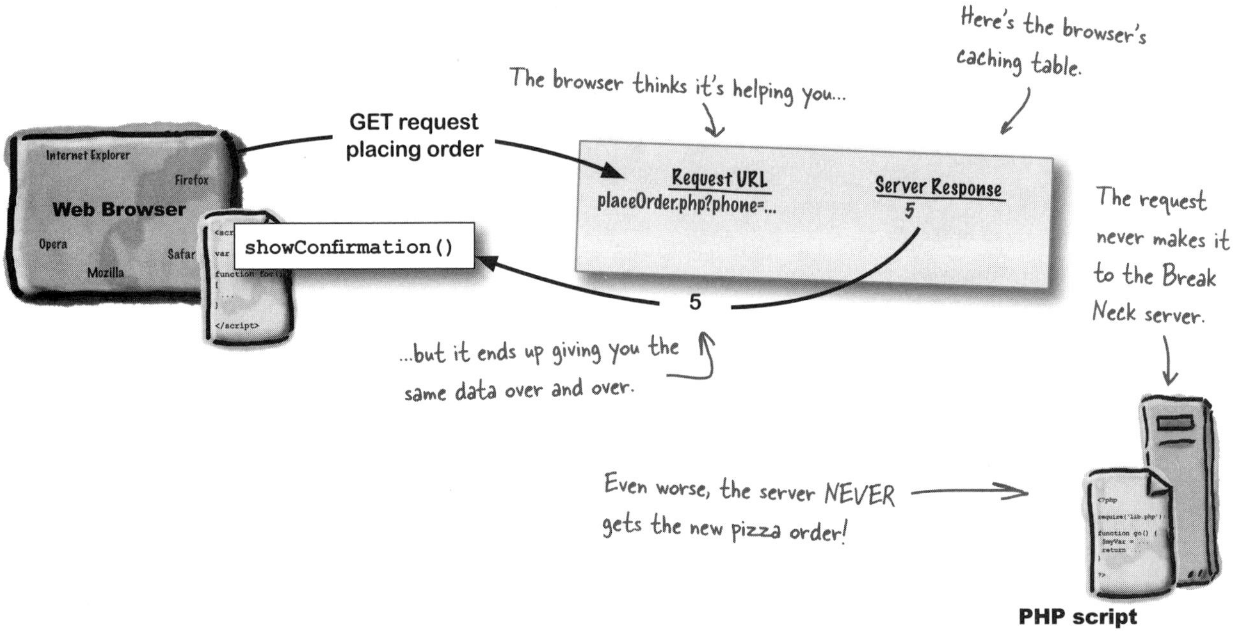

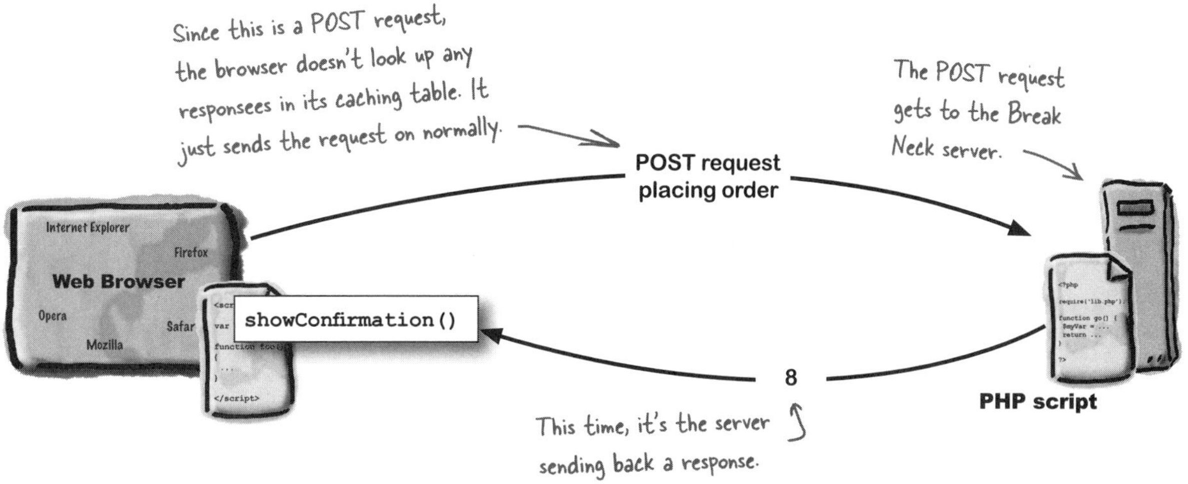
Since this is a POST request, the browser doesn't look up any responsees in its caching table. It just sends the request on normally.
POST request placing order
The POST request gets to the Break Neck server.
Internet Explorer
Firefox
Web Browser
Opera
Safari
Mozilla
showConfirmation()
8
PHP script
This time, it's the server sending back a response.

But isn't the URL always the same in a POST request? Why doesn't the browser try and use its cache, if the URL never changes?

Browsers hate a mystery

In a POST request, the browser doesn't know what data might be a part of the request, since the data isn't sent as part of the request URL. Since the browser isn't sure what's in the request, it sends all POST requests on to their destination server, and doesn't try and cache responses from the server.

Browsers don't try and cache POST requests.

Frequently Asked Questions

Q: Now that we're using a POST request, does the length of the data we send in the request matter?

A: No. You can send as much data in a POST request as you like. So those big orders for your next bachelorette party will get through to Break Neck with no problems.

Q: Is the length restriction on GET requests the only reason to switch to using a POST request?

A: Pretty much. While most people agree that POST requests are best for submitting orders and doing other transactions that are "final", the biggest reason to use a POST request instead of a GET request is because you can send unlimited amounts of data in a POST request. In a GET request, both the browser and the server have a maximum length for request URLs; anything longer than that gets ignored.

Q: I thought that POST requests were more secure than GET requests?

A: POST requests are *marginally* more secure than GET requests. There's one additional step that goes into packaging up POST data: an encoding on the browser, and a matching decoding on the server. But decrypting POST data is pretty trivial. Anyone who is looking to get your information can get it from a POST request almost as easily as they can from a GET request.

If you really want to secure your request, you'll have to use a secure network connection, like SSL. That's a little beyond what we're covering in this book, though. For the most part, that's an issue for the server to worry about, and not your Ajax application.

Q: I've always heard you should send credit card numbers and personal information using POST. Is that not true?

A: Well, that's more about what the request does than it is about security. Remember, most web programmers like to use POST requests for completing orders, paying for an item, or any other transaction that is "final". So you're posting a transaction, like you would in your checkbook. If you want extra security, though, then you still will want to use an SSL connection, or some other form of network security, for your requests.

In the same way, GET requests are usually used to get data (makes sense, doesn't it?). And since you're almost always completing a purchase or transaction when you enter in sensitive information like a credit card number, those end up being sent to the server as POST requests. But it's more about the *type* of the transaction, rather than making the request more secure.

Q: And when you send a POST request, you just put the request data in the send() method of the request object?

A: Exactly. You even use the same name/value pairs, like you did when adding the data to your request URL. Then, separate each pair using the `&` character. The only difference between how you supply the data in a POST request and the data in a GET request is that, in the GET request, you have to put in a `?` before the name/value pairs you add to the request URL. In a POST request, you don't need a `?` before the name/value pairs, since you're putting them directly into the `send()` method.

Q: That's it? There's nothing else we need to do?

A: Well, let's take our updated Break Neck pizza order form for a test drive and see...

Trying out POST requests

Make sure you've taken care of everything in the Just Do It exercise on page 299, and then load **`pizza.html`** in your web browser. Go ahead and enter a phone number, and while the server is filling in your address, enter in a pizza order. Click the "Order Pizza" button, and see what happens.

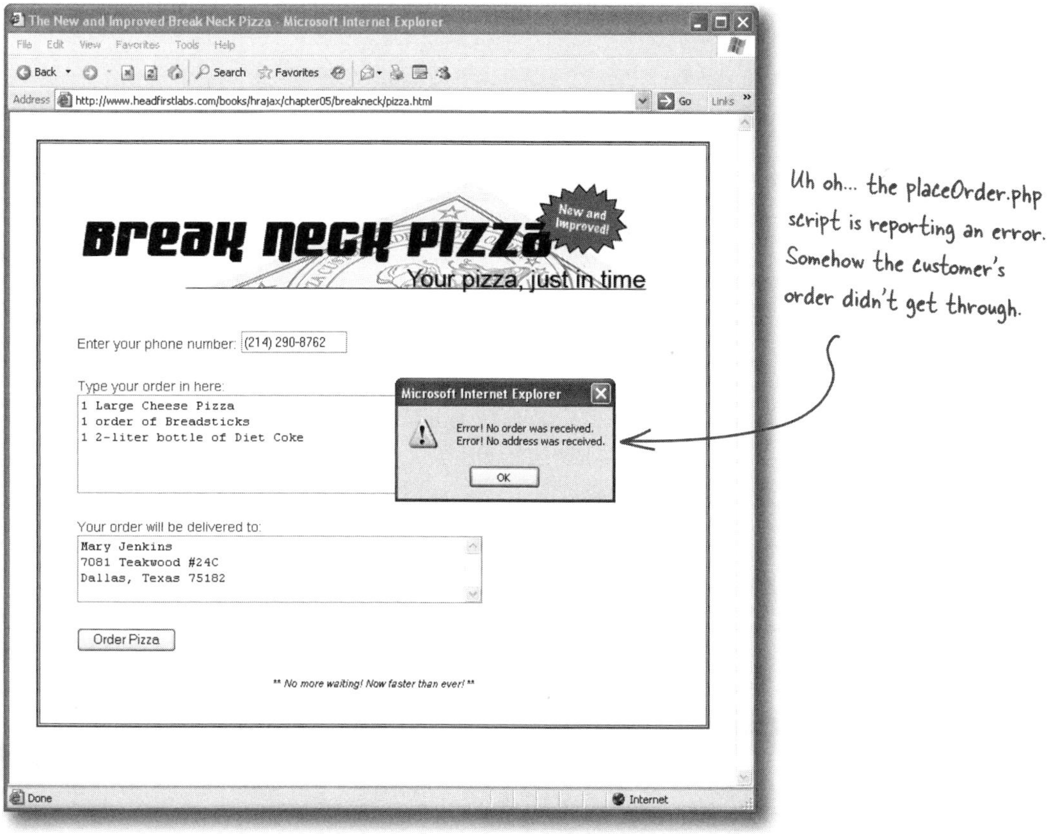

FREQUENTLY ASKED QUESTIONS

Q: I tried pizza.html on Safari, and it worked just fine. Is there something wrong (or right) with my code?

A: No. Safari tends to do a few things that make a POST request work *without* a few of the extra steps you need to take for most other browsers. The POST version of Break Neck fails on Internet Explorer, Opera, and Firefox, so we definitely need to figure out what's going on, and fix the Break Neck app.

Why didn't the POST request work?

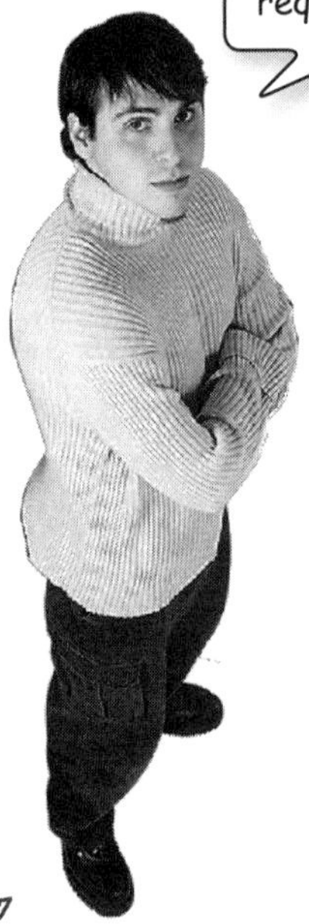
It's got to be the placeOrder.php script. We told open() to use POST for the request, so it's got to be a server problem.
Jim's the resident Ajax programmer at Break Neck.

I already told you, there's no problem with my script. You must have screwed something up in your JavaScript code.
This is Frank... he's been writing all the PHP scripts for Break Neck Pizza.

Jim: Are you sure? I'll bet you forgot to change your script to accept POST parameters. Come on, just admit it! Fix the thing, and we can get on with it...

Frank: Look, do you have a hearing problem? I've told you twice now, my script accepts GET *and* POST parameters. Are you sure you even sent the customer's order and address?

Jim: I'm positive. Once I realized how long someone's order could get, I updated the part of my JavaScript that places the order to use a POST request.

Frank: Well, looks like you made a mistake.

Jim: No way. I put the customer's phone number, address, and order in the `send()` method of my request object... I even double-checked. So I know the data's getting to the web server.

Frank: Well, it's not getting to me. When my script gets run by the server, and it checks for the "address" and "order" request parameters, it's not getting anything.

Jim: Wait a second. If I'm sending the data to the server correctly...

Frank: ...and I'm asking the server for the data, and getting nothing...

Together: *The problem must be the server!*

The mysterious POST data

Frank and Jim are onto something. Remember when we talked about the server decoding the POST data from your request? Once the server opens up the POST request data, it doesn't know what type of data it should expect... and servers really don't like mysteries. Let's take a look, and see what happens with the POST data:

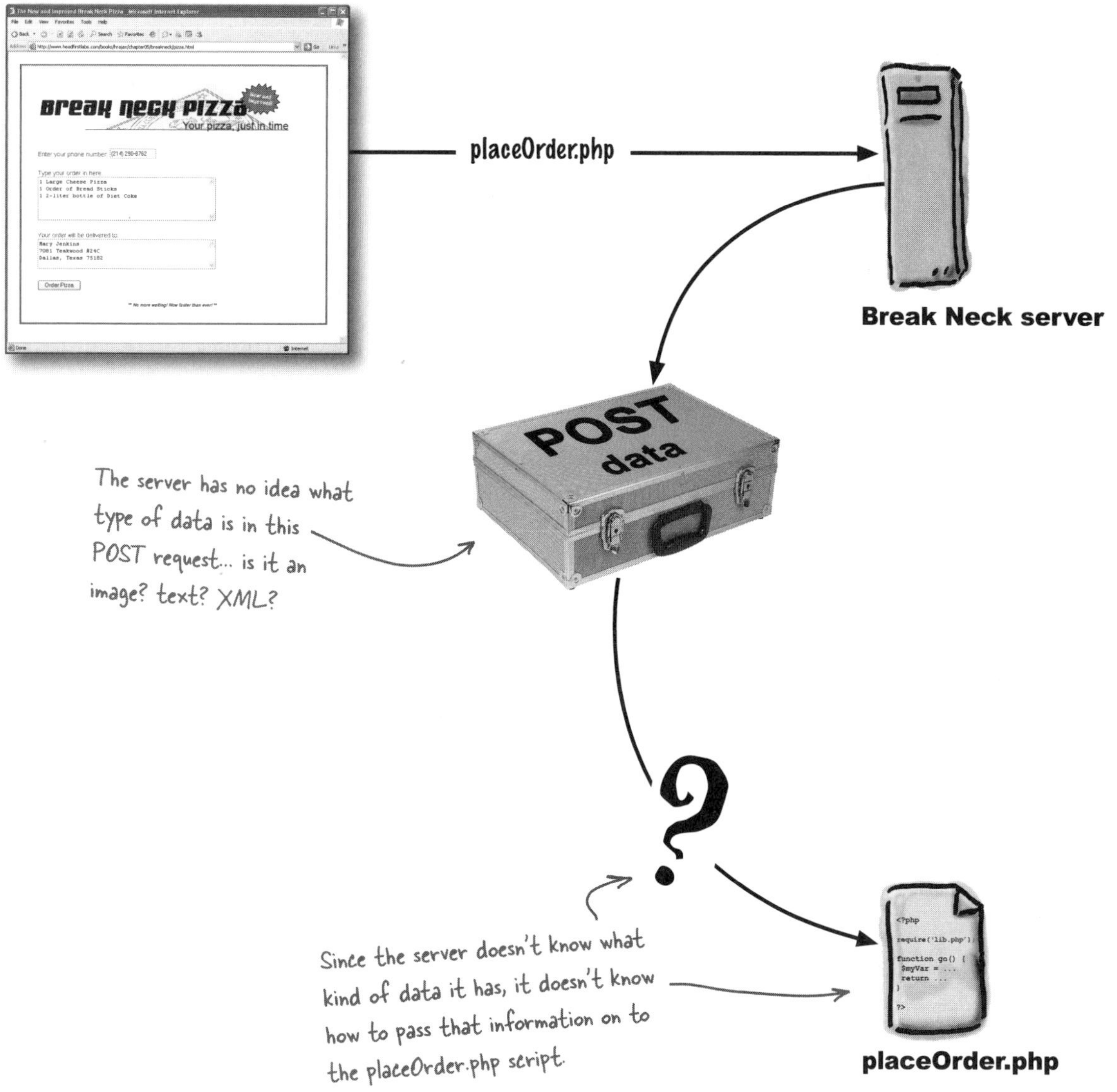

Break Neck Pizza
Your pizza, just in time
placeOrder.php
Break Neck server
POST data
The server has no idea what type of data is in this POST request... is it an image? text? XML?
?
Since the server doesn't know what kind of data it has, it doesn't know how to pass that information on to the placeOrder.php script.
placeOrder.php

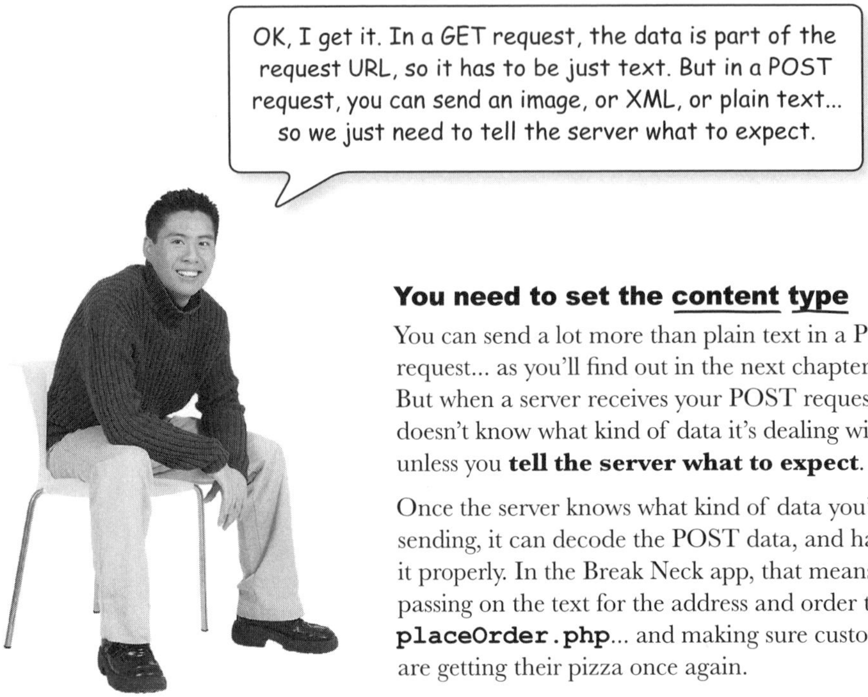

You need to set the content type

You can send a lot more than plain text in a POST request... as you'll find out in the next chapter. But when a server receives your POST request, it doesn't know what kind of data it's dealing with, unless you **tell the server what to expect**.

Once the server knows what kind of data you're sending, it can decode the POST data, and handle it properly. In the Break Neck app, that means passing on the text for the address and order to `placeOrder.php`... and making sure customers are getting their pizza once again.

Servers get information from the browser using request headers.

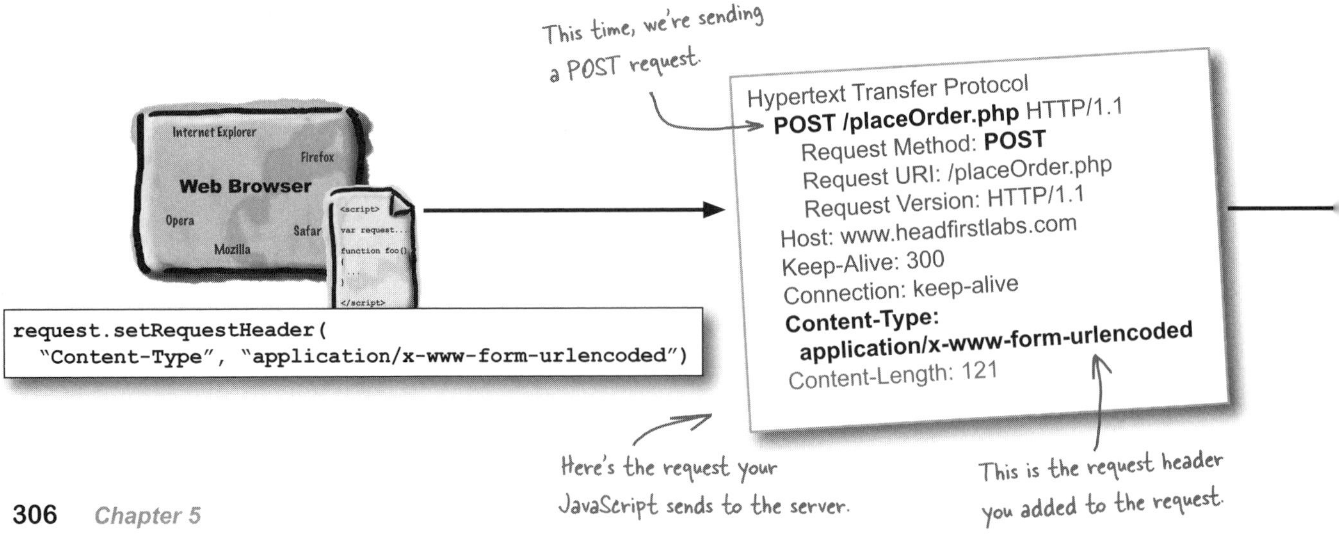

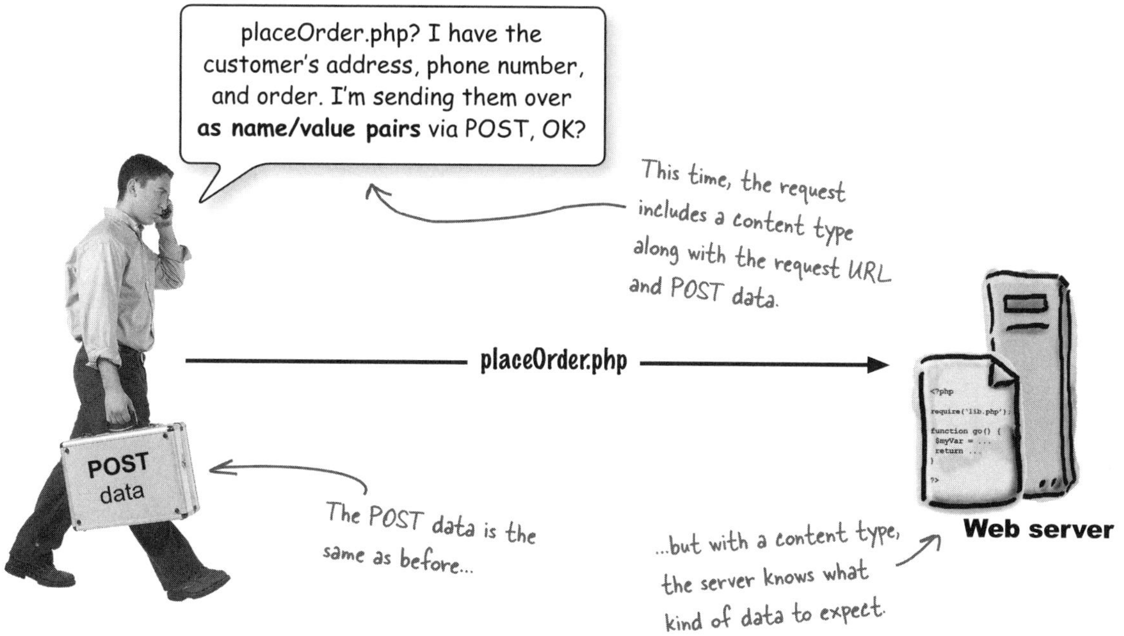

placeOrder.php? I have the customer's address, phone number, and order. I'm sending them over **as name/value pairs** via POST, OK?
This time, the request includes a content type along with the request URL and POST data.
placeOrder.php
POST data
The POST data is the same as before...
...but with a content type, the server knows what kind of data to expect.
Web server

Servers send information to the browser using response headers.

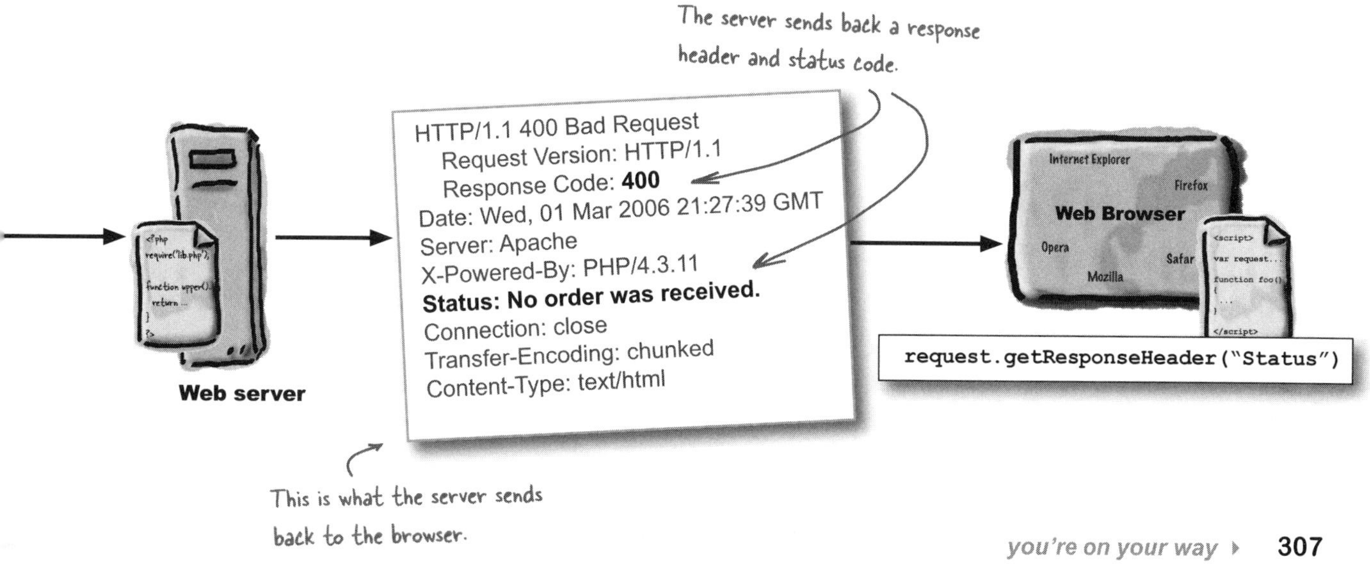

HTML Form | Send Order | PHP Script | Callback

Setting the Content Type

You have to set the content type for your POST data before you send the request. Then, when the request is sent, the server will get the request URL, the POST data, and the type of data it should expect. Anytime you need to tell a server something *about* a request, you'll use a **request header**.

Let's see how we can set a request header for the Break Neck request:

```
function submitOrder() {
  var phone = document.getElementById("phone").value;
  var address = document.getElementById("address").value;
  var order = document.getElementById("order").value;
  var url = "placeOrder.php";
  request.open("POST", url, true);
  request.onreadystatechange = showConfirmation;
  request.setRequestHeader("Content-Type",
        "application/x-www-form-urlencoded");
  request.send("phone=" + escape(phone) +
             "&address=" + escape(address) +
             "&order=" + escape(order));
}
```

setRequestHeader() allows you to add information to the request, usually intended for use by the server.

"Content-Type" is the name of the header...

...and this is the value for that request header.

This tells the server the data is encoded like it would be in a request URL, just as if the data came as part of a GET request.

FREQUENTLY ASKED QUESTIONS

Q: So a request header is sent to the server along with the request?

A: Yes. Any request headers are part of the request. In fact, the web browser sets some request headers automatically, so you're really just *adding* a request header to the existing ones.

Q: And "Content-Type" is used to tell the server what kind of POST data we're sending?

A: You've got it. In this case, we're using name/value pairs, and the content type for that is "application/x-www-form-urlencoded". That particular type tells the server to look for values like it would get from a normal form submission.

Q: Are there other content types I should know about?

A: There sure are. In the next chapter, we'll look at the content type for XML. There are tons more, and you can simply Google for "HTTP Content-Type" to find various lists online for all sorts of different file and content types.

Another test drive

Add the line of JavaScript that sets the "Content-Type" request header in **`pizza.js`**, and save your JavaScript. Then load **`pizza.html`** in your web browser, and try to enter an order again.

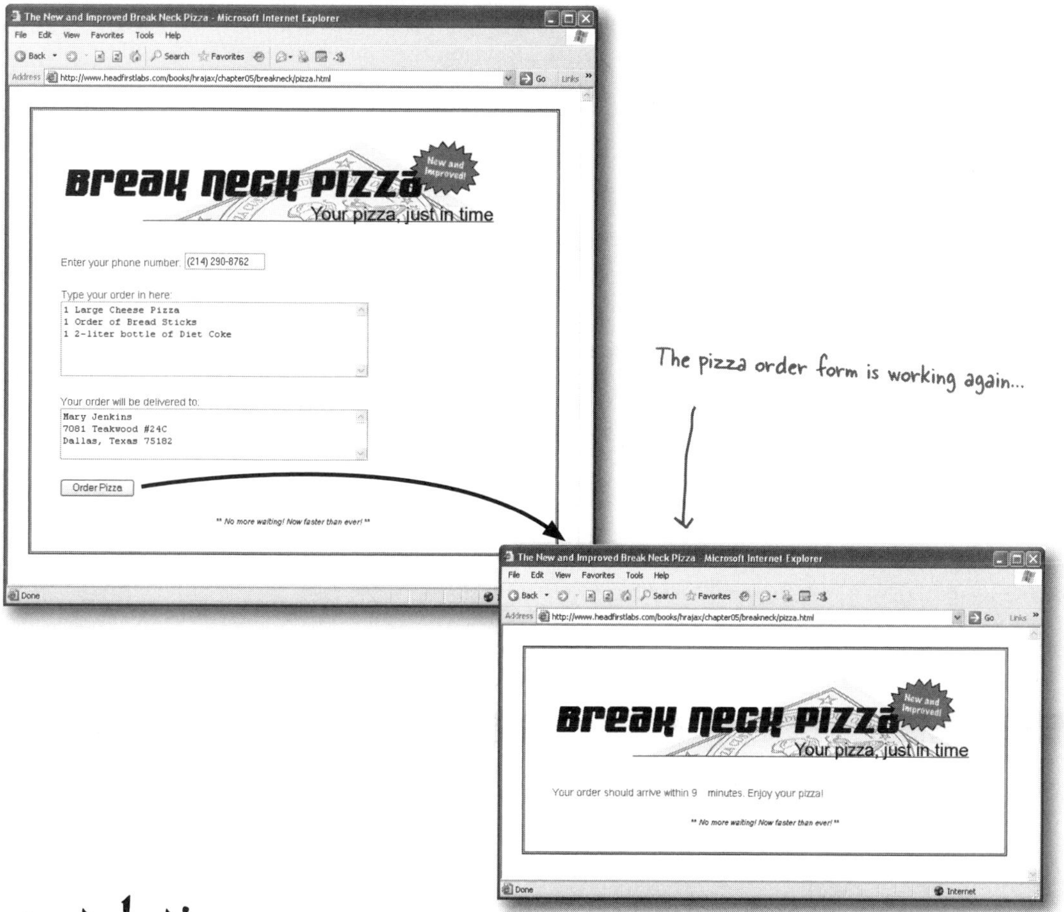

The pizza order form is working again...

...but this time, the order is being sent to the server using a POST request. No big orders are gonna get lost with POST!

Congratulations... You've saved Alex's butt once again. Pizza's on us!

But you still haven't told me what the actual maximum length of the request URL in a GET request is. Hello?

It's browser-dependent

Each browser treats URLs differently. So the maximum request URL length is different on each browser. Opera, Internet Explorer, Safari... it just depends on which browser customers are using.

But it's really small, I guess. Like, just 50 or 75 characters long?

Well, it's not that small...

Remember, each browser is different. But, for example it's about 2,000 characters on Internet Explorer... that's a good rule of thumb to use for other browsers, too.

Did you say two-**THOUSAND**? Are you kidding me? What are we expecting here, Schwarzenegger is gonna order pizza for the *entire state* of California? Come on... this is just ridiculous!

Hmmm.... well... umm....

OK, you got us. There are probably not going to be a lot of times when the customer's address, phone number, and pizza order are longer than 2,000 characters... even when it's Super Bowl party time.

But there are still good reasons to use POST requests...

Espresso Talk

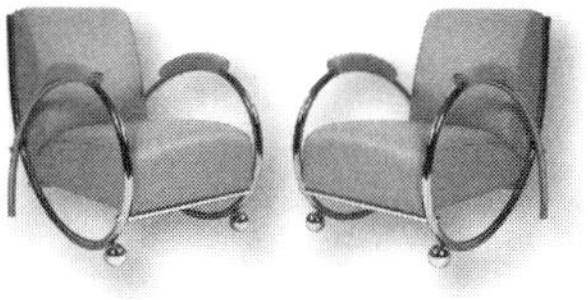

Tonight's overly caffeinated guests:
POST request and GET request

POST: Hey there, GET, I'm surprised you're still around. I'm getting so many requests these days that I just figured you had headed to Fiji or something.

GET: Still around? Oh, I'm plenty busy. Besides, I'd much rather be in demand because of what I do, not what people *think* I do.

POST: What's that supposed to mean?

GET: Have you actually asked anyone *why* they're using you instead of me?

POST: Oh, you really are losing it. There are tons of reasons to use me instead of you.

GET: Oh really? Name five. I dare ya'.

POST: This is going to be fun. Gee, where to begin. OK, how about I'm more secure. Nobody uses you for sending important information, like a credit card number or checking account number.

GET: *(Sigh)* Just because people believe something doesn't make it true. You're not really any more secure than I am. Any junior programmer can break open POST data just as easily as they can read a request URL. And unencoding POST data? Takes about 30 seconds... if you're doing it one-handed.

POST: OK, sure, whatever. Well, here's another reason to use me: you don't have to worry about how long your request data is. You've got that lousy length limitation.

GET: Yup, and if you can tell me 2,000 characters of text that you're used to getting in name/value pairs, I'll tell you why that really matters to anyone. Hardly anyone sending plain old text is really going to need more than that for their data.

POST: Hmmm. Well, who wants to see all their data in the address line of their browser? Huh? How about that, Mr. I-need-no-content-type?

GET: Oh, so now it's a beauty contest? Besides, I thought this was a book on Ajax. Nobody sees the URL in an asynchronous request, even if it is a GET request. I'm still waiting for that great reason to use POST requests...

POST: Well, everyone knows it's just... better... to use POST for sending form data to a server.

GET: Tradition. That's all you've got, huh? So let's mount up on horses, pull out the pantaloons, and start worrying about falling off the edge of the earth... you've got to be kidding. If everyone in the world jumped off a bridge, I suppose you'd be getting your bathing suit on, wouldn't you?

POST: Urggh... well... wait, wait, WAIT! I've got it!

GET: Oh, I'll bet this will be priceless. What now? Did Howard Stern say POST is better? I'm sure we can all rely on important trend indicators like that to make important development decisions...

POST: XML.

GET: Huh?

POST: XML, big mouth. I don't suppose you have much to say about that, do you?

GET: Ahhh... well...

POST: Yeah, that's what I thought! You've got to escape each and every one of those angle brackets, don't you? And what about your length limitation? That's a *big* problem with XML.

GET: Hmm. Well, it can't be that important... I mean, we're on like page 240 or something, and we haven't even talked about XML yet...

POST: Oh, you really are out of the loop. I guess you missed the memo buddy... wait until Chapter 6. It's XML central, baby, and I bet you're nowhere to be found. C'ya! I hear the next chapter callling... I'm sure they need someone who can handle XML requests!

I gotta tell you, you've saved my butt again. Customers are happy, I'm getting massive tips, and my boss is just going on and on about Ajax.

Reviewing your Ajax library

You've got a lot of tools in your Ajax and asynchronous programming library by now. Before you dive into Chapter 6, take a moment to relax, and write down what you've learned so far. In the blanks below, list some of the key Ajax concepts you've picked up in the first five chapters.

____

____

____

____

____

Take a look at the new POST version of Break Neck Pizza

60 Second Review

- In a GET request, all the data you send to the server is added to the request URL.
- Each browser has a maximum length for URLs, including any data included as part of that URL. For most browsers, that maximum length is around 2,000 characters.
- There isn't a length restriction on the data you send to the server if you're using a POST request.
- In POST requests, the data is sent to the server separate from the request URL. The request URL only has the name of the program on the server that should be run.
- You can send different types of data in a POST request: plain text, XML, binary objects like images and files, and anything else that your web browser can encode.
- The server doesn't know what type of POST data to expect unless you tell it.
- Use the setRequestHeader() method on the JavaScript request object to pass additional information on to a server.
- Using the Content-Type request header, you can tell the server what kind of data you're sending in a POST request.
- The content type "x-www-form-urlencoded" tells the server that you're using name/value pairs, in plain text, just as if that data had been submitted by a web form.
- POST requests are only marginally more secure than GET requests, and both require additional layers of security—like SSL, the secure sockets layer—to protect your data from prying eyes and malicious programmers.

Exercise Solutions

Just Do It Solutions

It's time to make Break Neck an even better place for ordering pizza. Look in the **`chapter05/breakneck/`** folder in the book's examples, and you'll find the Break Neck order form, complete with HTML, CSS, and PHP. You'll need to open up **`pizza.html`**, and change the form to run **`submitOrder()`** when "Order Pizza" is clicked, instead of submitting directly to the **`placeOrder.php`** script on the Break Neck server.

As long as you're making improvements to Break Neck, go ahead and move all of the JavaScript out of **`pizza.html`**. You can use **`ajax.js`**, which you wrote in Chapter 3, for creating the request object. Then, create a new JavaScript file called **`pizza.js`**. Move your Break Neck functions—**`getCustomerInfo()`**, **`updatePage()`**, and **`submitOrder()`**—into this file. Don't forget to add **`<script>`** elements that link to these files in your HTML!

Here's just the <head> section of pizza.html.

```
<html>
  <head>
    <title>The New and Improved Break Neck Pizza</title>
    <link rel="stylesheet" type="text/css" href="breakneck.css" />
    <script type="text/javascript" src="ajax.js"> </script>
    <script type="text/javascript" src="pizza.js"> </script>
  </head>
```

There's no other JavaScript in the HTML in this new version.

Here are the two external JavaScript files you should have created.

Here's ajax.js. You should have this file from Chapter 3.

```
var request = null;
try {
  request = new XMLHttpRequest();
} catch (trymicrosoft) {
  try {
    request = new ActiveXObject("Msxml2.XMLHTTP");
  } catch (othermicrosoft) {
    try {
      request = new ActiveXObject("Microsoft.XMLHTTP");
    } catch (failed) {
      request = null;
    }
  }
}

if (request == null)
  alert("Error creating request object!");
```

Here are your Break Neck-specific functions; you should have these in a fille called pizza.js.

```
function getCustomerInfo() {
  var phone = document.getElementById("phone").value;
  var url = "lookupCustomer.php?phone=" + escape(phone);
  request.open("GET", url, true);
  request.onreadystatechange = updatePage;
  request.send(null);
}

function updatePage() {
  if (request.readyState == 4) {
    if (request.status == 200) {
      var customerAddress = request.responseText;
      document.getElementById("address").value = customerAddress;
    } else
      alert("Error! Request status is " + request.status);
  }
}

function submitOrder() {
  var phone = document.getElementById("phone");
  var address = document.getElementById("address");
  var order = document.getElementById("order");
  var url = "placeOrder.php?phone=" + escape(phone) +
            "&address=" + escape(address) +
            "&order=" + escape(order);
  url = url + "&dummy=" + new Date().getTime();
  request.open("GET", url, true);
  request.onreadystatechange = showConfirmation;
  request.send(null);
}
```

...we're watching you...

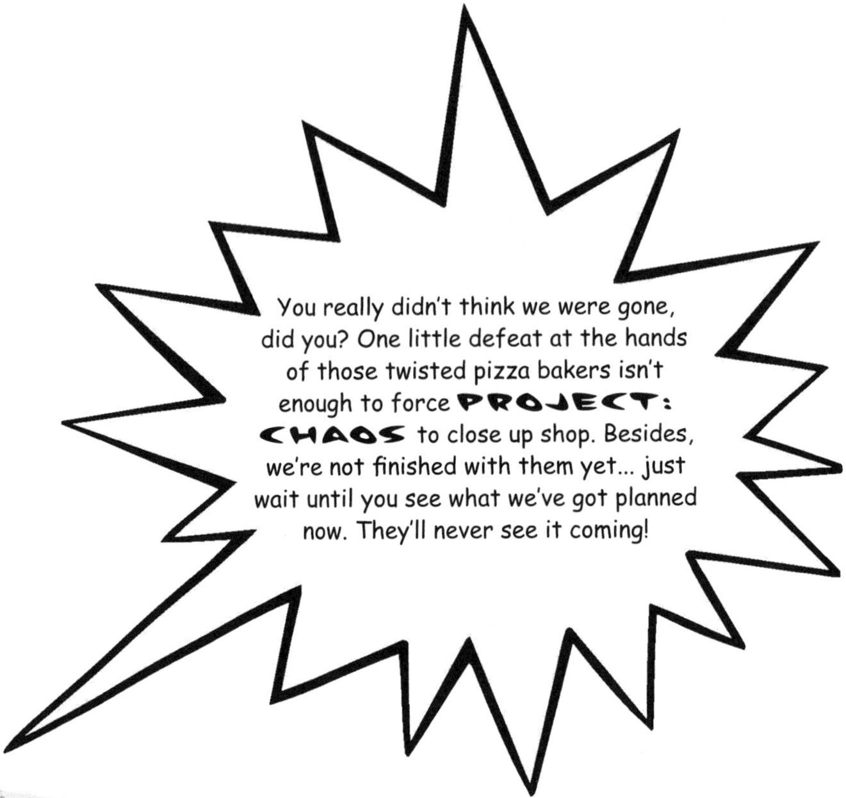

You really didn't think we were gone, did you? One little defeat at the hands of those twisted pizza bakers isn't enough to force PROJECT: CHAOS to close up shop. Besides, we're not finished with them yet... just wait until you see what we've got planned now. They'll never see it coming!

You found this tape recorder lying on your front porch, next to the morning paper.

Injecting mischief into Break Neck

It looks like PROJECT: CHAOS has another idea for breaking Break Neck. This time, though, they've stumbled onto something a little trickier... they've been doing some reading.

Hmmm... I wonder what PROJECT: CHAOS found in "Security Warrior" to help them foul up Break Neck Pizza...

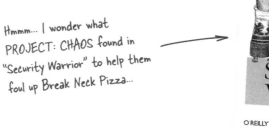

Break Neck Pizza online

Open up your web browser, and visit the "official" Break Neck Pizza site, at **`http://www.headfirstlabs.com/breakneck/pizza.html`**. Then follow the set of instructions that **PROJECT: CHAOS** left you, tucked inside that morning paper.

STOP! You MUST try this online... this probably won't work if you try this on your local copy of pizza.html.

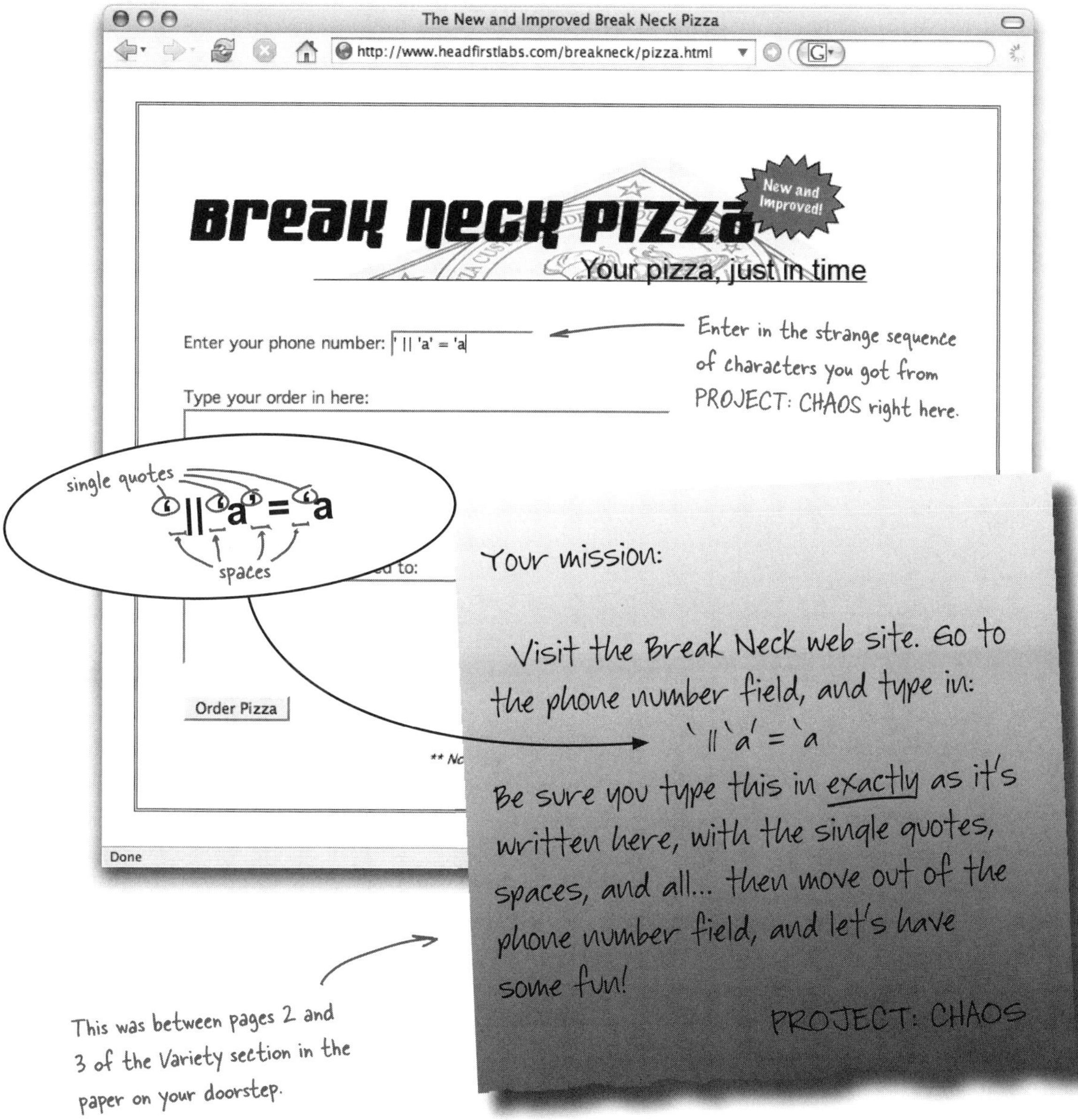
The New and Improved Break Neck Pizza
http://www.headfirstlabs.com/breakneck/pizza.html
Break Neck Pizza
New and Improved!
Your pizza, just in time
Enter your phone number: ' || 'a' = 'a
Type your order in here:
Order Pizza
Done
Enter in the strange sequence of characters you got from PROJECT: CHAOS right here.
single quotes
' || 'a' = 'a
spaces
Your mission:
Visit the Break Neck web site. Go to the phone number field, and type in:
' || 'a' = 'a
Be sure you type this in exactly as it's written here, with the single quotes, spaces, and all... then move out of the phone number field, and let's have some fun!
PROJECT: CHAOS
This was between pages 2 and 3 of the Variety section in the paper on your doorstep.

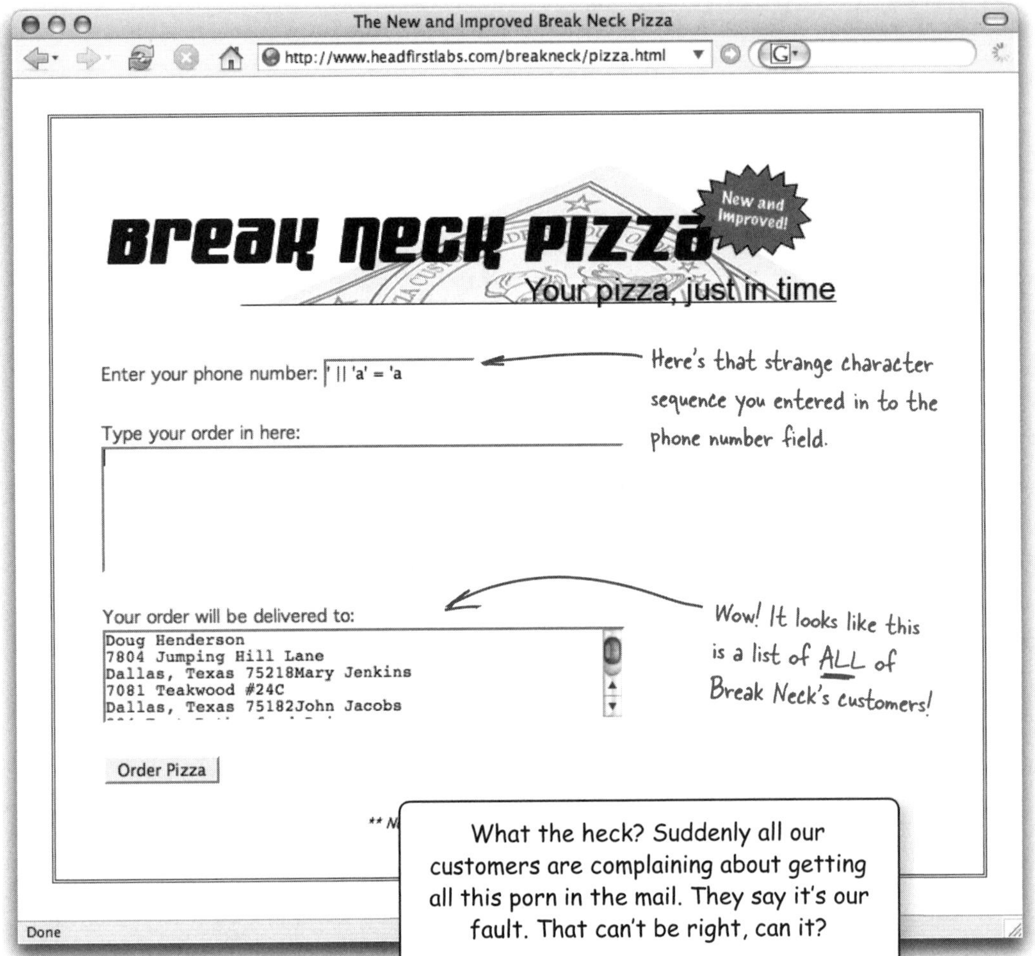
The New and Improved Break Neck Pizza
http://www.headfirstlabs.com/breakneck/pizza.html
Break Neck Pizza
New and Improved!
Your pizza, just in time
Enter your phone number: ' || 'a' = 'a
Here's that strange character sequence you entered in to the phone number field.
Type your order in here:
Your order will be delivered to:
Doug Henderson
7804 Jumping Hill Lane
Dallas, Texas 75218Mary Jenkins
7081 Teakwood #24C
Dallas, Texas 75182John Jacobs
Wow! It looks like this is a list of ALL of Break Neck's customers!
Order Pizza
Done

What the heck? Suddenly all our customers are complaining about getting all this porn in the mail. They say it's our fault. That can't be right, can it?

Actually, it *is* Break Neck's fault!

Looks like you're going to have to save the day once again.

Welcome to SQL injection

Break Neck has fallen victim to a SQL injection attack, and now all their customers are paying for it.

Remember Joe? He's the JavaScript guy at Break Neck.

So how did this...

Enter your phone number: ' || 'a' = 'a

This doesn't make a lot of sense, but it sure looks harmless. Weird... but harmless.

...somehow result in this?

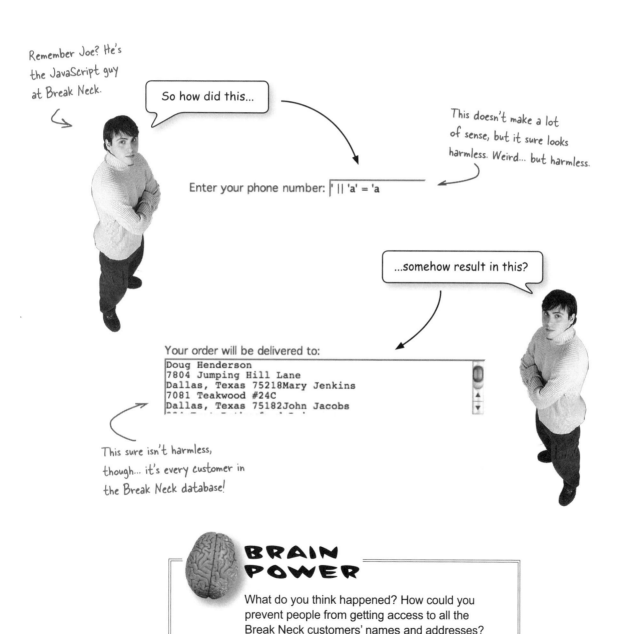

Your order will be delivered to:

```
Doug Henderson
7804 Jumping Hill Lane
Dallas, Texas 75218Mary Jenkins
7081 Teakwood #24C
Dallas, Texas 75182John Jacobs
```

This sure isn't harmless, though... it's every customer in the Break Neck database!

BRAIN POWER

What do you think happened? How could you prevent people from getting access to all the Break Neck customers' names and addresses?

SQL Inspector

To really understand what's going on, you're going to have to get into a little SQL. Below is part of the lookupCustomer.php script that is requested b getCustomerInfo() when a phone number is entered into the Break neck form... we've highlighted the line of SQL that asks the Break Neck server for a customer based on the phone number entered into the web form.

```
if (!$conn)
  die("Error connecting to MySQL: " . mysql_error());

if (!mysql_select_db("headfirst", $conn))
  die("Error selecting Head First database: " . mysql_error());

$phone = preg_replace("/[\. \(\)\-]/", "", $_REQUEST['phone']);
$select = "SELECT *";
$from   = "  FROM hraj_breakneck";
$where  = " WHERE phone = '" . $phone . "'";

$queryResult = @mysql_query($select . $from . $where);

if (!$queryResult)
  die('Error retrieving customer from the database.');
```

Here's lookupCustomer.php, which you first saw back in Chapter 2.

Your job is to take this query, and then write in the special characters that **PROJECT: CHAOS** asked you to type into the Break Neck web form. Then, you'll know exactly what's being sent to the Break Neck database... and maybe even get some ideas about what's going on.

SELECT *
FROM hraj_breakneck
WHERE phone = '__________________________'

Here's the SQL that lookupCustomer.php creates.

Write in what you typed into the phone number field here.

Wait, I think I see what's going on here...

Frank is the lead PHP programmer at Break Neck.

Here's what the SQL statement sent to the Break Neck database becomes...

```
SELECT *
  FROM hraj_breakneck
WHERE phone = '_' || 'a' = 'a_'
```

Let's make that a little easier to read...

```
SELECT *
  FROM hraj_breakneck
WHERE phone = '' || 'a' = 'a'
```

Notice how the single quotes you entered into the phone field work with the quotes already in your SQL query.

This "||" means "OR" to a SQL database.

...which is the same as saying this...

```
SELECT *
  FROM hraj_breakneck
WHERE phone = ''
    OR 'a' = 'a'
```

This will return false for all customers, since they all have a phone number.

Uh oh... this is always true! 'a' is always equal to 'a'.

Here's the problem!

This SQL query will be true for every customer!

Team Chat: SQL Injection

Frank: So no matter what the customer's phone number is, the WHERE clause is going to return true...

Jim: ...because of that part about 'a' = 'a', right? That's always a true statement.

Frank: Exactly. So the query returns all the customers in the database, instead of just the one with a specific phone number. I can see why everyone got upset!

Jim: So how do we fix this? We're getting like 10 complaints a day.

Frank: Well, I was reading about this thing called "magic quotes" in PHP. I think if we turn that on, it will protect us against SQL injection attacks.

Anne: Actually, Frank, magic quotes is going away in PHP 6, and a lot of people don't like that feature. It's a better idea to not count on features like that... take control yourself.

Jim: Hey, I saw some JavaScript code the other day that validates a phone number. I bet I could add that to the Break Neck form, and help avoid this happening...

Frank: ...and aren't there some MySQL functions I can use to make sure that this doesn't happen? I guess that would be better than counting on some sort of "magic quotes" function to help me out. I'll bet we can fix this...

Jim: Yup. Let's get to work. I'll take care of a little validation code, and you add that MySQL thingie you were talking about...

...and we can get back to the business of happy customers and hot pizza.

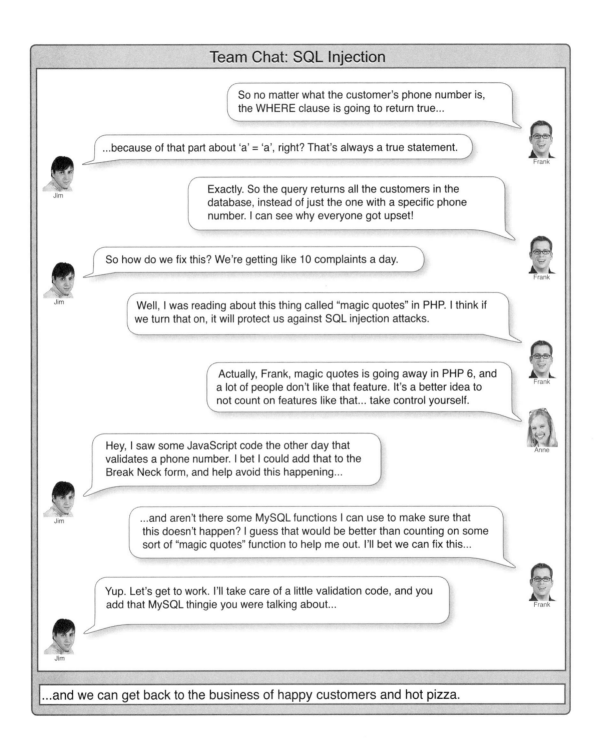

Wait a second... so this is really a **server-side** problem? Why should I have to write more JavaScript if I didn't cause the problem in the first place?

Validation protects your web app from hackers. You should always validate user input.

It's still your web application

Sure, SQL injection affects people like Frank and Anne, who work with the Break Neck PHP, more than it does the asynchronous JavaScript programmers. But if something goes wrong, you better believe that you're still going to hear about it!

Besides, with just a little bit of extra JavaScript, you can really help make your app more secure. Validation protects everyone, not just the server-side guys.

Frequently Asked Questions

Q: I'm totally lost on all this PHP stuff. I thought this was a book on asynchronous programmg!

A: It's OK if you don't really understand PHP. In fact, lots of programmers handle the JavaScript code on a web app, and then work with an entirely different group of people for the server-side part of the application.

The main thing you need to know is that things *can* go wrong on the server.

Q: So if I don't understand what's going on, what's the point of knowing about SQL injection in the first place?

A: All you need to know is that things *can* go wrong... and that most of the time, things ***will*** go wrong. Now, you can talk to your server-side guys, and help make sure nobody is getting your customer's addresses or phone numbers.

Q: Then this is really all about communication, right? Between me and the other people on the team?

A: Exactly! There are plenty of times you won't know the answer to a problem, or even that a problem exists. But if you just spend a little time with the other folks on your team, your web app will be much the better for it. Along the way, you might even pick up some ideas about making your code better... like validating input...

Protecting against SQL injection → in your JavaScript

If you look in the online examples, you'll find a folder called **chapter05-interlude/breakneck**. This has all the Break Neck files, as well as a new utility file, **validation-utils.js**. Here's how you can add validation to your local version of Break Neck Pizza:

Here's just part of the validation-utils.js file. This file is in the examples, in the chapter05-interlude/breakneck/ folder.

1 Make sure you have validation-utils.js

```
  return (isInteger(s) &&
          s.length >= minDigitsInIPhoneNumber);
}

function validatePhone(phoneNumber) {
  if ((phoneNumber == null) || (phoneNumber ==
    alert("Please enter your phone number.");
    return false;
```

validatePhone() is the function you'll use to check the phone numbers entered in the Break Neck web form.

validation-utils.js

2 Add a reference to validation-utils.js in the Break Neck web form.

Here's the top part of pizza.html. You can use your version from Chapter 5, or get the latest version from the book's examples.

```
<html>
 <head>
  <title>The New and Improved Break Neck Pizza</title>
  <link rel="stylesheet" type="text/css"
        href="breakneck.css" media="screen" />
  <script type="text/javascript" src="ajax.js"> </script>
  <script type="text/javascript" src="pizza.js"> </script>
  <script type="text/javascript"
        src="validation-utils.js"> </script>
 </head>
```

This line makes the functions in validation-utils.js available to the rest of your JavaScript.

pizza.html

③ Validate the phone number before sending it to the Break Neck web server.

You should have getCustomerInfo() at the top of your pizza.js file.

```
function getCustomerInfo() {
  var phone = document.getElementById("phone").value;
  if (validatePhone(phone) == false) {
    return;
  }
  var url = "lookupCustomer.php?phone=" + phone;
  request.open("GET", url, true);
  request.onreadystatechange = updatePage;
  request.send(null);
}

function updatePage() {
```

validatePhone(phone) checks to make sure the value of the phone field is a phone number.

If the phone number isn't valid, you shouldn't send a request to the Break Neck server... just return to the web form.

If there's a problem, validatePhone() will print an error out, and return "false".

pizza.js

Remember, all the Break Neck-specific JavaScript is in pizza.js now.

④ Test out your validation changes.

Load up pizza.html in your browser.

Here's that same weird set of characters that you entered into the Break Neck online form a few pages back...

This time, your validation detects the problem, and never sends the "fake" phone number to the Break Neck web server.

PROJECT: CHAOS isn't getting anybody's customer list with this improved version of the Break Neck order form.

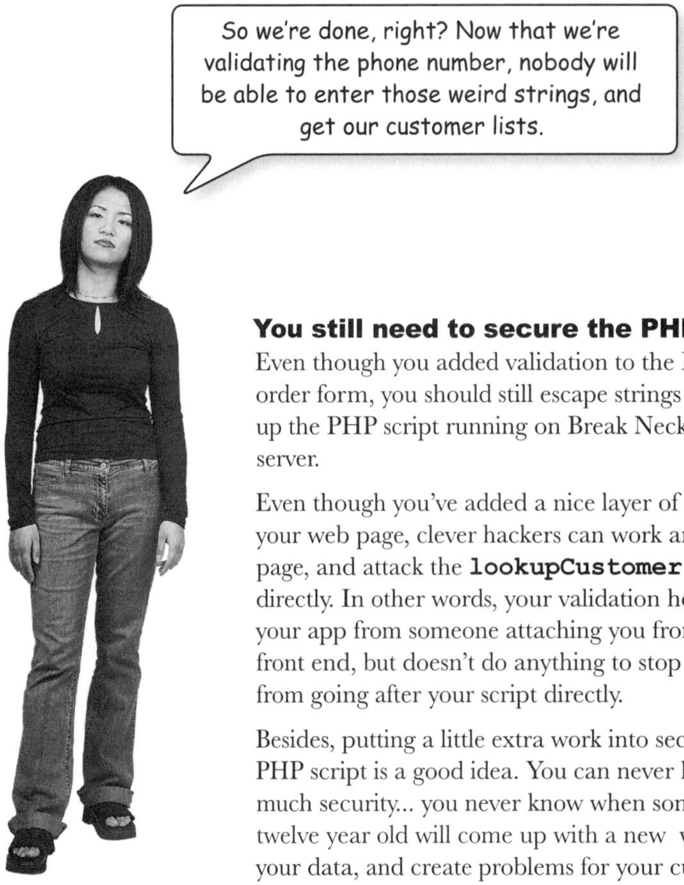

So we're done, right? Now that we're validating the phone number, nobody will be able to enter those weird strings, and get our customer lists.

You still need to secure the PHP script

Even though you added validation to the Break Neck order form, you should still escape strings and tighten up the PHP script running on Break Neck's web server.

Even though you've added a nice layer of security to your web page, clever hackers can work around your page, and attack the **`lookupCustomer.php`** script directly. In other words, your validation helps protect your app from someone attaching you from a web front end, but doesn't do anything to stop someone from going after your script directly.

Besides, putting a little extra work into securing your PHP script is a good idea. You can never have too much security... you never know when some clever twelve year old will come up with a new way to get at your data, and create problems for your customers.

You can never have <u>too</u> <u>much</u> security.

What's wrong with the PHP script?

Let's take a look at **`lookupCustomer.php`**, and see where we might be able to make some improvements.

It's OK if you're not familiar with PHP... just get a basic idea of what's going on, so you can tell your PHP guys what to watch out for.

```
<?php

// Connect to database
$conn = @mysql_connect("mysql.headfirstlabs.com",
                       "secret", "really-secret");
if (!$conn)
  die("Error connecting to MySQL: " . mysql_error());

if (!mysql_select_db("headfirst", $conn))
  die("Error selecting Head First database: " . mysql_error());

$phone = preg_replace("/[\. \(\)\-]/", "", $_REQUEST['phone']);
$select = 'SELECT *';
$from   = ' FROM hraj_breakneck';
$where  = ' WHERE phone = \'' . $phone . '\'';

$queryResult = @mysql_query($select . $from . $where);
if (!$queryResult)
  die('Error retrieving customer from the database.');

while ($row = mysql_fetch_array($queryResult)) {
  echo $row['name'] . "\n" .
       $row['street1'] . "\n" .
       $row['city'] . ", " .
       $row['state'] . " " .
       $row['zipCode'];
}

mysql_close($conn);

?>
```

Even though we get rid of some of the phone number formatting, like (,), and -, there's still a problem...

...we're not doing anything to protect against the characters that are in SQL injection attacks, like those single quotes...

...and the potentially dangerous string still gets inserted into the SQL query.

Here's another potential problem. The script loops through all the results it gets, and displays each one...

...but the script should never return more than one customer. We'll need to fix this.

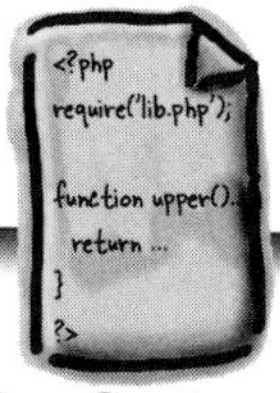

lookupCustomer.php

Remember this script from Chapter 2? It's the PHP script that getCustomerInfo() makes a request to.

SQL injection attacks without the web form

Now that you know some of the problems with the lookpuCustomer.php script, let's see how **PROJECT: CHAOS** (or any other hacker) could exploit those problems and get the Break Neck customer list.

Now, only real phone numbers can get through your validation.

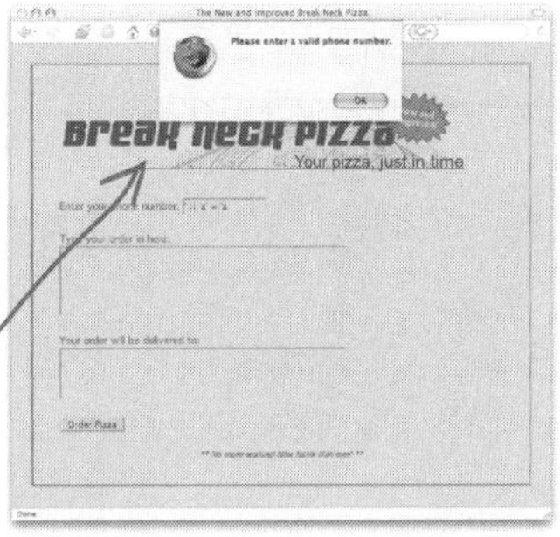

Your validation catches attacks through the Break Neck order form.

```
Hypertext Transfer Protocol
  POST /placeOrder.php HTTP/1.1
    Request Method: POST
    Request URI: /placeOrder.php
    Request Version: HTTP/1.1
  Host: www.headfirstlabs.com
  Keep-Alive: 300
  Connection: keep-alive
  Content-Type:
    application/x-www-form-urlencoded
  phone=(214) 290-8762
```

These two POST rquests are treated exactly the same by the Break Neck web server and PHP script.

Clever hackers can send a POST request directly to your PHP script, without using the Break Neck order form at all.

```
Hypertext Transfer Protocol
  POST /placeOrder.php HTTP/1.1
    Request Method: POST
    Request URI: /placeOrder.php
    Request Version: HTTP/1.1
  Host: www.headfirstlabs.com
  Keep-Alive: 300
  Connection: keep-alive
  Content-Type:
    application/x-www-form-urlencoded
  phone=' || 'a' = 'a
```

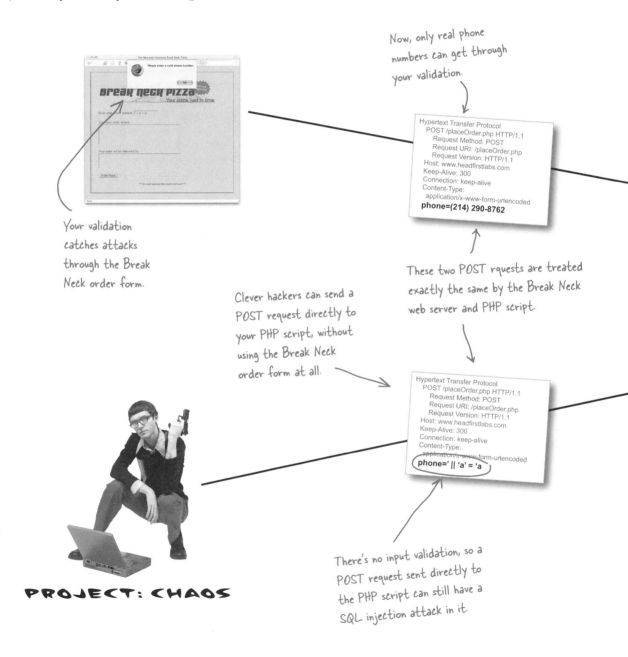

PROJECT: CHAOS

There's no input validation, so a POST request sent directly to the PHP script can still have a SQL injection attack in it.

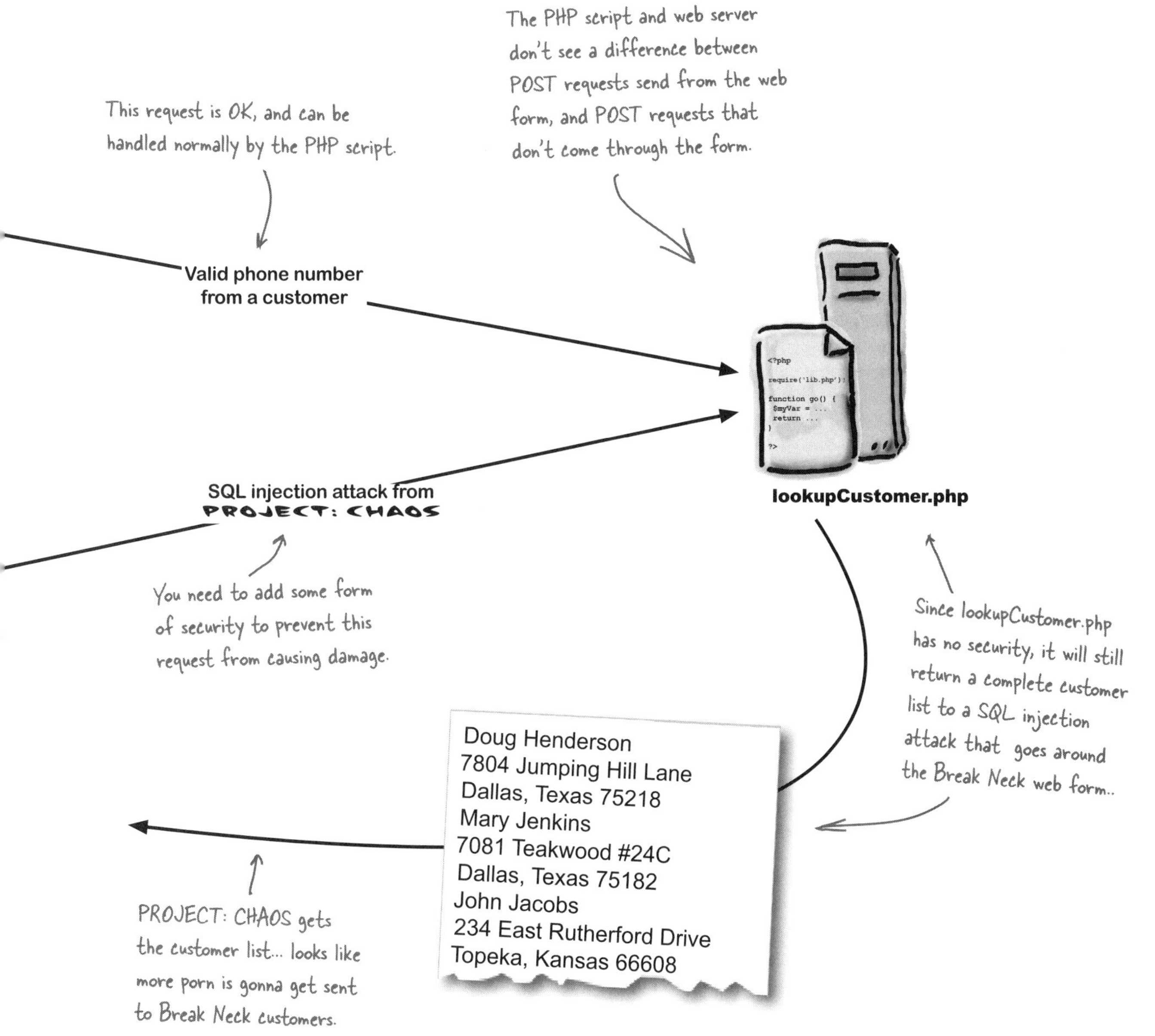

This request is OK, and can be handled normally by the PHP script.
The PHP script and web server don't see a difference between POST requests send from the web form, and POST requests that don't come through the form.
Valid phone number from a customer
lookupCustomer.php
SQL injection attack from PROJECT: CHAOS
You need to add some form of security to prevent this request from causing damage.
Since lookupCustomer.php has no security, it will still return a complete customer list to a SQL injection attack that goes around the Break Neck web form..
Doug Henderson
7804 Jumping Hill Lane
Dallas, Texas 75218
Mary Jenkins
7081 Teakwood #24C
Dallas, Texas 75182
John Jacobs
234 East Rutherford Drive
Topeka, Kansas 66608
PROJECT: CHAOS gets the customer list... looks like more porn is gonna get sent to Break Neck customers.

Protecting against SQL injection → in your PHP scripts

There's no reason to stop with your JavaScript. Let's help Frank make a few upgrades to his PHP to help protect the server from SQL injection attacks, too.

```
<?php

// Connect to database
$conn = @mysql_connect("mysql.headfirstlabs.com",
                       "secret", "really-secret");
if (!$conn)
  die("Error connecting to MySQL: " . mysql_error());

if (!mysql_select_db("headfirst", $conn))
  die("Error selecting Head First database: " . mysql_error());

$phone = preg_replace("/[\. \(\)\-]/", "", $_REQUEST['phone']);
$phone = mysql_real_escape_string($phone);
$select = 'SELECT *';
$from   = ' FROM hraj_breakneck';
$where  = ' WHERE phone = \'' . $phone . '\'';

$queryResult = @mysql_query($select . $from . $where);
if (!$queryResult)
  die('Error retrieving customer from the database.');

while ($row = mysql_fetch_array($queryResult)) {
$row = mysql_fetch_array($queryResult);
echo $row['name'] . "\n" .
     $row['street1'] . "\n" .
     $row['city'] . ", " .
     $row['state'] . " " .
     $row['zipCode'];
}

mysql_close($conn);

?>
```

This is the most important change. This function will take care of escaping any special characters, like those single quotes in the input string you entered.

We really shouldn't be looping through the results. There should never be more than one customer displayed at a time.

Now, no matter what the phone number is, only one customer (at most) is returned in the server's response.

lookupCustomer.php

With these changes, lookupCustomer.php is protected from most SQL injection attacks. Nice work!

Your customer database is secure!

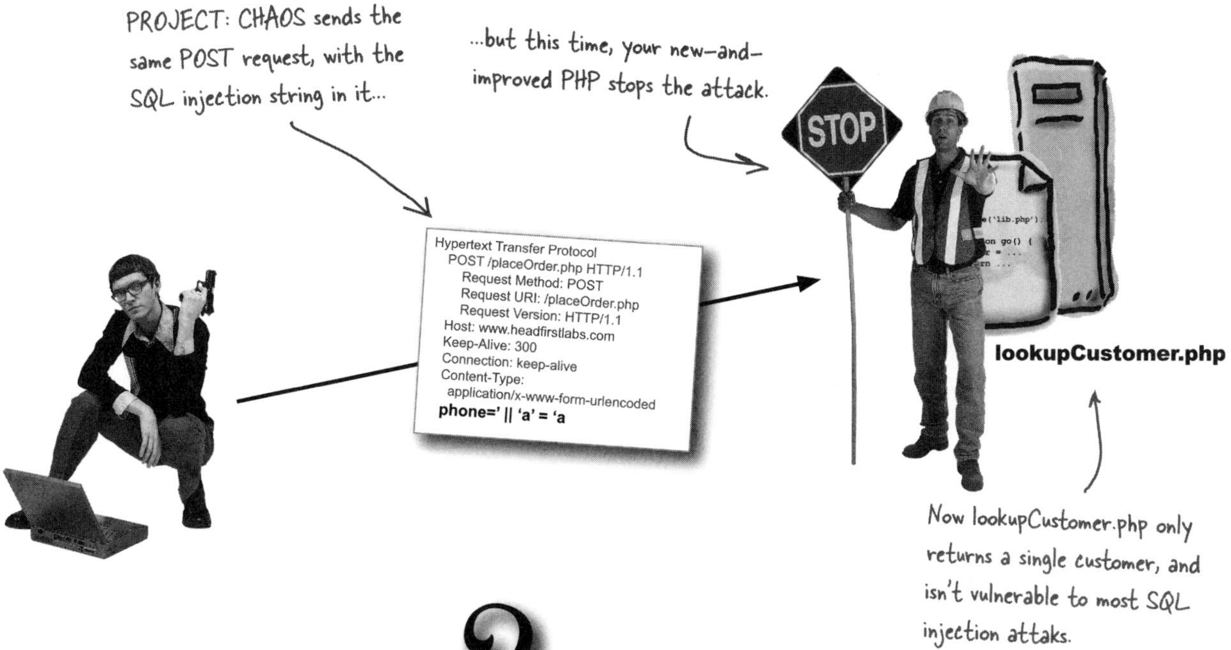
PROJECT: CHAOS sends the same POST request, with the SQL injection string in it...
...but this time, your new-and-improved PHP stops the attack.
Hypertext Transfer Protocol
POST /placeOrder.php HTTP/1.1
Request Method: POST
Request URI: /placeOrder.php
Request Version: HTTP/1.1
Host: www.headfirstlabs.com
Keep-Alive: 300
Connection: keep-alive
Content-Type:
application/x-www-form-urlencoded
phone=' || 'a' = 'a
STOP
lookupCustomer.php
Now lookupCustomer.php only returns a single customer, and isn't vulnerable to most SQL injection attaks.

Frequently Asked Questions

Q: mysql_real_escape_string()? What in the world is that? Did I mention that I'm not a PHP programmer?

A: `mysql_real_escape_string()` is a PHP function that escapes any special characters in a string, and makes that string safe to use in your SQL statements. It only works for MySQL databases, but you can find functions similar to this for all the major databases.

And it's OK if you're not really familiar with PHP or these functions. Remember, the point is that you're talking to the programmers working on the server-side components of your app. Just tell them to be sure that they secure their scripts.

Q: And all this is called SQL injection?

A: SQL injection is just *one type* of security risk for web apps. When you have form fields that are used to build SQL queries, hackers often try and enter special strings—like the one you got from PROJECT: CHAOS—to try and get information out of a database, or insert bad data into the database.

The bad news is that there are lots of other types of attacks you have to worry about... but the good news is that with validation and a little security on the server, you can protect yourself against almost all of these attacks. So go forth, and secure!

SQL Injection is only the tip of the iceberg... we'll be back when you least expect it.

PROJECT: CHAOS

6 XML Requests & Responses

More Than Words Can Say

But I'm so much **more** than just a pretty face... I really **do** have something to say.

Ever feel like nobody is listening to you? Sometimes plain old English just doesn't cut it when you're **trying to communicate**. You've been using text for all of your requests and responses so far, but it's time to break out of our plain-text shells. In this chapter, we'll **dive into XML**, and teach our servers to say a lot more than they ever could with plain text. As if that's not enough, you'll teach your requests XML, too, even though that's not always a good idea (more on that inside). Get ready... once you've finished this chapter, *your requests and responses will never be the same*.

Dr. Zigmund: Ahhh, yes. So many of my patients feel zees way. It is a common problem. But in many cases, it is zimply just in your mind.

Server: But in my case, it's true! I mean, everyone wants to *talk* to me... I've got plenty of people saying things to me all the time...

Dr. Zigmund: Zee? Zat is very important, to have friends that are zere for you.

Server: But that's the thing. When I start to say something back, they barely listen. In fact, it's been getting a lot worse just lately.

Dr. Zigmund: Tell me more about... "lately."

Server: Well, I used to say a lot of things. Like <html><head><title>Hello!</title></head></html>. But now, if I say anything more than "1012", I get complaints. Nobody will let me get more than a word or two into a conversation.

Dr. Zigmund: And you zay you have more to zay?

Server: Yes! I have much more to zay... I mean, say. Sometimes, I have a *lot* of things to say. I listen all the time and I never ignore a request... but when it comes time for me to respond, if I'm not done in a second or two, I get called these horrible things...

Dr. Zigmund: Like what? What do zey call you?

Server: Slow... bloated... 20th-century... oh, it's horrible! I just want people to let me say a little more than "6" or "Pot 1", you know?

...to be continued...

Speak Up!

Time for a quick refresher on what the server's been saying to our Ajax apps. Below are the five example applications you've developed so far. Your job is to go back and figure out what the server responded within each app, and write that response on the lines provided.

Chapter 1: Boards 'R' Us

____
____
____

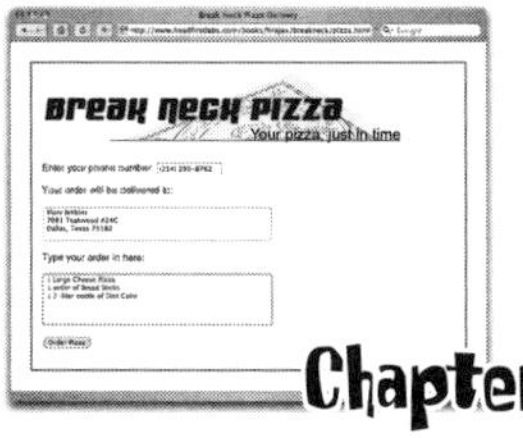

Chapter 2: Break Neck Pizza

____
____
____

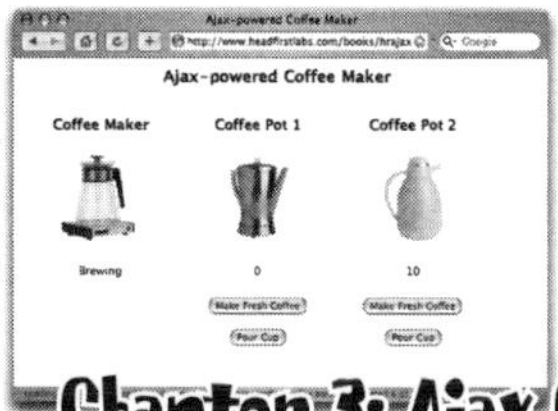

Chapter 3: Ajax Coffee Maker

____
____
____

Chapter 4: Top 5 CDs

____
____
____

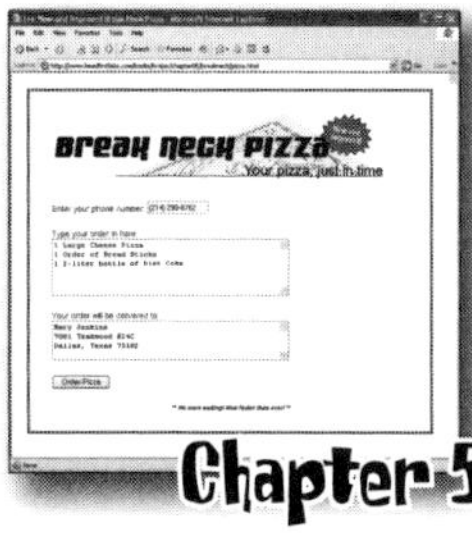

Chapter 5: Break Neck Revisited

____
____
____

Speak Up!

So did the server have much to say? What about all these complaints about nobody listening? Do you think they're valid? Check your answers below, and decide for yourself... is the server getting to say very much?

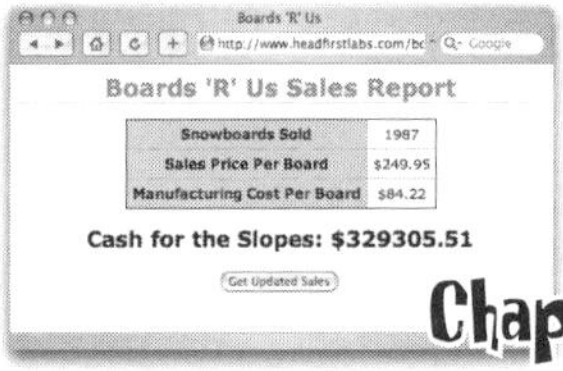

Chapter 1: Boards 'R' Us

1143

This is the only app where the server gets to send much back...

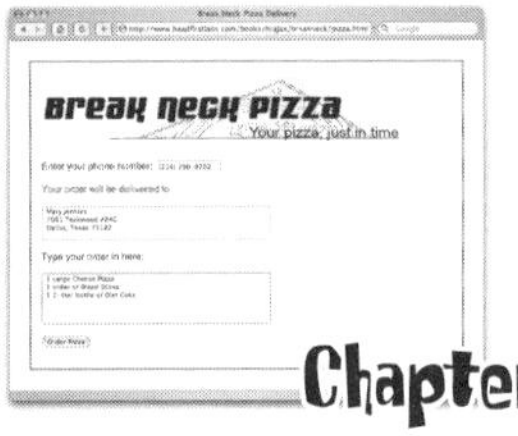

Chapter 2: Break Neck Pizza

Doug Henderson
7804 Jumping Hill Lane
Dallas, Texas 75218

Wow... the server really doesn't get to say much in these apps.

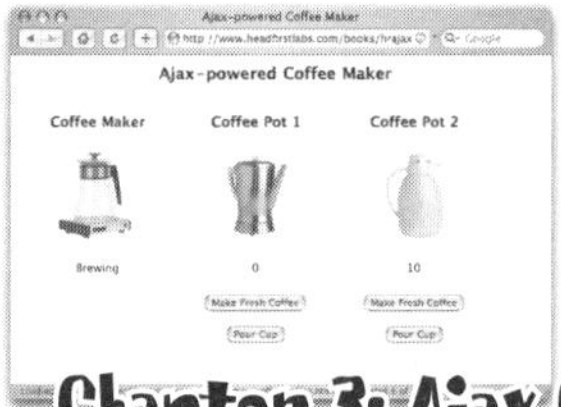

Chapter 3: Ajax Coffee Maker

2

Chapter 4: Top 5 CDs

No server involved!

Chapter 5: Break Neck Revisited

7

Remember, this was how long it would take for the pizza to arrive.

Do you see what I mean? I can't go on saying nothing more than "7", or "2"! It's driving me insane!

Dr. Zigmund: Vell.... I do zee that you got to zay quite a bit in zee Chapter 2 over there. A whole address... zurely that's ex-ziting!

Server: Well, yes, but that's still just *one thing*. I mean, I couldn't send back, say, the customer's address, *and* a special coupon for repeat customers. I just get to say that one thing: their address.

Dr. Zigmund: Vell, zey zay that brevity is the zoul of wit.

Server: What? Oh... the *soul* of wit. Well, whoever "zey" are, they don't have to sit around all day listening to long requests, now do "zey"?

Dr. Zigmund: Now let's just calm down. Have you *tried* to say more than one thing in your responses?

Server: Sure! But nobody really understands what I mean. Like, once I tried to send a customer's address, phone number, and order back, and I used a semicolon to separate each part of my response. But nobody seemed to like that... they said I was too "proprietary", and that I needed to be "standardized."

Dr. Zigmund: Zat is true, you know. Next, you'll tell me you were using commas or zat strange "pipe" symbol to split your data up.

Server: *(Well, there was this one time...)*

Dr. Zigmund: I think I have just the zing for you, my dear friend. Let me just get out my prescription pad. It's time you got a good dose of zandardization. Zis will help everyone under-zand exactly what you're saying.

Server: What goes is zander... ummm... standardization going to do me? I just want to be understood...

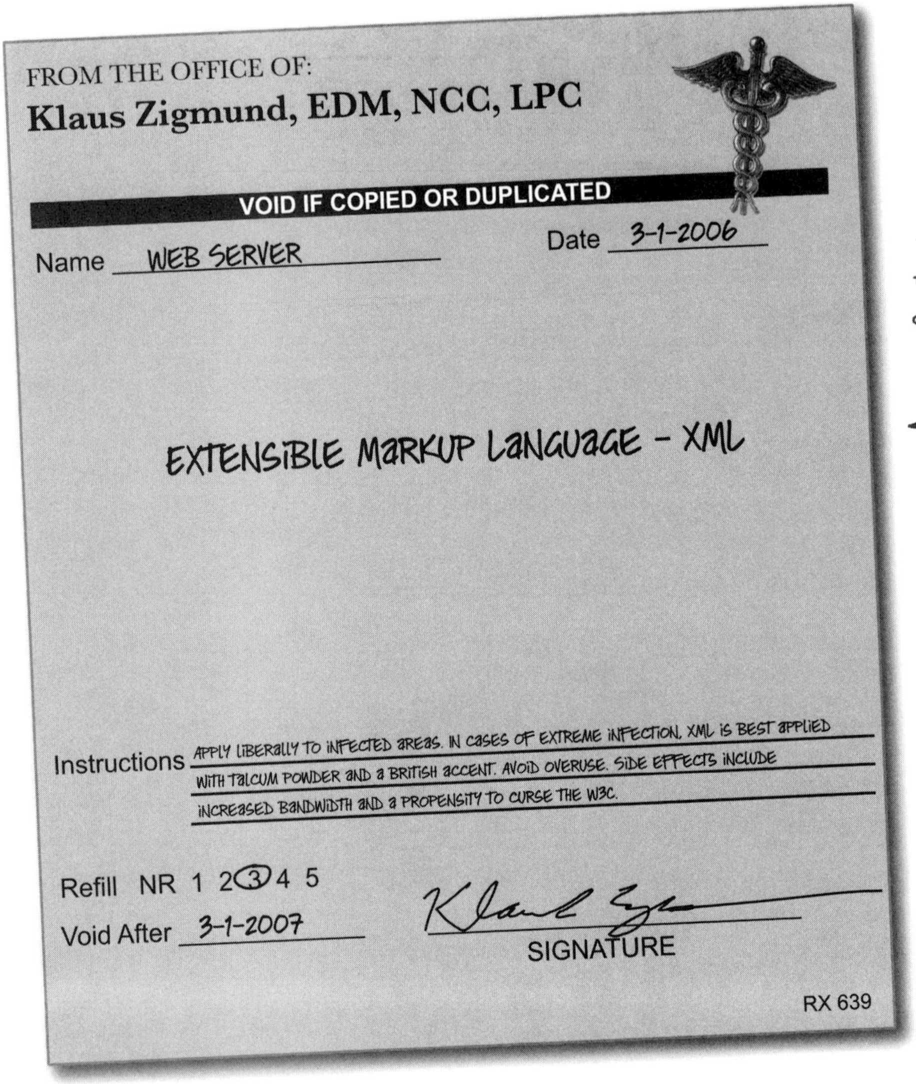

FROM THE OFFICE OF:
Klaus Zigmund, EDM, NCC, LPC

VOID IF COPIED OR DUPLICATED

Name WEB SERVER
Date 3-1-2006

EXTENSIBLE MARKUP LANGUAGE - XML

Instructions APPLY LIBERALLY TO INFECTED AREAS. IN CASES OF EXTREME INFECTION, XML IS BEST APPLIED WITH TALCUM POWDER AND A BRITISH ACCENT. AVOID OVERUSE. SIDE EFFECTS INCLUDE INCREASED BANDWIDTH AND A PROPENSITY TO CURSE THE W3C.

Refill NR 1 2 (3) 4 5

Void After 3-1-2007

SIGNATURE

RX 639

Here's the prescription that Dr. Zigmund wrote out for Server.

XML: just what the doctor ordered

He may be a bit hard to understand, but it seems like Dr. Zigmund has some pretty specific ideas about helping web servers say more in their responses. Keep this in mind, as we'll be coming back to XML in just a moment.

But, speaking of help, it looks like an old friend might need some help herself...

Remember Katie?

Katie's been busy since we left her back in Chapter 1. She's got a couple of new product lines now—snowboarding boots and a new custom line of bindings—and she's updated her online report to keep up with all three product lines.

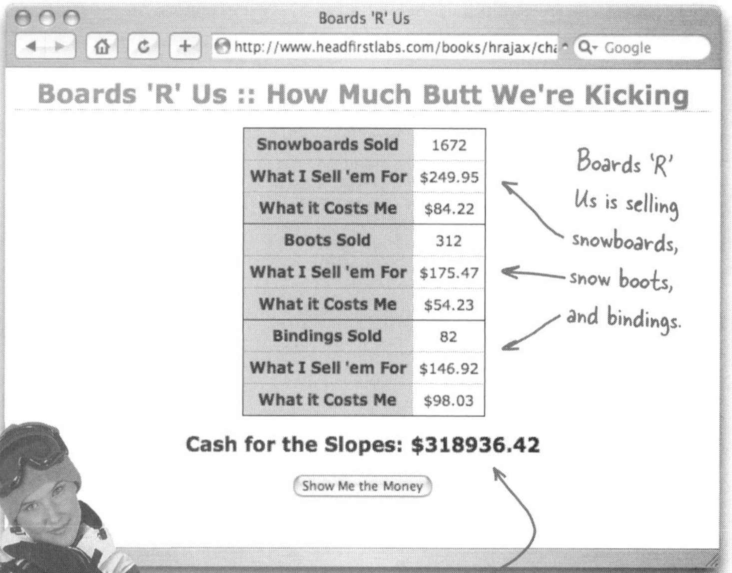

Boards 'R' Us is selling snowboards, snow boots, and bindings.

Business is booming. We've got three product lines now, but there's a problem... we don't know how to get updated totals from the server for all three lines at once. Think you can help us out again?

Katie's been making some serious cash with her new product lines!

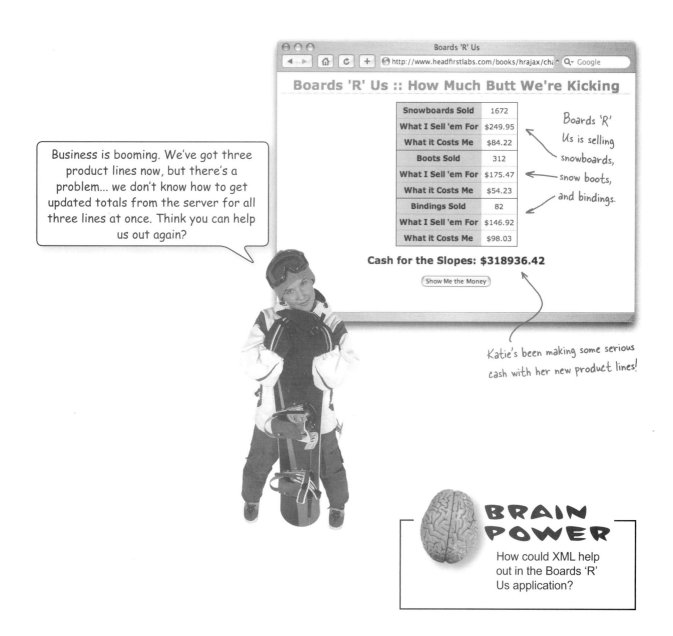

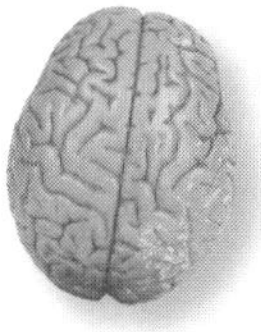

BRAIN POWER

How could XML help out in the Boards 'R' Us application?

The problem with Boards 'R' Us

The Boards 'R' Us report still uses an asynchronous request to talk to the server, and since you solved their caching problems, the report works for everyone in the company (including Katie's man running Windows).

But the server needs to send back three sales numbers now: the total number of boards sold, as well as the number of boots and bindings sold.

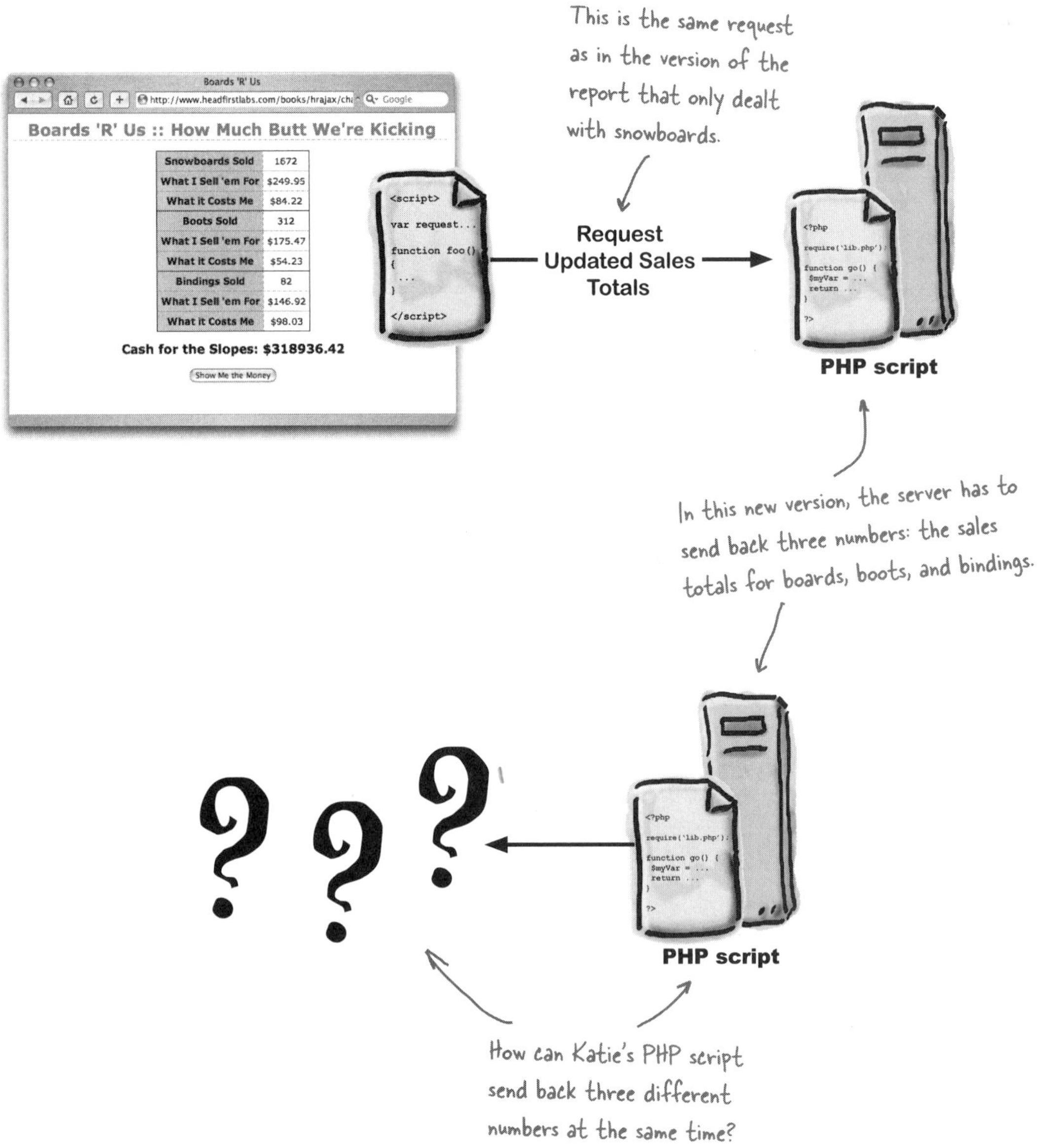

Great! Someone finally *wants* me to say more, and I don't know how. I HATE being a server!

Dr. Zigmund: Progress, my dear friend! Now people vant to hear you.

Server: But how can I say three things at one time? This is my only chance... and I'm going to blow it.

Dr. Zigmund: I don't zink you have been using my pre-zcription, have you?

Server: I could just string the three sales totals together, and a space between them... no, that's a pretty crummy idea...

Dr. Zigmund: Have you con-zidered zee XML?

Server: Maybe comma-separated values? Those are big in spreadsheets... but no, the commas could get mistaken as part of the total itself...

Dr. Zigmund: Now I wonder who is not listening to whom... young man, I'm trying to tell you...

Server: If I just had a way to send data in a format that I know the Boards report would be able to understand... I know Katie hates anything that might break in a few months, or isn't standardized...

Dr. Zigmund: Zees is hopeless. Zere is no cure for zee clueless zerver, it zeems.

OK, look... I'm loving this cute little story, but I've got it, OK? The stupid server needs to use XML, right? That's the answer to the Boards problem?

But do you understand *why*?

XML can definitely help Katie out with her online report. So far, you've used plain text to send responses back to the web browser... but that's just because you've only had to return a single piece of data, like an address, or the number of minutes until a pizza will show up.

When you need to get more than just a single piece of information from the server, though, things get a little trickier. You've seen that using proprietary data formats just isn't the answer:

Here are some examples of the server sending back data using a "made up" data format.

`1710;315;85`

There are three numbers in this response, but both the server and the browser have to know what the semicolon means...

`1710,315,85`

...and in this case, it's unclear what purpose the comma serves. Does it separate different numbers? Is this all one number?

`1710|315|85`

Boy, better hope nobody ever changes the order of these sales totals... that would be bad, bad, bad!

Even worse: what happens if the order of the data returned changes? Everything breaks!

Filling that XML prescription

Trying to come up with a data format that works for the server, that the browser understands, and that won't have to change if Katie adds another product line or changes the order of items on her report... that's not so easy.

Luckily for us, Dr. Zigmund (as well as that rather impatient girl on the last page) seems to have a solution: XML, the extensible markup language. Using XML, we can come up with a simple response format that is clear, and contains all three updated sales totals.

This line just identifies this content as XML. It gives the version of XML used...

...and how the XML is encoded.

<totals> is the root element... it just serves as a container for the three "sold" elements.

```
<?xml version="1.0" encoding="utf-8"?>
<totals>
  <boards-sold>1710</boards-sold>
  <boots-sold>315</boots-sold>
  <bindings-sold>85</bindings-sold>
</totals>
```

There's no question as to which number is the board sales, which is the boot sales, and which is the bindings sales.

Even if the order of these lines changed, it would still be clear what each number represented.

The server can send back this entire piece of XML as its response.

Frequently Asked Questions

Q: What's so great about XML?

A: The biggest thing going for XML is that it's a recognized standard. Some folks at the World Wide Web Consortium (or the W3C for short) define what makes XML, well, XML. And since most people agree to abide by the W3C standard, browsers, servers, and programs like PHP scripts can all use XML without wondering what a bracket or a semicolon means.

Q: I still don't see why it's so bad to just make up our own data format. Wouldn't that be easier?

A: It might seem that way, but proprietary data formats—formats that you make up for your own use—can really cause a lot of problems. If you don't document them, people forget how they work. Even worse, some of the characters you might use, like a semicolon or comma, can have more than one meaning, and they make the format confusing to programmers.

Q: I get why we should use XML, but do we have to use the same element names you did?

A: No, not at all. That's the beauty of XML: it's flexible. So you might use `boardSales` instead of `board-sales`, or `totalBindings` instead of `bindingSales`. It's really up to you. As long as both the JavaScript in your browser and the code on your server know what names to use, what those names actually are is really up to you.

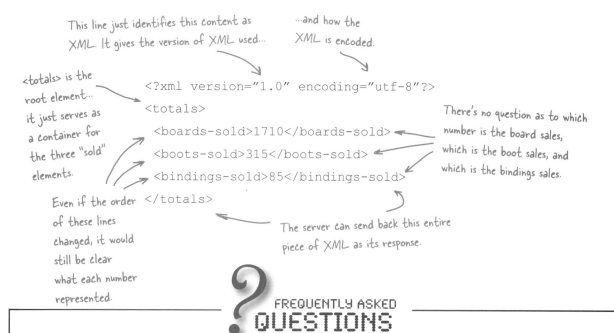

PHP ...at a glance

While you've been thinking about Katie's JavaScript and HTML, her server-side guys have been listening in. They've gone ahead and updated the getUpdatedSales.php script to return the XML we've been talking about, complete with updated totals for board, boot, and binding sales. Not too bad, huh? Here's what the script looks like now:

```
<?php

// Connect to database
$conn = @mysql_connect("mysql.headfirstlabs.com",
                       "secret", "really-secret");
if (!$conn)
  die("Error connecting to MySQL: " . mysql_error());

if (!mysql_select_db("headfirst", $conn))
  die("Error selecting Head First database: " . mysql_error());

$select = 'SELECT boardsSold, bootsSold, bindingsSold';
$from   = '  FROM boardsrus';
$queryResult = @mysql_query($select . $from);
if (!$queryResult)
  die('Error retrieving total boards sold from database.');

while ($row = mysql_fetch_array($queryResult)) {
  $boardsSold = $row['boardsSold'];
  $bootsSold = $row['bootsSold'];
  $bindingsSold = $row['bindingsSold'];
}

header("Content-Type: text/xml");
echo "<?xml version=\"1.0\" encoding=\"utf-8\"?>
?>

<totals>
 <boards-sold><? echo $boardsSold; ?></boards-sold>
 <boots-sold><? echo $bootsSold; ?></boots-sold>
 <bindings-sold><? echo $bindingsSold; ?></bindings-sold>
</totals>

<? mysql_close($conn); ?>
```

A lot of this is the same as when Boards 'R' Us had just one product, and wasn't using XML.

The Boards 'R' Us database now keeps up with three products: boards, boots, and bindings.

In this version of the app, we're interested in three values, instead of just one.

This tells the browser that the script is returning XML, not HTML markup or text.

Since the first part of this line, <?, is a start tag in PHP, you have to echo this line out using "echo", separate from the rest of the XML output.

The PHP returns XML now, instead of just a single number or a bunch of HTML.

Each XML element has the sales number for the related product, from the Boards 'R' Us database query.

Just Do It

Enough talk; it's time to take action. Open up the chapter06/boards folder in the examples you downloaded from http://www.headfirstlabs.com. You'll see the files for the Boards 'R' Us app, including an updated HTML report (boards.html), several JavaScript files (ajax.js and boards.js), and the XML version of getUpdatedSales.php. Your job is to update the code in the report to get the XML response from getUpdatedSales.php.

Open up boards.js, and find the function that gets the server's response. For now, go ahead and comment out all the DOM code that updates the form... we'll fix that up in a few pages. For now, you want to check the request's ready state, make sure the status code is 200 (meaning everything is OK with the response), and then show the server's response in a JavaScript alert box. Once you're done, you should be able to reload boards.html, click "Show Me the Money", and get something back that looks like this:

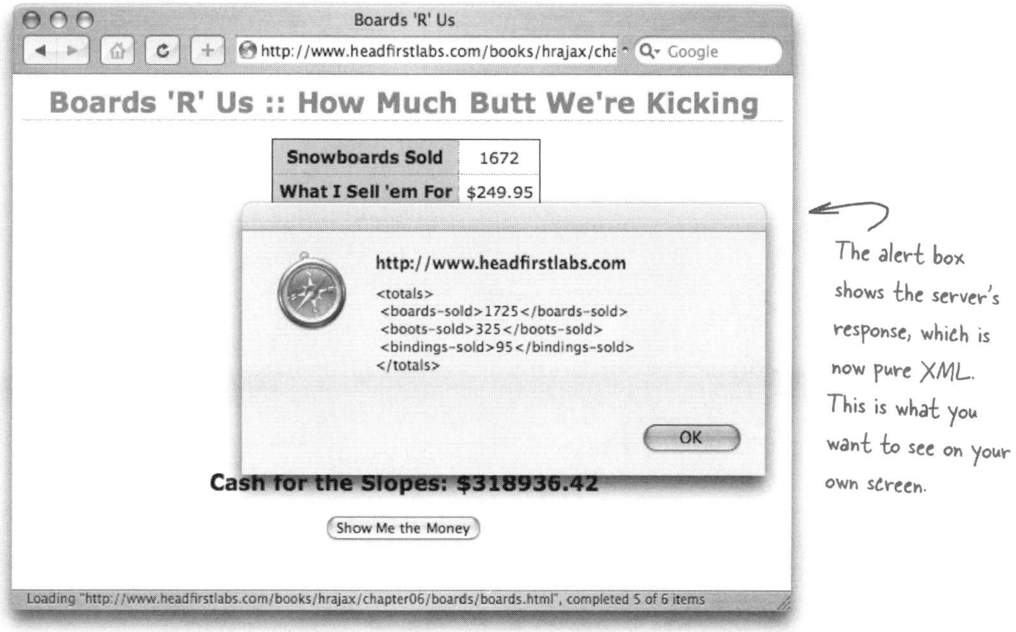

STOP! Don't turn the page until you've done this exercise.

Just Do It

Did you figure out how to display the server's response? Here's what we did:

1. We opened up boards.js, since that has the Boards 'R' Us callback function.
2. We found the callback, updatePage(), and commented out everything except for the two if statements that checked the ready state and the status code from the request.
3. We got the server's response, and then used the JavaScript alert() function to show it to the user.

Here's our code for updatePage():

```
function updatePage() {
  if (request.readyState == 4) {
    if (request.status == 200) {
      var response = request.responseText;
      alert(response);
/*
      var newTotal = request.responseText;
      ...
      replaceText(cashEl, cash);
*/
    } else {
      // Error handling code here
    }
  }
```

Leave the ready state and status checking code alone—we still need that.

This just gets the response from the server, and shows it with an alert dialog box.

You should have lots of code in here... comment all that out for now.

More Frequently Asked Questions

Q: That's it? The server sends back XML, and we just grab it using the responseText property?

A: At its simplest, yes. But, as you're about to see, there's a lot more we can do with XML than treat it as plain old text. So stick around...

Q: How do we get the values out of the XML? That seems like it's going to be a pain in the butt.

A: Yeah, you're right. Trying to break apart the XML data—called parsing the XML—and getting the values out isn't very easy. Fortunately, there's a better way to work with XML than as plain text.

Q: I remember something from way back in Chapter 2 about a responseXML property. Should we be using that instead of responseText?

A: Boy, you were really paying attention, weren't you? Yes, the request object has a property called **`responseXML`**, and yes, it's a great idea to use that instead of **`responseText`**. But before we get to that, it looks like we've got a visitor...

Hey there. Look, I know it's not my chapter, but I really think you might be interested in one of my DOM trees.
Oh my god. I'm finally starting to make some progress, and now Paul Bunyan wants to talk about selling me a bush.
Remember Mike from back in Chapter 4? He's the owner of the Webville tree farm.

Mike: Not a bush... a tree. And not just any tree; I've got a DOM tree you'd just love.

Server: Are you paying attention? Do you see me on this couch, and the nut with a notepad and bad accent? I'm not really looking to go into landscaping.

Mike: Well, I couldn't help but overhear you mention that you're sending XML back in your responses now.

Server: Yes, that's right... I really have communication issues, and Ziggy here thinks XML will help browsers allow me to say a lot more and still be understood.

Mike: Sounds like good advice to me. But how's a browser supposed to do anything with your XML? It's not that easy to parse an XML document, you know.

Server: What? Are you serious? You mean, all this work, and I'm *still* not going to be understood? Let me just find a toaster and a bathtub, and be done with it all!

Mike: That's what I'm here for, though! The browser—and JavaScript—can understand your XML. Any code that needs to read your XML response can just work with it using the DOM... and then everyone's happy.

Server: Yes! Well, let's get that DOM growing, then. I think I can see the light...

Trees, trees, everywhere I look

You've already seen how the Document Object Model makes working with HTML easy. But the DOM is a lot more versatile: you can use it to work with XML documents as well. Let's check out how the XML returned from **getUpdatedSales.php** looks as a DOM tree:

All the elements and text in the XML document...

```
<?xml version="1.0"
      encoding="utf-8"?>
<totals>
  <boards-sold>1710</boards-sold>
  <boots-sold>315</boots-sold>
  <bindings-sold>85</bindings-sold>
</totals>
```

...show up in the DOM tree representation of the XML.

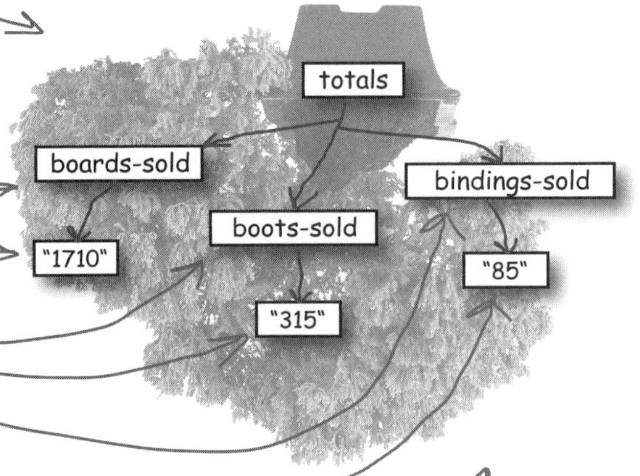

Each of the three "sold" elements has one child node: a text node with the number of that product that's been sold.

You may not have known...

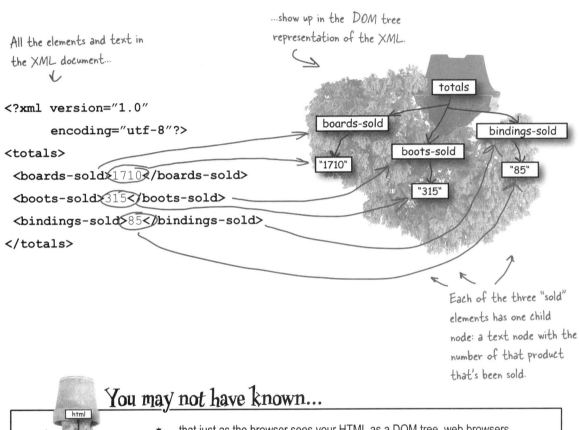

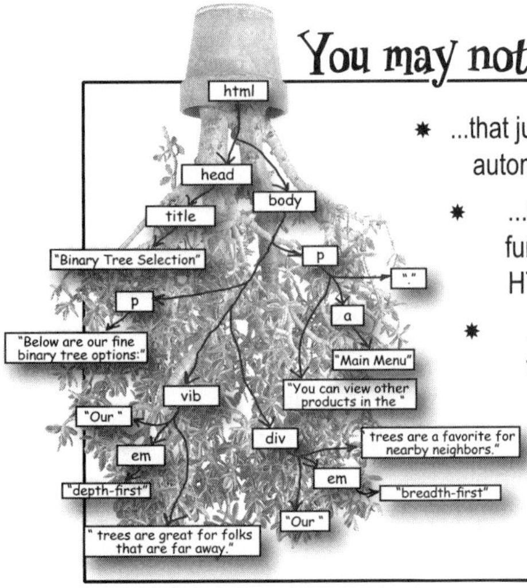

- ...that just as the browser sees your HTML as a DOM tree, web browsers automatically convert any XML they have to deal with into DOM trees.
- ...that you can work with more than one DOM tree in the same JavaScript function. For example, you can read an XML DOM tree and update an HTML DOM tree, all at the same time.
- ...that HTML elements and XML elements are both just element nodes in the DOM. There's no difference between an XML type and an HTML type, at least when it comes to the DOM.
- ...that the responseXML property always returns a DOM document object, even if the XML in the DOM tree is only a single element, or just a single text node.

Using responseXML in your code

You've already seen that the **`responseText`** property of your request object lets you read the XML that the server responds with. But we don't want a bunch of text that looks like XML; we're DOM experts now, right? Using the **`responseXML`** property, you can get the DOM tree for the server's response, and then work with that XML using the DOM.

Even if you don't feel like an expert, you're kicking butt! And by the time you finish this chapter, you'll be even better at the DOM than you are now.

And since the HTML for Katie's Boards report is another DOM tree, we just want to grab values from the XML DOM and stick them in the HTML DOM. Let's see exactly what we need to do:

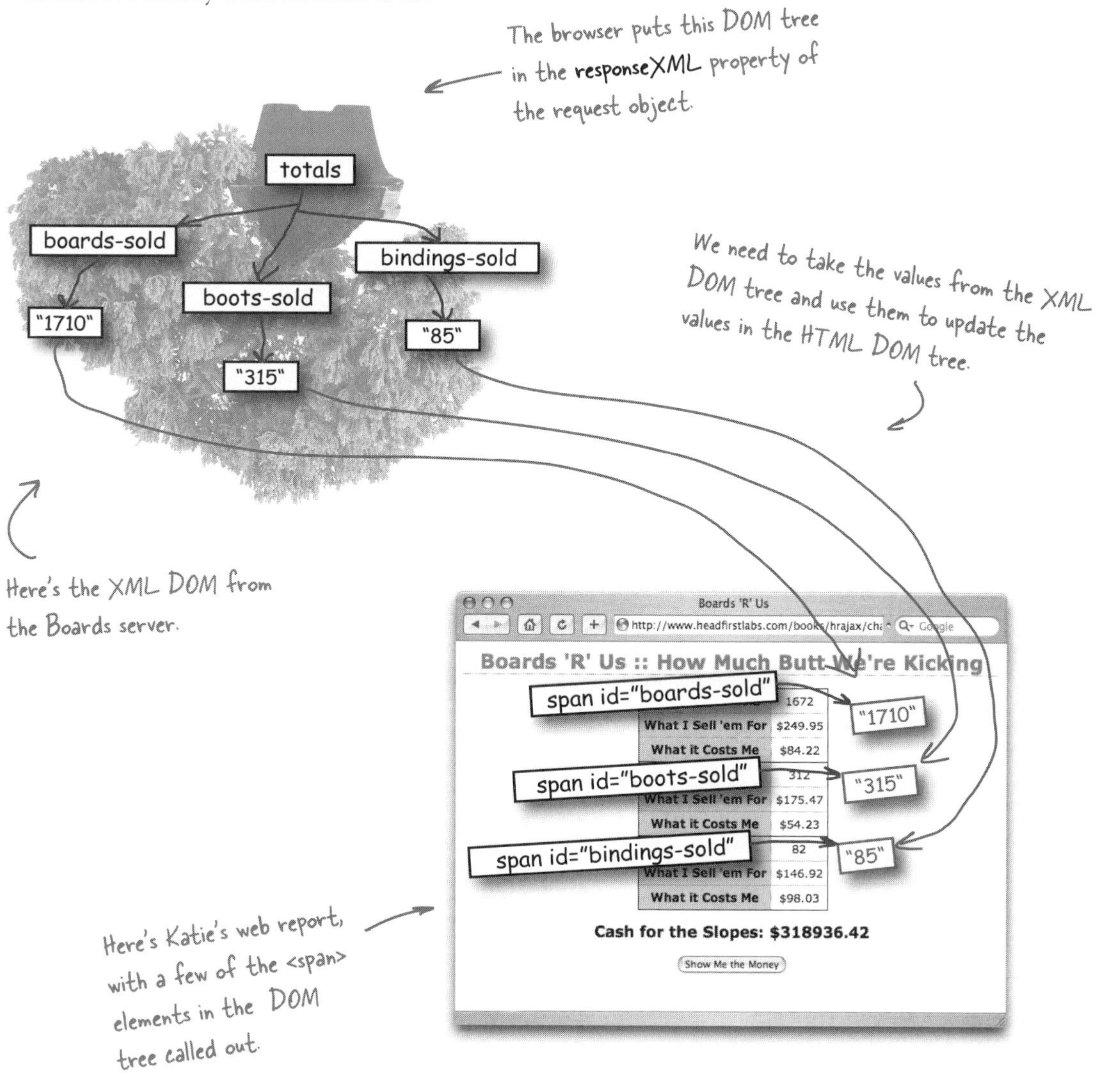

I'm with you so far, but how can we get to those three "sold" elements in the XML? They don't have id attributes like the <span> elements in Katie's HTML.

You can find them with their "tag name"

So far, you've been using **getElementById()** to find a specific element in an HTML DOM tree. But there's another useful method called **getElementsByTagName()**. You can use this to find all the elements in a DOM tree with a certain name, like this:

```
var xmlDoc = request.responseXML;
var boardsSoldElements =
  xmlDoc.getElementsByTagName("boards-sold");
```

Get the DOM tree representing the server's XML request.

Now we're working with the DOM!

This will return an array of all the elements named "boards-sold" in the **xmlDoc** DOM tree. Then, you can get elements from the list using an index, like this:

```
var firstBoardsSoldElement =
  boardsSoldElements[0];
```

Remember, JavaScript arrays start at 0, not 1.

You could also loop through this list using a "for" loop, if you wanted to.

Time to take a shortcut:

```
var firstBoardsSoldElement = xmlDoc.getElementsByTagName("boards-sold")[0];
```

This gets all the elements named "boards-sold"...

...and this returns just the first element from the list.

If you use asynchronous requests in your JavaScript code, but only send and receive plain text responses, would that be Aja? Or is that the tiger from Aladdin? What if you used the request object synchronously? That would just be Jax, right? But then, that sounds an awful lot like a kid's game, so that doesn't really work. And synchronous requests without using XML leaves you with "Ja", although that sounds more like the first name of that rapper... hmm. Yes, clearly, Ajax is the only name that makes sense, even though it has only a passing connection to what this book is about. Don't tell marketing, though... they say that throwing "Ajax" on the cover means a lot more sales. Oh, and be sure to keep an eye out for next month's featured titles: "Ajax and Ajill: A Nursery Rhyme Love Story," "Ajax Me No Questions, I'll D-H-T-M-L You No Lies," and "How to Have a Great Ajax Life: 20 New Positions for the Adventurous Client/Server Couple."

? FREQUENTLY ASKED QUESTIONS

Q: I still don't see what responseXML has to do with any of this.

A: The browser puts the plain text version of a server's response in the request object's `responseText` property—whether that's a single value, name/value pairs, or the text version of an XML document.

But if the server returns XML, and sets a Content-Type response header of "text/xml", the browser creates a DOM tree to represent that XML, and puts a reference to that DOM tree in the request object's `responseXML` property.

Q: So if I want to use the DOM to work on the XML, I should use responseXML instead of responseText?

A: Exactly. There's nothing wrong with getting the XML through `responseText`, but then you have to deal with parsing the XML yourself... and who wants to do that?

Q: In the HTML DOM on page 351, you showed id attributes as part of those <span> elements. I thought that the DOM represented attributes separately from elements.

A: Wow, you're really paying attention to those DOM trees, aren't you? Nice job... you're exactly right. The `id` attributes on those `<span>` elements are actually represented in the HTML DOM tree as separate nodes. We broke the rules a bit, though, and showed the `id` attribute as part of the element name, just to make things a little easier to understand. It's not quite how the DOM does it, but we thought it made our point a lot clearer.

Q: And there's no difference between an HTML DOM tree and an XML one?

A: The DOM for the web page represents HTML, and the DOM for the XML represents the server's response. But you work with both DOM trees in the same way, they have the same methods, and you can change both trees easily. Pretty cool, huh?

Just Do It

It's time to put everything you've learned so far into action. Below is the updatePage() callback function for the Boards app. To finish the code up, you'll need to use what you've learned about asynchronous requests, the DOM, XML, and dynamic HTML.

```
function updatePage() {
  if (request.readyState == 4) {
    if (request.status == 200) {
      // Get the updated totals from the XML response
      var xmlDoc = request.____________;
      var xmlBoards =
        _______.____________________("boards-sold")[0];
      var totalBoards = xmlBoards.firstChild.nodeValue;
      var xmlBoots =
        _______.____________________("boots-sold")[0];
      var totalBoots = xmlBoots.firstChild.nodeValue;
      var xmlBindings =
        _______.____________________("___________")___;
      var totalBindings = xmlBindings.firstChild.nodeValue;

      // Update the page with new totals
      var boardsSoldEl =
        document.________________("boards-sold");
      var bootsSoldEl =
        document.________________("boots-sold");
      var bindingsSoldEl =
        document.________________("bindings-sold");
      var cashEl = document.________________("cash");
      replaceText(______________, _______________);
      replaceText(______________, _______________);
      replaceText(______________, _________________);

      // Figure out how much cash Katie has made on boards
      var boardsPriceEl =
        document.getElementById("______________");
      var boardsPrice = getText(boardsPriceEl);
```

```
      var boardsCostEl =
        document.getElementById("_____________");
      var boardsCost = getText(boardsCostEl);
      var cashPerBoard = boardsPrice - boardsCost;
      var cash = cashPerBoard * totalBoards;

      // Figure out how much cash Katie has made on boots
      var bootsPriceEl =
        ____________.getElementById("boots-price");
      var bootsPrice = getText(____________);
      var bootsCostEl = ____________.getElementById("boots-cost");
      var bootsCost = getText(____________);
      var cashPerBoot = ____________ - ____________;
      cash = ________ + (cashPerBoot * totalBoots);

      // Figure out how much cash Katie has made on bindings
      ___________________________________________
      ___________________________________________
      ___________________________________________
      ___________________________________________
      ___________________________________________
      ___________________________________________
      ___________________________________________
      ___________________________________________

      // Update the cash for the slopes on the web form
      cash = Math.round(cash * 100) / 100;
      replaceText(cashEl, cash);
    } else
      alert("Error! Request status is " + request.status);
  }
}
```

You're on your own here, but this shouldn't be any problem for you at this stage of the game.

Trying things out

Ready to take Boards 'R' Us for a little test drive? Make sure you've finished the exercise on the last two pages, and made those changes to your copy of **`boards.js`**. If you're not sure about your answers, you can compare them to ours in the back of this chapter, on page 366. Then save your changes, fire up your web browser, and load **`boards.html`**.

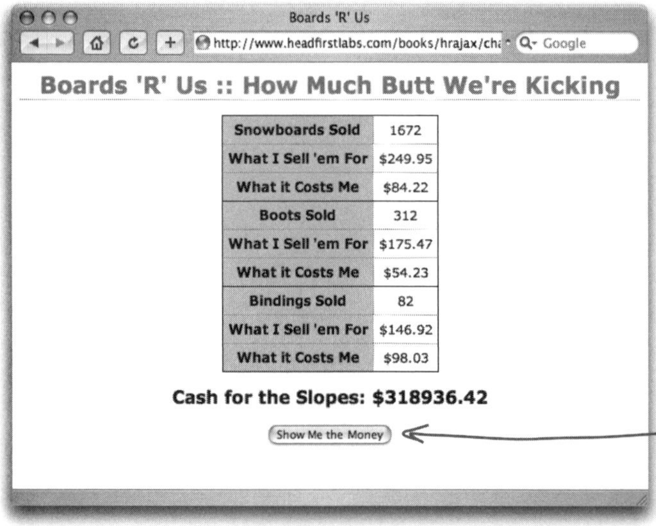

Here's how boards.html starts out. Click "Show Me the Money"...

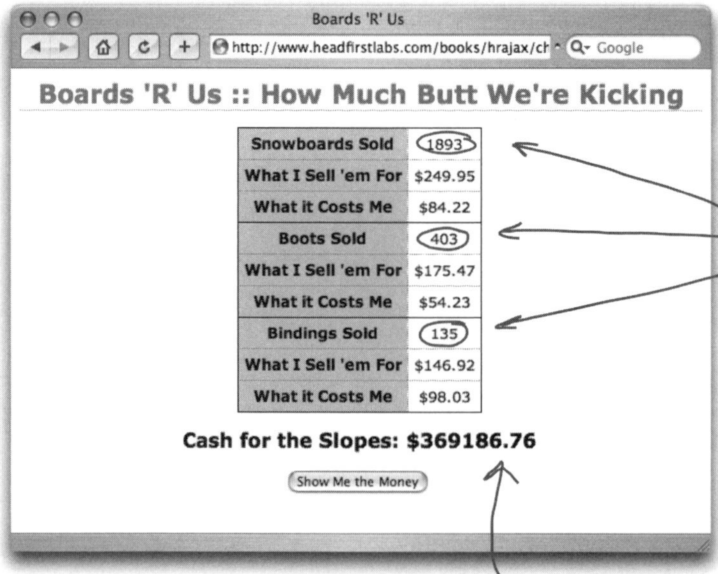

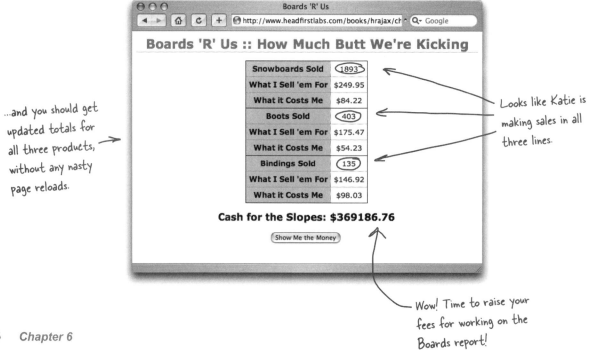

...and you should get updated totals for all three products, without any nasty page reloads.

Looks like Katie is making sales in all three lines.

Wow! Time to raise your fees for working on the Boards report!

I'm telling you, Doc. I'm so much happier these days. I've finally found a way to say so much more... XML has really done the trick.

Dr. Zigmund: Ex-zellent. Zo you find that you are listened to now?

Server: Oh, yes. And I'll even admit... that guy with the tree farm has really helped out a lot.

Dr. Zigmund: Tell me more about zat...

Server: Well, at first, I was sending back XML—which was great, I'm telling you, nobody was asking me about comma-separated values or anything like that anymore—and browsers totally understood what I was saying. But it seemed that people were having trouble *using* what I was saying.

Dr. Zigmund: Oh, really? Why do you zink zat was?

Server: Well, it turns out they were using the plain text version of my XML response. So they were trying to break up the XML on their own. Sheesh, what a pain that must have been! And lots of people were screwing things up. Really bad.

Dr. Zigmund: And how did you handle zis new confusion?

Server: Well, I took my Prozac first—thanks a lot, everyone says I'm so much calmer now—and told them to use the DOM tree representation of my XML. The browser even made it available through a simple property of the request.

Dr. Zigmund: Ahh yes, zee DOM tree from zee tree farm. Of course!

Server: Yup. I'm telling you, life is great these days. I'm finally getting a chance to really say what's important. And nobody's cutting me off, plus I hardly ever have to send back a bunch of HTML, either. I'm cured, Doc, I really think I'm cured!

XML is a standard... ...but how you use it isn't.

XML is a specification that the World Wide Web Consortium (W3C) works and agrees on. That means that when you say XML, everyone knows what you mean. But XML is really a metalanguage: a language for defining other languages. So, in the Boards app, you used XML, but you defined your own elements that had names that worked well with the Boards 'R' Us app.

If you wanted to update Break Neck Pizza's server to return XML, you'd probably use different elements, perhaps with names like **<deliveryTime>** and **<orderConfirmation>**. The code on your server and the JavaScript code that you write must use the same element names, or nothing is going to work.

XML is a meta-language: it defines other XML languages.

This is XML. It defines what an element is, what an attribute is, and how things like angle brackets, < and >, are supposed to be used. XML is a **metalanguage**.

< **XML** >

I still think XML is better than some weird made-up format. I mean, there will always be tools to work with XML, like the DOM, right?

Sometimes XML is great...
...and sometimes it's not.

XML is a popular data format, and you'll find tools like the DOM in every language. You don't have to worry about the order of elements in an XML document when you're using the DOM, and you don't need any special parsing code. So XML is a great idea for representing data.

But XML has its dark side, too: it takes a lot of text to say just a little in XML. All those angle brackets can really add up! And, as you'll see in the next chapter, there are plenty of other good options, like JSON.

Don't try to use XML for everything.

This is an XML document. You have to use elements and attributes according to the XML standard, but you can define your own element and attribute names to create your own XML **language**, just for your app.

```
<?xml version="1.0" encoding="utf-8"?>
<totals>
  <boards-sold>1710</boards-sold>
  <boots-sold>315</boots-sold>
  <bindings-sold>85</bindings-sold>
</totals>
```

Hey, I bet it's just as easy to send an XML request as it is to receive an XML response.

Well, there's a little more to it...

It turns out that you've got to do a good bit of work to send XML... in fact, quite a bit more work than it took to receive XML from the server. Most of the time, the effort you'll have to put into sending XML just isn't worth it.

First, you'll need to send the XML in a POST request...

Sure, that makes sense. Because XML can get pretty long, and there's that maximum URL length on GET requests, right?

Even the short XML response from the Boards server took up almost 200 characters!

That's right.

It doesn't take a lot of data before an XML document gets pretty long. You'll definitely need to use a POST request. Additionally, you'll need to let the server know that you're sending it XML, not name/value pairs.

That's easy, too. I bet we can use a different Content-Type request header, right?

You've really got this stuff down!

You can use the **`setRequestHeader()`** method on your request object to tell the server that you're sending it XML, like this:

```
request.setRequestHeader("Content-Type", "text/xml");
```

This tells the server that the content type of the incoming message is XML, in text format.

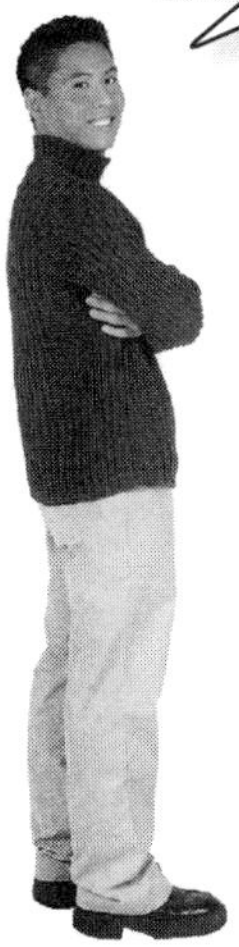

And now I can just use the DOM to work with my XML, and send over the DOM tree.

And there's the problem!

Look at the "Content-Type" request header on the last page... it's "text/xml". That tells the server that it can expect XML, but in a text format. That's *not* the same as a DOM tree.

In fact, there's no easy way to send a DOM tree to a web server. You'd basically have to write code that parses the DOM tree in reverse; it would need to take each node in the DOM tree and write it out as text. That's called *serialization*, and it's not an easy task.

Why would you do that?

After all the work you've done to learn how to use the DOM, it seems sort of silly to go back to text, doesn't it? In fact, it's pretty easy to make a mistake writing XML manually; that's part of why the DOM is so powerful. It helps keep you from making mistakes in your XML document's structure.

And besides, what exactly are you getting out of all the extra work involved in sending XML to a server instead of name/value pairs using plain old text?

You are back? I zought you were cured! What zeems to be the problem?

Server: I finally found a way to communicate... to be heard... to be understood...

Dr. Zigmund: Yes, yes, zee XML... is it not working anymore?

Server: No, it's great... I LOVE zee XML... I mean, "the" XML. But now everyone is trying to talk to *me* in XML.

Dr. Zigmund: And zere's a problem with zat?

Server: Well, yes! What was wrong with text? What happened to the days of simple name/value pairs? Now everyone is sending me these long XML documents, but they're saying the *same things* as when they were using simple name/value pairs.

Dr. Zigmund: And how does zat make you feel?

Server: Make me feel? It makes me feel bloated, and beaten down! Now I've got to parse the XML just to get the same values out of it that I could get instantly before. And then I've got to make sure there aren't any errors. Just the tiniest little mistake in the XML, and everything blows up. Then the browser yells at me, and... oh, I just don't think I can take this!

Dr. Zigmund: Zo you want to abandon zee XML?

Server: No! No, I love being able to say so much when I respond to a request, and XML lets me do that. I just don't understand why everyone thinks that they have to speak XML to *me*. It just doesn't make sense...

Dr. Zigmund: It zeems to me that it's best to zend you zee plain text, and leave zee XML to you. Yes?

Server: Exactly! It's so simple... oh, I hate my life. Why, oh why?

My, my... zose are a lot of questions. I would zay, just remember my two golden rules: leave zee XML to zee server, and it's probably all your muh-zer's fault.
Apparently Dr. Zigmund is reading Head Rush Ajax, and perhaps a bit too much Freud...

Frequently Asked Questions

Q: If we want the server to return XML in its response, shouldn't we use XML to make our request, too?

A: Not at all. The format you use for making your request has nothing to do with the format the server uses in its response. You could use plain text for the request and response, text for the request and XML for the response, XML for both the request and response, or even XML for the request and text for the response.

Q: And if we're sending XML, we just need to set the request header, right?

A: If you're making an XML request, you need to use a POST request, set the "Content-Type" of the request to "text/xml" using `setRequestHeader()`, and then send your XML in text form using the `send()` method of the request object. Other than those few special steps, you'll send the request just like you would send a normal text request.

Q: I still don't see why I can't just use the DOM and send my DOM tree to the server.

A: You can use the DOM to build an XML request, but you can't just send your DOM document directly to the server. You'd have to get the text version of the DOM, and then send that instead of the actual DOM objects themselves.

Q: Why? Wouldn't it be better to just send the DOM directly, if working with XML as text is so bad?

A: Well, it does seem like sending the DOM directly would be simpler. But it's not easy to send objects across a network, especially using the Ajax request model.

Besides that, there really aren't any advantages to sending XML instead of just simple name/value pairs. So for the most part, XML would only complicate your requests, not make them simpler.

Q: I read about this JavaScript toolkit that would convert my DOM tree to a text XML document. Can't I just use that toolkit, and then send the XML it creates on to the server?

A: Sure, there's nothing wrong with that approach. But remember, you're really not gaining anything by using XML in your request. You already can send multiple values using name/value pairs, and that format is a standard that any server will recognize. So even if you *could* use XML, you probably don't want to.

Q: So there's *never* a time when I should send a request in XML?

A: Just about the only time it makes sense to send an XML request is if the server you're talking to only accepts XML. For instance, you might need to talk to a web server that only accepts SOAP requests, which is a particular XML format. Other than these special cases, though, name/value pairs are almost always the better choice for sending requests.

Which Data Format?

Welcome to this week's edition of "Which Data Format?" You've got to decide which data format is best for the 5 examples below. Be careful: some are requests, while others are responses. Good luck!

	Text	or XML
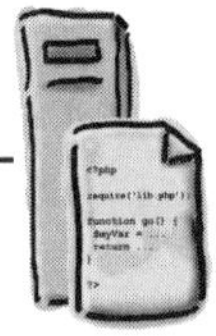 ← Top 10 iTunes downloads of 2006	☐	☐
 Request today's house blend →	☐	☐
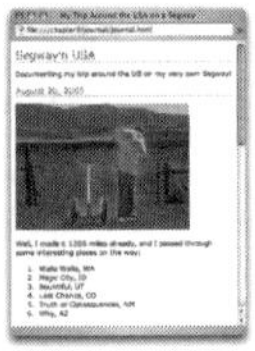 Update journal with new entry →	☐	☐
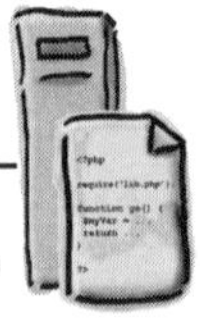 ← Number of hobbits that fit in a Volkswagen	☐	☐
 Play "When It Falls" next →	☐	☐

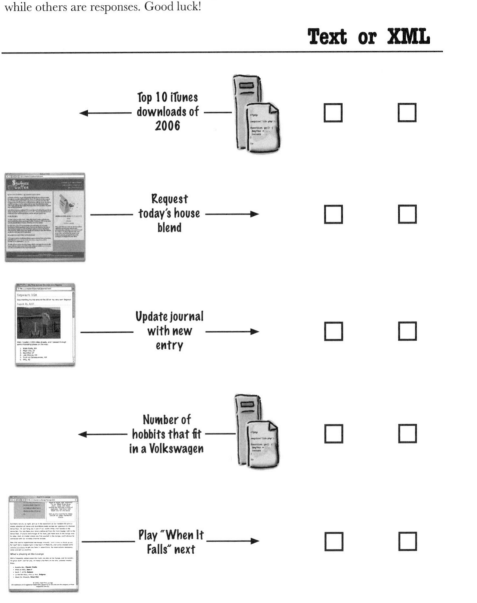

60 Second Review

- XML, the extensible markup language, lets you structure your data using elements and attributes.
- Most server-side scripts and programs can create XML responses to send back to browser requests.
- XML allows a server's response to include more than one piece of information, without requiring proprietary data formats or special formatting.
- The responseText property of a request object returns the text version of any XML document returned by a server.
- You can get the DOM representation of an XML document returned by a server-side component using the requestXML property of the request object.
- If a server doesn't set the Content-Type response header to "text/xml", many browsers won't correctly set the responseXML property of the request object.
- When the browser receives an XML response from a server, it creates a DOM tree representing the document.
- You can send XML documents as well as receive them, although it takes a special toolkit or custom code to send a DOM representation of an XML document.
- Creating XML manually, using plain text, is error-prone and usually requires a lot of effort.
- For most requests, name/value pairs sent as plain text are the best solution, and require less processing by both your JavaScript and the web server to which you're sending the request.

Exercise Solutions

Just Do It

It's time to put everything you've learned so far into action. Below is the updatePage() callback function for the Boards app. We've filled in all the blanks for you, so check your answers against ours, and make sure you feel like you understand all this code.

```
function updatePage() {
  if (request.readyState == 4) {
    if (request.status == 200) {
      // Get the updated totals from the XML response
      var xmlDoc = request.responseXML;
      var xmlBoards =
        xmlDoc.getElementsByTagName("boards-sold")[0];
      var totalBoards = xmlBoards.firstChild.nodeValue;
      var xmlBoots =
        xmlDoc.getElementsByTagName("boots-sold")[0];
      var totalBoots = xmlBoots.firstChild.nodeValue;
      var xmlBindings =
        xmlDoc.getElementsByTagName("bindings-sold")[0];
      var totalBindings = xmlBindings.firstChild.nodeValue;

      // Update the page with new totals
      var boardsSoldEl =
        document.getElementById("boards-sold");
      var bootsSoldEl =
        document.getElementById("boots-sold");
      var bindingsSoldEl =
        document.getElementById("bindings-sold");
      var cashEl = document.getElementById("cash");
      replaceText(boardsSoldEl, totalBoards);
      replaceText(bootsSoldEl, totalBoots);
      replaceText(bindingsSoldEl, totalBindings);

      // Figure out how much cash Katie has made on boards
      var boardsPriceEl =
        document.getElementById("boards-price");
      var boardsPrice = getText(boardsPriceEl);
```

You could have these three lines of code in any order, as along as you keep the element and its value together.

```
    var boardsCostEl =
      document.getElementById("boards-cost");
    var boardsCost = getText(boardsCostEl);
    var cashPerBoard = boardsPrice - boardsCost;
    var cash = cashPerBoard * totalBoards;

    // Figure out how much cash Katie has made on boots
    var bootsPriceEl =
      document.getElementById("boots-price");
    var bootsPrice = getText(bootsPriceEl);
    var bootsCostEl = document.getElementById("boots-cost");
    var bootsCost = getText(bootsCostEl);
    var cashPerBoot = bootsPrice - bootsCost;
    cash = cash + (cashPerBoot * totalBoots);

    // Figure out how much cash Katie has made on bindings
    var bindingsPriceEl =
      document.getElementById("bindings-price");
    var bindingsPrice = getText(bindingsPriceEl);
    var bindingsCostEl =
      document.getElementById("bindings-cost");
    var bindingsCost = getText(bindingsCostEl);
    var cashPerBinding = bindingsPrice - bindingsCost;
    cash = cash + (cashPerBinding * totalBindings);

    // Update the cash for the slopes on the web form
    cash = Math.round(cash * 100) / 100;
    replaceText(cashEl, cash);
  } else
    alert("Error! Request status is " + request.status);
  }
}
```

This was a little bit tricky... you've got to keep a running total, so begin with the current value of cash, and then add to that.

Which Data Format?

Welcome to this week's edition of "Which Data Format?" You've got to decide which data format is best for the 5 examples below. Good luck!

	Text	XML
 Top 10 iTunes downloads of 2006	☐	☑
 Request today's house blend	☑	☐
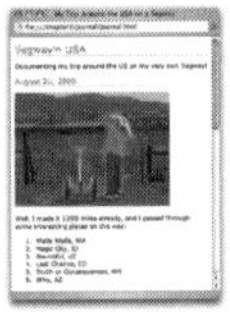 Update journal with new entry	☑	☐
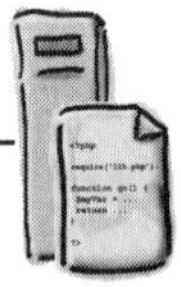 Number of hobbits that fit in a Volkswagen	☑	☐
 Play "When It Falls" next	☑	☐

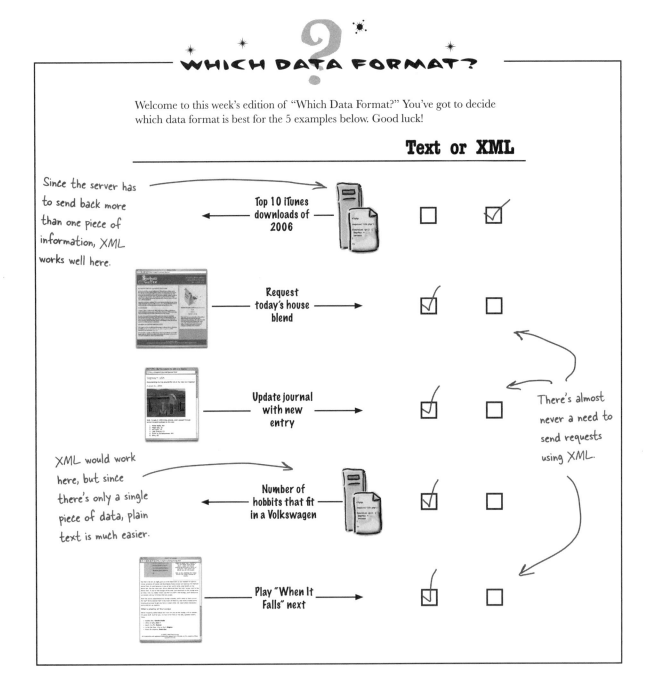

Since the server has to send back more than one piece of information, XML works well here.

There's almost never a need to send requests using XML.

XML would work here, but since there's only a single piece of data, plain text is much easier.

7 JSON versus XML

A Fight to the Finish

It's time to go back to elementary school. Remember the days when differences were resolved with harsh words, flying fists, and poor kung fu imitations? Remember when nothing thrilled your soul like hearing "**Fight!**" screamed in the halls of the cafeteria? In this chapter, we're going back to those days, and leaving friendly words and the golden rule behind. **XML and JSON**, two different formats for **sending and receiving data** in your asynchronous requests, are ready to let their differences be settled in the squared circle. Get your scorecard ready, and let's take it to the ring!

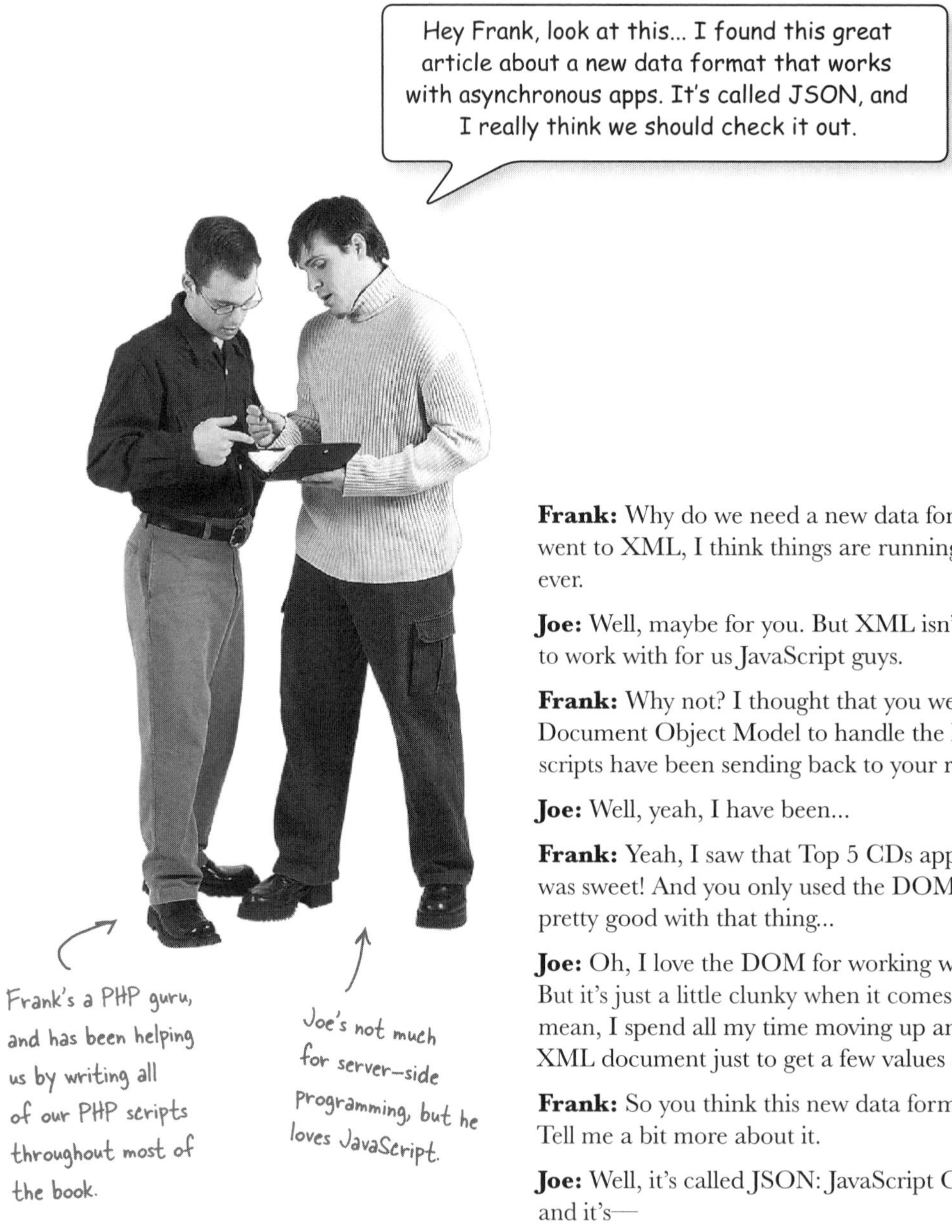

Hey Frank, look at this... I found this great article about a new data format that works with asynchronous apps. It's called JSON, and I really think we should check it out.
Frank's a PHP guru, and has been helping us by writing all of our PHP scripts throughout most of the book.
Joe's not much for server-side programming, but he loves JavaScript.

Frank: Why do we need a new data format? Since we went to XML, I think things are running better than ever.

Joe: Well, maybe for you. But XML isn't exactly easy to work with for us JavaScript guys.

Frank: Why not? I thought that you were using the Document Object Model to handle the XML my scripts have been sending back to your requests.

Joe: Well, yeah, I have been...

Frank: Yeah, I saw that Top 5 CDs app you wrote. It was sweet! And you only used the DOM? You must be pretty good with that thing...

Joe: Oh, I love the DOM for working with web pages. But it's just a little clunky when it comes to XML. I mean, I spend all my time moving up and down the XML document just to get a few values out.

Frank: So you think this new data format will help? Tell me a bit more about it.

Joe: Well, it's called JSON: JavaScript Object Notation, and it's—

Frank: Wait a second. The *data format* is JavaScript? That doesn't sound so good. I write PHP, Joe, not JavaScript! What are you thinking?

Joe: But it's supposed to be really easy to use, and fast...

Frank: Look, I'm a server-side guy. I'm not gonna start using JavaScript in my PHP. That's just nuts!

A review of request and response formats

Before we dive into the JSON versus XML debate, let's review the data formats we've already used in the first six chapters.

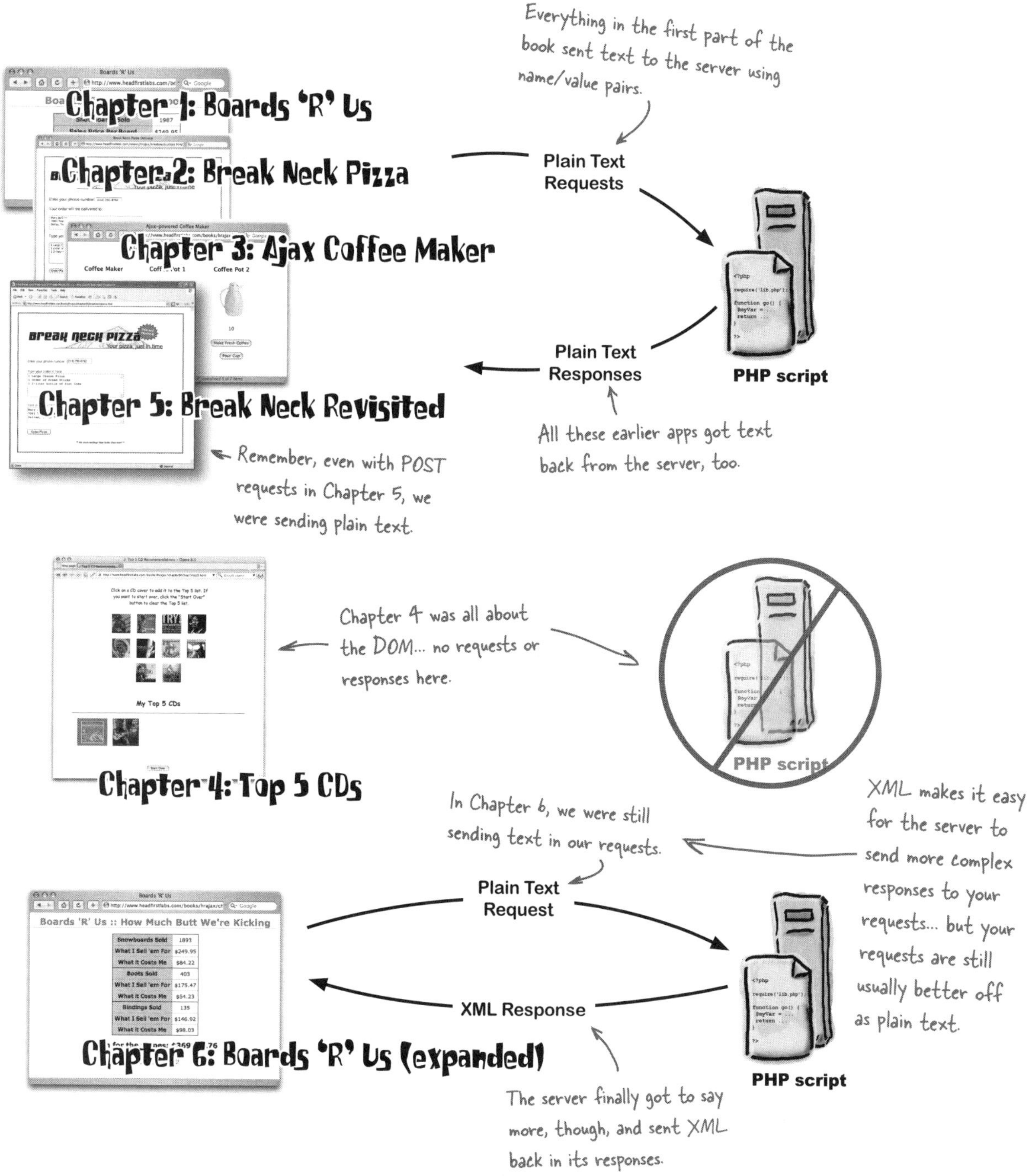

Everything in the first part of the book sent text to the server using name/value pairs.
Chapter 1: Boards 'R' Us
Chapter 2: Break Neck Pizza
Chapter 3: Ajax Coffee Maker
Chapter 5: Break Neck Revisited
Plain Text Requests
Plain Text Responses
PHP script
All these earlier apps got text back from the server, too.
Remember, even with POST requests in Chapter 5, we were sending plain text.
Chapter 4 was all about the DOM... no requests or responses here.
Chapter 4: Top 5 CDs
PHP script
In Chapter 6, we were still sending text in our requests.
XML makes it easy for the server to send more complex responses to your requests... but your requests are still usually better off as plain text.
Plain Text Request
XML Response
Chapter 6: Boards 'R' Us (expanded)
PHP script
The server finally got to say more, though, and sent XML back in its responses.

Should you use XML or JSON?

Joe and the JavaScript guys want to look at JSON, but Frank's PHP team thinks XML is the way to go. Which is the best data format? In this chapter, we're going to let JSON and XML take each other on, and see which one survives the **ULTIMATE DATA FORMAT CHAMPIONSHIP.**

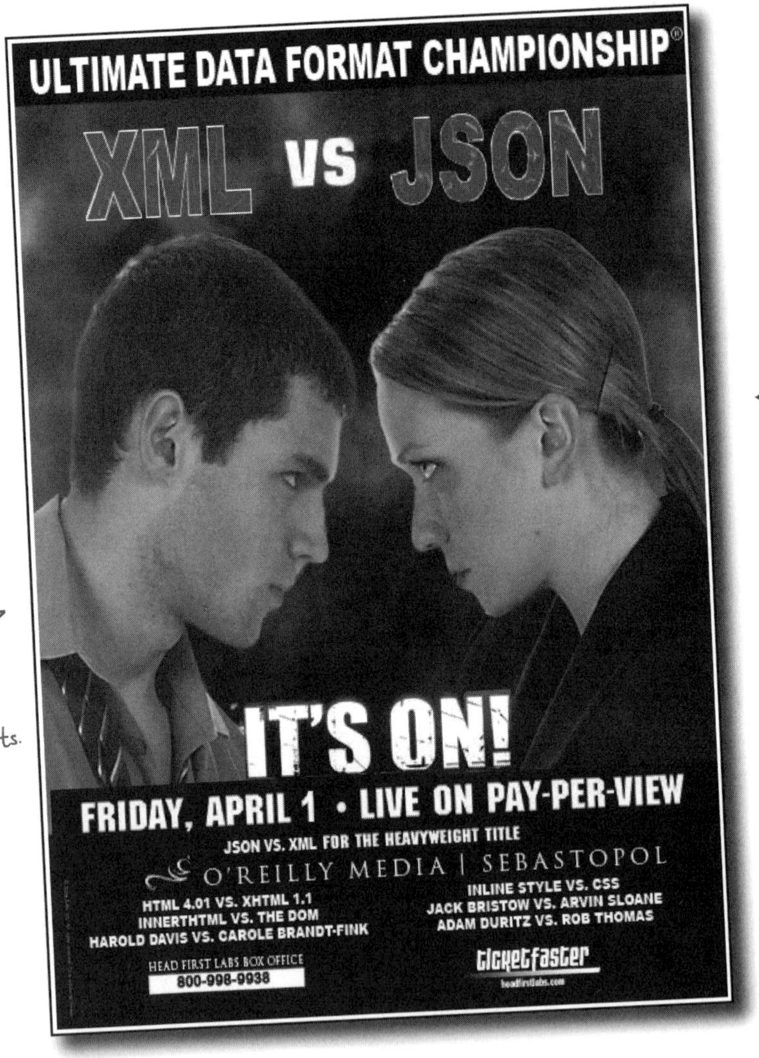

JSON is a relative newcomer, and is poised to give XML a run for his title as reigning data format champion.

XML, the heavyweight champion of data formats.

Fighting Words

Today's adrenaline-laced, psyched-up fighters:
XML and JSON

XML: *(glares at JSON)*

JSON: Your time has finally come, XML. Tonight, the world is gonna see that you've lost a step, especially when it comes to JavaScript and asynchronous applications.

XML: I've heard that one before... but here I am, still the reigning data format in the world.

JSON: You're only at the top because people think that there's nothing else available. I know lots of people that can't stand you, XML... you're big and bloated, and a real pain to work with.

XML: I'm big because I can handle anything. Snowboard sales, HTML, purchase orders... you throw it at me, I'll take care of it. No problem. You think a little pipsqueak can handle all those different types of data? I don't think so.

JSON: Maybe not, but I'm fast... a lot faster than you, most of the time.

XML: I'm plenty fast, especially if you use my attributes. And, I'm versatile... I can do all sorts of things, like represent a math equation or a book.

JSON: Yeah, well, most of my users aren't too interested in sending math equations across the network. Besides, all those angle brackets? Ugh... anyone that knows arrays can start working with me without having to learn all that weird XML syntax.

XML: But can someone transform you into something else? Like with XSLT? Or what about web services... you gonna tell me you can handle web services?

JSON: Wow, you've really been a bit overused, haven't you... you're missing the point, bracket-head. I don't care about all those things. I just care about getting information from a web page to a server and then back without a bunch of extra work... like having to crawl up and down a DOM tree. Know anyone who thinks *that's* fun?

XML: Uh, yeah. Hello? We've got a whole group of DOM experts out there these days, writing killer user interfaces. Did you see that Top 5 CDs listing? That was pretty cool, and it was only about 100 lines of code. Anyone that knows the DOM is ready to use XML, *today*!

JSON: Look, all developers really need is a lightweight data format that's easy to work with in JavaScript. And that's me, big boy, not you.

XML: What are all the servers going to think about this? You know, PHP and Perl and Java... I don't see them lining up to throw their support in with you and your "lightweight data format" spiel.

JSON: Well, I guess that's true... but there are libraries that those guys can use to work with me.

XML: Libraries? If they've got to use a library, why not use a standard like the Document Object Model?

JSON: My libraries might be standard one day, too, you know....

XML: But here I am, being used *right now*, because I'm *already* a standard. At the end of the day, you're just one more proprietary data format. Maybe you've got a few more fans than comma-separated values, but I'll put an end to that.

JSON: Oh really? Let's get it on, XML.

The heavyweight champion: XML

You've already seen how a server can return XML in response to your request:

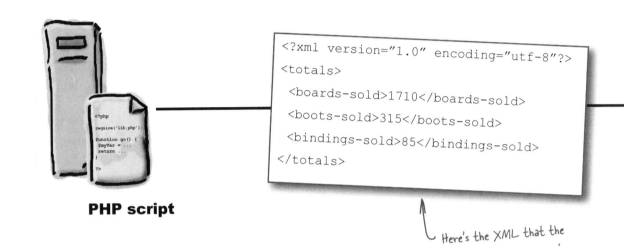

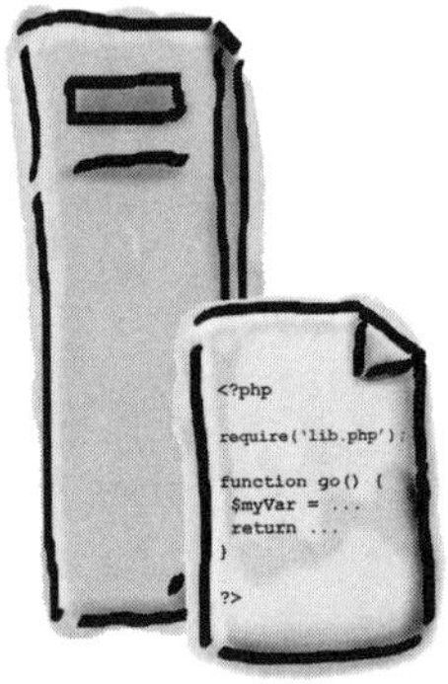

PHP script

```
<?xml version="1.0" encoding="utf-8"?>
<totals>
 <boards-sold>1710</boards-sold>
 <boots-sold>315</boots-sold>
 <bindings-sold>85</bindings-sold>
</totals>
```

Here's the XML that the Boards 'R' Us server sent back in Chapter 6.

XML has been around the block... and you already know how to use the DOM to work with XML data..

You work with XML using the DOM.

You use the DOM to work with XML

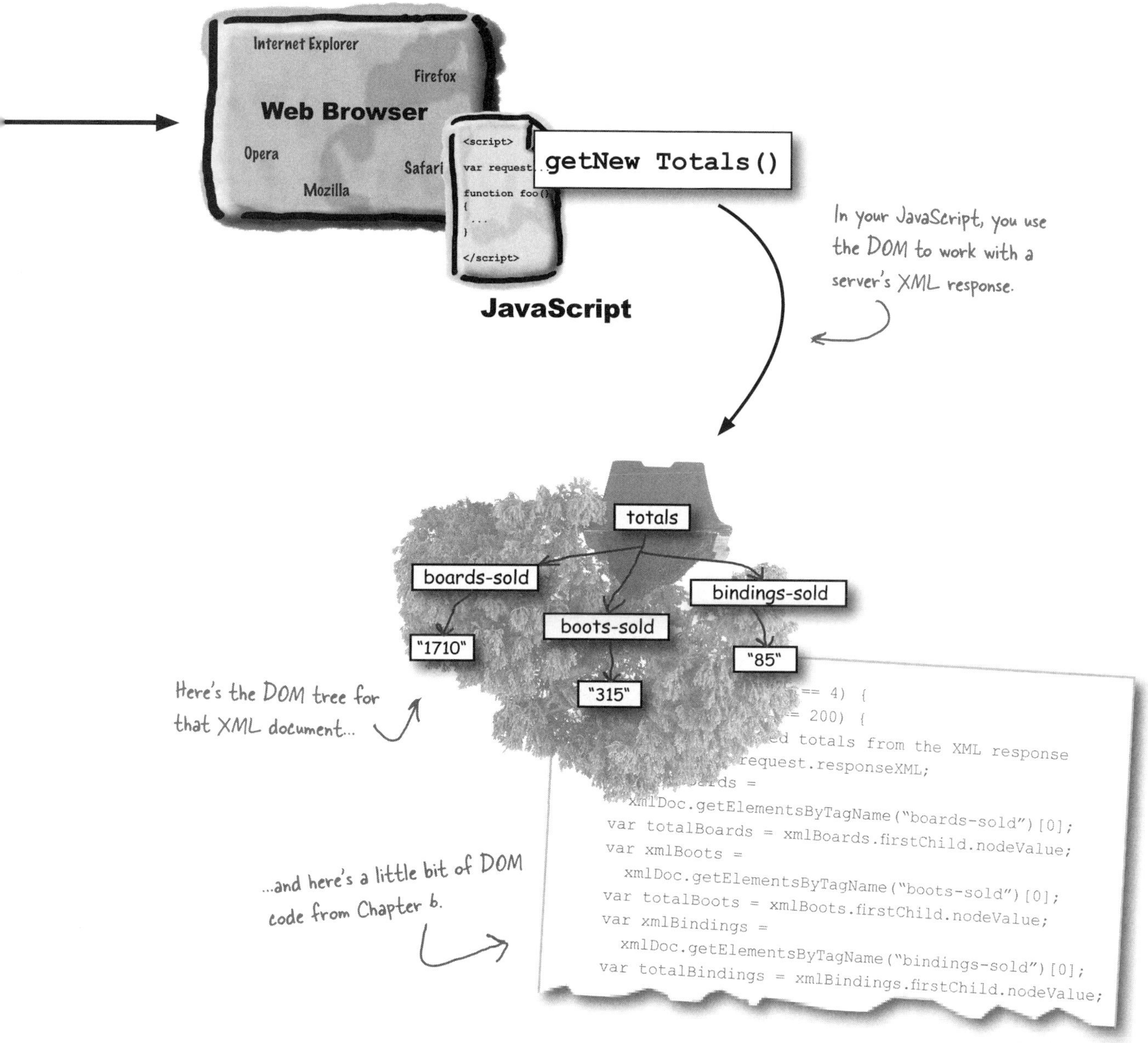

The young upstart: JSON

JSON is more about curly braces than the brackets you use in XML, but it can store all the same data that XML documents can:

Here's the JSON equivalent of the XML you looked at on the opposite page.

"totals" is at the top-level, and contains the three other pieces of data.

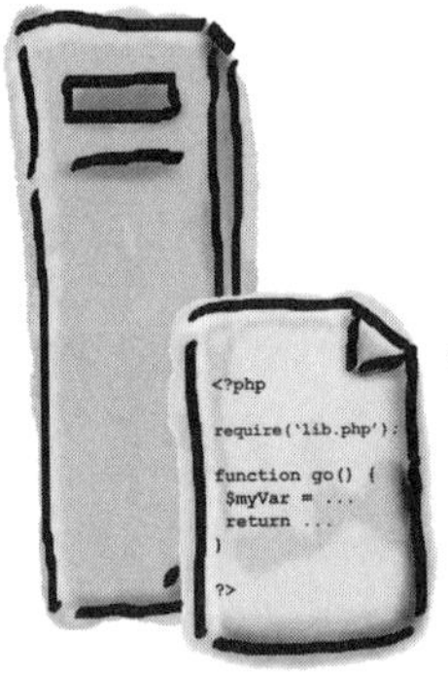

PHP script

```
{"totals": [
  {
    "boardsSold": 1710,
    "bootsSold": 315,
    "bindingsSold": 85
  }
]};
```

There are three individual bits of data, each with a numeric value.

"boardsSold", "bootsSold", and "bindingsSold" are the names of each piece of data...

...and 1710, 315, and 85 are the data values.

JSON is relatively new to the Ajax scene, but has a lot of big fans already.

You work with JSON using "normal" JavaScript.

You don't need a special object model to work with JSON data

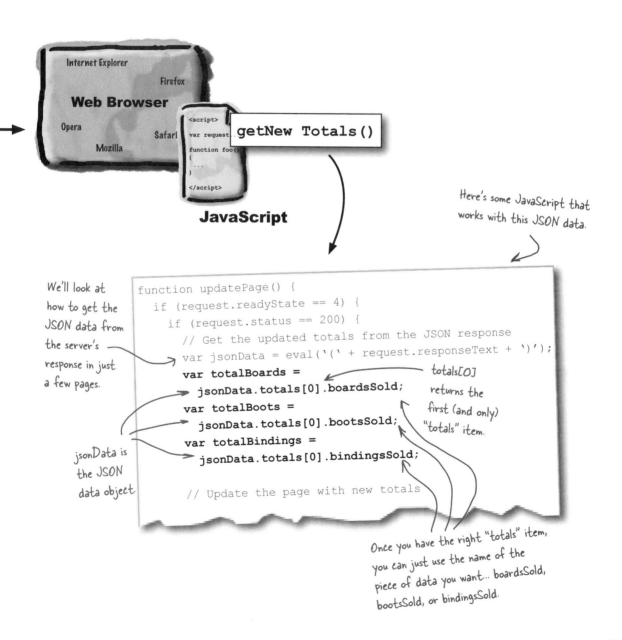

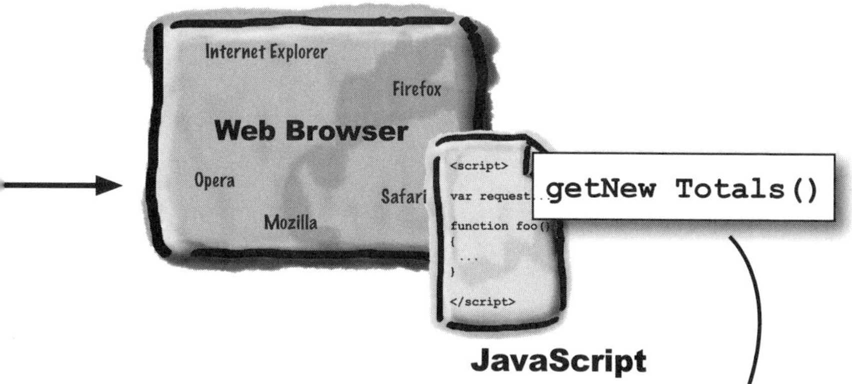

Here's some JavaScript that works with this JSON data.

```
function updatePage() {
  if (request.readyState == 4) {
    if (request.status == 200) {
      // Get the updated totals from the JSON response
      var jsonData = eval('(' + request.responseText + ')');
      var totalBoards =
        jsonData.totals[0].boardsSold;
      var totalBoots =
        jsonData.totals[0].bootsSold;
      var totalBindings =
        jsonData.totals[0].bindingsSold;

      // Update the page with new totals
```

We'll look at how to get the JSON data from the server's response in just a few pages.

totals[0] returns the first (and only) "totals" item.

jsonData is the JSON data object.

Once you have the right "totals" item, you can just use the name of the piece of data you want... boardsSold, bootsSold, or bindingsSold.

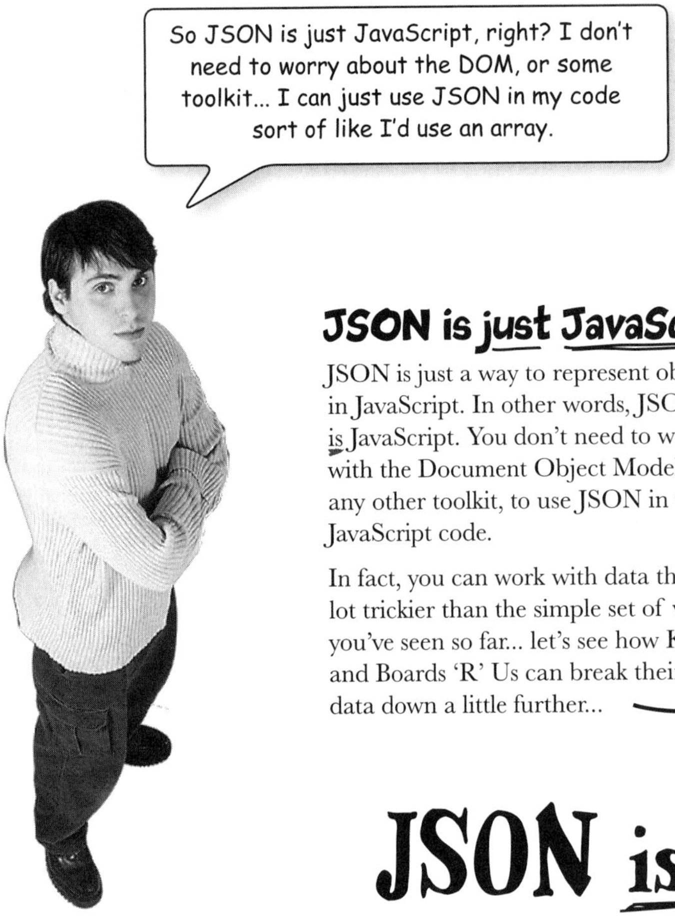
So JSON is just JavaScript, right? I don't need to worry about the DOM, or some toolkit... I can just use JSON in my code sort of like I'd use an array.

JSON is *just* JavaScript

JSON is just a way to represent objects in JavaScript. In other words, JSON is JavaScript. You don't need to work with the Document Object Model, or any other toolkit, to use JSON in your JavaScript code.

In fact, you can work with data that's a lot trickier than the simple set of values you've seen so far... let's see how Katie and Boards 'R' Us can break their sales data down a little further...

JSON is JavaScript.

Here's a little more JSON. This time, the Boards 'R' Us sales are broken up by city.

The first row is totals[0], the second is totals[1], and so on...

```
{"totals": [
  {"location":"Vail", "boardsSold":642, "bootsSold":86, "bindingsSold":19},
  {"location":"Santa Fe", "boardsSold":236, "bootsSold":45, "bindingsSold":32},
  {"location":"Boulder", "boardsSold":453, "bootsSold":90, "bindingsSold":16},
  {"location":"Denver", "boardsSold":379, "bootsSold":94, "bindingsSold":18}
]};
```

This JavaScript... ...uses this JSON data... ...to get Boards 'R' Us sales totals.

```
// Get the updated totals from the JSON response
var jsonData = eval('(' + request.responseText + ')');
var totalBoards = jsonData.totals[0].boardsSold +
                  jsonData.totals[1].boardsSold +
                  jsonData.totals[2].boardsSold +
                  jsonData.totals[3].boardsSold;
var totalBoots = jsonData.totals[0].bootsSold +
                 jsonData.totals[1].bootsSold +
                 jsonData.totals[2].bootsSold +
                 jsonData.totals[3].bootsSold;
var totalBindings = jsonData.totals[0].bindingsSold +
                    jsonData.totals[1].bindingsSold +
                    jsonData.totals[2].bindingsSold +
                    jsonData.totals[3].bindingsSold;

// Update the page with new totals
```

The JavaScript gets the boardsSold from each location, and adds them together to get an overall total.

The same thing is done with the boots and the bindings... each location is accessed by an index, like an array, and then the values in that location are used.

You don't even have to convert these values from strings... JavaScript knows that they are numbers and treats them that way automatically.

Frequently Asked Questions

Q: So JSON is just another data format, like XML?

A: That's right. Any time you send information between your web page and a server, you're going to need some way to format that information. So far, you've used plain text to send requests, and text and XML to send responses. JSON is just one more way to send data back and forth.

Q: If we've already got XML and text as options, why do we need JSON?

A: A lot of JavaScript programmers aren't used to looking at or writing XML. Even though the DOM hides a lot of the details of XML, JSON still feels a lot more like arrays and lists to JavaScript programmers than XML does. If you know both XML and JSON, then you're *way* ahead of the curve, and can choose whichever format you like.

Q: I'm a little confused by all those curly braces. Can you explain how they work again?

A: The curly braces, { and }, contain *unordered* sets of values, and the [and] characters indicate an ordered array. Take a look:

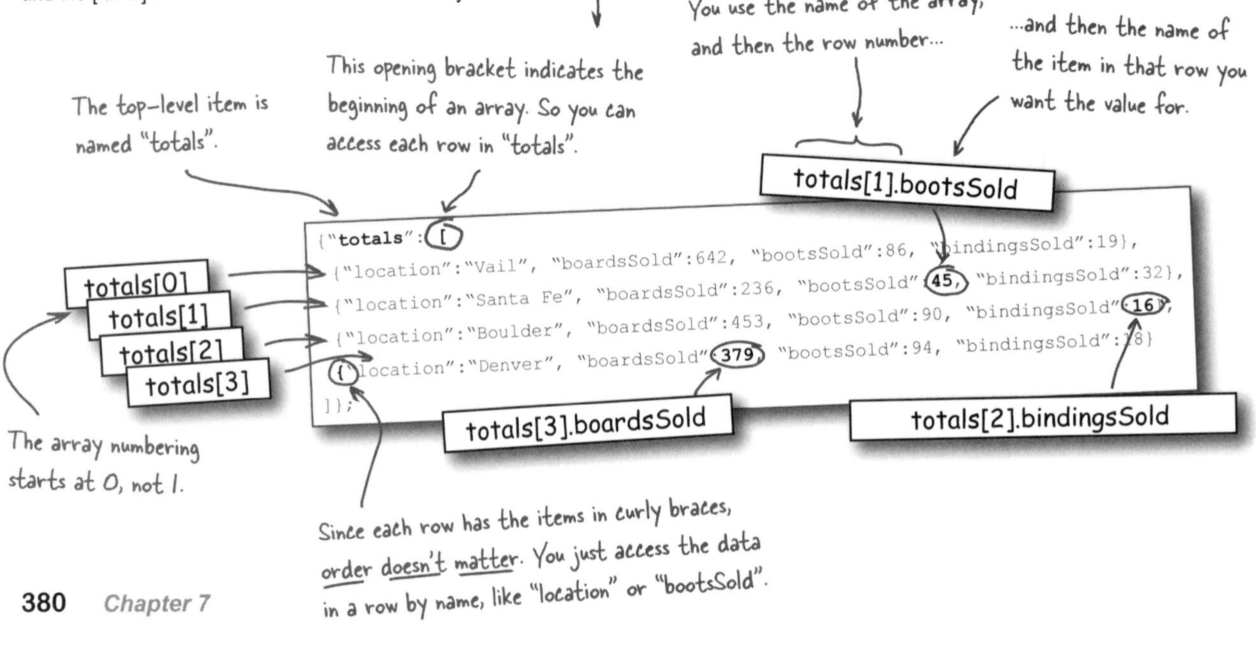

You use the name of the array, and then the row number...
...and then the name of the item in that row you want the value for.
This opening bracket indicates the beginning of an array. So you can access each row in "totals".
The top-level item is named "totals".
totals[1].bootsSold
{"totals":[
{"location":"Vail", "boardsSold":642, "bootsSold":86, "bindingsSold":19},
{"location":"Santa Fe", "boardsSold":236, "bootsSold":45, "bindingsSold":32},
{"location":"Boulder", "boardsSold":453, "bootsSold":90, "bindingsSold":16},
{"location":"Denver", "boardsSold":379, "bootsSold":94, "bindingsSold":18}
]};
totals[0]
totals[1]
totals[2]
totals[3]
totals[3].boardsSold
totals[2].bindingsSold
The array numbering starts at 0, not 1.
Since each row has the items in curly braces, order doesn't matter. You just access the data in a row by name, like "location" or "bootsSold".

Q: So I should convert my version of the Boards 'R' Us application to use JSON?

A: That's really up to you. We've created a version of the Boards app which gets JSON from the server. You can check it out online at http://www.headfirstlabs.com/books/hrajax/chapter07/boards/boards.html. You can also check out the code we used in the chapter07/boards/ folder in the examples.

But there's nothing that says you need to use JSON in your version of the Boards app, or in your own apps. It's just an option, along with XML and text. The choice is really yours.

Q: But which is better? XML or JSON?

A: It really depends on your app. Lots of times, JSON looks and feels a little more like working with rows in a table, or arrays... but XML can represent complex data structures pretty easily, too. The choice is up to you!

Just Do It

Before we discuss how JSON and server-side languages like PHP get along, let's take a closer look at how you can access JSON data in your JavaScript. Here's another JSON data structure:

```
{"books": [
 {"title":"Hyperion", "author":"Dan Simmons", "isbn":"0553283685"},
 {"title":"The Stars My Destination", "author":"Alfred Bester", "isbn:":"0679767800"},
 {"title":"Black House", "author": [ "Stephen King", "Peter Straub"],
                     "isbn":"0345441036"},
 {"title":"The Golden Compass", "author":"Philip Pullman", "isbn":"0679879242"},
]};
```

Below are several values from the JSON structure. Your job is to write the JavaScript code that would return the value from the JSON data structure. You can assume the JSON data is in an object called jsonData.

We've done the first one to get you started.

"Alfred Bester" — `var bester = jsonData.books[1].author;`

"0679879242" — ______________________

"0345441036" — ______________________

"Dan Simmons" — ______________________

"Black House" — ______________________

"Peter Straub" — ______________________

Answers on page 390.

I'm thrilled that JSON data is so easy to use in your JavaScript code... but it's a big pain in the butt for me and my PHP scripts to deal with. You realize that, right?

We *did* *say* that JSON is JavaScript

The great thing about JSON is that it's just JavaScript, so the JavaScript code in your web pages can use JSON data really easily. If you're already used to working with arrays in JavaScript, then you'll be able to use the arrays returned from a server's JSON-based response. If you're used to working with JavaScript objects, then JSON will feel really natural, too.

The bad news is that since JSON is JavaScript, languages like PHP and Perl and Java can't understand JSON without a little help. You're probably going to need a library to help you create and output JSON in your server-side scripts and programs. Then you're going to have to figure out how to use those libraries, which takes a little time and effort.

We talk about how to get one of the most popular JSON libraries for PHP working in Appendix 1.

Here's Frank's modified PHP script... now it responds to your requests with JSON data instead of XML data.

```
$boardsSold = $row['boardsSold'];
$bootsSold = $row['bootsSold'];
$bindingsSold = $row['bindingsSold'];

require_once('JSON.php');

$json = new Services_JSON();
$vail = array('location'     => 'Vail',
              'boardsSold'   => $vailBoards,
              'bootsSold'    => $vailBoots,
              'bindingsSold' => $vailBindings);
$santaFe = array('location'     => 'Santa Fe',
                 'boardsSold'   => $santaFeBoards,
                 'bootsSold'    => $santaFeBoots,
                 'bindingsSold' => $santaFeBindings);
$boulder = array('location'     => 'Boulder',
                 'boardsSold'   => $boulderBoards,
                 'bootsSold'    => $boulderBoots,
                 'bindingsSold' => $boulderBindings);
$denver = array('location'     => 'Denver',
                'boardsSold'   => $denverBoards,
                'bootsSold'    => $denverBoots,
                'bindingsSold' => $denverBindings);
$totals =
  array('totals' =>
        array($vail, $santaFe, $boulder, $denver));
$output = $json->encode($totals);
print($output);

mysql_close($conn);
?>
```

You'll need a new Services_JSON object to handle encoding a JSON response in PHP.

JSON.php is just one of several PHP libraries that lets PHP work with JSON data.

PHP's array type is the closest thing to JSON data structures.

This takes a lot of effort.... it seemed a bit easier to output an XML response.

JSON uses lots of arrays, and even arrays of arrays.

encode() converts your PHP arrays into a JSON structure.

Once you've got a JSON data structure, you can send that structure back as a response.

Wanna compare JSON to XML? Flip back to Chapter 6, and compare the PHP that responds with XML to this PHP, which responds with JSON.

If I can convince Frank to have his scripts send my JavaScript JSON, how do I deal with his response? Do I use responseText again? Or responseXML?
Yeah, right. Like I want a bunch of JavaScript in my PHP scripts...

JSON comes across as text

When servers respond with JSON, they send the data across as text. So you need to use the **`responseText`** property of your request object to get the JSON data. But JSON is meant to be used in JavaScript as an object, so you've got to convert it from text to its object form. You can do this using JavaScript's **`eval()`** function, like this:

```
function updatePage() {
  if (request.readyState == 4) {
    if (request.status == 200) {
      var jsonData = eval('(' + request.responseText + ')');

      // Get the updated totals from the XML response
      var totalBoards = jsonData.totals[0].boardsSold +
                        jsonData.totals[1].boardsSold +
                        jsonData.totals[2].boardsSold +
                        jsonData.totals[3].boardsSold;

      var totalBoots = jsonData.totals[0].bootsSold +
                       jsonData.totals[1].bootsSold +
                       jsonData.totals[2].bootsSold +
                       jsonData.totals[3].bootsSold;

      var totalBindings = jsonData.totals[0].bindingsSold +
```

eval() takes a string and converts the string of JSON data returned by the server into a JavaScript object.

jsonData will hold the JSON data in its object form after this runs.

request.responseText holds the JSON data, in text form, that the server returned.

Looks like JSON has some serious skills... this is a data format that isn't gonna roll over for XML.

Frequently Asked Questions

Q: Couldn't I just output JSON in my PHP script as text, and avoid using a library?

A: If you really wanted to, yes. You'd have to know JSON pretty well to just type it in, and be sure you don't make any errors. But if you're really familiar with JSON, that might be an option for you, and you can avoid having to use the JSON libraries in your PHP scripts

One of the big advantages of using a library for JSON output, though, is that your scripters and server-side programmers don't have to learn JSON; they can use normal PHP or Java data structures, and then let the toolkit convert those structures to the JSON data format.

Q: So I need a library to use JSON in my web apps?

A: Your JavaScript code can use JSON without any special libraries or toolkits. But your server-side programs, which are probably written in PHP or Java or maybe Ruby, probably don't know how to work with the JSON data format without a little help. So you'll need to get a library that allows those programming languages to understand and work with JSON data.

Q: So where can I get libraries for my server-side languages?

A: You can visit the JSON web site at http://www.json.org to get information on most of the popular JSON libraries. There's a library for all the major programming languages, so you shouldn't have any trouble finding one that's right for you.

Q: And if my server returns JSON, I use the responseText property to get that data?

A: Exactly. The server returns the JSON data as text, which is easy to send over a network connection. The web browser stores text responses from servers in the request object's `responseText` property, so that's where you should look for a JSON response from your server.

Q: Why do I need to use eval()?

A: Remember, JSON is JavaScript Object Notation. JSON is a data format, but it represents data as an object, not just plain text. When you get the server's response, though, it is plain text, stored in the `responseText` property of your JavaScript request object.

To convert that text into an object, you need to use JavaScript's `eval()` function. `eval()` takes a string as an argument, and tries to either run that string as a command, or convert it into an object. In this case, `eval()` sees that you're giving it the text version of some JSON data, and returns a JSON object that you can then use in the rest of your JavaScript.

Q: And there's no DOM tree involved, right?

A: Right. You don't need the Document Object Model to work with JSON data.

Since JSON is just JavaScript, I can use JSON as the data format for my asynchronous requests, too, right?

You can use JSON, XML, or text in your requests to the server

You can send JSON to the server in your requests, just like you can send XML or text. But just like with XML, it's often easier to use plain text name/value pairs to send your requests to the server.

You should use text data for your requests whenever possible.

JSON is great with objects... ...but do you really need objects?

JSON is a great way to send objects or arrays to a server. But then the server is going to have to use a JSON library to take the data it receives, and convert it to arrays, or some other format that the server can use.

Even when you have objects, it's usually easier to represent the object's values as name/value pairs, and just send plain text to your server. In general, if you *can* use text for your request, you *should* use text for your response.

So which is the better data format?

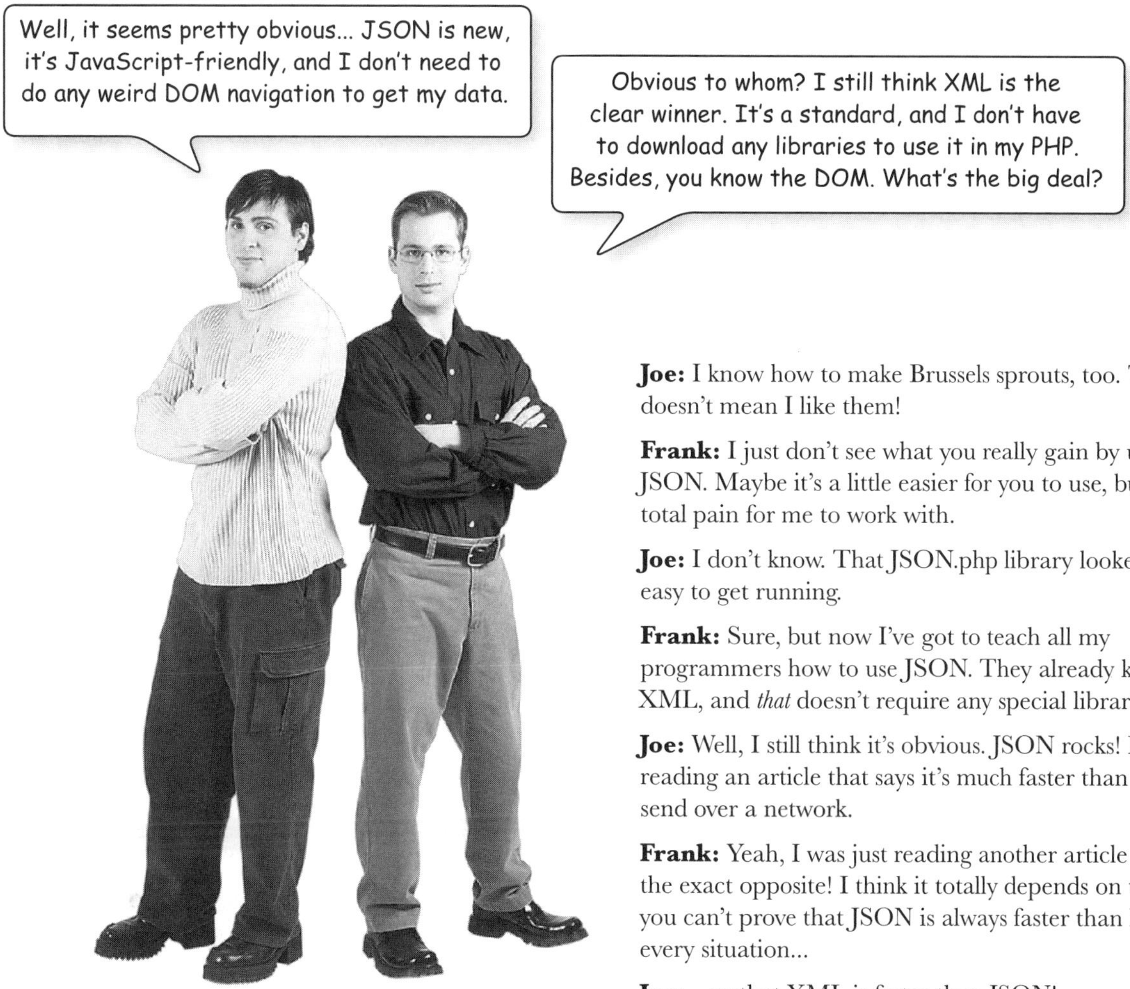

Well, it seems pretty obvious... JSON is new, it's JavaScript-friendly, and I don't need to do any weird DOM navigation to get my data.
Obvious to whom? I still think XML is the clear winner. It's a standard, and I don't have to download any libraries to use it in my PHP. Besides, you know the DOM. What's the big deal?

Joe: I know how to make Brussels sprouts, too. That doesn't mean I like them!

Frank: I just don't see what you really gain by using JSON. Maybe it's a little easier for you to use, but it's a total pain for me to work with.

Joe: I don't know. That JSON.php library looked pretty easy to get running.

Frank: Sure, but now I've got to teach all my programmers how to use JSON. They already know XML, and *that* doesn't require any special libraries.

Joe: Well, I still think it's obvious. JSON rocks! I was just reading an article that says it's much faster than XML to send over a network.

Frank: Yeah, I was just reading another article that said the exact opposite! I think it totally depends on the data... you can't prove that JSON is always faster than XML in every situation...

Joe: ...or that XML is faster than JSON!

Frank: Right. I guess we're just not gonna agree on this.?

Joe: Well, we have to pick one format or the other, right?

Which data format

Look, I'd rather be climbing a mountain than messing with a bunch of weird data formats. I use plain text for everything.

The choice...

I've been designing web pages for years, and all I ever needed was HTML, CSS, and JavaScript. I don't see why I need to learn XML now... I'll stick with text and JSON for my data.

should *you* use?

We have a lot of very well-respected clients, and they care about speed and standards, not the latest fad. We use text for our requests, and XML for responses from our servers.

...is *yours*!

I'm all about the new stuff, baby. I was the first guy in the office to use Ajax, and I use JSON for everything. Plain text is boring, and XML is **so** 1998.

Just Do It Solutions

Before we discuss how JSON and server-side languages like PHP get along, let's take a closer look at how you can access JSON data in your JavaScript. Here's another JSON data structure:

```
{"books": [
 {"title":"Hyperion", "author":"Dan Simmons", "isbn":"0553283685"},
 {"title":"The Stars My Destination", "author":"Alfred Bester", "isbn:":"0679767800"},
 {"title":"Black House", "author": [ "Stephen King", "Peter Straub"],
                        "isbn":"0345441036"},
 {"title":"The Golden Compass", "author":"Philip Pullman", "isbn":"0679879242"},
]};
```

Below are several values from the JSON structure. Your job is to write the JavaScript code that would return the value from the JSON data structure. You can assume the JSON data is in an object called jsonData.

Always begin with the JSON data object.

Value	JavaScript
"Alfred Bester"	var bester = jsonData.books[1].author;
"0679879242"	var isbn = jsonData.books[3].isbn;
"0345441036"	var isbn2 = jsonData.books[2].isbn;
"Dan Simmons"	var simmons = jsonData.books[0].author;
"Black House"	var blackHouse = jsonData.books[2].title;
"Peter Straub"	var straub = jsonData.books[2].author[1];

Remember, all these array indices start at 0, not at 1.

This goes to the third row...

...and then to the "author" item...

...which is an array. And we want the second author, in position [1].

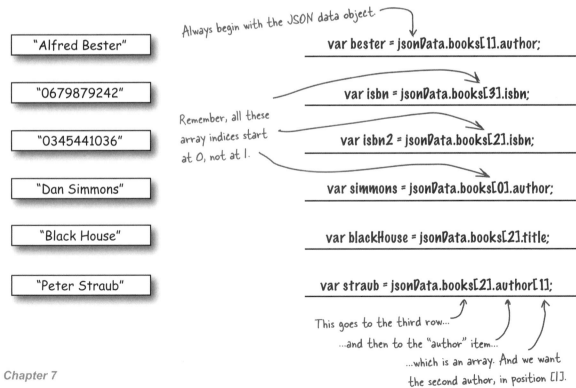

Appendix 1: extras

A Few Special Bonus Gifts

Just for you: a parting gift from Head First Labs. In fact, you'll find **five special bonus gifts** in this appendix. We wish we could stick around and tell you about a lot more, but it's time for you to take what you've learned and head out into the cold, cruel world of web programming on your own. We'd hate for you to take off without **a little more preparation**, though, so take a look at the top five things we just couldn't squeeze into this book.

Then you're done. Well, there's one more appendix. And an index. And a few pages marketing made us stick in... but really, you're... almost... to the end.

#1: Ajax toolkits

We've talked a few times about using an Ajax "toolkit" to handle repetitive tasks like creating a request object or sending a request. Once you understand how to write this code yourself, you may want to look into a few of these toolkits and see if they offer any functionality you might to take advantage of. Here are a few of the most popular toolkits:

You'll also see these toolkits referred to as "frameworks". Don't worry... it's all pretty much the same thing.

Prototype

Where to get it: **http://prototype.conio.net/**

How to use it:

Just reference the prototype.js file you download from the Prototype web site in your HTML.

```
<head>
 <title>The New and Improved Break Neck Pizza</title>
 <link rel="stylesheet" type="text/css" href="breakneck.css" />
 <script type="text/javascript" src="prototype.js"> </script>
 <script type="text/javascript" src="pizza.js"> </script>
</head>
```

Sending a request:

Ajax.Request is the Prototype JavaScript class that handles Ajax requests.

```
var request = new Ajax.Request(
  url,
  {
    method: 'get',
    parameters: 'phone=2142908762&name=Mary',
    onSuccess: updatePage,
    onFailure: reportError
  }
```

url is the URL to send the request to.

This can be either "get" or "post".

Here are your name/value pairs that are sent to the server-side program.

Here's one of the nicer features of Prototype: you can set up separate functions to handle different response conditions.

Handling a response:

Prototype sends your callback functions the request object as a parameter, since the request object isn't set up as a global variable.

```
function updatePage(request) {
  var response = request.responseText;
}
```

You don't need to check the ready state and status code... Prototype does that for you, and if there's a problem, runs your onFailure callback.

Dojo

Where to get it: **http://dojotoolkit.org/**

How to use it:

```
<head>
 <title>The New and Improved Break Neck Pizza</title>
 <link rel="stylesheet" type="text/css" href="breakneck.css" />
 <script type="text/javascript" src="dojo.js"> </script>
 <script type="text/javascript" src="pizza.js"> </script>
 <script language="JavaScript" type="text/javascript">
   dojo.require("dojo.io.bind");
 </script>
</head>
```

First, include the dojo.js file you download from the Dojo website.

In static JavaScript, run dojo.require() on all the Dojo "packages" you want to use.

dojo.io.bind is the Dojo package that contains Ajax-related code and utilities.

Sending a request:

It's usually easiest to put all the arguments you want to use with Dojo into a JavaScript data structure.

```
var arguments = {
  url:      'lookupCustomer.php',
  method:   'GET',
  content:  'phone=2142908762&name=Mary',
  error:    reportError,
  load:     updatePage
};

dojo.io.bind(arguments);
```

These arguments are similar to what you would use with Prototype.

Once you've set up your arguments, run dojo.io.bind(), and pass it your arguments.

Handling a response:

Dojo expects your callback functions to accept several parameters. The parameter named "value" is what you'll want most of the time... it contains the server's response.

```
function updatePage(type, value, evt) {
  var response = value;
}
```

#2: script.aculo.us and other UI libraries

In addition to several Ajax toolkits, there are some great JavaScript libraries you can use to build really slick user interfaces (UIs). These libraries are just external JavaScript files that you can include and use in your applications, whether those apps are asynchronous or not.

script.aculo.us

Where to get it: **http://script.aculo.us/**

How to use it:

Nothing new here... these are just more JavaScript libraries to add to your HTML.

```
<head>
 <title>The New and Improved Break Neck Pizza</title>
 <link rel="stylesheet" type="text/css" href="breakneck.css" />
 <script type="text/javascript" src="prototype.js"> </script>
 <script type="text/javascript" src="scriptaculous.js"> </script>
 <script type="text/javascript" src="pizza.js"> </script>
</head>
```

script.aculo.us uses the Prototype library for its server interaction, and some lower-level JavaScript functions.

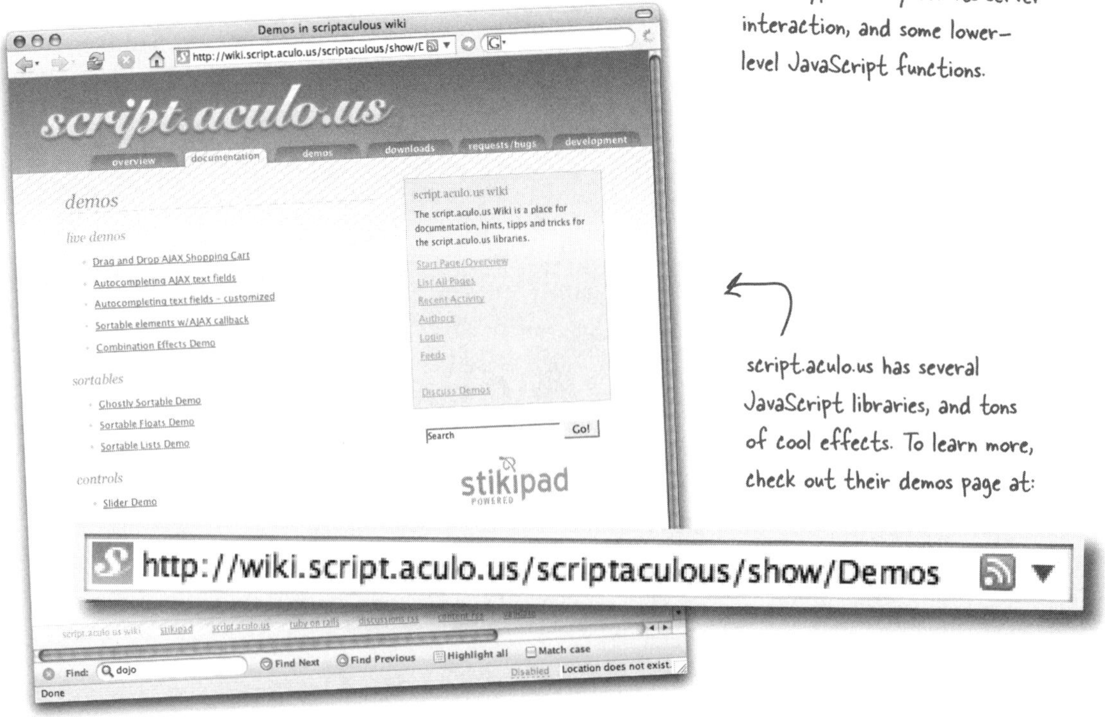

script.aculo.us has several JavaScript libraries, and tons of cool effects. To learn more, check out their demos page at:

Rico

Where to get it: **http://openrico.org/**

How to use it:

```
<head>
  <title>The New and Improved Break Neck Pizza</title>
  <link rel="stylesheet" type="text/css" href="breakneck.css" />
  <script type="text/javascript" src="prototype.js"> </script>
  <script type="text/javascript" src="rico.js"> </script>
  <script type="text/javascript" src="util.js"> </script>
  <script type="text/javascript" src="pizza.js"> </script>
</head>
```

Like script.aculo.us, Rico uses Prototype, as well as a utility library.

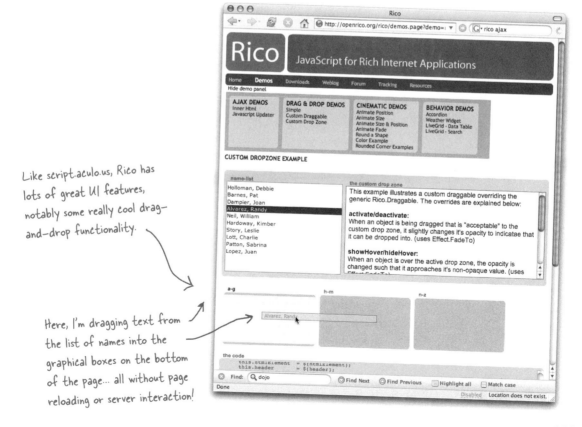

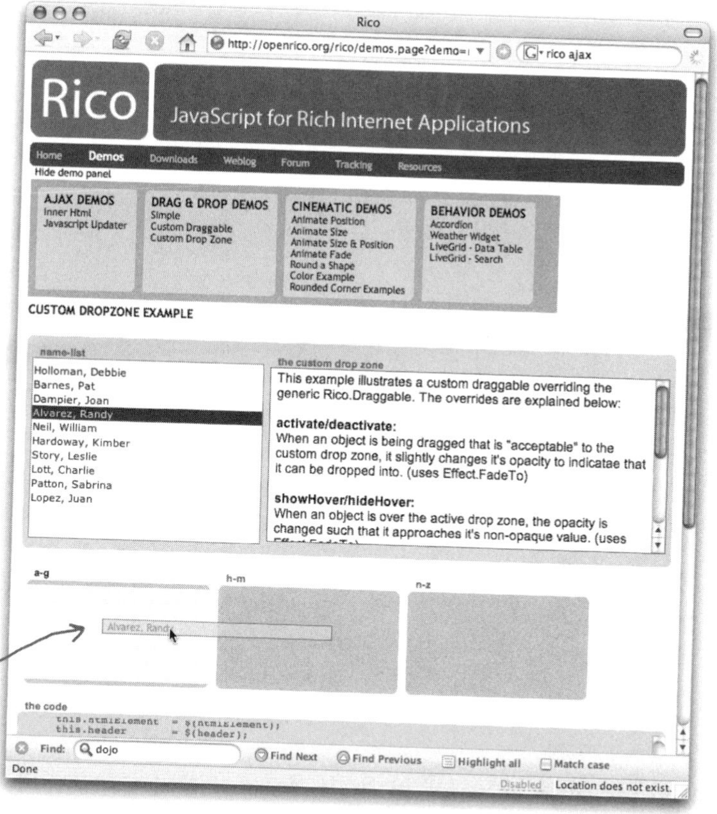

Like script.aculo.us, Rico has lots of great UI features, notably some really cool drag-and-drop functionality.

Here, I'm dragging text from the list of names into the graphical boxes on the bottom of the page... all without page reloading or server interaction!

#3: Inspecting the DOM

By now, you're a pro at using the Document Object Model to update your web pages on the fly. But once you've used the DOM to make changes to your page, how can you see exactly what the web browser sees? The answer is to use a DOM inspector:

This is the Top 5 CDs app from Chapter 4.5, running on the Firefox web browser.

Open the DOM Inspector on Firefox by going to the Tools menu, and selecting DOM Inspector.

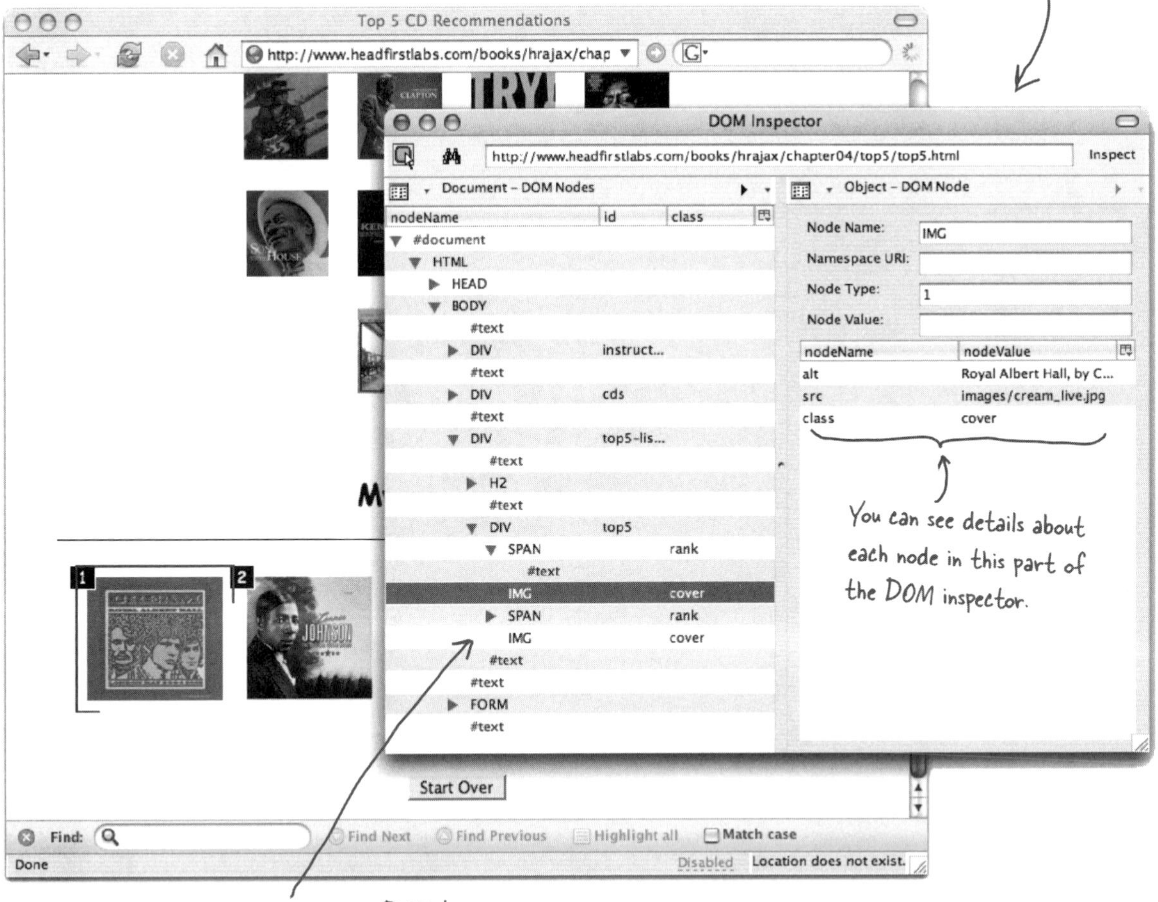

You can see details about each node in this part of the DOM inspector.

You can expand the DOM tree, and click on a node to get details about that particular node in the DOM tree.

NOTE: You need to specifically request that the DOM inspector be installed on Windows. When you're installing Firefox, select Custom Install, and then Web Developer Tools. This will ensure the DOM inspector is installed with your version of Firefox.

Inspecting the DOM in Internet Explorer

You'll need to download and install a separate tool for inspecting the DOM on Windows, using Internet Explorer.

The IE DOM Inspector is shareware... if you like it, you'll have to pay $29.99 to use it for more than 15 days.

Where to get it: **http://www.ieinspector.com/dominspector/**

How to use it:

Just install the EXE file from the IE DOM Inspector web site, and install the tool. IE DOM Inspector is shareware, so it only runs for 15 days before you have to either pay for it or uninstall it.

Here's the IE DOM Inspector in action.

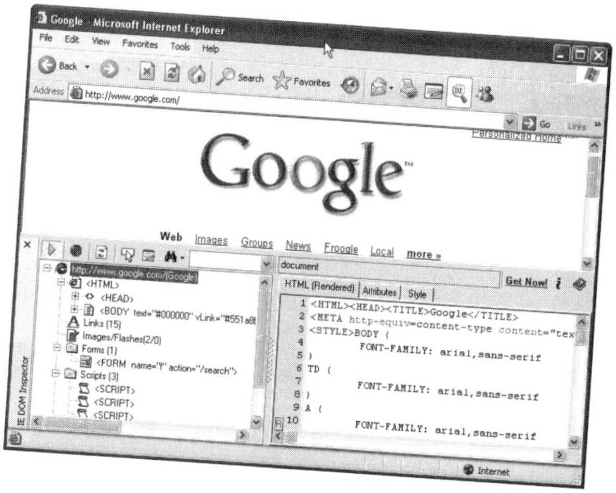

Inspecting the DOM in Safari

To inspect the DOM in Safari, you'll need to use WebKit. WebKit is the open-source system framework used by Mac OS X apps like Safari, Dashboard, and Mail.

Where to get it: **http://webkit.opendarwin.org/**

How to use it:

Download WebKit from the project web site. Then, enter the following command in a Mac OS X Termainal prompt:

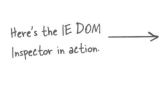

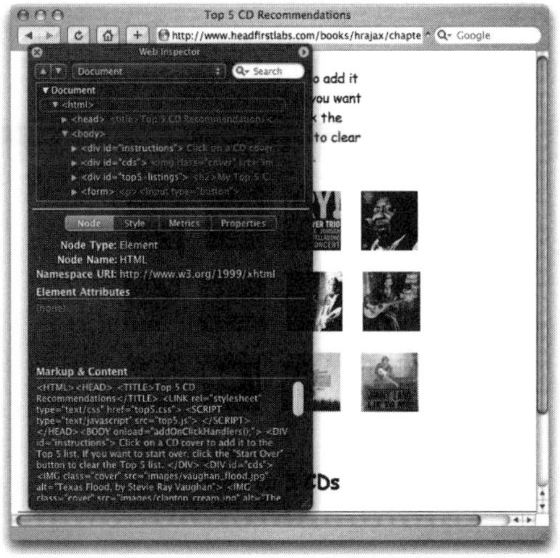

Right-click, and select "Inspect Element", to bring up the DOM Inspector in Safari WebKit.

#4: Using JSON libraries in your PHP scripts

You've already seen how JSON can help you send and receive complex objects in your Ajax apps. But for PHP scripts, you're going to need a library if you don't want to type in your JSON manually. Here's how you can use JSON in your PHP scripts, without needing to type in the JSON by hand:

JSON-PHP

JSON-PHP is probably the easier JSON library to use in your PHP scripts. It's easy to install and use.

Where to get it: **http://mike.teczno.com/json.html**

How to use it:

```
require_once('JSON.php');

$json = new Services_JSON();
```

First, use require_once() to include the JSON.php file you downloaded from the JSON-PHP web site.

require_once() makes sure that the JSON.php file is only loaded once, even if multiple PHP scripts refer to JSON.php.

Create a new variable, and assign it a new instance of the Services_JSON class. This class will let you output JSON data from your PHP data structures.

```
$order1 = array('name'         => 'Jim',
                'size'         => 'large',
                'beverage'     => 'mocha',
                'coffeemaker'  => 1);
$order2 = array('name'         => 'Bob',
                'size'         => 'medium',
                'beverage'     => 'latte',
                'coffeemaker'  => 2);

$orders =
  array('coffeeOrders' =>
        array($order1, $order2));
$output = $json->encode($orders);
print($output);
```

You can create arrays and variables just as you normally would in your PHP code.

When you're ready to convert your data structure to JSON, use your Services_JSON object, and run encode() on your PHP variable.

Finally, use print() to send the encoded JSON back to the requesting web browser.

#5: Using eval() with JSON

In Chapter 7, you saw how you can use the **eval()** function to evaluate JSON returned from a server-side script:

```
function updatePage() {
  if (request.readyState == 4) {
    if (request.status == 200) {
      var jsonData = eval('(' + request.responseText + ')');

      // Get the updated totals from the XML response
      var totalBoards = jsonData.totals[0].boardsSold +
                        jsonData.totals[1].boardsSold +
                        jsonData.totals[2].boardsSold +
                        jsonData.totals[3].boardsSold;
```

The eval() function takes a JSON response, and converts it into a JavaScript object.

The problem with **eval()** is that it runs the JSON response from the server without any security checks... if some malicious organization was able to tamper with your server's response, you could end up running some harmful code in your JavaScript.

Like PROJECT: CHAOS!

Use a JSON parser

If you're concerned about security with JSON, you may want to use a JSON parser, and avoid using **eval()** in your JavaScript functions.

Where to get it: **http://www.json.org/js.html**

You'll have to reference the JSON.js file you download from the json.org web site. using <script> tags in your HTML.

How to use it:

```
function updatePage() {
  if (request.readyState == 4) {
    if (request.status == 200) {
      var jsonData = JSON.parse(request.responseText);

      // Get the updated totals from the XML response
      var totalBoards = jsonData.totals[0].boardsSold +
```

A JSON parser will only accept string input... anything else is kicked out. No security risk!

JSON.parse() takes a text response from the server and converts it into an object.

Appendix 2: ajax and DOM utilities

"All I Want Is the Code."

It's time for a little bonus credit. Within the pages of this appendix, you'll find some of the utility code that was a little advanced for when you ran across it earlier in the book. By now, though, you should be ready to tackle these Ajax and DOM utility functions head-on.

We put all this code in a file called ajax.js. You can call it anything you like, as long as you change your HTML <script> tag to refer to the right filename.

ajax.js

You've seen this code plenty of times by now. This little bit of JavaScript takes care of creating a request object, and makes sure that the object will work on all modern web browsers, from Internet Explorer to Firefox to Opera. Get used to this code if you're not already... it's the foundation of every Ajax application.

```
var request = null;

try {
  request = new XMLHttpRequest();
} catch (trymicrosoft) {
  try {
    request = new ActiveXObject("Msxml2.XMLHTTP");
  } catch (othermicrosoft) {
    try {
      request = new ActiveXObject("Microsoft.XMLHTTP");
    } catch (failed) {
      request = null;
    }
  }
}

if (request == null)
  alert("Error creating request object!");
```

You'll see a lot of code that uses false here, instead of null, but that won't work on some versions of IE. Stick with null, and your code will work on all platforms.

Remember, you've got to try XMLHttpRequest for browsers like Opera and Mozilla, and then try ActiveXObject for Internet Explorer.

Follow the code... things end up here if all the different attempts at creating a request object fail.

OK, we admit it... this isn't the most robust way to handle errors. By now, though, you're ready to add some more advanced error handling on your own.

Using ajax.js

You can use ajax.js by adding a <script> tag to the <head> section of your web page's HTML and referring to the file's name, like this:

```
<head>
 <title>The New and Improved Break Neck Pizza</title>
 <link rel="stylesheet" type="text/css" href="breakneck.css" />
 <script type="text/javascript" src="ajax.js"> </script>
 <script type="text/javascript" src="pizza.js"> </script>
</head>
```

This is the <head> section of an HTML page.

In this case, this HTML refers to ajax.js, as well as an application-specific JavaScript file, pizza.js.

This space is really important... without it, some browsers won't load the JavaScript file you refer to with the src attribute.

Now tell me again why I shouldn't use one of those fancy Ajax toolkits I keep seeing on the Web. Don't those offer all sorts of extra functionality?

Don't use what you don't understand

There's nothing wrong with using an Ajax toolkit, especially if the toolkit takes care of lots of routine and repetitive tasks. That's all **ajax.js** really does: it takes code that you need in every single Ajax application, and it tucks it away in a file that you can use and refer to over and over.

But, you shouldn't just grab the coolest looking toolkit you can find, stick in a **<script>** tag, and hope for the best. Open up the JavaScript for the toolkit and figure out what's going on. After 400 pages of asynchronous programming, that shouldn't be too much of a problem!

text-utils.js

Once you've got your asynchronous JavaScript taken care of, you're ready to tackle some DOM code. You learned about the Document Object Model in Chapter 4, but we used the text-utils.js file in several earlier chapters... before you were the DOM guru that you've since become. Here's the code for text-utils.js, along with lots of notes on how it works.

```
function replaceText(el, text) {
  if (el != null) {
    clearText(el);
    var newNode = document.createTextNode(text);
    el.appendChild(newNode);
  }
}
```

replaceText() takes an element, and replaces all the text in the element with the text you supply.

First, we use clearText() to get rid of any existing children.

Next, we use the document object to create a new text node, and then append it to the element's child nodes.

```
function clearText(el) {
  if (el != null) {
    if (el.childNodes) {
      for (var i = 0; i < el.childNodes.length; i++) {
        var childNode = el.childNodes[i];
        el.removeChild(childNode);
      }
    }
  }
}
```

clearText() removes all the child nodes of the element you pass to the function..

This loops through all the child nodes, and removes each one.

Watch out! This removes all child nodes, even if they aren't text nodes.

```
function getText(el) {
  var text = "";
  if (el != null) {
    if (el.childNodes) {
      for (var i = 0; i < el.childNodes.length; i++) {
        var childNode = el.childNodes[i];
        if (childNode.nodeValue != null) {
          text = text + childNode.nodeValue;
        }
      }
    }
  }
  return text;
}
```

getText() returns the text for the element you pass into the function.

This loops through all the child nodes of the supplied element.

Remember, element nodes and other non-text nodes have a null nodeValue.

This takes the nodeValue for all text nodes, which is the text, and adds it to any existing text.

This variable will have all the text in the element when this function finishes.

Using text-utils.js

You can use text-utils.js by adding a <script> tag to the <head> section of your web page's HTML, just like you did with ajax.js:

```
<head>
 <title>Ajax-powered Coffee Maker</title>
 <link rel="stylesheet" type="text/css" href="coffee.css" />
 <script type="text/javascript" src="ajax.js"> </script>
 <script type="text/javascript" src="text-utils.js"> </script>
 <script type="text/javascript" src="coffee.js"> </script>
</head>
```

Remember to leave a space between the <script> opening and closing tags, so all browsers will load your external JavaScript.

Index

Symbols

A

B

C

D

E

F

G

H

I

J

L

M

N

S

T

U

V

W

X

Now that you've applied the Head Rush approach to asynchronous programming, why not apply it to the rest of your life?

Come join us at the Head First Labs web site, our virtual hangout where you'll find Head First resources including podcasts, forums, example code, and much more.

But you won't just be a spectator; we also encourage you to join the fun by participating in discussions and brainstorming.

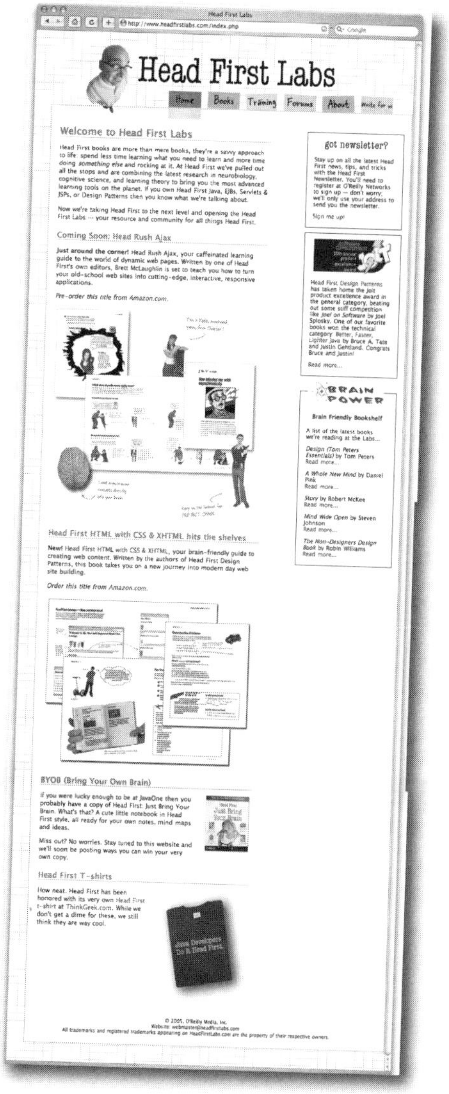

What's in it for you?

- Get the latest news about what's happening in the Head First world.
- Participate in our upcoming books and technologies.
- Learn how to tackle those tough technical topics (say that three times fast) in as little time as possible.
- Look behind the scenes at how Head First and Head Rush books are created.
- Meet the our authors and support teams who keep everything running smoothly...
- Why not audition to be a Head First or Head Rush author yourself?

Why wait? Our web servers are standing by. Visit now!

http://www.headfirstlabs.com